BRISTOL CONNECTICUT

In the Olden Time
New Cambridge

WHICH INCLUDES
FORESTVILLE

Eddy N. Smith, George Benton Smith
and Allena J. Dates
Assisted by G. W. F. Blanchfield

HERITAGE BOOKS
2013

HERITAGE BOOKS
AN IMPRINT OF HERITAGE BOOKS, INC.

Books, CDs, and more—Worldwide

For our listing of thousands of titles see our website
at
www.HeritageBooks.com

A Facsimile Reprint
Published 2013 by
HERITAGE BOOKS, INC.
Publishing Division
100 Railroad Ave. #104
Westminster, Maryland 21157

Originally published by
Eddy N. Smith, George Benton Smith and Allena J. Dates,
Assisted by G. W. F. Blanchfield

Hartford, Conn.
City Printing Company
1907

— Publisher's Notice —
In reprints such as this, it is often not possible to remove blemishes from the original. We feel the contents of this book warrant its reissue despite these blemishes and hope you will agree and read it with pleasure.

International Standard Book Numbers
Paperbound: 978-0-7884-5458-5
Clothbound: 978-0-7884-6959-6

THIS WORK is respectfully dedicated to the memory of those Bristol men and women of other days, whose steadfast integrity and undaunted perseverance, has made it possible for Bristol to become the eminently prosperous community that it is today.

APPROACHING BRISTOL ON A
WINTER'S MORNING.

THIS WORK is respectfully dedicated to the memory of those Bristol men and women of other days, whose steadfast integrity and undaunted perseverance, has made it possible for Bristol to become the eminently prosperous community that it is today.

APPROACHING BRISTOL ON A
WINTER'S MORNING.

Introduction

By Frederick Calvin Norton.

BRISTOL is less fortunate than some other towns in the state in that its complete history has not as yet been written by any one living within its borders. This work offers a very fruitful field of investigation for some historical student of the future, and it is the fond hope of all natives and residents of the town that such a history of Bristol will be produced within the memory of men now living. Fragmentary historical sketches of Bristol have been written with ability in the years that are past by Bristol men or women, and they have served their purpose. The real history of the hustling town among the hills of Hartford County, from the time that the hardy settlers of Farmington pushed their way through the woods and underbrush to what is now Bristol, to the present period of great commercial and social prosperity, has yet to come from the press.

When an effort is made to gather what has been written by Bristol people about their own town, and present it in a substantial, permanent form for posterity to look at, it is a matter of satisfaction to all those who have the welfare of Bristol at heart. If we have no completed history of the place any effort to collect what has been written and to present it in an attractive manner ought to meet with the appreciative support of all the people of the town. This book is such an undertaking; and it has been carried through with signal success. All that is of interest to the many inhabitants of this hill town has been embodied by the publishers between these two covers; and if anything has been omitted, it is the result of oversight. The book is most comprehensive and ambitious in its detail; it has been revised and rearranged several times, so that all departments of Bristol's life may find a place in the volume and the publishers may feel proud of their real success in the undertaking.

Many articles that have been printed in years past are here reproduced for the purpose of placing them on record permanently.

To the people of this town the work will be interesting for years to come, and will serve its mission, even if not a complete history of the subject; and, to coming generations, it will stand as a monument of the history of present day Bristol.

NEAR PIERCE'S BRIDGE.

INDIANS
Of BRISTOL and VICINITY

By Milo Leon Norton

THE Indians who frequented Bristol before its settlement by the English, were of the Tunxis tribe, of Farmington, and there is no evidence that there were ever any dwelling places other than temporary camps of individuals, or, at most, small parties of the aborigines, within what are now the boundaries of the township.

In the early history of the town of Farmington, mention is made of that section now divided into the towns of Bristol and Burlington, under the general name of the "West Woods." It was the resort of the white hunters of that early period, by virtue of a treaty with the Indians by which hunting and fishing rights were to be equally enjoyed by whites and Indians; and so plentiful was the game in the forests which then covered the hills and valleys of Bristol and Burlington, that venison and bear meat sold at a very low price in the Farmington market. Dr. Noah Porter said in an address at the celebration of the two hundredth anniversary of Farmington, in 1840, "There are men now living, who remember when venison was sold in our streets at 2d the pound."

Previous to the discovery of the beautiful meadows at the great bend of the Tunxis River, which the early records name, "Tvnxis Sepvs" (literally the little river, to distinguish it from the great river, the Connecticut), nothing was known of the territory west of the Talcott range, except as it may have been penetrated rarely by a few daring hunters and explorers. When a treaty was ratified with the Indians, in 1650, and the lands opened for settlement, two well-defined trails led westward through the woods, one practically where the first colonial road was built from Chippen's Hill to Farmington; the other southwestwards crossing the mountain west of the sewer beds diagonally; crossing the present town of Wolcott also in a southwesterly direction; thence through the southeast corner of Plymouth to Waterville, then in the territory known as Mattatuck. Over this trail to Mattatuck the early settlers of Waterbury travelled; taking the first millstones ever used in that town on horseback. At the reservoir on South Mountain, southwest of the Allen place, near the south end of the pond, and not far from the town line, the trail crossed what was then a swamp over a causeway of loose stones and earth, the nearest approach to a roadway ever made by the aborigines.

The trail crossed Mad River near the beaver dam which then existed

JACK'S CAVE.

near the south end of the Cedar Swamp reservoir, continuing southwesterly, the present highway following it for some distance. A cave, near Allentown, known as Jack's Cave, is but a short distance from the old trail. The Indians made it a stopping-place on their journeys to and from Mattatuck. It was afterward inhabited for many years by a negro, named Jack, who had a squaw for a wife, and who subsisted by basket making. There is a fireplace which has a natural flue extending to the top of the cliff. The open side of the cave was protected by slabs and earth, forming a comfortable dwelling. At Allentown, upon the farm of Walter Tolles, were open fields, which were cultivated by the squaws in summer; and corn and beans, and perhaps tobacco for the pipe of peace, were grown there.

It seems to have been the custom for certain of the huntsmen of the tribe, in their communistic form of government peculiar to the race, to hunt in certain areas which were either assigned by the chief, in his patriarchal capacity, or were held by common consent during the pleasure of the individual hunters. At any rate trespassing upon each other's hunting preserves was looked upon with disfavor; and encroachment by the white hunters, notwithstanding treaty privileges, was not entirely satisfactory to the dusky huntsmen who claimed certain tracts as their private territory. This state of affairs was the more aggravated, doubtless, by the gradual disappearance of the game caused by the inroads made by the white hunters, with their superior weapons, the skillful use of which, however, was soon acquired by the red men.

Thus previous to the first settlement of Bristol by the Whites, after this part of Farmington had become somewhat famous as a huntingground, hunters from Farmington, Hartford, Wethersfield, and even Wallingford, which then included Meriden and Cheshire, penetrated these dense woods and returned laden with trophies of the chase. It ought to be mentioned in passing, however, that there was then no undergrowth, the Indians annually burning over the woods, so that one could see quite a distance through the standing timber, and pass rapidly and easily through.

Among these early hunters were Gideon Ives, of Middletown, and Capt. Jesse Gaylord, of Wallingford. They were companions in hunting expeditions, both being famous hunters. It is a tradition in the Ives family, that their ancestor was, like Nimrod, a mighty hunter; his proud boast being that from these "West Woods" he had taken between four and five hundred deer, eighty or ninety bears, and a large amount of other game. On one occasion the two were stalking a deer which they saw upon the summit of the hill since known as the Rock Lot, just south of the residence of James Peckham, near the Cedar Swamp. The deer was making toward the east, and the two hunters agreed to separate, one going around the hill on the north side, and the other on the south side, the one who sighted the deer first to shoot it. Just as Mr. Gaylord reached the eastern extremity of the hill, which slopes to the edge of a swamp in that direction, he saw an Indian taking deliberate aim at Mr. Ives, who, unaware of his danger, was taking aim at the deer. Mr. Gaylord instantly leveled his rifle, and, being a quick shot, dropped the Indian before he had time to fire. Mr. Ives, in astonishment, asked why he had shot the Indian, and was told that it was done to save his life. They decided to dispose of the Indian's body by stamping it into the soft mud of the swamp near by, and kept the matter a profound secret for many years, for fear that it would become known to the tribe, and that revenge would be taken for the death of their kinsman; the very simple code of the red men requiring blood for blood, an eye for an eye, and a tooth for a tooth. The reason for the attempt upon the white man's life was supposed to be because he was trespassing upon the private hunting-ground of the red man, which his sense of justice caused him to resent. The same sense of justice, when an Indian found a carcass of deer or other game, hung up out of reach of prowling wolves, until the hunter could return with assistance to take it away, prevented him from molesting it, and also filled him with wrath when

INDIAN ROCK OR ROCK HOUSE.

RUINS OF CAPT. JESSE GAYLORD'S HOUSE IN 1907.

this confidence was broken by the unscrupulous white hunter, and no doubt kept alive a bitter animosity against the white invaders. The Indian was known to the Whites as Morgan, and the swamp where he was buried, as Morgan's Swamp, to this day. It would be interesting to know what became of the deer.

There are other versions of this story. One given by Deacon Charles G. Ives, at the celebration of the fiftieth anniversary of his deaconship, in 1859, has it that the shooting was done by his ancestor to save Capt. Gaylord; that they discovered the Indian trying to get a shot at them, that they separated with the understanding that if the Indian pursued either the other was to shoot him down. But this account does not agree with the one handed down in the Gaylord family, which is substantially as related It was told to the father of the writer by Capt. Jesse Gaylord, grandson of the hero of the story, who also stated that the Indian's rifle, powder horn and bullet pouch were preserved many years in the family; but other traditions, including that of Deacon Ives, assert that the rifle and other accoutrements of the red man were buried with him. It may have been this adventure which determined Capt. Gaylord's choice of location for a residence, for he afterward purchased land and built upon it, in the immediate vicinity, his first house being a few rods south of the big bowlder, known as Indian Rock, or Rock House, from the fact that it was the temporary home of Morgan, who occupied the grotto underneath it when hunting in the vicinity. He afterward built a quarter of a mile south, the large, red farmhouse being occupied by his descendants until 1870, when Jesse, his great grandson, moved to Bristol village. The old house was torn down a few years afterward, and only the picturesque cellar and chimney stack remain.

Aside from occasional infractions, such as the foregoing incident, there always existed friendly relations between the white population and the Tunxis tribe, of Farmington. It has been stated that a man named Scott, was murdered in a brutal manner at what is now known as Scott's Swamp, in the western part of Farmington, by Tunxis Indians. But Julius Gay, who has made the history of the Tunxis tribe a subject of much research, says that there is not a particle of evidence that Scott was murdered by the Tunxis. He ascribes the deed to a prowling band of some outlying tribe, who skulked around for the purpose of carrying off any stray white people they might encounter, holding them, bandit like, for ransom. He says that Scott was captured while at work in a field, and because he made an outcry, which the captors feared would bring assistance, his tongue was cut out, and he was afterward brutally murdered. This was about the year 1657. The traditional massacre of the Hart family, near the present Avon town line, Mr. Gay regards as mythical. The house was burned, accidentally, at midnight, and all but one of the family perished in the flames. The Indians had nothing whatever to do with it. There was a murder of some person by the Indian, Mesapano, which may have been the Scott incident, and which is mentioned in the records of April, 1657, of the General Assembly, as "a most horrid murder by some Indians at Farmington." But the Tunxis were not mentioned as the guilty parties, for messengers were sent to the Norwootuck and Pocumtuck Indians, of Hadley and Deerfield, demanding the surrender of Mesapano, to be tried and punished for the crime. The Tunxis were peaceable, treaty-keeping and tractable Indians, many of the young attending school, and their parents attending church, with their white neighbors. There is reason to believe that they were never very redoubtable warriors, as their own version of a battle between themselves and an invading armed force of Stockbridge Indians, at Indian Neck, near the bend of the river, admits their defeat and retreat to their village on Round Hill, where they were saved from extinction or capture by the bravery of the squaws, who armed themselves and so ably defended their homes and supported their brothers in arms, that the intruders were driven off with great loss. This was but a short time before the settlement of the Whites at Farmington. No doubt the proximity of the more invincible whites, was a strong inducement to them to permit white occupation of the beautiful valley of the Tunxis; and for many years thereafter, when there was a threatened attack by the Mohawks, whom all the Connecticut Indians feared, the Tunxis tribe, men, women and children, would rush pell mell across the river and place themselves under the protection of their white allies.

There are but few purely Indian names which now cling to the haunts of the red men in this vicinity. Chippen's Hill is a contraction of Cochipianes, which the old records give as the name of the red hunter who made that part of the town his hunting preserve. In my boyhood it was invariably pronounced Chippeny, which was much nearer the original. Another Indian, called Fall, gave his name to the mountain of that name. Morgan, whose tragic end has already been related, has his name preserved by the swamp in which he was buried. Zach was the name of the Indian who made what we now call Mine Mountain, but which the early settlers called Zach's Mountain, his hunting place. Bohemia and Poland are names applied to two Indians who held reserved lands, including Poland Brook and the Bohemia Banks, in Forestville. Poland Brook flows through what is known as Todd's lot, and the Bohemia Banks are the bluffs extending from Poland Brook to the Plainville town line. Poland lived in a tepee on the banks of the brook; and Bohemia lived on the flat south of the Sessions Clock factory, or in that vicinity. Compound, who gave his name to Compound's Pond, now known as Compounce, was the most important, historically, of the Bristol Indians whose names have been handed down to us. His history is fully set forth in another place. Presumably the European names given to some of the Indians by the Whites, were so given because the real names were unknown or unpronounceable; and, for purposes of identification, one name was as good as another.

One interesting incident may be worth relating in connection with the Indian, Zach. When Capt. Newton Manross was a lad in his teens, he was fishing one day in the brook that flows into the mine pond west

BALANCED BOULDER, NEAR WITCH ROCK.

of Zach's Mountain, where he took refuge under a shelving rock to escape a shower. Being of an inquiring turn of mind he noticed what appeared to be a white stone in the earth floor of the cavern, which proved to be a skull. He returned the next day with a spade and unearthed an entire skeleton of an Indian, a full-grown male. The bones were taken by him to his father's clock shop in Forestville, where the skull was long used as a recepticle for small parts of clock movements. When the factory was burned the bones shared the general cremation. The skeleton was undoubtedly that of the old hunter, who may have been murdered and concealed by his enemies, or he may have died a natural death, and was buried by his friends. How many tragedies, unwritten and unknown, may have taken place on these hills in the far-off centuries, when the red men hunted each other with the ferocity of panthers, and the cunning of foxes!

My grandmother, who was born in 1783, remembered the Indians distinctly. They were in the habit of calling at the farmhouses for cider, on their way from Farmington to Waterbury, and *vice versa*. But one Indian would call at the house, the others, when there were several in the party, invariably sitting on the ground by the roadside until their companion returned with the coveted beverage. She lived in the old house now occupied by the Tymerson family, then the home of Elijah Gaylord, which stands on the summit of Fall Mountain. A locality about a mile to the westward has been known as Indian Heaven, since the first settlement of that neighborhood by the Whites. It is not known how the name originated, but presumably because of the abundance of game in that vicinity. A region where game was abundant would naturally excite the admiration of the red huntsmen, whose highest ideal of heaven was expressed by the words, "Happy Hunting Ground."

The name Pequabuck, which is applied to the stream flowing through Bristol, is of Indian origin, taking its name from the Pequabuck Meadows, mentioned in the early records of Farmington, which lay near the beau-

tiful spot where the Pequabuck joins the Tunxis. Its name, according
to Trumbull, would indicate that it flowed out of a clear pond, being
a variant of Nepaug, which means the same thing, having reference to
Sheherd's Pond, in New Hartford. But there was no such pond from
which it could flow, until artificial ponds were constructed by the white
people. About the year 1863, an educated Indian physician, of the
Chippeway tribe, Dr. Monwadus, pitched a tent in winter north of the
house of Mr. Wetmore, on Park street. That was before the street was
opened or a house built there. The doctor was very skillful, and treated
many cases during the few weeks that he remained in town. He was
familiar with the Indian tongue, not only of his own tribe, but with
other dialects, and asserted that the name, Pequabuck, meant stony
river; but that it should be spelled, Pequabock. That interpretation
certainly applies to this part of the stream with greater propriety than
the one favored by Trumbull; but at Farmington, where the stream
was best known to the Indians, who probably applied the name to the
meadows at its confluence with the Tunxis, and not to the river itself,
stony would be as inappropriate as clear pond. Therefore, as yet,
the name is not satisfactorily accounted for.

Bristol has the distinction of being the place where the rude pottery
of the aborigines was manufactured from the cotton-stone, or foliated
talc, which is found upon the eastern slope of Federal Hill, where Joel T.
Case built a machine shop. As late as 1876 fragments of this pottery
were common about the fields of the vicinity, laid up into stone fences,
or doing duty as corner stones for the zig-zag rail fences of the locality.
This stone, a variety of soap-stone, being easily worked, was hollowed
out by chipping with hard, sharp-edged stones, into round and oval
dishes, and kettles of various capacity, ranging from a pint to several
gallons. Other Indians beside the Tunxis may have come here to re-
plenish their supply of crockery and cooking utensils, camping, perhaps,
for weeks while they were patiently chipping away at the soft stone.
The same formation crops out in other places on the same range of hills;
one near the Liberty Bell shop, where there was once a saw mill for sawing the cotton-stone into jambs for fireplaces; another at Edgewood,
near the Bartholomew factory. But this Federal Hill quarry seems to
have been the only one known to the Indians. When the machine-shop
was built, and the debris was cleared away from the ledge where the
cotton-stone was quarried, a large bowl or kettle was found, partially
completed, but undetached from the rock. It may easily be imagined
that as the Tunxis potters were busily at work, there was a sudden
descent of the dreaded Mohawks, and a precipitate retreat.

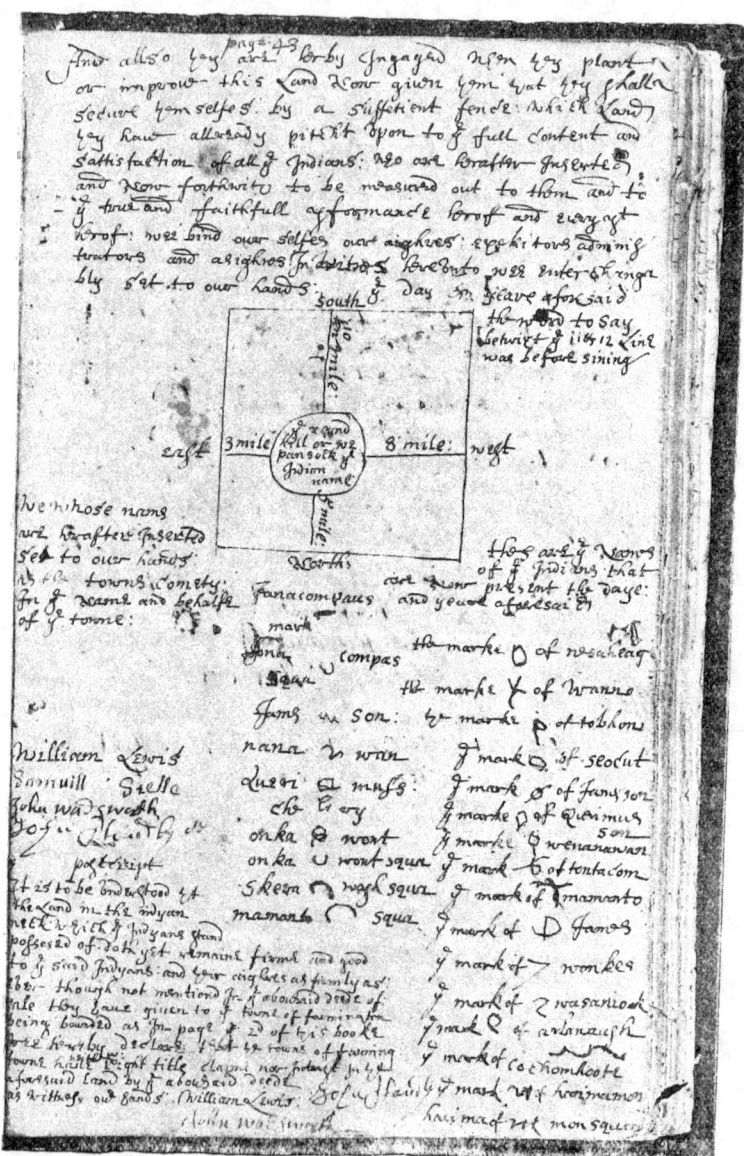

FACSIMILE PAGE.

Old Town Record Book of Farmington, Conn., showing signature of Jon a Compaus (Compound) and Compas "Squa" to the Indian agreement of May ye 22, 1673.

"Compound"
A TUNXIS CHIEFTAN

By Miss Alice Norton*

ABOUT the middle of the 17th century, a tribe of Tunxis Indians and their chief, Compound, occupied the land adjacent to the lake now known as Compounce, in what was then a part of Farmington, now Southington.

The old deeds preserved in Farmington and Waterbury furnish the evidence in regard to this chief. His name is variously given as Compas, Compaus, Compowne, Compoune, Compound and appears with those of other Indians who gave to the white settlers titles to the Farmington and Waterbury lands.

There are three original deeds containing his autographic mark. The first of these, among the Farmington records, is dated May ye 22, 1673, and is of extreme interest.

It confirms to the men at Farmington, 33 years after its first settlement, previous grants of land made to them by the Indians. On the deed is traced a crude map of the land in question, beneath which are the names and marks of twenty-six Indians, written in two columns, each column beginning respectively with the names and marks of "Nesaheg" (Neasaheagun, sachem of Poquonnock, in Windsor), and of Jon a Compaus (Compound).

Here is revealed the interesting fact that "Compas squa" (squaw) was present and by her mark upon this deed, bequeathed to us with her own hand the only record we have of her existence. Her mark and that of "Compaus" are, queerly enough, transposed, thus revealing their simple ignorance of the King's English.

By the deed of August 26, 1674, the Tunxis Indians conveyed a large tract of land in Mattatuck (Waterbury)—to the whole of which territory they laid claim—to the first white settlers of that town. This deed is signed by the "universal Nesaheagun," John a Compowne and twelve other Indians.

In 1890 a happy chance brought to light among the ancient records stored away in one of the oldest houses in Waterbury, the original deed of December 2, 1684, by which another tract of Mattatuck land was transferred to the English settlers, and the grant of 1674 was confirmed, "with all and singular rode timber rocks quorys broocks rivers swamps medows" the same to be discharged from all "former bargins sales, titles morgages, leases fins fes joynters dowrys suts or encumbrans whatsoever."

In this deed 1684 the name Compound stands first in the list of signatures.

Could romance itself conjure up a group of names more picturesque than these of the original owners and proprietors of Mattatuck: John a Compound, Hacketousuke, Atumtoco's mother Jemse dafter (daughter)

---

*Extract from "Compounce." Published by Miss Alice J. Norton, 1902.

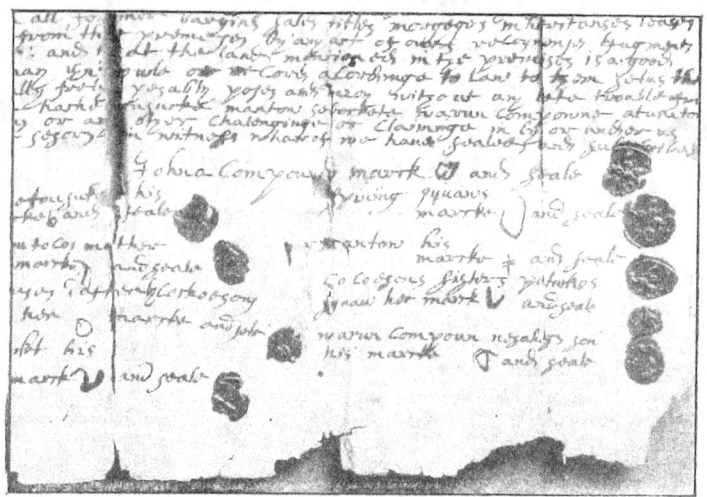

FACSIMILE OF A SECTION OF THE DEED OF DEC. 2, 1684.
With Autographic Mark of Compound.

by Cockoeson's sister, Abucket, Spinning Squaw, Mantow, Cocoeson's sister's Patucko's squaw, Warun-Compoun Nesaheg's son, Atumtockco, Cockeweson's sister's dafter, all of whom "parsonally aperd" (before John Wadsworth * * * ist) "and acknoleged this Instrument to be their free and volentery act."

One looks upon this ancient document, rescued from the oblivion of over two centuries, with a sentiment of profound veneration, and pictures to himself the group of swarthy faces as, to the names written, the Indians added with their own clumsy fingers, each, his or her individual "marck" or totem. This deed is valuable not only for its Indian signatures, but for the autographs of men famous in the early history of Connecticut; Thomas Judd and John Standly, Benjamin Judd and John Wadsworth, Timothy Standly and John Hopkins, "freemen of farmentowne" and most of them among its eighty four proprietors.

A wide field of speculation regarding the chief, Compound, opens before us as we contemplate these records.

Nesaheagun was the Sachem who with others signed away to the white settlers much of the territory of Farmington and Waterbury, and thousands of acres in Simsbury, Windsor, Wethersfield and Middletown. Warun-Compound is described as Nesaheagun's son, but it is John a Compound whose name stands second to that of Nesaheagun in the deeds of 1673 and 1674 and first in the deed of 1684.

Quoting from Orcutt's history of Derby,—"This fact suggests that John a Compound, whose name stands next to Nesaheagun's may have been an elder son of the same chief."

According to another authority (Rev. Joseph Anderson—History of Waterbury), he may have been a nephew or brother, and as such succeeded Nesaheagun in the sachemship, as among some tribes the succession of chiefs was through a brother or nephew instead of a son.

However, that may be he was a "native prince" and identified with the Indians who from time to time occupied the territory of Mattatuck.

"The name Compound," says one historian (Mr. Anderson) "although not of English origin, has been forced into a strange resemblance to English. There is reason to suspect it as an Indian name in disguise, or possibly that the Indian proprietor who here comes before us, may have been named from the 'other side falls,' wherever these may have been. At all events, acompwn-tuk would mean the 'falls or water on the other side.' " It is therefore not improbable that his name was a place-name, and derived from his connection with the water or lake "on the other side" of the mountain.*

For the tragic story of the chieftain's fate we are indebted to tradition, which tells us that his home was the cave near the shore, and that while crossing the lake in an iron kettle he was drowned, finding his grave beneath its waters. Various additions have been made in recent years to this brief but graphic tale, but all such are utterly without foundation, and detract from the simple pathos of the traditional story.

A singular coincidence in connection with the legend, is that Compound's mark, as seen in some of his signatures, resembles the outline of a kettle, which suggests the pleasing fancy that this may have been his device or emblem.

As to his personality, we may have seen that he had influence and standing among the native tribes, and there is nothing in history or tradition to prove that he was other than a noble specimen of his race such an one as the imagination loves to associate with the "beautiful glacial lake that he owned."

One sees how naturally the term "Compound's" became in time Compounce and the early records give us the musical "Compounce Pond Water" transformed now into Lake Compounce.

The torture of the white man by the Indians (not of the Compounce tribe) has been a tradition of this neighborhood from the earliest times.

An old Indian trail, later the first traveled road between Farmington and Waterbury, passed through the borders of the neighborhood. Here have been found traces of an Indian encampment and burying ground, and the frequent finding of arrow-heads, pottery and rude

BIRCHES AT LAKE COMPOUNCE.

---

*"The oldest families north of Compound Lake had the traditions certainly 100 years ago (1775) that the Indians that visited there came from over the mountain west."—*Timlow's History of Southington.*

stone implements in the past, testifies that here in this little valley were their hunting and camping grounds, and here were buried their dead.

An authentic story has traveled down the years, of the recollection of a family of Indians, that, about the year 1760, lived in a wigwam in the woods east of the lake. They tarried only a summer and then disappeared.

Thus vanished from the land the last remnant of this ancient race, leaving only the memory and the magic of a name.

Before the coming of the white man, who diverted the streams to other channels, Lake Compounce was one of the sources of the Quinnipiac river. Cuss Gutter brook ran into it through the valley above, and a small stream below connected it with Cold brook, a tributary of the Quinnipiac. White and gold fish, now extinct, lived in its waters, and wild ducks and geese, the loon and other water birds found here the solitude they loved.

On the distribution of the Southington division in 1722, the lake and adjacent land became the property of Samuel Steel and Thomas Orton, both men of prominence among the proprietors of Farmington.

The property appears to have frequently changed owners until December 7, 1787, when it was purchased from the estate of Daniel Clark, of Wallingford, by Ebenezer Norton (grandfather of the late Gad Norton), whose adjoining property had descended to him through several generations, from his ancestor John Norton, also one of the Farmington proprietors.

The lake property is referred to in the earlier deeds as "a parcell in that division of land lying between Panthorn and Watterbury, bounds not yet surveyed and layd out;" and in the deed of 1787 as "one certain Piece or Parcel of land situate in Southington at a Place called Compound's Pond."

The oldest inhabitant remembers Lake Compounce as a lonely place, scarcely known beyond the limits of the town, frequented only by an occasional hunter or fisherman, and the neighboring children who went there to padddle about in the old dug-out, hewn from a chestnut log, which had replaced the birch-bark canoe of the Indians.

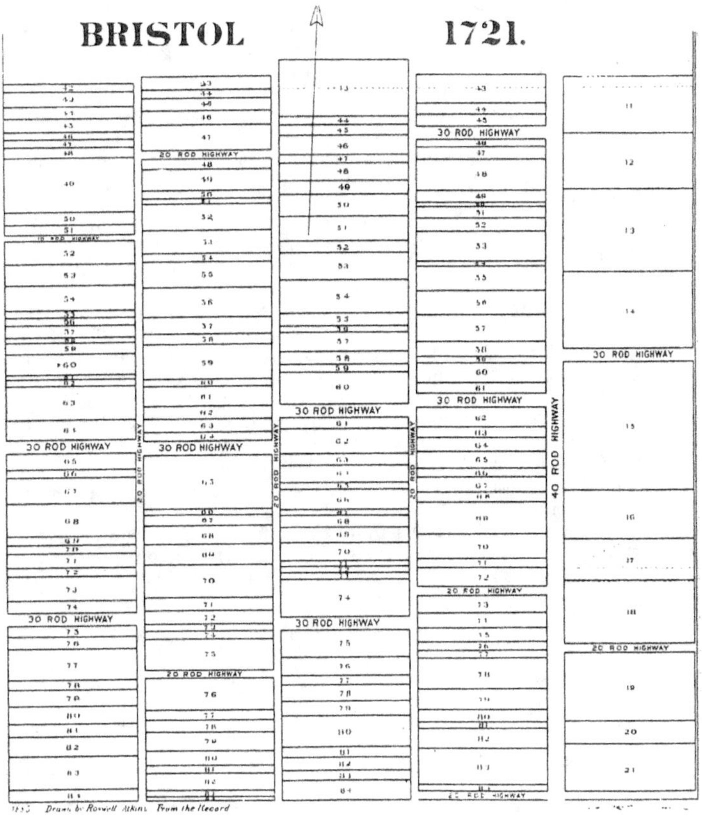

OR "NEW CAMBRIDGE."

BRISTOL 1721.

This Chart was prepared by the late ROSWELL ATKINS with great care and shows the original division of the land in Bristol.

BRISTOL IN 1721

Mr. Atkins made the following statement in connection with the chart which he prepared:

"On account of the mutilated condition of the original records, I have been obliged, in preparing the accompanying chart, to depend, to a great extent, upon such memoranda as I could find among the papers of county surveyors, and deeds of transfer of lots and parts thereof, covering a period of seventy-five years immediately following the layout.

"For the highways running north and south I have had to depend, to ascertain the width, entirely upon the descriptions to be found in recorded deeds.

"No two perambulations agree as to the position of the boundary line on the north. I have, therefore, placed this boundary at five miles and fifty-three rods from the boundary line on the south, and indicated the line on the map by a dotted line.

"The reservation for the Indians, Bohemia and Poland, is indicated by two sets of dotted lines in the first tier of lots, No. 17. The southern parallel line and the broken western line are fixed by means of a survey recorded in 1723, and include a tract of one hundred fifty-two and one-half acres. This record, however, is not sufficiently full to determine positively the exact location. The parallel lines are fixed by means of memoranda of Tracy Peck, County Surveyor made in 1808 from a copy in the hands of Noah Byington, County Surveyor.

"There are undoubtedly some errors in the chart, but, in the main, I think it is correct."

The following table shows first, the number of lot numbered from Simsbury line; second in parenthesis, the width of lot from north to south in rods and feet, e. g. by 84.04 is meant, 84 rods, 4 feet; and third, the name of owner:

First or Eastern Tier of Lots.

No. 11 (127.08). Daniel Porter, Mr. Newton, James Bird, Widow Orvis.

No. 12 (132.15). John Clark, John Woodruff, John Smith, Mathew Woodruff.

No. 13 (186.12). Thomas Gridley, John Langton, Samuel Gridley, John Root, Sen.

No. 14 (172.06). Richard Brownson, Thomas Barnes, Moses Ventrus, John Brownson, Jr.

No. 15 (289.10). John Norton, Thomas Orton, Captain Lewis, Isaac Moore.

No. 16 (112.06). John Thompson, John Steel, Jobanah Smith, Widow Smith.

No. 17 (97.10). Zachariah Seymour, Samuel Steel, Sen., Abraham Andrus, Thomas Richardson. (30.02). Indian Reservation.

No. 18 (145.04). Robert Porter, John Porter, Samuel Cowles, John Cole.

No. 19 (176.09). Obadiah Richards, John Scovil, Joseph Hecox, Mr. Haynes.

No. 20 (54.00½). Samuel Steel, Jr., Benoni Steel, David Carpenter, John Carrington.

No. 21 (105.09). Thomas Thompson, Richard Seamour, Samuel North, Thomas Hancox.

Second Tier of Lots.

No. 43 (63.13), John Langton; No. 44 (29.11), John Steel; No. 45 (26.15½), James Bird; No. 46 (17.13½), Jonathan Smith; No. 47 (32.06), Thomas Bull; No. 48 (69.04½), Thomas Orton; No. 49 (2812½), Thomas Hancox; No. 50 (9.10), Benoni Steel; No. 51 (25.09), Samuel North; No. 52 (29.14½), Isaac Brownson; No. 53 (71.09), John Norton; No. 54 (9.10½), Samuel Steel, Jr.; No. 55 (54.11), Thomas Barnes; No. 56 (53.12½), Daniel Porter; No. 57 (63.13), William Judd; No. 58 (33.05), Moses Ventrus; No. 59 (15.01), John Porter; No. 60 (42.06), John Andrus; No. 61 (27.06), Thomas Thompson; No. 62 (45.01), Thomas Judd; No. 63 (22.13½), John Brownson, Jr.; No. 64 (33.05), Thomas Porter, Jr.

No. 65 (38.04), Joseph Woodford; No. 66 (18.11½), Obadiah Richards; No. 67 (31.00½), Widow Smith; No. 68 (25.09), John North, Jr.; No. 69 (75.11), John Root; No. 70 (57.14½), Isaac Moore; No. 71 (23.00½), Abraham Brownson; No. 72 (44.03), John Lee; No. 73 (41.00), Mathew Woodruff; No. 74 (33.12½), John Clark; No. 75 (33.11), Thomas Judd, Jr.; No. 76 (20.01½), John Carrington; No. 77 (16.14½), Joseph Hecox; No. 78 (72.00), Mr. Howkins; No. 79 (48.05), Stephen Hart, Jr.; No. 80 (30.09½), John Stanley, Jr.; No. 81 (14.10), David Carpenter; No. 82 (44.03), John Warner; No. 83 (85.04), Captain Lewis; No. 84 (15.01), Phillip Judd.

Third Tier of Lots.

No. 43 (131.15), Mr. Hooker; No. 44 (20.05), John Carrington; No. 45 (24.07), Thomas Gridley; No. 46 (44.13), John Lee; No. 47 (21.04), Zachariah Seymour; No. 48 (41.09), Mathew Woodruff; No. 49 (33.12), John Thompson; No. 50 (48.15½), Stephen Hart, Jr.; No. 51 (54.07½), Daniel Porter; No. 52 (28.02½), Widow Orvis; No. 53 (60.15), Stephen Hart, Sen.; No. 54 (72.15), Mr. Howkins; No. 55 (30.04), Isaac Brownson; No. 56 (12.00), John Root, Jr.; No. 57 (48.00), Capt. Thomas Hart; No. 58 (30.04), Jacob Brownson; No. 59 (18.15½), Obadiah Richards.

No. 60 (72.08), John North, Sen.; No. 61 (23.01½), John Brownson; No. 62 (59.01½), Richard Brownson; No. 63 (25.14), Samuel North; No. 64 (33.12), Capt. John Hart; No. 65 (15.04), Phillip Judd; No. 66 (46.10), John Brownson, Sen.; No. 67 (9.11½), Benoni Steel; No. 68 (23.01½), John Welton; No. 69 (32.13), Thomas Bull; No. 70 (44.13½), John Warner; No. 71 (17.01), Mr. Newton; No. 72 (16.02½), Abraham Andrus; No. 73 (17.01), Joseph Hecox; No. 74 (84.08), Mr. Wadsworth; No. 75 (64.10½), John Langton; No. 76 (43.06½), Samuel Cowles; No. 77 (21.11½), Daniel Warner; No. 78 (38.05), John Woodfuff; No. 79 (37.03) Thomas Judd, Sen.; No. 80 (76.10), John Root, Sen.; No. 81 (23.01½), Thomas Porter, Jr.; No. 82 (31.14), John Judd; No. 83 (33.05), Abraham Brownson; No. 84 (44.09), Samuel Steel, Jr.;

Fourth Tier of Lots.

No. 43 (30.00), John Steel; No. 44 (18.06), John Scovel; No. 45 (28.02), Widow Orvis; No. 46 (31.11), Thomas Porter, Sen.; No. 47 (58.10), Isaac Moore; No. 48 (23.01), John Brownson; No. 49 (46.10), John Brownson, Jr.; No. 50 (20.05), Daniel Andrus; No. 51 (9.10), Benoni Steel; No. 52 (60.11), John Stanley; No. 53 (55.06), Thomas Barnes; No. 54 (21.04), Zachariah Seymour; No. 55 (60.15), Stephen Hart, Sen.; No. 56 (64.10), William Judd; No. 57 (38.12), Joseph Woodford; No. 58 (23.01), Samuel Hecox; No. 59 (77.09), Mr. Wyllis; No. 60 (18.15), William Higason; No. 61 (45.11), Thomas Judd, Jr.; No. 62 (31.06), Mr. Wrotham; No. 63 (33.12), John Thompson.

No. 64 (16.02), Abraham Andrus; No. 65 (121.08), Mr. Haynes; No. 66 (12.00), John Root, Jr.; No. 67 (24.07), Thomas Gridley; No. 68 (44.09), Samuel Steel, Sen.; No. 69 (44.13), John Lee; No. 70 (84.08),

Mr. Wadsworth; No. 71 (25.14), Samuel North; No. 72 (29.01), Thomas Hancox; No. 73 (15.04), John Porter; No. 74 (20.05), John Carrington; No. 75 (76.10), John Root, Sen.; No. 76 (72.15), Mr. Hawkins; No. 77 (23.01), John Welton; No. 78 (30.15), John Stanley; No. 79 (46.15), John Andrus; No. 80 (32.13), Thomas Bull; No. 81 (17.01), Mr. Newton; No. 82 (38.05), John Woodruff; No. 83 (14.12), David Carpenter; No. 84 (9.11), Samuel Steel, Jr.

Fifth or Western Tier of Lots.

No. 42 (15.04), Phillip Judd; No. 43 (33.11), Thomas Porter, Sen. No. 44 (28.02), Widow Orvis; No. 45 (33.11), Moses Ventrus; No. 46 (17.01), Joseph Hecox; No. 47 (18.05), Obadiah Richards; No. 48 (23.01), Samuel Hecox; No. 49 (121.06), Mr. Haynes; No. 50 (29.01), Benjamin Judd; No. 51 (23.05), Abraham Brownson; No. 52 (51.11), Robert Porter; No. 53 (46.10), John Brownson, Sen.; No. 54 (60.11), John Standley; No. 55 (16.10), Jobanah Smith; No. 56 (18.16), William Higason; No. 57 (31.06), Mr. Wrotham; No. 58 (9.11), Samuel Steel, Jr.; No. 59 (25.14), John North, Jr.; No. 60 (48.00), Thomas Hart; No. 61 (9.11), Benoni Steel; No. 62 (14.12), David Carpenter; No. 63 (77.10), Thomas Newell.

No. 64 (48.15), Stephen Hart, Jr.; No. 65 (38.05), John Woodruff. No. 66 (17.01), Mr. Newton; No. 67 (58.10), Isaac Moore; No. 68 (76.10); John Root, Sen.; No. 69 (21.11), Daniel Warner; No. 70 (20.05), Daniel Andrus; No. 71 (30.04), Isaac Brownson; No. 72 (22.10), Richard Seymour; No. 73 (60.15), Stephen Hart, Sen.; No. 74 (31.06), Widow Smith; No. 75 (23.01), John Brownson; No. 76 (31.06), John Warner, Jr.; No. 77 (72.08), John Newton; No. 78 (23.01), Thomas Porter, Jr.; No. 79 (39.11), Edmond Scott; No. 80 (41.09), Mathew Woodruff; No. 81 (30.15), John Standley, Jr.; No. 82 (45.11), Thomas Judd, Jr.; No. 83 (72.15), Mr. Hawkins; No. 84 (30.00), John Steel.

BRISTOL

AN ADDRESS.
Prepared by Roswell Atkins and Epaphroditus Peck.

Delivered at the Centennial Celebration of the incorporation of the Town of Bristol, Connecticut, June 17, 1885, by Epaphroditus Peck.

HISTORY is but fragmentary at best. We say, "Bristol is a hundred years old to-day," but these hills and valleys are many centuries old. Men and women had their homes, and institutions, and rude manufactures here, for how many centuries we can hardly guess; but their savage lives left no record, except the rude weapons or tools which they casually dropped, and which we casually find.

The Indian tribe of this neighborhood was the Tunxis. But their sparse population, and their indolent natures, prevented any attempt to subdue these rugged forest-covered hills. Along the river at Farmington, where the soil was level and mellow, they had their principal village; in the open fields, which are now Plainville, they had another settlement; but these woods—the "Great Forest" they called it—were more valuable to them as a hunting-ground, stocked with all manner of game and fish, than they could have been as a village site. The ledge of Cotton-

The Pierce Homestead, built by Ebenezer Barnes, the central third in 1728, the north and south wings later upon the marriage of a son and daughter. Bought by the Pierce Family in 1797, in whose hands it still remains, and is at present the residence of Mrs. Julius E. Pierce. A remarkable fact that, although nearly two hundred years old, it has only been owned by two families.

*The James or Gad Lee place, later known as the "MUZZY PLACE."
Residence of L. O. Norton.*

Stone, running along the crest of this hill, they discovered, and put to practical use; and the vessels, finished and unfinished, together with the still evident traces of work on the ledge itself, show that a quarry of considerable importance was located there. Vessels from this quarry are said to be found in many parts of the state.

Without doubt, the Indians who came here to work this quarry, or to hunt in the "Great Forest," built wigwams for their temporary use; and there were certainly a few isolated Indians who lived here permanently.

The name of Cochipianee, who lived on the hill to the northwest, has come down to us in the name of Chippin's Hill; Morgan Swamp, on Fall Mountain, preserves the name of another Indian, who died, and is said to have lived there; the claims of Bohemia and Poland to their land in the Stafford district were respected by the whites in the layout of 1721; there was probably an Indian wigwam near the James Lee house, and a group of them near the Compounce cemetery. But the tribal center was at Farmington, and there was nothing within our limits which could be called even a village.

The same causes which determined the choice of the Indians, operated also upon the early white settlers of New England, and tracts of arable land, lying near water-courses, were everywhere first chosen for settlement. So when the Massachusetts settlers began to think of colonizing the wilderness around them, and heard from the friendly Indians of the fertile and open valley of the Connecticut, Wethersfield, Windsor, and Hartford, on the riverbank, became the first village sites. So again in 1639, when the river towns had sent out a committee to explore the surrounding country for the most inviting spot for settlement, they selected, as the Indians had done, the fields along the Farmington River, and began there the settlement of our mother town in the next year.

Thirty-seven of the Hartford settlers received a charter from the

General Assembly, and also bought from the Tunxis Indians the right to settle on the land included therein. Among these proprietors we find the familiar names of Hart, Lewis, Barnes, Brownson, and Wilcox. In 1672 the Assembly fixed the length of Farmington at fifteen miles, and its width at eleven miles, extending west from the Hartford line. The western boundary thus fixed is now the western line of Bristol.

As the Farmington settlers in turn began to push beyond their original location, the level land along the Pequabuck attracted their attention, and in 1663 the town granted to John Wadsworth, Richard Brumpson, Thomas Barnes, and Moses Ventruss, a tract described as "fforty acors of meddow Land Lying att the place we comonly Call Poland." Twenty acres more were granted to John Langton and George Orvis in 1664. This Thomas Barnes was an ancestor of our townsfolk of that name, and the sixty acres then granted lay on both sides of the west branch of the Pequabuck River, extending nearly as far west as to the rolling-mill. These two grants seem to have exhausted the arable land in this direction, and no settlement was made upon them.

In 1672, the Farmington proprietors, then eighty-four in number, took formal possession of the territory which had just been assigned to them by the General Assembly. They laid out a parallelogram a little over eight miles long, and four wide, for the home settlement, and called it "the reserved land." The remaining land they divided among themselves in proportion to their assessment lists, giving to Mr. Hooker, the minister, a double portion. The actual survey of the western land was not made until 1721. Six tiers of lots were laid out, each three hundred and five rods wide, and about eleven miles long, with reservations between them for twenty, thirty, and forty rod highways; so that each "division," with its adjacent highway, was a little over a mile wide. The first two of these tiers were each divided into twenty-one lots, and each lot assigned to four proprietors; the last, or westerly, four were each divided into eighty-four lots, and assigned to individual owners; so that each Farmington proprietor had a lot, or an undivided quarter-lot, in each division. The widest of these lots were one hundred and thirty-one rods, four feet wide, and the narrowest nine rods, ten and a half feet; each one, of course, being three hundred and five rods long. These allotments were made to the men, and in the proportions, which had been fixed by the vote of 1672, and most of them were actually taken by the heirs of the men in whose names they were allotted. Narrower highways were reserved, running across the divisions, and a reservation of about one hundred and ninety acres was made to the Indians, Bohemia and Poland. The westerly five of these divisions now constitute the towns of Burlington and Bristol.*

The actual settlement was begun six years later by Daniel Brownson of Farmington. He bought the seventy-first lot in the fifth division in November, 1727, and in that year, or early in the next, built a house at Goose Corner, so called. This house has long been gone, and Mr. Brownson seems to have left the village very soon.

The second settler, and one in whom we feel more interest, because both his house and his family still remain, was Ebenezer Barnes, a descendant of the Thomas Barnes already mentioned. He built, in 1728, the house, which, having since been added to at both ends, is now the central part of Julius E. Pierce's residence in East Bristol. In the same year, Nehemiah Manross of Lebanon, the ancestor of our present Manrosses, built a house north of Ebenezer Barnes, and on the west side of the road. Perhaps in this year, Abner Matthews built a house on the East Fall Mountain road.

During the next score of years a little group of houses was built on the East Bristol road, north of the Barnes and Manross houses, another hamlet on Chippin's Hill, a still smaller one on Red Stone Hill, and isolated houses stood on Fall Mountain, in the present Stafford district, and in the centre of the town.

---

* See Chart, Page 21.

The only present Bristol families which settled here before 1742 are the Barnes, Manross, Gaylord, and Jerome families. Joseph and David Gaylord came here between 1740 and 1742, and both became prominent citizens; David was one of the first deacons of the Congregational church, and Joseph equally prominent in the Episcopal church. David Gaylord's house stood about where Henry A. Pond now lives; Joseph's, southwest of the Brownson house, on the slope of the mountain.

William Jerome bought land in the second division in 1741, and his son Zerubbabel moved here. The farm which the family still occupy they bought in 1748, from Caleb Palmer, who had already built a house on the present site of Horace O. Miller's.

The distinctive symbol of New England Puritanism has been said to be a meeting-house fronted by a school-house. Our ancestors very early established both these institutions. Prior to 1742, they had felt the distance to the Farmington church a heavy burden. In that year they sent a petition to the General Assembly praying for permission to hire a preacher of their own during the winter months. This petition, bearing the signatures of all the residents, is among the legislative archives at Hartford.*1 It was promptly granted, and the first society meeting
*1.

PETITION FOR WINTER PRIVILEGES, OCTOBER, 1742.

To the Honour^{ble} the Gou^r Councell, and Reprefentatiues, of his Majeftys Colony of Conecticott In New England, In General Court, to be Affembled, the 14th Day of octob^r A.D: 1742 — The Humble memorial of us the fubfcribors Inhabitants In ye Townfhip of Farmington In ye County of Hartford, &c., Humbly fheweth, that we are fettled In A Certain place, within ye Bounds of f^d Townfhip, Called by the Name of ye 2^d, 3^d, 4th, 5th, & 6th Diuifions of Land In f^d Townfhip Weft from the Referued Land, and are fo Remote, from any meeting Houfe, In any minifterial fociaty In f^d Town, as Renders it exceeding Difficult for us to attend the publick Worfhip of God, In any place where it is fett up, and efpecially, In the winter feafon — and allfo that there is fuch a Number of perfons fettled in f^d fiue Diuifions of Land as that we are Compitently able to hire A minefter, to preach ye Gofpel to us In faid winter feafon — Wee Do therefore Humbly pray this Honble Affembly to Grant unto us who are or fhall be fettled on the f^d fiue Diuifions of Land, Begining att ye fouth end of ye faid Diuifions of Land; and from thence to extend North fiue miles Liberty of hireing an Authordox and fuitably Quallifyed perfon to preach ye Gofpel amongft us, for ye fpace of fix months In ye year Annually, viz, Nouemb^r Decemb^r Janu^r feb^u march & april more or Less accordings as we Can and Do hire fuch A preacher, with ye powers and prieuledges by Law belonging to fuch A fociaty—Hoping that it will not be Long Before we fhall be able to be A fociaty fully Conftituted — and your memorialift as In Duty Bound fhall euer pray, &c ——

octob^r 6th Day A.D: 1742: —

Ebenezer barns, Jofeph gailord, ben'mman brooks, Gid peck, John Brown, ebzer gailord, John hicox, Zerubbabel Jearom, Mofes Lyman, Joel mitchel, edward gailard, John gailard, Stephen Barns, Gerfhum Tuttle, Jofeph benham, Dauid gylord, Nemiah manros, Samuel Gaylord, Jofeph Gaylard, Timothy Brown, bifh (?) manros.

[This petition and the following one were evidently drawn up by a professional scrivener. The records which follow, were, of course, written by the various clerks of the society. The petitions may be regarded, therefore, as representing the literary style of a practiced writer, and the records that of an average village clerk of the period.]

was held November eighth, 1742. This is an important date, for then first, did this tract, which we call Bristol, and the settlers living upon it, assume individuality and corporate existence, as "the Southwest winter society."

In December it was voted to hire Mr. Thomas Canfield for the coming winter. This Reverend Thomas Canfield, a young man of twenty-two, our first gospel minister, disappears from our local history at the end of this winter. He went to Roxbury the next year, and preached there till his death in 1795. His epitaph concludes with the following lines:

> "O what is man, poor feeble man
> Whose life is but a narrow span.
> Here lies intomb'd in earth and dust
> The Reverend, meek, the mild and just."

The Congregational church at Roxbury have in their possession a record in Mr. Canfield's hand-writing, containing the following statement: "I having an Invitation to go & Preach at ye Mountain, now called Cambridge in Farmington, wch I accepting accordingly Preachd yre ye next Sabbath it being ye 6th of Decr & from yt time till the latter end of Octobr 1743."

It is difficult to reconcile this statement as to the length of his service here either with our society records, or with the powers granted to the society by the Assembly.

The Reverend Ichabod Camp probably preached during the next winter, though no positive record of that fact exists.

The poverty of the settlers, and the hardships which they underwent to support preaching, are shown by the levy of a sixteen pence tax, that is, a tax of six and two-thirds per cent., in 1743, to pay the society expenses, which cannot have been more than a very small sum. But the people were not daunted, and at the same meeting at which this sixteen pence tax was laid they voted to apply to the Assembly for a complete ecclesiastical organization.*2 The town assented, and in

THE "LOT JEROME PLACE."—Since destroyed by fire.

*2. See page 30.

1744 the Assembly again changed the "Southwest winter society" into the "New Cambridge society," with power to lay taxes, and support preaching and schools. The name "Cambridge" appears from the Canfield record to have been already given to this section of the town in popular speech, but the reason is unknown.

This society had hardly begun its record, when the universal contest between orthodoxy and liberalism broke out. One party, made up principally from the settlers on Chippin's Hill, was more inclined to the milder doctrines of the Church of England, while most of the settlers in the valley were rigid Calvinists. During the fall of 1744, Mr. Samuel Newell was invited to preach three months, and his vigorous support of the Westminster theology caused a speedy outbreak of the latent differences. The majority voted to settle Mr. Newell, but seven members were so pronounced in their opposition that his coming was deemed unwise. Mr. Camp then preached again, and a Mr. Christopher Newton, both of whom, I think, were more acceptable to the minority, and both of whom afterward became Episcopal clergymen. After these futile

*2.

PETITION FOR ECCLESIASTICAL INCORPORATION, APRIL, 1744.

To The Honorable General Assembley to Be Holden att Hartford on ye Second Thurfday of May Next   The Memorial of us The Subfcribers Hereunto all Inhabitants Liveing Within ye Bounds of Farmington & County of Hartford Humbley Showeth y^t your Honours Memorialifts Liveth on That Tract of Land in f^d farmington Commonly Called ye fecond, 3^d 4th 5th & 6th Divifions of Land Lying Weft of ye Referved Lands fo Called & at about feven or Eight Miles Diftants from ye Publick Worfhip of God in farmington firft fociety to ye Which Wee Belong & Wee Haveing Obtained Liberty of ye Honorable Affembly to Hire an OrthoDox Minifter among Ourfelves fix months in a year for ye Space of two years Which Term of Time is Expired & Wee Having Obtained a Voat of ye faid firft Society in farmington to Be A Diftinct Society, By and With ye Bounds & Limits of five Miles fquare of ye Divifions aforefaid Begining at ye Northweft Corner of Southington Parifh Bounds at Waterbury Line from Thence North With f^l Line five miles & from Thence Eaftward five miles & from Thence Southward five miles & from Thence Weftward five miles to ye firft mentioned Bounds Which f^d Tract of Land is Generally good & Wee are of Opinion is Sufficient for A Diftinct Society & Wee Being fo Remote from ye Publick Worfhip of God y^t it is Impracticable to attend ye same With our families unlefs it be When Wee Have preaching among ourfelves Wee Therefore Humbly Pray your Honours to Take our Circumftances into your Paternal care & Wife Confideration & make us a Diftinct Eclefiaftical Society With ye Limits aforefaid or In sum Other Way Grant Relief unto your Memorialifts & Wee as In Duty Bound fhall Ever Pray

Farmington Aprill ye 12 Ano Domini 1744.

ebenezer Barns, beniamin gaylard, Hez: Rew, Dauid Graues, Abel Roys, John Hikcox, Edward gailard, Nehemiah manros, Daniel mix, Ebenezer Barns iuenor,* Jofeph Graues Moses Lyman, Caleb Abernathy, daniel roe, Caleb Palmer, Dauid gaylard, Jofeph Gailard Juner, Jofeph Benham, Stephen Barns, Abner Matthews, Jofeph Gaylord, Nehemiah Manrows iuner,* Simon Tuttel, Zerubbabel Jearom, Gershum tuttle, John gailard, William Jearom, Zebulon frifbe, Benjamin brooks, Edward ———†, ben mix, Daniel mix, Thomas Hart. Samuel Gaylord.

---

* Junior.   † This name is entirely illegible.

attempts to secure agreement, the majority again voted to hire Mr. Newell, and he was settled accordingly in 1747.

The opposition had now increased to ten, and they, Caleb and Abner Matthews, Stephen and Benjamin Brooks, John Hickox, Caleb Abernathy, Abel and Nehemiah Royce, Daniel Roe, and Simon Tuttle, "publikly declared themselves of the Church of England, and under the bishop of london." The relations of these churchmen, as they were called, to the society, became somewhat peculiar. They at once refused to pay their ecclesiastical taxes, and for some time took no part in society affairs. It was finally agreed that they should be entirely relieved of the "meeting-house rate," and should pay one-half of the "minister rate" so long as they had no rector of their own.*3 After this compromise the churchmen began again to share in such society business as did not directly concern the management of the Congregation church; after an Episcopal rector was located here, separate assessment lists were made, a separate collector appointed, and a due share of the tax paid to their rector. The two churches lived in harmony until the Revolution, when the political hostility became much more fierce than the religious had ever been.

Mr. Newell was installed in August, 1747, and it was evidently a great day for the society: Joseph Benton, Nehemiah Manross, Joseph Gaylord, David Rich, Ebenezer Barnes, Jr., and as many more as chose, were instructed by a vote of the society to keep open a public house of entertainment on the day of the ordination.

The society gave Mr. Newell £500 "for his settlement," payable within three years, and a permanent salary of £300, beside building him a house (since known as the Dr. Pardee place).*4 These sums were payable, however, in colony bills of credit, which were worth only about one-sixth of their face value. The influence exerted upon the village by this clergyman can hardly be over-estimated. He was a strong-minded, strong-spoken man; holding to the rigid old doctrines of theology, and exerting a great influence even in secular matters. He was pastor for forty years, till his death in 1789. The following epitaph is inscribed upon his tomb in the South grave-yard:

"Here Lyeth Interred the Body of ye Rev. Samuel Newell, A. M., Late Pastor of the Church of Christ in New Cambridge. A gentleman of Good Genius, Solid Judgment, sound in the faith, A fervent and experimental Preacher of unaffected Piety, kindest of Husbands, Tenderest of Fathers, the best of Friends and an Ornament of the Ministry. And having served his generation faithfully by the Will of God with serenity & calmness he fell on sleep February ye 10th 1789, in the 75th year of his Age, And the 42nd of his Ministry.

Death, Great Proprietor of all, 'tis thine
To tread out Empires, and to quench ye Stars."

*3.   *4 See Page 32

("Jenewary" 4th, 17$\frac{49}{50}$.)

It was agreed upon and Voted between the prefent Churchmen that are amongſt us . . . . . . that they paying all their miniftearel Rates to us for the year paſt and half their mineſtearel Rates for the futer untill they haue a lawful minefter acording to the Cannons of the Church of England which may Requir and Recouer their Rates by laws of the gouerment ſet ouer them we the ſofiaty would forgiue or Relinquiſh to them two Rates which was laid the year paſt viz a two ſhiling Rate and a four ſhiling Rate and all other Charge that ſhall ariſe for ye finiſhing the meeting houſe and mr Newels Wood —

In spite of the heavy burden which the support of a pastor had imposed upon the little society, and in spite, too, of the severe loss which the Episcopal schism had caused, they almost at once began to plan for the building of a meeting-house. In December, 1746, the site, which had been chosen by a committee from the General Assembly, was bought of Joseph Benton for £4. They began the work at once, and, I think, began to hold services in the new building early in 1748, though it was not entirely finished till 1753.

The sacrifice which the people made to build this house and support preaching is strikingly shown by the heavy taxation. Before it was begun the society taxes had never been less than five per cent., but in May, 1748, a ten per cent. tax was laid, in December of the same year a twenty per cent. tax, and another ten per cent. tax in December, 1749! It must be remembered, too, that this was for ecclesiastical purposes alone, and did not include town or state taxation. It was against these ten and twenty per cent. taxes that the protest of the Churchmen had been especially directed. This first meeting-house stood a few feet northeast of the present one, and was furnished partly with the old-fashioned pews, and partly with seats. Sittings were assigned according to the wealth, age, and official rank of the congregation, and this "dignifying the meeting-house" was a most delicate operation. To

*4

(July 20ᵗʰ, 1747.)

At a fofiaty meeting of the Inhabnitants of the 4 fofiaty in yᵉ town of farmington Called new Cambridg viz of fuch Inhabitants of fᵈ fofiaty as are leagly Qualifid to Vote in the Choice of a minefter and to make an agreement with them being held by ajᵒrnment in fᵈ fofiety on the 20ᵗʰ day of july Ad 1747

Whereas this fofiaty haue maid Choice of mr famˡˡ newil to be our minifter and haue giuen him a call to fettel in the gofpel mineftry amongft us of which call he hath excepted it is therefore Voted and agreed by this fofiaty that if yᵉ fᵈ mr famˡˡ newil fhall become our ordaind and fetteld minifter that then we will and fatiffy unto him for his yearly falery befides what hath been allredy Voted him for his fettelment viz for what Remains of this year fixty feuen pound ten fhiling in bills of Credit of this Coleney in old tener on the firft day of next enfewing febury and the firft day is the time at the which we agree and couenant with him the fᵈ mr famˡˡ newil to pay him his falery yearly from year to year

And we agree and Couenant to pay and fatifħe unto him for his falery the firft day of febuary A d 1749 one hundrd and fourty pound and in the 1750 one hundred and fifty pound 1751 one hundred and fixty pound and in the year 1752 one hundred and eighty pound and in the year 1753 two hundred pound and in yᵉ year 1754 two hundred and twenty pound and in the year 1755 two hundred and forty pound and in the year 1756 two hundred and fixty pound and in the year 1757 two hundred and eighty pound and in the year 1758 three hundred pound which we couenant and agree to make as good to him then as 3 hundred pound is now for his yearly salery which is to be his ftanding falery and is to be paid and fatiffied to him the fᵈ mr famˡˡ newel for his yearly falery during his continance amongft us in the gofpel miniftry and is to be paid to him in bills of Credit of this Coleney of the old tener or in good and marchantable grain fuch as Wheat Rie and Indian corn which grain is to be Rated and paid to him according to the Curant market prife that fuch grain fhall bair at hartford in the county of hartford yearly on the firft of jenaury deducking Reafonable Carage (They were also to furnish him "a fufifhantcy of firewood for his famely.")

each man's grand list was added fifty shillings for each year of his age, and twenty pounds additional for the rank of Captain, ten for that of Lieutenant, and five for that of Ensign.*5   All over fifty years of age were seated in front, the young folks in the galleries, the children on benches in the aisle. The children were to be seated in the pews, "menkind at 16 years old, and female at fourteen." One pew, doubtless the least desirable was assigned to the slaves; for some of the good people held slaves in those days, and the Jerome family still have a bill of sale of "a negro boy, Job," signed by no less reverend a person than Parson Newell himself.*6   Deacon Gaylord appears to have been the musician of the society, and for fourteen years he was elected to "set the psalm."

Attendance at church, and proper behavior while there, was enforced with all the rigor of the law, as some light-minded youths of Parson Newell's flock found to their sorrow. In 1758 Nathaniel Messenger, "for whispering and laughing between meetings," was fined three shillings and costs, and in 1762 John Bartholomew, "for playing with his hand and fingers at his hair in meeting," paid a like penalty.

This meeting-house was replaced by a larger one in 1771, and that by a third, which is the main part of the present building, in 1831.

*5.

(December, 1771.)
    Voted Chufe a Committe to Dignify the New meeting houfe
    Voted that but one head fhall be allowed to any mans Lift
    Voted that it fhall be allowed in the Lift fifty fhillings a year for age
    Voted that no Commiffion fhall be allowed in feating any man
    Voted that all that are above Sixty years of age fhall be Seated at the Difcrefion of the Seators

[The rules for dignifying the first meeting-house are stated in the text The second line of this record means that only one allowance for age shall be made to a family, and the fourth that military titles shall not be considered]

*6.

SLAVE BILL OF SALE.

Know all Men by thefe Prefents That I Sam'll Newell of Farmington in the County of Hartford & Colloney of Connecticut in New England, for & in Confideration of four Hundred & Seventy pounds Money of the old Tenour by me in hand Received & to me well Secured by William Jearom of Farmington, in the County of Hartford & Colloney of Connecticut in New England, Do give grant Bargain Sell Convey & Confirm unto the aforef'd William Jearom his Heirs & affigns forever, one Certain Negro boy Named Job, of about fourteen year's of Age to have & to hold the f'd Negro, forever & Deliver the faid Negro Boy found & well — & further I the fd Sam'll Newell Do by thefe prefents bind myfelf my Heirs Executor's & adminiftrator's to Warrant & Defend the abovef'd Negro to f'd Jearom, his Heirs & affigns, forever againft all claims & Demands whatfoever in witnefs whereof I have hereunto Set my hand & Seal this Seventh Day of Jannuary A: D: 1755.

Signed & Delivered in prefents of   Sam'll Newell [SEAL.]
    Hezekiah Gridly Juner
    Abigail Gridly

GRAVE OF REV. SAMUEL NEWELL, IN THE SOUTH OR DOWNS' CEMETERY.

Of the early Episcopal church much less can be related. The ten "churchmen" left the Congregational church in 1747, and three years later they seem to have been under the care of some Episcopal clergyman. In 1754, they built a small church building, opposite the Congregational meeting-house, north or northwest of the present first district school-house. Here occasional services were held by missionaries from another parish, among whom were Messrs. Camp and Newton, who had formerly preached in the Congregational church.

In 1774 the Reverend James Nichols took the care of this parish, probably in connection with others. Soon after his coming, the ecclesiastical differences, which had separated his people from the rest of the society, began to develop into political differences. The excited and patriotic feelings of the Revolution were largely directed against the Episcopalians, nearly all of whom were supporters of King George. Chippin's Hill, where many of them lived, became quite a Tory centre, and meetings were held there of Tories from all parts of the state. Mr. Nichols is said to have been several times shot at, and the popular indignation at the position of his people was so markedly shown that many of them left New Cambridge for more congenial neighborhoods. Mr. Nichols himself stayed in the western part of the state, and his loyal people continued to collect their separate taxes, and send them to him. These were received by him in 1778 at Salisbury, and in 1779 and 1780 at Litchfield. The society refused to recognize these payment of taxes to the absent rector as a sufficient discharge, and made some collections by legal process. Of course this intensified the bitter feelings between the two parties, and the Episcopal services were suspended for several years.

After the Revolution Mr. Nichols returned to New Cambridge, and the church in 1784 reorganized with twenty-nine members. Services were held by several successive rectors until 1790. In that year the parish united with the Episcopalians of Plymouth and Harwinton to build a church mid-way between the three parishes. This is still standing, and is now a mission of the Bristol church, called Plymouth

East church. The vacated church building was sold to Abel Lewis, was used by him as a barn, and was afterward destroyed by fire. Many stones are still standing, hardly decipherable.

The school-house, the second great institution of New England Puritanism, was not wanting in New Cambridge. Three years after the first incorporation as a winter society in January, 1745, a school committee was chosen "to git in the school mony," and from year to year it was voted to have a lawful school. This early school was kept during the winter only—probably in some private house. In 1749 it was "voted, that would haue a school kept in this sosiaty six mounths viz 3 mounths by a master and 3 mounths by a dame."

In 1754 the town gave liberty to build two school-houses, of which one stood east of this green, near the Roman Catholic parsonage, and the other on Chippin's Hill, thus accommodating the two principal sections of the town. In 1764 a third school-house was built, in what is now the Stafford district. Within a few years these divisions of the town had grown to five, and in 1768 a formal division and designation of the district lines was made.

These five districts may be roughly described as follows:

The house of Royce Lewis, on Maple street, lately pulled down by W. P. Stedman, was taken as a central point. All the territory north of that constituted three districts; the North, extending from the old road, now King street, a mile and a half to the west, and including everything north of that line; the Northwest, including Pine Hollow (so called in the original layout), and Chippin's Hill; and the Northeast,

THE ABEL LEWIS STORE, LATER KNOWN AS THE "STEARNS PLACE." (The windows were formerly used in the old Episcopal Church.)

From Photograph loaned by Miss C. L. Bowman.

Stafford and North Forestville. The land south of Royce Lewis's was divided into two districts, called South and Southeast, by a line drawn from Maple street over the hill to the main mountain road. The Red Stone Hill settlement was excepted from this division, and kept a school in common with Plainville.

The three school-houses already built accommodated three districts, and the South district now built one near the South grave-yard, and the North district one near the Parson Newell house. Thse divisions proved to be only temporary; Chippin's Hill was soon divided into two districts, and constant changes have been made in the number and boundaries of the districts ever since.

These early schools were not free schools in the modern sense of the term. The school-houses were built, and a part of the running expenses were paid, by the society, but each scholar paid a certain sum for tuition in addition.*7 The instruction included principally reading, spelling, writing, and ciphering, with careful training in the Westminster catechism, which was personally superintended every Saturday by Parson Newell.

The school-houses were all small, and built on the ancient model, with a bench running around three sides of the room, on which the scholars sat facing the wall for study, and which they climbed over, so as to face the centre of the room in recitation.

Our school system now includes twelve districts, emplyoing twenty-eight teachers, and paying for all ordinary expenses nearly $17,000 per annum. The recent adoption of a common course of study, the holding of common graduation exercises, and the establishment of a partial town high-school course, have done much to consolidate and benefit our educational interests.

When the French and Indian war broke out, Parson Newell urged his people to their duties in the field, and a small body of New Cambridge volunteers entered the British army and served during the war. The date of this war is so remote, and there is such a dearth of records in regard to it, that the names of the individual volunteers, or the part taken by them, have almost entirely passed beyond the reach of history. The Revolutionary war was of so much greater importance, and retained so much stronger hold on the popular memory, that the part taken by the New Cambridge settlers is a little more possible of ascertainment.

In 1774, when the enrollment of "minute men" was made, sixty-eight Farmington men signed the compact to march to the relief of Boston at a moment's warning, armed and equipped. Among these, at least four—Isaiah Thompson, Obadiah Andrews, Samuel Peck, and Wise Barnes—were New Cambridge men. A count, somewhat conjectural, and which doubtless falls below the real number, gives eighty-

---

*7.

(December 28th, 1749.)

Voted, That all the Children that ſhall enter the ſchool whether maile or female ſhall pay the ceuril* part of the charge of the ſᵈ ſchool . . . .

Voted that a ſchool ſhould be kept in this ſoſiaty untill our ſchool mony all Redy laid is ſpent or Run out

*Several.

nine New Cambridge men as having served in the Revolutionary war.[*A]
Many families sent more than one member to the field. Of these the
Allen family sent two; Andrews four; Barnes seven; Bartholomew eight,
including Abraham Bartholomew with three sons, and Jacob with two;
Gaylord three, one of whom shall be mentioned particularly hereafter;
Hotchkiss three; Hungerford two; Hart three; Jerome two; Lewis four,
of whom Lieutenant Roger Lewis left to his family his sword and canteen,
the latter of which still bears a dent made at the battle of Monmouth
Court-house; Lee two; Matthews three; Manross two, of whom Elijah,
enlisting at sixteen years of age, acted as a musician and became fife-
major; Norton two; Peck four; Roberts four, of whom Gideon, afterward our first clock-maker, with Jacob Bartholomew, became a captive
in the famous British prison-ships; Thompson three; Wilcox two; and
Warren two, sons of Elisha Warren, who, visiting his sons in camp at
Boston, contracted the small-pox, and was buried back of his house,
where the fragments of a grave-stone still remain.

Many other families were represented in the army by a single member. One New Combridge volunteer, Ira Hooker, is known to have
been a witness of the execution of Andre.

Aaron Gaylord and his family had a peculiarly distressing experience of the horrors of war. In 1775 he removed to Wyoming county
with his family. At the beginning of hostilities he was elected commander of the fort, which was scantily guarded, most of the men being
absent in the army. The fort was attacked by Indians, and against
Gaylord's judgment a sally was ordered by a council of the soldiers.
The massacre which resulted is a matter of history. The single soldier
who escaped brought back the hat of Lieutenant Gaylord, and helped
the women of the settlement to flee for their lives. Several weeks later
the wife arrived at New Cambridge, exhausted, impoverished, and
widowed. Two years later, however, she sent her only son, then fifteen
years of age, into the army.

The great national struggle, which most of us remember so distinctly, obscures in our mind the earlier and more desperate one, but
our fathers made far greater sacrifices in 1776 than did we in 1861, and
the enlistment and drafts almost stripped the hamlet of adult men.

In December, 1780, the first action was taken looking towards a
town incorporation. Committees were appointed to confer with the
West Britain society as to terms of union, and to apply to the Assembly
for an act incorporating the two societies as a town.

The people of New Cambridge meant to secure the precedence to
which their greater size entitled them, and made it a condition of the
union that New Cambridge should always be called the first society,
and should have the town sign-post within its limits. This negotiation
failed, and in 1781 it was voted "to make another tryal with West Britan."
This, was no more successful, however, and the matter was dropped
for three years.

---

* A. This list of soldiers in the Revolutionary War, who went from Bristol, was prepared with great care by Mr. Roswell Atkins.

Abel Allen, Samuel Allen, Noah Andrews, Obadiah Andrews, Joseph Andrews, Gideon
Andrews, Amos Barnes, Daniel Barnes, Thomas Barnes, Wise Barnes, Josiah Barnes,
David Barnes, Simeon Barnes, Abraham Bartholomew, Abraham Bartholomew, Jr.,
John Bartholomew, Jacob Bartholomew, Charles Bartholomew, Isaac Bartholomew,
Lemuel Bartholomew, Jacob Bartholomew, Jr., Joseph Byington, Daniel Curtis, Noadiah
Clark, Samuel Deming, Oliver Dutton, Hezekiah Gridley, Samuel Gaylord, Aaron Gaylord,
Daniel Johnson, Calvin Judd, William Lee, Samuel Lee, Josiah Lewis, Roger Lewis, Abel
Lewis, David Lewis, Caleb Mathews, Jesse Mathews, John Mathews, William Mitchell,
Elijah Manross, Theodore Manross, Timothy Mix, Joseph Norton, Ebenezer Norton
Zebulon Peck, Lament Peck, Samuel Peck, Abel Peck, Moses Parsons.

William Richards, Stephen Rowe, Gideon Roberts, David Roberts, William Roberts,
Samuel Roberts, Nehemiah Rice, Lemuel Gaylord, Josiah Holt, Stephen Hotchkiss, Lad-
wick Hotchkiss, Samuel Hotchkiss, Samuel Hickox, Ira Hooker, John Hungerford, Mathew
Hungerford, Benjamin Hart, Thomas Hart, Jason Hart, Daniel Hill, Enos Ives, William
Jerome, David Jerome, James Stoddard, Joseph Spencer, Joseph Stone, Daniel Thompson,
Josiah Thompson, Isaiah Thompson, John Thomas, Asa Upson, Elisha Warren, Abraham
Warren, Benjamin Wilcox, John Wilcox, James Wilcox, Elias Wilcox, William Wheeler

HISTORIC OAK, ON PEACEABLE STREET, WHERE EARLY TOWN MEETINGS WERE HELD.

It will interest us all, I am sure, to know that a vital point of dissension was the building of a town building, which New Cambridge desired and West Britain opposed. Truly, history repeats itself.*9

In 1784 negotiations between the two societies were renewed, and in February, 1785, a conference was had, at which the town-building plan was finally dropped, and a full agreement was reached. I think that this meeting, or some similar one, must have been held under the old oak on Peaceable street. It has long been tradition that our first town-meeting was held under this tree, but this certainly is an error. It seems natural, however, that some of the meetings of the two societies in conference might have been held there, and that such a meeting could have been confused with the formal town-meeting in the popular memory.

A petition for incorporation was drafted, signed by committees of the two societies, and sent to the Assembly which met in May, 1785. This petition was promptly granted, and the name of Bristol given to the new town. This name nowhere appears to have been suggested or asked for by the settlers; for all that can be learned to the contrary, it was selected by the General Assembly on considerations of convenience and euphony alone.

The first town-meeting was held, in obedience to the act of incorporation, June thirteenth, 1785, in the New Cambridge meeting-house, a few hundred feet from where we now stand. This first board of selectmen was then elected, consisting of Joseph Byington, Deacon Elisha Manross, and Zebulon Peck, Esq., of New Cambridge, and Simeon Hart, Esq., and Zebulon Frisbie, Jr., of West Britain.

It was voted that the selectmen should do the business free of cost

---

*9At the time of the delivery of this history, an animated contest between Bristol centre and Forestville, in which the former advocated, and the latter opposed, the erection of a town-building, had just been temporarily disposed of by indefinite postponment.

to the town. This economy was given up the next year, however, and
the selectmen were paid three shillings a day. Jacob Bartholomew
was elected treasurer, Judah Barnes collector for New Cambridge,
Abraham Bartholomew collector for West Britain.*10

The grand list of the town amounted to £17,000, and of this about
half belonged to each society. It was provided in the act of incorporation that town-meetings should be held alternately in the New Cambridge and West Britain meeting-houses, and this arrangement was
followed during the twenty-one years of the union. But the union
of two societies of so nearly equal size was productive of continual small
jealousies, and as early as 1795 the town declared its wish to be divided.
The troubles were patched up for a time, but soon broke out again.
New Cambridge appears to have claimed the right to always have three
of the five selectmen, and West Britain to have the majority of the
board taken from each society alternately. The claims of West Britain

*10.

EXTRACTS FROM THE BRISTOL TOWN RECORDS.

(June 13th, 1785, first town-meeting.)

In Compliance with, and at the direction of the General Affembly in their Bill in
form incorporating the Town of Briftol: the inhabitants of faid Town being duly
warned as ordered by the Bill to attend a Town meeting on the fecond monday of
June: Ano Domi 1785 at the meetinghoufe in New Cambridge at 9 o' the Clock in
the morning. And being fo met at Time & place, faid meeting proceeded to the
choice of a moderator and Simeon Hart Efqr was Choofen Moderator to Lead in fd
meeting at the fame meeting Jofeph Byington was Choofen Town Clerk — voted to
adjourn fd meeting to 2 o' the Clock P. M. Meeting opened according to adjourn-
ment — voted that the Selectmen Shall do the bufinefs for the Town free of coft To
the Town — Voted that Jofeph Byington Den Elifha Manrofs Zebulon Peck Efqr
Simeon Hart Efqr and Zebulon Frifbie Jr be Selectmen for the prefent year ——

- voted that Judah Barns be Conftable & Collector to gather the State Tax and account
  with the State Treafurer for the prefent year —
- voted that Capt Daniel Barns Zebulon Frifbie Jr and Seth Peck be Conftables for the
  prefent year
- voted that William Lee Benjamin Willcox Nathaniel Mathews Thomas Brooks
  Stephen Hotchkifs Jr & Capt Ichabod Andrus be Grandjuriors for the prefent
  year —
- voted that Abel Lewis Jacob Hungerford John Gaylord Noah Andrus Samuel
  Smith Othnial Mofes Jr Ezra Yale and Ambrofe Hart be Tythingmen for the
  prefent year —
- voted that Jofiah Holt Jacob Bartholomew Capt Jeffe Gaylord Amafa Hart Samll
  Hecox Dan Hill David Lewis Reuben Ives Samll Brooks Jofeph Hayford Rice
  Lewis David Marks Timothy Woodruff Blifs Hart Joel Hitchcock Capt Titus
  Bunnel Ezra Cleaveland Lemuel Potter Samuel Warner Jr and Samll Andrus be
  Surveyors of Highways for the prefent year —
- voted that Capt Thomas Hungerford Jofeph Byington Jofiah Peck Capt Ichabod
  Andrus Capt Yale & Philip M. Farnfworth be Lifters for the prefent year —
- voted that Jofiah Holt Capt Afa Upfon David Newell Seth Wiard Benjamin Belden
  and Seth Peck be a Committee to Exchange Highways & remove Neufances and
  to do it without Coft to the Town
- voted that the Selectmen . . . be a Committee to agree and Settle with the
  Town of Farmington in all matters of Claim refpecting the Two Towns —

MAIN STREET, LOOKING NORTH, IN 1873.

in this respect were generally successful, as they were able to carry the meetings held in their society.

The election of representatives to the Assembly was also a cause of rivalry, and the town tried in vain to obtain the right to send two representatives.

In 1804 the New Cambridge voters carried another resolution to have the town divided, which the West Britain meeting promptly voted to oppose. The General Assembly divided the town in May, 1806, giving the old name, Bristol, to the New Cambridge society, and calling the northern society Burlington. The organization and limits of the town of Bristol have since been substantially unchanged.

One hundred years ago this hill-top had already become a public spot. A little to the northeast of the present site stood the Congregational meeting-house, in which the town had just completed its organization, radiant in "spruce yellow" sides, white doors and windows, and "Spanish brown" roof. Across the road was the still smaller Episcopal church building, with its cemetery in the rear. Farther south stood the "Sabba'-day" houses, a most necessary institution in those days of stoveless churches; little houses belonging to different families of the congregation, where each kept a Sunday fire, and during the noon intermission filled their foot-stoves, ate their lunch, and warmed themselves for the afternoon service. These were built in the highway, by permission from the town, as early as 1754, and were still standing in the present century.

Near the head of this green were the whipping-post and stocks, neither of which, I think, was often used. Close by the whipping-post stood a tree, on which the Whigs had hanged a Tory caught at one of the meetings at Chippin's Hill, during the stormy times of the Revolution. The arrival of an early traveler, who cut down and resuscitated this man, saved the instruments of the law from being over-shadowed by the victim of popular violence.

On the east side of this green stood, probably, the school-house, then some thirty years old, which had originally served for the whole society except Chippin's Hill.

This ground itself had been already dedicated to public use, and was a militia training-ground. A company of "trainers" had been formed in 1747, of which Caleb Matthews was the first captain. Judah Barnes was afterward elected captain, and the trainings were held back of the Barnes tavern; but before the Revolution the members of the society bought this land for that purpose, and it has ever since been public ground. The principal distinction attained by the Bristol militia was a century later than the first organization, when the attempts of this company to evade training, by a succession of ingenious and successful devices, made Bristol a terror to the state officers, and finally, it is said, led to the downfall of the state militia system.

The two roads inclosing this green were already laid out, but in what condition they were it would be difficult now to tell. The road-making was then done by special tax, which one might pay, or work out, at his option, receiving in wages, if he chose to work out his tax, three shillings a day in the spring, and two in the fall, and a like amount for a yoke of cattle. Until some time after the town's incorporation the roads leading out of town were hardly better than the Indian trails which had preceded them. When the Lewis family came to Bristol, Josiah Lewis was a week in traveling from Southington with his family and goods, having to cut his way through woods, and to find a ford

* 10—Continued.

voted that Jofiah Holt Gideon Roberts & Judah Barns be rate makers for the prefent year —

voted that Rice Lewis & Zebulon Frifbie Jr be Key Keepers for ye prefent year —

voted that Capt Hez^k Gridly & Hez^k Weft be Sealers of Leather ye currant year

voted that Luke Gridly Rice Lewis Juftice Webfter and Daniel Bunnel be fence viewers for the prefent year

voted that Capt James Lee & Seth Wiard be Sealers of weights for the prefent year

voted that William Lee & Capt Ichabod Andrus be Sealers of Meafures

voted that Jacob Hungerford be infpector & packer of pot afhes

voted that Judah Barns be infpector & packer of flour for prefent year

voted that Seth Wiard be infpector & packer for the prefent year

voted to Lay one penny on the pound on the Lift 1784 payable by the firft day ot October next to the Town Treafurer for defraying the Charges of fd Town —

voted that Jacob Bartholomew be Town Treafurer for the prefent year

voted that Judah Barns be Collector for that part of the Town rate that Belongs to New Cambridge & account with the Treafurer —

voted that Abraham Pettibone Jr be Collector to Collect that part of the Town rate that Belongs to Weft Briton and account with the Town Treafurer —

voted that the Sign Poft fhall be Erected in the moft Convenient place Between the meeting houfe in N Cambridge & the Church.

voted that a white Oak tree by the pound in Weft Briton fhall be the Sign Poft thair

voted that the Swine Shall run on the Commons with a good fufficient yoke on their necks & ring in their nofes

voted to adjourn this meeting —

or make a bridge across the brooks. The turnpike, which was laid out in 1805, taught people how to make roads for the first time. Before that, "corduroying" muddy places, and removing stumps and stones to some extent, as in our cart-paths, had been all that was attempted on most of the roads.

The opening of the Abel Lewis tavern, in 1794, in the house now occupied by Miss Stearns, completed the quartette of public buildings —meeting-house, church, school, and tavern—and made this green a well-equipped village centre.

The number of taverns which were then kept is one of the curiosities of the time. Ebenezer Barnes had very early begun to keep a tavern, and when the Pierce family bought the Barnes house in 1795, they continued the business. About 1750, Zebulon Peck opened a second tavern near the old Brownson house. At the beginning of this century there were in Bistol, besides the old Pierce tavern, and the Lewis tavern just mentioned, one on Fall Mountain, kept by Joel Norton, one on West street, kept by Austin Bishop, a deacon of the Baptist church, one at Lewis's corner, by widow Thompson, one at Parson Newell's former residence, the Dr. Pardee place, by his son's widow, one on Chippin's Hill, by Lemuel Carrington, one in the north part of the town, by Asa Bartholomew, and possibly others. Each one of these had its pole and sign, consisting of a tin ball with decanter, foot-glass and punch-bowl painted thereon. Their principal business was the supply of liquor to the neighbors, and probably only one or two of them exceeded the lawful requirements for the entertainment of travelers, namely, one spare bed and stable-room for two horses.

They supplied in some degree the place not only of our hotel and eating-houses, but of clubs, newspapers, and postoffice, for not even a weekly mail came nearer than Farmington till 1800, and what little general news ever reached the town was circulated by the nightly gatherings at the taverns. The Bartholomew tavern ("Barthomy tavern" as it was called), was the most important one, situated as it was midway between the two societies, and there the meetings of town officers were generally held, and much of the public business was done.

My limit of time and your limit of patience must greatly condense this sketch as to the history of the century which has elapsed since the town's incorporation. The building of the stage-route, and the estab-

* 10—Continued.

(November 12th, 1787.)

At a meeting of the Inhabitants of the Town of Briſtol Aſſembled by ſpecial Reſolve of the General Aſſembly on the 12th day of November AD 1787 for the purpoſe of Chooſing a Delegate to ſet in Convention in the City of Hartford on the firſt Thirſday in January next to Ratify and aſſent to the Conſtitution propoſed by the Delegates of the United States Lately Aſſembled in the City of Philadelphia—

Simeon Hart Eſqr Choſen Moderater to Lead in ſd Meeting

Zebulon Peck Jr Eſqr Choſen Delegate by the major part of the members preſent . . . voted to Ratify the Conſtitution propoſed by the Convention of Delegates from the United States Lately Aſſembled at the City of Philadelphia by a Majority as Eight is to five nearly of the members preſent

(December 14th, 1789.)

Voted, that the Overſeers ſhall alow three ſhillings a Day per man for Labour in mending the rodes in the ſpring & two ſhillings per day in the fall of the year—

MAIN STREET, LOOKING SOUTH, IN 1873.

lishment of a weekly mail, about 1800, which fixed the business centre at the north side, the building of the railroad in 1850, which changed the business centre again to the south side, the establishment of the Baptist, Episcopal, Methodist, Roman Catholic, and Adventist churches, the settlement and growth of the village of Forestville, and the establishment and steady development of our clock and other manufacturing interests, have been the principal features of this history.

The Baptist church has the oldest continuous history of any except the Congregational. In 1791 the Baptists of Bristol, Wolcott, and Plymouth united to organize a church, and for eleven years meetings were held in the three societies alternately. Elder White Osborne was the first pastor, then Isaac Root and Daniel Wildman. In 1802 this church built a meeting-house on West street, forty-two feet by thirty-two. This building is now a part of the Barnes Brothers clock factories. The church still standing on the old site was built in 1830, and the handsome brick one on School street in 1880.

* 10—Continued.

(April 8th, 1793.)

Voted to Set up the Onockeolation * in Each Society of fd Briftol in the month of September next under the Enftruktion of the Civil Authority and Selectmen of fd Town they procuring Surficient Bonds to prevent the Enfection Spreding among the Inhabitants of fd Town the naturel way —

THE DANIEL ROBERTS HOUSE, ON WEST STREET. THIS IS THE OLDEST HOUSE ON THE STREET, BEING BUILT IN 1783. SINCE REMODELLED AND NOW KNOWN AS THE SETH BARNES PLACE. (See page 45.)

The early history of this church included a curious contest with the supernatural powers. A witchcraft excitement of very considerable extent broke out in the town, and Elder Wildman, Deacon Dutton, and others of that church became the especial victims of the evil deeds which tradition has reported. Elder Wildman boldly invited to his house, and tried to cure, a girl who had been afflicted by witches, and, as the story goes, was not only unsuccessful, but was grievously tormented himself. Deacon Dutton's ox was bodily torn in pieces before his eyes, after he had uttered some expression of unbelief, and others on West

* 10—Continued.

(April 13th, 1795.)

this meeting haveing taken into confideration a Bill Paffed in October Laft by the Honorable Upperhoufe directing that Application of the monies that fhall arife from the fale of the Weftern Lands belonging to this State which bill was continued and ordered to be printted by the Honorable General Affembly and having confidered the Great advantages which may be Derived to the community by promoting moral and religious Inftruction and a liberal Support of fchools of education — Voted unanimoufly that this meeting Do fully approve of the mode propofed in and by faid Bill for the Application of faid monies and in this Method do manifeft a Defire that the faid bill may meet the concurance of the Honorable Lower-houfe in may next

THE SETH BARNES PLACE IN 1907.

street and Fall Mountain told marvelous tales of demoniac possession. This witchcraft excitement was begun and kept up by a young man named King, who was studying for the ministry with Elder Wildman. On his departure, the activity of the evil spirits ceased.

The present Episcopal society was organized in 1834 with twelve members. Services were held at first in the Congregational and Baptist chapels. In 1835 the Reverend George C. V. Eastman was settled, and a church built on Maple street. This was occupied until 1863, when they moved to the Main street church which they now occupy, and sold their old building to the Forestville Methodist society.

The Methodist Episcopal church was organized in April, 1834, and meetings were held for a while in the West street school-house. Great hostility was felt toward this church by the other religious bodies, and they could only buy land for their meeting-house by concealing the purpose for which it was intended. They completed a meeting-house on West street in 1837, which they vacated for their present Summer street church in 1880. The Reverend Albert G. Wickware was the first pastor, and the church at organization had twenty-seven members.

* 10—Continued.

(May 5th, 1796.)

Voted, that the Treaty between the united States of America and Great Britton be put into full Efect by a unanamus Vote not a Defenting vote —

Voted to Prefer a memorial to Congrefs in favour of Retifiing the Treaty between the Britannic Majefty & the United States of America — with but one Defenting vote —

Voted that the Town Clerk Shall make a Copy of the memorial and Send it to Hartford to put it into the Publick Prints —

The Forestville Methodist church was formed in 1855, and in 1864 bought the Maple street Episcopal church building, which they still use.

The first Roman Catholic services were held about 1840, near the north copper mine, by missionaries from other parishes, to accommodate the workmen there. When the mine was abandoned, and railroad work began, many of the workmen moved to Bristol centre, and the services of the church followed them. In 1855 a church building was erected though the parish was still a missionary one. It was made an independent parish in 1866, and the Reverend M. B. Roddan, who is still its pastor, began his labors.

Occasional services were held in town from 1842 to 1858, by Adventist preachers. In the latter year a church was organized, and in 1880 they bought the old Methodist church building, and began to employ a regular pastor.

The people of Bristol early began to develop the mechanical taste which has been so remarkable a feature of the town ever since. Even before the beginning of the clock business, small shops in various parts of the town were making goods for the towns-people, and to some extent for market.

A grist-mill, that necessary incident of a farming community, had been started by Deacon Hezekiah Rew before 1745, near the Barnes tavern. This was sold to Joseph Adkins, who built a saw-mill at the same place, and afterward sold them both to the Barnes family. Mr. Adkins also built a mill on what is now the Downs site.

A distillery, saw-mill, and grist-mill were also running in Polkville in the early part of this century on the Bartholomew site, but were probably started half a century later than the Barnes mill.

Tin-shops were especially numerous, both in Bristol and in North Forestville, and I suppose that the huge tin-carts were then our principal medium of export trade.

William and Thomas Mitchell early made cloths, it is said in a shop near Goose Corner. It seems very likely that this family owned the

THE OLD DOWNS' MILL, ON RIVERSIDE AVENUE.

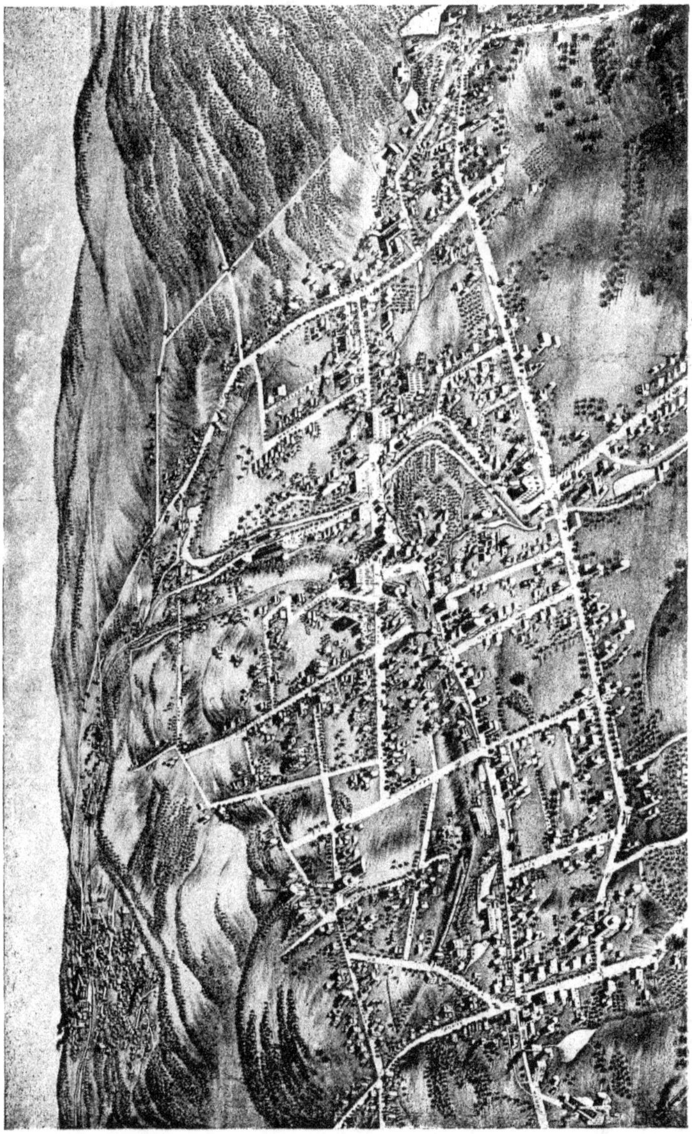

BIRDSEYE VIEW OF BRISTOL IN 1871.

cotton factory at the north side, which was afterward used in the clock business by George Mitchell, and is now used by the Ingraham Company. Another cloth mill stood on the river, near the Barnes tavern. William Mitchell was one of the first makers of cloth in America.

An account-book is still in existence of the tannery business carried on by Jabez Roberts from 1761 to 1770, in a shop near Albert Warner's, and Zebulon Frisbie probably built, during this period, the old tannery building still standing, long unused, on West street.

Before the town's incorporation a partnership built a forge at the falls on the Terryville road, where scrap iron, and iron from the ore, was puddled and wrought for use. The original plan of this company was to extract and use the iron ore found at this locality, but, though abundant, it was found to be too brittle for use, and the experiment was finally abandoned.

Other small shops were early established, but, as the clock business developed, all the capital and skill of the town was drawn into that. The pioneer of clock making in Bristol, and indeed in this country, was Gideon Roberts, who lived in what is now the town house, on Fall Mountain, and began in a crude way before 1790 to make clocks. His clocks were made entirely with hand tools at first, and peddled by him about

* 10—Continued.

(April 10th, 1797.)

Voted, that the Onoceolation * of the enfection of the Small Pox may be Set up in Briftol under the enftruction of the Civil Authority and Selrctmen of fd Town & During the pleafure of the fd Town —

* Inoculation.

(December 13th, 1802.)

Voted that the Inhabitants of this Town Make up their Nomanations for Town Officers in Each Society in Open School Society meeting anually for the futer —

[This seems to indicate that each society commonly presented its own "ticket" for town officers.]

(May 21st, 1804.)

Voted that Col'n Abraham Pettibone John Fuller Jeremiah Grifwold Jeffe Fuller Giles Humphrey and Job Mills be a Committee to Draw the Remains of the New bridge socalled back to the place where it was Carried from by the late flood Either by a Spell or any other way as they think beft —

(May 24th, 1804.)

Voted that Blifs Hart Bryan Hooker Efqr and David Marks be a Commttee to make a Draught of by Laws Refpecting Hogs Sheep Geefe turkies &c. going at Large and make Report to Sum Futer meeting —

(June 16th, 1806.)

Voted, that thofe who go to work on the County road next monday fhall have it difcounted on their tax provided that one fhould be laid for the purpofe of makeing fd road —

Voted, the felect Men fhall provide liquor on fd day at the expenfe of the Town —

FORMERLY THE NORTH SIDE TAVERN.

the country on horseback; after his sons grew up his business was increased, so that at one time in 1812 he had four hundred movements in process of manufacture, and his goods found a regular market, especially in the South. He became well off, is said to have owned the first chaise used here, and left a considerable property. During the latter part of his life he was known as a Quaker, and wore the garb of that society. Some of his clocks are still in existence in this neighborhood. Like all other clocks of this early period, they were made to hang on the wall; and at a later date were put into the familiar tall cases.

Joseph Ives began making clocks about 1811 at the Laporte Hubbell site in East Bristol, and, soon after, he and his brothers started small shops, one on Peaceable street, one on the brook near the Noah Pomeroy site, and one near the Dunbar spring-shop site. In this latter he made a clumsy metal clock of his own invention. Dunbar and Merriman were also located on the Pomeroy brook during this decade. About 1813, Chauncey Boardman, in a little shop still to be seen near Ashworth's factory in North Forestville, began making clocks of the primitive wall pattern.

The invention of the shelf clock, by Eli Terry of Plymouth, prostrated the trade in the long clocks that were made here, and our makers all stopped business about 1820. They soon adopted the new pattern, however, and during the score of years before the panic of 1837, the first Jerome factory, on the spoon-shop site, the Samuel Terry factory, farther east, south of the river, where the Bristol Brass and Clock Company's dam now crosses it, the Eureka shop, built by a large partnership, the Bartholomew factory in Polkville, the Burwell shop, built by Charles Kirk, the old Baptist Church building, converted into a factory by Rollin and Irenus Atkins, the Ephraim Downs shop, on the "Bone and Ivory" site, and the George Mitchell factory, which, originally the West Britain meeting-house, then moved to Bristol for a cottonmill, is now a part of the Ingraham case shop, were all occupied in the making of wooden thirty-hour clocks, or expensive brass eight-day clocks.

In this Mitchell factory Mr. Elias Ingraham, the founder and head of the E. Ingraham Company, learned the clock trade.

These factories, with the older ones, and the three at Forestville, were making in 1836 nearly one hundred thousand brass and wooden clocks a year.

The completion of the Farmington canal in 1826, by greatly increasing the facilities for transportation, had been a great assistance to our local prosperity. Before this all goods had to be hauled to and from Hartford or New Haven in horse-teams. These facilities were further increased in 1850 by the opening of the railroad. The panic of 1837 generally prostrated business, but the invention of the small brass one-day clock by Mr. Chauncey Jerome revived it on a stronger basis than before. Mr. Jerome himself sent an agent to England, established a market there, enlarged his business, and in 1843 built two large factories, one on each side of Main street just below the bridge. Both these factories, and the Terry factory, the three largest in town, were burned in 1845, and Mr. Jerome moved his business to New Haven. But his cheap brass clocks had given an impetus to business which lasted until the great panic of 1857. Then almost every clock-maker in town failed, or suspended business. Since the revival of prosperity which

* 10—Continued.

EXTRACTS FROM THE NEW CAMBRIDGE SOCIETY RECORDS.

(October 14th, 1742 : — First society meeting.)

At a general Affembly holden at New hauen octob'r 14 1742 they granted us ye memorail of farmington firſt ſofiaty liueing in the ſouthweſt part of ſd ſofiaty Beginning at the ſecond third fourth fifth and ſixth diuiſions of land to begin at the ſouth end of ſd diuifion and to extend fiue miles North a liberty of Winter preuiledges to hire an othurdox miniſter to preach amongſt us ſix mounths

it being Neſſeary for us to Chooſe ſutabel men to cary on our Neſſeary Concerns

We haue at a ſofiaty by legal Warning on the Eighth day of Nouember in the year 1742 Maid Choice of thoſe offercers as foloweth

firſt we uoited* maid Choice of Ebnezer Barns for our Moderater furthermore at the ſame meeting they maid Choice of moſes Lyman to be their ſofiaty Clark

At the ſame meeting they maid Choice of edward galord Neimaah manroſs and ebnezer hamblin to be their Commitee for their ſofiaty concerns

At the ſame meeting maid choice of Samuil gaylord a Collecter to Colect their mineſter Rate

At the ſame metting they maid choice of John hikox for our ſofiaty Treſurer

At the ſame Meeting they paſt by Voite that we Will hire preaching as long as the Court has giuen us Liberty

At the ſame Meeting we paſt by Voite that we Would meet at John browns for the Winter ſeaſon for the preſnt

At the ſame Meeting We Voted that any two of the Comitee ſigning of the bills of Charge going in or Coming out ſhall be ſufiſint

(January 28th, 1744⅓.)

At the ſame meeting Neamiah Manros Caleb Abernathy and famil. gaylord choſen School Commitee and to take care to git in the ſchool mony

At the ſame meeting it was Voted that our ſofiaty meeting ſhould for the futer be warnd by notifications ſet up in writeing one at the tavern door one at daniel Roes ſhoop and another at the door of the corn mill

---

* voted.

MAIN STREET—LOOKING SOUTH—IN 1906.

followed, the business of our clock factories has gone, on, with no such crushing disaster as came in 1837 and again in 1857.

The Joseph Ives shop in Forestville, which has been mentioned, was afterwards occupied in making small wooden articles, and finally in making clock-parts by Elisha Manross. He built in 1845 the factory near the railroad, which was burned and replaced by the Welch and Spring movement-shop in 1870. Hendricks, Barnes and Company went into the old Ives shop, and made there the first marine clocks ever made. This location, after several changes, passed into the hands of Laporte Hubbell, who is still manufacturing in a new building on the same site. Soon after 1820, Chauncey Boardman and Joseph Wells built a factory in North Forestville, near the turnpike. This was one of the most important factories of that time.

Fifty years ago, besides the old houses on the turnpike, and a little settlement near the Boardman and Wells shop, there were only about a dozen houses in Forestville, and the neighborhood of the station and of the Welch Company's factories was still unbroken forest. In 1835, William Hills, J. C. Brown, Jared Goodrich, Lora Waters, and Chauncey Pomeroy built a factory, and began work where the Welch company is now located. Mr. Hills built a house on the south side of the river, and Eli Barnes on the north side, in the same year. The name Forestville, which has been already used by anticipation in this address, was then selected for the locality; so that this centennial year of the town is also the semi-centennial of the village of Forestville. Mr. Brown bought out the rest of this firm, and in 1853 built what is still called the J. C. Brown shop. Upon his failure, this passed to Mr. Welch, and from him to the E. N. Welch Manufacturing Company, organized in 1864, now our largest clock-makers.

After the panic of 1837, there was a general feeling that our investments had been too rigidly confined to one line of business, and the result has been the gradual establishment of hardware, woolen, and other factories, which now nearly or quite equal the clock business in importance. The Bristol Manufacturing Company, formed in 1837, the Bristol Brass and Clock Company, founded in 1850, and now doing, in its three factories, the largest business of any manufacturer in town, J. H. Sessions and Son, whose business was begun in 1869, and the Sessions Foundry Company, organized in 1878, N. L. Birge and Son, the Dunbar Brothers, Wallace Barnes, the Roots, Bartholomews, Warners, and other smaller concerns, engaged in various kinds of manufacture, give our prosperity a far more solid basis than it could have in the growth of any single business. There are now about thirty factories in town, many of them of considerable size, making in the aggregate nearly or quite three million dollars' worth of goods annually, sending and receiving by the railroad over thirty-five thousand tons of freight, giving the direct means of support to two-thirds of the inhabitants, and creating a ready market for all the produce our farmers can raise.

* 10—Continued.

(March 14th, 1745.)

At the fame meeting it was Voted that Bills of Publick Credit of the old tener fhould pafs or be ftated at thurty two fhiling per ounce in filuer

At the fame meeting it was Voted that meafuyers fhould be taken in order to our being fet off for Training

(May 17th, 1745.)

At the fame meeting more then two thirds of the fofiaty declard be their Vote they Would build a meeting houfe as foon as with Conueniancy may be

At the fame meeting Mofes lyman was Chofen our agent to Peition to the general Affembly for a commitee to ftate the place for the meeting house

(July 2d, 1747.)

At the fame meeting it was uoted that we will giue mr famll newel for fettelment as followeth one hundred pound in half a year and one hundred pound more at the years end and one hundred pound the fecond year and two hundred pound the third year to be paid one half in mony of the old tener and the other half in prouifion pay if he will fettel with us in the gofpel mineftry

(January 16th, 1748⅜.)

uoted that our Collectors fhall Collect the Rates of them thofe that call themfelues of the Church of england amongft us and we will defend them

(December 4th, 1749.)

Voted that Thomas hart fhould haue his bill of Charges with Refpect to his Colecting the minifteral Rate of those that yt Call themfelues Churchman amongft us as it was laid before the fofiaty

SOLDIERS' MONUMENT—ONE OF THE FIRST TO BE ERECTED IN THE NORTH

The civil war, and the part taken in that contest by this town, are too recent to need any detailed mention. To most of you that period is not a thing of history, but of memory. I will only say that of the early Connecticut regiments there were Bristol men in nearly every one, and during the first year of the war over one hundred enlisted. Company B of the Fifth, and C of the Fifteenth, contained little bodies of Bristol men, and companies K of the Sixteenth, and I of the Twenty-fifth, were principally made up from here. Many of our soldiers fought through the entire war, and entered Richmond with Grant at the close: many died in battle, or by disease,

* 10—Continued.

(December 12th, 1750.)

Jofeph Benton de† hez Rew was Chofen prifers to prife mr Newl wood at his house

† deacon.

'omen fhall fit togather in the pews in the meeting houfe

(December 3rd, 1753.)

Voted to ad to mr newels Rate on hundred pound mony of the old tenei prouided he will find himfelf with firewood

Voted to fend a pition to the general Affembly next may for the mony or the uefe of the mony norfolk is to be fold for to fuport of fchooling amongft us and other yong fofiatys if they will joyn with us

deⁿ ftephen Barns Benjamin hungerford and Capt galord was Chofen to dignify the meting houfe and Zebulon peck thomas hart and de dauid gaylord was Chofen featers to feat the meeting houfe

and were buried in unknown graves; the large body who belonged to Company K of the Sixteenth had almost a harder experience than either for after two years' service they were captured at Plymouth, N. C., and sent to Andersonville prison; and there, or in other prisons, there died twenty-four of the original seventy-four who had gone out with the company.

The entire number of enlistments credited to this town's quota was three hundred and eighty-seven. Deducting re-enlistments and non-resident substitutes, the number of separate men, resident here, who entered the service cannot have been less than two hundred and fifty. Of these, fifty-four, over one-fifth, died in the service; sixteen of wounds in battle, twelve of disease, two at sea, and twenty-four of the unspeakable horrors of Andersonville, Florence, and Libby prisons.

When the war was nearly over, the grief of our citizens at these severe losses, and their respect for the memory of their slain townsmen, found expression in the building of our soldiers' monument, which was completed in 1865, one of the very first in the country.

Another notable monument, in the Forestville cemetery, is the tribute paid by Amherst students to their Professor, Newton S. Manross

* 10—Continued

(December 17th, 1753.)

Voted that the pews next the pulpit fhould be the firft in the dignification the firft feat and the 2 pews next the gret door the 2 the 2 feat and the 2 piler pews the third the corner pews the fourth the light pews the 5 the 2 pews under the ftars the 6 ———

At A fofiaty meten holden on jeaneury ye 12 : in y^u year 1767 at the meten hous hezekiah griddelye afq was chofen mooddrater thomas hart m^t robbard cogfwell Afa upfon was chofn commitee to A juft the Acounts with the tax gather and Like wife to in speét & ajuft the acounts with the formor collectrs and commitey and fettel y^u fofieatys acount with euery own

uoted to meet on ye faborth days at ten a cloock in ye morning and ye inter mifhon is to be but own our from this time to ye fuft of march nex

the above meeten was befolued by a uoot *

at the above meete notted uneafesnefs with the committies doouings

(September 25th, 1769, in the matter of the second meeting-house.)

Voted to get the flore Bords and Roof Bords amoung our felves

Voted to get the singles amoung our felves

Voted that En : Samuel Adams fhall Cull and pafs his Judgment upon the fingles that are Brought for the Meeting houfe whether they are fit for fuch houfe

Voted to Give 4 pence hapeny p^r foot for all the Hewed timber Great and Small for the above f^d meeting houfe Delivered at the place where f^d houfe is to be Built Good timber Hewed fit for fuch Building

* Vote.

(May 17th, 1770.)

Voted to Raife our Meeting houfe By a free-will offering ' and was Chofen Liew Jofiah Lewis Lieu Ebn : Barns Rachel Barns wid : Afahel Barns Ens Gerfhom tuttle Samuel Brockway Royce Lewis to keep publick entertainment in the time wee are Raifing our Meeting houfe

who enlisted with the Sixteenth, was elected the first Captain of Company K, and fell at the head of his company, at the first meeting with the enemy.

In 1785, the grand list of the town was	$83,309.27
In 1797, this had decreased to	61,715.38
And in 1806, still further to	54,446.52

A corresponding decrease in population took place during the same period. The division of the town in 1806 divided nearly in halves both property and population, and a loss even from that is shown by the census of 1820. Then, it will be remembered, began the especial development of the clock business, and from that time the town has steadily increased in population, and more rapidly in wealth. The increase reported by the census during the decade from 1870 to 1880, from 3,788 to 5,347, was over forty per cent., a gain equaled by very few Connecti-

* 10—Continued.

(August 7th, 1770)

Voted to Colour our new meeting houfe

Voted to Colour the above f'' meeting houfe viz : the Body of f'' houfe fpruce yellow and the Dores and windows of faid houfe white

Voted to Colour the Roof of our new meeting houfe Spanifh Brown

(December 3'd, 1770.)

Voted that the Meeting houfe Committy fhall give £o=3=6 p' Gallon for the rum they had of the fociety.

(December 6th, 1773.)

Voted that the Society fhall take the Land that was purchafed for a place of perade fouth of the Meeting houfe and pay to thofe that Bought f'' Land the fum of ten pounds two fhillings And Set f'' Land by for the Benefit of the fociety of New Cambridge

The above f'' vote is Detefted by Lieutn' Jofiah Lewis Ifaac hall Abraham Bertholomew Eli Lewis David Newell tim Mix Jacob Bertholomew Royce Lewis Ben willcox Jofiah Lewis Jnr abel Lewis Jofeph Row Seth Roberts Samuel Lewis

* Not an offering of money, but of labor

(March 16th, 1789)

voted that all Town Meetings that Shall happen out of the anual Courfe of the year fhall be warned by the Selectmens Seting up Notifications on the Publick fign Pofts in fd Town, and on the feveral Doors of the Tavernkeepers and griftmills in fd Town of Briftol

July 4th, 1776.

American Independence Was Declared by the General Congrefs

cut towns. Since 1880, we believe that this rate of growth has been fully maintained, and that the town has now more than six thousand inhabitants. This increase of population since 1870 has been accompanied by a marked development of the town; the two banks have been organized, the two newspapers started, most of our important business buildings erected, many business and residence streets laid out, and the general appearance of the town strikingly changed.

The record which we look back upon today is not one glittering with brilliant deeds, nor made illustrious by great names. But our fathers, with the honest, rugged virtues, that made early New England an unique power in the world, have laid for us a good foundation. Industry, integrity, wise conservatism of thought, the reverent fear of God, are

* 10—Continued.

(December 6th, 1779.)

Voted that the People be at their own Liberty to pay mr Newels Rate Either in Silver or Continental money Viz if in Silver their Equal part of 65£ * and if in this Courancy their Equal part of 1300£

April 12 1780 Southington these may Certify all whom it may Concern that Jacob Lindsly of New Cambridge is a member of the Baptist Society in Southington & Contributes to the Necessary Charges thereof & it is Desired he may not be Called upon Elswhere which is acording to law as

Witness my hand Stephen Gorton Elder

(April 15th, 1782.)

Voted that it is the Desire & request of this Parish that the Gen'l Asembly should apoint a Justice of the Peace in the Parish of N Cambridge at their Next Seshons

---

* £65 in silver had some time before been agreed on as an equivalent for the £300 promised in "old tenor" bills.

(December 7th, 1778.)

Voted that the Societies Comittee be impowered to Deal out the Salt that belongs to this Parish now in the hands of Dean Manross to the widows of Souldiers & other needy Widows & such other Needy persons as they shall think best

New Cambridge Decbr 1 1779

Altho the Society of New Cambridge as a Society have not rendered to me what was Justly Due by Covenant Febry 12 78 & Febry 12 79 yet a Number have been Just & Generous another Number have done Something Considerable a Considerable Number have done but a Small matter towards Justice   yet to prevent trouble in the present world I Do Give a free Discharge to sd Society for what was Due to me for my service at the two above named Periods & Refer them to the Last tribunal where impartial Justice will be Enquired after

Sam'l Newell

deeply implanted in the rocky soil of this hill. Let not this generation depart from these. Old-fashioned manners are disappearing; let not old-fashioned virtues also disappear. Let not the increase of our material prosperity produce, nor accompany, a decrease of intellectual or moral worth.

We cannot but wonder what will be the history read at our next Centennial Celebration, when the telegraph and telephone are crude curiosities for a loan exhibition, when the Great Rebellion is as remote to the thought as is the Revolution now, when perhaps our acts, and words, and names shall seem as quaint and antique as our fathers' seem now, when perhaps our thirty factories, and six thousand people, our churches, and schools, and institutions of every kind, shall be as petty and strange as the New Cambridge life is to us.

* 10—Continued.

(May 20th, 1782.)

At a Society meting of the inhabitants of the Parish of N Cambridge Legally warned for the Purpose of Nominating a man for a Juftice of the peace in sd parish & holden at the meeting house on the 20th of may A D 1782

Voted that the method for Nominating a perfon for sd ofice shall be by Each Giving in for the man that he would Nominate with his Name fairly written

The Nomination being brought in & Counted of as aforesd it apears that they were found in the following maner

Deacn Zebulon Peck	50
Lt Joseph Byington	22
Capt Nath Jones	2
Thomas Hart	1
Capt Afa upfon	1
Luke Gridley	1
James Lee	1
Benjamin Lindsly	1

INDENTURE OF SLAVE GIRL.

This indentor witnesseth, that I the widow Abigail Deming of Farmington in the County of Hartford & Colony of Conneticut in New England do Bind one Certain Negro Girl of nine years of age Named Silpah an apprentice to my son William Jearom of the Town & County affore-sd for and Duering the whole term of time of Sixteen years all of which sd term She the sd Silpah Shall faithfully Serve her Mafter & miftrefs in all their Lawfull Commands not abfenting from their bufinefs by night nor by Day their Secrets keep their Commands obey & behave in all points faithfully as a good Servant aught to do duering the whole term of sd time———

and all of which time her sd mafter is to provide for her in Sicknefs and health according to her Dignety & at the End of the above-sd Term her sd mafter is to give her two good Sutes of apparel fiting to all parts of her Body and for the well & faithfully executing this obligation we Set our hands and Seals this 22nd of June AD. 1771.

in prefence of us

Jofeph Byintun   Abigail Deming   [SEAL.]
Temporence Jearom   William Jearom   [SEAL.]

BLANKET, SPUN, DYED AND WOVEN BY ABIGAIL PECK, WHO SHOT THE LAST BEAR SEEN IN BRISTOL. LOANED BY MISS M. A. CARPENTER.

ABIGAIL PECK, "THE BEAR GIRL."

BY ALICE M. BARTHOLOMEW.

One summer Sabbath in seventeen hundred and forty-eight or nine, a bear came down Wolcott Mountain to the cornfields near Goose Corner.

There it was seen by the twelve year old daughter of Deacon Zebulon Peck, who was caring for her younger brothers and sisters, and preparing the family dinner, while the parents attended divine service.

The brother, younger, and Abigail, both wished to shoot it; but age and deputed authority won for her the distinction.

Later she married Hezekiah Gridley, Jr., who was captain of the Bristol militia during the Revolution, and led his men to New Haven to assist in repulsing General Tryon.

Their daughter, Abigail Gridley, wove the blue and white blanket seen on page 59.

It is of wool and linen in the "Double Bow-knot" pattern.

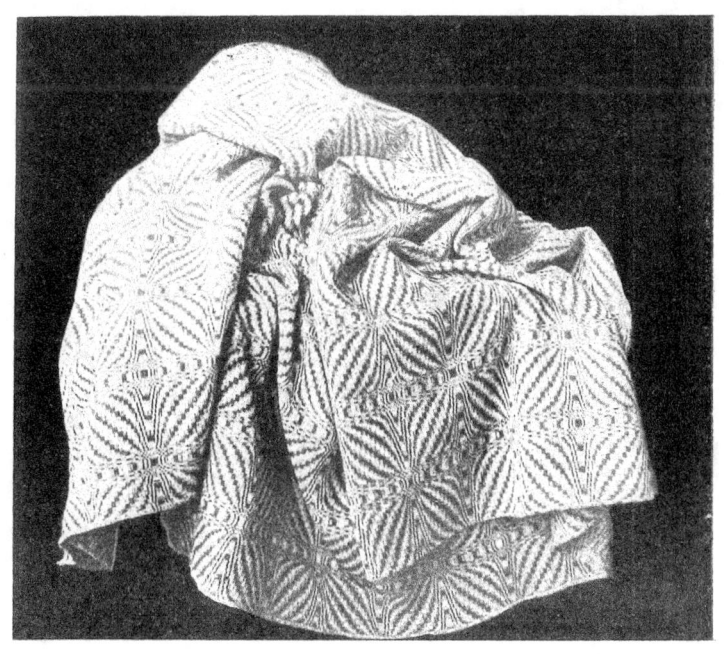

BLUE AND WHITE BLANKET WOVEN BY ABIGAIL GRIDLEY, OWNED BY MISS ALICE M. BARTHOLOMEW.

Katherine Gaylord, Heroine.

FIRST PRIZE, BIOGRAPHICAL SKETCH
NATIONAL SOCIETY
DAUGHTERS OF THE AMERICAN
REVOLUTION.

DEDICATED TO
KATHERINE GAYLORD CHAPTER.

BRISTOL, CONNECTICUT.

Written and Illustrated*
BY
FLORENCE E. D. MUZZY,
Organizing Regent.

---

* We regret that the limited space will not permit the reproduction of Mrs. Muzzy's charming illustrations that appeared in the original.

KATHERINE GAYLORD,
HEROINE.

BEAUTIFUL Wyoming—fair Wyoming! Not iron-bound, like these rocky New England shores; but smooth and fertile—easy to till, rich in harvest! Come, let us go!

How often, may we believe, did Katherine Gaylord listen to these and like persuasions before she could bring herself to say: "Whither thou goest, I will go!" and to leave the loved, rock-bound New England for the lovely but fearsome home in the wilderness. It could not have been an easy thing to do, for "only he is strong whose strength is tried," and the time had not yet come to prove her mettle.

The tale of much contention for this most desirable abiding place is oft-told. Over its beautiful woods and streams hovered an atmosphere of strife and hate. The aborigines fought for it among themselves, and when the white man came, fought for it with him.

Later, untrustworthy Indian sales, and ignorant, invalid grants by Royalty added to the confusion of property rights. Finally the country came to be claimed at one and the same time, by the Six Nations, Pennsylvania and Connecticut.

In 1768, Connecticut formed here a town, calling it by the suggestive name of Westmoreland.

This was divided into townships five miles square, each to be given to "forty" settlers who should agree to remain there, improve and protect the property. The first forty arrived in 1769 at Wyoming (called by the red man "Waugh-wau-wame," shortened by the white into "Wau-wame," and anglicized later into Wyoming).

In 1770 the forty began the famous "Forty Fort" at Kingston township, Westmoreland, but were interrupted by the Pennamite war. Five times were the Yankees expelled by the Pennsylvanians, and five times came back with true Yankee grit to "man their rights." The completion of Forty Fort followed the cessation of hostilities. This was built of upright timbers, closely set. A row of cabins, many of them containing several rooms, was ranged against the timbers within; while again within this circle of homes was an open space or parade large enough for the drilling of an entire company. In one of these cabins Katherine Gaylord had afterward a home.

The fort held one store, and a mill, consisting of a samp-mortar made of a burned log, with a pestle worked by a spring-pole. Before 1773, Westmoreland had called a minister, and a doctor had migrated thither. A tax was laid to support free schools; a land office was established, and military organization not neglected. The soil was prolific, sheep and cattle plentiful, food and clothing abundant. Peace seemed at last to brood over the beautiful valley, while back in New England the war-cloud hung low. No wonder one "Forty" followed another so rapidly.

In April-May, 1775, Katherine Gaylord, in her Connecticut home saw her husband, at the call for troops after Lexington Alarm, march to the front—Boston and vicinity. Detachments of the brigade to which Aaron Gaylord belonged took part in the battle of Bunker Hill. It is probable that he was among them, as he was afterwards appointed to

NOTE BY THE AUTHOR.

THE story of Katherine Gaylord, as here given, has been carefully compiled from every available source, in the attempt to present under one cover as complete and accurate an account as possible of this tragedy of the American Revolution. Dealing especially with Katherine Gaylord, Heroine, and the events with which she had personal connection, its scope must necessarily be historical and biographical, rather than genealogical. The Gaylord history shows the descent of Aaron Gaylord from William, who came to New England 1629–30.

The line of Katherine Cole Gaylord, from Henry Cole, is briefly traced as follows, by Mr. Milo Leon Norton:

1. Henry Cole, of Sandwich, Massachusetts (on Cape Cod), moved to Middletown, Connecticut, in 1643; married Sarah Ruscoe, 1646; had 4 children; removed to Wallingford, Connecticut, where he died 1676; Sarah Ruscoe Cole died in Saybrook, Connecticut, 1688.

2. William, youngest son of Henry Cole, born 1658; married Sarah ———, and lived in Wallingford.

3. James, son of William Cole, born March 7, 1707, in Wallingford; married Catherine Wood, of Windsor, Connecticut, January 20, 1742; lived in Harwinton and in New Cambridge, Connecticut; died in New Cambridge, September 16, 1803. He is often mentioned on the records.

4. Katherine Cole was born in Harwinton, Connecticut, November 28, 1745; her birth is given upon the Harwinton records as "Catheren," daughter of James and Catheren; and we find the name variously spelled, Catherine, Katherine and Caty. The Daughters of the American Revolution, upon the adoption of the name, voted also to adopt the spelling already put in print by her descendants, and to use the name Katherine. She married Aaron Gaylord about 1763; lived, after her marriage, at "New Cambridge in Farmington," now Bristol; moved to Wyoming Valley, Pennsylvania; returned to New Cambridge; and finally moved to Burlington, Connecticut, where she died, 1840, leaving three children, Lemuel, Phebe and Lorena. Nearly all of the facts concerning Katherine's life have come to us through the descendants of Lorena. A little was learned from Mrs. Sylvia Kirkpatrick, descendant of Lemuel; and an item or two from Mr. W. E. Frisbie, descendant of Phebe; otherwise, all facts come from the family and friends now residing in that part of the country where the last days of the heroine were spent.

Two of the descendants of Lorena, Mrs. Mary P. M. Brooks and Mrs. Helen M. B. Potter, have written personal recollections of the tale, as told them by their grandmother. The record of Mrs. Brooks is in print [see "Gaylord-Wyoming"] and it was from this, first of all, that the Katherine Gaylord Chapter, proved the worth of their heroine when her name was presented to them by their first vice-regent, Mrs. Mary Seymour Peck. Miner's History of Wyoming is authority for statements concerning the condition of affairs in the Valley at the time of Katherine's residence there.

The names of five of the eight men present at the funeral services of Katherine Gaylord have been found by Mr. Norton, as follows: Warren Bunnell, Martin L. Goodwin, David W. Goodwin, Lemuel Bunnell, John Buck.

Miss M. J. Atwood, first recording secretary, and Miss C. L. Bowman, first historian of the Chapter, have also rendered valued aid in this work. To all of these, and to any other who has extended the helping hand, the writer begs to express her sincere thanks.

FLORENCE E. D. MUZZY.

Bristol, Connecticut, December, 1898.

lieutenancy, this entry being found in Connecticut Records, May, 1777: "Aaron Gaylord established by the Assembly to be lieutenant of Third Company, Twenty-fourth Regiment." At the expiration of his term in December, he returned to his home in New Cambridge, now Bristol, Connecticut.

Early in 1776, hearing no doubt wonderful tales of fertile Wyoming, he moved to the "Far West," with his wife, Katherine Cole, and their three children, Lemuel, Phebe and Lorena—the oldest, Lemuel, being about eleven at that time.

It is supposed, though not recorded, that they joined one of the "Forties" continually going out. The journey, occupying about three weeks (time enough, in these rapid-transit days, to cross the continent itself three times, or travel half way round the world!) was made on horseback, with all their worldly goods.

Doubtless she found it hard enough, even with the strong arm of her husband to hew her path; but looking back upon it, in her terrible journey home three years later, Katherine Gaylord must have felt that, measured by suffering, the way out was ease and comfort, in comparison.

They settled in Forty Fort, and lived the usual frontier life of more or less poverty and deprivation. Katherine related in after years much of that life to her children and grandchildren, but many of her tales are faded and lost in the mists of the past. Viewing however, the self-sacrificing life of women as a whole, in those hard days, we may come better to understand her own; for surely she was never one to sit idly by, while others toiled.

From the remembered tales of her own lips, then, and from the recollections of others, we can see her, in addition to the care of her own home and family, toiling in fort or field, while the men were away upon public service; planting, garnering grain, husking corn, making hay; riding miles to mill, with laden steed, waiting for the wheat to be ground, and bringing it home at night through long stretches of darkening forest; and, later even making the salt-petre used in the manufacture of powder, for public defense.

When dry-goods were gone, and money failed, she fashioned garments from her own clothing, that her children might attend school. One hardly knows whether to laugh or cry over the untoward fate of Phebe's new gown, made from her mother's red flannel petticoat! This, having been hung out upon a line to dry, fell a victim to a lawless marauder from neighbor Roberts' pig pen, and Phebe was left lamenting! Let us hope that good Mistress Roberts possessed an extra flannel petticoat of brilliant hue, which was made a free will offering in behalf of Phebe's education. Every mother knows that there could have been no limit to the daily acts of self-denial which the frontier mother practiced.

Those who remember Katherine Gaylord unite in describing her as small and frail of build, or at least, of hardly medium stature; with blue eyes, brown or fair hair, delicate complexion, and fine features; hardly our ideal of a rugged pioneer woman. Power of spirit cannot always be gauged by power of body, nor force of character by outward seeming. In old age she is described by one still living, who knew her well, as a "very intelligent, agreeable and highly respected" person in her community.

It would seem that the family had friends in Wyoming for history states that a brother of Aaron "who died in the service" had settled there.

In December, 1777, six months before his death, Aaron Gaylord is upon the Westmoreland records as one of the appointed "fence-viewers" for the ensuing year. In those days of few and uncertain boundaries, this must have been an important work.

The valley now, 1776 to 1778, held hundreds of homes, with barns, stacks of grain and everything in plenty, agriculturally considered,

The commercial status is partly shown by the following list of prices:

Men's farm labor, three summer months, per day	5s 3d
Women's labor, spinning, per week	6s
Making horse shoes, and shoeing horse	8s
Taverners, best dinner	2s
Taverners, mug of flip, with 2 gills rum	4s
Good yarn stockings, a pair	10s
Beaver hats, best	4£
Tobacco, in hank, or leaf, 1 pound	9d
Good check flannel, yard wide	8s
Winter-fed beef, per pound	7d
Good barley, per bushel	8s
Dozen eggs	8d
Shad, apiece	6d

Wyoming was an extreme frontier, the key to a large territory beyond. The Six Nations were within a few hours' canoeing, and nearly all the able bodied men of the valley were now, 1778, called to help save their country—leaving their own homes to possible destruction. An outbreak seemed impending.

Given these conditions, it was an unaccountable fact that Congress did not respond to the appeals sent now by the helpless settlers for protection. Those remaining did all they could. They went to the field with rifle, as well as hoe. They sent out scouting parties to watch the Indian trails and report weekly. In this service Aaron Gaylord must have shared.

In May the scouts began to encounter the savages; although it had previously seemed the enemy's policy to remain in hiding, apparently fearing—as it proved—to alarm the settlers and cause the recall of the two companies from the seat of war before the Six Nations were ready for the attack.

Now and then small squads of Indians, covered with paint, would land before the fort, making warlike demonstrations, to the great alarm of those within.

People from the outer settlements began to come into the forts. Congress was again notified that an attack was imminent; but still the Wyoming companies were not allowed to return. Appeals to justice, mercy or policy seemed to have no effect upon Congress in its strange obtuseness to the dreadful peril of the colonists. About thirty Wyoming soldiers did return "with or without leave," but even then, the number of fighters was appallingly small.

It is probable that it was at this time of confusion and absence of regular officers, that Aaron Gaylord was appointed temporary commander of the fort, in accordance with the account given by Katherine to her children; but in the absence of official record, we are obliged to pass this by as tradition.

The last of June, the Senecas and other Indians to the number of six or seven hundred, with four hundred British provincials and a number of tories, descended the river, landed twenty miles above the fort, crossed the valley, and murdered several settlers.

A prisoner taken by them was sent to the fort, demanding its surrender, which was refused.

A council of war was immediately held at the fort, at which the majority argued that, as no help could be expected, the massacre of the fort's company was only the question of a few days; and that the only possible way of salvation was to attack and defeat the enemy.

A small minority, of which Aaron Gaylord was one, opposed this plan, feeling that it was worse than folly to venture out, knowing nothing of the strength of the invaders; but being overruled, Aaron Gaylord prepared to go with the others, saying: "*I will go, for I would rather die than be called a coward in such a time as this.*"

OR "NEW CAMBRIDGE." 65

WEST STREET, 1907

This street is two hundred and twenty-one years old, and is the only street in the borough which lies in the highway of the original layout, its generous width alone bearing evidence of its descent from the colonial assembly.* Probably through this thoroughfare Katherine Gaylord passed many times, and it seems fitting to illustrate this street first of all of the streets, and in this place. Great care has been taken to make the information as correct as possible. Each picture is numbered from 1 on, and then follows the street number (except in cases where the houses are not numbered). O signifies *owner*, R *resident.* This explanation applies to all of the street pictures which will follow throughout this work.

(1) No. 531, Seth Barnes *O;* (2) No. 520, Oscar Perrault *R;* Frank P. Dowd *R;* (3) No. 516, Mrs. Henry Hutchinson *O;* (4) No. 509, *rear* Sam'l Winchester *R;* (5) No 513, L. H. Mix *R;* (6) No. 511, John Le Febore *R;* Geo. Fortin *R;* (7) No. 509, Mrs. Jane Carroll *O;* (8) No. 504, L. Henderling *R;* Chas. Crocker *R;* (9) No. 501, Mrs. John Elton *R*, Edward H. Elton *R*, H. S. Elton *R*.

*Mary P. Root's *The Founders and Their Homes, or A Century Sketch of the Early Bristol Families 1663 to 1763.*

One account states that they started early the following morning, July 3, 1778, but the history of Wyoming says that they went out at noon, marched four miles, and formed a line of battle near Fort Wintermoot, where the fighting began at four in the afternoon; and the anxious listeners at the fort could tell that the battle was on. Miner's History gives this in detail.

During the half hour of open fighting they drew near to the river, and when about eighty rods away, with Menockasy Island a mile distant, it was suddenly discovered that they were surrounded by Indians who had remained stealthily in ambush until they had passed. They had fallen into the trap. A hideous battle yell, repeated six distinct times, coming from every side, told the dreadful truth.

An order to wheel and face the rear was misunderstood as an order to retreat to the fort, which was clearly an impossibility. In the confusion thus occasioned, resistance to such overwhelming numbers was fatal, and so the battle ended and the massacre began; while the helpless listeners at the fort, realizing a change and fearing the worst, waited in vain agony for those who would never come again. Only now and then an exhausted, bleeding straggler would stagger in to tell his heartrending story.

Menockasy Island offered their only hope, and many sprang into the river to swim across. A few escaped, but many were butchered as they swam, or shot in the thigh and reserved for torture, or happily, killed as they surrendered! In their frenzy, men shot old friends in cold blood, and one tory was seen deliberately to shoot his own brother.

The leaders of the two armies were of the same name—Butler—and were said to belong to one family.

Out of three hundred who went forth, over half were murdered; comparatively few falling in battle.

A detachment of thirty-five men arrived at the fort at evening, but too late. An attempt to concentrate the people of the valley at the fort was a failure, as fugitives were seeking the swamps and woods in every direction. With one company of one hundred women and children there was but one man. Few had provisions. "Children of misery, baptized in tears," were born and died in the wilderness and swamp.

About nine in the evening there came to Katherine Gaylord in the fort a worn-out fugitive—a neighbor of the fort cabins. He brought to her a hat, narrow brimmed, high crowned—with a bullet hole through the top—her husband's!

He told her all she ever knew of his death. Together the two men had crossed to Menockasy Island closely followed by the savages. It was nearly dusk, and the neighbor, running ahead, secreted himself under an uprooted tree, screened by bushes. An instant later Aaron Gaylord ran by, hotly pursued by the Indians. He was almost immediately overtaken and scalped. The savages returned, peering here and there, but in the gathering gloom soon gave up their search and disappeared.

The man in hiding dared not venture forth until after dark, although he knew by the sound that his friend lived for some time.

At length, creeping cautiously out, his foot struck against the hat of the comrade who had fallen a sacrifice to savage hate. Hastily securing it, he brought it with him to the heart-broken wife at the fort—a last relic of a life that was past!

Before he went out to his death Aaron Gaylord had counseled long with his wife, and had formed careful plans for her flight, should he never come back. Even after mounting his horse he had ridden back again to his own door, and, handing her the wallet which contained all the money he had in the world—a few dollars only—said: "Take this, if I never return it may be of some use to you."

That he never would return, seems to have been firmly impressed upon the hearts of both husband and wife. The children, Lorena and

(10) No. 502, C. F. Pettibone R, A. S. Pettibone R; (11) No. 492, Mrs. Wm. D. Bromley O; (12) No. 480, Mrs. Catherine Fish O; (13) No. 471, W. B. Chapin O, A. J. Rawson R; (14) No. 452, Leroy T. Hills O, Wm. M. Hills R (*No. 80 Race St.*); (15) No. 461, E. W. Gaylord O (at one time Methodist parsonage); (16) No. 449, Henry L. Hinman R, No. 451, Geo. R. Webster R; (17) No. 443, H. J. Forsyth R, No. 445, David Cormand R; (18) No. 441, Mrs. Lillia H. Linsley O, Henry L. Phelps R.

Lemuel, afterward related to their children his thoughtfulness in this planning. Lemuel remembered his father as he sat upon his horse giving final directions; and how, in obedience to his father's wish, he went at once to a distant pasture and brought in their horses to the fort.

"For," said Aaron Gaylord simply, but with a thought covering their entire future, "you may need them."

Katherine bade him good bye as a pioneer woman should bravely and hopefully without in spite of the sinking heart within; but she seemed to know they would meet no more in this life.

"Great strength is bought with pain." There was no time for tears.

Recalling his wishes and plans she hurriedly made ready for instant flight. Upon one horse she hastily packed clothing and provisions; upon the other the four were to ride alternately. Family tradition, however, records that, because of a sudden lameness, Lemuel was forced to ride much of the way, and Katherine herself walked.

Shortly after midnight they rode out of the fort into the horrible blackness beyond, into pathless woods, amongst "savage beasts and still more savage men;" a veritable hades through which they must pass or die! Long, weary, unmarked miles stretched out before her, while he to whom "her heart had turned out o' all the rest i' the warld" was suddenly gone to the land that is afar off; his body, that was so dear, lying uncared for, behind her in the wilderness. Think of it "oh, women, safe in happy homes."

Little Lorena never forgot that awful moment, and years after would vividly recall it to her grandchildren. "I was Lorena," she would say impressively, "and I was the youngest, only seven years old; and I remember but one incident of that night. As my mother, sister and myself, mounted upon one horse, and my brother (fourteen years of age) leading the other, went out from the fort into the darkness, mother turned, and speaking to her neighbors whom she was leaving behind, said: 'Good-bye, friends! God help us!' Her voice was so unnatural that I looked up into her face. I shall never forget the expression I saw there. It was white and rigid, and drawn with suffering that might have been the work of years instead of hours. It was so unlike my mother's face that I hid my own in her garments."

Others went out also, fugitives from their own; but from these Katherine and her pitifully helpless little group were almost immediately separated, each seeking safety in the way that seemed best to himself. Some elected to remain at the fort, and these were present at the surrender the following day. Investigation has proved that the many tales of atrocities done at the surrender are in a great measure untrue, as but one murder was committed, although the Indians could not be kept from plunder. After the withdrawal of the British forces, however, a few days later, the savages began an unchecked career of pillage, fire and murder; until those who had remained, hoping the worst was over, were forced to abandon the settlement, which was not fully re-established until December, 1799.

At daybreak Katherine had reached the thick recesses of the forest, but could see from afar the smoke of burning homes, and knew her flight had been none too hasty. All day long they hurried on. The first night they came upon a settler's deserted cabin, which sheltered them. The three succeeding nights and many others they camped under the primeval forest trees, where, said Lorena, "we tired children, feeling secure with our heads upon mother's lap, slept soundly, while she watched the long night through, listening to the howling of the wolves and hearing in every rustling leaf the stealthy tread of an Indian." How pathetic their trust! how overwhelming the burden thrust so suddenly upon the frail shoulders of the slender young mother!

After the second day one horse became so lame that they left it to its fate, and were thus obliged to plod wearily on foot, the remaining steed carrying their goods.

(19) No. 436, W. L. Weeks R, G. Lyons R; (20) No. 428, C. A. Garrett O, No. 430, Chas. F. Cable R; (21) No. 424, A. Bristol O; (22) No. 427, Fred W. Giddings O, 429, R. H. Elton R; (23) No. 401, H. G. Arms O; (24) No. 397, Mrs. E. Bradley O, Fred Day R; (25) No. 400, Jonathan Peck O; (26) No. 387, H. R. Beckwith R, W. B. Wheeler O; (27) No. 381, W. G. Graham O.

On the fourth day they arrived at a large stream. Here, either finding, or building a raft, they loaded nearly all of their precious stores upon it, intending to float them to a ford, which they knew must be somewhere below, hoping there to cross.

To their dismay, after starting the raft, they were told (perhaps by fugitives like themselves) that there were Indians below. Small wonder then, after hearing this, that even to save all they owned upon earth, they should not venture down the stream. So abandoning their goods, as they had previously their horse, they found a crossing elsewhere.

Their situation was now desperate indeed. They had their one horse with four to ride; one blanket strapped upon the saddle, for four to use; a precious box of tinder and flint; and one musket, with a small quantity of ammunition, which must be hoarded to the utmost and saved for defence. How many of those hard nights may we suppose that Katherine Gaylord slept under that solitary blanket? Not one, with her three children to be sheltered and comforted!

Their clothing must very soon have become worn and soiled enough; and this, to a person of Katherine Gaylord's natural refinement, must have been an added bit of distress—small though it was in comparison with greater burdens to be borne.

The bullet-pierced hat and leathern wallet were carried always in her hand, or about her person, and were in this way kept from disaster, and brought safely to her father's house. She treasured them as long as she lived, in an old chest, from whence children and grandchildren would reverently bring them forth to illustrate the never-old story of her escape from the Indians, and of the death of their heroic grandfather, Aaron Gaylord. After she was gone, these priceless relics were in some way most unfortunately lost.

And now for weeks they toiled slowly on and on, following the trail indicated by blazed trees, with many wandering aside into the pathless forest, with weakness and weariness, suffering and danger, ever on and on toward home.

After the loss of their provisions, they subsisted for several days upon berries, sassafras root, birch bark, or whatever they could gather by the way; not daring to start a blaze, or fire a musket so near the dreaded foe. Well for them that it was summer. Once they went from Thursday to Sunday afternoon without food. They met then a party of friendly Indians who fed them; but we can hardly imagine their terror at first sight of a red man! They afterward met other friendly Indians as they left Wyoming farther and farther behind, and were never once refused aid in all their terrible journey.

The country, however, was very sparsely settled, and many of the cabins they came across were deserted. As days grew into weeks, they no longer feared to kindle a fire at night, or to shoot game; although it was necessary to hoard their slender stock of ammunition with utmost economy.

They sometimes met stragglers from the army, or hunting parties but these were invariably kind and helpful; and such encounters must have sent many bright rays of hope and courage through the gloom, and unutterable loneliness of the vast primeval forest, in the dreary days when they saw no human face but their own.

One morning the little Lorena and her sister Phebe were running on in advance of mother and brother—though never out of sight—singing and chasing butterflies, gathering wild flowers, forgetting already the past, fearing nothing so long as they had mother, when they came upon two men sitting upon the ground. These proved to be hunters, who divided with Katherine their stock of food, as they heard her sad story; and helped her on her way.

But this incident made a great impression upon Lorena, owing to the fright of Phebe; who, screaming in terror, literally dragged Lorena back to her mother, scratching her face, tearing her garments (for the

(28) No. 368, Chas. Nagle R; (29) No. 360, C. M. Carrington O, Miss Louise M. Upson R, (Maples in front planted in 1845); (30) No. 350, E. L. Carrington O; (31) No. 352, H. B. Norton O; (32) No. 338, Lewis C. Morse O; (33) No. 307, H. A. Peck O; (34) No. 289, Wm. A. Terry O; (35) No. 275, Geo. C. Canfield R; (36) No. 271, F. S. White R, C. E. Potter R.

latter mishap there being no remedy, although Dame Nature would mend the former!) and greatly alarming the others. She remembered how her brother, the lad Lemuel, grown, since Wyoming, to man's estate, his mother's confidante, protector, and sole reliance—stepped boldly to the front, musket in hand, ready to defend his mother and sisters with his life, if need be. And the surprise and hearty sympathy of the two men remained always a warm memory with Lorena.

Another day, losing the trail, they came at nightfall, in sight of a large building with many lighted windows, which they took to be a wayside tavern. Within they could see a company of men seemingly soldiers, seated at a table, eating their supper.

Faint for want of food, and exhausted with travel, still Katherine Gaylord hesitated. With the memory of the British and Tory at Wyoming fresh upon her, how could she trust any man!

Desperation at last gave her desperation's courage; and entering a back room, she sank down in the darkness, with her little girls drawn close beside her; while her boy strode sturdily forward into the room where the men were gathered, and asked for food for his mother and sisters!

In a moment a light was brought, and they were surrounded by the astonished men, who with curious and pitying faces gazed at the forlorn little group, and listened to their pathetic story with manhood's unaccustomed tears. Nothing could exceed their kindness as they rivaled each other in giving comfort to the poor wanderers.

The unwonted luxuries of enough to eat, a bed to sleep in, with strong and ready protectors, were theirs that night; while the sense of security must have given to the poor mother such a rest as had not been hers for many long weeks.

"The gentlest woman," said Lorena in after years, "could not have ministered to our needs more thoughtfully and generously than did these rough, stalwart men."

In the morning they were loaded with provisions and sent on their way with many kind and hearty words.

They never forgot these friends, although they never knew who or what they were. Possibly, in the same way, their descendants may have heard this tale; and sometimes, even to this day, may ponder the fate of those hapless refugees whom their ancestors befriended in the wilderness!

They had often heard at night the howling of wild beasts, but had never been molested. Now, however, for several days an undefined feeling of unusual danger near at hand, had haunted Katherine, (who seems to have been one of those prescient souls, delicately susceptible to impressions which one of coarser fibre could not feel).

One night as they camped by their fire they caught a glimpse of a long, crouching, stealthy form in the underbrush, and knew that some savage creature was on their track. All the night long they could see his gleaming eyes in the firelight, but he dared not attack them. Neither dared he touch them by daylight, and in the morning they cautiously and fearfully went on their way, not venturing to stop for rest or food. Lemuel led, and the others followed, upon the staunch back of their sorely-tried friend—the one remaining horse. A driving rain set in, and the blanket formed but poor protection.

All day long they moved slowly on, with that fearful nightmare creeping ever softly, softly behind—biding his time!

When night drew near their outlook seemed hopeless. To go on in the darkness and storm would be impossible. The soaking rain precluded all hope of a fire, while to stop without a fire meant instant attack, and—a reward to the dogged determination of the brute behind them, of which they dared not think.

With the knowledge of all this and with a dreadful doom seemingly

(37) No. 261, F. W. Jacobs R, Mrs. C. B. Andrews O; (38) No. 251, G. Hendry R, L. L. Pierce O, Geo. Curtiss R; (39) No. 270, W. L. Hart O; (40) No. 262, G. C. Arms O; (41) No. 227, Mrs. Anna Wandle R, Geo Potter R; (42) No. 219, Chas. G. Eddy R; (43) No. 213. Geo. Kempster O, Alfred W. Kempster R; (44) No. 226, James Hayden O; 45) No. 216, J. H. Johnston R, No. 218, D. Sullivan. R.

so near, the faith and fortitude of the heroic mother did not fail. She drew her frightened children as closely as possible to her side, and, in her helplessness prayed ceaselessly for that help which to human vision could never come

Faith and works go hand in hand to fulfillment; and while she prayed she kept moving, straining her eyes in the darkness which settled so awfully upon them. And Katherine Gaylord never doubted that the Ever-Present Power in which she trusted, led their feet neither to right, nor to left, but directly into a little clearing, where the dark outlines of a deserted cabin with open door, appeared to their gladdened eyes!

Straight through the friendly portal—not stopping to dismount! Lemuel swung too the heavy door, dropped the bar into its place, and they were saved! Often in after years did Katherine say that she believed that they were directly led by Providence.

The cabin contained one room, with a small lean-to in which the horse found luxuries undreamed of in his recent philosophizing—warmth and shelter! The place had evidently been abandoned in haste; for they found stacks of firewood, with potatoes and corn meal in plenty.

A good fire soon warmed body and soul; and with safety, shelter, warmth, dry clothing and a hot supper of roasted potatoes and corn meal cakes, they felt a rush of fresh courage and new life. Their steadfast friend in the lean-to shared with them—(though whether or not, in the exuberance of their reaction, the children roasted for him the potatoes, history does not say).

And then they sat around the glowing fire, while Katherine thanked the Power that led them thither.

In the morning the panther had disappeared but fearing its return, they remained in their place of safety, and rested two days; then went on, doubtless strengthened by their enforced period of waiting.

Somewhere on this weary road, they must have met, but passed unseen, the brother of Katherine, sent out by her anxious father (who had heard of the Wyoming tragedy), to find and help her home. "Our unknown losses!" What a subject for thought. The brother, however, must have kept the trail, which she often lost; and so it came about that she was first to reach home. As after many weeks they saw once more the hills which compassed that dear home on every side, how tumultuous must have been her thoughts; while the mingled fear and suffering of the weary way by which they had come, must already have seemed as a troubled dream.

The news of their coming went before, and all through the familiar streets as they passed, old friends came out to greet them as those risen from the dead. Many went on with them to her father's house. As he came out to meet her, brave Katherine broke down at last, throwing herself into his arms, burst into tears—the first she had shed since that fatal night at Wyoming. And not the least touching of all, was her determined attempt still to keep up, prefacing her tears by the cheerful greeting: "Well, we are the worst looking lot you ever saw."

Love, home, and care were hers once more—even though that which was gone could never return. Here she found refuge at last; but she could not rest while her country suffered. Although she had seemingly given all—yet her patriotic heart consented to one more sacrifice.

In 1780, when Lemuel was about sixteen, she gave him to serve his country in its need, as he had upheld his mother in her own. Remember, he was her only son, and she was a widow. When we realize all that he was to her, we can more fully appreciate the intensity of her patriotism, as shown by this final offering. Lemuel was at the surrender of Cornwallis, and then, some time after the war, he left his mother at New Cambridge, and returned to Wyoming, drawn, perhaps, by more interests than one; for here he married Sylvia Murray, daughter of Noah Murray. They settled, finally, in Illinois and had a family of ten children.

(46) No. 212, H. Judd *O;* (47) No. 211, James McKernan *O;* (48) No. 200, Geo.Wissmann *R*, Miss Addie Judd *R;* (49) *No Number*, Mrs. Chas. Morway *R;* (50) *No Number*, Pierre Gaudreau *O*, Geo. Clayton *R*, P. Fucci *R;* (51) *No Number*, Wilfred Bourdeau *R*, Medard Bechard *R* (*was at one time Baptist Parsonage*); (52) No. 141, A. H. Buskey *R*, 143, James Barnes *R;* (53) No. 135, Wm. H. Merritt *O*, 137, H. S. Hintze *R;* (54) No. 114, Mrs. J. Shaw *R*, No. 110, Stephen O'Connell.

Phebe, Katherine's eldest daughter, married Levi Frisbie, and in 1800, moved to Orwell, Pennsylvania, where they had five children.

Lorena, the "baby," married, in 1799, Lynde Phelps, of Burlington, Connecticut, and was the mother of seven daughters.

So Katherine Gaylord lived, in spite of fate, to see twenty-two grandchildren. After her brood had flown and no longer needed the care which once was literal life to them she stayed on with her parents and cared for them. Her father, James Cole, living to be over ninety, was one day left for a short time alone in the house. In some way the roof caught fire and the building was burned to the ground. Almost nothing was saved, and again Katherine was homeless. It was with difficulty that Mr. Cole was rescued; and shortly after he died.

Katherine went then to live with Lorena, and for forty years she passed in and out among them, taking the liveliest interest in helping to "raise" the seven daughters of her daughter; who remembered ever her kind, motherly care, and the quiet, patient, Christian character she maintained.

In 1799, she had united with the Congregational Church of Bristol and she proved ever the truth of the beautiful thought, so suggestive of her spirit:

> "Our life is no poor cisterned store,
> That lavish years are draining low,
> But living streams that, welling o'er,
> Fresh from the living fountains flow."

Her sturdy independence was characteristic to the last. When in her nineties, her daughter Lorena begged her to lie down in the daytime to rest, she determinedly refused, giving as her reason, that she "did not wish to get in the habit of it!"

In extreme old age, later events faded from her mind, but Wyoming and its fateful memories were never dim.

She is said once to have been so overcome by the sight of a picture representing an Indian in the act of scalping a man, that she fell to the floor—so vividly did the horrible past return to her.

At the very last of her life here, she would sit for hours by the fire, lost to her surroundings, apparently living over the days gone by. She would sometimes start up in terror, calling to her children to hide from the Indians! Again she would seem to be in fear of wild beasts and cry out pitifully. Sometimes she would speak her husband's name, and smile—seeming to hold communion with him—perhaps she did—who knows? And at the last, after ninety-five years, she passed peacefully away; feeling no doubt in regard to the love of her youth, that while

> "Clouds sail and waters flow,
> Our souls must journey on,
> But it cannot be ill to go
> The way that thou hast gone."

The storm and tumult of her life seemed to follow her even unto death. At the time of her going a terrific snow storm occurred in New England, blocking the roads and shutting off all possibility of immediate interment. The village carpenter, who was also the village undertaker, had probably time to provide a suitable casket before the storm; but it was several days before the men could venture out even to break paths. Owing to a fierce wind, in many places the paths had to be twice cleared.

When at length the last storm which should ever rage over the head of devoted Katherine, had raved itself into calm, a handful of men left the "Center," to do for her the last service she would ever need at their hands. They started with horse and sleigh; but after going a few rods the plunging steed tore off a shoe, cutting his foot so badly as to disable him; and so they abandoned his help, even as Katherine had abandoned

(55) No. 109, Emory G. Gaudreau *O*, Ubald Foucault *R;* (56) No. 99, E. Osborne *R*, No. 101, H. Wellman *R;* (57) No. 93, Mrs. Ellen F. Judson *O;* (58) No. 86, Fred Smith *R*, Frank Wooster *R;* (59) No. 87, John Bousquet *R*, E. Christian *R;* (60) No. 80, Deborah C. Sanford *O;* (61) No. 63, J. B. Alexander *R;* (62) No. 44, Miss Ella Upson *O*, Edwin R. Thayer *R;* (63) No. 15, Mrs. Sarah A. Wandle *O.*

her steed near Wyoming long years ago. The men then drew the sleigh across the drifted fields to the place, two miles away, where, heedless of all tumult now, the body of the heroine lay in peace.

Greatly exhausted by the hard road and digging, the men were obliged to rest and take food before making further effort.

One still living, who as a boy, was present at this strange burial, recalls clearly the occasion, and how the body of Katherine was placed upon the sleigh, while her old friends and neighbors, with their own hands, drew it to its final place; even as in ancient times great heroes were borne upon the shoulders of those who would do them honor. Eight men were present at this final scene, but no woman was among them. A tragic ending to a tragic life!

"Never more, O storm-tossed soul—
Never more from wind or tide,
Never more from billows roll,
Wilt thou need thyself to hide!"

[SIGNED.] "CONNECTICUT."

Committee on Award of Prizes.
{ ELIZABETH BRYANT JOHNSTON, *Chairman*,
MARGUERITE DICKENS,
HARRIET M. LOTHROP.

GRAVE OF KATHERINE GAYLORD AT BURLINGTON, CONN.
(Courtesy of *Bristol Press*.)

Prehistoric Remains
Of the Tunxis Valley.

Illustrated With Photographs from Original Objects.*
BY FREDERICK H. WILLIAMS.

DR. F. H. WILLIAMS.

To the majority of men the Aborigine of Connecticut is less real than a vanished dream. The antiquarian finds him in musty deeds or forgotten laws. The etymologist traces him in the names of the mountains, brooks or vales that he loved, while here and there the thoughtless turn up his discarded arrows or his mouldering bones. But his wigwam has vanished with his council fires, the echo of his war-whoop is lost in the valleys and time has levelled the earth over his forgotten graves. Yet along with the disused tomahawk and the shaftless spear, the humbler implements of his domestic life everywhere betray to the patient seeker his ancient habitations. Sallust believed that the deeds of the ancient Romans were as illustrious as those whose praises were sung by the bards of Greece, but that they were so occupied with those deeds, that none thought to record them. So we may believe that some among

---

* All the articles illustrated belong to the writer except such as are marked with letters: *c* A. J. Churchill, Southington; *r* William C. Richards, of Bristol, who are here thanked for their use.

Students interested in Archæology may feel assured that all articles described are known to be genuine, and from this section tributary to the *old* Farmington Valley, and from Collinsville to Windsor.

THE SOAPSTONE QUARRY AT BRISTOL.

the early settlers of Connecticut were curious enough to have studied the domestic tools of the savage, but, if so, they forgot to record much of their knowledge. Besides we should remember that the metal tools of the white man were so vastly superior to the stone implements of the Indian, as to cause an almost immediate disuse of the latter, where metal could be obtained. Thus it happened that the students of ethnology, when attention became turned towards unravelling the domestic life of ancient savage man, some forty years ago, found it nearly a sealed book. Yet piece by piece the relics of ancient man have been collected, compared with each other and with what may now be found among existing savages. No longer held as mere curios to tickle a momentary fancy, these implements and ornaments have been used as the alphabets of a forgotten tongue, until now one can not only largely reconstruct the life of this vanished man, but, even entering his departed mentality, ask the reason of many of his ways and deeds.

It must, however, be the scope of this article to deal only with such visible remains as have come down to us from the pre-Columbian owners of the Tunxis Valley. Therefore, very many interesting topics must be left untouched.

POTTERY.

It has been said that, "articles of fictile ware are the most fragile and yet the most enduring of human monuments."* But owing to some cause, doubtless the alternate freezing and thawing in a country

---

* Jones' Antiquities of the Southern Indians, p. 441.

subject to heavy rainfall and shallow burials conjoined, perfect pottery is very rare in this valley. Small sherds are found, however, upon nearly all old village sites. They appear to have been well made and are often of a fine red color, but frequently blackened by fire and smoke. The clay is usually mixed with micaceous sands although some appears to have been mixed with ashes, and other sherds seem made of nearly homogenous clays. Externally the pottery is usually ornamented, sometimes with parallel lines, or with oblique detached lines, or series of punctures. Again we frequently find a net work of various patterns impressed upon it. In the American Museum of New York may be seen a very fine jar found near Windsor, belonging to the Terry collection. We know of no other perfect pottery from this section. In fig. 1 we illustrate a very rare pottery pipe and tube, which may or may not have been its stem, found in the bank of the Connecticut River, near the mouth of the Farmington, in 1884. Fig. 2 shows typical pottery sherds from Farmington, Plainville and Southington. A curious study is being developed by taking impressions in wax of the ornamental lines on both faces of pottery jars. One can thus often reconstruct, not only the forms of the matting or basketry upon which they were molded, but at times ascertain the nature of the fibres of which the netting or mats were made.

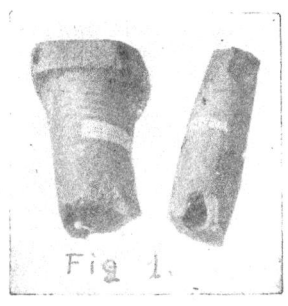

A POTTERY PIPE.

"It was a common practice among the aborigines to employ woven fabrics in the construction and ornamentation of earthenware. Im-

FRAGMENTS OF POTTERY.

SOAPSTONE DISHES.

pressions were thus left on the clay, and by baking they were rendered as lasting as if engraved on stone. From no other source do we obtain so wide a range of fabrics." †Fibre lines will be noticed upon the sherds illustrated in fig. 2.* From this we perceive how valuable any particular pot-sherd may be to science, and why each fragment should be carefully saved and shown to the nearest general collection.

STEATITE.

The working of soapstone is one of the oldest organized industries of the Tunxis Valley. In Bristol, Nepaug and Harwinton ledges have been found where the prehistoric Indian mined and roughly formed his pots and bowls. In 1892 a beautiful exposure of an aboriginal quarry was uncovered in Bristol, with many bowls in various stages of finish still attached to the ledge. For the Indian first marked out his dish and finished shaping its bottom and side before detaching it from the rock. This separation, owing to the general irregularity of cleavage and frequent faults in the steatite, was often disastrous, as the many broken rejects about the quarry show. When the bowl was once freed from the ledge it seems to have been taken to some village site and slowly finished, being generally smoothly polished, both within and without. The frontispiece shows the Bristol quarry from a photograph made by the Peabody Museum, and shown at the Columbian Exhibition at Chicago.

Fig. 3, one third natural size, illustrates a very fine two-handled bowl, found some thirty years ago, three feet deep in a sand bank at

---

† Holmes Prehistoric Textile Art, 13th Annual Report Bureau Ethnology.

* Since articles were illustrated for these papers the writer has read Prof. O. T. Mason's "Origin of Inventions." On page 58, we read speaking of clay jars, "but ninety and nine were made in nets, or baskets, or bags. In such examples the markings are on the *outside*." In fig. 2a, is shown the *inside* face of a potsherd from Plainville, which is exactly similarly ornamented on both *outside* and *inside* faces.

Plainville; few prettier bowls exist in the East. Fig. 4 shows a small drinking bowl from East Bristol. Fig. 5, one third natural size, is a cooking dish from Burlington, black with grease and smoke. There is also a banner stone in Terryville, and a unique, but unfortunately imperfect, bird amulet, belongs to the writer. Imperfect dishes and fragments are quite numerous. Some are found showing holes where they have been mended. Fig. 6.

The trap talus extending along the old valley from Southington north to the Massachusetts line, furnished the angular fragments from which were made the implements used in working soapstone. In comparing a collection of the implements with a collection of unworked stones it would seem as though nature had placed the models ready to the hand of man. The stones flake off into thin narrow pieces, often with such acute points that only a very little change is needed to produce the required tool. These tools are found on every village site from Southington to Congamond Lake in Massachusetts. And some have been found at Nepaug which retained the lustre of the powdered steatite. These implements were of four general types. Those rudely blocked out as axes and grooved, for helving. Of these some cut straight with the edge as our axes, some cut towards one like an adze, while others were pointed and acted more like a pick-axe. Examples of each are given, figs. 7, 8, 9. The second type is the most generally distributed; they are found from four to twelve inches long and all agree in having the worked edge beveled off to the left. They do not form very sharp points but nearly all show the polish of long use. If a number are placed in a row the general trend of the bevel will all be alike. Fig. 10.

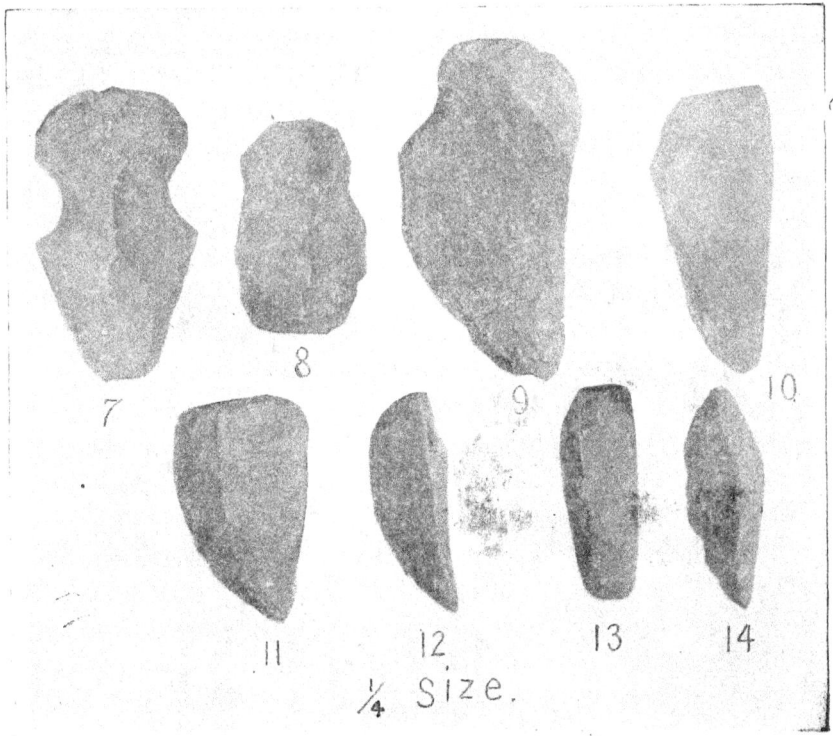

IMPLEMENTS FOR WORKING STEATITE.

The third type are smaller and more robust, rudely wedge shape except that the point is always acute. The blunt end is roughly shaped to fit the hand and take pressure from its palm. They seem to have been used as picks and gouges, being akin to the modern tool of the wood graver; figs. 11, 12, 13. They may also have been driven into the rock after the manner of wedges.

The fourth type resembles the third on its working point, but they are made of thin flakes of stone and often have a cutting point on both ends; fig. 14. It is not contended that these tools were used exclusively for working soapstone, but that soapstone was worked with them.

In attempting a description of the general remains of the Stone Age Art of the Tunxis Valley, a few explanatory remarks seem justifiable. European Archæologists divide their specimens into Paleolithic or ancient stone age, all the objects of which are chipped, and Neolithic, or newer stone age, in which many objects are polished. No such classification can be made applicable to American Archæology.* The writer would rather divide his description into domestic tools, largely used by women; implements of warfare and chase; religious or ceremonial, and ornamental. The prehistoric Indian himself may never have conceived that he possessed an art. Nature could never have seemed to him the kind and lavish mother that she does to us today. To him she was the stern and miserly controller of his destinies, from whom he only wrested, through strenuous and unceasing toil, those meagre gifts that never gave repletion. Therefore as one who strove hand to hand with nature on all sides, he walked closer to her nakedness than we. But his companionship was as that of a child who cannot wander far from the maternal font of being. He knew better than we how to read the external features of her presence; such secrets as she vouchsafed to him the knowledge, he learned with ready wit. But, unlike us of today, never having penetrated within the arcana of her mysteries, he could not stand aloof from

HAMMER STONES.

---

* As far as can now be seen the separation of a paleolithic from a later Indian tool in America is a question of its geological location. The writer inclines to accept the evidences of glacial man in America.

her as we may and make of those mysteries the ready slaves to work his will.

HAMMER AND PIT STONES.

Yet in consequence of this very close connection with nature, whatever he met with became a possible agent in his struggles with her for existence, and not having differentiated his arts, each tool may have had an hundred useful possibilities. Necessity is no more the mother of invention in tools than she is of variety in their uses. It must not then be expected that our names of his many implements, however useful to our study, always convey the Indian's conception of them. The simplest of all implements is the hammer stone. Wherever a brook rolled over the gravel beds, the Indian found it ready smoothed and shaped for his hand. On all his old camping grounds they may be collected in every sort of condition, from the plain stone showing no marks of usage, through various stages of elaborate working, down to those that have been pounded nearly to pieces. Wherever we find the spalls or cores of the arrow maker, we find the little "knockers" with which he worked his quartz or cherty pebbles; figs. 15, 16. In this locality the more common hammers are made of a hard quartz and quartzite. Some of these have been carefully pecked all around their edges and brought into a round (fig. 17), or oval shape, (fig. 18), a much used hammer. Many are beautiful objects; fig. 19. Others are made of a coarse but compact yellow quartzite and red sandstone. Irregular nodular stones of agatized material and quartz seem to have been prized for their great density and resistance to fracture.

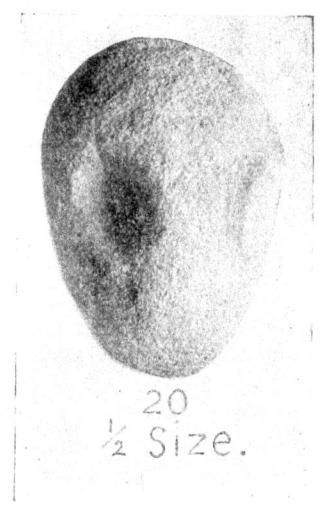

A PIT STONE WITH THREE "PITS."
(One opposite the two shown.)

Many of the objects in yellow sandstone, red sandstone and even compact quartzite are found with one or more little circular depressions or "pits." These pits are conical and usually about one quarter to one half of an inch deep.

Fig. 20 shows a rudely egg-shaped hammer of coarse red sandstone, in which the ingenious Indian, in addition to deep pits for thumb and middle finger, has made a third on the top of the stone for the index finger. This arrangement gives a firm hold. More commonly there is a pit upon the two flat faces of the hammer, opposite to each other. Sometimes there is only one pit, and again a stone may have five or more pits irregularly placed. Figure 21 shows a beautiful red sandstone that has the indescribable polish of long handling, with one pit on its long face and the other on its smaller end. These stones are found all over the world and are usually called hammers. The writer thinks many of them show no signs of having been used upon other stones. Simple as they are they possess a sort of beauty which endears them to their possessor. Fig. 22 is a one pit stone or "anvil." Figs. 23, 24, are two pit stones or "hammers."

It is conceivable that these simplest of tools, as the Indian came to comprehend their possibilities, worked as great a change in separating him from his ferine associates, as the discovery of iron and steam worked in advancing mankind from the stone age conditions. From striking

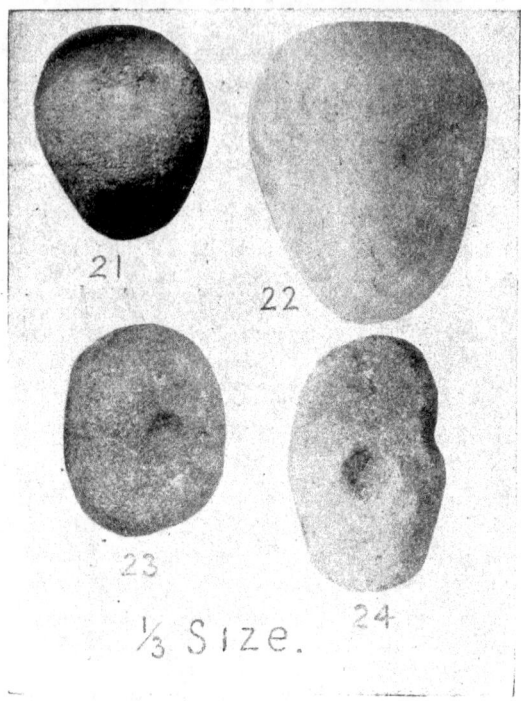

⅓ Size.

PIT STONES.

them together he may have gained his first conceptions of producing fire at his own pleasure. By striking them together he slowly discovered the different qualities of stones, the possibilities of the conchoidal fracture became manifest to him. From them he gradually evolved the whole art of chipping and pecking in stone. No thoughtful sudent can view these objects without emotion; their prototypes were the cornerstones of the portals of civilization; their discovery was the "open sesame" to those inventions to which man owes his present physical ameliorations. Whether it were apes or men that splintered the miocene flints of Thenay,* we can not doubt that when primitive man began to strike these stones together with a conscious purpose, he struck the blow that will be the ultimate death knell of all his savage animal associates, against which unarmed he waged an endless conflict.

POLISHERS.

The Stone Age artisan had three general modes of fabricating his tools and ornaments. Having discovered a stone suitable for his purpose, often one having a natural shape similar to the object desired, a few well directed blows with his hammer would roughly complete its outlines. Now he might slowly reduce it to shape by light and repeated blows of his hammer, wearing it away in coarse dust. This was pecking,

---

*The Abbe Bourgeois showed split flints from the miocene at Brussels, in 1873.

traces of which show upon nearly all large objects, except those made from flint or chert. Or he might grind it into shape by rubbing it upon a hard stationary stone of gritty nature, or by rubbing other gritty stones on it. This was polishing. Finally if the stone worked upon were of a proper nature to take the right cleavage, he might chip it away by direct blows from his hammer, or by sudden impulsion upon its edges with a hard object, wear it down in little flakes. This was flaking and chipping. Often several or all of these actions might be brought to bear successively upon one object. The little flakes produced by the ancient chipper are among the most distinctive of his vestiges. The eye of the practiced "relic hunter" trails their fabricator by these little spalls, much as the red man trailed the objects of *his* chase. By observing their variety, condition and abundance, he is often enabled to ferret out old and productive village sites. It seems probable that flaking was the earliest of all his arts in stone, and yet it ultimately reached the highest place among them. Besides the hammers described there have come down to us

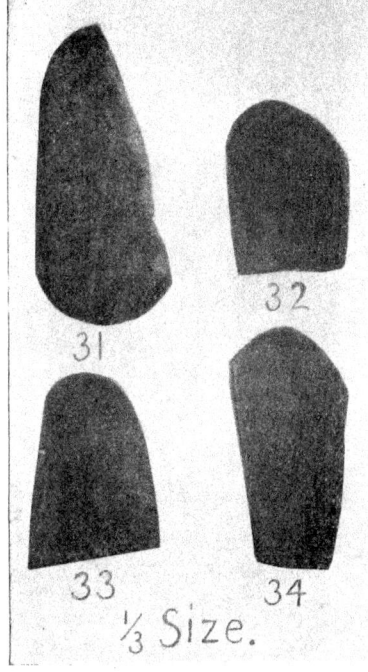

FLESHERS.

quite a variety of tools used in these processes. In figs. 25, 26, 27, one third natural size, are shown grinders or polishers of gritty red sandstone and quartzite. Fig. 27 is a red sandstone "pit" stone made into a polisher. Other curiously worked stones, whose use remains problematical, may be seen in figs. 28, 27. Fig. 30 is a beautiful stone of a dark chocolate color, carefully polished all over, which may have been used in perfecting the blades of axes and celts. The other tools are quartzite. All were found in Plainville or Farmington. The pitted stone, fig. 24, from Congamond Lake, has been used secondarily as a polisher.

FLESHERS.

Certain implements have been sparsely found around Farmington and Plainville which seem to have been made for removing skins from slain animals, and possibly bark from living trees, used in making basketry and mats. They all agree in being made from thin flakes of a very hard, dense and heavy stone. Roughly flaked out in chisel form they show no fine work except on one end. This end is always brought to a sharp edge from both faces, with the cutting edge prolonged in a curve to one side much like an old fashioned shoe knife. They all show the friction polish of long use, doubtless acquired from years of drudgery of the squaws. They are made from a silicious blue stone, but long weathering has made them a dull earth color, with a fine patina. In the Bristol Museum is one specimen with a straight blade resembling a chisel. We illustrate four specimens all from Farmington; figs. 31, 32, 33, 34.

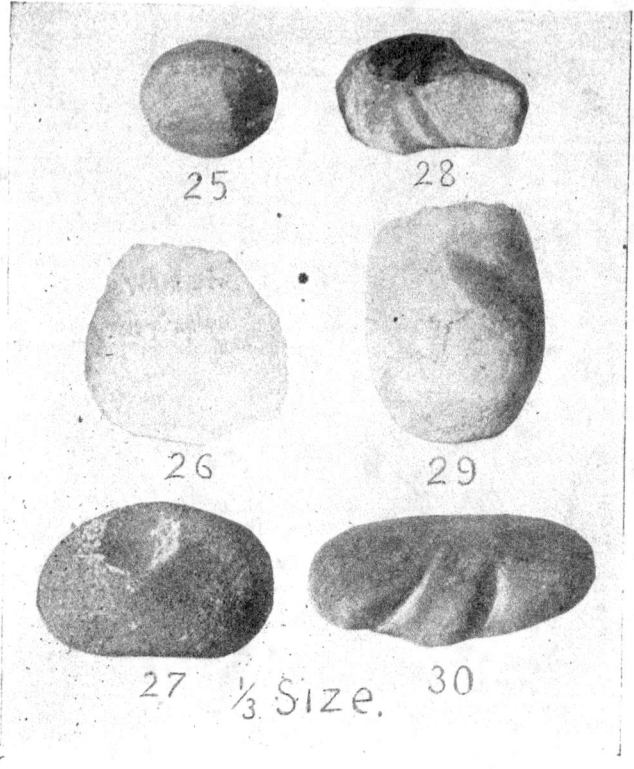

POLISHERS.

THE SCRAPER.

The writer believes that the scraper and its brother the flaked knife followed next after the hammer stone in the tide of evolution. Whether his environment were stone, bone or shell, wherever prehistoric man has left his traces, these most useful of tools are found. Among such simple implements we cannot be surprised that along with specimens of the highest art should linger others as rude and simple as may be found among the earliest vestiges of man. Fig. 35 represents such an object in yellow Jasper from Granby, that seems the counterpart of specimens from prehistoric France. Made from various cherty or quartzite stones, some were simply more or less chipped on one edge as in figs. 36, 37; some resemble arrow points ground off to a blunt edge. Others are merely round pebbles, split through their centers and then worked to such an edge that when drawn towards one they will rasp or cut any soft material. Figs. 38, 39, are fine examples. Many of these tools show signs of very prolonged use by the exquisite polish upon their working surface, and these are not always the ones that we would select for shape or beauty. Probably they were more used to soften skins and rub them flexible than for cutting; figs. 40, 41. Fig. 42, one half natural size, represents an uncommon form with unusual polish upon it. A great many seem to have been used as our cobblers use a piece of glass for rasping wood, horn, bones and hides, and doubtless also in preparing food and removing meat from bones; fig. 43. Some were doubtless hafted in wooden handles, the handles being split open, the tool was

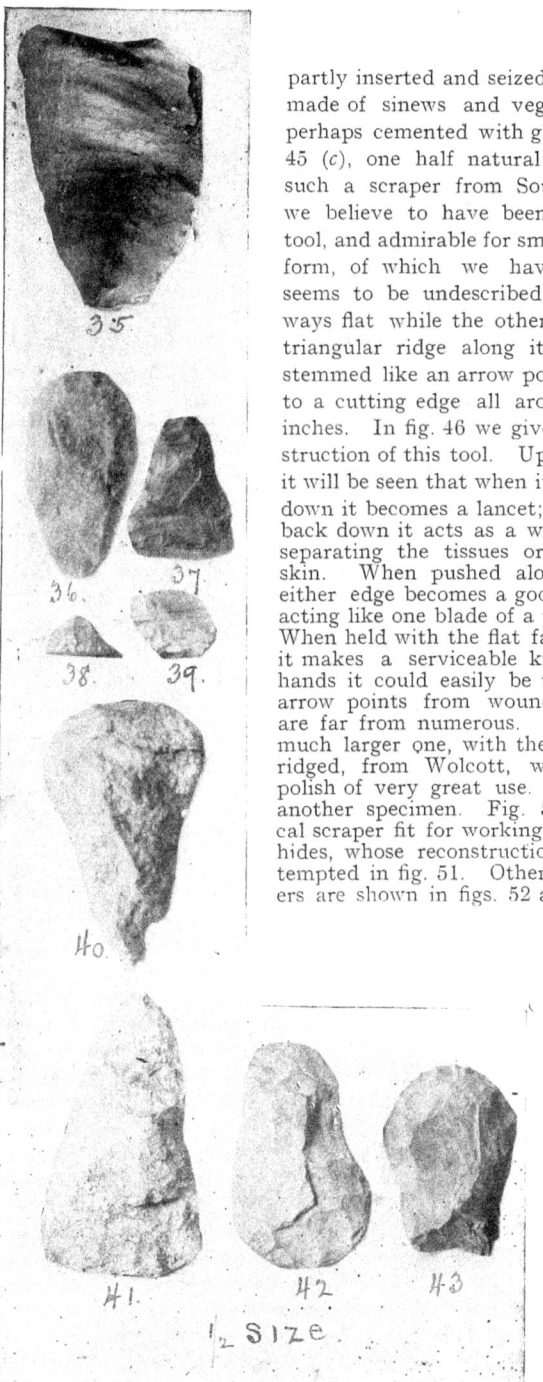

partly inserted and seized on with threads made of sinews and vegetable fibres and perhaps cemented with glue or pitch. Fig. 45 (c), one half natural size, represents such a scraper from Southington, which we believe to have been also a skinning tool, and admirable for small animals. This form, of which we have seen several, seems to be undescribed. One face is always flat while the other is raised into a triangular ridge along its center. It is stemmed like an arrow point and brought to a cutting edge all around; length 1¼ inches. In fig. 46 we give an ideal reconstruction of this tool. Upon careful study it will be seen that when it is used flat side down it becomes a lancet; with its curved back down it acts as a wedge or probe in separating the tissues or raising up the skin. When pushed along arrow shape either edge becomes a good cutting knife, acting like one blade of a pair of shears. When held with the flat face towards one it makes a serviceable knife. In skillful hands it could easily be used to extract arrow points from wounds. These tools are far from numerous. Fig. 47 shows a much larger one, with the back much less ridged, from Wolcott, which shows the polish of very great use. Fig. 48 gives another specimen. Fig. 50 gives a typical scraper fit for working both wood and hides, whose reconstruction has been attempted in fig. 51. Other forms of scrapers are shown in figs. 52 and 53.

SCRAPERS.

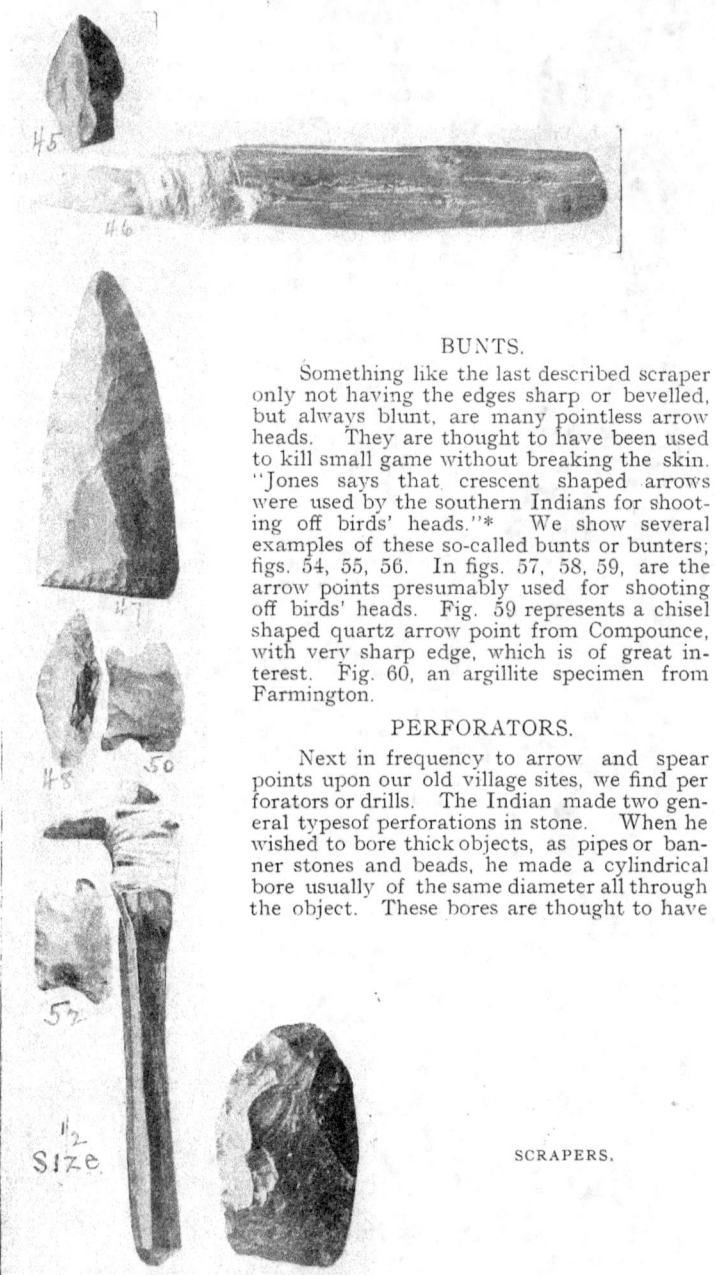

BUNTS.

Something like the last described scraper only not having the edges sharp or bevelled, but always blunt, are many pointless arrow heads. They are thought to have been used to kill small game without breaking the skin. "Jones says that crescent shaped arrows were used by the southern Indians for shooting off birds' heads."* We show several examples of these so-called bunts or bunters; figs. 54, 55, 56. In figs. 57, 58, 59, are the arrow points presumably used for shooting off birds' heads. Fig. 59 represents a chisel shaped quartz arrow point from Compounce, with very sharp edge, which is of great interest. Fig. 60, an argillite specimen from Farmington.

PERFORATORS.

Next in frequency to arrow and spear points upon our old village sites, we find perforators or drills. The Indian made two general types of perforations in stone. When he wished to bore thick objects, as pipes or banner stones and beads, he made a cylindrical bore usually of the same diameter all through the object. These bores are thought to have

SCRAPERS.

---

* "Fowkes" Stone Art. 13th Annual Report Bureau Ethnology, p. 168.

BUNTS.

been made with hollow horns or cane and reed stems with the aid of sharp sand. Concentric rings may be seen in many such perforations. Again, unfinished objects often have incomplete perforations whose condition shows that the drill was a solid tool. Many pipes seem to have been gouged out, but by what tool we cannot say. The most common form of perforation, however, is a conical bore which usually is made from both sides of the stone being worked. These holes meet at an angle about the center of the stone, and the opening is usually near one side of the perforation, showing that the drill was worked in obliquely from each side. In more carefully finished objects the center of the hole is later widened so that the whole diameter is more nearly equal, but only in a few does the peculiar conical appearance of the bore disappear. Some tools show a conical bore made entirely through from one side. Some investigators have doubted the possibility of drilling hard stones with such drills as have come down to us. For many of them are of such fragile material as red sandstone, shale and slate. Dr. Abbott† pictures a sandstone object of which he says: "By the aid of two stone drills we completed the perforation; accomplishing it after eleven hours of not difficult but rather tiresome labor." Two drills were used, one of jasper and one of slate. "The drill is of slate and comparatively soft, but it did not wear away more rapidly than the jasper specimen." We illustrate a number of typical forms from our valley. Fig. 61, one half natural size, is a double drill made from a moss agate. It seems almost incredible that such a tool could have been made from so hard a stone. It is one of the most beautiful objects we possess. Found in Farmington. Figs. 62, 63, 64, 65, represent drills with wide arrow like bases. Fig. 66 is a perforator made by rubbing. Figs. 67, 68, 69, 70, 71, 72, slender spear like tools, which were doubtless used as needles and awls as well as drills. Figs. 73, 74, represent large based perforators. Fig. 75, a small, very hard drill, resembling those from the Pacific coast. Some of these drills show the peculiar attrition polish that we noticed upon scrapers, and were doubtless used to perforate skins. They may have been hafted. Fig. 76 (c), one half natural size, presents a drill shaped tool that the writer believes to have been hafted and used as an awl to unravel stitches in skin robes, or possibly in fabricating baskets. It is not straight enough for a drill. Certain flaked tools of much larger size, whose edges are bevelled off sharply in opposite directions have been called reamers. When these were revolved to the left they would cut with both edges in succession, but the writer cannot understand what they were intended to cut. Fig. 77, shows a very fine example from Farmington.

KNIVES.

We find a large variety of implements which differentiate from scrapers and spears on one side and tomahawks, celts and fleshers on the other. Of the chipped class much the finer specimens were doubtless men's weapons, but in the polished types the highest evolution was in

---

† Stone Age in New Jersey, p. 326. Fig. 159, Smithsonian Pub., 394.

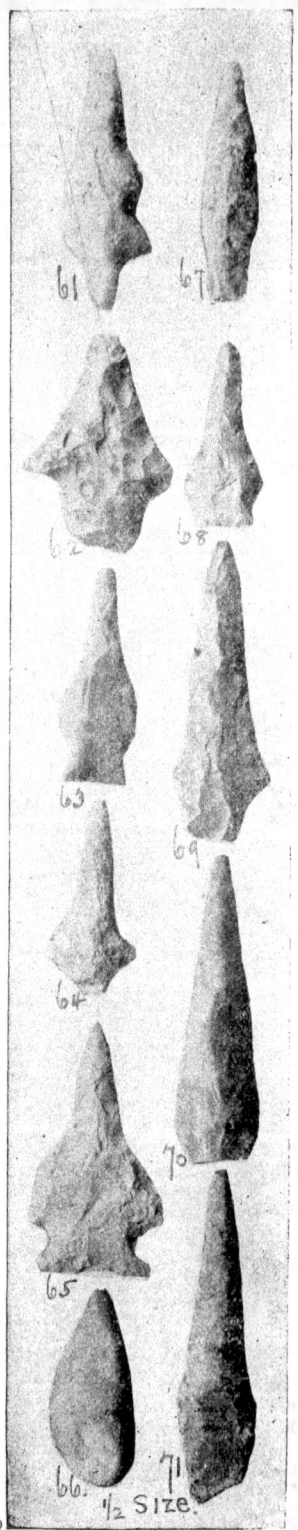

PERFORATORS.

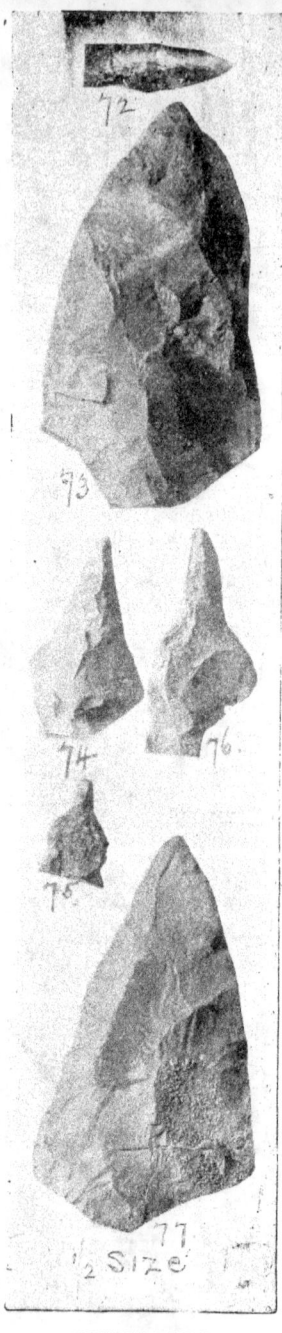

PERFORATORS.

woman's sphere of tools. Reserving a description of the weapon class for another heading, we will here outline those forms presumably domestic. The simplest of all were flakes struck off by one blow from a pebble, but the Tunxis Valley offers few suitable minerals for such flakes. We can only point to one object of a whitish opaque quartz, which was taken by the writer from the side of an excavation about three feet deep, during the trenching for the Bristol reservoir; fig. 78. Its artificial character is plain and its location very singular. A good many rudely made knives have been found, chipped mostly on one edge, some of which seem to foreshadow the later polished skinning knives; figs. 79, 80. Fig. 81, represents a most beautiful example of artistic chipping. It is of "hornstone," and chipped only on the blade, but work upon it is as fine as many specimens of Scandinavian art. Prof. Mason* illustrates one of these knives showing us the "primitive form of grip" or handle which we imitate; fig. 82. In fig. 83, we give a knife from Farmington exactly like it. Fig. 84 illustrates apparently a very ancient example in red sandstone. When one of these knives is held lengthwise, blade uppermost, along the hand, it will be seen to curve from one end to the other. When held properly the outlining of the edge sweeps from the

KNIVES.

forefinger in a gentle curve inward to the thumb. But if the knife is reversed the curve is away from the thumb. It seems only possible to cut a straight line when the curve sweeps along the natural curve of the hand from the thumb to the index finger, so we think this shape is *intentional*, not accidental.

---

* O. T. Mason, Primitive Industry, p. 46.

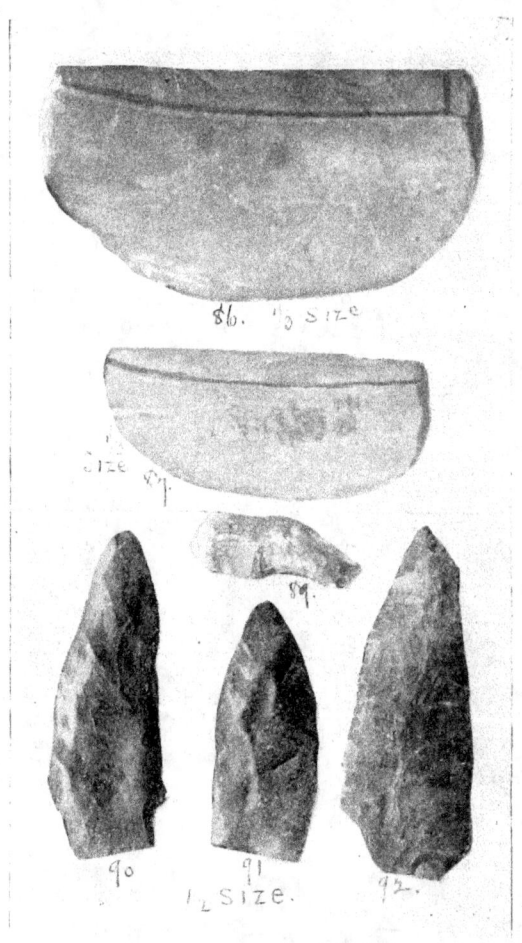

CELTS.

In fig. 86, one third natural size, we give a very fine example of a skining knife made of green slate from Plainville. The reader will readily see how closely it resembles a New England hash knife. These knives seem to have been made by grinding only and are pre-eminently the woman's tool. Fig. 87, represents another fine example from Plainville. There is another beautiful one made of black slate in the Bristol Museum. A very large example is shown in the American Museum of Natural History, New York, from Bloomfield. Dr. Abbot among many thousand |diverse tools only found one in New Jersey. Fig. 89, is a singular if not unique little knife from Burlington. It was obviously made to be hafted and would have cut up cooked meat very readily. A well made knife blade of such a curious substance as red shaly sandstone is shown in fig. 90. Fig. 91, seems very old. Fig 92, is from Bristol.

---

* Abbott, Stone Age in New Jersey, p. 303.

CELTS.

We now come to one of the most beautiful classes of all our Indian tools, the celt.‡ Upon these stones the ancient craftsman lavished some of his choicest skill. They are the most universal of all worked implements. A fine collection shows a wonderful variety of color and texture in stone, although all are made of heavy and tough materials. They were first pecked into shape and then polished more or less completely. The more common forms of Connecticut are quiteround in outline, yet many are oval or nearly flat. All typical celts agree in having a sharp blade, worked

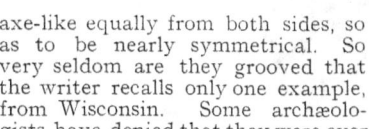

axe-like equally from both sides, so as to be nearly symmetrical. So very seldom are they grooved that the writer recalls only one example, from Wisconsin. Some archæologists have denied that they were ever hafted, yet one is exhibited in the American Museum, N.Y., found in a brook some fifty years ago. It is driven about half way through a well made handle and may have been either a tool or a weapon. These tools are generally thought to have been used in working wood. Probably they were employed also in rubbing down hard skins, as the Indian squaw doubtless used whatever tool came handy. As chisels they may have been pushed by the hand, but many show decided signs of having been vigorously pounded, as a joiner pounds his chisel. Working with no guide but his eye, no tool

¼ Size.

CELTS.

‡ From celtis—a chisel.

PESTLES.

but a stone hammer, and no measure but his hand, one is amazed to see how perfect some of these objects have been made. Fig. 93, one fourth natural size, is a very perfect black celt from Burlington. Fig. 94 (r), from Farmington, is more flat with its sides squared and beautifully polished nearly all over. Fig. 95 is almost a twin to 93. Fig. 96 shows a wider celt with expanding blade, made of a very dense black stone from Granby. Age has given this a beautiful "patina" of mottled bluish-grey and white. Only where a plow nipped one corner can the true color be seen. The depth of the weathering, while the polish of the stone remains as perfect as when made, would seem to indicate a great age. Its blade has been used until the edge is well battered down. Fig. 97, found by the writer in Plainville, differs from the others, in being flat and very thin. While perfectly shaped by pecking, only two inches of the blade has been polished. One side is flat while the other is beveled off after the manner of a plane. It would be a very serviceable tool in working charred wood, and capable of taking a very sharp edge. Implements of this class have been found made of quartz and simply chipped out, the extreme edge only showing the polish of long use. All such stones should be carefully collected for further study

THE PESTLE.

Schoolcraft* writes that Indian corn was raised along the Connecticut and tributary valleys, and coarsely reduced in mortars of stone and wood. This meal was our New England "hominy." The writer has never seen any mortars of stone from this section that he considered to have been used for such a purpose. He thinks our aboriginal mortars were made of hard wood, tradition says pepperidge trees. (*Nyssa Multiflora.*)

Schoolcraft§ pictures a Pennacook squaw of New Hampshire, pounding corn in a mortar, which is on the ground beneath a tree. Above it there is attached by a long cord to an overhanging limb a stone pestle. The rebound of the limb seems to *raise* the pestle and her hand gives it the downward blow. The writer cannot help the suspicion that some of Schoolcraft's pictures of life are quite imaginary; still he has seen numerous pestles with projections or grooves on the end perfectly adapted to such suspension. Schoolcraft† also pictures a pestle with an animal's head on the upper end, saying that it was "a family name wrought by a symbol," what we should call a "totem." Two such pestles are in the Bristol Museum, but not from the section we are describing. Pestles are quite frequently found, and being such conspicuous objects, usually reported to collectors. They never seem to have been polished, except from use on their working ends. Therefore in them we may see the art of pecking brought to its highest elegance, and many such objects are indeed most fair to look upon. In fig. 98, is shown a pestle from Bristol, found by the late Caleb Matthews on Chippins Hill, seventeen inches long. Fig. 99, depicts an extra fine pestle from Farmington. Made of a dark material it is evenly pecked into a perfect shape all around. In another respect this pestle may be unique. It certainly is a novel example of ancient stone art. Although made of a very hard stone, a hole of unknown depth about one half of an inch in diameter, has been drilled into its working end. Into this hole another stone of yet harder nature has been perfectly fitted, the whole being ground off evenly smooth. We have also another pestle in which a similar hole has been begun but left unfinished. The perfect pestle was found perhaps fifty years ago by an old negro who dwelt upon the site of the old Indian village. This old fellow had an exceedingly verdant memory, which reached backward several centuries while describing *his remembrances* of the ancient red men, as *he saw them* shooting their arrows across the primeval reaches of the meadows. The writer must now redeem a pledge made to the old man a decade ago when the pestle was reluctantly given into his keeping—to immortalize both the pestle and its finder. Jacob Sampson Freeman, for half a century the custodian of this last vestige of some Sagamore, cherishing it almost as a Fetich, he became involuntarily an humble disciple of science. May his memory remain as green as his imagination, as his shade gambols through the happy hunting grounds. Our pledge is fulfilled. *Requiescat in pace.*

* "Archives of Aboriginal Knowledge," Vol. I, p. 84.
§ Ibid, Vol. 4, p. 174.
† Ibid, Vol. 3, p. 466.

"The devices of primitive man are the forms out of which all subsequent expedients arise. The whole earth is full of monuments of nameless inventors."—*Mason.**

The general similarity of the culture existing among the Tunxis Indians to that of the natives of other sections of North America, as shown by their remaining implements, points to their common origin. Yet the dissimilarity of speech and the extent to which special forms of art and customs had differentiated in different sections, point also to a very ancient origin of man in America. In judging the advance and skill of any people by their artefracts, we must consider their surroundings, their food supply, and especially those materials upon which their skill might be expended. The comparative ease with which the more tractable materials could be obtained must ever have had as large an effect upon the expansion of special arts as the pressure of that necessity called the "mother of invention."

Yet a comparison of such worked objects as we possess shows the Tunxis†Indian to have been capable of work equal to most any people of America—unless it be claimed, which we shall not consider, that his better objects were the result of barter. The Indians of this section are believed to have always been few in number; for, except he attach himself to some food supply that is either by nature or through his own efforts made regular and unfailing, man never multiplies rapidly nor emerges from a savage state. All the great Oriental civilizations grew up around the wheat, barley, rice or date fields, or in the pastures of domesticated animals. So in America the nuclei of budding civilizations were found amid the maize or cocoa fields, or attached to the buffalo or the llama. Elsewhere existed only different degrees of a baser savageism, and even that a largely degenerate and apparently a disappearing people.

Of the Connecticut Indians we are told, "The women of an ordinary family cultivated and harvested two or three heaps of maize in a season

---

* Origin of Inventions, p. 413.

† We know nothing of prehistoric migrations of tribes. Those Indians whose relics we are discussing may have been of a hundred successive nations.

AGRICULTURAL TOOLS.

of from fifteen to twenty bushels each," and also raised beans, pumpkins and tobacco.* In their agricultural labors we are told that they used largely their fingers as tools. "The only other implements which the Indians seemed to have used were spades rudely constructed of wood, or a large shell fastened to a wooden handle."† As it must have been easier for the Indian to have made a stone spade than one of wood, such a conclusion seems hardly tenable.

Our early settlers were more interested in converting the Indian, when not killing him, than in studying his physical surroundings, to which we must owe the poverty of their descriptions.

It is only the span of three generations since the learned men of Europe considered their prehistoric relics to be either the weapons of fairies or the thunderbolts of the god of lightning.

---

* DeForest, Indians of Connecticut, p. 5, quoting Roger William's key.
† Ibid.

While the ungrooved celt was a universal tool, curiously enough the grooved tool, excepting a few hammer forms, seems to have been mostly confined to America. The prehistoric dwellers of the Tunxis Valley left us many grooved implements, ranging from the rudely notched picks of the steatite miners, through more or less perfect axe-like forms, to little hatchets or tomahawks. These are mostly classed as axes, but from many years' study of the ruder forms the writer cannot consider them either rejects or unfinished axes, but believes many of them were used as earth picks and hoes in cultivating maize. The agricultural tools are more rudely made than celts, often merely coarsely flaked into shape. Showing no signs of hammer pecking, their only polish is that of use, and this shows chiefly on the bit and in the groove. When we examine such a tool it will be seen that a line drawn from the center of the head to the center of the blade shows the blade curving

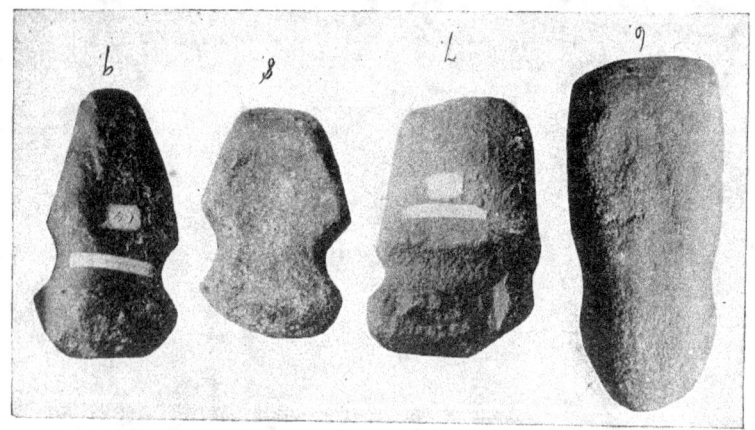

GROOVED AXES.

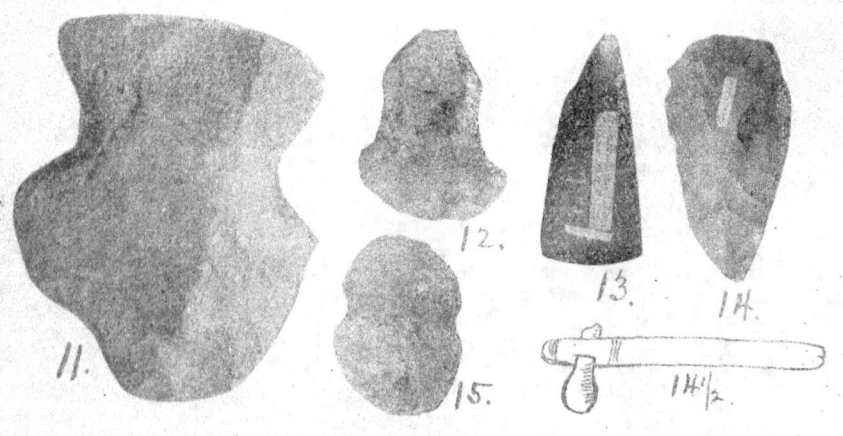

TOMAHAWKS.

away to one side. Fig. 2 (Farmington). No one could direct a straight blow with such a tool used axe fashion.

Fig. 3 (Plainville) gives us a side view of this form of tool which shows the point contended. Various leaf-shaped tools seem to belong in the section of digging implements. Fig. 4, from Windsor meadow, shows a fine and ancient example. Chipped spades of quartzite, somewhat resembling those from Illinois, only much ruder and smaller, have been found at Congamond Lake. They show a fine polish from use. Figs. 5, 5 (2).

The real grooved axe was built upon a straighter line than the hoe. Usually pecked into a more perfect shape, it was often laboriously polished all over. The nomadic nature of our aborigines and the vast forests full of partly decayed timbers must have rendered a great number of these tools unnecessary, yet we find some fine examples. Fig. 6c illustrates one from Southington. Fig. 7 is an unusual specimen from Farmington Ornamented with a ridge around both sides of the groove, it was once polished all over, but has been roughened anew by the unrelenting fingers of time. Fig. 8 shows a fine flat axe from Plainville. We also illustrate another example in fig. 9.

We may here speak of the tomahawk, which doubtless served to break up wood and bones on the march as well as for purposes of war. Some of these are very axe-like, as the specimen, fig. 11 c from Southington. Fig. 12 shows a very rare tool, a chipped quartzite hatchet from Farmington. Fig. 13 shows a beautiful object of the celt type, from Burlington, which we consider a typical tomahawk. In fig. 14, from Farmington, we have a third type which must have been used exclusively for war or chase. We believe this to have been much the more common form. We read of the torture of captives by the Indians, who were said to have tied the victims to a tree and thrown tomahawks with such skill that they remained attached to the tree around the captive's head. The futility of such a use of the prehistoric tomahawks needs no comment. The curious reader can find in Vol. 2, p. 16, of Winsor's "Narrative and Critical History of America," a Caribbean form of tomahawk, showing how they were helved, as given by Oviedo in his book, edition of 1547; fig. 14½. In this section we must include certain grooved stones found in Farmington and Southington, fig. 15 c. These stones were doubtless firmly fastened to a slightly elastic handle by a strap of rawhide and used as war clubs. We cannot agree with those who style them hammers.

GOUGES AND ADZES.

Closely connected with the celt and axe and having the same dua development, grooved and ungrooved types, are the gouge and adze They are among the most remarkable of ancient tools. Made of very hard stones they are always finely polished, and the cutting edge is always nearly perfectly symmetrical. They all agree in having one face flat and the other more or less acutely rounded. The gouges are hollowed out more or less deeply on the flat face and brought to a sharp curvilinear blade; some representing nearly a half circle, while others are more expanded, a few being nearly flat.

Examples: from Farmington, fig. 16; Granby, fig. 17; Plainville, 18, and Bristol, 18 a, are shown. Fig. 19 shows a chipped quartzite gouge from Congamond Lake, which recalls the pleolithic implements of Sweden.* It is the general opinion that gouges were used in making canoes. The adze differs from the gouge in being made for a helve. It is usually less deeply hollowed, has a more curved back, with a flatter face. The arrangement for helving is often exceedingly ingenious, especially when we consider that it must have been planned before the stone was worked down to its final shape. Some are merely flat celtlike forms with the blade brought to an edge even with the lower surface

---

* In the writer's cabinet are two similar tools from Sweden.

and only slightly curved to the sides. Fig. 20 shows a rare style from Granby, three inches long. Fig. 21 represents a typical form of adze, with a curved back and two ridges forming a raised groove for helving.

THE GOUGE-ADZE.

This implement combines the features of gouge and adze and is more common than the flat forms. The cutting edge varies the same as gouges and the raised back is sometimes grooved, and at others has carefully made ridges for attaching the helve, often so arranged as to protect the withe or strap used in seizing on the handle from the friction of use. Figs. 22, 23 R, 24, 25 illustrate the several forms.

In fig. 23 the mode of attachment is a small nipple-shaped protuberance. Fig. 26 R, from Plainville, is a very peculiar form, only 2½ inches long. It is exceedingly well made and deeply gouged on its face; upon its back is one very sharply made ridge. This tool must have had a small handle, probably of bone, and been driven chisel-fashion by a mallet. The illustrations show the several forms. This whole series of implements is of the highest interest but lack of space forbids further individual descriptions. This form of implement seems to have had a fuller development in New England than to the South or West.

GOUGES AND ADZES.

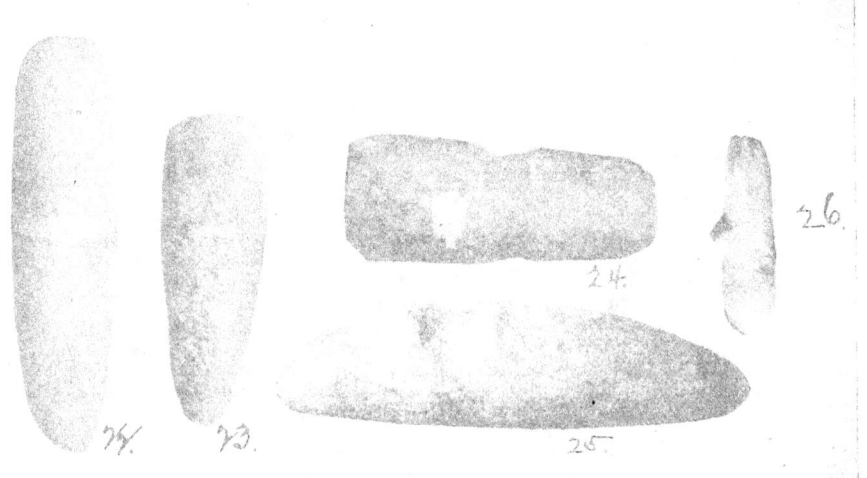

GOUGE-ADZES.

THE PLUMMET OR SINKERS.

Stones shaped like various styles of plummets are found all over the United States. Very elaborate forms in soapstone have been taken from the Florida mounds. The writer has collected them made from the central column of great sea shells (Busycon) on the shell mounds around Tampa. They were probably used as ornaments, although their use is a disputed point among many archæologists. We illustrate two local examples, fig. 27, Farmington; fig. 28, Plainville.

(A late writer in the Antiquarian contends that they were weapons to use as slings. We should enjoy seeing him using some of the plummets of shell, pottery and soapstone from the South.)

ORNAMENTAL AND CEREMONIAL OBJECTS.

That the ancient red man was not insensible to the seductions of pleasing shapes and colors is easily shown when we study their vestiges. Arrow points are found which today are valued for jewelry. No one can look over a good collection of these points without a feeling of wonder, not only at the great variety of shapes and materials, but also at the skill with which the beauties of the stone are made manifest. In all manner of implements we find uncommon and curiously marked stones, laboriously worked into shape. Upon the pottery we have already shown the love of ornamentation. The love for color expended itself also upon mats and basketry, of which we possess no prehistoric examples from this valley. Tanned skins and barks were dyed and painted. Teeth and claws of animals were made into necklaces. Bones and shells were largely made into beads both for use as ornaments and for money. But we know only of a few long beads from a grave in Farmington. These long beads are considered as of greater antiquity than the wampum forms.† The Indian was also lavish in the use of paints upon his own person. We are able to illustrate two small paint cups, one of which was dug up by Mr. Jacob Mesrole, of Southington, near Wonx spring, and when found was partly filled with red paint powder, fig. 27 *a*, and

---

† Although these beads came from a grave in Farmington, the writer is not satisfied of their being prehistoric. He would be pleased to hear of any others from this section of the state.

fig. 28 a, also from Southington. Lumps of red and yellow paints are not uncommon in Florida shell mounds. Aside from this use of paint and beads upon himself and his trappings, the subject of ornaments appears to have been closely allied to religious and ceremonial observances. The Indian made various ornamental objects of stone, bone and shells. The stones were mostly beautifully grained slates or crystalline forms. The use for which the varied objects were intended is yet buried in the oblivion that overwhelmed their makers. They no doubt filled a place in his imagination and helped to satisfy a craving, which, if it were not a love of art and beauty, was at least its embryonic form. They also doubtless had a further reason for being, some probably may have been the badges of official or priestly rank, and used as ceremonial accessories, while others may have simply ministered to the pride of their possessors, as mankind today takes pride in possessing painting and sculpture. Whatever may have been their use, they are found all over the United States east of the Rocky Mountains, more or less sparsely in New England, and becoming more numerous and varied in shape as we approach the ancient centers of denser populations. Uncommon forms have more restricted areas, and there is quite a perceptible difference in special arts among the Southern Indians, where certain forms unknown to New England are found. Various names are given to these objects, according to the imagination of the describer. Curiously enough the older authorities in ethnology, such as Schoolcraft, seem to be the poorest. Comparative study has proven more valuable than tradition.

GORGETS AND PENDANTS.

Flat objects with two perforations whose opposite faces are always beautifully polished and which are usually symmetrical, that is if cut into two equal parts each would be the counterpart of the other, are called gorgets. Fig. 29 shows a beautiful specimen in green banded slate from Plainville. Similar objects with only one perforation, more usually near one end, are called pendants. Fig. 30 gives one of an unknown lightish colored material from Granby, and fig. 31 one from Southington of black slate. Broken and decayed fragments of gorgets are frequently found on village sites.

AMULETS.

These are long and narrow stones, always highly polished, usually made of black or banded slate, having one face flat and the other either convex or triangular. They appear in two types, the plain bar; called bar amulet, or with the upper face more or less resembling a sitting bird, with an expanded tail, and head with projecting eyes, called bird amulet. Both forms agree in having one conical perforation at each end passing from the flattened base obliquely upward and outward. Fig. 32 shows a beautiful bar amulet of banded slate from Bristol. Fig. 33 shows a bird amulet from Ohio to illustrate the type. Fig. 34 represents a bird amulet, the head broken off, made of soapstone, from Terryville. These objects are exceedingly rare in New England. Their use is unknown. The writer imagines them to have been connected with the operations of the shamans or priests called pow-wows. Fig. 35 and 36 portray a very different form of ornament from Burlington. This handsome relic is a perfect specimen, and its perfection seems more wonderful when we consider that it was made with no other rule or square than the eye and hand of the artisan. It has two perforations passing up from the center of the central boat-shaped groove at such an angle that a cord passed through each suspends the object on a level. It is made of banded slate. These stones are called shuttles, but of their use we know nothing; they are quite rare. Never bored except in the center, their perforations are always cylindrical and very small for an Indian tool. Fig. 37 shows a singular and well polished object from Bristol of no apparent use. This may be a clay stone, but it has

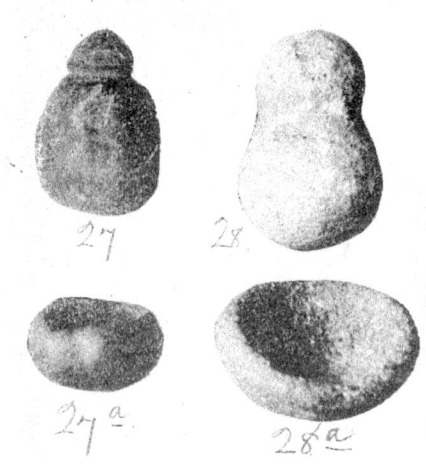

PLUMMETS AND PAINT CUPS.

the greasy polish of long handling, which seems to cling to an Indian implement for ages in the earth.

BANNER STONES.

The banner stones differ from other objects in this class in having one large perforation through the center. In this section all bores are round; west and south a few are found with oval perforations. Examinations of a number of large collections seem to prove to the writer that all symmetrical forms have round bores, while those with a symmetrical wing have oval bores. The writer would be pleased to learn of exceptions to this statement for New England.

These are among the choicest examples of prehistoric art. While mostly made of slate, many are found in very hard materials. Fig. 38 represents one from Columbia, Conn., worked from crystal. They seem to have been blocked out and shaped before being bored, as is shown in fig. 39 R from Farmington. They are thought to have been badges of office or ceremonial flags, borne upon handles which were doubtless painted and gayly bedecked with colored feathers and carried in dances and processions. The finished specimens are always very highly polished and almost perfectly symmetrical. Fig. 40 R represents a fine "butterfly" banner from Bristol. In fig. 41 we illustrate an immense arrow-shaped stone found some twenty years ago in Southington. One face is of light gritty sandstone, the other of a smooth red shale almost slate. It is fully seventeen inches long, thirteen inches wide, and less than one inch thick. Its great size precludes any useful purpose. We must believe that some figure was painted on its smooth face, and that it was used as a banner stone. Yet it may have been a totem. When shown to Prof. Otis T. Mason, the curator of ethnology of the National Museum, he told the writer that he knew of but two such objects, both being in Washington. They were much smaller, and came from the Apache country.

It opens a curious conjecture what the occurrence in so widely separated districts of such singular stones may mean, more especially when we consider that the Tunxan and Apache Indians probably represent different phylogenetic stems.

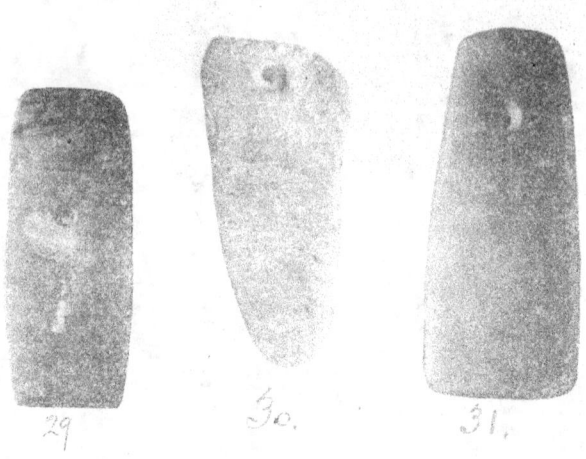

GORGETS AND PENDANTS

THE RELIGIOUS IDEA AMONG THE ALGONKINS.

It is not the scope of this paper to discuss the moral and religious life of our Indians. But a better appreciation of certain objects may be obtained by a slight glimpse into the workings of the later Indian's mind. Dr. Daniel Brinton[1] has published a learned book upon Indian myths and religious traditions. Cushing[2] is also publishing a singular attempt at describing the ancient Zuñian system of religious ceremonials. These works give us the remaining opinions of the higher minds, among the Indians and their traditions. It seems hardly probable that the common people comprehended what glimpses of ethical or cosmic truths might underlie their myths or ceremonials. For instance, the great divinity among the Algonkin people was Michabo—the great white rabbit. This word was compounded from *michi* (great) and *wabos*, the little grey rabbit of our woods. Now the Algonkin root word for white was *wab*. Dialectic forms occur, as *waupan*, the morning; *waubon*, the east, the dawn. The name *michabo* probably was really the great white dawn, the creating light, the morning and sunlight, which was a common form of Nature God among many people. But the Indian, confused by the similarity of the root form of the words, degraded the conception to a big white rabbit and made this nonsensical being his god.[3] Such misconceptions are not unknown in modern religious cults. Having no real monotheistic conceptions the Indian supplicated such local superstitions as his fancy feared or hoped to bribe. Brinton[4] gives an Algonkin[5] prayer overheard by the Jesuit Brebœuf, anterior to 1636: "Oki thou who dwellest in this spot I offer thee tobacco. Help us; save us from shipwrecks; defend us from our enemies; give us good trade; bring us back safe to the village." This contains no moral principle: recognizes no relation above that of barter.

---

1. Myths of the New World. Phil., 1896.
2. 13th Annual Report, Bureau of Ethnology, Washington.
3. Brinton, Ibid, p. 196.
4. Ibid, p. 339.
5. The historic Tunxans were of Algonkin stock.

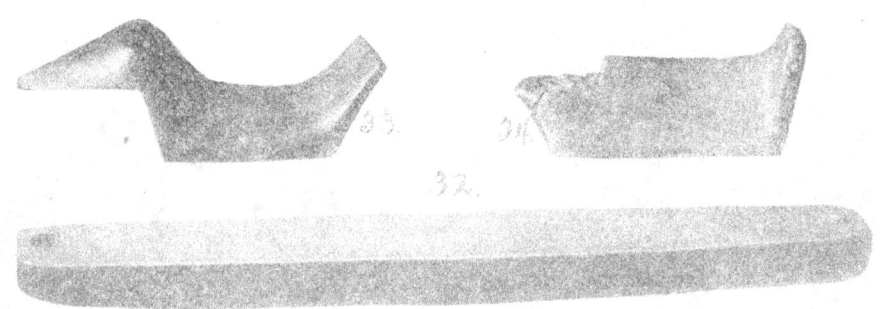

AMULETS.

The Indian gave tobacco in exchange for that which he thought that the invisible could yield to or deny him. And yet is not this even a higher standard than that of some of our modern sagamores of trade who seek to bribe the demiurge of legislation for power to prey upon their fellowmen? Those ceremonial relations that grew out of the etiquette of contact, or which were woven around the individual by tribal conservatism, modified by and intermingled with a belief in the incantations and conjurations of the Shamans, bounded the religious horizons of the common Indian. The Shamans or Pow-wows were the priests among the Indians; also the jugglers, nature-doctors, rain-makers and witch-finders. Incapable of comprehending the phenomena of nature, he lived in a superstitious fear of unseen influences and sought to propitiate or deceive the forces that he supposed were behind them. But it is nowhere shown that he worshipped devils, any more than that Saul worshipped a devil when he besought the witch at Endor. Yet, even if certain esoteric truths may have been conveyed along the centuries through the initiations of those secret societies which seem the common property of a certain stage of savagedom, they seemed to have exercised no ennobling power over the individual.* He was hopelessly entangled amid the meshes of an hundred ancient remembrances and customs whose beginnings and causations had been lost in the mist of ages, but whose power to enthrall him grew ever stronger with the procession of the years. We are irresistibly led to the conclusion that among the red men the religious idea had become completely submerged in the ceremonial. The spontaneity of the individual had been lost in a debasing web of ceremonial communism. Their myths indeed remained like those shining planets which science teaches us are dead and yet nightly parade the glittering but soulless shadows of once life-sustaining orbs. Communism invaded every walk of the Indian's life. Whatever he possessed, it forced him to share with others,† although among some tribes horses and probably arms and personal adornments belonged to individuals, male and female owning their own implements. The land, however, was held in common. When he died his chiefest possessions were commonly destroyed at his burial. His wife and children were usually left nothing. Religion demanded prolonged and shameful mourning among many tribes for the poor woman whose husband had departed for the happy hunting grounds. In every direction he seems to have been compassed about with customs that he dare not violate and yet which forbade the possibility of individual progress beyond fixed lines. hence everywhere we found the Indians a degenerating people.

---
* Vide Churchill, Pop. Scie. Mon., Dec. 1890, "The Duk Duk Ceremonies."
† See Lucian Carr, Antiquarian for 1897, page 92.

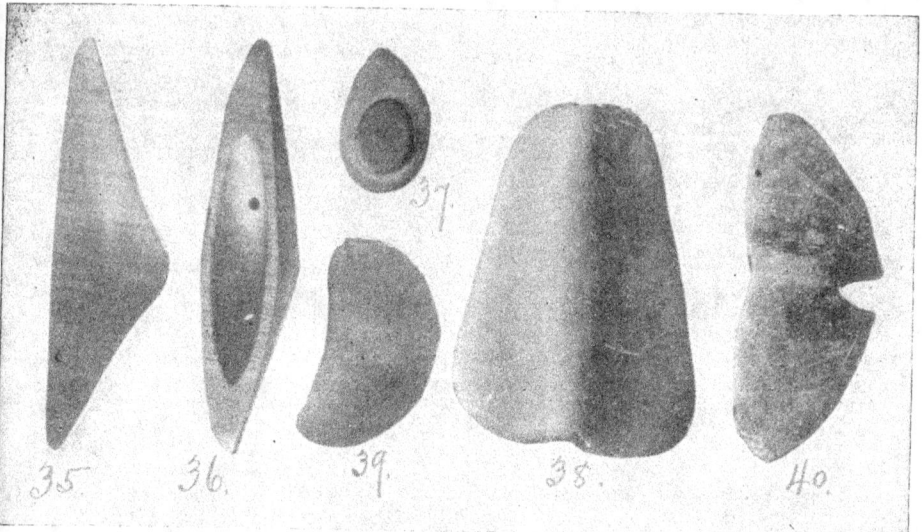

AMULETS AND BANNER STONES.

A civilization blasted in its generous youth by the deathly germ of socialism, its age ever "looking backward" into the night of tradition, the future of the Indian had no hopes of ultimate amelioration. His highest efforts at civilization could not escape the ban of socialism. The priestly classes who ruled Mexico and Peru maintained the most elaborate forms of prohibitions and debasing paternalisms, ever the obverse sides of socialism.

All mankind, be it red, black or white, dream of an Arcadia where labor is not needed and selfishness unknown. The modern followers of Balaam, cursing at present progress, point to this golden age in a communal past. But the finger of investigation, ever delving deeper into the mysteries of the ages, always finds the golden age of socialism receding yet deeper into the elusive obscurity of the past. Along the centuries time has printed the immutable law of evolution. It is in the liberty to variation and the guaranteed integrity of the individual effort that progress plants her seeds. Whatever unduly restrains the individual under the bonds of a forced uniformity ultimately blights the whole collection of individuals. Such Aryan people as cast off socialistic communism progressed. The Indian retaining communism sank ever deeper in its hopeless enmeshments.

An interesting treatise might be elaborated upon this subject, but to our present purpose it limits itself to the uses of tobacco, the occurrence of images and totemism. The manner in which the religious idea was undoubtedly connected with the ceremonial objects just described is at present too much involved in obscurity for any description. Regarding images Dr. Brinton says, "Idols of stone, wood or baked clay were found in every Indian tribe without exception so far as I know."* We must not conclude from this that idols were largely venerated among the half-nomadic Connecticut aborigines. And we should hesitate to believe that such images as have been found represented any fixed attributes or definite divine qualities, as they seem to have done in Mexico. In the Western States very many curious pieces of pottery representing

* Myths of the New World, p. 343.

often old hunchbacked squaws are found among the mounds and called idol mugs. In the middle South, stone and clay images and heads occur. For the curious we insert a clay image, fig. 42, with the peculiar flat face seen upon the larger idols in stone, and a stone head, fig. 43, which we consider as very ancient, both from Nagooche, Ga., and never previously illustrated. The student will find a very ancient and probably pre-aztecan idol in the Bristol Museum, found in Central America. The writer possesses a quartzite mealing stone, or round pestle from Farmington which has been elaborately worked into a perfect shape, whose upper face shows a bird plainly scratched out, but not suitable for pho-

FIGURE 41.

tographing. We also show in fig. 44 a singular flat head exhumed on Union Hill, Bristol, some ten years ago. This is the only representation of a human head, we have ever known from this valley, except some pipes, which are obviously intrusive and apparently of post-Columbian Cherokee manufacture.

TOTEMS.

Among all peoples we find individuals or families with animal names, and among some remain beliefs or traditions which associate these people with animal ancestors. The ancient Jews possessed these Totemic animal names,* which was one among the many singular resemblances of rites and customs that led many theoretical writers to

---

* "Israelite and Indian," by Garrick Mallory. Pop. Scie. Mon., 1889—Nov. and Dec.

consider the Indians as the veritable lost ten tribes of Israel.† We now recognize that such resemblances do not indicate any necessary blood relationship or previous intercommunication, but that similar mental states when meeting similar environmental conditions develop similar expedients. It is hardly probable that the Indian actually believed himself to have descended from any brute such as he saw about him, but rather from some transcendant and spiritual animal, which possibly he may have considered as a common ancestor of both himself and his animal namesake. Among some tribes a belief was said to have prevailed that at death they would return into their totemic animal, and probably some animals were held as sacred from this cause. It seems probable that all animal worship may have grown out of this idea of metempsychosis allied with the veneration of ancestors. When an Indian found a natural object which he believed to resemble his supposed totemic ancestor he was led to venerate it, either as a reminder of his ancestral form, or perhaps as the veritable abode of the ancestral spirit, for the Indian in his ignorance of nature's laws was not troubled to explain the manner of things. The local Manitos we read about were often doubtless these totems, while others represented the mysterious forces of nature, as the noises at Moodus. We are able to present a fine totemic image of a duck which was found on the Indian trail that ran from Bristol to Burlington. It is now in the cabinet of W. C. Richards at Bristol, a venerable and respected relic. [See frontispiece.]

TOBACCO AND PIPES.

To elaborate the use of tobacco alone would be more than sufficient to occupy all our allotted space. A great deal has been written upon it since the time when the earlier visitors from Europe were amazed upon seeing smoke pouring out from the nostrils of the naked Indians. Amid much that has been fancifully written about tobacco we may safely reach a few conclusions. The Indians believed the smoke to be agreeable to his invisible gods, and wafted it to them as an incense. He seems nearly everywhere to have connected the cardinal points with his creating spirits and to have wafted smoke to the four quarters of the horizon as well as to the east at sunrise. In the more agricultural sections where a sedentary population had bred up more elaborate ceremonies the pollen of maize was used as a holy sprinkling, or emblem of fructification. Large pipes with long stems gaily painted and elaborately adorned with the heads, and more especially the wings of birds, were used by heralds and other travelers as passports or safe permits when approaching strange tribes. Treaties of peace or alliance and all social compacts seem to have been ratified and sealed, so to speak, by the general successive smoking among the contracting parties of one of these pipes. War is also said to have been proclaimed by sending a red pipe adorned with red feathers. Says the Jesuit Charlevoix:* "The custom is to smoke the calumet when you accept it, and perhaps there is no instance where the agreement has been violated which was made by this acceptation. To smoke in the same pipe, therefore, in token of alliance, is the same thing as to drink in the same cup, as has been practiced at all times by many nations." We have no calumet pipes from this section, but illustrate a noble specimen from Nagooche, Ga., fig. 45. What would we not give could it only tell us the story of all the lips that have pressed it. Among all peoples where the social compact has not yet acquired the force of definite and general laws and an efficient police, we find these singular substitutes, which stand to our laws as do hieroglyphics to our modern alphabets. The cities of refuge among the Semitic nations, the eating of salt among the Bedouin, blood brotherhood among the African, taboos in Australasia, and church sanctuary in mediæval Europe, seem various ways of attaining a common idea. Yet it remains probable that the Indian ordinarily had nothing

---

† See "Peruvian Antiquities." Von Tschudi, pp. 8 to 12. New York, 1855.
* "Voyage to America," Vol. I. page 130. Dublin, 1766.

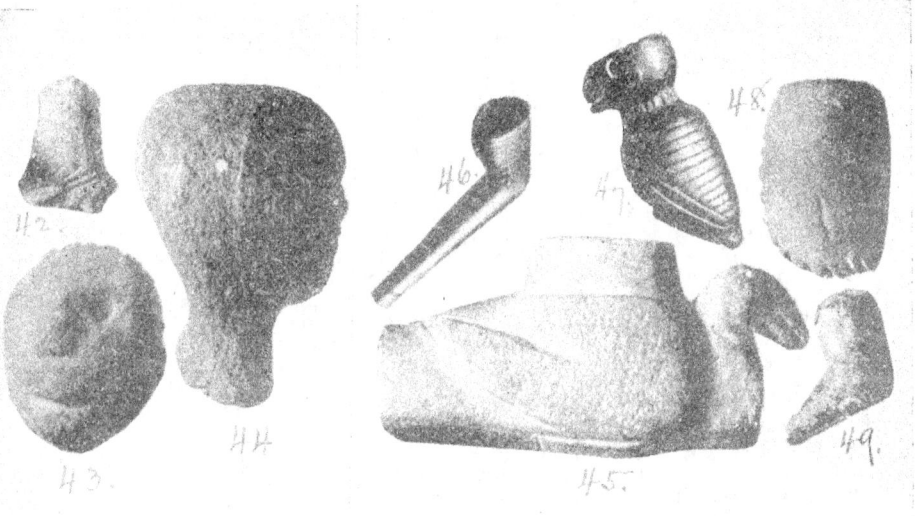

IDOLS.   PIPES.

more than a sensual love for its narcotic qualities in using tobacco. It gave him dreams, and dreams are ever the cherished mentor of the savage, and assisted him in acquiring the frenzy necessary to incantation and prophecy. The pipes which have been found in this section all differ one from another, so that we cannot assign to any the honor of being a local form. In the American Museum of New York is a magnificent greenstone calumet pipe from near Middletown, Conn., of the platform type, which has been called the mound-builder's pipe. Fig. 46 shows a pipe of steatite with a long stem, resembling a modern briar pipe. At the union of bowl with stem is a hole which has been luted with cement, a common Indian expedient rendering it easy to clean. Found in Plainville it represents a type thought by some to be common to the dreaded Mohawks. Fig. 47 m shows a very peculiar and elaborately carved pipe of black slate found on the west mountain of Southington. It has a hole in the rim of the bowl for suspension. It resembles a raven. In the Algonkin myth of the deluge the raven took the place of the Jewish dove. This pipe also reminds one of the thunder bird of the Vancouver Indians. In fig. 48 we present a pipe made of red sandstone, the mate of which we have never seen. The superb collection of Commodore Douglass in New York contains nothing like it. It is certainly genuine, and was dug up in Bristol about ten years ago. Fig. 49 shows a small steatite pipe also found near Bristol. A pottery pipe was shown in the April paper. Several other pipes have been found in this valley. Such as the writer has seen are manifestly intrusive, and not prehistoric. Among them is one genuine Haidah black pipe and several green slate pipes from the Cherokee artisans.

We now turn to the red man's art as we find it embalmed in his offensive and defensive weapons. We believe the primitive man was by choice an eater of meat, although made by his oft necessities, omnivorous. We are led more closely to this opinion from the belief which grows upon us that all our edible grains and fruits have been modified toward perfection by man, even by this naked savage man, from primitive forms not capable of sustaining human life. As they journeyed and jostled together along the slow and rugged course of evolution, man gave such plants as were useful to him his protection, and they returned his care with an ever increasing harvest. It was also the spirit of primitive man to be cruel, for was not all nature cruel and pitiless unto him? He recognized nothing of that pity of our modern conceptions of the brotherhood of life, and having the universal instinct of savageism which considers all mankind without the pale of its own clan as an enemy, war was, if not his pastime, at least his frequent necessity. Hence we find the highest development of his skill in those weapons devoted to the destruction of life, and in the manufacture and adornment of those ceremonial objects whose functions were closely interwoven with the pomp and panoply of war. It is our privilege today as at no other known epoch of the world's history to attempt a review of a people in their entirety. To seek man out ere he was able to record his achievements and to follow him where his deeds were no longer worth recording. The Indian lived in the present, forgetful of his true past, and knowing nothing of his future beyond those unanswering fears and fancies which attend both the weakness of infancy and the decrepitude of age. But we may view him from the swaddling clothes of the primitive troglodyte, through the robust adolescence of invention, to the miserable senility that closed his epoch. It is this priceless privilege of forcing from the past a mental biograph of the progress of mankind and his inventions which contributes the truest zest in our study of man. .

The bow and arrow of the Indian furnished his most effectual weapon, both in war and chase, to which he added for closer thrusting the spear or lance and the knife or dagger. These arrows and spears, while sometimes headed with bone or wood and canes tempered hard by heating in a fire, were mostly tipped with points of chipped stone. In the

FIG. 50 IS PROBABLY A FLAKER. FIGS. 51 ARCHAIC FORMS OF ARROWS.

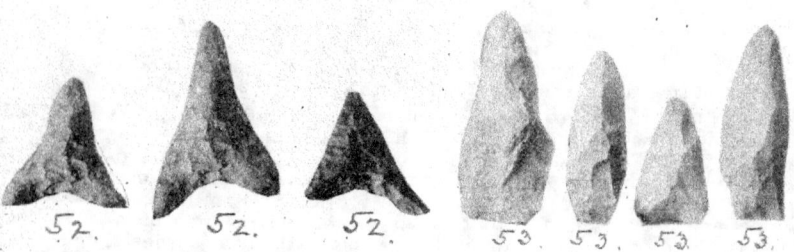

ARROW POINTS.

"Story of the Pilgrim Fathers," by Arber, 1897, page 432, we find the following in "Governor Bradford's Relation," which was printed in 1622, referring to the first conflict with the Indians: "We took up 18 of their arrows, which we sent to England by Master Jones (of the Mayflower): some whereoff were headed with *brass*, others with hart's horns and others with eagle's claws." Not a word spoken of stone heads. Some modern archæologists are beginning to believe that our historic Indians made none of such weapons as we now find. In the first interview with Samoset, we read, "He had a bow with three arrows, one headed and two unheaded." I find no mention in stone arrow points in use, in the Relations of Governor Bradford. Hence it is that we find the art of stone chipping, which we have classed as the eldest of his inventions' ultimately carried by the Indian to the highest point of perfection. The bows themselves that gave the Tunxan arrows force have turned to dust along with the arms that drew them; the shafts of the spear and arrow have melted in the pitiless crucible of nature. But the stones that gave them their cruel effectiveness remain, eloquent witnesses of their fabricators' skill. When we handle these beautiful objects of inanimate stone, we feel speaking from them an epitome of the Indian's civilization. When we compare the rude and almost formless figurines taken from the early tombs of Asia Minor with the finished works of a

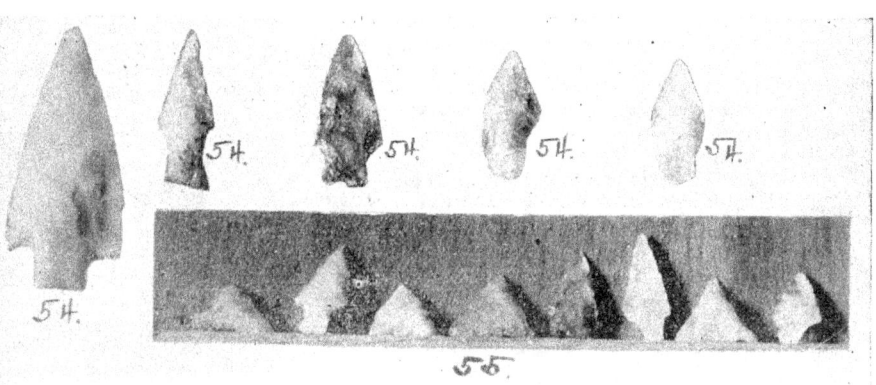

FIGS 54.   ROCK CRYSTAL POINTS.   FIGS. 55.   MINUTE POINTS.

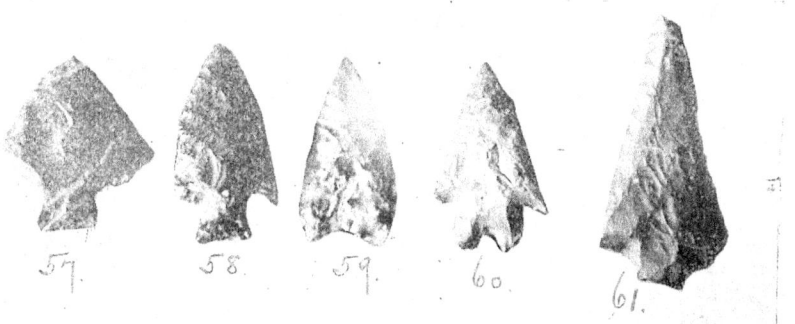

ARROWS.

Phidias we may compass the evolution of Grecian art.* So here we find entombed the fruits of the entire evolution of the red man's art in chipping in stone. From the timid and uncertain blows of the paleolithic savage, step by step the acquired skill of assured art was imperceptibly welded with the conscious hand, until we behold here such results as the white man with all his tools has nowhere been able to imitate. Stone chipping is now believed to be a lost art. The ethnologists of the Smithsonian Institute have never found an artisan who, even when supplied with all the tools of modern art, was able to imitate some of the leaf-shaped implements of prehistoric man. And the most skilful of the flint knappers of Brandon, England, men whose occupation is making gun flints also failed after months of effort to produce the forms made by a savage whose only tools were stones and bone.

It is not certainly known how the Indian made these arrow points, working such a brittle material as white quartz into the exquisite forms here portrayed. It is the general belief that chert jasper slate and quartz cobbles were first split into narrow flakes with stone hammers. Possibly they were heated in pits and split by cooling suddenly with water. Partly made implements were often buried in considerable quantities. It is supposed that these stones were thus softened and rendered more tractable. Such a cache was found some years ago near Hadley, Mass., containing sixty arrow and spear blocks. These blocks are so old that they were turned to an ashy white, they resemble the St. Acheul blocks in shape and coarse chipping. The flakes were gradually chipped down into shape with the little knockers. When the stone had thus been partly outlined, it was finished by another process. Either some hard object as stone, bone or horn was used as a chisel driven by a hammer to force off little flakes from either side alternately, or the so-called flakers† were used to push suddenly against the arrow, being worked from alternate sides, each impulsion of the tool taking off a little splinter opposite the point of impact. Various arrow flakers have been found among surviving savages. The only tool resembling these from this section that we have seen is shown in fig. 50, which

* Vide De Cesnola Collection of Central Park. New York.
† See figs. 15 and 16.

ARROWS.

resembles the alleged bone flakers from the prehistoric cemetery of Madisonville, Ohio. We are able to conceive no other use for the above implement. Skillful men in all tribes where suitable materials were obtainable seem to have made a business of arrow chipping, and it is known that points were sent in barter to great distances from the places where they were fabricated. Some twenty-five years ago a cache of perfect jasper arrow points was found near Compounce containing seventy-eight fine specimens.

These chipped implements divide naturally into two orders, those notched or tanged for attachment to a shaft, and those with no perceptible arrangement for hafting. By general consent archæologists separate them into three divisions—arrow points, usually under two inches in length; spear points, two inches and upward, and knives. The arrow point differentiates into the drill, the bunter, and the tanged knife or scraper, as shown in our first articles. We shall here consider only those forms used in war and chase. Space forbids a consideration of the many curious forms, and speculations upon the manner of their development from some presumably primitive ideal. The inquiring reader will find the general type forms carefully worked out in a recent monograph by Mr. Gerard Fowkes.* A glance at the forms here illustrated will readily convince the student that no one people had a monopoly of arrow forms, as we can show here every type of Mr. Fowkes except the long lozenged shape tang which we find from Arkansas and Mississippi. Anyone familiar with large collections of arrow points learns to distinguish certain peculiarities of finish and material by which the probable source of any individual point may be guessed. There is a distinct individuality which distinguishes the fossi chert points of Florida from the same colored type of Wisconsin. The white quartz of Connecticut are easily separable from those of Virginia or Carolina. Yet this shows more in the material and the way it takes a finish than in the skill of the artisan. If there is any form more common than others in this region, we think it is the small points of white quartz. Upon some workshops, notably at Compounce, nearly all are found of this substance and upon the near mountain may be seen the veins and pits from which the Indian has pounded out his material. Also red sandstone and shale seem to have been largely used, as they are the most abundant of our workable stones; very many decayed fragments are found in every considerable workshop. If the writer were to express an opinion as to the more ancient forms in this valley, it would be for the type here illustrated, fig. 51, of which many are found so very old that all trace of the chipping has been eroded, and they look as though they had been rubbed into shape. Most of the forms occur universally, but occasionally local workshops are found with nearly all the points of one type, notably in Granby, where all the specimens are triangular; figs. 52. In one place in Farmington were found a number of very rude arrows of an intractable metal which may be very old; we have seen nothing like them elsewhere, either in shape or material; figs. 53. Basanite and red and yellow jasper pebbles were found in the bed of the Farmington and made into beautiful forms. Argillite occurs in older types. Also some exceedingly beautiful points are found of the clearest rock crystal, equal to anything from North Carolina, fig. 54. Many arrows occur in materials of whose source we know nothing.

FIGURE 62.

---

* 13th Annual Report, Bureau of Ethnology.

Arrows have been divided into war points and hunting points, the former inserted into the shaft so loosely that when the shaft was pulled out the head would remain in the wound; such a wound would be very serious in Indian surgery. While those styled hunting arrows are notched or tanged so as to secure firm attachment to the shaft and be easily recovered by cutting the dead animal. It is also possible that some of the smallest points were used in a blow tube made of a hollow reed. In such cases the point was probably poisoned. Venomous serpents were made to bite raw flesh, and when this had become partly putrescent the arrows were thrust into it and made highly poisonous. Fig. 55 shows these minute points from this valley. Fig. 56 shows eight war points of various shapes. Fig. 57 is a very curious shaped tanged point. Fig. 58 is a beautiful object of smoky quartz. Fig. 59 is of smoky quartz, and may have been a knife; it has sharp edges. Fig. 60 has serrated points with long barbs and a deeply notched tang, a rare and beautiful object in greenish stone. Fig. 61 is bevelled off on opposite sides like a reamer.

Many other forms are illustrated, which our space forbids us to classify.

THE SPEAR OR LANCE.

The spear was made both for war and chase, and used also for fishing. The long slender points are commonly called fish spears, but the writer has not found them as often on the banks of brooks as on the uplands. Spears represent some of our most beautiful objects of the Indian's handicraft. We believe that many were used for diverse purposes of which we know little. The spear is usually tanged for hafting similarly to the hunting arrow and was probably attached in the same manner. In fig. 62 we present a marvelous implement of black chert from Southington, fourteen inches long, and a small part, probably two inches, has been broken off and lost from one end. This tool has that peculiar elongated diamond shape which may be noticed in some large obsidian implements from Mexico, called sacrificial knives. Some

SPEARS.

twelve years ago we saw two similar implements in white chert at Palatka, Fla., which were unfortunately lost in the great fire a few years later. The occurrence of such aberrant types of implements in such diverse regions opens many conjectures. We illustrate nine typical spears. Fig. 63 is an immense leaf-shaped blade of yellow slate from Plainville. This is our rarest form. It is probable that some of the leaf-shaped implements were intended to be finished in this shape. Figs. 64 and 65, beautiful black chert, Bristol. Fig. 66, fine arrow-shaped spear, Farmington. Fig. 67, red jasper, Plainville. Fig. 68, magnificent white spear, almost like noraculite, from Granby. Fig. 69, red sandstone, Bristol. Fig. 70, large awl-shaped spear, from Bristol.

We know nothing how the shafts of these spears were made, and possessing neither spear nor arrow shafts or bows from this region, shall not attempt to discuss their forms. Those interested in the subject of Indian bows should read the splendid monograph of Prof. Mason.*

KNIVES AND DAGGERS.

The earlier explorers of America, especially those who touched along the coast of Florida, described the Indians as using knives of shells with which they cruelly cut and mangled their victims. It is probable that similar implements were used by all Indians dwelling near the seas, but none have come down to us from this section. We also believe that very many of the sharp points which we class as arrow heads, were inserted into split wooden handles, securely fastened with fibres, glue or pitch, and used as knives.

It is also more than probable that some of our long slender spears were used with very short handles as daggers. In fig. 71 is given an ideal restoration of a fine red jasper knife from Farmington, which would serve equally for a scalping knife or a dagger. In figs. 72, 73, 74, we show three typical forms. Fig. 75 is a curious implement which both curves on the edge and bends sideways upon itself.

In fig. 80, from Granby, is a magnificent specimen of the leaf-shaped implement which represents the highest perfection of the art of stone chipping. Made of a fine yellow chert, it is absolutely perfect in all directions. Near the edge of the broad end is a crystal that sparkles like a nest of diamonds. This tool was dug up from apparently undisturbed gravel in digging a well six feet below the surface. It is believed that many of these leaf-shaped tools were wrapped in pieces of fur or rawhide for handles and used as daggers. Fig. 81 is a beautiful chert dagger from Bristol.

We have shown what vestiges of the prehistoric man have come down to us. There yet remain many articles which undoubtedly are Indian—notably a fine canoe found at Plainville, and now in the Bristol Historical rooms. There is also a large stone mortar which tradition associates with an old Indian who gave his name to Chippen's Hill in Bristol, and the traditionally historic cave dwelling of one Compounce, whose name lingers in the beautiful glacial lakelet that he owned. But the writer intended only a description of prehistoric remains. There are many graves in Farmington of unknown age. On the highway from Bristol to Burlington, in the edge of Edgewood, there is a hill of glacial debris that rests upon stratified gravel. On this hillside have been seen low mounds which were undoubtedly artificial, and which had not been constructed since the white man settled in Bristol. Of this, the owner of the adjoining land, Mr. Jerome, is sure. Some years ago, Mr. William Richards and the writer met Mr. Jerome and dug into one of these mounds. Digging down about two feet through soil that showed plainly marks of previous disturbance, we came to a level floor made of round cobble stones, perhaps three feet long by two in width. When these stones were removed, we found yet another layer beneath, which

* "North American Bows and Arrows." by Otis T. Mason, Smithsonian Report, 1893, p. 631. et Seq.

showed plain evidence of a severe heating. Between the two layers of stone was an inch or more of charcoal. The lower floor rested upon undisturbed and stratified gravel. No tool of any kind was found. A specimen of the charcoal was sent to Washington, but the Government microscopist found no evidence of animal matter in it. The nature of the pits or altars, or whatever they may have been, remains a mystery.

The preparation of these papers has been a labor of love to the writer, in hoping to help rescue from oblivion some few remaining vestiges of those who once roamed these valleys in their pristine beauty; if he thus helps to hinder their further dispersion, he has his full reward.

We, in all the pride of our higher civilization, owe it to the memory of these races, whose very savageism kept the hills and dales of America a rich and virgin soil that we might wax strong upon them. They gave untold centuries to the development of the maize from a wild grass of Florida, those golden grains that are richer to us than all the golden cliffs of the Rockies. Let us then garner into museums those vestiges that yet remain. Time, ever envious of the sole perogative of immortality, seeks their sure effacement. The earth and air wage unrelenting warfare for the destruction of these unprotesting witnesses of a vanished people. In their history as left us in these stones, silent no longer to those who interrogate them aright we may read the story of our own ancestral struggle in the long, dark, awful night which left no verbal record. The winged spirit of thought goes backward into those prehistoric, abysmal depths, and shows us the sure origin, both of what remains to us of savage instincts and that tenacious, ever upward, aspiring spirit which through invention seeks the mastery of nature

KNIVES AND DAGGERS.

Bronze Medal awarded to Dr. F. H. Williams, at Chicago, 1893 (designed by August St. Gaudens).

A SUPPLEMENTAL NOTE BY THE EDITOR.

Dr. Williams exhibited his collection of aboriginal relics at the Columbian International Exhibition in Chicago, in 1893, and received a bronze medal for his exhibit. This is very beautiful, and we illustrate it, full size. The diploma accompanying the award is worded in the following strong manner, and should be a matter of local pride.

Frederick H. Williams, Bristol, Connecticut.

Exhibit—Ancient Stone Implements from Bristol, Connecticut.

Award—This collection well represents an ancient village site, in the town of Bristol, Connecticut. It is carefully arranged, and shows clearly a majority of the implements which were used in this village; these are intelligently gathered, and carefully exhibited, of historic value, and the zeal shown in the effort made to collect and present these objects is worthy of imitation in other localities.

The following illustrations have been made from specimens in Dr. Williams' collection since the preceding article was written, and are shown because they are of much interest in connection with the subject. The editor can think of nothing that could be said in this work that would afford him such genuine pleasure as to be able to here inform the citizens of Bristol that Dr. Williams has made arrangements to give his unique and most valuable collection of prehistoric relics to the Town of Bristol, and that it is to be placed in the Public Library, when the building is completed. Probably a more comprehensive collection does not exist outside of our largest museums, and it is doubtful if there is a collection anywhere that will afford the student such an opportunity for the study of the habits of the American Aborigine, for Dr. Williams made his collection with this object in view. Certainly Bristol is to be congratulated upon this valuable acquisition to its Public Library, and we feel honored to be allowed to announce Dr. Williams' valuable gift at this time.

A CORNER IN ONE OF DR. WILLIAMS' CABINETS

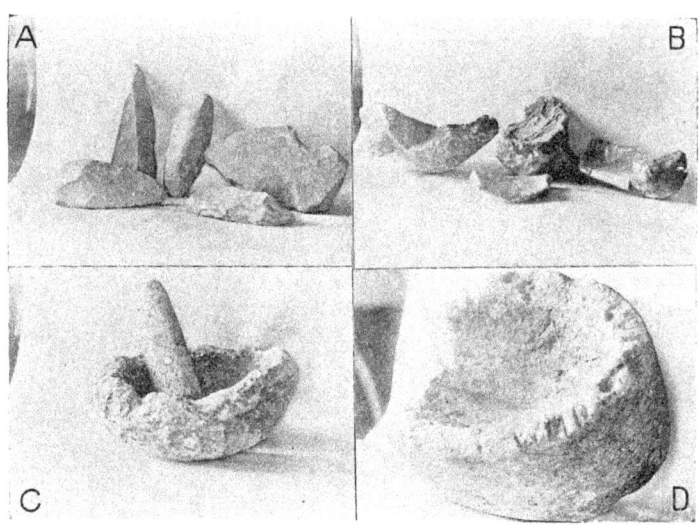

A.—Implements used in working *Bristol* Soapstone Quarries, by the Indians. B.—Fragments of vessels found on *Federal Hill*. C.—Unfinished dish, and a soapstone roller, like a pestle. D.—Very large dish from *Terryville*. (All about one seventh natural size.)

E.—A chipped quartzite tomahawk, Rare. F.—Axe, from *Compounce*. G.—Rare form of hoe, from *Farmington*. H.—Woman's chipped knife, from *Lewis' Corner, Bristol*. (All about one fourth natural size.)

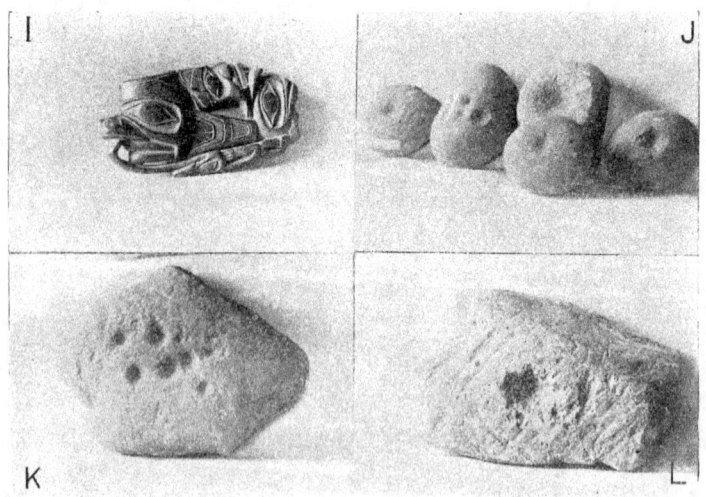

I.—Pipe found in *Southington*. This is Haidah Indian work of the northwest coast. Probably a relic of aboriginal intertraffic. J.—Fine pit stones, from *Bristol*. K.—A so-called anvil. L.—A pit stone or anvil of soapstone. (All about one fifth natural size.)

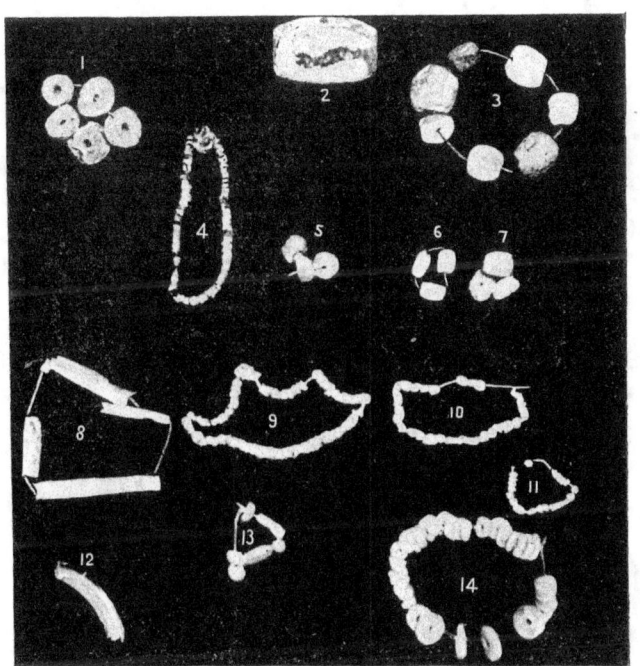

VARIOUS FORMS OF INDIAN WAMPUM OR MONEY,

Beads of various forms were in use among the Indians for several purposes. They were made from stone, clay and shells. The shells were sometimes those having natural holes as some from California. Bones and teeth were also made into strings of beads for ornamental purposes. Nos. 4, 9, 10, 11, 14 of the figures were so-called, wampum, or money beads, and were made from clam shells. The different parts of the large clams, having different colors, making different values. The purple beads being the highest values. No. 13 of the figure represent ornamental beads. Nos. 1, 2, 3, 5, 6 and 7 are beads made from larger parts of the central columns of conch shells, used for ornament.

No. 2 is a very large bead from the great mound that used to stand opposite St. Louis, on the east side of Mississippi River. No. 8 is made from bones. No. 12 is made from a bear's tooth.

The finer kind of wampum beads was used to form the wampum belts, which were used in all great ceremonies, and which conveyed to the initiated historical facts for immemorial remembrance.

FLAKED SERAPUS FROM LICKING CO., OHIO.
Showing the "conchoidal fracture" (see page 86).

This head of death is from Mexico, and is said to be the emblem of Death in the pictography of the Aztec people. Representations of the gods of Mexico, both the great gods and the small local divinities, which answer to the saints of modern liturgical cults, seem to have been made commonly in clay. Along with these are many evidently grotesque figures, the signification of which we do not know.

The Story of Fall Mountain

By Milo Leon Norton

THE first settler of what may be called Fall Mountain, though the site of the house is a few rods east of the district line, was Edward Gaylord, of Wallingford, whose house stood in the open field a little south and west of the cabin occupied by Nelson Decker, on land now owned by Eliada S. Tuttle, and which was known to the residents of the vicinity a generation ago, as the Gaylord orchard. Only two or three of the original trees of the old orchard now remain, and they have attained to a great size and venerable appearance.

Mr. Gaylord had a family of sturdy sons who became mighty hunters, and tillers of the soil, some of whom, and others of the name, settled on the heights to the southwest of the old homestead. Benjamin Gaylord settled on the place known as the Barnum farm, now owned by F. H. Wood; John Gaylord lived where William Fenn now lives; Elijah Gaylord built a small house farther up the road toward the Cedar Swamp reservoir, where the cellar may be seen, just north of the house built by James Scarrett; Samuel Gaylord built in the lot adjoining the Cedar Swamp reservoir, nearly opposite Indian Rock; a daughter, Lucy married Alpheus Bradley, a carpenter, who built the house occupied by

WITCH ROCK, OR FALL MOUNTAIN SCHOOL, DISTRICT NO. 12.

THE JESSE GAYLORD HOMESTEAD, FROM A SKETCH

James Peckham; Jesse Gaylord built the large house which stood east of the Cedar Swamp, which was torn down about 1880. He was the hero of the tragedy resulting in the death of the Indian, Morgan, related in another chapter. About 1800, Elijah Gaylord moved from the house he built south of the Fenn place, to the Orrin Judson place, now owned by the Tymerson family. From him it came into the possession of his son, Elam, and from him to his daughter, Anna, who became the wife of Orrin Judson. The house vacated by Elijah Gaylord was sold to Luke Adams, removed to its present site, where it was the life-long home of his son, James Adams, familiarly known to his neighbors as Uncle Jimmy.

The old-fashioned cider mill, which was housed under a shed southwest of the house, was an institution long to be remembered by the children of the district, whose delight it was to suck cider through a straw as it trickled from the cheese, made up in the old-fashioned way of pumice and straw, and pressed out by long levers operating a huge wooden screw. To this mill the farmers of the region round about took their cider-apples in fall to be ground, doing the work themselves, and leaving a certain proportion for the proprietor as toll. How many miles I traveled, when a boy, while riding on the long sweep, driving the old horse on the endless journey around the ring, while the apples were being crunched in the cogs of the mill beneath the hopper, I shall never know. But I do know that cider-making was an event in the annals of farm life in that period "before the war," which I shall always recall with pleasure.

Luke Adams was a revolutionary soldier, and James was a soldier of the war of 1812. In his early married life "Uncle Jimmy" used to take his family to church every Sunday in his ox-cart, cleanly swept for the purpose. He had a habit, which all who knew him will recollect, of constantly humming the old tune of Durham, when slowly plodding up the mountain, with his oxen, often with a load of cider-apples which he had bought somewhere in the village. Sometimes he would hire one of us boys to help him pick up apples; and I have picked up many bushels for him in orchards about town, where now are streets full of houses, and where electric lights are aglow at night, and where electric cars speed by in a manner which would have made his patient oxen stare in amazement. The honest old farmer was killed by the cars at the crossing then situated just east of the present railway station, in 1871.

The following poem, which I wrote about this old cider mill, and which I reproduce by courtesy of *The New England Farmer*, may be of interest in this connection:

THE CIDER MILL.

Oh memory loveth ofttimes to recall
    The scenes that occurred in the sweet long ago,
When the fruit-laden boughs of the orchard in fall,
    Their blessing of fruitage on man did bestow.

White, golden and red, as they lay in the pile,
    Were the apples just garnered from under the trees,
Where they ripened in Autumn's beneficent smile,
    And their nectar distilled for the wasps and the bees.

And rapture was mine when the cart-body's rim
    Overflowed with the many-hued apples it bore;
But my joy was completed when full to the brim,
    The cider-press channel with juices ran o'er.

When I stood by that press with a straw in my mouth,
    As I sipped the sweet flood that abundantly fell,
I was buoyant and flush with the vigor of youth--
    But now, 'tis a tale of the past that I tell.

The mill and its owner have long passed away;
    No longer the apple-cart climbeth the hill;
E'en the orchard itself has long gone to decay,
    And naught but their memory lingereth still.

Yet sometimes at even, when sunset is red,
    And my routine of work for the day is complete,
My thoughts will revert to a weather-worn shed,
    And the press and the cider, delicious and sweet.

Fall mountain was made a school district in 1798, when the School Board defined its boundaries as follows: "Voted that the inhabitants living on Fall mountain, beginning at Bazaleel Bowen's, and extending to Chauncey Jerome's, including those from Capt. Jesse Gaylord's, Mr. Hinman's,* and including all in that quarter of the society as far as the lane that goes to Capt. Gaylord's orchard, be made into one school district, and be known by the name of Fall mountain district."

Bazaleel Bowen lived in a house which stood near the Wolcott town line, a short distance south of the Andrew Rowe place on the east side of the road. He had two boys whose exploits have been handed down, so notorious were they, as examples of youthful depravity. Early in the last century, Nathan Tuttle kept a country store in a building that stood until recently, when it was destroyed by fire, on the corner at Indian Heaven, a locality lying on both sides of the Bristol-Plymouth town line, on the western boundary of the district. One of the tricks of the Bowen boys was the purchase of some article, whether gunpowder or tobacco I have forgotten, of Tuttle, for which they agreed to bring a certain number of eggs in payment. They then proceeded to rob a number of birds' nests, securing the required quantity, which they took to the corner store. The proprietor could not dispute that they were eggs, or that there had been no specification as to the kind of eggs which were to be brought, and was therefore obliged logically to cancel the indebtedness. But thereafter, under all circumstances, he was careful to specify that *hens'* eggs should be exchanged for his merchandise. It may seem surprising, but it is a fact, that many people from the village of Bristol, traveled all the way to Indian Heaven to do their trading. The Bowen family, much to the relief of the other residents of the Mountain, emigrated to Ohio, probably about 1830, together with several families from the vicinity, some of them travelling the entire distance with ox teams.

Chauncey Jerome lived on the brow of the hill west of the residence of Mr. Dillon, formerly the Capt. Wooding place. There is no trace of the cellar remaining, but the house stood on the south side of the road, in an open field at that place. He was a tory during the revolution, and was so outspoken in his denunciation of the course of his patriot neighbors in rebelling against the authority of the English crown, that he was made the object of much persecution on the part of the "Sons of Liberty," as the patriots called themselves. The apple tree was standing until a few years ago, to a limb of which he was suspended by the thumbs, stripped to the waist, in order that he might receive a severe thrashing at the hands of the patriots. But being extremely agile in his motions, he managed to reach the ground with his toes, when he sprang up, liberated his thumbs from the cords that held them, and ran like a deer, pursued but not overtaken by his would-be disciplinarians. The tree stood just back of the barn on the Barnum place before mentioned. He took refuge in the house of his brother-in-law, Jonathan Pond, who lived in the next house below his, just over the Plymouth line. Pond met the pursuers with a loaded gun and held them at bay until Jerome made good his escape.

About 1760, Isaac Norton, of Durham, a descendant of Thomas Norton, one of the original settlers of Guilford, settled upon the summit of the mountain, on the site of what is now known as the Weeks' place.

CURIOUS BOULDER NEAR CEDAR SWAMP.

(1) RUINS OF THE LYMAN TUTTLE, JR. PLACE AT "INDIAN HEAVEN,"
WHERE THE FIRST BAPTIST MEETINGS WERE HELD IN 1791
From photo taken by Milo Leon Norton.
(2) CELLAR HOLE OF THE SAME IN 1907.

The log house he built stood a little south of the Weeks' house, recently burned, a tamarack tree, at the foot of the garden, denoting the spot where the well may still be seen. He had a numerous family, some of whom moved to Norfolk, another to Westfield, Mass., while his sons Aaron and Joel remained in Bristol. Joel built the house still standing, south of the log cabin, where, at one time, he kept a tavern. Aaron built the old house opposite the home of Gideon Roberts, the pioneer of the American clock industry, in 1786. Both Aaron and Joel were soldiers of the Revolution, Aaron serving under that gallant leader, Col. Nodiah Hooker, of Farmington. He was a large land owner, having a tract of land extending from the old road west of A. T. Bunnell's to the Plymouth town line, near the Beecher Perkin's place, on the Waterbury road. He was my great grandfather, and upon a part of his immense landed estate my ancestral home was located.

The neighborhood to which I have previously alluded, known as Indian Heaven, has a historical interest as being the birthplace of the Bristol Baptist Church. A small colony of Baptists, from new Haven and vicinity, settled in the vicinity, William Tuttle building on the cellar near the present club house, on the Plymouth side of the line; Joel Matthews building the house a short distance east, until within a few years the home of George William Matthews; Lyman Tuttle building a quarter mile west of the corner; Edmund Todd, Elam Todd and Truman Prince, also living in the neighborhood. It was in Mr. Todd's new barn, just north of the Tuttle homestead, on the Plymouth side of the line, on April 13, 1791, that the Bristol Baptist Church was organized. Preaching services were held in this barn, and also in the Tuttle house, near the club house, before its completion; a part only of the chamber floor being laid, the preacher, Elder Daniel Wildman, of Danbury, standing on a joiner bench in the kitchen, could address his audience seated upstairs and down. It was intended at first to build a church in this vicinity, but afterward it was decided to build in the village of Bristol, where the first Baptist church edifice was erected in 1802. Not only was this a thrifty farming community, but maufactur-

LOG CABIN AT "INDIAN HEAVEN," USED AS A CLUB HOUSE.

ing was also carried on at a two-story factory, the wheel-pit of which can still be seen just below the old dam, which was located a few rods below the dam of recent construction. Here wood turning was engaged in by the Tuttles, and afterward tack hammers were made by a firm in which Charles Swasey and Timothy Atwater were interested. This was in the forties. The shop was burned and was never rebuilt. Previous to this Nathan Tuttle(2) carried on the manufacture of combs in the building which he afterward enlarged and used as a store. Austin Sheldon, who married one of the Tuttle girls, also had a blacksmith shop opposite the Lyman Tuttle house, west of the Lucas Lane place. Lane also ran a shingle mill for sawing out shingles, half a mile south of Indian Heaven, as the crow flies, near the Castle Prince place, now marked by old cellar holes. The life of Austin Sheldon, who was widely known as the Pennsylvania hermit, has about it a tinge of sad romance. He had purchased a tract of land, without seeing it, in Lehman, Pa., and upon going there found it almost worthless. He was disposed to make the best of the situation, however, and to go there to live with his young wife, thinking that between farming and blacksmithing he could make a comfortable living. But his wife's family persuaded her to refuse to go with him, and he lived there many years alone, in a cave, partly closed in with lumber, quite a distance from any human habitation. He was a gentle, inoffensive man, enjoying the society of the birds and animals about his forest home, which became very tame and sociable; and many children were welcomed to his cabin-cave as visitors. He attracted much attention from newspaper men and others, and be-

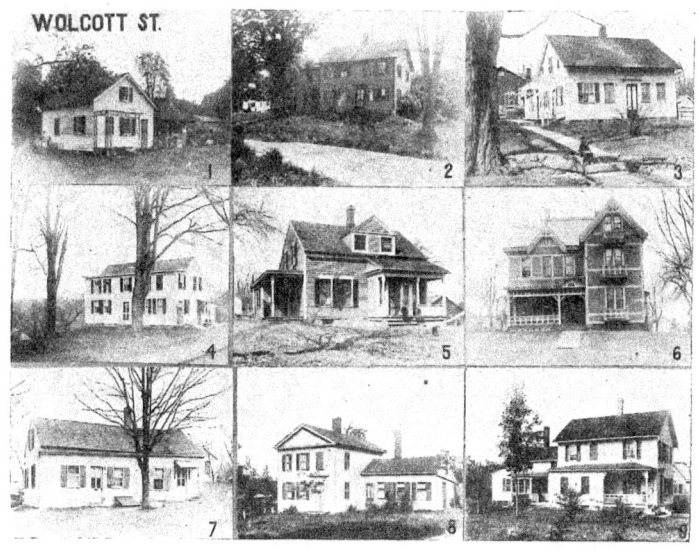

WOLCOTT ST.

(1) No. 5, Frank Wilder R, formerly the Edward Norton place; (2) No. 4, Mrs. L. Seisswert R, Wm. Litke R, formerly the Gordon Clark place; (3) No. 24, Joseph C. Russell O, formerly the John Sutliff place; (4) No. 35, George A. Rowe O, Edward O. Watrous R, Patrick J. Doyle R, formerly the Chandler Norton place; (5) No. 38, Roy Crittenden R, No. 40, Joseph F. Ryan R; (6) No. 48, Ernest T. Belden O, Mrs. Elizabeth Belden R; (7) No. 43, George H. Day O; (8) No. 51, James Hinchliff R; (9) No. 64, Noble Peck O, George W. Denny R.

WITCH ROCK.

came quite a noted hermit. He was always neatly dressed, and was extremely neat and genteel in his habits. During his last days he was a frequent visitor in Bristol, where he had relatives. For many years he was very deaf.

An awful tragedy occurred in New Haven, on Christmas, 1855, when Justus Matthews, a brother of George William and Henry N. Matthews, who was born in the Matthews home at Indian Heaven, was murdered by a sect of religious fanatics, known as the Wakemanites. It is one of the strangest tales that religious fanaticism is responsible for, showing to what lengths the religious devotee may be tempted to go. Rhoda Wakeman, the leader and founder of the sect, having, it is believed, murdered her husband, came to New Haven from Fairfield, and gathered a small company of believers about her, who accepted her statement that she had died and gone to heaven, where she had been commissioned by Jesus Christ to return to the earth to redeem mankind, or at least all who would listen to her. She professed to have power to kill and to raise the dead, to heal diseases, and to cast out devils. Justus Matthews, his wife and sister, and his sister's husband, all of Hamden, were among those who accepted the "Divine Messenger," as she was called. She professed that Justus had backslidden and had become the man of sin, it is thought because of a debt of three hundred dollars that she owed him, and which he thought should be secured. At any rate she impressed upon the little company the importance of having Justus put out of the way or she would die, and if she died the world would instantly be destroyed. This they firmly believed. Justus was sent for, and persuaded that it was his duty to be killed that the world might be saved. Sam. Sly, a half-witted fanatic, did the deed, after Matthews' own sister had tied his hands behind his back, and blindfolded him, "in the fear of the Lord." He was first beaten into insensibility by a club, and then his head was nearly severed from his body by a jackknife. The perpetrators were acquitted on the ground of insanity, but were kept under restraint during the remainder of their lives.

In a pasture lot on the Barnum farm, which has always been known as the Cole lot,(3) directly north of the residence of Sereno Nichols, is a heap of moss-grown stones, near which stands one or two pear trees. This was the childhood home of Katherine Cole, wife of Aaron Gaylord, who was massacred with nearly all the settlers at Wyoming, Pennsylvania, in 1778. Katherine escaped with her children, and made her way back, through the forest, to her father's house. The house was destroyed by fire early in the last century, and upon the death of her father, Katherine went to live with her daughter in Burlington, where she ended her days. Another victim of that terrible tragedy was Elias Roberts, a neighbor of the Cole family, and father of Gideon, the clock maker. His widow, Fallah Roberts, made her way back to Bristol on foot, carrying her babe in her arms the entire distance. An old potato grater, which Fallah Roberts used in after years to make starch for the family, and to raise small amounts of pin money for her own use, is preserved in the collection of historic relics of Bristol. The process was a very simple one. The potatoes were grated to a pulp and then placed in a vessel of water, when the starch settled to the bottom, the residue was poured off and the starch dried, when it was ready for use.

Fall Mountain is not without its traditions of witchcraft, which date back to the early years of the last century. Witch Rock, a short distance above the schoolhouse, received its name from the story that whenever Elijah Gaylord drove his ox team down the hill past the rock, the cart tongue would drop to the ground, no matter how securely it

(10) No. 78, T. B. Robinson O, John Streigle R, formerly the Lora Waters place; (11) No. 88, Samuel A. Hubbard R, Clarence B, Atkins O, formerly the Rufus Sanford place; (12) No 105, Mrs. John A. Bradley R; (13) No. 109, Charles T. Thrall O, formerly the Bud Sutliff place; (14) No. 115, E. R. Brightman R, formerly the Hezekiah Lewis place; (15) No. 118, George B. Evans O, Herbert L. Kern R; (16) No. 126, Edward W. Bradley O; (17) No. 136, Geo. H. Miles O; (18) No. 167, M. J. Rockwell O, Edward E. Andrew R, formerly the James Holt place.

SITE OF KATHERINE GAYLORD HOMESTEAD.

was fastened. As it was reputed that he had in some manner incurred the ill will of Granby Olcott, as she was known, a reputed witch who lived in the adjoining town of Wolcott, it was supposed that she was the cause of the trouble. But a still more serious case was reported at the house of Joseph Byington, now occupied by J. H. Clemence. A young woman living there was grievously tormented, night after night, by having pins and needles stuck in her flesh by invisible hands. Seth Stiles was employed to watch with the afflicted girl, and as fast as the pins were inserted in her flesh he would draw them out and stick them in a silk handkerchief. When the pins ceased to be inserted in the human pin cushion, he held the handkerchief over the hot coals in the fireplace until the pins became so hot as to burn themselves out of the cloth and to drop into the fire. She was never troubled afterward, but the witch suspected was found the next day, so it was reported, terribly burned. Another case bordering on the supernatural was reported and thoroughly believed by those who witnessed the phenomenon. In 1822, a woman named Stiles, who lived in the Gideon Roberts house, called one evening, at the home of my father, who was then nine years of age. Later in the evening her family heard groans outside the door, and found her in an unconscious state from which she never rallied, but died soon after being taken into the house. Medical aid was summoned, but nothing could be done to relieve her. A postmortem examination revealed the fact that she had been assaulted and outraged by a number of fiends in human shape, the scene of the assault being traced to an orchard some distance north of my father's residence, in what has long been called the Bunker Hill lot, on the Barnum farm. That she had been carried from the orchard to her home was shown by her shoes having been removed and left under the trees, while her stockings were not soiled. The criminals were never detected. Some time afterwards, at night, when any one came up Peck Lane past the scene of the crime, a light would appear, which would keep along abreast of the traveller, but inside of the fence, and when nearly out to the corner of the mountain road, it would turn eastward toward the deceased woman's home, and disappear. I have talked with one or two persons who solemnly declared they had seen this light, beside my father, who remembered it distinctly. The lane ceased to be used as a thoroughfare for some time afterward, by the timid, after nightfall.

Joel Truesdell, who lived on the place afterward owned by the late Andrew R. Rowe, was a type of the old-time self-made American nobleman. Descended from an English farmer who had settled in the Mohawk country, he was the son of a seafaring man who lost his all in a ship wreck, including his life from the freezing and exposure that he endured. The widow left with five small children to support had enough to look after, so the two oldest boys, James and Joel, started out from New London, their home, to seek their fortunes in the wide world. They drifted to Wolcott, but there the town officials much alarmed lest the boys should become public burdens, bade them move on. Bristol offered them a refuge, and here Joel spent the remainder of his long life. He purchased the Rowe farm in the southwest corner of Bristol, working at his trade as a shoemaker as well as at farming. His three sons settled in the west, but his two daughters married and remained in the vicinity, one of them becoming the wife of Seth Gaylord, and the other the wife of Ransell Brockett. He held various offices of trust, being elected selectman in 1807, afterward holding minor offices, and becoming a Justice of the Peace, from which he obtained his title of Esquire. As a justice he was always strictly upright, but a terror to evil doers. He was twice married, his second wife surviving him. He died of a rose cancer in 1856, in his eighty-eighth year. I well remember the one-story red house in which he lived, and the immense granite

(19) No. 172, Mrs. Flora J. Clark R, formerly the A. H. Rood place; (20) George Lawley, Jr. R, formerly the William Nichols place; (21) Mrs. Harriet L. Root, O; formerly the Smith Dart place; (22) Wm. H. Coons O; (23) "Woodlawn," Frank M. Gaylord O, formerly the Nancy Horton place; (24) Averitt E. Hare O, formerly the Cyprian Elton place; (25) Edward H. Allen O, formerly the Garry Allen place; (26) Allen T. Bunnell O, formerly the "Jake" Wright place (a still at the rear in the olden time); (27) Henry A. Way O, formerly the John Peck, Sr. place.

boulder in front. The rock was broken up and removed by the last owner of the place, Mr. Rowe, who also replaced the old house by one of modern design. It was recently burned, and has not been rebuilt.

One of the most interesting natural objects of Fall Mountain, was the Cedar Swamp, which was flooded early in the seventies, and used as a storage reservoir for Waterbury factories. In the earliest times, when the swamp first became known to the white men, there was a beaver dam at the southern end, which can now be seen at low water. The entire swamp was covered with a dense growth of white cedars, except an open channel near the eastern edge. When a dam for a sawmill was built, soon after the first settlement of the vicinity, and the water begun to rise, it was found that the whole growth of cedars rose with the water, and fell again when the water was drawn down— a floating forest. It was a natural lake which had become overgrown with the cedars, the matted roots forming a raft, through which spliced rods were driven, in places, to the depth of forty feet without striking bottom. At one time there was a movement on foot to drain the swamp and to remove the peat, which exists there in enormous quantities, for fuel. But the flooding of the swamp prevented this from being carried out.

To the east, and near the head of the pond, is a natural curiosity, in the shape of a bowlder, the formation of which has been declared by experts to be very peculiar. Several geologists have examined the rock and declared themselves at a loss to account for it. It was discovered by my father about seventy-five years ago, who thought that he had

(28) Mrs. Cora M. Eddy *O*, J. J. Mulpeter *R*, formerly the Aaron Norton place, built about 1786; (29) A. C. Bailey *O*, formerly the Gideon Roberts place; (30) B. G. Nichols *O*; (31) Mrs. Drusilla Blakeslee *O*, formerly the John R. Peck place; (32) O. J. Bailey *O*, formerly the Burton Allen place; (33) S. T Nichols *O*; (34) Trank H. Wood *O*, formerly the Barnum place; (35) Peter G. Gustafson *O*, formerly the Wentworth Bradley place; (36) Wallace H. Miller *O*, formerly the Leonard A. Norton place.

found a bowlder of limestone. The rock is composed of thin layers, or veneers, of quartz, cemented together with lime. Broken off the interior has one color, and resembles limestone, or marble. But the edges of the veneers, where they have been exposed to the weather, show where the lime has been eroded, leaving the layers of quartz exposed. Fragments of this rock are scattered for a mile to the south, being laid up in cellar and field walls, but I never have been able to find it elsewhere. When in New Hampshire and Vermont, I have looked in vain for the rock *in situ*, for somewhere to the north of us there must be the original ledge from which it came. It was not until recently that I obtained a clue that may lead to the discovery of its starting place on its long pilgrimage over the New England hills. A1 friend who is of an observing turn of mind, and a student of the natura sciences, when shown this rock, said that when exploring the geological formation along the St. Lawrence River, known as the Laurentian formation, he discovered the thin edges of protruding quartz, precisely as they exist in this bowlder. The place of his discovery was near the mouth of the Saugenay river, which would be rather too far east to be the home site of this rock; but the same formation may exist farther up the river St. Lawrence, and more in range with the path of the glaciers.

The first schoolhouse built in the district, stood on the corner opposite the Barnum place, near the present guide board. On the opposite corner stood a blacksmith shop, where, early in life, Capt. A. Wooding worked at blacksmithing. The second schoolhouse stood at the four corners at the top of the mountain, on the east side of the road that runs north and south, and on the south side of the road to Bristol. Later it was moved to its present site. There may be a few people now living who can remember when the schoolhouse was heated by a fireplace; and when the benches were made of logs hewn flat on the upper side; legs, driven into auger holes on the underside, serving for supports. The schoolhouse (20) of my boyhood had advanced far beyond this primitive stage. It was provided with plank seats running around three sides of the room, the teacher having a table and chair at the front end of the room, between the two entrances opening into the entry. Some of the schoolhouses of that period had a dungeon in one end of the entry, where refractory pupils were shut in to reflect upon the enormity of their misconduct. But ours was not so provided. A desk of wide boards, sloping inward, and having a shelf underneath for the storage of books, slates, and the like, took up the room between the seats and the wall. In the middle of the room was a box stove, and two benches for little tots. A blackboard, much out of repair, occupied the wall space back of the teacher's chair. An incident connected with this blackboard, may be worthy of mention.

It was the custom for the teachers to board around, in those days, and when one of the lady teachers was boarding at our house, she was shown a pair of double-lens, green spectacles, which had the peculiarity, by means of reflection, of enabling the wearer to see what was transpiring behind him, as well as in front. She borrowed the spectacles, explaining to the school that weak eyes were the cause of her wearing them. When she stood with her back to the school to oversee the writing of exercises on the board, was the signal for a general, but silent outbreak of grimaces, whisperings, and swapping of knives or trinkets dear to the juvenile heart. But this day, as she stood with her back toward them, she not only called out the name of every culprit, but told exactly what mischief was being done without taking her eyes off the board. This convinced the urchins that she was gifted with supernatural powers, and resulted in much better conduct during the rest of the term. It was not until the last day of school that the secret was divulged. The effort on my part to keep a secret that length of time was a severe strain, but I did it.

The old schoolhouse was repaired, long after I had graduated, was burned about 1881, and the present (7) schoolhouse was built in its stead, the following year. It has the modern improvements in the way of chairs and desks, but I doubt if the three R's are more faithfully drilled into the minds of the pupils than they were fifty years ago.

Sherman Johnson, early in the last century, came into possession of the place now owned by William Fenn. He was a mechanic of much originality, and constructed upon the brook southeast of the house, a saw mill, a still, a turning shop and a cider mill. East of the residence of James Peckham, he built a dam, flooding over a large tract of land known as Morgan's Swamp, which served as his reservoir. The dam can still be seen. At the brook where the shops stood can be seen the wheel pit and foundations. Henry Bradley succeeded to the title of the farm by inheritance, and lived there the greater part of his life. He was a manufacturer of clock hammers, which were cast of zinc, in a little shop which stood west of the house of F. H. Wood, but which now stands east of the house, and is used as a carriage house. Mr. Bradley also manufactured that part of clock mechanism known as lock work, a specialty that was in the hands of his sons, Wentworth and Harlan P. Bradley, for many years afterward. The lock work was made in the chamber of his house. The front chamber of this house was in use for some time as a meeting place for Second Adventists, Mr. Bradley and his family being early converts to the Advent

(37) The Samuel McKee place, Miss Julia Potter *O*, and used as a laundry by Jason H. Clemence; (38) Built by Truman Norton, later known as the Jerry Thomas place. In the ell of this building Gideon Roberts had the first clock shop in America, Jason H. Clemence *O*; (39) ruins of the H. A. Week's place, the original Isaac Norton homestead; (40) S. P. Harrison *O*, the Joel Norton Tavern; (41) Mrs. Edwin Gomme *R*, the Eli Norton place; (42) Richard E. Dillon *O*, the Captain Alviah Wooding place; (43) Adam Schragder, *O*, the Charles Graniss place; (44) Louis Moulaski *O* (Allentown Road), the George William Mathews place; (45) the Orrin Judson place (at present unoccupied).

faith. He sold out about 1862, and removed to Divinity street, where he ended his days.

The land upon which stands the red house, known to older residents as the McKee place, was purchased of John Gaylord, who owned the Fenn place, in 1805. It is now used as a laundry. Samuel McKee was of Scotch descent, came from Derby, and was a soldier of the Revolution, having had many interesting experiences, and some narrow escapes from death and capture. His daughter married Eli Terry, the Father of American clock-making, and the entire family became identified with the industries of Terryville.

The small shop once used by Gideon Roberts, and which is undoubtedly the original (8) clock shop of the United States, was built for a tin shop a few rods north of the house of the late Alonzo Rood. It was bought by Roberts and placed in the southwest corner of his front yard, where, by means of a foot-lathe and hand saws, he made the first Yankee clocks. The building was bought of Hopkins Roberts, and removed to its present site, by my uncle, Asahel Hinman Norton, where it now forms the L of the house now occupied by J. H. Clemence.

Fall Mountain has suffered, like many other rural districts, from the removal of the descendants of the original families to other localities, as well as by the abandonment of homesteads, a condition prevailing to a great extent all over the State. There are now but two persons,

(46) Alverda J. Tymerson *O*, the Enos Blakeslee place (Witch Rock Road); (47) Alexander Morin *O*, the James Adams place (Witch Rock Road); (48) David Y. Clark, the Thos. Prince place (Witch Rock Road); (49) Cabin, (Witch Rock Road); (50) Theron A. Johnson *O*, the Leander B. Norton place (Witch Rock Road); (51) James H. Peckham *O*, the Aunt Lucy Hotchkiss place; (52) Wallace A., Emily M. and Rachel E. Allen *O*, the Lyman Bradley place; (53) Clark Hare *R*, the James Scarrett place; (54) Wm. M. Fenn *O*, the Henry Bradley place.

THE TRUMAN NORTON PLACE,
Showing ell, in which Gideon Roberts had the first clock shop in America.
From photo by Milo Leon Norton.

James Peckham and a widowed sister, descendants of Samuel Gaylord, now remaining on the mountain, within the boundaries of the district, of the old stock. I have not tried to trace the history, or even mention all of the old families, because of the lack of time and space needed to do the subject justice. Since 1860 five houses in the district have been burned and were never rebuilt, and two were abandoned and were torn down. In 1860 there were living in the district, with all of whom I was personally acquainted, the following families: Henry Bradley, James Scarrett, Lyman Bradley, Isaac Hotchkiss, Jesse Gaylord, Lorenzo Thomas, Leander B. Norton, Thomas Prince, James Adams, Enos Blakeslee, Orrin Judson, Benajah Camp, Eli Norton, George Plumb, Capt. Alvah Wooding,   Moulthrop, Charles Granniss, Miles Sanford, George William Matthews, Charles Peck, Jeremiah Thomas, Leonard A. Norton, Garry Nettleton, and George Nettleton. Of all these persons there is only one now living, Lorenzo Thomas, who resides in another part of the State.

Moses Dunbar,
LOYALIST

By Judge Epaphroditus Peck.

THE history of Moses Dunbar seems to me to be a story full of interest to all students of Connecitcut's history, because he was the only person who has ever been executed for treason against this state; and full of interest to all who love heroism and high-minded devotion to principle, because of the fidelity and consecration with which he served the church and the King to whom he believed his loyalty to be due, consecration alike of the affections and the activities of life, fidelity even unto death.

Moses Dunbar was born in Wallingford in June 14th, 1746, the second of a family of sixteen children. When he was about fourteen years old, his father removed to Waterbury; that is, I suppose, to what is now East Plymouth. The present town of Plymouth was then a part of Waterbury, afterward set off as a part of Watertown in 1780, and set off from Watertown by its present name in 1795.

In 1764, when not quite eighteen years old, he was married to Phebe Jerome or Jearam of Bristol, then New Cambridge. In the same year, "upon what we thought sufficient and rational motives," he and his wife left the Congregational Church, in which he had been brought up, and declared themselves of the Church of England.

The Rev. James Scovil was then located at Waterbury as a Church of England missionary of the "Society for the Propagation of the Gospel in Foreign Parts," Connecticut being foreign missionary ground, from the standpoint of the English Church; he was also in charge of the little Anglican Church in New Cambridge, which perished in the storm and stress of the Revolution.

To his Episcopal surroundings we are undoubtedly justified in tracing Dunbar's later toryism, and particularly to the influence of Mr. Scovil, and of the Rev. James Nichols, who succeeded him in charge of the New Cambridge Church.

When the war of the Revolution broke out, the King's cause had no other such zealous supporters, in Connecticut at least, as the Anglican missionaries stationed in the state.

We can easily see the reasons for this. These men, brought up in the English Church, accustomed to look on the King as the head of the church, and by the Grace of God, Defender of Faith, came to New England only to find here the despised separatists, who in England were entitled to nothing more than contemptuous toleration, and who had not always had that, ruling in church and state with a high, and not at all a gentle, hand. Their own church, which at home had every advantage, political and social, whose Bishops sat in the House of Lords, whose services were maintained in splendid pomp by the public funds, which was the spiritual governor of England, as King and Parliament were its civil governors, was weak and despised and suffering great legal disadvantages, as compared with its Puritan rival.

RESIDENCE JUDGE EPAPHRODITUS PECK, SUMMER STREET.

To give an extreme instance of the hardships which the Episcopal clergymen sometimes suffered, William Gibbs, of Simsbury, who was the first Anglican minister to officiate in New Cambridge, was required by the authorities of Simsbury to pay taxes from his own scanty income to support the Congregational ministry. When he refused, he is said to have been bound on the back of a horse, and in that harsh way carried to Hartford jail, where he was imprisoned as a delinquent taxpayer. He was then an old man, became insane, and continued so until his death. (1.)

Our own church records show that legal compulsion was used to make the churchmen, who doubtless had a heavy burden to carry in their own church, pay taxes for Mr. Newell's support.

While the law for the support of the Congregational churches by taxation was finally relaxed for the benefit of Episcopal dissenters, and their treatment probably tended to become more friendly, as their numbers increased, the position of constant inferiority and occasional oppression in which they found themselves must have been very galling to the clergymen of the English church, who doubtless felt that they were entitled by English law to be the dominant, instead of the inferior, church.

The Puritan government was not one likely to be beloved by those who were out of sympathy with its theology and practice; still less by those who devoutly believed it to be both schismatical and heretical, and who constantly felt the weight of its oppressive hand upon them.

But the churchmen had always the crown, and the powerful mother church at home, to look to as their backer and defender; and, though neither church nor crown seem ever to have interested themselves much in the lot of their co-religionists here, the distinguished connection there was at least a matter of pride and fervent loyalty to the ostracized churchmen here.

---

1. Welton's sermon and notes concerning the Episcopal Church in New Cambridge. Bristol Public Library.

And, naturally enough, they believed that the fear of the wrath of the powerful church at home was all that restrained the Puritans here, and feared a withdrawal of all privileges, and an attack on the very existence of their churches, if the Puritan colony should succeed in establishing its independence.

"It was inferred from the history of the past that, if successful, few would be the tender mercies shown by the Independents in New England to a form of Protestant religion which was in their eyes 'dissent,' and which nothing but the want of power hitherto had prevented them from fully destroying. It was the remark of a Presbyterian deacon, made in the hearing of one who put it upon record, 'that if the colonies should carry their point, there would not be a church in the New England states.' " (2.)

And so, when the hated rulers of the colony openly defied the King, denied the authority of Parliament over them, and finally determined to make their Puritan commonwealths independent altogether, it is not difficult to understand how bitter the opposition to the revolutionary movement must have been among the churchmen, and what firebrands of tory zeal the missionary clergyman, in their circuits through the state, must have been.

The position of active hospitality to the colonial cause taken by the Episcopal clergy led to their being specially marked out by the intolerant patriotism of the day for prosecution; and this in turn, no doubt, reacted to increase their hatred of the colony, its Puritan religion, and the possibility of its acquiring independence.

Nineteen days after the Declaration of Independence, the clergy of the state met to determine their course; one point of peculiar difficulty was the prayer for the King, and that he might be victorious over all his enemies, in the prayerbook.

At least one Congregational minister in Massachusetts suffered embarrassment from a similar cause. He had prayed so long for "our excellent King George," that, after the war commenced, and independence had been declared, he inadvertently inserted the familiar phrase in his prayer, but, recollecting himself in time, he added: "O Lord, I mean George Washington."

But the Church of England clergy could not so readily evade their prescribed prayer for the King. They could not omit it without unfaithfulness to the canons of the church, nor include it without incurring the wrath of their neighbors, and the accusation of open disloyalty. They, therefore, resolved to suspend public services, until the storm of revolution should blow over; which they probably thought would be but a few months. (3.)

But one old man, John Beach, of Newtown and Reading, absolutely refused his consent to this resolution, and declared that he would "do his duty, preach and pray for the King, till the rebels cut out his tongue." The doughty old loyalist kept his word, and yet died peaceably in his bed, in the eighty-second year of his age, just in time to escape the bitter news of Cornwallis' surrender. (4.)

But he had some exciting experiences in the meantime. While officiating one day in Reading, a shot was fired into the church, and the ball struck above him, and lodged in the sounding-board. Pausing for the moment, he uttered the words, "Fear not them which kill the body, but are not able to kill the soul; but rather fear him which is able to destroy both soul and body in hell." He then proceeded with the service, without further interruption.

At another time, a party of men entered his church, and as he was about reaching the prayer for the King, pointed a musket at his head,

---

2. Beardsley's History of the Episcopal Church in Connecticut, vol. 1, p. 312. Beardsley, 1, 313.
2. Welton's sermon, cited before. Also see Beardsley.
*   Welton's sermon, and Beardsley.

"OVERLOOK," RESIDENCE S B HARPER.

He calmly went on, and, whether they did not fire, or missed, he escaped injury. (5.)

But many of his brethren, though less bold than he, suffered more.

Dunbar's last days in jail were confronted by the sacred offices of the church administered by Rev. Roger Veits, a fellow-prisoner, who had been tried at the same term with Dunbar and convicted of assisting captured British soldiers to escape, and giving them food.

Nor was Dunbar's own pastor, Rev. James Nichols, treated much better. Rev. James Nichols appears by the records of his church to have administered baptism five times in 1776 after July 4th, once in 1777, and four times in 1780, Rev. X. A. Welton says that these sacred offices were performed in a cave, and adds: "Once, says reliable tradition, he was discovered hiding in a cellar near the residence of the late Sextus Gaylord, captured, tarred and feathered, and dragged in the neighboring brook." (6.) At the same term of court at which Dunbar was convicted of treason, this Mr. Nichols was also tried, but was acquitted. (7.)

A new convert to the religious faith of the Church of England, under the teaching of its persecuted ministers, a man evidently of courage and resolute energy, we can hardly wonder that Moses Dunbar was a devoted and fearless supporter of the royal cause. In his own words, "From the time that the present unhappy misunderstanding between Great Britain and the Colonies began, I freely confess I never could reconcile my opinion to the necessity or lawfulness of taking up arms against Great Britain." (8.)

His adherence to the Church of England had already caused a

---

5. Beardsley, 1, 319.
6. Welton's sermon.
7. Connecticut Courant, Jan. 27, 1777.
8. Dunbar's statement, in The Town and City of Waterbury, vol. 1, page 435

breach between himself and his father, in which he seems to have been practically driven from home, and it was then probably that he began living near his wife's home in New Cambridge. He continued to pay toll-taxes in Waterbury as a resident, and describes himself in deeds as of Waterbury; but both a strong local tradition, and the early printed accounts of him, speak of him as having lived in Bristol, that is, of course, of Farmington, and he is so described in his formal indictment. A house that used to stand on the east side of Hill street, a little way north from the South Chippins' Hill schoolhouse, was known to every one about there as the house where Moses Dunbar lived.

Probably after his father cast him off, the young husband of eighteen took himself to the more friendly society of his wife's family, who lived in this Chippins' Hill neighborhood.

He certainly attended schurch in the little church building on Federal Hill, and there his four children were baptized, Bede, in 1765, Zeriah in 1773, Phebe in 1774, and Moses, of whom I shall speak again, in December, 1777.

During the twelve years from his marriage in May, 1764, to his wife's death, he had seven children, of whom four survived their father. On May 20th, 1776, his wife died, as wives and mothers usually did in those days, when they reached the age of thirty or so.

Not many months afterward, he was married again to Esther Adams. The Revolutionary War, with its accompanying divisions of neighborhoods and families, was now in full progress, and Dunbar was already an object of suspicion. "Having spoken somewhat freely on the subject," he says, "I was attacked by a mob of about forty men, very much abused, my life threatened and nearly taken away, by which mob I was obliged to sign a paper containing many falsehoods." (9.)

The family of which he was a member by marriage was as much

RESIDENCE EDSON M. PECK, SUMMER STREET.

---

9. Dunbar's statement, *ut supra*.

divided politically as any could be. Zerubbabel Jerome, the father, and his three sons, Robert, Thomas, and Asahel, were all four soldiers in the American army. Asahel died in the service. (10.) Chauncey and Zerubbabel, Jr., were tories, and were, in 1777, imprisoned for some time in Hartford jail for disloyalty, and finally released on profession of repentance, and taking the oath of allegiance to the state. (11.) Chauncey was also once flogged, or escaped flogging only by slipping out of his shirt, by which he was bound, and fleeing to shelter. (12.)

Phebe married Dunbar; Ruth married Stephen Graves, who was a notorious tory leader, and lived for a time in the "tory den," where his wife, then nineteen years old, carried him food at night; Jerusha married Jonathan Pond, who, Mr. Shepard says, was probably a tory, and the other danghter, Mary, married Joseph Spencer, whose political position is now unknown. (13.) Of Stephen Graves, Mr. Welton speaks as follows:—"Stephen Graves, a young churchman residing in the southeast corner of Harwinton, was drafted for the continental army, and sent a substitute. The next year, while he was paying wages to the substitute, he was drafted again, an act so manifestly oppressive and cruel that he refused any longer to maintain his substitute, and thenceforth became the object of relentless persecution by the lawless band who styled themselves the 'Sons of Liberty.' Once they caught him and scourged him with rods, tied to a cherry tree, on the line between Plymouth and Harwinton, at the fork of the roads. Again he was captured in Saybrook, whither he had gone to visit his grandfather's family, and brought back, but when within three miles from home he escaped, while climbing 'Pine Hollow Hill,' and reached home safely; but did not enter his house till his pursuers had come and gone without him. The loyalists of the neighborhood for a while worked together on each one's farm for safety. Their wives kept watch for (the Sons of Liberty) and she who first sighted them, blew her tin horn or conch; all the others in turn repeating the warning, till the men had time to get well on their way to their cave, which the men-hunters never discovered." (14.)

After his first wife's death, Dunbar says:—"I had now concluded to live peaceable, and give no offense, neither by word nor deed. I had thought of entering into a voluntary confinement within the limits of my farm, and making proposals of that nature, when I was carried before the Committee, and by them ordered to suffer imprisonment during their pleasure, not exceeding five months. When I had remained there about fourteen days, the authority of New Haven dismissed me. Finding my life uneasy, and as I had reason to apprehend, in great danger, I thought it my safest method to flee to Long Island, which I accordingly did, but having a desire to see my friends and children, and being under engagement of marriage with her who is my wife, the banns of marriage having been before published, I returned, and was married. Having a mind to remove my wife and family to Long Island, as a place of safety, I went there the second time, to prepare matters accordingly. When there I accepted a captain's warrant for the King's service in Colonel Fanning's regiment.

"I returned to Connecticut, when I was taken and betrayed by Joseph Smith, and was brought before the authority of Waterbury They refused to have anything to do with the matter. I was carried before Justices Strong and Whitman of Farmington and by them committed to Hartford, where the Superior Court was then sitting. I was tried on Thursday, 23rd of January, 1777, for High Treason against the State of Connecticut, by an act passed in October last, for enlisting men for General Howe, and for having a captain's commission for that pur-

---

10. The Tories of Connecticut, by James Shepard, Connecticut Magazine, IV., 262.
11. Records of the State of Connecticut, Vol. 1, p. 259.
12. Welton's sermon, *ut supra*. The Tories of Conn., *supra*, p. 260.
13. MS. notes of Mr. James Shepard. See Conn. Magazine, IV., 260.
14. Welton's sermon, *ut supra*.

RESIDENCE J. R. HOLLEY, BELLEVUE AVENUE.

pose. I was adjudged guilty, and on the Saturday following was brought to the bar of the court and received sentence of death." (16.)

Several things in this statement attract attention; firstly, the great powers stated to have been exercised by the "committee," who could imprison a man at their pleasure, not exceeding five months, without trial; again, the persistent activity in the royal cause, which even his marriage hardly interrupted. During his very honeymoon, he was pledging himself irrevocably to the King's cause, and receiving the formal commission, which would necessarily condemn him, if it were discovered upon him. The regiment in which he was commissioned was made up of American loyalists, and Rev. Samuel Seabury, afterward the first American Bishop of the Episcopal church was its chaplain.

The refusal of the Waterbury authorities "to have anything to do with the matter," for which Miss Prichard in the history of Waterbury already cited, expresses herself as thankful, evidently thinking that it denoted greater moderation on their part, seems to me to mean simply that, in inquiring into the facts the Waterbury magistrates found that the specific acts charged were committed in Farmington, and, therefore, sent him thither for trial. It was only the usual and necessary procedure, since a criminal trial must always be had in the jurisdiction where the criminal acts are committed.

Judge Jones, in his History of New York, a bitterly loyalist book, says of the charge against him:—"His commission and orders from General Howe were in his pocket. There happened to be no existing law in the Colony which made such an offense punishable with death. A law was therefore made on purpose; upon which *ex post facto* law he was indicted and tried for treason." (17.)

This charge that the law was passed after the criminal acts were committed, if well-founded, would be a serious one; for such legislation is universally recognized as contrary to natural justice. By the Consti-

---

16. Dunbar's statement, *ut supra*.
17. Jones's History of New York, Vol. 1, page 175.

tution of the Uinted States, not then in force of course, any *ex post facto* law is invalid and null. But I do not believe that the statement is true.

The act defining treason under which he was convicted was the second act, the first having been a ratification of the Declaration of Independence, passed by the General Assembly which met October tenth, and adjourned November seventh, 1775.

Jones himself says that Dunbar was taken up early in 1777; Dunbar says that by the justices he was committed to Hartford, *where the Superior Court was then sitting*, by which he was tried on January 23rd, 1777. This was the January, 1777, session of the court, The indictment charges his treasonable acts to have been committed on November 10th, 1776, and January 1st, 1777; very likely the latter date was charged because he was arrested on that day, and the royal commission was then found in his possession.

So that it is quite clear that his arrest, and the acts for which he was tried, were a considerable time after the passage of the act against treason.

Doubtless this is true; that he and other tories had been arrested and imprisoned as dangerous characters, and there had been no sufficient statute under which to punish them; and the Legislature, at the earliest possible moment after the Declaration of Independence, supplied the omission. But when they instituted a prosecution under the act, they clearly set up acts occurring after its passage.

The indictment of Dunbar read as follow: "The Jurors for the Governor & Company of the State of Connecticut upon their oaths present that one Moses Dunbar of Farmington in said county being a person belonging to and residing within this state of Connecticut not having the fear of God before his Eyes and being Seduced by the Instigation of the Devil on or about the 10th day of November last past and also on or about the 1st day of January Instant, did wittingly and feloniously wickedly and Traitorously proceed and goe from said Farmington to the City of New York in the State of New York with Intent to Join to aid, Assist and hold Traitorous Correspondence with the British Troops and Navy there Now in Armes and Open Warr and hostilities against this State and the rest of the United States of America and also that the said Moses Dunbar on or about the said 10th Day of November last and 1st day of January Instant Did wittingly and knowingly feloniously wickedly and Traitorously at New York aforesaid Join himself to the British Army and Enter their Service and Pay and did Aid and Assist the said British Army and Navy Now in Arms and Enemies at Open Warr with this State and the rest of the United States of America and did Inlist and Engage with said British Army to levy Warr against this State and the Government thereof and Did Traitorously Correspond with said Enemies and Give them Intelligence of the State and Situation of the State and did plot and Contrive with said Enemies to Betray this State and the rest of the United States of America into their Power and hands against the peace and Dignity of the State and Contrary to the form and effect of the Statute of this State in Such Case lately made and provided."

His sentence was: "that he go from hence to the goal from whence he came and from thence to the place of execution and there to be hanged up by the neck between the heavens and the earth untill he Shalle be Dead." (18.)

The name of the man whom Dunbar was charged to have persuaded to enlist, John Adams, suggests that he was probably a father or brother of the Esther Adams, whom he had just married. Apparently Dunbar carried on his courtship and his loyalist campaign together; and won the heart of the daughter for himself, and of the father or brother for the King, at the same time.

---

18. Superior Court Records, Secretary of State's Office, vol. 18.

There were quite a number of other trials and convictions under the same statute; but no one was executed but Dunbar. I presume that the colonists felt it necessary to make an example of some one, to show that the law had teeth, and to drive the tory sentiment of the state into concealment and silence. For this purpose they may have desired a shining mark, and selected as the victim a man of high character rather than the reverse.

He was ordered to be hanged on March 19th, 1777. On March first, with the aid of a knife brought him by Elisha Wadsworth of Hartford, he cleared himself of his irons, knocked down the guard, and escaped from the jail. Wadsworth was indicted for his part in this escape, and was sentenced to be imprisoned for one year, to pay forty pounds fine, and the costs of his prosecution. Half of his term of imprisonment, and his fine, was afterward remitted.

Dunbar was soon recaptured, and was executed on March 19th, 1777, according to the sentence. The gallows was erected on the hill south of Hartford, where Trinity College now is. "A prodigious Concourse of People were Spectators on the Occasion," said the Connecticut *Courant* of March 24th.

"It is said that at the moment when the execution took place a white deer sprang from the near-by forest, and passed directly under the hanging victim. This tradition," says Miss Prichard's History of Waterbury, "is pretty firmly established."

Two official sermons were preached on the occasion of Dunbar's execution; one by Rev. Abraham Jarvis, of Middletown, afterward Episcopal Bishop of Connecticut, at the jail, to Dunbar himself; and one by Rev. Nathan Strong, of the First Church in Hartford, in his church. Mr. Strong says: "For reasons we must in charity hope honest to himself, he refuses to be present at this solemnity; my discourse therefore will not be calculated, as hath been usual on such occasions, to the dying creature who is to appear immediately before the Great Judge; but to assist my hearers in making an improvement of the event, for their own

RESIDENCE MILES LEWIS PECK, SUMMER STREET.

RESIDENCE HENRY L. BEACH AND PHILIP H. STEVENS, PROSPECT PLACE

benefit." It is reasonable inference that Dunbar's refusal to listen to a Congregational minister let to Mr. Jarvis, a leading clergyman of his own faith, who was also a loyalist, being invited to preach the sermon to him. His treatment would not seem in this matter to have been harsh or inconsiderate.

Mr. Strong's references to him in his sermon are also entirely free from bitterness of tone; he ends thus:

"With regard to the dying criminal, while you acquiesce in the necessity of his fate, give him your prayers. Though public safety forbids him pardon from the State, he may be pardoned by God Almighty. As Christians, forgive him; let not an idea that he hath sinned against the country keep alive the passions of hatred and revenge.

Remember the instruction of Christ, forgive our trespasses as we forgive them that trespass against us, forgive your enemies, and pray for those who use you wickedly; commend his spirit to the mercy of God, and the Saviour of men's souls." (19.)

The text was I Tim. F, 20. "Them that sin rebuke before all, that others also may fear."

The excitement among the loyalists by Dunbar's sentence and impending death appears very clearly in this statement by Judge Jones, in the history of New York, already cited: (20.)

"No less than four expresses, at four different times, were sent to General Howe between the condemnation and the execution, to each of which the most faithful promises were made, that an application of such a serious nature should be made to the Government of Connecticut, as should insure his discharge.

There were about four hundred rebel officers and five thousand soldiers at this time prisoners within the British lines at New York.

---

19. Strong's sermon, Conn. Hist. Library.
20. Vol. 1, page 176.

No application was ever made, and while the general was lolling in the arms of his mistress, and sporting his cash at the faro bank, the poor unhappy loyalist was executed. This is a fact, and the General knows it. His word, his honour, and his humanity were all sported away in this affair."

Jones goes on to accuse the Connecticut authorities of barbarous treatment of Dunbar's wife:

"Dunbar had a young wife, big with child. On the day of execution the High Sheriff, (by orders no doubt) compelled her to ride in the cart, and attend the execution of her husband. This over, she left Hartford, and went to Middletown, about sixteen miles down the river, where a number of loyalists lived, and where several British subjects were living upon parole.

Her case being stated, a subscription was undertaken for her comfort and relief. No sooner was this hospitable act known to the committee at Middletown, than they sent for the poor woman, and ordered her out of town, declaring at the same time, that if she should thereafter be found in that town, she should be sent instantly to jail.

The unhappy wretch was obliged to leave the town in consequence of this inhuman order, and had it not been for the hospitality of a worthy loyal family, who kindly took her under their roof, she would in all probability have been delivered in the open fields. A striking instance this of *American lenity*, which the rebels during the war proclaimed to the world with so much eclat." (21.)

As to this, of course there is now no contrary proof; but few classes of statements are so unreliable as to the counter-charges of severity in a civil war. Jones's authority is very small, as I was assured by the late President of the Connecticut Historical Society, and State Librarian, Mr. Charles J. Hoadley, he certainly is wrong in his previous statement that Dunbar was tried under an *ex post facto* law, and the treatment by the authorities in other respects does not seem to have been unkind.

RESIDENCE MRS. N. S. WIGHTMAN, SUMMER STREET.

21. Jones's History of New York, vol. 1, page 177.

RESIDENCE CHARLES T. TREADWAY, BELLEVUE AVENUE.

If Mrs. Dunbar rode with her husband to execution, I think it much more likely that it was from her devoted wish to stay by him to the last, than from any compulsion put upon her by the sheriff. That she may have been subjected to persecution afterward is likely enough, from all that we know of the usual treatment of the tories.

A reference to the date of the baptism of Moses, son of Moses Dunbar, on the New Cambridge church record, December, 1777, confirms Jones's statement as to Mrs. Dunbar's condition. Mr. Welton says that this son came to an untimely end; how, I do not know. Mrs. Dunbar went within the lines of the British army for protection, but afterward returned to Bristol, and married Chauncey Jerome, the brother of Dunbar's first wife, with whom she went to Nova Scotia. After the peace, they returned to Connecticut, and were the parents of several children. (22.)

Many years afterward Mrs. Jerome, then an old woman, was driving by the hill where Trinity stands, with Erastus Smith of Hartford; pointing out to him an apple tree, she said, "That is where my poor first husband was buried." Smith related this to Mr. Hoadley, who told it to me.

More than a century after Dunbar's execution, when an old house at Harwinton was destroyed, papers were found in the garret and examined, among which were two papers written by Moses Dunbar on the day before his death.

The first was addressed to his children, and was as follows:

MY CHILDREN: Remember your Creator in the days of your youth. Learn your Creed, the Lord's prayer, and the ten commandments and Catechism, and go to church as often as you can, and prepare yourselves as soon as you are of a proper age to worthily partake of the Lord's supper. I charge you all, never to leave the church. Read the Bible. Love the Saviour wherever you may be.

---

22. Sabine's American Loyalists, under *Moses Dunbar*.

I am now in Hartford jail, condemned to death for high treason against the state of Connecticut. I was thirty years last June, the 14th. God bless you. Remember your Father and Mother and be dutiful to your present mother.

The other paper is an account of his life, and a statement of his faith. I have already quoted from it. It concludes as follows:

"The tremendous and awful day now draws near, when I must appear before the Searcher of hearts to give an account of all the deeds done in the body, whether they be good or evil. I shall soon be delivered from all the pains and troubles this wicked mortal state, and shall be answerable to the All-Seeing God, who is infinitely just, and knoweth all things as they are. I am fully persuaded that I depart in a state of peace with God, and my own conscience. I have but little doubt of my future happiness, through the merits of Jesus Christ. I have sincerely repented of all my sins, examined my heart, prayed earnestly to God for mercy, for the gracious pardon of my manifold and heinous sins. I resign myself wholly to the disposal of my Heavenly Father, submitting to His Divine will. From the bottom of my heart I forgive all enemies and earnestly pray God to forgive them all. Some part of T—S—'s evidence was false, but I heartily forgive him, and likewise earnestly beg forgiveness of all persons whom I have injured or offended.

"I die in the profession and communion of the Church of England.

"Of my political sentence I leave the readers of these lines to judge. Perhaps it is neither reasonable nor proper that I should declare them in my present situation. I cannot take the last farewell of my countrymen without desiring them to show kindness to my poor widow and children not reflecting upon them the manner of my death. Now I have given you a narrative of all things material concerning my life with that veracity which you are to expect from one who is going to leave the world and appear before the God of truth. My last advice to you is, that you, above all others, confess your sins, and prepare

RESIDENCE MRS. CHARLES S. TREADWAY, BELLEVUE AVENUE.

RESIDENCE OF THE LATE EDWARD B. DUNBAR, SOUTH STREET.

yourselves, with God's assistance, for your future and Eternal state. You will all shortly be as near Eternity as I now am, and will view both worlds in the light which I do now view them. You will then view all worldly things to be but shadows and vapours and vanity of vanities, and the things of the Spiritual world to be of importance beyond all description. You will then be sensible that the pleasures of a good conscience, and the happiness of the near prospect of Heaven, will outweigh all the pleasures and honours of this wicked world.

"God the Father, God the Son, and God the Holy Ghost, have mercy on me, and receive my spirit, Amen, and Amen."

Moses Dunbar.

Hartford, March 18, 1777.

As we read these high-minded words, in which there is neither any retraction nor attempted excuse, any effort at denial of the facts, nor any bitterness of complaint against the authorities who had condemned him, but a calm statement of his opinions, his acts, and his sufferings and a reiteration of his devotion to the church of his choice, as we think of this young man of thirty, leaving four children to be fatherless, motherless, and exposed to hatred and persecution for their father's sake, a wife married but a few months, and a child yet unborn, and meeting death for the faith to which he had been converted, and the King and country to whom he believed that his loyalty was due, I hope we can see that there was devotion, heroism, and martyrdom on the loyalist, as well as on the patriot side.

The rightfulness of Dunbar's execution, in itself, may be a matter of fair debate. Of course he was within the terms of the act for the punishment of treason, "which prohibited levying war against the state or aiding its enemies, by joining their armies or by enlisting others;" but the law of England also prohibited the levying of war against the King, or assisting his enemies, and the question which was his lawful ruler, to whose laws he owed obedience, was the very question at issue in the contest. From the British standpoint, all the Revolutionary soldiers were guilty of treason against the crown, just as in our recent civil war every Confederate soldier, was, by strict construction of law, subject to be hanged as a traitor.

But in civil contests, which take on the dimensions of war, it is not usual, in civilized communities, for the parties on one side or the other to apply the civil penalty of treason, but rather to regard captured enemies as entitled to the treatment of prisoners of war. So the British army treated its prisoners in the Revolution, as did both parties in the Civil War.

Nathan Hale, whom the British put to death, was a spy, and subject to the death penalty by all the usages of war; Andre, whom the Americans executed, was also a spy in the American lines, and, besides, assisting in an act of nefarious treason by an American officer; these cases are quite different from that of a man who, when rival governments were demanding his allegiance, decided for the King, and honestly fought for him, as his neighbors did for the state.

The fact that the state government, though a number of other tories were convicted of treason, executed none of them, seems to show that they had doubts of the propriety of their action.

And yet Dunbar was not carrying on open war, in the King's uniform, but acting secretly, and in the territory of which the state government had possession; by the acts of himself and his associates the British army was getting secret information and assistance from within the enemy's lines; that kind of service is much like that of a spy, and we can hardly blame the state authorities severely for not making fine distinctions in favor of those who were assisting the hated enemy in their own neighborhood, secretly winning recruits among the young men of their own communities, and, by all the means in their power bringing invasion, conquest, and royal vengeance, upon their fellow-citizens of the state.

RESIDENCE P. H. CONGDON, LAUREL STREET.

Records of the State of Connecticut, vol. 1, page 4.

RESIDENCE REV. HENRY CLARK, CHURCH STREET.

The burning of Danbury by a British detachment, guided by Connecticut tories, the month after Dunbar's execution, showed how far the loyalists of the state were ready to go in their bitterness toward their fellow-citizens. Isaac W. Shelton, said to have been one of the guides of the Danbury expedition, was a member and officer of the Bristol Episcopal church in 1736, and it is not unlikely that he and Dunbar were acquaintances and associates in the cause.

Shelton was certainly across the line, and Dunbar, at least, very near to it, that divides open enemies, entitled, when captured, to be treated as prisoners of war, from traitors and spies, who, however, sincere may be their conviction of the justice of their cause, subject themselves knowingly to the penalty of death if they are taken.

But as to the outrages committed upon the tories by their neighbors, nothing can be said in justification. War does not justify nor excuse, among civilized people, the whipping, tarring and feathering, or hanging, of non-combatants, even if they hold and express opinions obnoxious to the prevailing sentiment of the community. That such excesses are not the necessary outcome of excited patriotic feeling was shown in the Civil War, three generations later. Our communities were no less stirred then by the emotions of a great conflict than they had been in the days of the Revolution; but, unless in isolated cases, the most odious of the "Copperheads" were not subjected to personal violence and outrage.

The struggle of a brave people for independence is not ennobled or advanced by acts of riotous violence.

And yet, though the circumstances offered no justification, they do afford some mitigation and excuse. The position of the weaker and invaded party inevitably arouses more bitterness of feeling than that of the invader. To illustrate again from the Civil War, a northern sympathizer at the south would probably have been in much more danger of personal injury than a rebel sympathizer at the north. The language and acts of the northern Copperheads while they tended to produce national disaster and disunion did not excite any real fear of the invasion of our towns, the burning of our homes, or our subjection to a foreign yoke.

But the real explanation of the harsh and cruel treatment of the tories and their families was in the narrower, more intolerant spirit of the time and the place. The spirit of intolerance was perhaps the worst defect, so far as the outward life was concerned, of the Puritan character. The Puritans had learned to be firm, devoted, tenacious even to death, for the truth as they saw it; they had not learned to be considerate, charitable, or even tolerant, to the different views of others. The very adherence to Episcopacy had seemed to them a scandalous wickedness and offense; and when the religious schismatics also opposed them in their cherished ambition to establish an independent commonwealth, and dared to defy public sentiment, and to maintain loyal allegiance to King George, the dominant party could admit neither any soundness in their reasoning, any purity in their motives, nor any right to differ so widely, and on such vital questions, from the majority.

Dunbar's own father is said to have declared when his son was arrested that he would furnish the hemp to make a rope for him; and I have no doubt that brutal utterance, so unlike in temper to the son's words, which we have read, was applauded as patriotic firmness by his neighbors.

The revival of historic patriotism of these past few years ough to bring an increase of knowledge, as well as of zeal; certainly after a hundred and twenty years we can afford to look at the great struggle from both sides; and so I have taken pleasure in drawing the picture of a man highminded, devout, and heroic, and yet a determined and obdurate tory, whom the state of Connecticut hanged as a traitor.

RESIDENCE WILLIAM E. SESSIONS, BELLEVUE AVENUE.

THE TORY DEN.*

IN THAT section of the country where the towns of Harwinton, Burlington, Plymouth, and Bristol touch, is situated a wild tract of wooded land known as "The Ledges." There is one cliff among many that faces the south and at its foot lies the "Tory Den." Large bands of Patriots in Revolutionary times sought for this hiding place in vain, and there are few even to this day who can find it.

By climbing to the top of the cliff you may picture the country to the south as it was in those stirring days. In 1775, the Chippens Hill section, that rolling land seen at the left, was one of the flourishing parts of the town of Bristol. There were houses there many more than now and where there are now strips of woodland was rich meadow. East Plymouth at the right was also good farming country. Even Fall Mountain upon the southern horizon had patches of good land. Bristol and Plymouth were sections of a state which had the proud distinction of being the granary of the Revolution. Occasionally in a patch of woods there is discovered a cellar of one of the old time houses.

The people living in the region spread out before the eye, were an industrious class of farmers and their religion was in an overwhelming proportion that of the Church of England. Originally Congregational, and of Puritan stock, they had been converted by missionaries of the Society for the Propagation of the Gospel in Foreign Parts to the Episcopal faith. They had paid with their own money the expenses of a student from Yale, James Nichols, and sent him over to England to be ordained as their minister. This divine, a Waterbury youth of wealthy family, became filled with the enthusiasm for the mother country and returned to take up his work in Bristol and Plymouth in 1774, being the last Church of England clergyman to come across the water for service in Connecticut. He held meetings in the mission house in Bristol Center and also at Plymouth Hollow now Thomaston.

With the coming of war the Church of England people were in a predicament. Though more tolerant perhaps to individual thought than the Puritan church, the established church preached strong loyalty to church and king. Rev. Mr. Nichols was not hesitant in his utterances upon the controversy. He was arrested as an instigator among his people, which he undoubtedly was, and brought before the court at Hartford. At one time he was caught in an East Plymouth cellar and tarred feathered and dragged in a brook. It became so warm for him that he fled to Litchfield whence he made occasional visits to administer baptisms in his parish and possibly to attend to his real estate transactions, for some of his money was invested here.

The staunchest friend of Rev. Mr. Nichols was Stephen Graves of Harwinton. It was upon or near his property that the Tory Den was located. His log house at Upton, where the Prof. John C. Griggs house now stands, was the meeting place of the Tory leaders. Upon high ground, in the very ledges themselves, it was the safest council chamber that could be found. The Tory Den in fact was much used as a refuge from this place and was probably first hit upon for this purpose. Ruth Graves, a bride not more than 19 years old, furnished food for the men of the den, clambering nearly a mile through the wooded crags. As her husband became more and more suspected, he was compelled to

---
Reprinted from Hartford Courant April 25, 1907.

THE TORY DEN.   PHOTO BY BRISTOL PRESS.

resort oftener to the den. Once returning from Stratford he escaped from his captors near Pine Hollow hill and spent some time in the cave before he dared enter his home.

The traditions in the Graves' family give us the best information of any about the "Sons of Liberty," and it is probable that the Graves homestead was the most frequent recipient of their unwelcome raids. "Captain Wilson's Sons" they are in one place called. Who Captain Wilson was is left to conjecture, but Wilson is a Harwinton name and a name found to fit the description is that of Captain John Wilson, who during these troublesome times, was Harwinton's deputy to the General Assembly. From the Graves family may be learned the precautions that the Tory families were compelled to resort to; how, while the men worked together on the farm of one of their number with their guns near at hand for protection, the women each with her children at home, listened for the sound of a horn and watched for a glimpse of the "Sons;" how upon sight of the marauders she blew a loud blast upon a conch or horn and then laid it in its hiding place, prepared to receive the entire band, or how, when she heard a blast sounding in the air, blew an even louder one herself, that the signal might pass along to her neighbor. The story told that Captain Wilson once presented his pistol to the head of a young girl in the Graves' household and threatened to shoot her if she did not tell him where the noisy conch shell was concealed.

That these bands of searchers were large is evidenced by the words of Moses Dunbar, who says that he was grievously abused at the hands of about forty men. Flogging and beating were apparently methods of chastisement frequently used. Hanging and stringing up were resorted to. Nichols, the minister, it is said, was shot at. Stealing of food supplies was a source of great annoyance if not suffering.

The story of Moses Dunbar should be so familiar as to need no comment. Somewhere in the Chippens Hill district it is probable that he lived with his wife's people, for the home of his father, a Congregationalist in Plymouth, was shut against him. A nobler minded man it would be hard to find. In returning from Long Island to transport his family thither, he was caught with a commission as captain in the King's army, found guilty of enlisting a man for that army, and was hanged at Hartford, March 19, 1777, being the only Tory executed as such in Connecticut. On South Chippens Hill lived probably Isaac W. Shelton, who at the time the war began, was about 19 years of age. Judging by his later life, he was a man of ability. He left the section early and went to the British, being one of the guides that assisted at the destruction of Danbury.

Furtherest of any from the cliff, in the Fall Mountain section, on the top of Todd Hill, lived Chauncey Jerome, the most picturesque of the Tories. The house in which he lived is supposed to be the place known as Nathan Tuttle's store, which burned a few years ago, on the three corners near where the fishing club of Bristol has recently constructed a small lake. Erect in bearing, fully six feet in height, and of muscular build, he was a man of spirit and filled with the courage of his convictions and was not afraid to express them. A crowd captured him, pulled his shirt up over his head, tied him to a tree, and preparing to flog him, when he wrenched himself away, leaving his shirt on the tree, and ran to the house of his brother-in-law, Jonathan Pond, who stood at the door with gun in hand, forbidding any to enter.

The Tory Den was familiar ground to Jerome and it is probable that he was one of the leaders at the secret councils. He lived to be an old man and is described as often walking toward Chippens Hill with dignified, but resolute step with the aid of a stout staff, his nose slightly aquiline, his eyes as keen as an eagle's and almost fierce, when unexpectedly overtaken upon the roadway by any whose faces were not familiar to him, his forehead high and broad, with thin white locks falling gracefully nearly to his shoulders.

He was one of the seventeen prisoners from Bristol who were found to be under the influence of one Nichols, a designing church clergyman, and to have refused to go in the expedition to Danbury. Of his sisters, Ruth was the wife of Stephen Graves, Phebe was the wife of Moses Dunbar, and Jerusha was the wife of Jonathan Pond. Jonathan Pond lived at the foot of Fall Mountain, in the house now owned by Martin Konopaski, in the town of Plymouth. He bought the place from Rev. Mr. Nichols. He was a blacksmith and formerly lived on Chippens Hill, which accounts for his intimate relations with the people there. He was not of the Episcopal faith. He paid for one substitute to fight for him in the war and owned a half interest in another and was a member in good and regular standing in a Bristol military company.

The troublesome times of '77 passed away and as American success became more pronounced the Tories disappeared or became Patriots, some of them fighting nobly for the patriot cause. Stephen Graves and Chauncey Jerome remained Tories to the end of the war, and the name clung to them. Those who left their homes and were less remembered as Tories, as Isaac W. Shelton, or as Mark Prindle of Harwinton, returned and were restored to influential positions in the communities in which they lived. The question of whether to stay or flee must have been a difficult one to solve. The moving of a family of such size as they had in those days was no easy matter and the prospect of losing all one's properties was not alluring. Captain Abraham Hickox, a deputy sheriff in Waterbury, withdrew to the British lines and his Hancock property was confiscated, including the mill at Greystone, and was developed in the interests of the state. To a man unmarried such as is supposed was the case with Isaac Shelton, flight was the natural solution. To one having property, flight was also feasible. Yet Moses Dunbar tried it and didn't succeed. General Washington, during his six months' dictatorship, after the battle at Princeton, issued a proclamation promising no molestation to Tories who would leave the country. It was on this proclamation that Moses Dunbar was relying when he left the safe confines of Long Island and returned for his family.

In 1791, St. Mathew's parish was founded at East Plymouth, and the church was built, which is now standing within two miles of the Tory Den. This parish was made up of the Episcopolians of Bristol, to whom were united some from Harwinton, and some from Plymouth, who it is said were displeased that their new meeting house had been built at Plymouth Hollow, rather than on Town Hill. The members chosen to present the petition for the formation of this new parish to the Legislature, was the prosperous Isaac W. Shelton, and he, with Stephen Graves, were two of the four upon the building committee. The church was dedicated in 1795, by Bishop Seabury, which dedication, together with one in a nearby parish, was his last official act before his death. Alexander Viets Griswold, the first minister, became later a noted bishop. The name of Stephen Graves appears once as selectman in Harwinton, showing that his Tory reputation was being forgotten. Chauncey Jerome, to the day of his death, was known as Jerome, the Tory.

The populous nature of the country in those times can be guessed today by the size of the church. Services are held in the building occasionally during the summer months, with no heating apparatus but a low wood stove, with stiff backed seats and creaky floor, a living remnant of the past. Certain of the old families have clung to it through thick and thin, until hardly a one remains and no services not of the Episcopal form has ever been held within its walls.

A tradition which is probably reliable states that Eli Terry J ,r, wished to purchase from Luman Preston the Marsh mill and property for manufacturing purposes, "having found out that Poland brook could be turned into the Old Marsh pond," but Preston, who was a strong churchman, would not sell. One reason given was that the building up of a factory village would ruin the church.

The shops of Bristol and Terryville are drawing away the life of what was once a thriving community of farmers, but as the Tory Den reminds one of the warlike attitude of some of the church's ardent supporters, the church building also reminds of their intense religious loyalty, a people of whom Bishop Griswold quaintly writes were "mostly religious and all comparatively free from vice."

THE LEATHER MAN.

By Alice M. Bartholomew.

IF NOT a resident, the "Old Leather Man" was a regular visitor in Bristol for many years.

His well-known route of travel brought him from the west through the north part of the town, and to Forestville journeying east.

It is said he went to a Connecticut coast town, and turned westward again through the southern part of the State, ending his trip at the Hudson River, whence he returned by a second road.

This routine, summer sun or winter's wind were seldom allowed to interrupt and usually occupied thirty-four days for the circuit.

In 1884 and '5, he made nineteen consecutive trips of thirty-four days each, but during the last years of his life the periods grew longer, even forty days, but more often thirty-six or thirty-eight.

Clad in a suit entirely constructed of old bootlegs laced together, trousers, coat, cap and sack, even moccasins of the same home make, and naturally of swarthy complexion, but blackened still more by wind and weather, he was a terrible object for little girls to meet on the sidewalk and even some little boys rather shunned the honor.

The picture given above is very good. It was taken without his knowledge from the shield of a good woman's washing hung out to dry.

She habitually fed the traveler and knew what noon to expect his

THE TORY DEN, WHERE THE OLD LEATHER MAN USED SOMETIMES TO STOP

THE OLD LEATHER MAN.

call. It is thought he never would have consented to be photographed, had he known it.

Much romance has been circulated about this traditional Connecticut character. It is even true that more than one man has worn the costume and title. An earlier, more gently-bred person was known in Waterbury and Litchfield, whose death was a mystery, but our traveler died of cancer in the mouth, some twenty years ago. He was found in a cave, where he had habitually spent the nights, near Mount Pleasant, New York.

It has been said that he was a Frenchman, by name Jules Bourglay, who lost a fortune in the leather business and his fianceè with it, but it seems much more probable that the account of him offered by Mr. John Welton, a local historian of western Connecticut, is more trustworthy. Mr. Welton calls him a fugitive from justice and a negro.

"Years ago," he says, "there was a notorious resort not far from New Hartford known as the Barkhampsted lighthouse."(There was always a light there at night.) "It was the rendezvous for a gang of thieves, white men and colored who committed all sorts of crimes. At last the authorities broke up the place; and would have been glad to capture more of the people."

This man, in Mr. Welton's opinion was one of the half breed negroes, who had settled into this apparently lawful, if wandering life. It is possible that the other leather-man was the Frenchman.

There was always a small package in the bottom of our traveler's sack, which he would not allow any curious friend to even touch. This led to a little suspicion that he might possibly be the bearer of some valuable, in a business way. The regularity and persistency with which he traveled, would be thus accounted for. It was noted that no such package was found in his sack, in the cave. It must have been delivered before he lay down to die, and the wonder expressed at the time, whether a successor would some time follow him, has apparently been answered in the contrary.

THE LOG CABIN, On Wolcott Mountain After An Ice Storm

BITS OF PEQUABUCK SCENERY.
(*Photographs by Milo Leon Norton.*)

THE PEQUABUCK RIVER

By Milo Leon Norton.

MILO LEON NORTON

SHE was born of the hills, of the royal hills,
And the nymphs of the fountains and laughing rills,
Poured out their treasures of jewels rare,
To deck the couch of the princess fair.

Queen Summer came from her leafy bowers,
To crown the babe with a wreath of flowers;
And the Frost King brought her a diadem,
Inwrought with many a beautiful gem.

'Twas a peaceful valley she wandered through
Where the supple willows and alders grew.
Through meadows where daisies nod and bend,
And trees their welcoming arms extend.

Or, lingering oft in some silent pool,
She would sleep and dream in the shadows cool;
Then dancing and tripping from stone to stone,
She would sing in a mellow undertone.

But, oh! an enemy came one day,
As she leaped and laughed in her innocent play;
And he, in his sordid soul, decreed
Henceforth she must minister to his need.

He reasoned that if, in the Calvinist plan,
To be damned is the fate of degenerate man,
Were it foreordained, then it might be true,
This stream to be dammed was predestined too.

So they piled up a barrier huge of stone,
Which directly athwart her path was thrown;
And she beat and struggled against it in vain,
Her liberty fearing she ne'er would regain.

But at last, with a rage that she could not conceal,
She sprang at the flukes of the miller's wheel.
With a dash, and a crash, and a deafening sound,
The brimming buckets spun round and round.

Then quickly again she flowed along,
And filled the air with a gleeful song;
Through dingle and dell wound in an out,
Or leaped o'er the rocks with a joyful shout;

Or, dallying oft in some quiet nook,
She would welcome a tribute-bearing brook.
And thus she journeyed for many a mile,
With a rhythmic flow and a happy smile.

But along her course, again and again,
She was made to toil for designing men,
Who would seek her lithesome steps to stay,
And make her a prisoner day by day.

But the wily river would quiet keep,
And gather strength for a final leap,
Their barriers clear with defiant roar,
Then flow on her winding way once more.

Sometimes when the clouds their burden shed,
And the brooks and the rills had been overfed,
She would give full vent to her pent-up wrath,
And sweep the offending walls from her path.

But she came at last to mourn and grieve,
For the tranquil life she used to live;
And the East Wind chanced to hear her sigh,
And it touched his heart as he hurried by.

So he stopped in his flight, and whispered low:
"Wouldst thou escape from thy human foe?
Then hasten away to yonder plain,
And there thy emancipation gain."

So she sought the plain and found, at last,
Her lot in delightful places cast.
And she hastened not but took her ease,
'Mid the fragrant flowers and the stately trees.

And oft she lingered in peaceful rest,
With the shadows flickering on her breast,
Meandering hither and yon at will,
With a current placid, deep and still.

ALONG THE PEQUABUCK.
(*Photographs by Milo Leon Norton.*)

THE UNITING OF THE PEQUABUCK AND TUNXIS RIVERS, NEAR FARMINGTON
CONNECTICUT.

    And thus she came to an ancient town,
    Where the Tunxis was pouring his waters down;
    And he bade the gentle river to come
    And find in his bosom her future home.

    She blushed with the glow of the sunset red,
    When she heard what her fluvial lover said;
    For King of the rivers, grand, was he,
    And she his beautiful Queen would be

    So down where the clerical elm tree stood,
    His chancel the marge of the shadowy wood,
    Where the ash and the linden stood side by side,
    There the sycamore gave away the bride.

    Then the blushing bride and the bridegroom gay,
    Went joyously, lovingly, on their way;
    While the oaks and maples along the bank,
    To the health of the bridal waters drank.

History of First Congregational Church

AN HISTORICAL ADDRESS DELIVERED OCTOBER 12, 1897, BY EPAPHRODITUS PECK.

JUDGE EPAPHRODITUS PECK.

WHEN Rome was imperial mistress of the world, the people used to say, "All roads lead to Rome;" and Thomas Carlyle, in Sartor Resratus, repeats the thought with the sentence, "Any road, this simple Entepfuhl road, will lead you to the end of the world."

It is a like thought that fills with interest the study of the history of an old New England Congregational Church. Not so much the charm of landscape or variety of incident along the way, but that the road leads back to those great, unique, pioneer days of Puritanism, when, here in New England, such a people lived and fought and worshipped God as the world has never seen elsewhere.

Not that like earnest and strenuous strains of character have not appeared in many nations and in all times; but never elsewhere, unless

CONGREGATIONAL CHURCH—1907.

in Hebrew history, has a country been populated and institutions established by a community in whom a natural earnestness and an intense desire for the strenuous things in character and life had been intensified by persecution and exile, until the Kingdom of God and His righteousness had become the supreme interest of the state, the foundation of society, and the constantly controlling thought and purpose of all individual life.

The little Independent churches which had been formed in England represented in themselves the advanced left wing of Protestantism, in which not only papal, but also royal, episcopal, and presbyterian supremacy was denied, and the pure simplicity of apostolic days sought after, with that intensity of purpose which those who sympathize with its aims call godly zeal, and others call fanaticism. Persecution, even to poverty, imprisonment and death, purged away all indifferent adherents and exile sifted out the most stalwart and heroic as seed for the new country.

A pioneer population is always made up of daring and adventurous spirits; but what other land ever saw a pioneer population whose daring was daring to leave all for the service of God, whose radicalism was in earnestness of consecration, whose search was not for gold, nor for the fountain of perpetual youth, but for treasure in heaven, and assurance of eternal life.

The narrow and unlovely sides of the Puritan character were evident enough to inspire hatred and ridicule from their contemporaries, and to make them the object of much satire and criticism in later historical writing; but in spite of an ideal of character which largely omitted the gentler and more amiable qualities, in spite of a sense of duty to others which included little charity for weakness or toleration of differences of opinion, in spite of a conception of God based on the Hebrew ideal of the Old Testament rather than on the Christian ideal of the New Testament, the Puritan immigrants laid in New England such granite foundations of individual character and of church and state, that, with all the changes of time, we can still feel that our house will not readily fall before the winds and floods, for it was founded upon a rock.

The settlement of this community does not, of course, date from the very beginning of the Puritan colonial life. We are of the fourth generation. Newtown begat Hartford, Hartford begat Farmington, and Farmington begat New Cambridge.

The first settlement here, in 1728, was a century after the coming of the Mayflower. And, in that century, the intensity of the Puritan spirit had no doubt much moderated. The days of persecution in England had passed by, and settlers had begun to come to New England for many other reasons than to find a refuge for the safe exercise of their religion. A century of quiet prosperity on this side of the water was of itself likely to take the edge from the fierceness of the early Puritan zeal.

But, time then moved far more slowly than now. The ox-cart fairly symbolized the intellectual movement of the time, as the locomotive, the bicycle and the electric fluid do that of today; and I think the new Cambridge settlers of 1728 and 1747 were still closely akin in spirit to their fathers of early Plymouth and Salem.

The idea of a total separation of church and state, so fundamental in our modern system, would have been abhorrent to them To their thought the first concern of every community was to set up and unitedly carry on the worship of God; the minister must be found even before the schoolmaster or the constable; and no evil behavior was more offensive to the feelings of the community, or deemed more harmful to its good order, than neglect of the services of the sanctuary. Everywhere the Congregational church was the established church in the fullest sense; having its house of worship built by the community, its minister called by vote of the legal voters, paying its expenses by public taxation, and punishing any neglect of its services by processes of criminal law.

I shall not go over the familiar story of the settlement. In 1728, the first house was built, and in 1742, fourteen years later, when the first ecclesiastical organization was sought, the petitioners for it were twenty-one, probably almost or quite the entire body of legal voters.

What the road to the old church in Farmington was like, who can tell? Doubtless a mere bridle path, winding among the trees and over the streams. So in 1742 the little body complained to the General Assembly that they were "So Remote from any Meeting House in any ministerial sociaty in sd Town, as Renders it exceeding Difficult for us to attend the publick Worship of God In any place where it is sett up, and especially in the winter season," and with stalwart courage declared "that there is such a Number of persons as that we are Compitently able to hire a Minester, to preach ye Gospel to us In said winter season;" and therefore begged that they might be allowed to hire "an Authordox and suitably Quallifyed person to preach ye Gospel amongst us for ye space of six months in ye year Annually;" that is, to be a winter society, as the phrase was. This permission was granted, and on November 8, 1742, the community met in society meeting, and from that day, by good fortune, we have the full records of the ecclesiastical society, until its dissolution in 1897.

"At the same Meeting we past by Vote that we would meet at John browns for the winter season for the present." This John Brown house was on King Road, north of Pierce's Bridge. Later they met at Stephen Barnes's, west of the Bristol House, at Abner Matthews's, on the South Mountain road, at Joseph Benton's, near the John Moran house, at Ebenezer Barnes's, now the middle of the Julius Pierce house, and at John Hickox's on Chippin's Hill.

The search for the "Authordox and suitably Quallifyed" minister at once began, and Mr. Thomas Canfield was engaged to preach for the first winter. He first preached here on December 6, 1742, and that was undoubtedly the first church service held in this community. The

INTERIOR OF CONGREGATIONAL CHURCH—SHOWING PULPIT.

little company of some twenty families, gathered at John Brown's house to hear the preaching of God's word, must have had a service meagre and simple enough to satisfy the most extreme advocate of Puritan simplicity; but what a depth of joy there was in the fulfilled desire of their hearts, how clear the divine presence was to them in that crowded dwelling house, who, in these days of increased wealth and lessened faith, can truly appreciate?

Mr. Canfield two years afterward began his life pastorate in Roxbury. He was but twenty-two years old when here, graduated three years before at Yale College. In a record existing in Roxbury, he mentions his winter's preaching here, referring to the place as "ye Mountain, now called Cambridge in Farmington."

The next fall the society left it to the committee to hire a minister, and there is no record stating who was hired. But the people were already eager for more gospel privileges, and appointed one committee to apply to the town and another to the General Assembly that they might be a "distinkt sosiaty." The Farmington society had already consented, and the act of ecclesiastical incorporation was promptly passed. Then, being a legal society, they might settle a minister and so become a fully organized church of God, and to this their thoughts at once turned.

A few days after the act of incorporation was passed, they met, chose society officers, and "Voted that we would apply ourselves to the next association for advice in order to the bringing in a minister amongst us as soon as Convenontly may be." Three days later they called Mr. Joseph Adams "as a probationer or candidate in order for a setlement amongst us in the gospel minestry."

The Adams candidacy came to nothing, and in September a committee was appointed to procure preaching till December, and it was "Voted that mr Newel should be invited first to preach with us." Probably he was hired for the two following months, and the varying opinions which people formed of him led to the long contest over his settlement, and finally to the division of the church; for this church's history began with a schism instead of ending with one.

On December 3, 1744, it was "Voted that we would hire mr samll Newel for our minester in Case it should be the advice of the assosion and theire was seven on the negitive." This negative vote of seven is the first appearance of the breach in the society. In January, 1745, the vote to hire Mr. Newell was again passed, and negotiation about the amount of his settlement and salary was begun. In October, 1745, a third vote was passed "that we would have mr samll Newel seteled amongst us in the gospel minestry—there was 28 in the afarmitive and 2 in the negitive." Whether the vote was taken on this resolution before the opposition had arrived, or whether the arguments against Mr. Newell were not given a fair hearing we do not know; but this at least appears on record, that "Moses lyman John hikox Abel Royce Abner mathews Stephen Brooks and Caleb Palmer have hear entered a protest against the management of sd sosiaty meeting." In the difficulty, recourse was had to the peculiar Congregational tribunal, a "counsel of Minesters to hear and determine any deferences that are amongst us with Respect to our seteling mr samll Newil as our gospel minester." That council met on November 13 and the same day, doubtless after it had advised them to agree on some other man, and adjourned, the majority submissively voted to "pay and satisfi unto mr samll newil the ful and just sum of three pounds mony of the old tener per sabbath he hath preachd" and to square up all his board bills.

Then follows for two years a trial of other candidates, but the hearts of the majority evidently remained steadfast to their first choice, and no one but Mr. Newell gave satisfaction. At length they would no longer be deprived of the minister of their choice by a refractory minority, and in March, 1747, he was again called to settle among them, if the association advised. The vote was thirty-six to ten.

In the next resolution there is a tone of despair and exhausted patience: "if the above assosiation dont advise us to mr samll newel as

RESIDENCE WILFRED H. NETTLETON AND WILLIAM E. WIGHTMAN, MAPLE STREET.

abovesd our committee shall ask there advice Who we shall apply ourselves next to preach the gospel to us."

But manifestly the council felt that if the little society could agree on no one in three years they could never agree, and that the majority were entitled to have their so long deferred wish; they approved the society's action, and in July, 1747, the society voted to proceed with settlement of Mr. Newell.

And then the long growing opposition culminated and eight men made their formal revolt. "And here it must be noted that at the same meeting Caleb mathews Stephen Brooks John hikox Caleb Abernathy Abner mathews Abel Royce danell Roe & simon tuttel publikly declard themselvs of the Church of England and under the bishop of london." Nehimiah Royce followed in a few weeks.

This revolt must have been no trifling matter to the little society. Caleb Matthews was chairman of the society's committee and also of the building committee, which was then making plans for a meeting-house. Abner Matthews was also on the building committee. John Hickox had been the first society treasurer, and the others were men of prominence in the community.

The real ground of difference between the two parties was undoubtedly theological; with the passage of time a feeling of dissent to the rigid Calvinism of the Puritan church had spread in the New England colonies. This more liberal element, Arminian in theological tendency, found a refuge in the Episcopal church, then having a precarious foothold in Connecticut and the only rival religious body to the dominant Congregationalism. Parson Newell was certainly a stalwart exponent of old-fashioned, thoroughbred, Calvinistic doctrine; and it is a curious fact that two ministers who had been preaching as candidates for the Congregational pastorate, apparently the choice of the minority, were very soon after serving the Episcopal church as its rectors, Messrs. Ichabod Camp and Christopher Newton.

The people now had a pastor, to whom their fidelity had been confirmed by opposition and intensified by the long delay, and with the preparations for his ordination were united preparations for "gathering the church." The society, which had thus far been acting, was the legal, municipal corporation, but now the spiritual body of Christ's covenanted followers was to be formed.

"The church was gathered at the lecture preparatory to the ordination of and consisted of about twenty male members:" exactlv twenty of each sex, if our present roll is correct. The ordination was on Tuesday, August 12, 1747, and the formation of the church on the lecture day (probably Friday, August 8,) previous. Three neighboring ministers, Messrs. Whitman of Farmington, Colton of Hartford, and Curtiss of Southington, were invited to assist at the solemn fast by which the membership of the new church consecrated themselves to God's service in this new relation, and the same ministers, with two others, and representatives of their churches, assisted at the ordination.

I do not know what was the ceremonial of formation of the church; doubtless it was simple in the extreme, with only a pioneer dwelling house for sanctuary, and little to exalt the imagination except the consecrated joy of the people and their sense of the divine presence and benediction, as with fasting and prayer they set up in this community, for all time to come, the altar of the living God.

The long uncertainty about a minister had not prevented the little community from making early plans for a meeting-house. In March, 1745, the society had asked the General Assembly to fix the site for a meeting-house, and, in May, had voted by a large majority that they would build a meeting-house "as soon as with Conveniancy may be," and in December, that it should be forty feet by thirty in size.

They bought of Joseph Benton the ground whereon we now stand, for four pounds, and by the united efforts of the people, who got out

RESIDENCE WILLIAM J. TRACY, BELLEVUE AVENUE.

RESIDENCE JOSEPH B. SESSIONS, BELLEVUE AVENUE.

the timber and together raised the building, paying for the finishing by taxation, the little house was built. It seems to have been occupied in 1748 or early in 1749, but was not completed until 1753.

Nor did the church's exertions cease with having assumed the support of a minister and the erection of a meeting-house; at the same meeting at which the ordination was arranged for, they appointed a committee to build Mr. Newell's house; and it was no mean one, either. Thirty-eight feet by twenty-three on the ground, lathed and plastered in the parlor and bedroom, and ceiled int he dwelling-room, it was intended to be fit for the occupancy of the man whose superiority in consideration over any other man in the community would be unquestioned.

And a year later it was resolved "that we would have a lawful school in this sosiaty."

No wonder that the taxes were appalling in their size; an eight penny rate was laid in October, 1748, to finish the meeting-house, in December a two shilling rate for the same purpose, and in the same month one of four shillings "besides what we have already laid." Six shillings and eight pence on the pound is thirty-three and one third per cent! What do degenerate later days think of a tax like that? No wonder that "at the same meeting Benjamin Brooks declared himself to be of the Church of England," and that Stephen Brooks, Jr., and Joseph Gaylord followed soon after, and no wonder that the residents the next month petitioned the General Assembly for a tax on the land in the society "only on the unresidents."

Of this first meeting-house we have no picture or full description. It was undoubtedly a plain, unadorned, rectangular building, with steep roof; it had galleries, though they were not finished for several years. The floor was divided into twelve pews; not narrow, low affairs like our present pews, but large high-walled divisions, almost rooms, in each of which the adults of several families might sit. There were also two "seats," probably benches, filling spaces left vacant by the pews.

It stood some sixty feet northeast of this building, and stood north and south, the front end to the north.

On the west side was the high pulpit with its approaching stairs. No sounding board is mentioned, and it would hardly seem that it could have been necessary in so small a building; but in Puritan church architecture the sounding board served to give dignity and solemnity to the pulpit, rather than to supply an acoustic necessity. There certainly was one in the second church, and I have little doubt that it was also in the first.

One important function of the old church that has been entirely dropped in our modern democratic days was the dignification of the meeting-house, and the seating based on that dignification. The committee to dignify the meeting-house was appointed as soon as the building was complete and annually reappointed. They determined the relative dignity of each pew; and then the seating committee had the infinitely more delicate task of determining the dignity of each family, or rather of each adult person, for the entire family did not sit together, and of assigning the most worthy person to the most worthy pew, and so on in regular order down to the pews under the stairs, which were the lowest in rank. What a strain on Christian fellowship and on social friendships that must have been! Think of having it officially determined who was superior to you and who inferior, in regular order of the entire community; and of the ignominy of being formally decided to be the least worthy family in the entire congregation! Fortunately for the peace of the committee, the rules for fixing the dignity of each man or unmarried woman (I think the wives went according to the rank of their husbands and sat with them) were definitely fixed. The grand list was taken as the starting point, (let no one say that reverence for wealth is a modern invention,) and it was the adopted rule "to alow every person fifty shillings per year for his age, all so a Captain twenty pound,

MAIN STREET, 1907, NORTH FROM R. R. BRIDGE.

MAIN STREET, 1907 SOUTH FROM HIGH STREET.

to a leut ten and to an ensign five." Still further deference was paid to age by providing that all over fifty years of age should be seated at the discretion of the seaters, and within this discretionary class I should think that the duties must have been delicate indeed. Even children were seated by the committee, "men kind at sixteen years old, and females at fourteen."

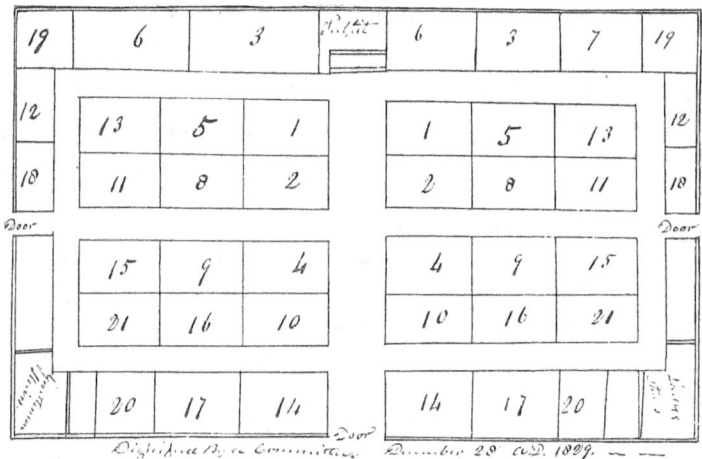

PLAN OF CHURCH DIGNIFICATION—FROM ORIGINAL NOW IN POSSESSION OF JUDGE EPAPHRODITUS PECK.

The following is the detail of the Congregational Church Dignification of about the year 1830 (exact date not known). The spelling of the original has been followed. In the case of many of the women's names, it is impossible to tell whether the title is Wid. (widow) or Mrs. Each group of names represents the occupants of one pew or seat as indicated:

No. 1, N. OF THE PULPIT, Wid. Munson, Wid. Muzzy, Wid. Hulda Churchill, Wid. Sarah Newell.
No. 1, S. OF THE PULPIT, Rev. Jona. Cone, Dea. Ira Hooker. Dea. Bryan Hooker.
No. 1, N. OF THE ALLEY, James Lee, Eli Lewis, Reuben Ives, Thomas Barns, Hubbell Stephens, Mrs. Rachel Gaylord.
No. 1, S. OF THE ALLEY, Wife of Abel Lewis, Wm. Lee, Asa Upson, Isaac Norton, Lament Peck.
No. 2, NORTH, Aron Norton, Wid. Mary Pierce, Elezer Norton, Enos Ives, Esq.
No. 2, SOUTH, James Steele, Joel Norton, Abel Allen, James Holt, Mrs. Martha Lewis, Mrs. Philene Wilcox, Mary Beckwith.
No. 3, NORTH, Oliver Gridley, Roger Lewis, Wm. Jerrome, Wid. Adams, Wid. Lomis.
No. 3, SOUTH, Luke Adams, James Frances, Bezaliel Bowin, Jesse Gaylord, Mrs. Root.
No. 4, NORTH, Abel Frisbi, Benj. Hart, Ithural Hart, Lydia Churchill, Stephen Rowe.
No. 4, SOUTH, Thos. Barns Jr., Elijah Manross, Ebenezer Darrow, Jabez Roberts, Wid. of I. Yale.
No. 5, NORTH, Noah Byington, Dr. Titus Merriman, Lazarus Hard, Solomon Payne, Mrs. Sarah Lee.
No. 5, SOUTH, Ira Churchill, Betsey Gridley, George Upson, Seth Hart, Wid. Jemima Peck.
No. 6, NORTH, Asahel Cowles, Wid. Tuttle, Selah Richards, James Hadsell, Wid. Eunice Beckwith, James Lee Jun.
No. 6, SOUTH, Seth Richards, Sam'l Gaylord, Wid. Woodard, Martin Byington, * Bradley, Wid. Rhoda Russell.
* Illegible.
No. 7, NORTH, Asahel Clarke, Wid. Sarah Gaylord, Sam'l Brooks, Noah Lewis, Wid. Boardman.
No. 7, SOUTH, Samuel Peck, Elisha Gridley, Calvin Hart, Elizabeth Johnson, Naomi Royce, Joel Baldwin, Wid. Hanna Mix.
No. 8, NORTH, Asa Bartholomew, Nath'nl W. Bishop, Seth Barnes, Abel Yale, Azariah Johnson.
No. 8, SOUTH, This is evidently omitted. Probably stairs, a stove, or something took its place. It may have been a "free seat."
No. 9, NORTH, Eli Lewis Jr., Luman Carrington, Jonathan Pond, Roxana Lewis Mrs. Mary Newell.
No. 9, SOUTH, Thomas Botsford, Eli Parsons, Renben Ives, Jun., Dodd Hungerford.

No. 10, NORTH, Ira Ives, Philo Pierce, David Norton Hannah Bradley, Chauncy Hooker.
No. 10, SOUTH, Sam'l Mackie, Wm. Torp, Damaris Lewis, Miles Lewis, Joseph Byington
No. 11, NORTH, Silas Gridley, Arron Norton, Mrs. Fanny Newell, Dea. Chas. G. Ives. Ephrain Cluver.
No. 11, SOUTH, Elisha Stephens, Joseph Ives, Sybel Steele,Wife of Asahel Norton Joel Norton Jr., David Root.
No. 12, NORTH, Isaiah Norton, Sheldon Rich, Roger Norton, Mark Norton, Sam'l Benham.
No. 12 SOUTH, John Case, Wm. Lee Jun., D. R. Wolcott, Seth Gaylord, Martin Hart, John Birge, Wife of Lemuel W Parker.
No. 13, NORTH, Clark Carrington, Elisha Horton, Shadrach Pierce, Wife of Lot Newell, Dan Hill, Rosannah Bradley, Levina Lewis.
No. 13, SOUTH, Chester Lewis, Tracy Peck, Alva Gridley, John Bradley, Sally Peck.
No. 14, NORTH, Sam'l Botsford, Truman Larcum, Cyrus Lewis, James Hart, Horace Adams, Betsey Bradley.
No. 14, SOUTH, Richard Peck, Benj. H. Rich, Alonzo Thompson, Chauncy Boardman, Lurena Brown.
No. 15, NORTH, Theodore Lewis, Reuben Hough, Jeremiah Royce, Newell Byington, Geo. Bulkley.
No. 15, SOUTH, Russell Richards, Wells R. Byington, Roswell Brainard, Chauncey Ives, Jerusha Johnson.
No. 16, NORTH, Dana Carrington, Orrin Hart, Chauncy F. Andrews, Wm. Rich. Dennis Rich.
No. 16, SOUTH, John Cowles, Dill Darrow, James Adams, Barnabas Churchill, Emily Hinsdale.
No. 17, NORTH, Major Churchill, Norman Lewis, Joel Root, Asahil Hooker, Bryan Richards.
No. 17, SOUTH, Eber. Hart, Elisha Brewster, Charles Sage, Wm. Darrow, Ephraim Wilcox.
No. 18, NORTH, Dr. Pardy, Wife of Alonzo Hart * David Munson, SHELDON LEWIS, Phillip Barns. * There is a word before David Munson which seems to be "& cts" (and others).
No. 18, SOUTH, Wm. Hubbell, Dana Beckwith, Asa Thompson, Titus M. Roberts.
No. 19, NORTH, Nehemiah Peck, Sylvester Peck, Asahel Mix, Alpheus Bradley, Major S. Wilson, Bryan Churchill, Benona Thompson.
No. 19, SOUTH, Allen Birge. Geo. Hooker, Harry Henderson, John Bacon, Theoph'ls Smith, Angustus Hart.

RESIDENCE R. K. LINSLEY, HIGH STREET.

Seats were made in the "alleys" for the children, and the young men were assigned the pew next the east door, till the galleries should be finished.

So you can form your mental picture of the quaint little room; the pulpit high in majestic dignity towering above all, the deacons and older men and women in the nearer pews, Deacon Manross and some other elders wearing white starched caps, the other pews filled with grave adults, young men in the gallery or rear pew, children in benches in the aisle; where the young women were the record saith not, but I suppose in the opposite side of the gallery from their brothers and beaux.

Even before the church was built, Joseph Benton and David Gaylord were successively elected choristers, and afterward, in 1761, Elisha Manross to assist Deacon Gaylord in setting the psalm; that is, I suppose, in announcing the tune to be used, after the minister had announced the psalm, giving the key and lining out the verses; in 1774, Gideon Roberts, the father of clockmaking here, was chosen chorister, "to serve upon the same Regulations & with ye same restrictions as appointed by the church in their Last act in that affair." What these regulations and restrictions were we know not, for the church records of that time are gone; but that they had to do with the conflict of that time between those who wished to sing by rote, that is, by their memory of the few familiar old tunes, and those who preferred to sing by note, that is, from printed notes of the music, we cannot doubt. To the conservatives singing from printed notes was as bad as reading from printed prayers.

I may add here that this first church was sufficient for the needs of the growing society only a few years. It had only been completed thirteen years, when in 1766, it was voted "to do somthing in prepration for building a new meeten hous." In June, 1768, it was voted to build at once, by a vote of sixty-three to six. New taxes were evidently coming, and a new departure to the Church of England took place.

In 1770 the second meeting-house was raised, and finished the next year. It was sixty-five by forty-five feet in size, had some striving for architectural beauty in its arched door and round window, and was of highly cheerful color. "Voted to Colour the above sd meeting-house viz: the Body of sd house spruce yellow and the Dores and windows of said house white.

Voted to Colour the Roof of our new meeting-house Spanish Brown."

There were forty-one pews on the floor, of the old-fashioned square type, reached by aisles that ran transversely, instead of from the door to the pulpit. The custom of dignifying the pews, and seating the congregation by their respective dignities, still existed and was continued as long as the second church was used. I have in my hand a "dignification" of that building, and a report of the seating committee of about 1830.* To this building a steeple was added, considerably altering its appearance, in 1797, and a bell for the first time called the people to divine service. This meeting-house was occupied till 1832, when additional room was again needed and the body of the present church building was built. Then for the first time the old-fashioned pews were given up, and the modern narrow pews, or "slips," as they were then called, were used.

If we could be taken back to the days of that first little meeting-house, its surroundings would seem no less strange to us than its interior. The little Episcopal church opposite, the sabba'-day houses where the worshippers might be warmed and refreshed during the noon inter-mission, the whipping-post and stocks at the head of the green, the vacant fields stretching in every direction, would make a picture quaint indeed to our eyes. Two dwelling houses at Doolittle's Corner, and three on Queen street, were the only ones within a circuit of nearly a mile. Parson Newell's house, at what you know as the Dr. Pardee place,

---

*See Facsimile of Plan and Designation List here mentioned on pages 179 and 180.

was quite handy to the meeting-house, according to the roomy ideas of the time.

Parson Newell served the church as its pastor forty-two years. He came here at the age of thirty-three, a recent graduate of Yale College, and died in the harness on February 10, 1789, at seventy-five years of age. His tomb is prominently situated at the very front of the old cemetery on Downs street, bearing an epitaph which has been often quoted for its stately beauty.

We have unfortunately no likeness, nor even a personal description of him.* But enough has been preserved by tradition, and can be read

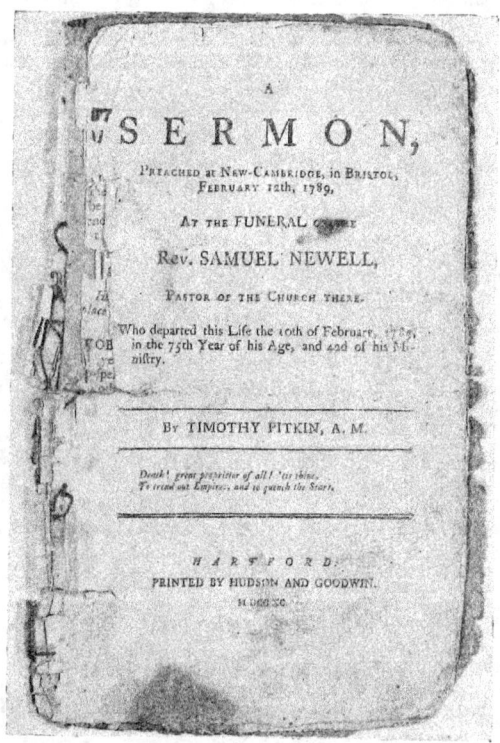

FACSIMILE OF PARSON NEWELL'S FUNERAL SERMON.
(*Owned by Judge Peck.*)

---

*Rev. Timothy Pitkin, in his sermon at Mr. Newell's funeral, thus characterized him:

"It was the pleasure of the Creator of all things to furnish Mr. Newell with a good genius, strong mind, and solid judgment; he was well acquainted with books, things, and men; a sociable and faithful friend, of a steady and firm fortitude of mind; yet had tender feelings in his own, and in the distress of others; was an open, plain-hearted, honest man; spake his opinion freely and without flattery, gave every one his due; and do not know that I ever saw the man who was a greater stranger to envy. As to his theological knowledge, was a good and thorough Divine, especially in practical divinity, and experimental. Sound in the faith, willing all should know his principles.

As a preacher, his sermons well composed and methodised, aimed not so much at the ornaments of language and beauties of style, as the truth, for he determined to know nothing among his people save Jesus Christ, and Him crucified. He did not daub with untempered mortars, nor play around men's consciences as if he was afraid to give them pain and uneasiness, but thundered forth the law to rouse up and alarm sinners, and displayed the glorious wonders of redeeming love; in short, was a plain, fervent, experimental preacher; for he appeared to preach those truths which he felt in his own heart, and that Jesus whom he knew."

between the lines of the record book, to give a good conception of his personal character. I think of him as the typical Puritan divine; strongly orthodox in a time whose liberalism would be thought almost medieval today, standing by virtue of his sacred office in a position of awful superiority to his flock, incarnating in his stately figure, human dignity and divine authority alike.

When he entered the church, the people rose and reverently saluted him, and he mounted the pulpit, and then gracefully returned the salutation; when he passed the children in the street they hushed their plays, uncovered, and made their deepest bows and curtseys; when his death was announced, an unspeakable solemnity filled the community, and one little girl is said to have asked her mother with trembling lips, "Mamma, is God dead, too?"

It is quite certain that he was not so absorbed in divine things as to neglect those of this world. He understood his rights and could assert them vigorously, as you will see. He was an extensive land owner, and made many purchases and sales. In his later days he seems to have been one of the substantial property owners of the town. At least one of his sales, evidenced by a bill of sale still in existence, was of a slave boy, Job, fourteen years of age.

His financial relations with the society were sadly tangled by the fluctuating currencies of the time. The salary offered him in the original negotiations of 1745 was fixed at a sliding scale to increase from one hundred pounds to two hundred and forty-five pounds, in bills of the old tenor, "which shall be mr Newels standing salery;" besides a settlement of five hundred pounds. At the next meeting the provision was added, that the bills should be rated at thirty-two shillings to the ounce of silver. This ratio of silver is at least four or five to one. At the next meeting a guarantee was added that they would always make good the discount of money, "so that thirty-two shillings shall be as good as one ounce of silver." These careful provisions against loss by the depreciation of the paper bills were, I have no doubt, required, or at least suggested, by the shrewd business sense of the pastor-expectant.

In 1747, when the final call was given, a new currency was extant, which for the moment was good, and a salary was offered of thirty pounds of the new currency, and to rise as the list rose until it reached seventy pounds, which might be paid in grain at stated prices. Probably Mr. Newell did not approve of the smaller amount and better money, for two weeks later the basis was changed to bills of the old tenor, beginning at one hundred and forty pounds a year, and increasing to three hundred pounds, "which we covenant and agree to make as good to him then as 3 hundred pound now is and further we agree that if mr newel and we shall not agree as to the value of our Paper bills on consequnely with Respect of the unstaidyness of our Paper bills that then and from time to time as ofen as occation shall Require will mutially Choose a Committee of uninterested persons to ajust the matter Between us."

It will be noticed that in changing from the new currency to the old the amount was increased nearly five times; and that there was an evident expectation of still further depreciation to be adjusted.

In 1759 the expected crisis had come, and the society appointed a committee of conference with Mr. Newell, and on their advice passed a new vote. "Whereas the medium of trade is altered," to pay him thereafter, instead of the three hundred pounds old bills to which he was then entitled, fifty-five pounds "Lawful Mony that is silver at six shillings and eight pence per ounce or an ekuevelent in Connetocut Late emishons."

With this scaling down to a hard money basis peace was restored till the early days of the Revolution, when Parson Newell demanded an equivalent for the new depreciation, and the people, who were doubtless just as much distressed by the shrinkage of their money as he, refused.

In 1778, he wrote in the society's record book, his receipt for "£65

(1) No. 5, Mrs. A. E. North *O;* (2) No. 19, J. E. Andrew *R*, No. 21, Wm. Muir *R;* (3) No. 23, M. B. Rohan *O*, No. 25, W. F. Stone *R;* (4) No. 31, Henry E. Cottle *R;* (5) No. 67, Geo. A. Thomas *O*, James R. Hughes *R;* (6) No. 77, Rev. Calvin B. Moody *R* (Parsonage First Congregational Church); (7) No. 78, Eugene Fairchild *R*, R. Baldwin *R;* (8) No. 83, Theo. C. Root *O;* (9) No. 84, G. E. Abbott *O*.

Continental bills, which is equal to about one-sixth part of what is justly due to me."

The next year they seem to have admitted the justice of his claims, and voted to pay him three hundred and ninety pounds "of the Present Curency" instead of the sixty-five pounds; but, alas for our financial record! a week later they reconsidered this vote, and resolved to pay sixty-five pounds of the present currency for salary.

The result was the following remarkable receipt:—"New Cambridge Decbr 1 1779 Altho the Society of New Cambridge as a Society have not rendered to me what was Justly Due by Covenant—yet a Number have been Just & Generous another Number have done Something Considerable a Considerable Number have done but a Small matter toward Justice yet to prevent trouble in the present world I Do Give a full Discharge to sd Society for what was due to me—& Refer them to the Last tribunal where impartial Justice will be Enquired after.
SAML NEWELL."

This summons of his parishioners to the bar of divine justice seems to have been effective with them, and in 1780 it was voted "that the People be at their own Liberty to pay mr Newels Rate Either in Silver or Continental money viz if in Silver their Equal part of 65£ and if in this Courancy their equal part of 1300£." Probably no one had any silver to pay, and Mr. Newell's receipt is for the magnificent salary of thirteen hundred pounds, received in money worth five cents on the dollar. Such is the history of depreciated money in the affairs of this society.

The nine men who seceded from the church before Mr. Newell's ordination, with their families, and some others who followed them later, formed the pre-Revolutionary Episcopal church whose history is so tragic and interesting, and so closely connected with the history of this church, that I will ask your indulgence in a digression of a few minutes to sketch it. The Episcopal church had at that time no American bishop, and but very few settled clergymen in New England. The church maintained a feeble existence by the labors of traveling missionaries and clergymen, who performed sacred offices in several parishes in rotation. Such offices were now obtained by the New Cambridge "churchmen;" a regular record of baptisms, beginning in 1747, is still in existence. The first of these officiating clergymen, who came here from Simsbury for several years, was Rev. William Gibbs.[*] Afterward, as has been said, Messrs. Camp and Newton, who had been candidates for the Congregational pastorate, served them, then Rev. Richard Mansfield occasionally from 1756 to 1759, Rev. James Scovel for about fourteen years, and, from 1774 until church services were suspended Rev. James Nichols. In 1754 they completed and opened for service a little church standing across the highway from the Congregational meeting-house where the north wing of the schoolhouse now stands. In 1758 they voted to have six days' preaching for the year ensuing, probably a bi-monthly communion; at other times they paid a quarter or a sixth of the salary of a clergyman, who gave them corresponding service.

For several years the society refused to release them from its ecclesiastical taxation; they evidently refused payment, and the society, in 1749, instructed its collector "to collect the Rates of them that call themselves of the Church of england among us and we will defend them." This instruction was evidently acted on, for, a year later, the collectors presented a bill of charges for collecting the rates of "those that call themselves Churchmen," and it was allowed.

Later, more peaceful counsels prevailed, and the churchmen were released from the "minester Rates as long as they do bring a Recept from their minester provided they will al of them Quit their Right in

---

[*] For the tragic history of his later years see "Historical Papers Concerning the Early Episcopal Church of New Cambridge," by Rev. X. A. Welton, Ms., Bristol Public Library

(10) No. 95, Titus E. Merriman *O;* (11) No. 96, Mrs. J. T. Peck *O;* (12) No. 104, E. E. Stockton *O;* (13) No. 115, W. H. Nettleton *O*, W. E. Wightman *R;* (14) No. 116, James T. Case *O*, A. B. Way *R;* (15) No. 126, D. T. Ogden *O*, H. G. White *R;* (16) No. 125, W. O. Perkins *O*, A. R. Nettleton *R;* (17) No. 130, M. H. Smith *R*, Andrew L. Carlson *R*, L. Norton *R;* (18) No. 139, F. A. Gates *O*, John Walton *R*.

the meeting-house;" they had already been released from the tremendous meeting-house rate. Thereafter, the relations between the two churches, were friendly, the churchmen still acting in society meeting and holding office on non-ecclesiastical subjects; in 1774 and afterward it even appears that the society appointed collectors for each body of believers, the churchmen's payments going to their rector and that of the Congregationalists to Mr. Newell; so that the society seems to have really acted as the legal ecclesiastical organization serving both churches.

But with the outbreak of the Revolution all this changed. The natural sympathies of the churchmen, who deemed themselves under oppression in the Congregational colony, and looked to the established church of England as their mother and protector, were with the crown. Mr. Nichols was an ardent loyalist, and his people almost unanimously followed him. Chippin's Hill, where most of them lived, became a rendezvous for Tory gatherings from all over the state, where soldiers were enlisted for King George, officers appointed, and information gathered to be sent to New York. Not far from there was the famous "Tory" den," where a few loyalists whose lives were not safe abroad, lay in concealment, their wives bringing them food at night.*

The Congregationalists, on the contrary, with Parson Newell at their head, were stout patriots.† Naturally, the flames of hostility raged against the church that was deemed the hotbed of toryism.

Let me read an extract from the printed state records of 1777, vol. 1, page 259: "On report of the committee appointed by this Assembly to take into consideration the subject matter of the memorial of Nathl Jones, Simon Tuttle, Joel Tuttle, Nathaniel Matthews, John Matthews, Riverus Carrington, Lemuel Carrington, Zerubbabel Jerom junr, Chauncey Jerom, Ezra Dormer, Nehemiah Royce, Abel Royce, George Beckwith, Abel Frisbee, Levi Frisbey, Jared Peck, and Abraham Waters, all of Farmington, showing that they are imprisoned on suspicion of being inimical to America; that they are ready and willing to join with their country and to do their utmost for its defence; and praying to be examined and set at liberty, as per said memorial on file, reporting that the said committee caused the authority, etc., of Farmington to be duly notified, that they convened the memorialists before them at the house of Mr. David Bull on the 22d of instant May and examined them separately touching their unfriendliness to the American States, and heard the evidences produced by the parties; that they found said persons were committed for being highly inimical to the United States, and for refusing to act in defence of their country; that on examination it appeared that they had been much under the influence of one Nichols, a designing church clergyman who had instilled into them principles opposite to the good of the States; that under the influence of such principles they had pursued a course of conduct tending to the ruin of the country and highly displeasing to those who are friends to the freedom and independence of the United States; that under various pretenses they had refused to go in the expedition to Danbury; that said Nathaniel Jones and Simon Tuttle have as they suppose each of them a son gone over to the enemy; that there was, however, no particular positive fact that sufficiently appeared to have been committed by them of an atrocious nature against the States, and that they were indeed grossly ignorant of the true grounds of the present war with Great Britain; that they appeared to be penitent of their former conduct, professed themselves convinced since the Danbury alarm that there was no such thing as remaining neuters; that the destruction made there by the tories was matter of conviction to them; that since their imprisonment upon serious reflexion they are convinced that the States are right in their claim, and that it is their duty to submit

---

* See "Historical Papers" above cited; also, "Moses Dunbar, Loyalist," by Epaphroditus Peck, Ms., Bristol Public Library.

† See his patriotic letter in the Connecticut *Courant*, Jan. 2, 1775, Conn. Hist. Soc. Library.

(19) No. 140, F. C. Wilcox *O*, (20) No. 149, H. J. Peck *R;* (21) No. 150, Mrs. A. D. Shiner *R;* (22) No. 155, M. D. Lardner *O;* (23) No. 162, J. H. Dunning *R*, J. C. Carroll *R;* (24) No. 165, E. F. Hubbard *R;* (25) No. 171, James H. Hoyt, *R*, C. F. Blanchard *R;* (26) No. 170, N. P. Stedman *O;* (27) No. 182, James Nicholas *R*, Rev. Gustav Gille *R;*

to their authority, and that they will to the utmost of their power defend the country against the British army; and that the said committee think it advisable that the said persons be liberated from their imprisonment on taking an oath of fidelity to the United States:—Resolved by this Assembly, that the said persons be liberated from their imprisonment on their taking an oath of fidelity to this State and paying costs, taxed at £22 7 10; and the keeper of the goal in Hartford is hereby directed to liberate said persons accordingly."

Of these seventeen names I can identify thirteen names as members of the Episcopal church of New Cambridge, and two others as having had children baptized there; and Mr. Nichols, the "designing church clergyman," was the rector. But imprisonment was not the worst of their suffering. The Joel Tuttle there mentioned was seized by a hand of over-zealous patriots, and hanged on the green east of this building, near the whipping-post; one of the party, seized by remorse or fear, returned and cut him down, and he revived; Chauncey Jerome narrowly escaped whipping; Mr. Nichols is said to have been tarred and feathered,* and was indicted for treason before the Superior Court at Hartford in January, 1777, but escaped conviction;† and Moses Dunbar, who was tried and convicted, and hanged for treason in March of the same year, was a brother-in-law of the two Jeromes, and four of his children were baptized in the New Cambridge church. Dunbar had been a resident of Waterbury; after his marriage to Phebe Jerome he lived in a house north of the South Chippen's Hill schoolhouse, east of the highway. He was the only tory hanged in Connecticut for treason. His dying statement and last message to his children, printed in the recent history of Waterbury, show him to have been a man of character, conscientious in his loyalist views, tender to his family, and of Christian spirit.‡

Church services were entirely discontinued here, and we may well believe the little church to have been the target of many bitter curses, and of more material missiles. After the storm of the war was over the little parish gathered itself together again, but the church appears to have been unfit for use. Occasional meetings were held in private houses for a time. In 1784, they voted, "that we are willing to meet again in the church which haith lain desolate for some time on account of the persecution of the times, and voted that we would repair the church house." But the load was too great for the weakened company to carry. In 1792 they united with the Episcopalians of Harwinton and Plymouth to establish the little church, midway between the three towns, which is now known as East Church; and Episcopacy ceased to exist here until Trinity Church was organized in 1834.

The record of this early Episcopal church was some twenty years ago in existence in East Plymouth, bearing on the cover the significant motto, "Fear God and Honor the King," but it has since dissappeared. By good fortune an authentic copy is in existence, and has just come into the possession of the Bristol Public Library. The church building was sold to Abel Lewis, who used it many years as a barn; and the arched windows were until a few years ago in the gambrel-roofed house which stood near the site of the Swedish Lutheran church. The churchyard, in the rear of the schoolhouse, had long lain neglected, until by the public spirit of one of my auditors,* it has very lately been cleared of weeds and rubbish, and the gravestones put in order. A boulder has also been set to mark the site of the church building, on which an inscription is shortly to be cut. Five of the nine original seceders from the Congregational church lie buried in that yard; and three of them are among those whose imprisonment I have spoken of.

The early history of this church is the part in which I have thought you would be chiefly interested, and I shall only very briefly touch upon the later history. Mr. Newell's successor, Rev. Giles H. Cowles, was a

---

* "Historical Papers," as cited before.
† Conn. *Courant*, Jan. 27, 1777.
‡ For a full account of him, see "Moses Dunbar, Loyalist," above cited.
* Mr. George Dudley Seymour.

A PEACEABLE STREET CORNFIELD.
Corn from seventeen to nineteen feet high.

"CUSS GUTTER" CULVERT—ICE EFFECT.
Photo by F. W. Giddings.

man of very similar views and character to his own. He says of his own settlement that "there was a considerable opposition, chiefly thro a dislike of Calvinistic doctrines;" his ordination sermon was preached by the great Jonathan Edwards. His ministry seems to have been eminently successful, marked by notable revivals, and he parted from the people bearing their warmest regard.

Rev. Jonathan Cone, the next pastor, was a man of great eloquence, the early part of whose ministry was singularly successful. But the latter part of it was clouded by persistent rumors and attacks affecting his personal character. Mr. Cone vigorously defended himself, and wielded the rod of church discipline unsparingly; but the result was most unhappy for the church. Four brief pastorates followed, those of Messrs. Leavenworth, Parmalee, Seeley and Goodrich; the church had never fully recovered a normal state of Christian harmony, and the Taylor-Tyler theological controversy of the time assisted to keep the breach of factional division open. So far did this contentious spirit go that Rev. Abner J. Leavenworth was at one time shut out from his pulpit by the nailing up of the door. Mr. Leavenworth had just been married, and his bride was present in church for the first time.

The great work which Dr. Leverett Griggs, eighth pastor, did for this church was by his genial and cordial temperament, and the spirit of fellowship and Christian fraternity which so marked him, to bring the church to a harmonious and united spirit again. His ministry of fourteen years, followed by his twelve years of residence here after his retirement from active work, entitled him to be mentioned in that culmination of the beatitudes: Blessed are the peacemakers, for they shall be called the sons of God. He is the only pastor of this church except Parson Newell who is buried in Bristol.

The latter pastorates of Rev. Messrs. William W. Belden, Henry T. Staats, Asher Anderson, William H. Belden, whose work ended so tragically, and Thomas M. Miles, are too recent to fall within the scope of history. They are matters of familiar memory and knowledge.

The early Puritan churches had a double pastorate, one minister officiating as pastor, and the other as teacher. In later days, the preaching of the sermons and the doing of pastoral work seem to have crowded out the teaching function with which they had been joined. In our century that office of the church has been revived by the Sunday school department of its work. Sunday schools began to be founded in this country about 1815, an adaptation to American needs of what in England had been a charitable work, and had borne the name of "ragged school" work.

In 1818, under the ministry of Mr. Cone, this church formed its first Sunday school. On September 13 of that year, after a general invitation to scholars, and a call for volunteers as teachers, ninety-six scholars and seven teachers were enrolled as a Sunday school. Of course the institution was in its infancy. The course during that year consisted of a "term" of eight Sundays only, and the principal work was the memorizing of verses of the Bible, and of the Catechism. At the end of the term prizes were given to the scholars who had recited from memory the greatest number of verses and answers. Of that first Sunday's enrollment, Henry W. Sage, who died recently in Ithaca, N. Y., was the last known survivor. The enrollment of 1819 included the names of Edwin S. Lewis and of Nancy Hooker (now Mrs. Hill), who are still living, and connected with this church.

Jonathan Cone was the first superintendent. Among those who have done notable service in this office have been Deacon William Day, Henry Beckwith, Esq., and Deacon Harry S. Bartholomew, who served twenty-five years continuously, and for a single year afterward.

The other great department of the modern church, the Society of Christian Endeavor, was organized here in 1886, by Rev. Mr. Anderson.

The church now has an enrolled and recognized membership of six hundred and one, the membership of the Sunday school is two hun-

Rev. Calvin B. Moody

dred and ninety-six, with a home department of ninety, that of the Society of Christian Endeavor one hundred and four, and that of its junior branch thirty-seven. The ladies' societies also carry on the work of contributing their money and labor to the home and foreign mission work of the church.

During the last ten years, the contributions of this church to benevolent and mission work have been $24,694.75; its expenditures in its own work about $45,000.

So I have tried to bring before your imagination the church of your fathers. As these one hundred and fifty years have passed, how all its surroundings have changed! Instead of the wide-stretching farms and forests is a busy, modern, manufacturing town; instead of the population of grave Puritan Englishmen, men of many languages and faiths fill our streets; instead of the ox-cart and the saddle and pillion, the electric car and the bicycle carry us; instead of a feeble colony of King George, we are citizens of a democratic republic, having twice the population of England herself; but the flame kindled here that August day on God's altar is burning still with steady and unaltered light.

The picture of the past seems strange and quaint, the language of the old records provokes a smile, if we could be sat down in Parson Newe's church, it would seem more foreign to us than anything we can find in foreign travel, and yet I am persuaded that in the altered body there is the same spirit. Just as President Washington and his three million followers, in the difficulties which encompassed the infant nation in 1789, were working under the same constitution, to uphold the same union, and preserve the same principles of democratic liberty which his successor of today, leader of seventy millions American citizens, is sworn to maintain, so our ancestors, strong and sturdy founders of institutions, had the same written guide, the Word of God, the same union, the Church of God, and the same eternal gospel of God's love and man's redemption, which form the foundation, and structure, and inspiration, of the Christian church today.

The present successful pastorate of the Rev. Calvin B. Moody commenced September 1, 1903, and continues at the present.

The Founders and their Homes

Or a Century Sketch of the Early Bristol Families, 1663 to 1763

Address at the One Hundred and Fiftieth Anniversary of the
First Congregational Church, October 12, 1897.

By Mary P. Root.

IF ANY explanation is needed for the presentation of this subject today, our explanation is that in the organization of every church the home comes first. In the history of the race, the home in Eden preceded, by many centuries, the building of a church. The church existed in the heart of the individual, and on the hearthstone of the home. With the coming of the first Christian family into this wilderness, came also the Christian church. And, like impartial historians, we wish to present to you today both sides of the story.

THE COMING OF THE WHITE MAN.

We are accustomed to date our town's origin with the first church organization (1747), with the first settler's arrival (1727), or with the earliest layout of the land (1721).

But when did the eyes of an Englishman first behold these hills? Certainly as early as 1663, when "three men strayed away into that portion of Farmington called Poland * * and * * selected lands to be laid out to them;" Richard Brownson, Thomas Barnes and another.*

Thus this section already had a name in 1663, first written poleland a name given it by Farmington coopers who came here for hoop poles. When then did the white man first set foot in Bristol?*

Six years earlier lead had been discovered in the hills west of Farmington. A rush for the lead mines followed. It was the Klondike of 1657. A result of this discovery was the founding of Waterbury, thirteen years later, by twenty-six Farmington men, who had been going back and forth along the Indian trails through Poland. Previous to the founding of Waterbury, the "long lots" of Poland had been taken up by the future Waterbury settlers: Thomas Newell, Abraham Brownson, Richard Seymour, Obadiah Richards, Thomas Barnes and others.*

Lastly, in proof that the white man's visit here was seventy years earlier than the settlement, is the record that, in 1686, there were already three roads between Farmington and Waterbury, one of which, believed to be the earliest, came over Fall Mountain.*

Then (1686) an event occurred which settled the destiny of Poland (Bristol). Sir Edmund Andros, that usurper of New England charters, was doing his utmost to get control of Connecticut. "The priceless charter was in danger." The freemen, by order of the court, assembled for public humiliation and prayer, and the assembly was in special session. Behind closed doors, the assembly transacted important business. The Charter, which gave authority to the colony to dispose of its land, was still in their possession. There were valuable lands in the north and west which there was yet time to save, in case Sir Edmund got the charter. The court, therefore, assigned all the unclaimed land in the colony, that portion included in the town of Farmington being assigned to the taxpayers of the town, and it was not deemed necessary

---

* The Town and City of Waterbury."—Miss Sarah F. Pritchard's Chapters.

(1) E. A. Mathews *O;* (2) G. W. Atwood *O;* (3) D. Larson *O;* (4) J. Dube *R*, formerly the Lemuel Peck afterwards Geo. Atwood Place; (5) Sylvester Ladd *O;* (6) I. Giles *O;* (7) Ed. Thomas *O*, Mrs. J. A. Clapp *R* (The Ed Barnes Place); (8) Wm. Thomas *O;* (9) John A. Anderson *O* (the Deacon Chas. Ives Place).

to make a minute in the public records of this transaction, nor to give reasons for this wholesale transfer of land.†

Years afterwards, it became difficult to settle estates, owing to uncertain titles to lands in this section, and, in 1721, by order of the general court assignments to individuals were made of the land here, in accordance wtth the act of 1686.

The original assignees were dead. Their heirs to the property here found a tract of land nearly five miles square, divided into five tiers of lots, with four parallel highways running from north to south. The lots were a mile long, the width depending on each man's taxable property in Farmington.

The largest grants to families whose names appear in Bristol history (the order being according to the size of the tract) were to the Brownsons, Harts, Judds, Roots, Steeles, Barnes, Thompsons, Nortons, Gridleys, Lees, Hooker, Lewis, Seymour, Newell, Richards.

All the land was assigned to the forty-nine original proprietors, a reservation of thirty acres being made for the Indians, Bohemia and Poland.

In connection with this land grant of 1686, there are several interesting items. The largest tract was a mile square, lying in central and east Forestville, and was assigned to four men, two of whom bear Bristol names, Captain Lewis and John Norton.

The smallest lots were of peculiar shape, being a mile in length by nine rods wide. Benoni and Samuel Steele of Hartford, sons of John Steele, owned lots here of this size.

The Brownson family (seven) owned nearly two square miles. The Hart family (four) and John Root, Sr., owned each one and one half square miles. The Barneses, Nortons, Gridleys and Lees each about one half square mile. Mr. Hayens and Mr. Wyllys, sons of the early governors, and residents of Hartford, owned lots on West street, Mr. Haynes being especially fortunate in his assignment, which lay in the corner between Divinity and West streets, including the present fair grounds, the Pequabuck flowing through it.

Mr. Samuel Hooker, the minister in Farmington, owned a lot on the present line of Burlington, then the center of the entire tract.

Thomas Barnes owned a half square mile, and the Widow Orvice three small lots, the only woman land owner here, whose descendants appear in the persons of Ebenezer Barnes and his wife, Deborah Orvice.*

THE SETTLEMENT.

Two generations passed away after the original grant before a settlement was made. In the meantime, Farmington youth, led by the Indian trail along the Pequabuck, came hither to inspect their possessions. And events proved that these hills possessed the same attractions for Ebenezer Barnes and Daniel Brownson that they had had for Thomas Barnes and Richard Brownson sixty-four years earlier.

The years 1726-7 witnessed their arrival, and the building of two houses, of which only one remained, Daniel Brownson having soon withdrawn. On the eastern slope of the nearest hills, at the opening of the range where the Pequabuck flows, Ebenezer Barnes built his home, a clearing in the forest, smoke rising from a solitary chimney, the beginning of a town.

Other settlers came, and along the base of the same hills, other homes were built, connected by a footpath, which determined the location of our earliest residence street, called by the settlers the Queen's Road.

John Brown's house stood on the hill north of Ebenezer Barnes's house, Caleb Abernathy's next, and above it Nathaniel Messenger's, all on the east side. On the west side were the homes of Ebenezer Hamblin and Nehemiah Manross,* houses rude in structure, dwellings

---

† "Two Hundredth Anniversary Farmington Church."—Noah Porter, also "The Town and City of Waterbury."

* Roswell Atkins' Chart. Page 21.

* Manual Congregational Church, Bristol.

of logs, perhaps, giving place soon to dwellings of frame. Would that we possessed the simplest sketch of those early homes on the Queen's Road, of which only Ebenezer Barnes's house has survived through a century and three quarters of time.

The Queen's Road! Truly it reminds us that the founders of Bristol were English subjects and that George II. and Queen Caroline were sovereign here as well as in the British Isles.

If we cannot gain access to their court where assemble Alexander Pope, Dean Swift, and Lord Chesterfield, let us get a glimpse of their majesties as they pass along in the procession of history. Prince George was a "choleric little prince" who used to "shake his fist in the faces of his father's courtiers," and called everyone thief and liar with whom he differed.

In the year 1727, on the death of the king, when Walpole came to announce the news to the prince, and to proclaim him King of England, Prince George, having never lost his German accent, and being awakened from his afternoon nap, roared out, "Dat is one big lie;" the first utterance of his majesty, George II.

His wife was Caroline of Anspach, a princess remarkable for her beauty, her cleverness, her learning, her good temper. They ascended the English throne June 14, 1727, the same time that the first settler took up his residence here, a coincidence which gives a special appropriateness to the name of the first residence street.

FALL MOUNTAIN SETTLERS.

MOSES LYMAN.

Having visited the houses on the Queen's Road, let us learn the meaning of the smoke rising from the wooded side of the mountain. Is it from an Indian wigwam? Or has the white man set up a home in the heart of the Indian hunting ground?

From the Queen's Road the Indian trail follows the river westward, and creeps on over the mountain to Waterbury. Half way up is the ample home of Moses Lyman, who came from Wallingford in 1736,

THE GIDEON ROBERTS HOUSE, BUILT BY MOSES LYMAN, 1736.

(10) G. F. Unefeld *O;* (11) The Baldwin Place (now owned by L. L. Gaylord); (12) Mrs. E. F. Gaylord *O* (the Luther Tuttle Place); (13) E. F. Gaylord *O;* (14) Chas. E. Gaylord *O;* (16) Henry E. Loveland *O;* (16) S. E. Scoville *R;* (17) Amos Beauty *R;* (18) S. D. Newell *O.*

and built a house which stands today, a monument to the substantial worth of this early householder, the second oldest house in town. Here he lived for years, with no sign by day or night to remind him of his nearest neighbor. The eastern hills hid the smoke from the chimneys on the Queen's Road, and the dense forests hid the lights of those who settled later on Fall Mountain and Chippin's Hill.

THE GAYLORDS.

The nearest neighbors of Moses Lyman were Gaylord families, whose arrival, next in order, is of importance because of their numbers, influence and service. There were five men with their families, four of whom were brothers, Samuel, Edward, Benjamin, and Joseph, and their double cousin David, all of whom came from Wallingford. The cousins Joseph and David were young men of twenty-two and came first. The oldest brothers, Samuel and Edward, were appointed to many positions of responsibility, and later became prominent in military affairs. Speaking in the language of royalty, the Gaylords made strong alliances here, and were connected by marriage with all the reigning families in the settlement. Joseph's wife was Elizabeth Rich, whom he married in the year of his arrival here. His eldest sister Mary married John Hickox, the first treasurer of the society. Thankful, another sister, was the wife of Hezekiah Rew, our first deacon. David's sister Mary married Stephen Barnes, the other deacon of the early church. Lois Gaylord was the wife of Caleb Abernathy. With the Gaylord brothers for society moderators, with three deacons and two officers of the militia, it is evident that the Gaylord family had a strong hold on public affairs.*

COLONIAL ROADS.

The origin of the colonial roads in Bistol, and their development into the turnpikes of a century ago and into the roads of today, is a chapter by itself, and too long to be given here.

There are several in our town, forgotten passageways of those early days, the most important of which is the colonial road to Farmington. It followed an old Indian trail of the Tunxis tribe, from their village there on the river to their hunting grounds here, and into the domain of the Indian Cochipianee on the Hill.

This first colonial road can be traced several miles both east and west from the north cemetery, which originally occupied a portion of it and which is still bounded by it on the north.

In a line due east from Lewis street is a stone wall which lies in the center of the colonial road. When the turnpike was built in 1806, it became necessary often to place obstructions of this sort in the old road, to force the traveler to use the turnpike and to pay toll therefor. Another obstruction on the Lewis property was the flax patch, which long ago obliterated one portion of the old road.

In the lots east of the stone wall, smooth rocks worn by the wheels of a century and a half ago, and depressions in the surface of the ground, guide us in the path of the colonial road into the woods beyond, known as "Poker Hole," and here the roadbed is easily recognized.

Taking another start, west from the cemetery, we see a grass grown path near the bridge at Rock Cut, in a line with the street beyond the bridge, which, like Lewis street, is identical with the old road.

Farther on, it is lost under the curve of the railroad embankment, but is found again in the woods west of the tracks. From here, it passes on through the Hoppers, and leads up the hill, coming out at the South Chippin's Hill schoolhouse, beyond which it is plainly seen in the lots of the place known as the Candee farm.

That portion of it which lies in the Hoppers is a good specimen of the old colonial road, and should be guarded by our historical societies as an interesting relic of the two earliest epochs in our history, the Indian and the Colonial.

---

*Ms. notes of James Shepard.

(19) W. F. Duncan *O;* (20) Mrs. Mary August *R;* (21) C. B. Brockett *O* (The Ransley Upson Place); (22) Geo. Manchester *O;* (23) Robt. Manchester *O;* (24) E. Manchester *O;* (25) Chas. Gastafson *O* (the Chas. Hines Place; (26) R. W. Williams *O;* (27) Geo. H. Turner *R.*

CHIPPIN'S HILL FAMILIES.

For the extension of the Farmington road to Chippin's Hill, we are indebted to two families by the name of Matthews and Brooks, who came between 1742 and 1747, and were soon joined by other families of the same names. They located at the top of the hill once owned by Cochipianee, and which commanded a magnificent view of the whole parish of New Cambridge and the valley of the Tunxis. The Chippin's Hill families took an active part for a few years in church affairs, but were strongly opposed to Mr. Newell's settlement, and in July, 1747, when the majority voted to call Mr. Newell, the minority, headed by Caleb Matthews and the Brookses, withdrew, and publicly declared themselves members of the Church of England.

THE FOUNDERS.

Having established the founders and their families in homes, let us observe the men who laid the foundations of this early church. The leaders in the movement which resulted in the establishment of the Parish of New Cambridge, were Ebenezer Barnes, Nehemiah Manross, Moses Lyman, and Edward Gaylord.

EBENEZER BARNES.

Ebenezer Barnes was born in Farmington and married, in 1699, Deborah Orvice. He was nearly fifty years old when he left Farmington for the hardships of a pioneer life. His family consisted of fifteen children, ten sons and five daughters, twelve of whom were born in Farmington.

For fifteen years, through summer heat and winter snows, he had taken his family to the meeting house nine miles distant, when he headed the memorial which obtained for himself and neighbors the privileges of a winter parish. He was approaching his seventies when he urged, with others, the establishment of a minister. In 1746, one year previous to the settlement of a pastor, his name appears for the last time when Ebenezer Barnes is appointed to lead in divine service.

MOSES LYMAN.

Moses Lyman was the first clerk of this society. On the coarse pages, stained with age, of the old church book, we can read the character of the man in the records he kept; we can judge him by the house he built, and by the part he took in the establishment of the parish. He served as scribe, moderator, on the society's committee, as agent to the town, and to the General Assembly. On November 10, 1745, when an important church meeting was held in his own house, where thirty voters were present, certain measures were adopted which led a minority of six headed by Moses Lyman to protest against the management of the meeting. Two adjourned meetings were held, and it was finally arranged that the differences should be settled by a council. For several years, he had acted as chorister in the church, but, after Mr. Newell came, he took no part in society affairs. Some time later, he moved away. In the cemetery of Goshen, Conn., is a monument bearing this inscription:

> Moses Lyman, Esq.,
> Who died Jan. 6, 1768.
> In the 55th yr. of his age,
> Lyman, so famed, so meek, so just, so wise,
> He sleeps in hope. Then cease from tears,
> When Christ appears his dust shall rise.

NEHEMIAH MANROSS.

Nehemiah Manross arrived soon after Ebenezer Barnes. His house was the second to go up on the Queen's Road. He came from Lebanon, Conn., the home of Jonathan Trumbull, who was perhaps his schoolfellow. At the second society meeting, Nehemiah Manross was chosen moderator, and seems to have been the most acceptable (and perhaps the most able) of any who filled the chair. During a period of twelve years, he was in continual service, adjusting the public accounts,

(28) Albert Hipler *R*, Wm. Blum *R;* (29) Capt. Ernest E. Merrill *O;* (30) Joseph Blum *O;* (31) R. Bachman *O;* (32) Jacob Molson *O;* (33) Jacob Gush (34) Pius Schüssler *O;* (35) Jos. Ehlert *O;* (36) B. Kather *O.*

JOSIAH LEWIS'S HOUSE, ON LEWIS CORNER.
Built 1766.

contracting for the erection of a meeting-house; and in 1754, when it was voted "that we take up the two 'pilar pews' and make three seats in their room," Nehemiah Manross was appointed to see that the work was done. With this he disappears from the scene. Tradition has kept alive the following explanation of his mysterious disappearance; one morning he left his home, according to his custom, on horseback for Hartford, and was never again seen. No trace of him could be found. His family believed that he had been attacked by the Indians, robbed and killed.

JOSIAH LEWIS.

Among the last to arrive, in the period preceding the founding of a church, was Josiah Lewis. He came from Southington, and tradition says he was a week on the way, cutting a passage through the forest for himself and family, which consisted of twelve children. Nine sons grew up and married, to each of whom he gave a farm of a hundred acres, a house, a barn, a cow, a hive of bees, and a Waterbury sweet apple tree. Five of these houses, including his own, were built on the Farmington road, three near the cemetery and two beyond the woods of Poker Hole. Four of the Lewis houses are still standing, built much after the same plan, all large, spacious houses, such as those early settlers used to build, when the heating of a house was not an important item in the yearly expenses. They were built before the Revolution and for years formed an uninterrupted row of Lewis possessions.

THE DEACONS.

Active in the spiritual life of the church during the first period were Hezekiah Rew and David Gaylord, both of whom, in 1747, were appointed deacons.

David Gaylord was thirty-one years old, and served twenty-eight years, outliving his brother in office and two successors and serving ten years with the third.

His home was an isolated one, built in the clearing on the slope

(37) August Mann *R;* (38) Adam Budosky *R*, Frank Sinks *R;* (39) Fred Bush *R;* (40) Adolph Sonstrom *O;* (41) E. A. Conlon *O;* (42) John J. Brennan *R*, John Johnson *R;* (43) J. J. Sullivan *R*, Arthur Wieonnet *R;* (44) Mrs. Philip Boos *O*, Oscar Thomas *R;* (45) John Henebry *R*, Mrs. Susan B. Holden *O*.

of the hill north of the Pequabuck, the house lot lying in the corner of East street and Riverside Avenue, and extending to the river, across which was the Indian trail to Waterbury, Deacon Gaylord's highway into the outside world.

Hezekiah Rew's name stands first on the church list. He was an older man than his brother deacon, and had served in the various offices of the society from sexton to moderator. He deserves special recognition for the service he rendered for ten years as society's clerk. Judging from his clerical work, he was a fair scholar—a man of good judgment too, appointed to the task of "dignifying the meeting-house," according to a custom by which the members were seated with reference to their age, position, and wealth. Four years later, he declined to act in this delicate business. His name appears no more. His burial place is not known, nor the date of his death. He lived on Peaceable street near Parson Newell, and his wife Abigail died in 1764.

Two early deacons, Stephen Barnes and Elisha Manross, were sons of the first settlers. Stephen Barnes was appointed in the place of Hezekiah Rew and, after a short term of service, died in his forty-fifth year. In his home on South street for several years previous to 1747, the settlers assembled for divine service, in which Hezekiah Rew and Stephen Barnes were appointed to lead.

Elnathan Ives succeeded Stephen Barnes in 1757, when his name appears for the first time, although he had been living here for ten years. He came from Farmington, and was the oldest son of Ensign Gideon Ives, "The Mighty Hunter," tales of whose hunts in these forests are a part of our history. Elnathan Ives lived to be seventy-one years old, but resigned his office of deacon thirteen years before his death. His house was on the Southington road near its union, at the bridge, with the Queen's Road. His son and grandson became members of this church, and two nephews followed him and settled here, Enos, father o Deacon Charles Ives, and Amasa, the father of the clock makers, Chauncey and Joseph Ives.

Elisha Manross, when only thirty-eight years old, followed Deacon Ives, and served forty-five years, the second longest diaconate. He is the best known of our early deacons, whose piety, dignity, and charity, belong to our church history.

REV. SAMUEL NEWELL'S FAMILY.

Reverend Samuel Newell, two years after his installation, married Mary Hart Root, widow of Timothy Root, and daughter of Deacon John Hart, all of Farmington.

Mr. Newell was thirty-five years old, and his bride thirty-two, the mother of three children, Timothy, Theodore, and Esther Root, who were nine, seven, and five years old, respectively.

Their father, Lieut. Timothy Root, had died three years before at Cape Breton, soon after the siege of Louisburg. (His father of the same name also died at Cape Breton, having been in the expedition which, thirty-three years earlier, set out for the conquest of Canada.) The children inherited the Root homestead property in Farmington, and did not come empty-handed into the home of their step-father.

Mr. Newell owned land here by inheritance from his grandfather, Thomas Newell, an original proprietor, and by the bequest of his brother Solomon who bequeathed to Samuel, Josiah and Mary Newell, several tracts of land, including the Indian reservation of Bohemia, valued at £807 or $4,000.

To this bequest we owe, perhaps, the arrival of the Upson family, between whom and the Newell family there was a double marriage. (Josiah Newell married Mary Upson of Farmington, and Mary Newell became the wife of Asa Upson.) Some time after Mr. Newell's settlement, Asa Upson and his wife Mary Newell took up residence on Peaceable street, between their brother the parson and the Royces, who had withdrawn from the Congregational church, because of their opposition to

(1) No. 160, North, Miss Lucy Beckwith O, James Geegan R; (2) No. 177, North, Leon C. LaCourse O, Wallace Calkins R, George Fortin R; (3) No. 189, North, Arthur T. Woodford R; (4) No. 179, Maple street, A. Croze R, P. J. Reddy R, J. Hassett R; (5) No. 183, Maple, W. H. W. Burns R; (6) No. 188 Maple, Rudolf Zhanke R, A. Schinman R, P. Tessman R; (7) Flag House, George P. Lyons, Tender; (8) No. 230, Peaceable, Chas. Sandstrom R, Emil Grotze R; (9) No. 235, Peaceable, Dennis O'Brien O.

Mr. Newell's settlement. In the bitterness of feeling which outlasted the century, the not unfriendly relations of these families may have given the name to the street they lived on, the goodly name of Peaceable street.

The new minister, in his contract with the parish, took care, not only that his salary should be paid but that the society should build him a house. (Mrs. Mary Root, who afterward became his wife, was then a recent widow, living in a substantial home left by her husband.)

The specifications for the house were drawn up with great precision even to cupboards and ovens, and, like the contract, show a knowledge of legal forms, which indicates that the Rev. Mr. Newell may have been a lawyer and architect as well as a minister and landowner.

For the detail of an interior of an early settler's home, we have a picture of the parsonage as found in the specifications drawn up by Mr. Newell.

The specifications follow the contract for settlement, and are as follows: "The condition of this obligation is such that if the above said Ebeneezer Hamblin, Mr. Samll Gaylord, Edward Gaylord shall within the space of one year and two months from the day above * * in good workmanship like manner erect build and set up one * * dwelling house for the said Mr. Samuel Newell upon his land in New Cambridge as he shall direct of thirty-eight feet long and twenty-three feet wide, and sixteen feet and one-half between joints with a lintow (leanto) adjoining the backside 20 feet long and sixteen feet wide, containing five rooms below, and shall workmanlike finish the lower rooms in the manner following, namely, well ceil the dwelling room and make suitable cobard (suitable cupboard) and shelves for such rooms and lath, plaster and whitewash the parlor and bedrooms, side and overhead, making all sutiable covenant (convenient) good and workmanlike doors and partions (partitions) * * stock and dig and stone * * a proper cellar at least seven feet deep from the lower floor, and the bignes of one end of the house from the chimney, and in good and workmanlike build * * a stack of chimneys consisting of three tunnels from the bottom and two more beginning at the chambers. Making at least two brick ovens of a sutiable bigness, and in a workmanlike manner make the window frames * * and glass the whole house, namely, nine windows, consisting of twenty-four squares of glass six and eight size, and one of eighteen square, and seven with twelve of the same size, all this to be done by the latter end of Sept., A. D. 1749.

And that the said Ebenezer Hamblin, Samuel Gaylord, Edward Gaylord, their exers and admid (executors and administrators) and assigns shall find and provide at their own cost and charge all and all manner of timber, stone, brick, laths, nails, iron, glass, lime, clay, sand, and all other materials whatsoever [as] shall be fit and necessary to be used in and about said building, and they, so doing, shall be quit of the above said written bond, obligation, etc., etc.

Signed and delivered this 20th day of July, A. D. 1747.

A parsonage was built on the knoll known as the Dr. Pardee place, and, during the first eleven years of the pastorate, five children were born, two daughters and three sons. Mary became a member of this church, and at twenty married Jacob Hungerford. Anna married Elnathan Hooker. The oldest son Samuel died when four years old. Two younger sons, Lott and Samuel, were sent to Yale college and the former died there; the latter, a graduate, was the only son to marry and perpetuate the name of his father.

Of Mrs. Newell's children, Esther Root died at fifteen. Timothy married, and settled on the homestead property in Farmington. Theodore married, united with this church, and settled here near his mother. Seven daughters were born in his family.

He appears in the records in various appointments, first when he is appointed to "git Mr. Newell's wood" and is allowed six pounds for the same. To supply Mr. Newell with wood seems always to have

(1) No. 47, W. H. Gladding *R*, Mrs. R. J. Jerrolds *R*, F. R. Parsons *R;* (2) No. 38, Burdette A. Peck *O;* (3) No. 38, Ernest C. Smith *R;* (4) No. 32, Edward L. Dunbar *O;* (5) No. 26, Hiram C. Thompson *O;* (6) No. 29, Mrs. Fanny W. Gowdy *R*, Mrs. M. Wilcox *R*, Mrs. C. Parsons *R;* (7) No. 23, Wilbur F. Brainard *O;* (8) No. 20, Cornelius T. Olcott *O*, R. C. Pease *R;* (9) No. 15, Hobart Booth *R*.

been an unpleasant task, no man in the parish undertaking it twice, young men being appointed to the place, as a kind of stepping stone into public life! And in 1767 the minister's stepson takes his turn with the rest.

Other houses scattered here and there were the homes of Joseph Benton, David Rich, Ebenezer Norton, the Tuttles, the Warrens and Daniel Rowe.

These are the glimpses we get of the little company, who, one hundred and fifty years ago, established this church in the wilderness, with its forty members, twenty men and twenty women. There were seventeen men with their wives; one old man, William Merriman, living in the family of his son-in-law, Caleb Matthews; two bachelors (Ebenezer Hamblin and Samuel Gaylord); the widow Sarah Bushnell; Miss Deborah Buck, whose brother Stephen married a daughter of Ebenezer Barnes; and Jacob Deming's wife, Abigail, who by her first husband, Timothy Jerome, was the mother of the Jerome families in Bristol, a distinguished member of which was Chauncey Jerome, the clock maker and autobiographer.

The congregation, however, included a larger number, men active in affairs but not church members, and many young people and children. Ebenezer Barnes brought fifteen grown up sons and daughters, and Josiah Lewis, twelve.

The year 1747 witnessed the fulfillment of their long cherished hopes, the establishment of an independent church. With this event, the first period of our history closes.

CHAPTER II.

The next period presents a different view. It is the period preceding the Revolution, a critical time in the history of the colonies, during which occurred the French and Indian war, 1755-1760, giving to the English race and Protestantism the destinies of a new world.

In Europe, the avaric or ambition of a king was sufficient to draw the nations into war. A fierce jealousy existed between George II. and Louis XV. of France, and, when France united with Spain to rob England of her commerce with her American colonies, New England was drawn in too. His majesty George II. forthwith fitted out an expedition for the conquest of the Spanish West Indies, and called on the colonies for men, money, and ships. The Connecticut assembly responded with cheerfulness to his majesty's demand, and lost nearly a thousand men in the expedition, which resulted in a total failure.

When France, a few years later, proclaimed war against Great Britain, the New England colonies, nothing daunted by their recent losses in the Spanish seas, cried out that Louisburg must be taken. At their own expense, they fitted out an expedition which captured that most important stronghold of France in the New World, in which expedition Connecticut played an important part. The town of Farmington contributed its quota of men, among whom were probably men from the parish of New Cambridge.

It remains to be proved that men of this society took part in the colonial wars, but it is noteworthy the number of names which appear with military titles attached.

The first militia company was formed about 1748, and, as the titles appear after 1760, it is possible that they indicate not merely militia rank, but rank in the colonial army.

Soon after the church was established, a second influx of settlers occurred. The following years witnessed many arrivals until the twenty houses of the first period had increased, in the next period, to fifty.

In the meantime, the early founders had retired from the stage and the new company appears whose character is distinctly military.

The Captains. Edward Gaylord, Caleb Matthews, Zebulon Peck, Zebulon Frisbie, Asa Upson, John Hungerford.

The Lieutenants, Josiah Lewis, Amos Barnes, Samuel Gaylord.

RESIDENCE ALBERT L. SESSIONS, BELLEVUE AVENUE.

Ensign Gersham Tuttle.
Sergt. Zebulon Frisbie, Jr., and Luke Gridley, a soldier in the French and Indian wars, whose diary recording his experiences in the war is still in the possession of his descendants.

Other new names which appear are, Jerome, Atkins, Churchill, Roberts, Byington, Mix, Stone, Andrus, Shepard, Clark, Smith, Rogers, Pearson, Cole. Lastly Hezekiah Gridley, father and son, both men of distinction in civil and military affairs.

The men of the second period took up not only the work laid down by the founders. They assumed other burdens, the miantenance of the church, a share in the colonial wars, the building of schoolhouses and roads.

THE VILLAGE ROADS.

When the church was built, there were four roads in the parish. The church on the hill was the only building in sight, except Joseph Benton's house in the lot southeast. Roads, connecting the church with the four corners of the parish, were soon opened. Peaceable street was extended up the hill to the church door, for the convenience of Parson Newell, Deacon Rew, and Josiah Lewis.

The Queen's Road people came over the ridge by a road running west and passing north of the Episcopal church property, a road unused for a century, but never closed up, which is today a grass-grown passageway guarded by stone walls, whose name of Lovers' Lane suggests its present use. Midway, and at right angles with this, was another leading south and coming out at the mill.

Center street connected the church with West street, which is our most interesting early road, on account of its origin. West street is two hundred and eleven years old, and the only one in the village which lies in the highway of the original layout, its generous width alone bearing evidence of its descent from the colonial assembly.

There is one other street which conforms with the highway of the original layout, the one running north and south on Chippin's Hill, which outrivals West street, being nearly twice as long and preserving, throughout its whole extent, the same generous width and having, in addition, magnificent views from the mountain.

THE EARLY ARCHITECTURE.

Of the twenty homes built during the first period, two still remain, Ebenezer Barnes's and Moses Lyman's. Of the former, the central portion with its stone chimney is the original house. The two ends, each with a brick chimney, which have been added, changed the dwelling house of the early settler into a commodious tavern. The wide roof, the three chimneys, the windows in long double rows, and the three front doors, give it a grave appearance, characteristic of early New England architecture.

The second oldest house in town, the home of Moses Lyman on Fall Mountain retains, except for the ell on the west, its original shape. It is one hundred and sixty years old, but shows no sign of age or infirmity, and will, probably, outlast many of its youthful neighbors. In its interior and exterior, it is a good example of a simple colonial house. The second story projects over the first, but there are no projections on the roof, no canopy over the door, no ornamentation, and hence no shadows, producing a severe expression, common alike to the homes and to the people of this early period.

Another interesting specimen of early architecture and the best of the kind known as the "leanter," is a Lewis house on Lewis corner. It belongs to the second period of our history and was built in 1766. It has a somewhat decrepit appearance, owing to the fact that, for several years, no one has lived in it, but, for picturesqueness in color, outline, and setting, nothing in Bristol surpasses it. The old well sweep in front, the long slope of the "leanto" roof, the double arched sheds, bordered by grape vines, like carved decorations of Italian arcades, and the jagged stone chimney, compose a picture perfect of its kind.

These represent the homes of the living. In the old cemeteries,

PROSPECT STREET, FROM R. R. BRIDGE.

we find the founders and their successors in their last resting places—homes of the dead, we say.

With few exceptions all are here, the minister and his wife, the deacons and their wives, the moderators and clerks, the captains and lieutenants, an honorable and venerable company in our old cemeteries.

But the spirit of the founders lives on, as this anniversary gives witness. The sacrifices they made, the labors they endured, bear perpetual fruit, for the healing our souls, like the tree of life in the garden. They worked out the problems of their day and they hand down to us the result. With every generation come new problems, to solve which we gain inspiration from the founders, and from the memories of those eventful early years.

[For their friendly interest, and for their most valued assistance in obtaining certain statistics and genealogical material used in this paper, grateful acknowledgments are due and are herewith tendered to Dea. F. O. Lewis, Bristol; James Shepard, Esq., New Britain; and Miss Sarah F. Pritchard, Waterbury.]

THE BAPTIST CHURCH.

The Baptist Church

Compiled Largely from a Sketch Prepared by Roswell Atkins in 1880

ON April 13, 1791, in the town of Plymouth, a small company of Christian people effected the organization which is now known as the Bristol Baptist Church. In exactly what building the organization took place is not now known. The first ordination of a minister occurred in the building afterwards occupied as a dwelling by Lyman Tuttle. When and by whom the building was erected is not now certainly known. In 1798, the church reported at the meeting of the Danbury Association that its membership list numbered sixty-six. Whether this is accurate or not is open to question. The membership roll of that date shows only twenty-six names. The additions for that year were reported to be twenty-one. The record, however, shows only eight. This confusion of numbers was not at all infrequent in those days when church bookkeeping did not receive as much attention as now.

In 1802, the membership of the church is given as one hundred and seven. Rev. Daniel Wildman was the minister. How long Mr. Wildman remained pastor of the church we do not know, but it must have been for a number of years, probably until 1817.

For twenty-six years, from 1791 to 1817, the records of the church are very scanty. Three pages in one book and six in another tell all that is now known of those years. Of the Ecclesiastical Society there are no records until 1814. The first entry in these records tells us that there was "A meeting for hiring a preacher and other necessaries." In the same month, November, it was voted "that we have preaching half of the time and that a committee be appointed to secure it; and that Austin Bishop, Ichabod Wright, and Samuel Atkins be the committee."

The first record of a preacher receiving a salary in this church is in 1816, when it was voted that the preacher be paid three hundred dollars per year. For a short time previous, five dollars a Sunday had been paid, but it is not positively known whether it was paid to a singing teacher or to the preacher.

In 1801, Rev. Daniel Wildman bought from his father, Captain Daniel Wildman, the land on the corner of West and School streets which for about eighty years held the meeting house of the Bristol Baptists. In 1809 this property was deeded to the Baptist Society. The meeting house had been built upon it some time before. In 1830, this house of worship was moved from its first site and was used for a clock shop. We cannot determine when the meetings were first held in the vicinity where this church stood, but previous to the building of the house, they were held in a hall standing where the parsonage afterwards stood. The evening meetings were held in a house a little south of this hall, afterwards owned by Theron Sandford. During these twenty-six years, from 1791 to 1817, the record gives one hundred and twenty-two to the roll of membership. There is reason, however, to believe that this is not a complete list. Fifty-two of this number were received

REV. HENRY CLARKE.

between October, 1815, and October, 1816. Elder Wildman was the preacher and he was assisted at times during this year by Elder David Wright and probably by Orra Martin. One of those received during this period was Asa Bronson, Jr., who afterwards entered the ministry and was a very successful preacher and pastor.

In 1817, Orra Martin was called from Wisconsin to be the pastor of the church. He continued in this pastorate until August, 1820, and maintained membership with the church for nearly a year later. In September of that same year, Elder Isaac Merriam was invited to preach for the church. He accepted the invitation and continued the regular supply until March, 1823, when he was settled as pastor, and he and his wife brought letters from the Baptist Church in Brandon, Vermont. He remained with the church until April, 1825, and continued a member of the church until October, 1826. During his ministry there were added to the church thirty-five by baptism. One of the number was Rollin H. Neale, D. D., who was licensed to preach, February 12, 1826. Two of those who until during this pastorate were Deacon George Welch and his wife, who came to the church by letter. The only ordination of a deacon that has occurred in the history of the church was in this period, when, on May 7, 1826, Irenus Atkins was ordained.

In January, 1827, the Rev. Henry Stanwood was invited to supply the church, and on May 2, 1828, he accepted the call to the pastorate and continued with the church as pastor until March, 1834. During his ministry seventy-six were added by baptism. Among them were B. F. Hawley and E. N. Welch. During Elder Stanwood's ministry, another house of worship was built. This occurred in 1830. The only record that has been found with regard to it is the following: "September, 1829, special meeting to take into consideration the expediency of building a new meetinghouse. George Mitchell, Truman Prince, and Daniel B. Hinman were appointed a committee to obtain subscriptions for building a new house for public worship, and also to ascertain the difference in expense of wood or brick and report at the next meeting. Adjourned to the 17th." Another record shows that the new house of worship was used for the first time about the last of December, 1830.

In 1832, a conference house was built. Sherman Johnson, Miles Norton, and Rollin Atkins were the building committee. In the same year occurs the first record of expenses being met by the rental of pews. Previous to this most of the money had been raised by subscription or property assessment.

After the resignation of Elder Stanwood, Elder William Bentley preached for the church until the spring of 1835. At that time Rev. Orsamus Allen was asked to preach for one year. The presumption is that he continued to preach for the church until 1837. During this time there were eighteen baptisms and fourteen additions by letter.

From October 1, 1837, until April 29, 1838, the church listened to the preaching of Elder Francis Hawley. After Elder Hawley, there seems to have been no settled pastor until June, 1841. Different preachers ministered to the flock. Among these was Rev. Simon Shailer. This period seems to have been one of hard trial to the church.

In June, 1841, Rev. James Squier became the pastor and remained until May, 1842. During his ministry there was a revival in which twenty-nine were baptised. The pastor was assisted by Rev. J. Robords, of Galway.

In April, 1842, Edward Savage, a recent graduate of Madison University, was engaged as supply, and in September of the same year was ordained pastor. He remained with the church until December 4, 1846. During his pastorate thirty-nine were added by baptism and twenty-one by letter. In 1844, the ill health of Mr. Savage compelled him to spend a few months in travel. The church, during the absence of Mr. Savage, was cared for by Rev. S. D. Phelps, D. D., who was then a student.

In 1843, the house which now stands on the southeast corner of

West and Meadow streets was built for a parsonage. The land was given for that purpose by Deacon George Welch. This property was sold in 1863 and a house which stood next to the church was bought with the proceeds, and for a number of years served as the church parsonage.

On January 29, 1847, the Rev. Leicester Lewis became pastor of the church. He continued the pastoral relation until September 25, 1853. There were added to the church during his ministry sixty-nine, of whom forty-six came by baptism.

On January 8, 1854, Rev. J. T. Smith of Sandisfield, Mass., accepted the pastorate He began his labors in the spring, and was installed June 28th. He continued in this pastorate until August 1st, 1856.

In September of the same year, Rev. Isaac H. Gilbert, a recent graduate of Brown University, was called as pastor. He was ordained November 26th of that year. He continued with the church until April 26, 1863, and then went to the church in Middletown. Sixty-nine were added to the church during his ministration, forty-seven of them by baptism.

From this time until January, 1866, the church was without a pastor. Among its supplies was the famous Jabez S. Swan, and also his son, Rev. C. Y. Swan. On January 26, 1866, Rev. George E. Horr of Orange, N. J., was tendered an invitation to the pastorate. He began his labors about the first of May of that same year, and continued with the church until November, 1868.

Until April, 1870, after the resignation of Mr. Horr, the church was again depending upon supplies. But, in March, 1870, the Rev. Charles W. Ray of Jewett City was urged to take up the pastoral relation. He accepted the invitation and began his work in April. He remained until August 31, 1873. During his ministry there was a revival of which mention is still made. Seventy-four united with the church in his pastorate, fifty-two of whom were by baptism.

On April 7, 1874, the church extended a call to Rev. Delavan Dewolf of Delavan, Wisconsin. Mr. Dewolf came in response to the call, and remained with the church until September 1, 1886. His ministry was a fruitful one and he was much beloved by the church and community. During this period, the present church building was erected, and also the present parsonage. The new building was occupied for worship for the first time in September, 1880. Both the church and parsonage are, in several respects, model buildings, and are associated in the minds of many with the ministration of Mr. Dewolf.

On October 21, 1886, Rev. F. E. Tower of Brattleboro, Vermont, was invited to the pastorate. The invitation met with his approval and his work with the church began on November 1st, of that year. Mr. Tower remained with the church until January 1, 1894. He was a student, an author, and a preacher of wide intellectual grasp.

The church extended a call to Rev. John S. Lyon, of Fair Haven, Vermont, on March 18, 1894. Mr. Lyon began his work in Bristol on May 1st of the same year. He continued with the church until the last Sunday in December, 1900. He at once took a very large place in the life of the community. His power as a public speaker was exceptional and his personality won for him a multitude of friends. His pastorate was successful from every point of view, and it was with the deepest regret that the church was compelled to accept his resignation. He is still remembered in Bristol with great admiration and affection. The notable revival under Evangelist Jackson occurred during this pastorate. It was an inter-denominational movement, and was far-reaching in its influence and results.

Rev. Henry Clarke of Stonington, Conn., on May 5, 1901, was voted a call by the church to become its pastor. His pastorate began in June of that year, and continues at the present time.

Rambles Among the Bristol Birds

By Frank Bruen.

"To business that we love
We rise betimes
And go to 't with delight."
ANTHONY AND CLEOPATRA—*Shakespeare.*

BRISTOL is well situated for pleasant walks, for bird and nature study. Go in whatsoever direction you will there is a great deal to charm the eye and ear; though the woodman's greed has done much in recent years to deprive Bristol of her assets of woodland beauty, and her birds of much needed homes, food and shelter. Let us hope that owners of woodlots may soon learn the principles and practice of common sense timber culture.

Space would forbid my treating in detail of rambles at all seasons, so I shall confine myself largely to May when the spring migration is at its culmination, with lapses backward perhaps, or leaps ahead as may be convenient.

It is five o'clock in the morning at Federal Green and the symphony of bird music thrills the ears of bird lovers and fills the novice with mingled pleasure and bewilderment.

The "Robin Chorus" is largely over at this time and different species like players in an orchestra give voice or withdraw when their turns come. The Robin is still most noticeable, but Chippy's little ditty almost unheard before is now quite prominent. The Rose-breasted Grosbeak's sweet, rich song is heard from half a dozen directions; the Least Flycatcher calls "chebec" from everywhere; the Bluebirds sound their sweet warble, the Purple Finch in ecstacy circles over head, pouring out delicious song, then goes fluttering to some perch, but unable to contain his happiness there he is up in the air again. His cousins, the Gold Finches in the elms, are equally happy and tuneful.

Up by the Congregational Church the Wood Peewee is calling plaintively and the Flickers are courting near by or drumming loudly on some dead branch, and the Downy Woodpecker is not backward in showing off his skill in the same way.

Over by St. Joseph's Church the Catbird is singing gloriously, showing that it is only a step from the sublime to the ridiculous, by ending his song with a miserable catcall.

The Purple Grackle from the colony nearby flies overhead with his hysterical call, a Humming bird buzzes by to some early blossom, the Baltimore Oriole sings from the elms where his pendant cradle is well under way, the Chimney Swift goes chattering overhead and in the distance we hear the Field Sparrow, Indigo Bunting, the Crow, Blue Jay and other birds which we shall see later on.

But who is this little fellow above our heads almost deafening us

NEST OF HUMMING BIRD.

with his "Hear me, see me, where are you?" It is the Yellow Throated Vireo and his cousin the Red Eyed Vireo is *preaching* away in the maple across the street; below the hill the Warbling Vireo, to me the sweetest of singers, is warbling out his joy. Earlier in the season we may hear the Solitary Vireo's fascinating song.

Warblers we hear in great variety, especially the Black and White's wheezy notes, the Redstart, Chestnut Sided and others, besides that quaintest of songs the "Ta, ta; ta, to, *how* do?" of the Black Throated Green Warbler.

ROBIN'S NEST AND EGGS.
(*An unusual place for a Robin's Nest.*)

But as *warblers* the warblers are a great failure, they should have been called *wood sprites* instead of *wood warblers*.

All this time the House Wren has been bubbling over with his explosive song and to appease his wrath for leaving him so long unnoticed I beg his pardon. The "Thank, thank, thank" or "Wet, wet, wet, wet" of the White-Breasted Nuthatch or "devil downhead" as he is sometimes called, will be seldom heard because his family duties forbid his showing himself much in public at this time. Otherwise he would be frequently seen going up or down the trees head up or head down as suited his convenience.

Other birds may be seen and heard here, but the sun is getting high and we must hasten away.

Our route is along Queen St., to the "Old Lane" entrance. Besides the birds just mentioned which seem to attend us on our way, we soon hear the Yellow Warbler or Summer Yellow Bird, and hardly have we entered the "Old Lane" than "Silver Tongue," the Song Sparrow, whose song we have been hearing, begins to scold, and near by in the grass among the briars nicely hid away, his nest is found with its speckled beauties or hungry little ones.

Now the Brown Thrasher's unrivalled song comes to us in full force from yonder tall tree and we stop to listen, breathless.

Next we come to "Chat Hollow," one-time favorite home of the Yellow-breasted Chat, White-eyed Vireo and a host of other birds, but its glories have largely departed because the swamp feeding ground above has been cleared away. But the place is full of the memories of former days and of the antics and queer noises of that clown in feathers, the Chat.

The bell-like song of the wood thrush and the *Buzz, buzz, buzz* of the Golden-winged, or the *Buzz, buzz* of the Blue-winged warbler, is generally heard. Chestnut-sided, Prairie, Nashville, Redstart, and other warblers are generally heard there yet, and the "*Teacher, teacher, teacher*" of the Oven-bird is sure to come from all sides, as does also the "Stick your peas" of the Towhee or Chewink.

WHITE-BREASTED NUT HATCH, HEAD DOWNWARDS.

A little farther along Phœbe used to call from above the old copper mine mouth, where year after year its nest was made, until unfeeling boys broke up the home.

Here we should hear the Grouse drum on the hill.

The Northern Yellow-Throat (formerly Maryland Yellow-Throat) is in forceful evidence with his "wichity, wichity, wich." Here, too, the Fox-sparrow may be heard early in the spring.

We wander on to the "Lone Pine," then leave the "Old Lane" and skirt along the woods below the standpipe, through alder and birch growths, noting here and there a new bird for our list or stopping to see or hear the old favorites. The Scarlet Tanager will be singing from some tall tree top and the Hairy Woodpecker giving his long roll from some dead limb and if we are *very lucky* we may hear a Red-headed Woodpecker calling from the "Maple Croft" woods. Through Maple-

THE LONE PINE AND THE OLD LANE.

croft we go to Lewis Corners and the Pines, we hear the Vesper, Grasshopper, and Savannah Sparrows sing, and the Barn Swallows twitter about us, and a troupe of Wax Wings may fly over us.

A Red Shouldered Hawk too is likely to leave her nest and circle about, screaming overhead. In the meadow the Bob-o-link is tinkling his metallic song and the Meadow Lark's song floats sweetly to us.

Here, too, the Kingbird loves to perch on some apple tree giving sharp calls between bites, and the Crested Fly-catcher's call is heard from the hillside, and from the distant swamp we may be fortunate enough to hear the wierd flute-like song of the Veery or Wilson's Thrush. Never shall I forget my endeavors to fasten that song to the right bird. Bob White's clear whistle was wont to be heard here but he is well nigh extinct about Bristol.

Up the valley to Edgewood, rounding the "Dumpling" we come to the ponds, and, where the foaming, dashing cascade begins may be heard the thrilling, wild song of the Louisiana Water Thrush. Here the Little Green Heron may be seen; the Red Wings will scold you from the alders, Sandpipers run along the shore, and Kingfishers sound their policemen's rattle as they fly from one favorite perch to another. A Swamp Sparrow may be heard in the swamp and on rare occasions a Great Blue Heron may fly out. Chickadee may be found already housed in some rotted stump, and at night the Whippoorwill will call from the "Dumpling" and sometimes a Night Hawk calls overhead.

Across the fields to Birge's Pond, through the Hoppers to "Cuss Gutter" over Fall Mountain to "Cedar Swamp" or down the Pequabuck to the Y, and around South Mountain to Compounce by way of "Purgatory" to hear the Water Thrush sing, the ponds below, the timbered lands east to Forestville, or up the river to Terryville, all are walks of beauty and interest.

But May is not the only month, for all seasons have their own peculiar charm and the somber days of winter are no exception. What can make one feel more sure of the Father's care over his creatures than to find a tiny Winter Wren living securely in the depths of "Cuss Gutter" when the Frost King has fettered the swift stream, save for a few breathing spots, and the earth is buried down in snow? One comes very near to Nature's God amid such scenes.

One great charm of the winter rambles is the finding of unexpected birds, those, who for some unknown reason, have remained North, when their comrades went South, or who are erratic in their movements, or who have become rare for the locality, they are as follows:

PHŒBE ON NEST, PHOTOGRAPHED FROM LIFE WITH THE AID OF MIRRORS

NEST AND EGGS OF THE SONG SPARROW.

Bluebird, Robin, American Crossbill, White Winged Crossbill, Purple Finch, Northern Flicker, Evening Grosbeak (1905 and 1907), Pine Grosbeak, Marsh Hawk, Red-tailed Hawk, Kingfisher, Ruby-crowned Kinglet, Meadow Lark, Red-breasted Nuthatch, Red Poll-linnet, Northern Shrike, Pine Siskin, Snow Bunting, Song Sparrow, White-throated Sparrow, Hermit Thrush, Towhee Bunting, Myrtle Warbler, Bohemian and Cedar Wax Wings and Winter Wren.

Bristol is both a popular summer and winter resort for birds; poor indeed would be our showing of birds if we had to depend upon our permanent residents.

The following birds may be called residents:

Bob White (almost extinct), Black Capped Chickadee, American Crow, Ruffed Grouse, Bluejay, White-breasted Nuthatch, Barred Owl, Screech Owl, English Sparrow, Downy and Hairy Woodpeckers.

Then there are those *species* which are constantly with us but of which the individuals may or may not breed to the north of us, these to coin a new term, I call resident-migrants.

They are the Crow, American Goldfinch, American Sparrow Hawk, Red-tailed, Red-shouldered and Marsh Hawks and Song Sparrow.

Another class is made up of winter visitants, birds that breed to the north of us and come to spend the winter with us. They are Brown Creeper, American and White Winged Crossbills, Evening Grosbeak, very rare, Pine Grosbeak, occasional, but then in force, American Rough Legged Hawk, Goshawk, Slate-colored Junco or Snow-bird, Golden Crowned Kinglet, Saw Whet Owl, Red Poll-linnett, Northern Shrike,

NEST AND EGGS OF THE PHŒBE, PHOTOGRAPHED FROM LIFE BY THE USE OF MIRRORS.

Pine Siskin, Snow Bunting or Snow Flake, Tree Sparrow, Winter Wren. Red-breasted Nuthatch and Bohemian Wax Wing.

A large class is migrant in the spring time going north, and returning in the fall on their way south.

These are Rusty Grackle, American Golden-eye Duck, Olive-sided Fly Cathcer, Yellow-bellied Fly Catcher, Canada Goose, Pied-billed Grebe, Broad-winged Hawk, Pigeon Hawk, Sharp Shinned Hawk, Great Blue Heron, Ruby Crowned Kinglet, Loon, Orchard Oriole, rare, Osprey, American Pipit, Solitary Sandpiper, Yellow-bellied Sapsucker, Fox Sparrow, Savanna Sparrow, White-crowned Sparrow, White-throated Sparrow, Gray-cheecked Thrush, Hermit Thrush, Olive-backed Thrush, Blueheaded or Solitary Vireo, Bay-breasted, Black Burnian, Black Poll, Black Throated Blue Canadian Flycatching, Connecticut, Magnolia, Myrtle, Nashville and Northern Parula, Wilson's, Black Cap and Yellow Palm Warblers, N. Y. Water Thrush and Red-headed Woodpecker.

The largest class is of summer residents, these are the ones that attract the most attention by their songs and these are the ones most of us mean when we say "the birds have come back again." Some of them lap over into the preceding classes. They are as follows:

American Bittern, rare, Red-shouldered Blackbird, Blue Bird, Bob-o-link, Indigo Bunting, Catbird, Cowbird, Crow, Black-billed and Yellow-billed Cuckoo, Mourning Dove, rare, Black Duck, rare, Purple Finch, Northern Flicker, Crested Flycatcher, Least Flycatcher, Purple Grackle, Rose-breasted Grosbeak, Coopers, Marsh, Red-shouldered and Red-Tailed Hawks, Black-crowned Night Heron, Little Green Heron,

NIGHT HAWK'S NEST AND EGGS.

FRANK BRUEN.

Ruby-throated Humming-bird, Kingbird, Belted Kingfisher, Purple Martin, Meadow Lark, Night Hawk, Baltimore Oriole, Wood Peewee, Phœbe, Robin, Spotted Sandpiper, Chipping, Field, Grasshopper, Henslow's, Swamp, Song and Vesper Sparrows, Bank, Barn, Cliff, Rough-winged and Tree Swallows, Chimney Swift, Scarlet Tanager, Brown Thrasher, Towhee Bunting, Red-eyed, Warbling, White-eyed and Yellow-throated Vireos, American Red-start, Blackthroated, Green, Black, White, Blue Winged, Chestnut-sided and Golden-winged Warblers, Northern Yellow Throat, Oven Bird, Pine and Prairie Warblers, Louisiana Water Thrush, Yellow Warbler or Summer Yellowbird, Yellow-breasted Chat, Cedar Wax-wing, Whippoorwill, American Wood Cock, and House Wren.

This list is probably far from complete but the writer, with one exception, has named only the birds seen by himself.

An intimate personal acquaintance with the birds is a lifelong joy and I hope that all Bristol people and others may try to emulate, in knowledge at least, Hiawatha, whom Longfellow thus pictures:

"Then the little Hiawatha
   Learned of every bird its language,
   Learned their names and all their secrets,
    How they built their nests in summer,
   Where they hid themselves in winter,
    Talked with them whene'er he met them,
   Called them 'Hiawatha's chickens.' "

History of School District No. 9

School District No. 7, 1796—School District No. 9, 1896*

RECORD OF HOMES IN NO. 7 FROM 1796 TO 1896, TO THE DIVISION LINE OF 1842.

BY MRS. H. S. BARTHOLOMEW.

REVIEWING the changeful years of a century in the history of No. 7, or the North East School District of Bristol, it is evident that its beginning as a distinct school district dates from one year after the Connecticut School Fund became available for free and public schools, 1795.

When in 1796, the town held its first school meeting in the "meeting-house," Joseph Byington, from the North East part of the town was moderator and David Lewis, from the same section, was one of the *nine* voted "to be school committee for the several districts to which they respectively belong."

The division of the town in 1768, into five districts, was thus made obsolete.

In 1798, Noah Byington, son of Joseph, Senior, received his appointment as Investigating or School Society's Committee and at the same time James Hadsell was made a District School Committee, one of *ten* in number. They were residents of No. 7, or the North East District.

Noah Byington served many years in his official capacity. Sometimes with Esquire Thomas or George Mitchell they constituted the entire board of examiners and school visitors, as in 1820. Usually several others were chosen also to perform the duties of the committee. Mr. Byington was a surveyor. His home was near and south of the first school house of the district No. 7, very near the present home of Franklin Yale, on the east side of the way. He was born 1762, and died 1834. His wife, Lucy, died 1798, age 32. The third wife, Ruth Manross, daughter of Deacon Elisha Manross of Forestville, died at the old home, 1867, aged 95 years. Of the children two sons, Noah Henry and Charles were physicians of Bristol and Southington, and Welles R., a deacon of Congregational Church, Bristol, 1830-1849. (All the Byingtons were large, strong men.) (From H. I. Muzzy.) After the death of Mrs. Byington in 1867, the house was last occupied by Michael Lyons, who removed soon to Farmington and built a house west of "the Meadows," near Bristol town line.

---

* The illustrations accompanying this article, have in all cases (where mention of the subject illustrated has been made in the text), been numbered to correspond with the number denoting their location on the MAP OF DISTRICT NO. 9.

For a few years previous to Oct. 10, 1896, the town conveyed pupils from No. 7 to the school in Edgewood. At that date it was voted in an adjourned town meeting "to form of No. 7, and No. 9, a new school district, called No. 9, to contain all the territory in both."

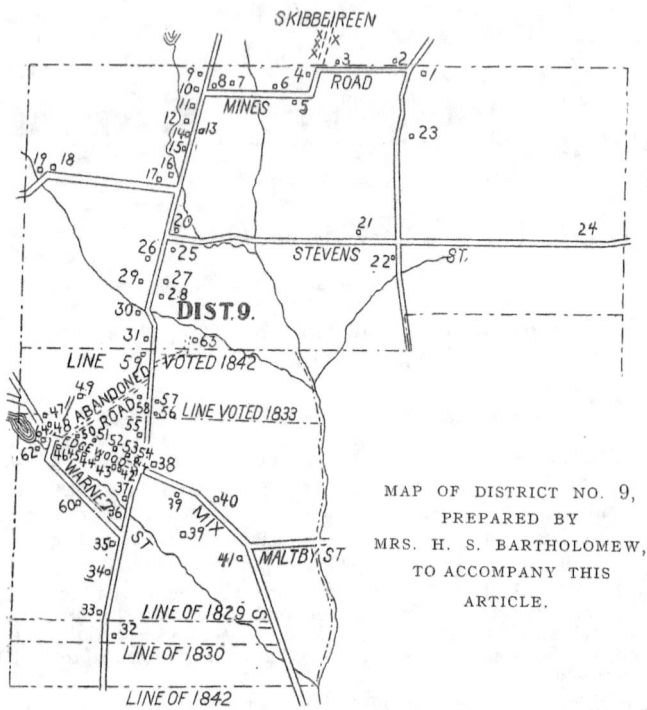

MAP OF DISTRICT NO. 9,
PREPARED BY
MRS. H. S. BARTHOLOMEW,
TO ACCOMPANY THIS
ARTICLE.

LIST OF BUILDINGS AND BUILDING SITES AS INDICATED ON ABOVE MAP OF DISTRICT No. 9.

No. 1, David Lewis and Joel Norton Places; No. 2, Hiram Norton Place; No. 3, Michael Critchley Place; No. 4, James Hadsell, Jr., Place; No. 5, Mining Company's House; No. 6, Ephraim Culver Place; No. 7, Mine Superintendent's House; No. 8, Store of Mining Co.; No. 9, Abel Yale (1st and 2d) Place; No. 10, Thomas Yale and Adna Hart Places; No. 11, John Bacon Place; No. 12, Schoolhouse No. 2; No. 13, the Joel Hart Place; No. 14, James Hadsell, Sr., Place; No. 15, Hadsell's Cooper Shop; No. 16, the Muzzy Saw Mill; No. 17, the Ward, Shane, etc., Place; No. 18, the Martin Hart Place; No. 19, Pest House, the Calvin Wooding Place; No. 20, James Hadsell, Sr., Place; No. 21, Philo Stevens Place; No. 22, Samuel Botsford Place; No. 23, Theophilus Botsford Place; No. 24, Henry Smith Place; No. 25, Schoolhouse No. 1; No. 26, Ashbel Mix Place; No. 27, Noah Byington Place; No. 28, Joseph Byington Place; No. 29, Luther Tuttle Place; No. 30, Wilson Sheldon Place; No. 31, Thos. Martin Place; No. 32, Mark Lewis and David Steele Places; No. 33, William Jerome, 3d, Place; No. 34, Simeon Curtiss Place; No. 35, Wm. Jerome, 1st, Place; No. 36, Horace O. Miller Place; No. 37, William Jerome, 2d, Place; No. 38, Wellington Winston, Sr., Place; No. 39, John London Place; No. 40, John London Place; No. 41, Asahel Mix Place; No. 42, Wm. B. Carpenter Place; No. 43, H. S. Bartholomew Place; No. 44, George W. Bartholomew Place; No. 45, Asa Bartholomew Place; No. 46, Wm. Jerome, 3d, and David Steele Places; No. 47, Lauren Byington Place; No. 48, Martin Byington Place; No. 49, John Conklin Place; No. 50, Moses Pickingham Place; No. 51, Allen Winston Place; No. 52, Jeremiah Stever Place; No. 53, Philo and Andrew Curtiss Places; No. 54, Schoolhouse No. 3; No. 55, Asa Austin Upson Place; No. 56, Charles Belden Place; No. 57, Ephraim McEwen Place; No. 58, Isaac Gillett Place; No. 59, Jerome B. Ford Place; No. 60, Grinding Shop; No. 61, Hardware Factory and Gristmill; No. 62, Saw Mill; No. 63, J. B. Ford's Machine Shop.

STORY OF NOAH BYINGTON RELATED BY H. S. BARTHOLOMEW IN 1901, TO HIS DAUGHTER.

"One night in early summer as Noah Byington lay in his four-post bed, in his little one story house (No. 27), with the lower half of his front door fastened, and the upper half open to admit the air, he heard a knock and called out: 'Who's there?' 'Mr. ——,' was the reply. 'I'm going to begin school tomorrow morning on Fed Hill* and want to be examined.' 'Why I can't do it now,' said Mr. Byington. 'Don't you see it's after eight o'clock and I've gone to bed? If you'll come back early in the morning I'll do it.' Then the visitor pleaded that he had something else to occupy the morning; it was a long walk and couldn't he do it then. 'Well,' said Mr. B., 'I can lie here and ask you some questions.' So there was a pause and the would-be teacher hung over the half door in the dim light waiting to make reply. 'How many sounds has A?' was the first question. 'Why A sounds like A', was the answer. 'Hasn't it any sound but just that one?' queried Mr. B. 'No,' replied the stranger. 'Well you don't pass,' was the announcement. 'Go home and study your spelling book.'

"School did not begin on Fed Hill the next morning."

David Lewis, son of Josiah, first School Committee of District No. 7, 1796, lived in the North East part of the town and District No. 7 of Bristol on Stafford Avenue at its junction with Mines Road. No. 1.) He married Martha Horsford of Canton. Doubtless he received from his father the invariable marriage gift to his sons—eight in number —viz.: a farm of one hundred acres, a house, a barn, a cow, a hive of bees and a "Waterbury Sweet" apple tree.

The children were Chester, b. 1785, Cyrus and Electa, b. 1791. They united with the church Feb. 4, 1816. Chester Lewis married Annah Beckwith, sister to Dana. She died 1833, aged 47. Their daughter, Angelina, died.

Almon Lewis, the son of Chester, married Orra Melissa Brown, who died 1889, age 70. Almon Lewis was a dry goods merchant, having stores at two places on North Street, Bristol. First, east of Doolittle's Corner on the south. The second store was west of the first on the north side of North Street, facing North Main Street. He built a house on Maple Street, Bristol, opposite his brother-in-law, Jonathan C. Brown, clock manufacturer of Forestville, now owned by Wilfred H. Nettleton.

Of his children (great-grandchildren of David Lewis), Irving, Ashburton and Emily, only Irving is married. He has a music store in Brooklyn, N. Y. Ashburton teaches music in Brooklyn public schools.

No data for Cyrus Lewis is at hand, later than 1816. Electa Lewis, third child of David Lewis, became second wife of Newell Byington. She died 1866, age 75.

Chester Lewis was killed by the cars at Doolittle's Corner, 1863, when returning from the funeral of Billy Hart, son of Calvin and Anne (Yale) Hart. He was 78 years of age.

David Lewis and his wife remained at this house for a season or more after its sale to Joel Norton, Jr., about 1815 the two families having fires in opposite ends of the large fireplace. The family having a fire in the end near the large brick oven, was obliged to put it out when baking was done. David Lewis died 1818, age 65. Martha, his wife, died 1836, aged 82.

---

* Years ago "FEDERAL HILL" was often called "FED HILL."

Joel Norton, Jr., b. on Fall Mountain, 1782. Married Jemimi, daughter of Jesse and Mary (Scott) Gaylord, 1805. Children, Henry G., b. 1806; Hiram, b. 1808; Ammi, b. 1810; Harriet, b. 1813; Rachel, b. 1815; Charles, b. 1821. Joel Norton died 1853. Jemimi died 1857. Henry G., b. 1806, married Parthenia T. True of Portland, Me., 1835. He was manufacturer, wholesale and retail dealer in all kinds of rubber goods in New York City with several stores in other cities. His only child, Mary E., married June, 1862. Alexander Würst, artist, son of Christopher, also an artist, natives of Dort, Holland. The son took, in 1866, the Royal Gold Medal in Brussells, Belgium, on the picture given by the heirs of Henry G. Norton to the Boston Museum of Art. The same year he took a medal at "The Hague" on a "Norwegian Torrent," now belonging to Luther S. Norton. There were other prizes besides two Prince of Wales medals. He died in Antwerp, 1876. Mary (Norton) Wüsrt died on her wedding journey in Geneva, Switzerland, August, 1862.

In 1864–5, Henry G. Norton built near the site of the David Lewis house (No. 1), the present Norton residence as a home for his brother, the late Deacon Charles Norton. When finished it was considered equal, if not superior, to any other dwelling in town, for richness and elegance of the building and furnishings. The barns were built in keeping with the house. They were across the town line in Burlington. One of them has been sold and moved to Whigville. Henry G. Norton died at this house, July, 1877. His collection of books in New York was presented to the Bristol Public Library. The family also gave $5,000 to the Bristol Library.

Ammi, third son of Joel, Jr., b. 1810, married Martha Smith of Burlington, 1837. She died in New Haven, 1860. M. second, Jane Gridley, now living in N. H. Ammi Norton lived in Forestville in the house now occupied by Geo. Doherty on West Washington St. He was of the firm "Manross, Norton & Welton," doing business in a factory built in 1836, where the Burner Factory now stands. Spool-stands, faucets, sand boxes and ink-stands were made. His children were Celia B., b. 1839, in Forestville. After the death of her mother and of her cousin, Mrs. M. E. Würst, she was adopted into the family of her uncle, Henry G. Norton. She died Dec. 24, 1903. Wallace, son of Ammi Norton, was in the Civil War. Later he became a salesman for Henry G. Wallace Norton died—.

Harriet Norton, b. 1813, m. Henry Gridley, 1840. Mr. Gridley was born and lived most of his life in Stafford district. Mrs. Harriet Gridley died 1878 at Maple St., Bristol. Henry Gridley married 2d, Rachel, fifth child of Joel Norton and widow of Richard Moses of Burlington, whom she married in 1836. Of her ten Moses children, Harriet, the oldest was an excellent district school teacher. School registers show the years she taught at the Mines and in Edgewood, then called Polkville. She finished her last term of school at the latter place in 1859, and soon after married Elias Baldwin, a nephew of Mrs. Franklin Newell of Peaceable St. During the recitation of passages from the Bible as usual in the school, the late John Henry Sessions, then a lad of ten years, repeated his text, chosen with care, Matthew 17:3, "And behold there appeared unto them *Moses* and *Elias* talking———". Adrien Moses (2), a prominent man and granger of Burlington; Ellen Moses (3) married Asa Upson of Peaceable St.; Bernard Moses (4), Professor of Languages in Berkeley College, California, accepted from President Wm. McKinley his appointment to the Philippine Commission of which Justice Wm. Taft was the head, and spent his term of years at the Islands. Other children of Richard and Rachel (Norton) Moses are in the West, if living.

Charles Norton, b. 1821, youngest child of Joel and Jemimi (Gaylord) Norton; married 1846, Martha G. Stocking of Kensington. Four children.:

Luther S. (1), b. 1847; married Sarah Frisbie, 1869. [Ch.: Charles, 1874; Parthenia G., 1888.]

Alfred (2), b. 1848; m. Adeline Lowrey, daughter of Alfred. [Ch.: Clara (1), Luella (2), Mary (3).

Henry C. (3), b. 1851; m. Florence Mooney of N. Y. C. He is now living in San Francisco, Cal. Manager of the Pacific Coast Rubber Company.

Elizabeth (4), b. 1862, who married Gilbert Blakesley of Bristol.

Charles Norton was a deacon of Congregational Church from 1867 until his death in 1882, aged 60. He attended the funeral of his brother Ammi in New Haven, where he contracted the fatal cold. Ammi Norton died 1882, aged 71.

Hiram Norton, second son of Joel, Jr., born 1808, lived at the next house (No. 2), west on the north side of the way, Mines Road. He married, 1831, Flora, daughter of Abel Yale, Jr., or third. One child, Edgar, born 1835. Hiram Norton died 1878, age 70. Mrs. Flora Norton removed to Divinity street, Bristol, where she died 1891. Edgar A. married, 1859, Julia A. Barnes, daughter of Jerry. Children: Walter M., William E., Eugenia B., Harland B. Edgar Norton died Nov. 21, 1892.

Hiram Norton's old home is now in use by Luther S. Norton as a farm and tenant house.

After 1860 Michael Critchley brought the old Whigville school house (No. 3), from near the Mines' Reservoir (where it had been in use by Keron Hyland as a dwelling) and located it west of Hiram Norton's house on the same side of Mines Road. His children were Christopher, David, Michael, Arthur, Maggie and Jemmie.

James Prior also had a home here and was the district's school committee, before 1887, when John Peterson, a milk dealer, purchased the place of George Steele. He enlarged the house and has occupied it until the present time. John and Matilda (Neilson) Peterson have

SCHOOLHOUSE (FOR MANY YEARS UNOCCUPIED) NEAR COPPER MINES.

RUINS OF THE ABEL YALE (1ST AND 2D) PLACE. (NO. 9.)

been the parents of fourteen children, including four pairs of twins. They now have six in life and health. When sixteen years of age, Frank, the oldest, enlisted for five years in the U. S. Navy, 1899–1905. With the Receiving Ship Vermont, he visited six European countries: France, Germany, England, Scotland, Spain and Portugal, with Canary Islands and the Danish West Indies. [His photograph in uniform is given.] Since returning he finds employment with the Stanley Rule & Level Co. of New Britain, at their works in the Bartholomew Factory at Edgewood. Other children of the family are Hulda, Edwin, Raymond, and the twins, Florence and Fanny.

On rising ground westerly from the last named place it was possible to obtain a view of the nondescript village of Skibbereen as seen in the distant field northwest. With its row of low white cottages following the lane at the eastern base of Zach's Mountain, it formed a rather picturesque sight. There in the copper mining days lived the Sullivans, Cunninghams, Collins, Fitzgeralds and others. It was named from the southern port Skibbereen of County Cork, Ireland, which was probably the last town in the loved home country on which their eyes rested. There is nothing remaining of this place with the exception of open cellars.

Skibbereen was across the town line in Burlington. The men were all laborers at the copper mines. The children, too, were educated at the school in No. 7, when there was room for them. Sometimes they were obliged to go the long distance to Whigville. One who sometimes was at school in the latter place was a fine scholar and later a Yale graduate, but not long lived—Cornelius Sullivan.

Outside Skibbereen bars or entrance, the Mines Road turns to the south for a short distance. At the north bend, facing the east, the last of the three large houses (No. 4), built by James Hadsell or his son,

James Hadsell, Jr., stood for many years. Chloe, wife of James Hadsell, Jr., was in the Church 1799. She died 1850, aged 83. After the Hadsell's an Englishman, whose name George Retfearn, was changed to Redfield, occupied it for a while. He married the widow of George Byington, son of Joseph, Jr. Still later Bryan Fitzsimmons lived there and may have bought it, as it is thought he took it away when he moved to Bristol Center.

His sons, Martin and James, were in the employ of G. W. & H. S. Bartholomew in the hardware factory some years, even after the family left this part of the town. Other children were Lawrence, Julia and Ann, five in all. It seems possible to have been either James Hadsell, Sr., or Jr., who was School Committee in 1798.

Around the southbend of Mines Road, as it turns to the west, was the double tenement house (No. 5), of the Mining Co., on the south side of the street. In it lived Wm. McCane, whose son, Thomas, is now in Forestville (Thomas McKaine), and a French family named Green, now living in Bristol Center and Plainville. Northwest of the last named house, on the north side of Mines Road was "The Bristol Copper Mine." For many years after the "Mine" was in operation or worked, the ancient Culver house stood on its grounds near the street, surrounded by huge piles of waste material (tailings). Sometimes its windows revealed to outsiders a row of extra fine specimens of copper and quartz crystals,

(1) No. 3, Mines Road, John Peterson O, *The Michael Critchley Place;* (2) No. 2, Mines Road, L. S. Norton O, *The Hiram Norton Place;* (3) No. 1, residence of L. S. Norton O, *Site of the David Lewis and Joel Norton Places;* (4) No. 23, Stafford Ave., (unoccupied) *The Theophilus Botsford Place;* (5) No. 21, Stevens St., Wm. H. Lugg O, *The Philo Stevens Place;* (6) No. 22, Cor. Stafford Ave. and Stevens St., Mrs. R. W. Fox O, *The Samuel Botsford Place;* (7) No. 24, Stevens St., Fred Carnell O, *The Henry Smith Place;* (8) No. 40, Mix St., J. B. Sanford O, *The John London Place;* (9) No. 39, Mix St., Mandus Carlson, *The John London Place.*

POOL AT COPPER MINE SITE.

with some silver. These were produced for the encouragement of those financially interested in the property. They were alluring to collectors and geologists. Ephraim Culver, who early owned the house (No.6), married Rhoda, daughter of Abel Yale, Sr., or second. Children of Ephraim and Rhoda (Yale) Culver:

Winslow (1), died 1830, age 23. Was church member 1824.

Aretus (2), whose descendants lived in Forestville, married, second, Jane Griswold, now living in Terryville. He was in the Civil War and one of those deputed to accompany the remains of Capt. Newton Manross to Bristol, after the battle of Bull Run. Died in Bristol, Feb. 9, 1865.

Abel Yale (3), who married Chloe Curtis, daughter of Salmon and died in Whigville 1878, age 63. His children, Rhoda and twins, Mary (Mrs. Wm. Fenn) and Martha (Mrs. John Talmadge), residents of Plainville, Conn.

Alice (4), who married Daniel Clark, son of Stephen, 1847. She died 1875, Mrs. Rhoda (Yale) Culver, died 1829, age 46.

Ephraim Goodenough next lived in the Culver house. He was the oldest of thirteen children of Levi of Peacham, Vt. He maried Martha Ladd, 1818, of Peacham, who died at Burlington, Conn., 1838. Ephraim Goodenough died in Bristol Center, 1873. He was in younger days a carpenter and wheelwright. Children (1), Lester, born at Burlington 1820. Died at Bristol Center 1898; Viola E. (2) [Mrs. Renslaer Raynsford], who died at West Hartford, Conn., 1876.

Orlando (3), b. 1824. Died at Burlington, 1844.

Rodney (4), b. 1827. A sea captain; went to California 1849. Died in Oregon, 1880.

Waldo (5), b. 1832, in Bristol. Is a printer in Leavenworth, Kan.

The last known family to occupy the small brown house was the

Woolworth, of whom older members were Philemon and Chester, then Azariah, Harvey, Leman, Philander P., who married about 1850, Sarah Candace, fourth child of David Norton (both dec.). He was in the Church 1840; Robert in Church 1843, and Franklin, Church 1844, now living in Thomaston.

A house (No. 7), was built in 1850 on the western part of the Mine grounds for Superintendents. It was known as the "Mine House." It was pleasantly shaded by locust trees and shrubs. H. H. Sheldon, said to be a relative of Dr. Nott of Union College, Schenectady, N. Y., the chief, if not only owner of the mines at that time, was the first occupant of the "Mine House." Laura P., wife of Mr. Sheldon, brought from Troy, N. Y., her letter of recommendation to Bristol Church, April, 1851. The children of Mr. Sheldon were two sons in school boy days and a very young daughter. Daily when schools were in session, the family ocnveyance, with pair of black horses driven by Patrick Iago, transported Dexter Sheldon and his brother to and from the Whigville school, while the youthful Iagos increased the attendance in No. 7. A store (No. 8), was added to the mining property on the north corner of Mines Road and Jerome Avenue, with Henry Roberts, son of Nelson of Burlington, installed as salesman at one time. The farmers of the vicinity found here a good market for farm and dairy produce and the miners a handy resort for the necessaries of life.

In 1848, Michael Hynds and his family came by stage to Bristol. They took up their abode in the Ambrose Hart "Old Mansion" house, in the Whigville district. He was a teamster at the mines.

The first house in the district south of the Burlington town line on Jerome avenue, was the old Abel Yale place (No. 9), on the west side of the way. Abel Yale, the builder, being sixth generation of the line of Yales from David and Ann Yale, in Wales, England; said to be progenitors of all the Yale families of this country. The name was originally spelled Yall, or Yell. Ann Yale, becoming a widow, married Theophilus Eaton afterward Governor of New Haven Colony (1638). They arrived at Boston, 1637, on board the ship Hector, accompanied by many emigrants, including the three children of Ann (Yale) Eaton: David (1); Ann (2), (wife of Gov. Hopkins, founder of the Hopkins Grammar School, New Haven, Conn.); and Thomas (3). David Yale, first child, settled in or near Boston, where his son, Elihu was born 1649. This family returned to Europe, 1652, and did not again visit America. Elihu, becoming wealthy in India*, sent a timely gift to the Collegiate School of Connecticut, which in time bestowed the name "Yale College" upon the school, in memory and appreciation of the service. The Charter of 1745 formally gave the name to the institution. (2 G.) Thomas Yale, second son of Ann, and uncle of Elihu, was one of the settlers of North Haven in 1660. He married Mary Turner, daughter of Nathaniel, famous in the Pequot wars. Capt. Nathaniel Turner's sword is preserved in the Hartford Atheneum. He was lost at sea in the ship of which the poet Longfellow wrote in "The Phantom Ship."

(3 G.) Capt. Thomas Yale, settler of Wallingford, 1670. (4 G.) Nathaniel Yale. (5 G.) Abel Yale, lived in the east part of Wallingford, now Meriden. (6 G.) Abel Yale, second or Junior, of Meriden, afterward of Bristol school district No. 7; b. 1733, married Sarah Jerome. They were admitted to the Church in Bristol, 1759. He died July 4, 1797, aged 64. Sarah, his wife, died 1816, aged 78. Children of Abel Yale second and Sarah (Jerome) Yale numbered twelve as follows:

Esther (1), b. 1760, married Oliver Phenton.
Thomas (2), 1761, married first Polly Beckwith, second Anna Northam.
Sarah (3), 1763, married Richard Russell.
Lydia (4), 1765, married Nathaniel Warner.
Anne (5), 1767, married Calvin Hart.
Lois (6), 1769, married Daniel Peck, and died 1812.
Ruth (7), 1771. Died 1791.

*See Illustration Page 240

Elizabeth (8), 1773, married Levi Boardman.
Abel (9), 1775.
Rhoda (10), 1778. Died 1781.
Mary (11), 1780, married Dudley Williams.
Rhoda (12), 1782, married Ephraim Culver and died 1829.

Abel Yale, 3d (7 G.), son of the preceding Abel Yale, 2d, born 1775, married first Lydia Barnes, daughter of Josiah, who died 1821, age 41. Their children were Julius, Henry, Flora, Elmore, Lydia and Sarah A.

Abel Yale, 3d, married second his cousin, Lorena (Jerome) Brown, widow of Abner. She had one son, Orrin Brown, of Forestville. Abel and Lorena (Brown) Yale's children were four daughters, Lorena, Fidelia, Mary Jane, Selina.

Abel Yale died 1847, age 73. Lorena, his wife, died 1869, age 73. Julius Yale (8 G.), oldest child of his father, Abel Yale, 3d, inherited the farm and spent there his life as a farmer as his father and grandfather had done. He was admitted to the church, 1844. He married late in life Lucinda North, who brought her letter from Farmington Church to Bristol, 1854. She died 1861, aged 44. Mr. Yale married second Pamelia (Barnes) Norton, widow of Franklin and daughter of Joel Barnes. Julius Yale died 1879, age 72. He left no family. Shortly afterward the house having temporary occupants, the odor of smoke was noticed, by those passing, for a day or two. It proved to proceed from smouldering timbers used in the construction of the old stone chimney. When the concealed fire broke forth the old brown house was very soon a thing of the past. The copper mine was opened on Abel Yale's land.

Lydia Yale (1), daughter of Abel Yale, 3d, and sister to Julius Yale, married John C. Root. Resided for a time in Harwinton, Conn. Returned to Bristol and the church, 1824. They had one or two children.

Sarah Ann Yale (2), married William Wilcox. Residence, Collinsville. He had grinder's consumption. She was in the church, 1838,

THE "HOME BY THE BROOKSIDE," *The Wilson Sheldon Place.* (NO. 30)
H. I. MUZZY O.

and returned to it from Collinsville, 1849. She died 1869, aged 52. Children of Wm. and Sarah A. (Yale) Wilcox were Ellen E. (1), [Mrs. Clarence Muzzy]; Franklin (2), who was a member of the 16th Regiment, Conn. Vol., and died in Washington, D. C., Nov. 9, 1862, interred in Bristol; Charles (3) lived with his uncle, Julius Yale, after his father's death. He joined the U. S. Regular Army in 1864 or '5 and was sent to the frontier. He returned after an absence of nearly fifteen years, when thought by his friends to be dead. Entered the army again, but left it in July of the year many sought gold at Black Hills, where he was supposed to have gone. His name, Charles Wilcox, was printed in a list of the "killed by Indians" at or near the Black Hills. His life and fortune continue an uncertainty to relatives. Lucelia (4), married Frank Colvin of Bristol.

Lorena Yale (3) married Burritt E. Barker, of Whigville. Her children were Anna E., [Mrs. Chas. Morris], (1); Marian (2), deceased, and Arthur (3). Mrs. Lorena (Yale) Barker died at the home of her daughter, 1903.

Fidelia (4), married Wm. Wadsworth of Hartford and died childless.

Mary Jane (5), married Don Evaristo Peck, 1846, and died 1897.

Selina (6), married Mr. Warner of New York State (deceased). She left a family. The children of D. E. and Mary J. (Yale) Peck were Don Cervantes (1); Burdette Abel (2); Mary Emma (3) [Mrs. F. L. Gaylord of Ansonia] and Ludella L. Peck (4), professor and A. M. of Smith College, Northampton, Mass., 25 years, who visited in 1903, the ancient seat of the Yales in Wrexam, Wales, England.

Thomas Yale, son of Abel Yale, 2d. b. 1761, lived in a house (No.10) adjoining the home lot of his father on the south. He married 1788, Polly Beckwith, who died 1795. Her children were Gad (1), b. 1791, and Polly (2), b. 1793, married Mark Perkins, 1811, lived in Oneonta, New York State. Mrs Polly Yale died 1795. Thomas Yale married second Anna Northam, 1796. Her children were Harriet (3), b. Sept., 1797, who married John Bacon. He died 1838, age 43. Roxana (4), b. 1799, married Adna Hart and lived at the Thomas Yale house. Gad, son of Thomas, married Hannah Barnes, 1817, of Josiah. Went to Kirtland, Ohio. Was converted to Joseph Smith. Sold a farm and gave $1,000 towards the erection of the Mormon Temple, 1836, at Kirtland, Ohio.

Thomas Yale died February 18, 1814.

Roxanna, daughter of Thomas Yale, married Feb. 23, 1821, Adna son of Ambrose of Simeon of Dea. Thomas Hart of Southington, Conn., son of Deacon Stephen Hart, settler, born at Braintree, Essex Co., England. Four children: *William Hart* (1), b. 1823, married, 1849, Emmeline Thayer of Mass., died at Foxboro, Mass., 1886, leaving a son, William T. Hart, b. 1850, married 1877, Ella Hatch of Hyde Park, Mass., died Feb., 1888, leaving two children, William S. Hart, b. 1878 and Mary D. Hart, b. 1885. *Caroline Hart* (2), b. 1824, married 1843, Edward Graham, died 1866. Edward Graham died 1886 aged 62. Five children: George A. (1), b. 1845 at Wallingford, Conn., died at Andersonville, Ga., 1864, age 19; Edward (2), b. 1848, died in Bristol, 1872, aged 24; Celia Caroline (3), b. 1850, married Nov., 1879, William D. Bromley of Bristol; Ida Julia (4), b. 1854, married Henry C. Butler of Bristol, Oct., 1876; William H. Graham (5), b. Dec., 1865, in Bristol Center, married first Florence Fenn. The Graham children were born in Edgewood with the exception of oldest and youngest.

John Gad Hart (3), third child of Adna and Roxanna (Yale) Hart, b. 1828, married, 1848, Abigal Benham of Burlington. She died in Lawrence, Kansas, 1894, aged 64. John G. Hart killed Feb. 24, 1868, at Black Rock crossing, New Britain, Conn., leaving one daughter, Helen M. Hart, b. May, 1850, married first William H. Carey, 1867, in New Britain, Conn. Two children: Henry W. Carey (1), b. 1870, died 1874; George Benham Carey (2), b. 1878, married, June 27, 1900,

RED DWELLING-HOUSE OF ASA BARTHOLOMEW IN 1807, (NO. 35). REAR OF THE SAME 1907—OWNED BY AUGUSTUS H. WARNER.

Charlotte Wells of New Britain. Mrs Carey married second, March 1902, John Hooker Hart of Farmington Conn., son of Dea. Simeon Hart, the time-honored instructor of boys at Farmington, Conn. John *Hooker* Hart was second cousin of John *Gad* Hart, b. 1828.

Fourth child, *Thomas Hart*, b. May 7, 1832, married 1855, Mary Elizabeth Dix of Wethersfield, Conn. He died of consumption, Oct. 30, 1862, in Meriden, Conn. He left a daughter, Cora A. Hart, born in Meriden, Dec. 26, 1859.

Erastus Bacon lived at this place after the Harts for a time and had a small store near. The house is now gone.

The next house south at about half the distance to the schoolhouse No. 2, of the district on the west was called the old Bacon house (No. 11). It had been empty since mining days, but before was the home of John Bacon, who married Harriet Yale, born 1797, daughter to Thomas and Anna (Northam) Yale. John and Harriet (Yale) Bacon were taken into the church, 1821. Mr. Bacon died 1838, age 43. Their sons are said to have been John and Erastus Bacon, both well-known in the town. The latter married Adeline Sessions, daughter of Calvin of Burlington and sister of the late John Humphrey Sessions of Bristol. He was in the Civil War; his fate unknown.

It was in this house that the first Roman Catholic masses in Bristol were held regularly, Father Daley coming monthly from St. Patrick's Church, Hartford, for the purpose, 1850. At first he caused crosses to be placed on fences near the house which made so much disturbance in the district it was deemed prudent to discontinue the practice. It is understood the meetings were with Mr. Riley, at the Bacon house, though there were occasional meetings before in the "mill" and schoolhouse. Afterwards Mrs. Shane had a home there and asserted herself as "the man of the house."

The second schoolhouse of No. 7 stands deserted south of the Bacon house (No. 12) site. The school which in the fifties had a daily average attendance of between 30 and 40 pupils with an occasional term still higher, became so small the town thought it wise to transport the remaining few to Edgewood. The school had been benefitted by excellent and well-known teachers of whom the names of a few are mentioned. Sarah Maria Rice, daughter of Jeremiah; Harriet Moses, daughter of Richard; Julia A. Barnes, daughter of Jeremiah; Sarah Foote, of Ira; Ursula M. Hart, of John; Celia B. Norton, of Ammi; Ellen E. Wilcox, of Wm.; Marietta Carpenter, of Wm.; Annie J. Brown, P. Frank Perry, J. Fayette Douglass, Hiram C. Cook, Lizzie Welch, of Constandt; Elizabeth Ives, of Deacon Charles G., besides several young teachers of the district or near; Adellah Yale, Helen Norton, Laura Curtiss, Eugenia Warner and others.

There were many families who sent children to this school before and after 1850, whose records and homes are not easily found. The school registers of the period afford the names of the children and serve to recall to mind some of the parents who left the place soon after the mine was abandoned. Capt. Wm. Williams' children were Elizabeth (1), John (2), Thomas (3), George (4), Ann (5), Johnson (6).

William Casey's were Michael (1), Sarah (2), Mary Ellen (3). They removed to Bristol Center. Marvin Young's children were Porter (1), who has been in Bristol and perhaps the others, who were Lydia (2), Edwin (3), Caroline (4).

L. Jones' daughter, 16 years of age, was in the school 1861, also her sister Elisabeth, 12 years, Wm. 8 years and George 6. The children of H. Roper were Hugh (1), Julia (2), Catherine (3), Ellen (4) and Ann (5). The Oulds' children were James (1), Samuel (2), Fanny (3), Richard (4), Children of Wm. Ward, 1852, were Thomas, 12, Jane, Elizabeth, John, Wm., Joseph and Maria. James Devine, whose home was in the *old* schoolhouse, sent to this the new one, Margaret, Mary Ann, Patrick. The Praed children were Nicholas, John and Jane.

Patrick Iago's own children and Mrs. J. Iago's were Margaret (1), Ann (2), Thomas (3): Lawrence (1) and Jane (2). Family names of some who furnished their quota for the school are Trewhella, Eustice, Gregor, McCall, Roach, Robinson, Donnovan, Gillern, Moren, Sullivan, Stone, Bolace, etc., etc.

Across the street from the schoolhouse stood the home of Joel Hart (No. 13), built for him by his father. Joel Hart, son of Calvin and Anne (Yale) Hart, married Sarah Bowers. Their six children were Lucy (Mrs. Elmore Yale), Sabina, Calvin, Cyprian and Almon. In 1838 he moved for five years to New Britain, when he returned to his old home where he died in 1844.

The son Calvin died at his grandfather's house (Calvin Hart, Sr.), in the south of Burlington where his son Louis now lives. His wife, Ellen, died the winter of 1906-7, at the home of her daughter, Mrs. Hiram Lowrey, leaving three children, William, who married Fanny Warner, Delia and Louis.

Cyprian Hart was the survivor of his father Joel's family. When young he was employed in the factory of Don E. Peck in Whigville, and others including the Corbin Manufacturing Company of New Britain before purchasing a farm in Wethersfield where he settled for life. He married in 1852, Eliza Perdue. Two sons are living as merchants in the town, C. C. Hart of the firm "Hart, Wells & Co.," wholesale seedsmen and Arthur. He was respected in the town and served eighteen years as selectman though not continuously. The Democrats sent him to Legislature in 1863. He was a member of the Wethersfield Grange. His death occurred since 1900.

In 1850 the Joel Hart house was well filled when the Williams brothers, sons and cousins came to take positions in the mining business. Captain Richard Williams and William Williams with his many school boys and girls, also two relatives of the name, lay preachers, who held Methodist services in several places.

Later Marvin Young lived there. His son, Porter Young, until recently a resident of Bristol has been an authority on matters concerning the "Bristol Copper Mine."

In 1872, Perley Buck, who married Ella Hart (deceased), elder

YALE MEMORIAL AT MADRAS, INDIA. *Photographed by George B. Smith.*

daughter of Calvin, Jr., resided at this place when engaged in the meat business with Sylvester Hart. Clarence Muzzy also lived there a while in his early married life. The house was long in disuse and is gone.

James Hadsell (Jeems Hedsel) (No. 14) built in the olden time a large house where now stands the two story white house of Henry I. Muzzy, south from the schoolhouse and well known as the Lyman Mix place. The church record of James Hadsell's wife, Huldah, serves to define the period in which he was a resident of the district No. 7. She was admitted to the church September, 1778. She died in 1827, aged 83 years. Mr. Hadsell was a cooper and had a shop for his work in the rear of his house He built at some time the cooper's shop south of the garden of the place (No. 15). It was standing on the bank, the narrow front near the street, until within a few years. Erastus Bacon had at one time a store in the building.

Mr. Henry I. Muzzy, now 83 years of age (1907), in reminiscence speaks of the sale of No. 14 to Mr. Bosworth, who in time and turn sold it to Lyman Mix. Mr. Muzzy was six years of age (possibly eight) when Lyman Mix drew off the Hadsell house and built the present two-story house. It was the year after the present Congregational Church was built. Lyman and Mary (Gaylord) Mix lived in this house until the death of Mr. Mix in 1872, aged 79. They had no children but adopted Rhoda Ann Wilmot daughter of Lucius H , who married an Osborne. Mrs. Mary Mix then purchased the old Episcopal parsonage, now on the north corner of Summer and Maple streets, Bristol, in which she lived till her death in 1855, age 85.

Mrs. Mary Mix invited the wife of her nephew (Dea. Charles Norton, dec.), Mrs. Martha S. Norton, to reside with her at Bristol Center, which she did, and remained at that place the remainder of her life. She died 1895, age 75.

Mr. Henry I. Muzzy lived at the Lyman Mix house after the death of Mr. Mix, until he sold it to the Mining Co., when he built his present home nearer Edgewood. Eventually he took back the house, which is the home of his farmer. Southward at the saw mill (No. 16) of H. I. Muzzy, a road not named, goes westward to Round Hill Road, in No. 8 district.

At a house (No. 19) near the western limit of No. 7, which Ira Hotchkiss, son of Elisha, built, and is remembered as a "pest house," Asa Bartholomew and twelve others are known to have been secluded, under care of a physician, to pass the ordeal of varioloid, according to custom. Calvin Wooding afterward lived in the house. He was somewhat noted as a "horse jockey." His skill enabled him to so metamorphose a horse that the honest man of whom it was purchased without a suspicion of having seen the animal before, would buy it back, allowing an addition of $50 or more to his previous selling price. Mr. Wooding moved to Hartford. George Byington, son of Joseph, Jr., then made this place his home. His children were Jane (m. DeWitt Winston), Margaret and James. The widow of George Byington, m. 2d Mr. Redfield.

The next house (No. 18) was owned by Martin Hart, son of Ambrose, and brother of Adna, b. June 10, 1783, died 1860, age 77. Sally Rowe, his wife, b. 1782, died 1853, aged 71. Their children were Richard Lemuel (1), b. 1800, d. 1809; Edward Ambrose (2), b. 1812; Julia Philena (3), b. 1809; Maria (4) 1855. Later they moved to the Mix house on Jerome Avenue, and always referred to the former home as "the old place." While there are no dwellings on this old road, and little or no travel, it is usable. On the hill near the west part of the saw mill a low building (No. 17), had plenty of residents at one time, Shanes, Wards, etc. Thomas Devine lived there alone the last of any one. He was drowned in the trench of the Stockinet Factory in Bristol.

Ascending a hill southward from the mill, we are at the second house built by James Hadsell (No. 20), on the north corner of Stevens St. and Jerome Ave. The Stevens family from Cheshire were living here before 1815, when Elisha and wife, Fanny (Brainard) Stevens, joined the church. He died 1847, aged 68. His sons, Deacons John, Edward and Harvey became fine and wealthy men of Cromwell, Conn. They were manufacturers of Britania Ware. They took pleasure in reviving old memories of home by visits to Bristol and friends. Mr. Stevens of Cromwell attended the 150th anniversary exercises of the Congregational Church, Bristol, October 12, 1894. About that time he presented to the church of his youth a handsome pulpit Bible. The next permanent resident was Isaac Muzzy, born in Spencer, Mass., 1803. The first of the family in Connecticut. He married, 1823, Hannah Minerva Mix, daughter of Ashbel. Children, Henry Isaac (1), 1824; Chloe Jane (2), 1825 (married Hiram Spellman); Hannah Minerva (3), 1828 (married Josiah Pierce); Franklin (4), 1832, died 1855; Lyman (5), 1836, died 1861; William Wallace (6), 1846 (married Anna Lee, 1872), child, Edward Winfield, who served in the Spanish War.

The son, Henry Isaac, also resided in this 2d James Hadsell house until the death of Lyman Mix, when he moved to the Lyman Mix house. John Peterson, previous to the purchase of his present home, succeeded Henry I. Muzzy in the place, where some of his children were born. Transient dwellers there have been since, in the old house, yet standing unfit for occupancy.

We now follow to the eastern-most house on the north side of Stevens St., nearly to Farmington line. A house had been for some years on

(10) No. 57, John Muir O, *The Ephraim McEwen Place;* (11) No 59, M. J. Ford O; (12) No. 30, "The House by the Brookside," H. I Muzzy O, *The Wilson Sheldon Place;* (13) No. 28, Frank Yale O, *The Joseph Byington Place;* (14) No. 26, H. I. Muzzy O, *The Ashbel Mix Place;* (15) No. 14, Axel Anderson R, *The James Hadsell, Sr., Place;* (16) No. 47, Seymour Reed R, *The Lauren Byington Place;* (17) Victor Avery O, (18) Amelia Kohl O.

the site of the present vine-clad stone house, thought to have been sold by a Mr. Cowles to Asahel Mix. It was occupied at one time by the Gladdens, who have descendants living in New Britain. Later school registers show the attendance of the children of Leverette Barnes, son of Elijah of Wise. Verona (1), Polly (2), Mary P. (3), and Martin Barnes (4). The latter was often a member of Julius Yale's family and liked in Peaceable St., where he sometimes lived.

The place was sold by Asahel Mix to Henry Smith, who with his wife came in the prime of life from England. They were both born, 1812. Their children were William (1), Susan (2), Emma (3), Annie (4), Ellen (5) (who died in childhood), Deborah (6), and Irna (7). They lived in the old house till 1862, when Mr. Smith built the present stone house (No. 24). These parents, anxious chiefly for the welfare of their children, taught them to choose good companions and to be true and faithful always. They drove with them on the Sabbath five miles to their church in Farmington, where they attended the Episcopal, or Church of England. The ministers of this denomination from Farmington and Bristol were welcome and familiar guests at the farm. Doubtless in the isolation of the home they had a strong influence for good upon the children of the household. The inspiration for life, of the son William may, however, have come from an unexpected event, when one day a fine looking old gentleman was brought to the house from Farmington Station by some one who could take him no farther. He wished to go to the Copper Mines where he was interested. It was Rev. Dr. Eliphalet Nott, President of Union College, Schenectady, N. Y. Mr. Smith was away with the family conveyance. Mrs. Smith, after giving the gentleman a cup of tea was (aided by her son) equal to the emergency. A farm wagon was cleared. A rug or piece of carpet spread, and lastly an arm chair placed in the wagon. Thus comfortably, Dr. Nott was taken by William Smith to view his mining possessions in Bristol.

During the drive Dr. Nott ascertained the wish of the young man for an education. He advised him to read, study, and prepare for college, and then come to him. These instructions were faithfully carried out. He first attended E. L. Hart's school in Farmington, and finished in Wilbraham. Dr. Nott then gave him his four years' tuition at Union College, and as long as William Smith lived was his firm and staunch friend. Dr. Nott often spoke of the beautiful hospitality and refinement he found in the quiet, modest home.

After Mr. Smith was 80 years old his daughter and her son found him one day in need of medicine. The son, then a medical student, now Dr. H. C. Spring of Bristol, fortunately had remedies which were given him. Mr. Smith expressed his pleasure, that the first medicine given him by a doctor was after he was 80 years of age, and also that it was administered by his own grandson. Mrs. Smith died 1881, age 69. William, oldest child, carried out his desire to become a minister of the Gospel, but died at the age of 42. He located in Pennsylvania. Mr. Henry Smith married second, Mrs. Carnell, mother of Frederick Carnell, the present owner of the farm. She survived him a few years. Mr. Henry Smith died 1896, aged 84. They are interred in the "*Scott's Swamp* Cemetery."

Frederick W. and Eliza Carnell came to the stone house in June, 1897, from New Haven. When the estate of the late Henry Smith was settled in the winter of that year, they purchased the interests of the heirs. Their children were May E. (1), Frederick J. (2), Arthur D. (3) and Robert S. (4), educated in New Haven, with the exception of Robert S., who was graduated from Bristol High School, 1904. Frederick James was graduated from Sheffield Scientific School of Yale University, 1900. He was a high stand student throughout his course, taking one half the prize for general excellence. Honorable in Physics, German, Chemistry, Mathematics (for which he had prize) and Mechanical Drawing, also general honors in Electrical Engineering. He was a member of Sigma Xi, a high stand society. Immediately after graduation he received the appointment as assistant in Physics in the laboratory of the Scientific School, and there continued his work and studies until his death at the New Haven Hospital, Nov. 15, 1902. Frederick James Carnell died as the result of a casualty, Saturday afternoon, Nov. 15, 1902. Accompanied by a friend and classmate, he went to Umbrella Island, near Short Beach, for an afternoon of duck shooting. In lifting his gun from the boat its accidental discharge shattered the arm at the elbow. More than an hour passed before a doctor could be reached, who decided that amputation was necessary. It was accordingly performed at the Hospital, but through shock, following loss of blood, he died a few hours afterward. He was 22 years of age. Arthur David married, June 20, 1906, Jennie M., daughter of the late Edward F. and *Martha (Tuttle) Gaylord.*

Returning to the four corners of Stevens St. and Stafford Ave. intersection, we go northward to the one house (No. 23) between the Joel Norton, Jr., house and the corners, where Theophilus Botsford, born 1758, resided. He married Dolly Bidwell of Middletown, Conn., born 1758, died 1828. He married 2d, Widow Whitmore, sister of Dolly. She had a daughter Elizabeth Whitmore. Theophilus Botsford died 1841, aged 83 years. He had six children: Daniel (1), born 1782; Samuel (2), born 1783; Dolly B. Norton (3), born 1786; Irene B. Atkins (4), born 1788; George Arthur (5), born 1790; Annis Botsford Winston (6), born 1792. He was one of the first who thought copper could be found in the vicinity by mining, and made some experiments to prove his belief. Some of the mining masters were domiciled here, and later the Gomme (Gum) family. The house is owned by John Peterson, but not inhabited.

At the southwest corner below, (No. 22), Samuel, second son of Theophilus, b. 1783, resided for a generation. He was a blacksmith. He married Betsy Clark of Meriden, b. 1782, died 1859, age 77. Samuel Botsford died 1862, aged 79. Their six children were as follows: Nancy (1) (m. Elias W. Perkins); Harriet (2) (m. Philo Stevens); Patrick (3), died in New York aged 61, unmarried; Hiram (4), b. 1813, d. 1875 aged

THE SECOND JAMES HADSELL PLACE, (NO. 20).

62, m. Jan. 16, 1839, Elizabeth Wetmore, daughter of his grandfather's 2d wife. She died Nov. 27, 1839, leaving an infant daughter, which his mother brought up. (Elizabeth, b. Nov. 27, 1839, m. Edwin Bristol of Cheshire. She died leaving several children, Edwin, Mary, etc.). Betsy (5), b. 1815, d. 1832 a. 17; Lorenzo (6), 1819, d. 1870, a. 51, m. Hannah Norton, 1842. She. born 1820, died 1853, leaving two children, *James* (1), b. 1845, d. 1889, m. Frances Barrows. Three children: Fanny A. (1), m. Albert Homewood; Hattie (2), m. Edwin Mitchell; Alice (3), m. James Connery. *Burdette Botsford* (2), brother of James, b. 1846, d. 1853, aged 7 years.

Harriet Botsford who married Philo Stevens, 1827, lived on the north side of Stevens St., near her father, Samuel Botsford. (A large house was built by the Lawsons on the site of the Philo Steven's house) (No. 21). The children of Philo and Harriet (Botsford) Stevens were eleven in number, Nancy (1); David (2); Franklin (3); Mary Ann (4); Harriet F. (5); Philo (6): Egligene (7); Josephene (8); Betsey M. (9); DeWitt Clinton (10); Charles (11). Philo Stevens, b. 1804, d. 1880, aged 76. Harriet his wife b. 1809, d. 1891, aged 82. Eliza (Gomme) Fox, widow of Simeon, now resides with her son, Thomas, a farmer, at the Samuel Botsford house. Her daughter, who married Wm. Lugg, resides on the site of the old Philo Stevens' house. He has been engineer at H. C. Thompsons' Clock Co. He has an oversight or the Mining Co's. property. They have four children, the oldest Herbert.

Having completed the tour of Stevens St., and going south on Jerome Ave., we come to the first and only schoolhouse (No. 25) of the district for nearly the first half of the century. It was situated on the east side of Jerome Ave., south of the house of Elisha Stevens. William Jerome 4th recalls his school days there, when he was taught by Enoch Marks of Burlington, a son of Lieut. David Marks, who became wealthy in New York State as inspector of salt at the extensive Syracuse Salt Works. William Elton, too, of Burlington, was his teacher. He practiced medicine in Burlington, where he lived with his wife and daughter. The former, Amelia Pettibone, of Choral; until some ten years ago the three, father, mother and daughter, in one week fell victims of pneumonia. A young son, Willard, was not at home. He is supposed to be living in Springfield, Mass.

Julia P. Hart, daughter of Martin, another teacher in the old school house, became second wife of Lauren Byington, son of Martin. They lived in Edgewood and died childless. She was called "Miss Julia" to her dying day, as known while teaching in her home district.

William Jerome 3d, father of William Jerome of today, attended at this school when Noah Byington was the instructor. The "scholars" sometimes tried his patience by not coming in promptly when the summons was heard. A loud rapping with a stick or ruler on the side of the door or house was the call to resume study of "reading, 'riting and 'rithmetic" in those days. Mr. Byington provided himself with a long whip for the treatment of his delinquent pupils. He gave each one who passed him entering the door a cut or lash with the whip. Young Jerome ran between the master's legs and escaped. About 1848 the school building was superseded by the new one near Mines Road. The old one "while staying after school" was purchased by a miner, James Devine, who had several children, attendants at the second, or new schoolhouse, and living in the old one. At last Luther S. Norton "carted it to Dublin Hill, Forestville." The Devines are now in New Britain.

A short distance southwest, Ashbel Mix, son of Timothy, built the large red house (No. 26), long a familiar landmark and home, with the tall pine trees at its south front. Ashbel Mix, son of Timothy, b. 1760, d. 1807, m. Hannah Byington, daughter of Joseph Byington, b. 1773, and died 1836. The Ashbel Mix farm was a portion of her father's estate. Their children were Lyman (1), b. 1793; Nancy (2) [Mrs. Ira Foote of Burlington, carded the wool, spun the yarn, and wove her wedding dress] b. 1794; Asahel (3), 1795; Noble (4); Ashbel, Jr. (5), 1801; Minerva (6), 1805, perhaps others.

Asahel Mix resided at this place until he built elsewhere in the district. He married, Jan. 13, 1820, Amna Judd. Martin Hart bought this place when for sale, to which he removed from his "old place" on the cross road, before mentioned with family data. In 1860 Martin Hart died. Simeon and Philo Curtiss, sons of Joshua of Milford St., Burlington, each resided here a few years, having the care of the property. The house finally went in much the same manner as the old Abel Yale place, consumed by fire in "the heart of the house," the old stone chimney; S. Curtiss living there at the time, about 1862. Mr. Henry Isaac Muczy later built on the site his present dwelling house, while the barns, nearly opposite, belonged to the old house. The fine old pine trees suffered in the fire which destroyed the house, and are nearly gone. H. I. Muzzy, b., 1824, still living, m., 1843, Mary Elizabeth Beach, daughter of Eli, of Plymouth, b., 1825, d., 1881. Their children, *Clarence Henry* (1), b., 1845, served in the Civil War, m. Ellen E. Wilcox, daughter of Wm., [children, Leila and Robert]; *George Franklin* (2), 1847, served in the navy in the Civil War, d., 1865, unmarried; Charles Edwin (3), 1849, m., Frances Emma Strickland (dec); Adrian James (4), 1851, m., 1873, Florence Emlyn Downes, 1851, [children, Leslie Adrian (a) (dec); Floyd Downes (b) (dec); Adrienne (c)], author of Prize Biography "Katherine Gaylord, Heroine;" Frederick (5), 1853, d., 1874, unmarried; Alice Elizabeth (6), 1855 [married Frank Winston, children, Ella (a), Ernest (b)], Ella Jane (7), 1856 [married Lewis Strong, child Roy]; Frank Lyman (8), 1858 [married first Emily Wilcox, child, died; married second Augusta Frinck, child, Dorothy]. Member of the firm A. J. Muzzy & Co.; Mary Minerva (9), 1861-1863; Mary Elizabeth

(1) No. 32, F. W. Holmes O, *The Mark Lewis Place;* (2) No. 33, Wm. Jerome (4th) R, D. I. Jerome R, *The Wm. Jerome (3d) Place;* (3) No. 34, Carl Peterson R, *The Simeon Curtis Place;* (4) No. 35, Theo. Lockenwitz O, *The Wm. Jerome (1st) Place;* (5) No. 36, Horace O. Miller O; (6) No. 37, Chas. H. Downs R, *The Wm. Jerome (2d) Place;* (7) No. 38, Chas. Hotchkiss O, *The Wellington Winston, Sr., Place;* (8) No. 55, A. H. Warner O, *The Charles Belden Place.*

(10), 1864–1873; Arthur George (11), 1866 [married Martha Ellen Thomas, child, Ruth]; Harriet Beach (12), 1868.

Southeast from H. I. Muzzy's present home (No. 27) were the old homes of Noah Byington, before mentioned, with his father, Joseph Byington (No. 28) very near on the south. The houses were much alike, small, unpainted, but pleasant appearing homes with gambrel or "curb-roofs." Joseph Byington, b. 1736, died 1798; married first, 1757, Jemima Hungerford, who died 1759. He married second Hannah Spencer, 1760. Children were: Isaac (1), b. 1761; Noah (2), b. 1762; Isaiah (3), 1764; Martin (4), 1767; Clarissa (5), 1770. Hannah (Spencer) Byington, d. 1771. He married third Hannah Warren, Feb. 20, 1772. Children, Hannah (6), b. 1773; Meliscent (7), b. 1775; Chloe (8), b. 1777; Joseph, Jr., (9), 1778; Asahel (10), 1780; Enos (11), 1781; Newell (12), 1787.

Hannah Warren Byington was born 1752, died 1819. Joseph Byington served as lieutenant in the war of the American Revolution. His name appears on the records from the "Lexington Alarm" in 1783. He was Justice of the Peace, doing much town business in Bristol.

His son Joseph lived after him in the house, and his grandson, Williams Byington, also lived there before Elmore Yale, son of Abel Yale, 3d, made it a home. He married Lucy A. Hart, daughter of Joel. Their children were: Adella (1), b. 1845, who lived to teach the district school, 1862, but died when aged about 20 years; Frances (2) Yale, b. 1850, was for ten or twelve years in charge of a sewing room at the Orphan Asylum in Hartford, where she was doing a good work at the time of her death from pneumonia in Dec., 1904.

Henry Yale (3) married Anna Ford, daughter of Jerome. Resides at Patchoque, L. I. They have eight children.

Franklin (4), who has a later home on the site of the old Byington house; married Melissa Ford, daughter of Jerome. They have a son, Alfred Yale, of the Tenth Generation from David and Ann Yale, of Wales, England, 1630.

Opposite Noah Byington's house was the old home of Luther Tuttle (No. 29). The well still of use in the field, is all that has marked the spot, as the site of the house, for many years.

Luther Tuttle, born 1774, was son of Ichabod Tuttle, one of the 28 men of Goshen, Conn., who enlisted 1775 in the Company of Capt. John Sedgwick, grandfather of Major Gen. John Sedgwick, of Cornwell Hollow, for Ticonderoga (captured May 10); married, 1772, Elizabeth Matthews; removed to Wyoming; was in the battle July 3, 1778, and killed by the Indians while running towards the river for escape. His name is inscribed with 159 others, victims of that atrocity, on the monument erected to their memory. His wife, with her three small children, Calvin (1), b. 1772; Luther (2), b. 1774 and Ichabod (3), 1776, escaped in a boat down the river, and made her way back to Conn. (Tuttle Gen.) She married second, 1792, Thomas Hungerford, and died aged 86.

Luther, the second son, born 1774, married 1796, Mary Bartholomew, daughter of Jacob, and resided at this house in District No. 7, of Bristol. Their children were: Chauncey (1), 1797; Betsey (2), 1799, married Carter Newell in 1820; Lemuel (3), b. 1801, d., age 3 years; Mary (4), 1803, married Orrin Moses of Burlington; Celinda (5), 1805, married Wm. Brown; Luther Lemuel (6), 1807, married 1830, Martha Lowrey, daughter of Thomas. Luther and Mary (Bartholomew) Tuttle died the same day of spotted fever, May 3, 1808. She, aged 29 years. Mary and Luther Lemuel were brought up by their Aunt Rosannah (Bartholomew) Cowles, wife of Asabel Cowles, who had no children, and lived in Peaceable St., where Luther spent his days, and the late Edward Fenn Gaylord, who married his daughter, Martha Tuttle, also died in 1905. Chloe, daughter of Mary, who married Orrin Moses, became wife of Andrew S. Upson of the Upson Nut Co., Cleveland, Ohio, and Unionville, Conn. Another daughter is wife of Thomas Brooks of

Unionville. Other daughters reside near Boston. The sons, John, etc., were large land owners in Burlington. The widow of Luther Moses, is living in Hartford.

On the south bank of the brook, Wilson Sheldon built his house (No. 30), west side of Jerome Ave., in 1854. He was one of the eleven children of Jerre and Katie (Lanfair) Sheldon of Pine Orchard, Branford, Conn. Children of Jerre and Katie (Lanfair) Sheldon: Nicholas (1), Truman (2), Austin (3), Asher (4), *Wilson* (5), Roswell (6), Betsey (7), Hannah (8), Safronia (9), Wealthy (10), Phebe (11). With his son Truman he started the present "Sheldon House" for summer sea-side guests. It is continued by descendants of Truman. The cottage recently in use at this resort, north side of the road, was originally the home of the family. It was covered with shingles. The daughter Sophronia, who married Mr. Burton, parents of Catherine Burton, sometime of Bristol, resided in the shingled house. Catherine Burton married Alonzo Welton, who died in Bristol, 1864, age 31.

The shingled house was afterwards moved and a modern cottage now stands on its site.

Of the eleven children of Jerre Sheldon only Asher survives. He is a resident of New Haven and 93 years of age, yet able to do light work. He takes pleasure in a walking trip of five miles, at one time, or writing an interesting letter in a clear, firm hand.

Wilson Sheldon was born in Branford, April 9, 1809. Died in Bristol, at the Brook-side home, Nov. 30, 1890, of pneumonia. When young he learned the wood turning business and became an expert workman of his time. His life work was chiefly in the clock-making industries of Bristol; beginning with Day & Brewster or Brewster & Ingraham and ending with the E. Ingraham Clock Co. He married Oct. 17, 1830, Phebe Rebecca Matthews, daughter of Joel and Abigail (Tuttle) Matthews of Fall Mountain, Bristol.

Mrs. Wilson Sheldon was of devoted, religious temperament. She

RESIDENCE OF WM. JEROME IN 1750 (NO. 35) THEODORE LOCKENWITZ O.

became a member of the Baptist Church, in Bristol, and a prominent soprano singer in the choir. In early married life, under stress of protracted religious services in connection with intense Bible study, her mind became unbalanced from which she never fully recovered. She died March 25, 1858.

Children of Wilson and Phebe R. (Matthews) Sheldon were nine in number: Jeremiah (1), 1831–1832; Andrew (2), 1833–1834; Mariette (3), b. Aug. 18, 1834; Emeline (4), b. April 4, 1836; Nancy Matthews (5), b. July 25, 1838; Orlando (6), June 24, 1841; Edward (7), Edgar (8) twins, b. 1845, died aged one year; Miles (9), b. 1848, lived about two years.

Mariette (3), b. 1834, married Ralph Merrills of New Hartford, Conn., a veteran in the Cavalry Service of the Civil War. Two daughters, Clara the elder is wife of Edward G. Peck, a foreman at P. & F. Corbin's, New Britain, Conn. The younger child died as the result of a fall in infancy. Mrs. Mariette Merrills died at the home of her sister, Mrs. E. M. Curtiss, Bristol, March 11, 1904, aged 70.

Emeline (4), b. 1836, married Edwin Miles Curtiss, son of Philo and Charlotte M. Curtiss of Edgewood. Their children were: Emerson W. (1), (blind from birth), married Emily Sheldon; Herbert (2), 2 years; Wallace E. (3); Elbert Everett (4), (drowned at Cedar Swamp Lake, 22 or 23 years of age); Ida May (5), married Will Cable; Linus (6), 10 weeks; Frank (7).

Nancy Matthews (5), b. 1838, died Dec. 16, 1906, of measles, age 68. Wife of Willis B. Wheeler of Bristol. No children.

Orlando (6), b. 1841. Enlisted when 22 years of age in the First Conn. Vol. Heavy Artillery. Received honorable discharge Oct. 9, 1865, after the close of the Civil War. The following winter took a course of instruction in the U. S. College of Business and Finance, New Haven, Conn. Has since been occupied in bookkeeping and mercantile pursuits. Married April 5, 1870, at Derby, Conn., Laura Maria Curtiss, daughter of Philo and Charlotte M. Curtiss. Three children were born to them in Bristol. Bertha Laura, a kindergarten teacher in New Britain, and twin daughters, who died in infancy. One son, Curtiss Lanfair, born in New Britain, Conn., Residence in New Britain, Conn. since 1884.

Later Axel V. Jacobson, who married Eliza Johnson, sister to John, Victor, Emma (Mrs. Max Christianson), Mary (Mrs. Axel Kalstrom), and others, bought the place. They were residing there in 1893. The death of Mrs. Jacobson, with subsequent poor health and finally death of Mr. Jacobson soon, again closed the home. It was purchased by Henry I. Muzzy, the present owner. It is seldom occupied and but for short periods.

At the hill top next south, Thomas Martin built a small house (No. 31). Only the well, 40 feet deep, with the nearly filled cellar are left of the former home. Thomas Martin married first a sister of the wife of Wm. Ward, who died leaving the children: Catharine (1), James (2), Mary (3), Patrick (4) The second wife had a daughter Margaret (Maggie). Only Patrick is known to be a resident of Bristol in 1907. When the house burned after 1860, the family moved to the Austin Wilcox house on Farmington Ave., on the mountain opposite the spring. Thomas Martin died Feb. 8, 1890, age 73.

SECOND DIVISION.

In 1829, the town voted that the northeast school district be extended south as far as the south line of the house lot of Wm. Jerome on the west side of the highway. 1830 the town voted that the northeast district be extended south to the south side of the dwelling house of David Steele.

October 6, 1828, is the date of a deed given to Asa Bartholomew by Selectmen of Bristol, Hartford Co., of land in two pieces of old highway. The lower piece called in the papers "Mill Road" was closed by

RESIDENCE BUILT BY WILLIAM (SECOND) AND BENJAMIN JEROME (NO. 37). SOLD TO ASA BARTHOLOMEW IN 1867, OWNED BY PHEBE (BRONSON) ALCOTT, OBERLIN O.

Mr. Bartholomew but reopened later when it was known as "the new road." When the first Bristol Directory was published, 1882, it was named Warner St., from its one factory owned by H. A. & A. H. Warner, (afterward burned). This piece was said "to contain all the old highway running easterly and westerly, beginning on the west line of the north and south highway a little north of the dwelling house of Polly Jerome" (now owned by Mr. Lockenwitz) (No. 35), "and from there running westerly a part of the way 2½ rods wide and the remainder of the way being 2 rods wide, until it runs to the east and west highway near the house now occupied by David Steele" (No. 46) [in 1907 by Alice M. Bartholomew as a studio], "reserving to Polly Jerome the privilege of a passage to and from her barn."

"The other piece is 2 rods wide and begins on the west line of the north and south highway, a little north of the house now occupied by Isaac Gillett (No. 58), and to extend west and south of the house of Moses Pickingham." The latter piece of old road has not been reopened. It came out on Jerome Ave., a short distance south of Jerome B. Fords' house on the west roadside. Asa Bartholomew then opened Edgewood St. from Jerome Ave. west to south of Moses Pickingham's place.

In March, 1833, an attempt was made to annex to the North School District the resident inhabitants of No. 7, south and southwesterly of the north dwelling house of Asa Bartholomew (No. 55), including that dwelling, or if best, to unite the two school districts in one.

The school meeting of March 11, 1833, to consider the subject in the Baptist "meeting house" adjourned till 3 o'clock, p. m., in the basement of the Congregational Church, and "Voted, that the petition of George W. Bartholomew and others, be referred to Joel Truesdale, Tracy Peck and Philip Gaylord, Esqs., as a committee to fully view and examine North and Northeast Districts with regard to scholars, distances, etc., and report to a future meeting their opinions; and if thought best to unite the two districts, to recommend a location for a schoolhouse." On April 1, 1833, the committee who were appointed at the last meeting, made a written report that in their opinion it would be expedient to unite the two districts, which report was not approved. Instead, it was "Voted, that all that part of the Northeast School District lying southeast and west of the north side of the red dwelling house of Asa Bartholomew (formerly the Upson house)" (in 1907 the residence of Augustus H. Warner) "be *annexed* to constitute a part of the North School District." October 3, 1836, at the annual meeting, "Voted, that all the inhabitants of that portion of this society upon which they reside be established and made a school district by the name of the *Middle North* to wit: beginning at the run of water passing the highway westward of the dwelling house of Lauren Byington and thence extending eastward to the north and south highway, North to include the red dwelling house owned by Asa Bartholomew and South to include the dwelling house of David Steele," (No. 32).

No. 7, called Northeast District.
No. 8, called North District.
No. 9, called Middle North.

In 1841, when the School Society's Committee were instructed to settle and define the boundaries of several districts agreeable to the law, it was done, and all written out in 1842. It was "Resolved, that all the territory within the following lines and boundaries shall form and constitute one school district, viz: Beginning at the center of the highway between the houses of Noah Lewis and David Steele, opposite the northeast corner of said Lewis' land, lying on the west side of the highway, and thence west on said Lewis' land north to his northwest corner, thence north in a direct line to the southeast corner of Rensselaer Upson's east line, and on the east line of land of David A. and Franklin Newell to the northeast corner of the ancient Newell farm, and thence across the lots and pond in a direct line to the bridge, across the small brook (or sluice) a little east of Byington and Graham's Factory, thence north across the lots to the original line between the old Byington and Camp farms, and thence east, following said line to the highway, and thence east across the highway and continuing east on the line between lands owned by Joseph Byington and Allen Winston to the center of the North Branch Stream and thence south in the center of said stream to the dividing line between the farm of Noah Lewis and the farm of the late Mark Lewis, deceased, and thence west on said original line to the highway and place of beginning. And all persons now residing within said lines and bounds, and all who may hereafter reside therein, shall be, form, and constitute one school district and be known and called District (No. 9) with all the rights, privileges and immunities that school districts by law enjoy."

Soon after this change in the districts was effected and supposed to be amicably settled, some of the residents of School District No. 8 urged that the "grist mill" be left in their district as they wished the income from the property tax; though considering its location, it seemed properly to belong to No. 9. A meeting was called, when a good man from No. 8 made a speech advocating the change. He requested No. 9 to remember the Golden Rule and do as they would be done by. "Fugh! Fugh!" said "Uncle" Asa Bartholomew, in reply, "we go by the Wooden Rule. Do as you agree," which seemed to settle the argument.

Having canvassed the north part of District No. 7, to the line as defined in 1842, to be the division between No. 7 and No. 9, making two districts of the one, No. 7, the record locates the remaining families now of No. 9, beginning with the southern-most house, (No. 32), which was early built by Josiah Lewis for his youngest son, Mark. It is said, if the date of Mark Lewis' marriage were known, it would correspond with that of the house building. The "house, with the farm of one hundred acres, a barn, a cow, a hive of bess, and a "Waterbury Sweet apple tree" being the marriage gift expected from the indulgent father, Josiah Lewis. Mark Lewis married Sarah Root, who died 1843, age 76. The children of Mark and Sarah (Root) Lewis were: Adna (1), who married Eunice Dutton and moved to Meredith, N. Y.; Theodore (2), married Phebe Rich, moved to Ohio; Sophia (3), born 1796, died 1827; Romeo (4), married George Lewis' widow; (5), Harry moved to Ohio; Willis (6), born 1800, married Lavina Bradley, died 1826; George (7), born 1802, married Miss North of Farmington, Conn., studied medicine and died of consumption in Florida, 1833, aged 31 years.

In 1830, David Steele, who married Nancy Wilcox, daughter of Benjamin, and sister to Chester, moved from his former home on the Mill Road to possess the Mark Lewis house. He brought his children, Samuel (1), Lucina (2), and Franklin (3), but Jane (4) was born in this second home. At that time the Hartford and Litchfield stages brought parcels of United States mail to the Noah Lewis corner south, which were thrown off without ceremony. Franklin Steele, then a young lad, would run down for the Weekly *Courant*. One time in particular he does not forget, when he hurried in without knocking, called out "I've come after the paper," and surprised the worthy people at family prayers. Mr. Steele removed the "lean-to" roof of the house and made other changes, so that frequently it is not recognized as one of the ancient Lewis homes. David Steele died Sept. 18, 1853. His widow became Mrs. Wm. Root and resided in Plainville, Conn. She died 1869, age 75. Afterward the Mix family owned and occupied the place the greater part of the time, until quite recently Judd Mix, son of Asahel of Ashbel of Timothy, with his wife, Anne (Palmer) Mix of Farmington, Conn.

Before there was an Advent Church in Bristol, meetings of that denomination were held often and regularly at this house, from 1860 to 1870. Worshipers from Hartford, including the wife of the mayor of the city, and from neighboring towns helped to swell the numbers in attendance. They were then called Millerites. When Judd Mix sold his place recently, an auction sale of household goods afforded to overs of "the antique" an opportunity to secure some desirable articles. The children of Judd and Anne (Palmer) Mix were Arthur, David and

THE OLD ASAHEL MIX PLACE.

Electa, who cared for the home chiefly after the death of the mother more than ten years past. The sons established gardens and built greenhouses which have developed into the Edgewood Gardens of today, owned and continued by E. W. Holmes.

Mr. Judd Mix and sons are in Bristol Center, 1907.

WILLIAM JEROME (JEROM).

William Jerome 4th, with his sister Mrs. Louisa Blood, and his brother Daniel with wife and daughter Harriet, reside at the next house north (No. 33), on the west side of the way. Their first ancestor in America was Timothy Jerome, who came from England in 1710, and became one of the first settlers of Wallingford, Conn. He purchased a large tract of land in Farmington which he gave to his son William, who had also a sale of land from Ebenezer Hawley of Farmington in 1741, and one from Benjamin Bronson in 1742, while yet he was William Jerome of Wallingford. The records and deeds show his first appearance in New Cambridge (Bristol) 1747, when he traded land with Caleb Palmer, who lived where the house of H O. Miller now stands. It is certain that William Jerome was admitted to the church in New Cambridge in 1750, and his brother Zerubbable, who settled in or near Pequabuc, in 1755, In 1752 the town of Farmington exchanged land with William 1st for a highway, the description of which in the papers, deeds, etc., indicates the location as that of the present thoroughfare appropriately named Jerome Avenue. It extends from Lewis' Corners to Burlington town line. William 1st, and his son William 2d, added to their landed property until it extended easterly as a continuous tract to nearly the present town of Farmington, and northward into Burlington.

William Jerome 3d married Charity Hotchkiss, daughter of Elisha and sister to Elisha, Jr., the clock maker of Burlington. In 1818, with David Steele, they built the house on Warner St. (now owned by A. M. Bartholomew) (No. 46) where the oldest child of Mr. Jerome was born. Soon after they left this place to spend a few years with the aged parents of Mrs. Jerome, in District No. 8. They returned to No. 7 about 1827, when they built the house (No. 33) in which the family have lived to the present time. It is thought to be 80 years old. William Jerome 3d died June 23, 1848, aged 56. Charity (Hotchkiss) Jerome died July 10, 1868. Children: Louisa (1), married Wm. Blood of Charlton, Mass. She has been a widow many years; William (2), not married, a farmer and fruit grower; Daniel (3), a farmer and fruit grower, married Mary Parker of Meriden, Conn. They have one daughter, Harriet Louisa Jerome, 6th generation from Timothy. While there were many of the older members of the Jerome family who were admitted to the First Congregational and only Church of Bristol at that time, this family are loyal members of the Prospect Methodist Church. The fervent prayers of Daniel Jerome have comforted many who have "passed away." They are not forgotten by those remaining as heard in the little schoolhouse of the village,

At the hilltop, north of the Jerome's, is a one-story house (No. 34) in which Simeon Curtiss, son of Joshua, was living before the middle of the last century and probably built. He was born 1816, and died April 3, 1882. He married Maria Hoskins. She brought a letter from Farmington, Conn., 1853, to Bristol Congregational Church. They had two daughters, Adeline (1) who died of consumption, 1862, aged 16, and Alvina (2) who married Julius B. Smith, son of Nelson. She died in Whigville, leaving her son Ernest, born 1874, a cripple from a fall when a babe. At Simeon Curtiss' death in 1882 the proceeds from his little farm were used in New York City, in medical treatment for the benefit of his grandchild and only living descendant, Ernest Robert Smith, who was a sturdy child to all appearances except for inability to walk. Though helped and able to attend school he was never cured of lameness. He went with the family when they removed to Geneva, Ohio, where he died of consumption Jan. 11, 1900, aged 26. A sister younger lived to the age of six years. For some years Simeon Curtiss,

1856 to '63, lived on the Martin Hart farm. He was in occupancy of the Hart house when it burned. While away, one of the tenants of his own house was Augustus H. Warner when living with his first wife, Eugenia (Smith) Warner. Their children were Henry D. and Fannie Warner, who married William Hart, son of Calvin 2d, living in Bristol Center.

The place then passed into the hands of Peter J. Lawson (Larson), who with his wife and youngest child, Carl Peter (Peterson), came from Sweden to America in 1882, and for the 26 years since has been with the Bartholomews in the factory. The father died March 14, 1907, aged 78 years. Carl Peter Peterson married Hilda E. Danielson (in America since 1891). They have two children, Mildred and Valdemar. Christina A. Peterson, oldest child of Peter J. Lawson, was the first of the family to cross the Atlantic. She came to America, 1879; lived in the family of the late H. S. Bartholomew until 1886 or 1887, when she married Charles Neilson of Bristol, Conn. They have a daughter and son living in Bristol. Her sister, Annie C. Peterson, came with the brother John August in 1880. She married Peter Neilson (dec.) brother of Charles. She has been a patient at the Middletown Hospital some years. Of her four children Albin and Elmer died, Ruby and a younger sister are in Hartford.

WILLIAM JEROME 1st

The ancient but well preserved house of William Jerome 1st (No. 35) is next north, on the west roadside also. Its last occupant to bear the name of Jerome was Polly, mentioned in the deed of old highways to Asa Bartholomew 1828, when a passage to her barn was reserved. The house once painted red is now looking youthful in a coat of white, unmindful of the burden of lives it has protected during its more than century and half of existence. There is no one to state the exact year of its building. From all the traditions of the continuous family it is learned that it is one of the oldest houses in Bristol built by the great-

SCHOOLHOUSE AT EDGEWOOD.

great-grandfather of Harriet Louisa Jerome of 1907. William 1st, son of Timothy, was born in Wallingford in the year 1717. He married Elizabeth Hart, Nov. 13, 1738. He removed to New Cambridge about 1745. He united with the First Congregational Church, 1750. He died in the year 1794, at the age of 77 years. Children of Wm. 1st and Elizabeth (Hart) Jerome were William 2d (1), Benjamin (2), David (3), Abigail (4), Sarah (5), Rhoda (6), and Anna (7).

William 2d married 1st Phebe Barnes [daughter of Josiah of Jediah of Ebenezer of Thomas, the pioneer]. He married 2d PollyAndrews. Benjamin Jerome married Sarah Andrews. Abigail married Josiah Lewis 2d. Sarah married Abel Yale 2d.

Benjamin Jerome brought up his family at the house of his father, Wm. Jerome 1st. His wife was Sarah Andrews. He was engaged in milling with his brother Wm. 2d, until his death, Sept. 18, 1803, aged 44 years. Children of Benjamin and Sarah (Andrews) Jerome: Lot (1), Hiram (2), Orrin (3), James (4), Sally (Sarah) (5) and Lorena [called in Congregational Church Manual "Irene, wife of Abner Brown"]. Her data are given in the Yale Genealogy of this record.

Lot was a resident of Bristol till old age. His house and farm were on Stafford Ave., a short distance north of Forestville on the west side of the street. Sylvia, wife of Lot Jerome (1), d. 1875, age 74; Hiram Jerome (2), b. Jan. 1802, m., 1829, Rachel Spencer, b. 1809, in Berlin, Conn. Hiram Jerome went to California at one time; was a brass worker in Bristol, 1861, and a member of the Congregational Church after 1816. He d. 1876, age 74. [Three daughters, Augusta (1), Abigail (2), Anna (3)]. Orrin Jerome (3), admitted to the Church, 1719, d., 1851, aged 60; artist, painter of miniature portraits of merit, as shown by work preserved, including a portrait of himself owned by his sister Lorena, 2d wife of Abel Yale 3d. James (4), joined Church, 1821; d., 1824, aged 26 years. Sally (Sarah) (5), joined the Church, 1815, with her husband Shadrach Pierce; Lorena (6) [Irene], m. 1st Abner Brown [one son Orrin Brown of Forestville]; m. 2d her cousin, Abel Yale 3d.

Other families resided in the house at different times, and often two at one time, before *Alanson, son of Lorenzo and Annis (Botsford) Winston* became permanent resident. Alanson Winston, b. 1816, m., 1839, Nancy Maria, b., 1818, daughter of Asa Bartholomew. Mr. Winston d., 1875, age 59, at Atlantic, Iowa. Mrs. Nancy M. Winston d., 1880, aged 62, at Atlantic, Iowa. Their children, born in District No. 9, Bristol, were: *Sarah Annis* (1), b., 1841, m., 1862, Julius Almeron Pond, son of Julius Rodney and Elizabeth (*Preston*) Pond, b., 1840. They have one child, Martin Almeron Pond, b., 1865, in Whigville, m., 1888, M. May Miller, daughter of David P. and Margaret A. (Bullis) Miller of Southington, b., 1867. [Ch., Infant (1), 1889, d., young; Leslie Miller Pond, (2), b., 1891]

DeWitt Alanson (2), b., 1843, m., 1867, Jane Elizabeth Byington, b., 1844, daughter of George. [One son, Nathan DeWitt, b., 1782] m., 1896, Emma Geneva Link, b., 1876. [Two children, the elder, Mabel Cynthia (1), b., 1897]. This father and son reside, Atlantic, Iowa. They are farmers.

Frances Maria (3), b., 1845, m., 1868, Peter J. Defendorf, b., 1847, at Pleasant Brook, Otsego Co., N. Y. Two children, Cora Rebecca (1), b., 1871, m., 1893, Charles Lawson Wooding, b., 1869, graduated from Yale College, 1892; librarian, Bristol Public Library. Children, Lois Frances b. Feb., 1895 (dec.); Helen b., 1897. Fred Winston (2), second child of Frances M. and Peter Defendorf, b., 1878, d., 1880.

Frank W. (4), of Pawnee City, Iowa, now of Bristol, Conn., b., 1852, m., 1875, Alice Muzzy of Henry, b., 1855 in Bristol, Conn. Two children [Ella M. Winston b., 1876, in Iowa; Ernest F., 1882; graduated Trinity College, Hartford, 1905].

George M. Winston (5), b., 1863, m., 1892, Edna May Todd, 1871. [Children b. in Nebraska; Charles J. (1), 1892; Fred D. (2), 1894; Martha E. (3), 1897].

FRANK PETERSON, U. S. N., 1899–1905.

Julius Rodney Pond of Martin, next bought the Wm. Jerome 1st house, in which also resided his only child, Julius Almeron Pond and family. Jullius Rodney Pond d., May 30, 1883. Mrs. Elizabeth (Preston) Pond, daughter of Luman, of Plymouth, d. Sept. 30, 1883. The son Julius Almeron Pond sold the place to Theodore Lockenwitz, the present owner, April 1, 1896. Mr. Lockenwitz has a large family of children and relatives.

Soon after 1860, Horace Osborne Miller built a house at the northwest corner of Warner St. and Jerome Ave., the site of the Caleb Palmer house (No. 36). "Caleb Palmer and his wife" were church members in Bristol, Aug., 1747. Wm. Jerome 4th, now living, was always told by his father, Wm. 3d, that Caleb Palmer lived at that place. Mr. Miller found in excavating for his cellar, the foundations of the old stone chimney, burnt stones, and a coin, several feet below the surface of the soil, which he did not long preserve. He also dug out from the terraces the stump and roots of a large pine tree, known for its size as a landmark from the beginning of the settlement. It was remembered by William and Daniel Jerome as a stump when they were children. Mr. Miller built his house in part of a building he had secured in Burlington of his father-in-law, Chester Bunnell. He purchased the old wagon shop, formerly used by Vincent Thompson and Lewis Bradley, in Burlington, near North Peaceable St., Bristol. The wagon shop, enlarged to nearly double the original size, stands west of his house on Warner St., and is his present barn. The house in use about a score of years (with the suggestion and encouragement of his son Luther) gave way to the present well-built home. Mr. Miller is a mason and brick-layer. He married first Henrietta Bunnell, daughter of Chester, the mother of his children. Mary (1), [Mrs. Hill of Bristol]; Henrietta (2), George (3), Luther (4), Emma May, (5) (dec.) and William (6). Mr. Miller m. 2d, Nancy Marvin of Goshen, Conn., who died after a residence of few years in Bristol. The 3d marriage was to Mrs. Electa M. (Curtiss) Hinman, of Plainville, Conn.

William Jerome 2d,, built and lived in the house of mansion style (No. 37), north of Mr. Miller. In 1788, with his brother Benjamin, he purchased of Amasa Ives an interest in the Gristmill where the Bartholomew Factory now stands. His brother died in 1803. In that year their interest in the mill was increased. In 1809, Wm. Jerome, 2d, was three quarters owner of the mill, with Isaac Graham, Sr., owning a one quarter's right. (Isaac Graham, Sr., was father of Edward (1), Alexander (2), George (3) and Isaac, Jr. (4)). He lived in a small house near the head of the Mill Pond in District No. 8. William Jerome married first Phebe Barnes, daughter of Josiah, of Jediah, of Ebenezer, of Thomas, the Pioneer. Married second, Polly Andrews. Children of Wm., 2d, and Phebe (Barnes) Jerome, were Alva (1), Sylvester (2), Daniel (3), William, 3d (4), Willis (5), and Willard (6), Amanda (7), Eunice (8), Hannah (9), Phebe (10). The children of the second wife, Polly Andrews, were Julina (Julia Ann) (11), Sophronia (12), Polly (13), William Jerome, 2d, died 1821, aged 65. Phebe, his wife, died 1804, aged 44.

William Jerome, 3d, married Charity Hotchkiss.
Eunice Jerome married Thomas Rowe.
Julina Jerome married Samuel Pardee (nephew of Dr. Jared Pardee).
Sophronia married Elizur Hart.
Hannah married Bryan Richards.

Phebe married Mr. Payne. Alva united with church, Feb. 17, 1811.
Wm. Jerome, 2d, died in 1821. The Gristmill was sold to Martin Byington and Isaac Graham (Byington & Graham). Asa Bartholomew, son of Jacob, bought the Wm., 2d (Jerome), place in 1807. In 1828, Polly Jerome, widow of Wm. Jerome, 2d, was living in the old home of Wm., 1st. It appears probable that the Jeromes went there to vacate the house bought by Asa Bartholomew in 1807.

Asa, son of Jacob and Sarah (Gridley) Bartholomew, was born at Bartemy Tavern, Peaceable St., or the old North School District of Bristol, March 25, 1776, where he lived until his marriage in 1801, to Charity, daughter of Isaac Welles Shelton. Charity Shelton had three direct lines of ancestry to Gov. Welles, of Connecticut. In 1805, they moved to Pleasant Valley, N. Y., for two years' residence. There they kept a tavern and the son George Welles, was born. Returning to Bristol they purchased the residence of Wm. Jerome, 2d, with 360 acres of land, establishing the home of many years. Eventually the place was sold to Frank Bishop of Avon, Conn., who sold it to Isaac Bronson, son of Deacon Irad about 1858. Mr. Bronson, with his second wife, Melinda (Price) Norton, adopted daughter of Eben Norton of Bristol, and Goshen, Conn., died in 1888 a tragic death by the hand of Mr. Bronson, while doubtless insane. They had no children.

Afterward Albert J. Hart engaged in market gardening here until the purchase of a home elsewhere. Others were residents for short periods. For the past nine years Charles Downs, son of Levi, of Northfield, Conn., has made it his home. He married Kate Scoville, daughter of Stephen E. Their children, born in this district, with exception of the oldest, who was born in No. 8, are: Elmer S. (1), Louise E. (2), (deceased 1893), Edna M. (3), Ella L. (4), Leroy E. (5) and Bertha L. (6), born 1906.

Mrs. Phebe (Bronson) Alcott of Oberlin, Ohio, is present owner of the property.

Children of Asa and Charity (Shelton) Bartholomew:

Emily (1), born Jan. 1, 1804; married Rensselaer Upson.

George Welles (2), born June 19, 1805; married first Angeline Ives, daughter of Deacon Charles.

Harry Shelton (3), born June 3, 1807; died Oct. 7, 1827, age 20.

Paulina (4), born June 18, 1809; married Alvin Ferry Alpress.

Jennette (5), born March 31, 1812; married Dr. Eli Todd Merriman.

Asa (6), born Feb. 5, 1815; married Mary Lydia Birge, daughter of John.

Nancy Maria (7), born Dec. 22, 1818; married Alanson Winston of Lorenzo.

GEORGE W. BARTHOLOMEW.

HARRY S. BARTHOLOMEW.

Jane Charity (8), born Feb. 22, 1821; married Wellington Winston of Lorenzo.

Asa Bartholomew, son of Jacob, born 1776, died at the home of his daughter, Mrs. Emily (Bartholomew) Upson, with whom he was living, Oct. 31, 1864, aged 88. Charity Shelton, whom he married, Sept. 10, 1801, was born 1784. Died at her home at the residence of her son, George Welles Bartholomew, Sept. 15, 1859, aged 75.

The house on north corner of Mix St. and Jerome Ave. (No. 38), was built by Wellington Winston, son of Lorenzo and Annis (Botsford) Winston, who married, Sept. 13, 1842, Jane Charity, daughter of Asa and Charity Bartholomew. He was born, 1818; went to California in 1849. He remained there but a year or two. Returning began a wood-turning business with his brother Alanson, lasting about five years. He died April 15, 1854, age 36. His burial was attended April 17, 1854, after the noted snow-fall of that year, on the 16th of April. Jane Charity (Bartholomew) Winston, his wife, died Jan. 28, 1888, age 67, at the Hospital in Hartford, where she had been ill some years. Interred at Forestville, her family residence. Three children born in District No. 9 are residents of Forestville. The sons, clock makers, many years. *Cora Annette* (1), b. Sept. 1, 1843, m. Chas. W. Bradshaw, May 13, 1872. He was born, 1842, d., 1886, age 44. [Children, Wallace L. (1), b., Nov. 13, 1873; Bertha Jane (2), b., Aug. 1, 1876, d. young.] *Wellington W. Winston* (2), b., July 7, 1847, m., Jan. 13, 1877, Mrs. Eunice L. (Smith) Wright, b., Oct. 13, 1853. She had a daughter Grace Wright, b., June 2, 1874. *Wallace F. Winston* (3), b., June 18, 1853, m., Oct. 16, 1881, Elizabeth Masters (dec.). She was b., March 27, 1850. [Ch., Bertha E. (1), b., Oct. 29, 1882; Howard W. Winston (2), b., Sept. 16, 1885.]

Dea. Irad Bronson bought the Wellington Winston house, 1858, where he lived with his wife Phebe till they died. He was third son of Isaac of Wolcott, Conn., b. Aug. 27, 1788. He was a deacon of the Congregational Church in Wolcott nine years, removed to Southington and brought letters to the Bristol Church from Holliston, Mass., 1858, also his daughter, Elizabeth T. Bronson, who died recently in Oberlin, Ohio, and is interred in Bristol. He married, Nov. 6, 1811, Phebe Norton, daughter of Isaac, who resided on the Isaac Pierce farm near Compounce Lake. Their children were *Phebe L.* (1), b. Nov. 8, 1812, m., June 14, 1836, Dr. Wm. A. Alcott (author), b. Wolcott, Conn., son of Obed and second cousin of Amos Bronson Alcott, the celebrated writer of the Concord School of Philosophy, and father of Louisa May Alcott and sisters. Dr. W. A. Alcott was author of over one hundred published volumes, of which nineteen were educational works, some of them in connection with Wm. Woodbridge, the author of School Geographies, etc. "His name is identified with some of the most valuable reforms in education, morals, and physical training of the present century." *Isaac* (2), b. May 15, 1815, d. 1888. *Elizabeth* (3), b. Jan. 27, 1818, d. at Oberlin, Ohio. Dea. Irad Bronson d. 1882, age 94. *Phebe (Norton) Bronson* died 1888, age 98.

Mrs. Phebe Bronson Alcott resides in Oberlin with her daughter, Mrs. Phebe (Alcott) Crafts, widow of Walter Crafts, a member of the American Institute of Mining Engineers, At the time of his sudden death, he was an official in the Columbus and Hocking Coal and Iron Co., 1883. The second child of Phebe (Bronson) Alcott is Wm. A., a clergyman of Mass., lover of nature, and pupil of Jean Louis Agassiz. He has a family near Boston.

Henry and Melissa (Brown) Leach followed the Bronsons in ownership and occupancy of the Wellington Winston house. Their oldest child, Edward Morrison, came with them. Other children born in the district were Ernest Brown (2), Nancy (3), Dora (4). The house burned on a morning of April, 1891. It was rebuilt the following summer. When last heard from Mr. Leach was living in the southwestern part of the state. (March, 1907). He was lineman for a telegraph co., with duties along railroad lines. The son Edward married, and is lineman for Southern New England Telephone Co. The mother of Mr. Leach was a nurse and planned, at one time, to build a sanitarium on Fall Mountain. The Leach family were originally from Maine. Albert John and Eunice M. (Belden) Hart removed from the Isaac Bronson farm, where he was a tenant and market-gardener, to the house vacated by Mr. Leach. He was son of John, of Ambrose, of Simeon, of Burlington; b. in Whigville, and m. Jane Chidsey, daughter of Dea. Chidsey of Avon, and sister to Thames Chidsey, purchaser of Dea. Charles G. Ives' farm in Peaceable St. They resided at the John Hart farm in Whigville, where Mary (1), Jenny (2), and Charles Hart (3), were born and the mother Mrs. Jane (Chidsey) Hart died of consumption when the children were young.

Mary Hart m. Dewey Lusk of Avon. She taught school before marriage and afterward resided in New Britain and Plainville. Her husband died after long continued ill health, when she canvassed for books, etc. Pursuing her avocation she called where exposed to measles and contracted the disease in most virulent form of black measles, a fatal case. Jenny died of consumption before the death of her sister Mary. Charles m. a niece of his step mother (Hutchinson by name). At the time of his father's death he was residing in Salisbury, Conn. Albert John Hart m. 2d, June 29, 1882, Eunice (Munson) Belden, b., 1848. They removed soon from Whigville to Unionville, where the daughter Jennie died and the sons, Ernest and John, were born. Ernest is a graduate, 1907, Williams College, Williamstown, Mass., and John is at Wesleyan University, Middletown. From Unionville, Conn., they came to District No. 9, Bristol, Conn. Albert John Hart died rather suddenly in the spring of 1896, age 62. Mrs. Hart removed to 27 Prince street, Bristol, where she now resides.

Wm. C. Bramhall and wife, Ruth Isabella (London) Mix, widow of Asahel Mix, then left the Mix house and resided in the Wellington Winston home until the death of Mrs. Bramhall in Oct., 1900, when they removed to another district. Their children are: Pearle (1), [married Frank Thomas, son of Theodore]; Ray W. (2); Laura L. (3); Paul E. (4); Wesley W. C. (5), and Beatrice M. (6). Ray and Paul are employed at the Stanley R. & L. Co. works in Edgewood. The last resident proprietor of the place is Charles W. Hotchkiss, son of Alfred C., employed at S. C. Co., Forestville. He married Myrtle Williams of Southington. They have two daughters, Pearle and Ruby.

At the place next east (No. 39) on south roadside is found the first house built by John H. London in this district, and formerly located in the field southeasterly from its present situation. It was convenient of access from Mix St., and not far from Asahel Mix's house, but facing Jerome Ave. John H. London, son of Hiram and Ruth (Curtiss) London, married Alice Terrill. Their children were: Maude (1), married Bryce; Lilian (2), married Harry Evans. She died in Waterbury, leaving one child (adopted by her sister Maude). Ruby (3), who died young, at this place; Mabel (4), married Perry Goodwin, a dentist, resides in Illinois, and Harold (5) and Alice (6), born in Bristol Center. Mrs. London died recently at their home, Mountain View, Plainville, Conn. (1907).

Edmund Root and family resided at the house in the meadow from 1882–1903, when they moved to New Hartford. He was a carpenter. His children: Elizabeth (1), Charles D. (2), Edmund (3). Mr. Leach bought the house intending to rent his home on the corner, and moved for a few weeks or months to the London place. He then returned to his house at the corner, but moved the London house to the street at present location. It is now owned by Mr. Friborg, of New Britain, who makes it a tenement. Recent occupants were the Olsons of Collinsville, whose 13th child was born during their life there. Amandus Carlson and wife, with children Eva and Alvin, are present habitants. When John H. London gave up his first built house he erected the second home on the north side of Mix street (No. 40), east of the former home, after its removal, in which he resided some years and sold it to Herman Ockles, who resided there about 20 years, including a visit to Germany

THE OLD MUZZY SAW MILL (NO. 16).

of several months, where he was engaged in carving a church interior at Hamburg. He is mentioned in directories as "furniture repairer." He seemed skillful in many occupations, factory operative, wood-carving, market-gardener, etc. His children were: Herman (1); Augusta Anna (2); Theodore (3); Oscar (4); a daughter (5) died young, named for her mother, *Florentina*. She was "laid to rest" in the yard. Mr. Ockles and family moved to Delaware, 1906. The place is the property of Maria L. Hotchkiss, widow of Alfred C., at Stafford Ave., above Maltby St.

Asahel Mix, son of Ashbel and Hannah (Byington) Mix, born Nov. 12, 1795, built the house near the junction of Mix and Maltby Streets (No. 41). It was his home 40 years. He left it for use of his second wife, who became Mrs. W. C. Bramhall. It was her home until the family went to the Wellington Winston house as stated. The records of the children of Asahel and Amna (Judd) Mix, born at the Ashbel Mix house on Jerome Ave., previous to the building of No. 41, are here given.

Asahel Mix, born Nov. 12, 1795; married Jan. 13, 1820, Amna Judd of Avon, b. July 2, 1795. Asahel Mix died 1878, aged 83. Amna (Judd) Mix died 1874, aged 79.

Cynthia (1), b. March 12, 1821; married March 25, 1840, Ephraim Scovel Maltby. She died April 13, 1865.

Alonzo (2), b. Sept. 20, 1822; not married. Resides 91 Summer St.

Asahel *Judd* (3), b. July 9, 1824; married Ann E. Palmer, Feb. 12, 1855.

Mary Elizabeth (4), b. Sept. 6, 1827; married July 20, 1844, James R. Mills. Died in Wisconsin, Dec. 8, 1865.

Lyman H. (5), b. July 5, 1829; died Oct. 9, 1831.

Nancy A. (6), b. July 1, 1831; married Sept. 4, 1849, Benajah Hitchcock. She died Nov. 30, 1906.

Ellen (7), b. Sept. 3, 1834; died April 2, 1856.

Emily (8), b. August 13, 1837; died Feb. 27, 1839.

Asahel Mix was an honest, energetic, business man of the district of "marked individuality." He united in 1816 with the Congregational Church, was later a Millerite and still later advocated some of the precepts of the Hebrew, in observance of the Seventh Day as his Sabbath, and the avoidance of the use of pork as food. Returning to Edgewood St., the house on the south side near Jerome Ave. (No. 42), was built in 1843, by *William Brown Carpenter*, who came to Bristol when about 21 years of age. His native place was that part of Massachusetts which became Pawtucket, Rhode Island, in the final adjustment of boundaries between the States. The family name of Carpenter is frequent in that vicinity. Copies of "armorial bearings" or coat of arms, as granted to one Wm. B. Carpenter and recorded 1663 at Herald's Col., London, Eng., may be found on tombstones in an old cemetery at Rohoboth, Mass. He was at first engaged in the cabinet business of this place—an industry of short duration. Then, in company with Benjamin Ray, making clock cases at Pierce's Bridge until the burning of that factory. He had charge of the case department of the Bartholomew clock making enterprise before 1840. Was captain of the popular military organization of "Bristol Blues," of which Richard Yale was drummer. The appointment of District School Clerk given him, 1849, was continued to the time of his death in the spring 1855, when David S. Miller was his successor. He resided before the building of his own house at the old home of Henry A. Warner on the same street, where two of his children were born.

Wm. B. Carpenter married Henrietta, daughter of Joseph and Almenia (Rich) Ives. Their children: Marietta A. (1), Henrietta E. (2), William B., Jr. (3). Mrs. Henrietta (Ives) Carpenter died June, 1851. Several families lived for a time in the Carpenter house before the son, Wm. B., Jr., became sole owner of the homestead. One of them, Oliver A. Beckwith, who was in Bristol, 1851, and in the church at that time. He had a position in store at the Copper Mines when resident of District No. 9.

Sarah J. (Thompson), wife of Oliver Beckwith, b. 1823; died Jan. 1891, age 67. Oliver Allyn Beckwith resides (1907), at Unionville, Conn. Children: Corinne (1), 1853; died July, 1902 (Mrs. J. H. Bidwell of Collinsville). Oliver A., Jr. (2), 1857; resident of Unionville, Conn. Marian Amy (3), 1858; died in childhood. [Data furnished by Oliver Russell Beckwith, Windsor, Conn., grandson of Oliver A., son of Oliver A., Jr.)]

James E. Ladd, who married Henrietta E., second child of Wm. B. and Henrietta (Ives) Carpenter, made this place their home until their removal to Bristol Center, about 1868. Their oldest child, Henrietta, called Hetty, died Jan. 8, 1865, nearly nine years of age; second child, Wyllys Carpenter; third child, Herbert Ives, was born in Bristol Center.

Wm. B. Carpenter, Jr., and wife, Fanny (Parsons) Carpenter, then resided at the home. They now are residents of New Britain. The firm of Warner, Carpenter & Alpress (A. H. Warner, Wm. B. Carpenter

LUCIUS S. BELDEN.

and Charles Alpress), were then doing a wood turning business in the old "grinding shop" on the "new road." The business was eventually sold to Mr. Warner, and the house to Clarence Muzzy, who did not occupy it but sold to the present owner.

Wyllys Carpenter Ladd, b. July 6, 1858; married Oct. 8, 1890, Edith Irene, daughter of Wallace and Eliza (Fuller) Barnes. He is a manufacturer of clock bells and light hardware on Wallace St., Bristol. Herbert Ives Ladd is commercial salesman, with home 83 Bellvue Ave.

Lucius Samuel Belden, son of Leroy and Catharine (Sessions) Belden, bought the house in 1875. He was born Sept. 26, 1843; married Ann Eliza Curtiss, daughter of Philo and Charlotte M. Curtiss. They have one daughter, born in Waterbury, Jan. 17, 1871. They reside at the place at present (1907). L. S. Belden is in the employ of Horton Mfg. Co.

House (No. 43) built in 1864-5 Occupied in the spring of 1865 by the owner, Harry Shelton Bartholomew, son of George W. and Angeline (Ives) Bartholomew. He was born March 14, 1832; married June 20, 1860, Sabra, daughter of Joseph Samuel and Rosetta (Fenn) Peck, b., May 15, 1837. He died in Pinehurst, N. C., Feb. 19, 1902, aged nearly 70 years. After attendance at his home district school, he had for a time the advantage of instruction at the Farmington School for Boys, taught by the eminent instructor, Deacon Simeon Hart. During several years of his father's stay in California, he cared for the mother and three younger children. When his father visited his family in 1851, he was pleased to return with him and spent nearly two years in visiting many localities, and in various occupations in California. Returning to Bristol he had mechanical instruction in Hartford and prepared for the manufacture of hardware. The firm of G. W. & H. S. Bartholomew was formed 1855, and used at first the little factory on "the new road," called the "grinding shop." It was the *cutlery shop* of former years. Later the business was transferred to the old clock factories where it continued till destroyed by fire in 1884.

Children of Harry Shelton and Sabra P. Bartholomew were: Alice (1), Harry Ives (2), Joseph Peck (3).

With the exception of one district school, Alice M. Bartholomew was educated entirely in private schools, with Prof. David N. Camp of New Britain, Rev. Charles V. Spear at Pittsfield, Mass., and Prof. Charles Bartlett of the Mass. Normal Art School, Boston, supplemented by a tour of European Art Galleries.

Harry Ives Bartholomew (2), Yale S. S., 1894, Ph. B. Mechanical and Construction Engineer, Portland Cement Works, Portland, Fremont Co., Colorado (1907).

Joseph Peck Bartholomew (3), Worcester Polytechnic Institute, Worcester, Mass., 1899, S. B. Superintendent Bit Brace Department, "Stanley Rule & Level Co.," Bristol and New Britain (1907).

Harry Shelton Bartholomew was clerk of School District No. 9 45 years (1856–1901). He was one of the oldest directors in service of the National Bank at the time of his death, 1877–1902. He was deacon of Congregational Church for nineteen years and superintendent of its Sunday School twenty or more years, and many times served the church in other official capacity.

At next number west (No. 44), the house built by George Welles Bartholomew, is now occupied by George S. Osborn. The building was done or completed 1835, William Darrow doing most of the labor by the day. The doors, pillars and outside carvings were done by his hand. It is estimated that he was employed about two years upon the done or completed 1835, Williams Darrow doing most of the labor by place. The outside work, fence, blinds, etc., being done after the family came there to reside from No. 55, on Jerome avenue. (The red dwelling-house of Asa Bartholomew that figured so prominently in the division of the school district.)

George Welles, son of Asa and Charity (Shelton) Bartholomew, b. June 19, 1805, married Jan. 14, 1829, Angeline, daughter of Deacon Chas. G. and Parthenia (Rich) Ives, b. March 30, 1807, died March 13, Chas. G. and Parthenia (Rich) Ives, b. March 20, 1807, died March 13, Jan. 23, 1828. She had one daughter, Hettie Julia, b. May 17, 1856.

Mrs. Julia (Cole) Bartholomew died May 2, 1896.
George Welles Bartholomew died May 7, 1897.
Children of George Welles and Angeline (Ives) Bartholomew:
Harriet Ives (1), b. Feb. 8, 1830; died Oct. 16, 1837.
Harry Shelton (2), b. March 14, 1832; died Feb. 19, 1902.
Frances Parthenia (3), b. Feb. 22, 1834; died Jan. 1, 1839.
Mary Elizabeth (4), b. March 28, 1836; died Jan. 18, 1839.
Jane Estelle (5), b. March 28, 1840.
Angeline (6), b. Dec. 22, 1843; died Aug. 28, 1893.
Emily S. (7), b. Aug. 31, 1846; died Sept. 13, 1848.
George Welles, Jr. (8), b. Aug. 24, 1848.

George Welles Bartholomew, Jr., married Oct. 18, 1876, Hettie Julia, daughter of Julia A. (Marvin) and Edwin Halsey Cole (first teacher of the High School Department in the Southside School House, Bristol). They reside in Denver, Colorado, and have had seven children. Five are living in the West.

Angeline, 6th child of George and Angeline Ives Bartholomew, married Oct. 24, 1871, Samuel Harvey Marvin. She died in 1893, leaving two daughters, of Columbus, Ohio. Her son, Percy Clarence Marvin, died Dec. 22, 1890, aged 17 years.

Mr. Bartholomew was engaged in a number of business enterprises in early manhood, chief of which was clock making, which he followed till about 1840. During his California life others were in occupancy and ownership of his home. After that time his associations were with his son, H. S. Bartholomew, until 1884, when *he retired* from business.

The family resided in the next house west, built in 1843, by his father, Asa Bartholomew, but returned and spent nearly half a century in the home he built with so great care. He was Justice of the Peace about forty years, Selectman ten years, Judge of Probate, Senator and Representative several terms; a Democrat. The place was sold after his death to Wm. J. Holden, who was resident a few years, when he sold to the present owner, Geo. S. Osborn, who came to Bristol from Hartford. He has a daughter, Gladys.

House (No. 45) built 1843 by Asa Bartholomew, Sr., on the site of David Steele's barn with *basement*, which Asa Bartholomew, Jr., utilized as a butchery and from which he sold meat. The present barn of the place is on the site of David Steele's blacksmith shop. Tenants of that time, 1843, and near, were Lucas Barnes, later of Bristol Center. (One of his daughters born here.) Henry Blakesley and Leroy Belden when they came to the district, 1851. It was sold to Franklin Steele, 1854. His children were born here. Tenants of the double house of that time and near: A. H. Warner, of whose children, Fanny and Henry Douglas, it was the birthplace. Mr. Steele began housekeeping in the Mark Lewis house (No. 32).

MISS A. M. BARTHOLOMEW'S STUDIO.

Mr. Steele *sold* to George Turner, Sr., for the use of the Ryals family. Charles Keyes, present P. M. of Southington and Axel V. Jacobson, were residents at some time. The widow of John Conklin (Mrs. Mary Madden Conklin) next owned the property, where she lost by death, her son John. Of her estate the present owner, John August Peterson, purchased the place.

John August Peterson, son of Peter J., came to America from Sweden, 1880. He married Anna Louise Peterson, sister to John and Adolf of Forestville, who died Nov., 1905. Children: Agnes (1), graduate B. H. S., and "Conn. Business College," Hartford, Ernest (2), and Oliver (3), who died aged one year. John August Peterson is employed in the "S. R. & L. Company" Works of Edgewood. Also has a farm, in charge of son Ernest.

The corner house (No. 46), junction of Warner and Edgewood streets, was built in 1818 by David Steele and Wm. Jerome, 3d. Louisa, oldest child of Wm. Jerome, 3d, was born at this place. The Jerome family soon removed to District No. 8 for a residence of few years. Most of David Steele's children were born in this house; Jane, only, at the Mark Lewis home, where they later removed. The place was sold to George W. Bartholomew, who made it the boarding place for his employees in the clock business. It was kept at one time by John Bacon, who afterward lived in Peaceable St., and was an honored member of the Prospect Methodist Episcopal Church.

Incomplete list of families that have lived in the boarding house.

1	Wm. Jerome, Sr.,	24	Mr. Doolittle,
2	David Steele,	25	Leroy Belden.
3	Elijah Williams,	26	Samuel Russell,
	with three brothers,	27	Samuel Russell, 2d,
4	Mr. Eustice,	28	Geo. Bartholomew,
5	Mr. Glaston,	29	Uriah Russell,
6	Mr. Frie,	30	Fred Russell,
7	"Sher" Lewis,	31	Almeron Pond,
8	Warner MacIntire,	32	Mrs. Emma Downs,
9	James Mills,	33	Peter Diefendorf,
10	Mr. Sanford,	34	Charles Keyes,
11	Major Case,	35	Wm. Hart,
12	Ai Bunnell,	36	Edward Porter, Sr.,
13	Nathaniel Cramer,	37	James Hodges,
14	Mr. Gilbert,	38	Charles Justin,
15	Henry Warner,	39	Wm. Griffin,
16	Eli Byington,	40	James Ryals,
17	Isaac Graham,	41	John Carroll,
18	Porter Warner,	42	George Turner,
19	Mr. Marsh,	43	Patrick Deegan,
20	David Clark,	44	Mr. McCloud,
21	John Bacon,	46	Thomas Lord,
22	Jeduthan Clark,	47	Charles Anderson.
23	Horace Miller,	48	Herbert Loveland,

Incomplete list of men who boarded in the Co. boarding house.

1831
    Albro Alford,   Allen Winston,

1832
    W. B. Carpenter.

1833 House kept by John Bacon.
  May 1st.
      A. Alpress (Alvin),   O. Weldon (Oliver),
      Wm. Courier,   Henry Bancroft,
      Emery Moulthrop,   Wm. Fancher,
      Nathan Wildman.

1835 House kept by Jeduthan Clark.
Jan. 1st.

Wm. B. Carpenter,	Harman Stedman,
Ephraim McEwin,	David B. Clark,
Harry Thompson,	Benjamin Barnes,
Sherman Barnes,	Sylvester Lyman,
Joseph Thompson,	O. P. McKinney,
T. B. Kibby,	Geo. Alpress,
S. Smith,	W. W. Wintenbury,
H. H. Newcomb,	Wellington Winston,
R. Johnson,	J. Breakenridge,
Luther Carter,	Wm. Carter,
Lucas Barnes,	Timothy Bradley,
Gad Roberts,	Isaac Muzzy.

1847 House again kept by John Bacon.

Alexander Graham,	Monroe Barnes,
Richard Sansome,	Amasen Smith,
Patrick Fox,	E. L. Welton,
James Creighton,	George Nichols,
E. Woodruff,	Isaac Graham,
——— Olny,	Enos Hart,
Ara Hawley,	Nathan Wildman,
John Rudd,	Richard Yale.
Orrin Thompson.	

The house changed owners and shared the fortunes of other Bartholomew property. It came again to them in the purchase of the factory property from the Hotchkiss Brothers of New Haven, by the G. W. & H. S. Bartholomew Co., about 1860. At the retirement of G. W. Bartholomew from business in 1884, it was bought by Harry S. Bartholomew, whose daughter purchased the old house, in which she is fitting rooms as a "Studio" for her pleasure in art work. An addition reaching easterly was built after 1818 in which now resides Chas. Anderson, wife and daughter Ebba. He is employed by the "Stanley R. & L.Co.," Edgewood.

"THE DUMPLING," SOUTH OF BARTHOLOMEW FACTORY.

Lauren, son of Martin and Amy Manross Byington, born 1797, married first Honor Graham. They had no children, but were guardians to the minor sons of Isaac Graham, Sr. Elisha Hotchkiss, Jr., also was a guardian to some of them, 1829. Lauren Byington married second Julia Philena, daughter of Martin Hart. She built the home (No. 47) in which they resided west of the home of the father, Martin Byington. Her father, Martin Hart, spent his declining years at this house, where he died 1860, age 77. Mrs. Julia P. (Hart) Byington died about 1862.

Lauren Byington married third Mrs. Eliza F. (Colvin). Mr. Lauren Byington united with the church with his third wife in 1871. He was the third husband of his last wife. The first left a son, Wm. Nichols, who made Edgewood his home. Mrs. Byington had other sons, Frank (1), Fred (2) and Eugene Colvin (3), possibly others. Lauren Byington died 1889, age 92. He was a farmer. Mrs. Eliza Byington resides in Avon (1907).

The place was next owned by Warren Smith (unmarried), who provides a home for his aged parents, Benjamin F. Smith and wife. The father is feeble and blind, 'Seymour Reed, son-in-law (of B. F. Smith), also resides with them. He is R. F. D. carrier, Route No. 1, the first route in the County of Hartford. Children of Seymour and Viola (Smith) Reed: William (1), Arthur (2), Joseph (3), Rollin (4), Ruby (5).

Martin Byington, fourth son of Joseph, Sr., and Hannah (Spencer) Byington, born 1767, married Amy, daughter of Deacon Elisha Manross, of Forestville, sister to Ruth, wife of Noah Byington. His home (No. 48), opposite the "gristmill," where Bartholomew Factory now stands, was on the steep part of the bank with a flight of wide and long stone steps or terraces leading to the house. Lauren Byington, the only son, lived here with his mother after the death of his father, Martin Byington in 1821, aged 54, till marriage to second wife, Julia P. (Hart) Byington, and the new residence. Martin Byington had been owner with Isaac Graham, Sr., in the gristmill and manufacturing of framed mirrors, some of which can be seen in Edgewood houses. Their factory was in No. 8, where George Turner, Jr., is doing business, in 1907. Children of Martin and Amy (Manross) Byington: Lauren (1); Rowena (2), who married William Curtiss [Angeline (1), Almira (2), Wm., Jr. (3)]. William and Rowena (Byington) Curtiss resided in the old house after Lauren occupied the new one. Williams Byington also made it his home and a Mr. Atwood.

Asahel Mix bought the old house. He carried it to some of his own land on the hill northwest from its former site, reconstructed it and sold, with the land, to John Conklin, who made it his home. (No. 49).

It is thought Mr. Conklin was employed at the copper mine in his first years of life here. He was certainly in the employ of the Ingraham's Clock Co. several years before he enlisted in the Twenty-fifth Regiment for the Civil War. He died of consumption. The children of John and Mary (Madden) Conklin were: Daniel (1), John (2), William (3); a daughter (4), who died before her father, at the house on the hill.

Later Mrs. Conklin bought a place on Edgewood St., as has been stated, where her son John died and was interred at New Britain. Mrs. Mary (Madden) Coughlin died at the home of her son Daniel, in Bristol (North Side), Aug. 28, 1896, age 60. The son William died later. The children have now all "passed away," but grandchildren are residing in the town. The name of John Coughlin is very familiar to residents of No. 9, in notes from the baseball field.

The home of Moses Pickingham (No. 50), at the south end of the old abandoned road, comes next in course of record. The name slightly shortened since the deed of 1828, to Peckham, is known to belong to his descendants, residents of Bristol on Wolcott Road. Moses Peckham married Thankful Gaylord, March 26, 1823. Moses Peckham had a son, who was schoolmate of Samuel, oldest son of David Steele, and Wm. Jerome, 4th, at the old schoolhouse near Noah Byington's home.

This house was rented to several families before its purchase by Henry A. Warner, one of which was Selah Steele, Jr., from New Britain, whose first wife was Phebe Baldwin, of Phineas, of Milford, Conn. Their only child, Harvey Baldwin, born Feb. 23, 1827, was playmate of the children of District No. 9. He was in 1862, Dr. Harvey B. Steele, a celebrated physician of West Winsted, Conn. He married 1861, Mary Mather of West Winsted. It is said Selah Steele also resided a while in the Wm. Jerome, first, house. Wm. B. Carpenter lived some years in the Peckham house. It was the birthplace of some of his children.

Henry A. Warner was born in Plymouth, Conn., 1814. His father's family moved to New Hartford when he was 9 years of age, or in 1823. He worked at clock making in Hotchkissville for a time; came to Bristol for a year or two and returned to his home in Plymouth Hollow, now Thomaston. He married in 1835, Miss Eliza Roberts, daughter of John of Burlington. Two years later he came to the place (District No. 9, Bristol), which was his home residence till his death, which occurred May 27, 1890.

His wife died in 1859. Children of Henry A. and Eliza (Roberts) Warner were: Augustus H. (1), b. 1838; Sarah (2). The first home was in the "Boarding House" (so-called), where the son was born.

(1) No. 53, Mrs. S. E. Curtiss *O, The Philo and Andrew Curtiss Places;* (2) No. 42, Luther S. Belden *O, The Wm. B. Carpenter Place;* (3) No. 43, Mrs. H. S. Bartholomew *O;* (4) No. 52, Mrs. J. E. Russell *O, The Jeremiah Stever Place;* (5) No. 51, Franklin Steele *O, The Allen Winston Place;* (6) No. 44, George E. Osborne *O, The George W. Bartholomew Place;* (7) No. 50, Mrs. Sarah Weed *O, The Moses Pickingham Place;* (8) No. 45, August Peterson *O, The Asa Bartholomew Place,* (9) Miss A. M. Bartholomew's Studio, Chas. F. Anderson *R, The Wm Jerome (3d) and David Steele Place.*

Mr. Warner purchased the Peckham place and lived in the house some years. About 1860, he built the present home, on the site of Moses Peckham's house. The old house was divided. The better portion used in the rear of the new dwelling forming an L. The remainder constitutes the shed attached to barn of the place at present. Henry A. Warner married second, 1865, Mrs. Jane (Clark) Butler, daughter of Gordon. She died in Hartford, date May 14, 1896. Mr. Warner was engaged most of his business life in the wood-turning business. In 1854, formed a partnership with John H. Sessions, turning knobs and job turning. The firm of Warner & Sessions continued until 1865, when he sold his interest to Mr. Sessions. Mr. Warner bought a Dunbar factory, where he made travelling bag frames a short time, which was sold to Turner & Clayton. The following autumn he bought the interest of C. H. Alpress in the wood-turning company of Alpress & Carpenter, of which his son, A. H. Warner, was a partner. The firm name continued, Alpress, Carpenter & Co., but a few months, when Mr. Warner and his son bought the whole business, which was continued till his demise as H. A. & A. H. Warner.

Mrs. Sarah (Warner) Weed, daughter of Henry A. and widow of Julius, of Hartford, Conn., now owns the place, where she spends the summer months.

Allen Winston, 9th child of John and Sarah (Bartholomew) Winston, b. 1808, died Oct. 25, 1848, age 40; married Eunecia Foote of Burlington, Conn., b. Aug. 25, 1812, died when in Virginia with her daughter Helen. Children were Helen (1), b. 1834, who married Sept. 4, 1850, in Bristol, Conn., her cousin Granville Winston of Lynchburg, Va.; Dwight (2), b. about 1837, went to California. Allen Winston built the house numbered 51 in 1833. He was a farmer, and also a manufacturer early in the history of the village. Stray papers and accounts of the late G. W. Bartholomew note the firm "Winston, Hale & Carpenter," probably of short duration. The barn first built by Allen Winston not meeting his requirements as to size, was changed into a dwelling and located at No. 53 of the Map. It was replaced with a larger one to which Alanson Winston, nephew of Allen, added the shed, all now standing.

Alanson Winston was next occupant and owner of the Allen Winston house. With his brother Wellington they were woodturning manufacturers of knobs, door stops, etc., for about five years, during which time Alanson lived at this house. Frank Winston was born at this place. They returned at the close of the business to the old Wm. Jerome 1st house, the property of Mrs. Maria (Bartholomew) Winston, wife of Alanson.

David Miller was next owner, who sold to J. H. Sessions, who lived there 1855 to 1869. During the time of his residence the "Warner & Sessions" firm were doing a prosperous business, following the Winstons, by whom Mr. Sessions and A. H. Warner had been employed. Later Mr. Sessions owned it all, and built a factory on the site of the Byington & Graham shop in District No. 8, which was used after he removed to the center of the town by George Turner, Sr. It was burned 1884.

John Humphrey Sessions, son of Calvin, born in Burlington, Conn., March 17, 1828, married Emily Bunnell, daughter of Allen and Rhoda (Atwater) Bunnell, b. Jan. 30, 1828. Children born at this place are John H. (1), (deceased), Caroline (2) [Mrs. George W. Neubauer]; William Edwin (3), who was twelve years of age, when the family moved to Bristol Center, 1869. Mr. Sessions sold the residence to Edward Alpress who married Sarah Root (dec.). He sold to Franklin Steele, the present owner, in Feb., 1871. Edward Alpress now resides in New Britain, Conn. He married second, Mrs. Adelaide (Tolles) Porter, b. Dec. 25, 1883, widow of Geo. Henry Porter, who died 1882. [Son Henry Tolles Alpress, b. Feb. 4, 1889.]

The present owner, Franklin Steele, son of David and Nancy (Wilcox) Steele, b. May 27, 1829, married Nov. 24, 1852, Caroline Bunnell,

b. Jan. 13, 1827, daughter of Allen and Rhoda (Atwater) Bunnell, who died Dec. 9, 1898. Children, Frank W. Steele (1), died age 2½ years; Samuel Wilcox Steele (2), sexton of the West Cemetery, Bristol; Franklin William Steele (3), died aged 16 years; Thomas Bunnell Steele (4), resides at Bristol Center; twins, Sterling James Steele (5), died Jan. 19, 1889, and Estella Jane Steele (6), resides Edgewood.

Franklin Steele, who has spent his active life in the factories of his brother-in-law and sons, John H. Sessions, retired some years since. He is undoubtedly the only person, whose birthplace was District No. 9, who has lived continuously within its limits to the age of 78 years. He is engaged at his convenience or pleasure in agriculture.

The house (No. 52), now owned by Mrs. Jane E. Russell, east of Franklin Steele, was built by Jeremiah Stever about 1850. He was formerly one of the firm of Stever & Bryant, Clock Makers of Whigville. Jeremiah Stever, married first Mary Welton of Waterbury. She died in Whigville, leaving one daughter named Mary. Mary Stever married first Samuel Beckwith of Canton, brother of Oliver A. Beckwith. Samuel Beckwith died in a few years, when she married John Carroll (dec.). [Two daughters, Sarah Carroll, a teacher, Grace Carroll, stenographer.] Mrs. Carroll resides on Woodland, St., Bristol. Mr. Stever married second Jane Smith of Derby, Conn., who died 1873. Children of Jeremiah and Jane (Smith) Stever: Helen (1); Charles (2). Helen Stever married Reuben Frost of Marion, Southington, Conn. (one daughter, Helen, married —— Beckley). Charles Stever resides in California. He has a family. Mr. Stever married third, Louisa, daughter of Wm. Smith, cousin of the second wife. She died in a few years, when Mr. Stever married fourth —— (name unknown). There was one or more children in this family, when the parents died in one week of pneumonia.

Edward Graham, who married Caroline Hart, daughter of Adna lived in this house at one time. Children, William H. (1); Lucelia (2);

THE GEORGE W. BARTHOLOMEW PLACE, FROM AN OLD PHOTOGRAPH

Ida (3) [Mrs. H. E. Butler, 79 Summer St., Bristol]. The place was purchased by Uriah Russell, 1876. He married Jane E. Bartholomew, daughter of Geo. W., b. March 28, 1840. Uriah Russell was born March 29, 1831, died Sept. 21, 1891, aged 60, after a long illness. Four children.

Fred Warren (1), b. Nov. 22, 1862, married Nov. 18, 1885, Margaret Sullivan, b. April 10, 1866. Children [Marguerite (1), (dec.); Fred Ives (2); Elsie (3); Faye (4)].

Herbert Archer (2), b. April 23, 1866, died April 16, 1869, age 3 years.

Grace Edna (3), b. Jan. 7, 1868, married Oct. 23, 1895, Mortimer Cole Keeler, b. Aug. 10, 1868; four sons, Robert Russell Keeler, b. Aug. 22, 1898; Raymond Mortimer Keeler (2), b. 1902; Irving Welles (3), b. May 25, 1904; Harvey Hickok Keeler (4), Oct. 24, 1906.

Helen Louise Russell (4), b. July 28, 1872, married June 14, 1899, Elbert Elmer Smith, b. Dec. 30, 1860. One son, Russell Robbins, b. 1905.

WM. B. CARPENTER, JR., (AT NO. 42).

Uriah Russell, whose family settled in Andover and Boston, came from Mass., to Bristol, Conn., to engage with Jeremiah Stever and Julian Pomeroy in making "old-time" sewing machines. J. Stever was an ingenious man, who secured many profitable patents. One of his inventions was a precursor of the bicycle and tricycle, but not developed at Byington & Graham's factory.

Philo Curtiss, son of Joshua of Burlington, married Sept. 3, 1829, Charlotte Curtiss, daughter of Aaron Curtiss of Burlington, Conn. Their children were Lucius (1); Jonas (2); George (3); Edwin (4); Ellen (5); Laura (6); Andrew (7); Ann Eliza (8); Emma (9). The residence was the first house (No. 53) east of Jeremiah Stever's home. For a few years, Mr. Curtiss, with his brother, Simeon Curtiss lived on the Martin Hart farm (No. 26). During Philo Curtiss' absence, Isaac Graham, Jr., occupied the house at this place (No. 53), in 1860 and after. They removed later to Hiram Norton's house on Mines Road (No. 2). Isaac Graham married Lucy, daughter of Henry Hotchkiss of Burlington,

Lucy (Hotchkiss) Graham died of cancer at the Hiram Norton place. Isaac and Lucy (Hotchkiss) Graham had children, Alexander (1); Lauren (2) and others.

Philo Curtis resumed his residence at this place, where he lived till his death, June 10, 1875.

Mrs. Charlotte Curtiss died Oct. 27, 1883 at her daughter Emma's [Mrs. Downs] in Waterbury.

Andrew Jackson Curtiss, b. Oct. 26, 1844, married Jan 1, 1873, at Troy, Penn., Sarah Elizabeth Ayers, b. July 14, 1843. One daughter, Miriam Curtiss, b. Oct. 25, 1873, married Dec. 2, 1903, E. Samuel Gillette, b. Oct. 21, 1874. Andrew J. Curtiss built a house on the site of his father's, 1892, occupied October of same year. He died Jan. 27, 1907, as the result of a fall some years before. Emma J., youngest child of Philo and Charlotte Curtiss married first George N. Downs, May 14, 1872; married second Charles H. Monroe, Dec. 6, 1898, and resides at Mill Plain, Waterbury, Conn. Children, Edith A. Downs (1), b. Aug. 2, 1877 (dec.); Harry C. Downs (2), b. Dec. 8, 1883, resides in Bristol (married); Paul A. Downs (3), b. March 4, 1891, Waterbury, Conn.

The schoolhouse (No. 54), built when District No. 9 was formed in 1833, is east of the Andrew J. Curtiss residence. Asahel Mix was appointed Committee of District No. 7, after the division in 1833, the former Committee Samuel Pardee being resident south of the "red dwelling house of Asa Bartholomew" was not available for No. 7. David Steele, first School Committee of No. 9, provided for the school its first instructor, David Alford.

Franklin Steele of David, began at this time his school-education. Other early teachers were Benjamin F. Hawley, one of whose pupils was Harry S. Bartholomew.

Miss Louisa Jerome (Mrs. Blood) has the distinction of first summoning the pupils to study, or opening of school by using, instead of a stick or ruler, a *bell*. In 1837, Miss Almira E. Peck, daughter of J. S. Peck, of Whigville was teacher. During the term the "inocculation" for of Whigville was teacher. During the term the "inocculation" for prevention of smallpox was performed by Dr. Camp, for the school. It was in the early years of this shool that Wm. Jerome, fourth of the name, carried live coals between two pieces of board from his home to knidle the schoolhouse fire. When they caught fire, causing a blaze, he sometimes ran backward to prevent burning his face. Matches were invented but the use of them was not familiar. People were suspicious and afraid of them.

It would be possible, if best, to present the long list of teachers to 1907. The mention of a few will suffice. Harriet Moses, 1859. Lizzie Welch, 1860, Rev. Mr. Seeley, Visiting Committee. The schools have at this date changed from the simple study of the three R's to the following curriculum: Reading (1), Spelling (2), Geography (3), Grammar (4), Arithmetic (5), Algebra (6), History (7), Philosophy (8), Latin (9), Composition (10). (Penmanship not mentioned.) Average attendance, eight pupils. (Miss Welch now Mrs. Bevin of East Hampton, Conn.) School taught 1868, by Laura M. Curtiss, number of pupils, 33. (Miss Curtiss now Mrs. Orlando Sheldon of New Britain.) In 1871 taught by Marietta Carpenter of Edgewood, number of pupils, 32. Mrs. Rosie E. Barnes taught the years Oct. 14, 1872–Dec. 15, 1873. In 1882, Miss S. E. Howlett. The Visitor's report contained the following: "The record shows this to be the banner school of the town in point of regular attendance the per cent. for the year being 96.01. Though a small school, still the material is not wanting here on the part of the pupils to make it the banner school in other respects."

1885 the Visitor reports: "The Visitor, the teacher and the scholars are very much gratified by the new desks. This is another of our schools where there is no room for criticism and no opportunity for aught except commendation. The point especially to be noted is, perhaps, the pervasion of a gentle and what may be called family spirit in the school."

The desks of the schoolhouse were made purposely rather high for the acommodation of adults at evening meetings, etc. Mr. J. J. Jennings declaring it was not a house of public worship and that the arrangement was injurious to the health of the young, at last secured the proper seats for a schoolroom, if not for a prayer meeting or singing school.

From about this time, 1885, there have been but three teachers. Pupils were taught about ten years by Mrs. R. E. Robotham and Miss Minnie Moor about the same length of time. Miss Bartlett has filled out the remainder of the years until 1907. Mrs. Robotham died at her home in Northampton, Mass., Nov. 27 (Thanksgiving Day) 1903. Her daughter, Georgia I., is a teacher at the Willimantic High School, Windham Co., Conn. That the schoolhouse of District No. 9 served the purposes of a Village Hall, Lyceum, Religious Chapel, etc., may be shown in part by the following:

ITEM FROM THE *BRISTOL PRESS.*

Dec. 31, 1891.

"The thirty-fourth annual New Year's meeting will be held in the 'No. 9' schoolhouse tomorrow afternoon at two o'clock.

There will be present the following named ministers, who have been stationed in Bristol since these meetings were first established:

Rev. John Simpson, now of Plainville, who will preach the sermon, as he has done every year but one, when called to attend the funeral of a parishoner.

Rev. Charles H. Buck, of Brooklyn.
Rev. C. E. Miller, of Brooklyn.
Rev. Geo. L. Thompson, of New York City.
Rev. A. C. Eggleston, of Waterbury.
Rev. A. H. Wyatt. of Bristol.

ANDREW J. CURTISS (NO. 53).

AUGUSTUS H. WARNER (NO. 55).

Some of the ministers with their families will be the guests of Mr. Sessions for two or three days and tomorrow will start at one o'clock from his house to the meeting.

One 'buss will take M. H. Perkins and the old choir, of which he was leader for a number of years, and two 'busses will be required for the ministers and their families and Mr. Sessions and his family, who will go with him.

On New Year's day thirty-four years since, following a revival of great interest, a number of residents near gathered in the little schoolhouse, and voted to meet there annually for religious services, and that Rev. Mr. Simpson be the preacher so long as he was within one hundred miles, and with the exception noted he has been the preacher all these years.

Rev. Arza Hill, a much beloved minister, will be missed this year, he having died last April.

Another familiar face no more to be seen is that of Mrs. Catherine Belden, who died during the summer.

At five o'clock the annual New Year's dinner will be served in the ample dining room of Mr. Sessions on High street."

There were forty meetings held in all. Mr. Simpson's death occurred suddenly on the 13th of February, after the fortieth meeting. They were then discontinued.

The "red dwelling-house (No. 55) of Asa Bartholomew" would hardly be recognized by former residents, clothed as it is in a dress of delicate *gray*. It once belonged to Asa Austin Upson, and was a part of his "east farm." At his death in 1807, this portion of his estate was alloted to his sister, Sophia Upson. The deed of 1815 of a piece of land belonging to the farm was signed in Bristol by Philip and Sophia (Upson) Barnes. In 1828, when ninety acres were deeded with a house and shed comprising the whole of the "so-called" "east farm" Philip Barnes and wife were residents of Athens, Georgia. It is not known that Asa Bartholomew resided there. He was well established at the house of William Jerome, 2nd, south. His son, George Welles, who married Jan. 14, 1829, Angeline Ives, daughter of Dea. Charles, lived there in early married life. It is the birthplace of their son, Henry Shelton Bartholomew, born in 1832. Afterward Mrs. Paulina (Bartholomew) Alpress had a home in the house many years. The size of the dwelling allowed the occupancy of two families at the same time, which was a frequent arrangement.

Early families known to have lived at the place are James Hall, who had three sons, one born before 1829, and two later, Edward Hall, etc. Oliver Weldon, another tenant had a store in part of the house for a time. Eli Byington, father of Henry Newell Byington, also made it a home something more than fifty years since. The latter a resident of Walnut Grove, Minn., visited Bristol in recent years, with great enjoyment, returned to his family in Minnesota, where he died June 17, 1906. He was born in Wrentham, Mass., and son of Eli of Joseph, Jr., of Joseph, Sr., Bristol, Conn.

Paulina (Bartholomew) Alpress, b. June 18, 1809, married Sept. 12, 1832, Alvin Ferry Alpress, b. June 2, 1806, and died Jan. 6, 1850. He was a "Forty-niner." He died while journeying for his health, at Honolulu, S. I., aged 44. Mrs. Paulina Alpress died Feb. 9, 1894, age 84.

Children, Ellen Alpress (1), b. Dec. 11, 1833, died Jan. 13, 1839, age 5 years; Charles H. Alpress (2), b. Dec. 31, 1835, died unmarried; Edward A. Alpress (3), b. May 1, 1840; George T. (4) b. July 14, 1846; Alvin Ferry Alpress (5), b. Oct. 25, 1849, died Oct. 31, 1897, unmarried.

George Theodore Alpress, b. July 14, 1846, married Anna Bell of Defiance, O., Dec. 27, 1870, b. April 25, 1852. Her father, an architect, was killed by Indians near Pikes Peak. Children of George T. and Anna B. Alpress, Gertrude (1), b. Oct. 30, 1871, married June 12, 1894, Edward Keyes Ives, b. Feb. 12, 1870, son of Byron and Aurelia (Jones)

Ives; Harry Alpress (2), b. March, 1873, died 1875; Charles Edward (3), b. Nov. 2, 1878.

Mrs. Paulina Alpress sold her house to Augustus H. Warner, the present occupant She purchased a home in Race St., Bristol, where she died. Augustus Henry Warner, b. June 11, 1838, married Oct. 6, 1858, Eugenia Louisa Smith, b. Oct. 26, 1839, died Oct. 7, 1865. Married second Mary Elizabeth Siddell, b. July 18, 1846.

Children of first marriage, Fanny Eliza (1), b. Sept. 15, 1859, married Sept. 15, 1880, Wm. Goodale Hart, b. July 14, 1855. He is a mechanic and lives in Bristol. [Children, Maude Louisa (1), b. June 7, 1881. Employed in office of American Silver Company, Bristol; Percival Warner (2), b. July 7, 1884, employed as shipper by Coe Brass Co., Torrington, Conn.; Wesley Eugene (3), b. Feb. 28, 1887, died July 4, 1887; Ella Marion (4), b. Aug. 3, 1888, employed in office of American Silver Company.]

Henry Douglass (2), b. March 31, 1861, married March 5, 1895, Lucy Morgan Smith. One daughter [Grace Eugenia, b. March 13, 1901].

Children by second marriage.

Eugenia Estelle (3), b. Aug. 8, 1868, married Charles Edward Dennis, Ph. D., Aug. 17, 1865.

Anna Maria (4), b. Jan. 27, 1872, employed in office of Swift & Sons, Gold-beaters, Hartford, Conn.

Bessie Sarah Warner (5), b. May 26, 1874. Smith, 1905, A. B. Brown University, 1901, A. M. Teacher of Latin in Hope St. High School, Providence, R. I.

Edna Isabel (6), b. July 26, 1878. Brown, 1900, B. P. Married Lester B. Shippee, A. M., Aug. 2, 1905, Edna graduated at Whitmarsh

SOME CHARITY SHELTON'S DISHES.

"Turtle" shaped teapot, belonging to Charity Shelton in 1801; bowl of her grandmother's descending some generations; and cup and saucer from her early home. *Owned by Miss A. M. Bartholomew.*

FRANKLIN STEELE. (AT NO 51)   HENRY A. WARNER (AT NO. 50).

Surgical Hospital, 1903. She was Superintendent there of nurses, one year. Augustus H. and Henry D. Warner (A. H. Warner & Co.) have a wood-turning business at Federal near North St., Bristol, Conn.

Charles, son of Leroy and Catharine (Sessions) Belden, b. March 5, 1854, married Harriet, daughter of Henry C. Ruic. He built the house (No. 56) opposite A. H. Warner in 1882, making a barn for the place of the former home of Philo Curtiss. They have one son, Edward, born 1877, married June, 1900, Nelly, daughter of James and Rhoda (Porter) Hodges. They have two children [Clara Susanna Harriet (1)] [Charles Samuel Leroy (2)]. Edward was graduated at the Bristol High School, pursued his studies at Wesleyan, Middletown, Conn., and Boston, Mass. Was a member of New York East Conference of Methodist Episcopal Clergymen, 1903. Rev. Edward L. Belden is located (1907) at St. James and Lake Grove, Suffolk Co., Long Island. Charles L. Belden built a second dwelling-house at 50 Merriman St., Bristol, where he resides (1907). He is employed at Horton Mfg. Co.

Carl Peter Peterson rented the Edgewood house a few years, boarding some of the employees of Stanley R. & L. Co.

Ephraim McEwen was a resident of the Distric some years before building the house (No. 57) north of Charles Belden. He was first a tenant of "The Boarding House" so called possibly elsewhere. He built after the Carpenter House, which was in 1843. His children, whose approximate dates of birth are given from School Register 1858-9, were Mary (1), 1845; David (2), 1847; Martha (3), 1854; Susan (4). The parents were "deaf mutes." The mother, "Harriet, wife of Ephraim McEwen," united with Congregational Church, March 13, 1842. The family removed to Bridgeport, Conn.

A family of Sullivans, also one of Owlds (Olds) had residence at the place before its purchase by Samuel Leroy Belden, who married Catherine Sessions, daughter of Calvin. There was no barn on the premises, which were involved and depreciated in value. Mr. Belden came to the village, 1851. He resided in the Alanson Winston house on Jerome Ave., at the double house No. 45, on Edgewood St., and possibly at "The Boarding House," when he removed to the house, where himself and wife spent the remainder of their lives.

Mrs. Catharine (Sessions) Belden died Aug. 23, 1891. Samuel

Leroy Belden died May 4, 1899. Children, two sons Lucius and Charles (data before given). The house was sold to Everett Barnes, who sold in a very few years to the present owner, John Muir, son of Henry, who also resides at this home. John Muir married Alice Linden Durward. Children, Ruth (1), aged 5 years; Donaldine (2), 1 year. Mr. John Muir employed Horton Mfg. Co.

At this place (No. 58) there is no trace of a building. *Memories* of an old well in the "plain lot," owned by John August Peterson are the only reminders of the facts, as learned from deeds of 1828, when one Isaac Gillett lived where the now "abandoned road" came out to Jerome avenue from Moses Pickingham's dwelling southwest. There is a strong probability of this Isaac Gillett's identity with Isaac Gillet who formerly lived on the southern part of "Johnny Cake Mountain" in Burlington on a farm before owned by Edward Marks, an uncle of Esq. Wm. Marks. If proved, he had three daughters. The oldest married Rev. David Marks, third of the name, son of Esq. Wm. Marks, who died suddenly at the home of his son, Rev. David Marks, when stationed in New York City. The youngest daughter of Isaac Gillett, Rebecca, married Lucien Bunnell.

In 1876, J. B. Ford purchased a small farm partly in District No. 7, the remainder in No. 9, on which he built the ell of his present house (No. 59). Later he added on the south the Superintendent's house from the Copper Mine. Jerome Bonaparte, son of Omri C. of Somers, Conn., and Caroline Kent Ford, b. Oct. 5, 1845, in Collinsville or Burlington married June 17, 1866, Mary Jane Barclay, b. in Farmington, Conn., Dec. 18, 1843. Children: Roselia S. (1), b. July 2, 1867, died 1885 interred in family cemetery, Burlington, removed, 1906, to Forestville; Melissa (2), b. Jan. 19, 1871, married Franklin E. Yale [one son, Alfred]; Anna Barclay (3), b. July 31, 1875, married Henry Yale, eight children. Mr. Ford has a Machine Factory at No. 63.

DEACON CHARLES GRANDISON IVES DISHES.

Pflip Glass of Deacon Ives; pewter and china from home of Deacon Ives; coffee urn of Angeline Ives Bartholomew. *Owned by Miss A. M Bartholomew.*

DIATOMS OF BRISTOL

By Wm. A. Terry

DIATOMS are very small, one celled organisms, which are among the primal forms of life, and have apparently existed with little or no change from the earliest appearance of life upon the earth. They are bivalves, with shells of glass instead of lime, held together by side hoops of the same material instead of hinges. For many years after their discovery they were supposed to be animals, chiefly because of their power of locomotion, a very large proportion of them being rapid travelers during their whole lives. Several eminent scientists still hold to this opinion, but they are now generally regarded as belonging to the vegetable world. They vary greatly in size and

WILLIAM A TERRY.

outline, and are elaborately ornamented with sculptured markings, alae, striæ, costae, etc., many of them being among the most beautiful forms in nature. Their shells being so largely silex they are comparatively indestructable, and where the conditions are favorable they often accumulate in vast quantities. Nearly every permanent body of water, however small, contains them in greater or less abundance; when this water disappears the diatoms are left as a fossil deposit.

Quite a number of these deposits are found in Bristol. A little over the line west of the lower reservoir of the Bristol Water Company is one of these deposits; the stratum of diatoms is about two feet thick and covers one or two acres. It contains numerous species, many of them large and interesting. When this reservoir was made another fossil deposit was removed. On the farm of Silas Carrington is another deposit notable for the abundance of Frustulia Saxonica, well-known as a test object for the microscope; its markings are so minute as to require high powers and perfect lenses to resolve them. On South Mountain, north of Cedar Swamp, is a deposit containing numerous species, and an abundance of remarkably spiny spiculæ of fresh water sponges.

On the Hubbard farm on Chippen's Hill is another deposit showing an abundance of the large form of Stauroneis acuta, which should have a better name as it is not the same as the St. acuta of European writers. I do not find this variety shown in any European publication. On the Atwood farm on Peaceable Street is a small deposit.

On the old Lazarus Hird farm is a deposit showing an abundance of the very rare Achnanthidium flexellum; and north of this on the Mix farm is perhaps the largest deposit in Bristol. It covers fifteen acres and perhaps more, and is of unknown depth. I have material brought up from a depth of 10½ feet, showing seven feet thickness of diatoms to this point, which probably continues down several feet more, but we could get no farther down on account of the rapid inflow of water.

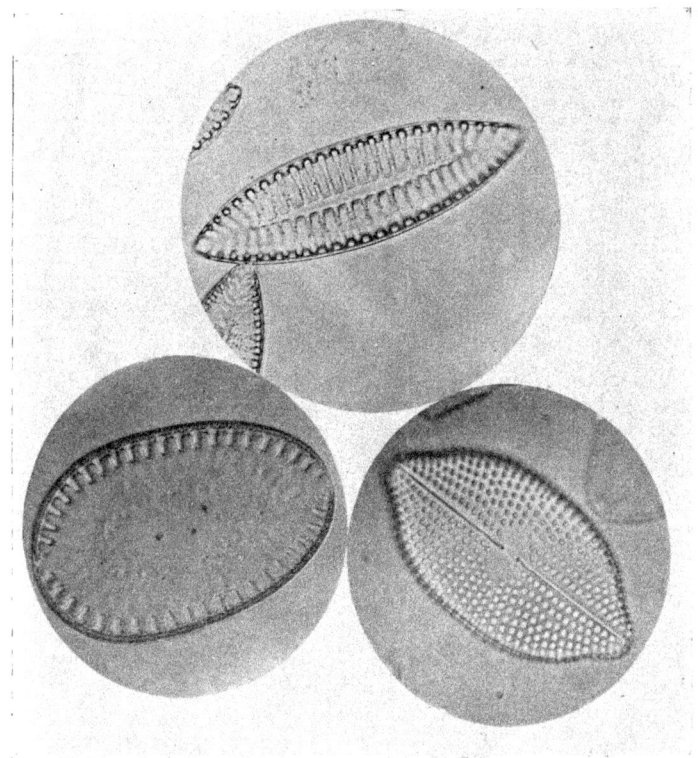

SURIELLA BISERIATA, Tacoma, Wash.

SURIRELLA BISERIATA, n.sp. Terry. NAVICULA MACULATA,
Port Townsend, Wash. Mobile, Ala.

This deposit is remarkable as containing the beautiful little Cyclotella antiqua, which has never before been found in this country as far as I can ascertain. I have sent specimens to the most experienced collectors but none of them had ever seen it before. This Bristol form is more beautiful than any of the European specimens that I have seen. This deposit also contains the rare A. flexellum, the very rare Navicula follis, the rare Fragillaria Harrisonii, and others.

At the old Tamarack Swamp on the head waters of the East Bristol Poland Brook, is a deposit in which the diatomaceous stratum is two feet thick and covers several acres; this is also rich in species. There are more small deposits in town, and probably many others that have not yet been discovered. Of living diatoms many of the larger and most remarkable of the fresh water species are found in Bristol. Those ponds that are swept by freshets seldom contain a large amount, but most others are rich. South Mountain Reservoir has abundance, of which very large specimens of Surirella biseriata are noticeable.

On Bunnell's lot the boiling spring is full of filamentous varieties of many species, and has also abundance of Fragillaria Harrisonii which is rare. Bunnell's Pond is rich; has many species of large surirella, of which Surirella cardinalis is interesting, as it is considered rare in many sections, though abundant in Bristol. Dunbar's Pond and Clayton's Pond show many species among them very numerous specimens of Cymbella cuspidata, which is remarkable as being of a decided green color, while other diatoms are a red brown color while living.

Birge's Pond is particularly rich. Surirella elegans and S. splendida are very large and much elongated. S. cardinalis is very large and abundant. S. nobilis and S. robusta are plentiful. Abnormal valves of these are numerous, two valves being grown together with a large corrugated opening in the center. Their great numbers seeming to show that this deformity was hereditary. Prof. Brun's new species, "Navicula peripunctata" is more numerous here than in Crane Pond, Mass., where it was first found. Spring's Pond has many species, the predominating one being a new Surirella, which is also abundant in the pond hole formed by the elbow cut off from the river when the railroad company moved the highway east of the saw shop. Down's Pond also shows the *new* Surirella, together with many other species in great abundance, among them a small Stauroneis with exceedingly slender and sharp pointed euds, this is probably *new*, as I cannot find it described anywhere.

The *new* Surirella is also abundant in Thompson's Pond, and in Allen's Pond in Stafford district. Outside of Bristol it appears in an ice pond east of Shuttle Meadow, New Britain, and in an ice pond at Leete's Island. So far it appears to be found only in Connecticut, and Bristol is its headquarters, it being abundant here in five different ponds. This new Surirella is about the size of S. gracilis, but has more rounded ends, the cross bars reach the median line, and it is frequently much elongated, and has a distinct spiral twist. I sent a quantity of these to Dr. Ward, he sent out numerous slides of them labeled "Surirella Terryi, n. sp. Ward."

Many of the small streams, ditches in marshes, and springy mountain rills are rich in diatoms. In a rill on Fall Mountain is a remarkable colony of the large Stauroneis acuta previously mentioned, with them is a *new* Stauroneis, one of the largest and quite peculiar. It is more cylindrical and elongated than any other stauroneis, and the upper valve has large saucer-shaped psuedo-nodules near each end. *No other stauroneis has anything like this.* The lower valve has no nodules. Dr. Ward also sent out slides of this labeled "Stauroneis Terryi, n. sp. Ward." Farther up the mountain Mr. Wm. C. Richards found a rill containing a notable colony of Navicula elliptica, very abundant, and much larger and heavier than those of the Connecticut shore. On Chippin's Hill is a small pond which contains Stauroneis Stodderii, which is quite rare.

All these fossil deposits, the ponds and streams mentioned, and many others, contain hundreds of species, a full description of which would require a large volume; a mere list of their names would cover many pages. Very many of these are among the most remarkable and beautiful of the fresh water varieties. The filamentous kinds are found nearly every where in Bristol, and the species are very numerous. They resemble the Algæ, except that they are brown instead of green, and each joint or cell is an individual organism with an independant life of its own.

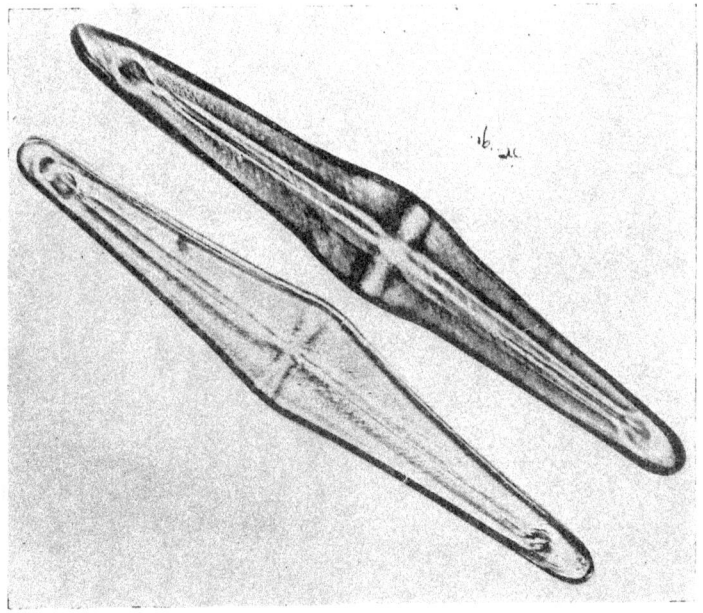

THE BRISTOL STAURONEIS. Stauroneis Terryi, n. sp. ward.

PROSPECT METHODIST EPISCOPAL CHURCH.   Photo by Gale Studio

Prospect Methodist Episcopal Church

METHODISM is educational and evangelistic. Methodism is one of the largest branches of the universal Church of God. This religious body had a humble beginning in Bristol, but for a couple of decades at least, it has been one of the most powerful factors in the progress of the place and the higher life of the people.

The first sermon in Bristol by a Methodist preacher was delivered

Rev. Arthur H. Goodenough.

in the old Baptist Church and was preached by Rev. Nathan Bangs, who later became president of Wesleyan University. His text was "But we desire to hear of thee what thou thinkest; for as concerning this sect, it is known to us that it is everywhere spoken against." Occasional meetings were held in the schoolhouse on West Street, and were frequently conducted by the traveling preachers from the Burlington Circuit. In the spring of 1833 the Bishop placed Rev. Albert G. Wickware in charge

His first important work was to organize a class, which, in those days was the foundation of every local church. The persons constituting the class, were Mrs. Hill Darrow, Mrs. Lord Hill, Leander Hungerford, Sidney Burwell and wife and Mrs. Polly E. Burwell.

The formation of a church organization commenced in April, 1834. Tracy Peck, Justice of the Peace, issued a warrent authorizing Rev. Mr. Wickware and others who might be interested in the movement, to form themselves into a religious society to be known as the Methodist Episcopal Society of Bristol, said organization to take place in the schoolhouse, on West Street. This instrument was dated April 23, 1834, and was made returnable, with the indorsement of the doings of said meeting, to the Subscribing Authority. All requirements were promptly met. The first society had 27 members. The few energetic and devoted people resolved to build a church edifice. Steps were taken immediately to secure a site for such building. This was found not to be an easy matter. The prejudice against the new sect was strong and persistent. The early Methodists had become accustomed to that kind of thing, but it only fanned their enthusiasm into mightier flame. Mr. Evits Hungerford and Mr. Philip Gaylord were the committee to purchase the necessary land. Mrs. Chloe Daniels was ready to sell. The committee hastened to the residence of Justice Peck, found him at dinner; he was compelled to leave the table and execute the legal document of sale, for fear the enemies of the Society should upset the bargain. The structure was erected and dedicated within a year. People came to the services from fifteen miles around.

The young society was served in turn by noble and faithful ministers. The church multiplied and prospered. During the years 1857-8 the pastor was Rev. John W. Simpson. During this period a revival commenced on Chippins Hill, extended to Polkville (Edgewood) and other places. Conversions were many. On New Year's Day, 1858, Mr. Simpson preached in the schoolhouse at Polkville. John Humphrey Sessions, who had previously "professed religion" attended the service, and before the meeting closed he was so impressed by a divine power that he here made a complete consecration of himself to God and precious results soon followed. That fact, simple in itself, has meant much to the town of Bristol and to the Methodist Church in particular. Mr. Sessions was an able, vigorous and successful business man. As he prospered the Methodist Church prospered.

From that time on the records show a gradual increase in the minister's salary and in the contributions to the Conference benevolences. By 1879 the Society had so prospered and grown that the church edifice on West Street was altogether inadequate to accommodate the people who came to worship. It was also felt that the new church should be built in a more central part of the town. A more eligible and commanding site on the corner of Summer and Center Streets was purchased. A brick structure was erected and the people were happy in their new church home. This was done during the pastorate of Rev. Dr. George P. Mains.

In 1888 again the congregations had outgrown their building and large additions were made. Rev. Albert H. Wyatt was then the pastor.

In 1893 a new and more commodious building was felt to be an absolute necessity. The late John Humphrey Sessions resolved to build a new church and present it to the society. This he did. The building is of granite, of modern architecture and is one of the most commodious and handsome church buildings in the state of Connecticut. The audience room will accommodate over one thousand persons; with the chapel opened it will seat two thousand people. Mr. Sessions' two sons, John Henry Sessions, gave the carpets and upholstering, and William Edwin Sessions, presented the costly and elegant organ. Their united gifts meant an expenditure of $75,000.00. The entire plant is valued at $100,000.00. A handsome and artistic window adorns the building, the gift of the congregation, as a testimonial to the munifi-

"Enter into his gates with thanksgiving, and into His courts with praise."—*Psa., c., 4.*

"Praise waiteth for thee, O God, in Zion."—*Psa.*, *lxv.*, *1*.

cent donor, John Humphrey Sessions. The handsome structure was dedicated by Bishop R. S. Foster of Boston, assisted by many clergy. Rev. M. W. Prince, D. D. was the pastor.

On Sunday, June 4, 1904, the tenth anniversary of the dedication of the new building was observed. The sermon was preached by the present pastor. The following is a quotation from his sermon:

"Ten years ago today this edifice was dedicated to the worship of Almighty God. The benevolent man who gave the building, and the distinguished bishop who dedicated it, have both gone to the temple not made with hands, and to their eternal reward. The time between that day and this, measures a decade of years.

Amid all the changes that have taken place we are spared. We are permitted the privilege of reviewing the past, and also to enjoy the worship of this hour. No greater gift could be made to a community, or to a people than the gift of a church. The gift of a library, the gift of an orphanage, the gift of a home for the indigent poor, would be a blessing indeed. That would be a work worthy the munificence of the noblest and best. But no gift, in the scope of its influence, in the permanency of its work, in the quality of its good, can compare with the gift of a church. All philanthropy, the best and wisest legislation, the potency of human friendship, are all inspired and strengthened and made effective by the influence and spirit of the church. For this reason the people, rich and poor, men and women give their money to build and support churches. This church was the gift of one of your own brothers, to you, for you, to use for the glory of God. How well it has been used I shall show you presently. A church debt is a burden,

"Peace be within thy walls, and prosperity within thy palaces.—*Psa., cxxii., 7.*

TESTIMONIAL WINDOW, inscribed as follows: "As a testimonial to the liberality of JOHN HUMPHREY SESSIONS, by whom this church was built, this window was contributed by a grateful congregation, Anno Domini MDCCCXCIII."

"For He loveth our nation and He hath built us a synagogue."—*Luke, vii., 3.*

REV. CHARLES H. BUCK.

"Feed the flock of God."—*I Peter*, v., 2.

"Beyond my highest joy
I prize her heavenly ways."

THE LATE JOHN HUMPHREY SESSIONS.

and is to be deplored. The only way, however, that some communities can have a church is to go in debt for it. The members of this church have not been hampered and burdened in that way. John Humphrey Sessions lifted that load forever from your shoulders. And on this anniversary day you hold him in loving and grateful remembrance and for decades and generations to come this beautiful and commodious structure will stand here as a silent but eloquent sermon of God's love to men, and of man's love to God. And here you and your children will congregate to sing and praise and pray.

For ten years the gospel has been preached here every Lord's Day. That is a great thing to begin with. God's minister has come with a message of salvation, of forgiveness, of good-will, of hope of heaven. The duty of the pulpit has been to give no uncertain sound. My predecessors failed not to give the Truth. They have fed you with the finest of the wheat. They have been faithful and safe teachers as well as earnest and successful preachers."

The Bristol Methodist Episcopal Church is one of the most generous in the New York East Conference in its support of its own pastor and in its contributions to the Conference benevolences. For a single decade prior to 1904, to the local church, to missions, education and philanthropy, the church gave over $100,000.00.

The present membership of the church is 710. The Sunday School has 745 members, with 85 in the Home Department and 80 on the Cradle Roll. William Edwin Sessions is the indefatigable and devoted superintendent.

The society owns an excellent parsonage which is a source of much delight to the pastor's family. The first pastor to occupy it was Rev. A. C. Eggleston some twenty-four years ago.

The Rev. Charles H. Buck, D. D., has the honorable distinction of having served this society three full terms as pastor, making eleven years in all. The present pastor, Arthur Henry Goodenough, is on his eighth year and has accepted a unanimous call for the eighth year.

The Epworth League, Ladies' Aid Society, Woman's Foreign Missionary Society, Woman's Home Missionary Society, Pastor's Guild, Men's Club and other branches are active and vigorous.

FREDERICK CALVIN NORTON.

That Strange Yankee Game, Wicket*

By Frederick Calvin Norton.

WHEN it was announced a few weeks ago that Bristol had held the wicket championship for three or four years back, it caused a ripple of laughter to go over the town where, for sixty years or more, no man living knows of a wicket team that has defeated the players from Bristol. Bristol men and boys take to wicket playing as a duck will to water and there has never been a team organized in this State that has defeated the men who represent the Clock Town.

This game was popular before baseball was heard of and in the different sections of the town there are always a half dozen or more players that could be relied on to make a record when the time came. Farmers' sons, mechanics and everybody, in fact, would gather at night on the hill green opposite the Congregational Church, and play their favorite game. In the district known as Polkville, two miles north of the borough, there always lived some excellent players and some of them are still living.

To those of today there is little known about the ancient and honorable game of wicket. Look where you will, you cannot find any

---

*Published in Hartford Courant in 1904.

work on the subject. Yet this game enjoyed a popularity locally that baseball will never attain.

During the past thirty years, Bristol has never thought of playing a game of wicket without "Gus" Smith for bowler. This position corresponds to the pitcher in a baseball game and to play successfully a man has to possess a lot of ability. "Gus" always had the trick of bowling the ball in such a manner that the man at bat was uncertain whether he could hit it and the result was in the majority of cases, that he didn't make runs enough with "Gus" to win the game.

Mr. Smith, many years ago became slightly unbalanced mentally and was sent to the Connecticut Hospital for the Insane at Middletown, where he remained for a long time. All the time he was there he kept the game of wicket in his mind and whenever Bristol had a game on, "Gus" was sent for and did the bowling The unusual feature of a man from an insane asylum, bowling for a wicket game could be seen in Bristol for the last dozen years or so. Later "Gus" went to the Soldiers' Home at Togus, Me., and is there yet, but if there is a game here this fall he will be sent for and will do the bowling.

When the New Britain-Bristol contest took place last fall the management sent to Maine for Smith and he came here bright as a daisy for the game. His work was of the same character as in the old days. He is only slightly demented, but that does not in any way interfere with his ability to bowl a ball that will befuddle the most intellectual man

The center of this ball is tightly wound wool yarn. It was spun and knit by Charity Shelton, the grandmother of Harry Shelton Bartholomew, and she gave it to him for the ball. It has worn out three or more leather covers, and has always been re-covered by Mr. Cook. Always used by the Bristol players at their games with out-of-town people, they rarely used it in practice—and it retired from games with Mr. Bartholomew—so it happens that this ball was never beaten.

in Bristol or New Britain. He is now between fifty and sixty years old, but is as lively as a cricket on the day of a wicket game.

A feature of Bristol's wicket history is that the teams have always been composed of Bristol players, while the teams that had striven to gain the championship have been made up of players from several towns. In Wethersfield there are a few good players and in New Britain there are a few, but the team representing that city at the last game with Bristol was made up from at least four towns. The fact is that wicket runs in the blood in Bristol. The men take to it naturally and where opponents have to spend weeks in practice, Bristol players simply accept the challenge and in nine cases out of ten never practice before the game.

DESCRIPTION AND HISTORY OF WICKET.

The origin of the game of wicket is obscure. Different authorities say that the men who settled New England brought with them the game of cricket, but as this savored so much of the English aristocracy, the hardy men of New England gradually changed the features of the game. It is safe to assume that wicket is practically cricket in an abridged form. In the Yankee game a batsman defends a wicket which a bowler attacks and the largest number of runs that a side gets in two innings wins the game. When a stranger sees a game of wicket for the first time he is struck by the crowd of men on the field, as there are about thirty players at once. It seems impossible for anybody to do anything with such a crowd around, but if the spectator watches long enough he will change his mind.

The field is laid out with what is known as an alley, a smooth space of ground, at each end of which is the wicket. This consists of two pyramids of wood on top of which is a slender stick about five feet long. At the other end of the alley stands the bowler outside of the other wicket. The bat resembles a lawn tennis bat except that the part where the net work is on a lawn tennis bat is made of wood. At the other end of the alley seventy-five feet away, is another batsman of the same side and at each end also is a bowler. The bowler can throw the ball from either end as many times as he wishes, and at times a good bowler will completely mix up a batsman.

The business of the batsman at all times is to defend the wicket and if the wicket is not knocked off its pyramid the man is not out. Sometimes a man will stay at his place at bat for a long time. The special business of the bowler, on the other hand, is to get the wicket off its perch as soon as possible The bowler takes a ball and starts at a point considerably beyond the end of the opposite wicket and runs toward the batsman. When he reaches the wicket he jumps over it and then throws the ball along the ground towards the other end of the alley in an effort to prevent the batsman from hitting the ball and getting a run and to displace the wicket. If the wicket is knocked off, either by the ball or some fumble of the man batting he is out and the next man in the batting order takes his place. Then, on the other hand, the man at the bat is anxious to get runs for his side, but an observer would think it well nigh impossible for any man to knock the ball far enough so that he could reach the other alley and thus count a run.

With thirty agile players standing around the batsman to prevent the ball from going far it would seem impossible for one to get a run, but they are piled up with an ease which makes one wonder whether it is all luck or not. When he hits the ball and one of the other side does not catch it on the fly, the batsman runs to the other end of the alley, and if the ball is not thrown to the wicket tender before he gets there a run is counted. The bowler can change from one end to the other at any time and there are various tricks which are resorted to to put the batsman off his guard. The ball can be delivered by either bowler from either end.

The placing of a field for wicket is similar to that of a cricket field for swift bowling, as the fielders are placed around the wicket. The batsman who puts the ball out of the reach of the thirty alert fielders is performing a more wonderful feat than the man who gets a home run in a baseball game. There are many rules in the game, one of which is that the ball when bowled along the ground must touch the ground before it passes the central line of the alley, or it is called no ball. It is only when the ball happens to hop up a little just before it reaches the batsman that he is able to hit it so as to send it into the field and over the fielders' heads. The batsman cannot run on a bye or a wide as in cricket, but only after the ball has been hit. The batsman can run and meet the ball if he wishes.

In baseball the decisions of close plays are always left to the umpire but in wicket there are really three umpires. There are two referees, one for each side and there is a judge appointed to be a sort of supreme court for the other two. Last fall when Bristol played New Britain, Governor Chamberlain was the judge, but he did not have to go to the field but a few times.

MEMORABLE GAMES OF WICKET.

One of the important games played many years ago in this town was that against a team from Waterbury on the Federal Hill Green on September 9, 1858. Big preparations were made in each town, for the game and the Waterbury players hired a special train to bring them to Bristol. The *Waterbury Journal*, long since defunct, issued the day following a special in which it told the story of the game. The greater part of the day was spent in playing and a band from Forestville rendered music. There was no ill feeling and when the game ended the Waterbury team was defeated by 110 runs. When the contest was over, the players went to the hall and dressed for a banquet which followed at the Kilbourn House. The band headed the procession down Main street hill and the wicket players marched behind to the center of the town, where they were roundly cheered.

The game not only attracted attention in this section of the State, but it assumed such proportions that New Yorkers became interested and it was reported with much detail in the New York *Sunday Mercury* a few days later. That newspaper remarked at the time that Bristol had a wicket team to be proud of. The New York newspapers had a chance to tell the same story twenty-two years later when the Bristols went to Brooklyn and defeated the club of that city.

The most important game ever played in this town was with New Britain on Monday, July 18, 1859, for the championship of the State. For some time previous to the game the Bristols had advertised that they were willing to meet a team from any town or city in the State or any combination to determine which was the better one. After a while New Britain accepted the challenge, although a well-known Bristol man said a few days ago that there were some Hartford players on the team when it reached Bristol. The leading men of each town were as interested as the players themselves and the affair was arranged with a much detail as any sort of public celebration would be in these days. Monday morning dawned clear and hot and it turned out to be one of the warmest days of a warm summer. The whole town was afoot early and a holiday was practically declared. The game was to be played at Federal Hill Green and that plot of ground at ten o'clock on that day presented a scene that will never be forgotten by those who saw it.

Interest had also grown in Hartford to such an extent that a special train was made up in that city for the event. The train left Hartford at 7:30 A. M., with one carload of Hartford people and when it reached New Britain, four cars were quickly filled with excited people. Every car was trimmed with flags and bunting and as the train reached the local station about nine o'clock it presented a grand appearance. The visitors had a band with them and the crowd that greeted them at the station was a large one. It is estimated that when the game commenced there were fully 4,000 people in and around the grounds. Every window of the Congregational Church was filled with people who stood there all day; every available window in houses of the neighborhood was also filled, while thousands stood in the hot sun watching for ten hours the contest that was to decide the supremacy.

A large ring was reserved for the players and the ground was "clear, hard and fine" according to a newspaper of that day. The two teams had elected Judge Charles S. Church of Wolcottville as umpire of the game and Charles G. Thompson of Bristol and E. H. Porter of New Britain were the referees. The game lasted most of the day and was watched by the great crowd of spectators as if the lives of the players depended on their work. The New Britain men were dropped behind early in the game and although they made a heroic effort to win they could not get enough runs to outclass the Bristols. The *Hartford Press* said that "the most remarkable order prevailed during the game and the contestants treated each other with faultless courtesy, the good-natured cheers at each others' mishaps being given and received in the best of spirits. The judges required the umpire but few times during the game and the decisions were yielded to promptly. Toward the close of the day a number of outsiders were unnecessarily vociferous towards the New Britain players but they were an exception." Said the *Press:*—"The sole drink of the day was cold water for the New Britain club and mixed water and milk for the Bristols. Rum was at a discount." New Britain was defeated by a score of 190 to 162, which wasn't a very large margin but enough to determine who were the better players. The score of the game printed in the *Press* at the time is here given for the purpose of showing who took part in that memorable contest:

SETTLING A DISPUTED POINT.

SCENE AT GAME OF SEPTEMBER 4, 1903.

INNINGS.

BRISTOL	FIRST	SECOND	THIRD
George Hendrick,	0b	0b	0b
Elijah Manross,	2b	0c	7b
Franklin Wordworth,	0c	4b	6b
Charles Alpress,	0b	1b	12c
Russell Fellows,	1b	0b	0c
Lucius Osborne,	1b	0b	0b
George H. Mitchell,	0b	0b	0b
J. Fayette Douglass,	0b	0b	5b
Eli Manross,	8c	0c	0
Harry S. Bartholomew,	11c	2b	1c
Franklin Steele,	4t	2t	0b
William Jerome,	5b	7c	0c
Hiram Wilcox,	1c	0t	0b
Henry I. Muzzy,	1c	0c	4c
John Williams,	3c	4c	6c
T. B. Robinson,	4b	0b	1c
Henry A. Peck,	5b	5c	0c
Volney Bradley,	0b	0c	1
Josiah Tracy Peck,	1c	4c	2c
Rufus Sherman,	1b	0b	3b
Hobart A. Warner,	7b	0b	0b
Orrin Tuttle,	2t	1b	0b
Warren McIntire,	2c	12c	0b
Albert Woodruff,	0b	0b	0b
William Carpenter,	0b	0b	1c
Horace Grey,	0b	0b	4c
Charles Smith, Jr.,	0b	6c	3
John Manross,	5	0b	0b
John C. Mack,	5b	1	2c
	75	55	60

NEW BRITAIN

William Maitland,	4c	0b	5b
William H. Hart,	2c	0c	0b
Charles W. Andrews,	2b	4b	1t
Samuel Moore	3b	0b	2c
Henry Mather,	7c	9c	5b
William Burritt,	4t	0c	0c
Andrew E. Hart,	11b	1c	0t
Monroe Stannard,	0b	0b	0b
W. H. Riley,	2b	1b	1c
William Hotchkiss,	0b	0b	2b
John Stannard,	1t	1c	1c
Charles Gilbert,	1c	0b	5c
Daniel Gilbert,	0b	1b	7c
John Burritt,	2b	0b	0b
Walter Parsons,	2b	0b	0b
Philip Corbin,	0c	0b	0b
C. Myron Talcott,	0c	0	2b
Andrew Corbin,	0c	2b	0b
Thomas Brigham,	0b	1b	0b
George Gilbert,	1t	3b	0b
Frank W. Beckley,	0b	5b	0b
Robert Kenyon,	0b	15	1c
Walter Stanley,	4b	2	2c
F. W. Stanley,	0b	0c	0c
Valentine B. Chamberlain,	0b	0b	5b
Edward Stanley,	0c	3c	1c
Thedeus Butler,	4b	5t	3
I. S. Lee,	0b	0b	0b
Walter Judd,	0b	0c	0b
Thomas Hart,	1	0b	5c
	51	53	48

Grand total, Bristol, 190; New Britain, 152.

"b," bowled out; "t," ticked out; "c," caught out.

When the game was over the New Britain enthusiasts marched to the passenger station with their band and boarded the special train. They were a crestfallen lot, although nothing had taken place except the defeat to make them sad. The train that was so gayly decorated in the early morning was now changed to a different garb, for the men from New Britain now dressed the cars in mourning. A generous supply of black bunting had been secured so that the train looked as though it were carrying the body of some famous man to its last resting place. The members of the New Britain club remained behind for the customary banquet, which was served in the Kilbourn House. Those who participated in this feature were the officials of the game, Church and Porter, Philip Corbin, Josiah Tracy Peck, Valentine B. Chamberlain of New Britain and Elijah Manross of Forestville.

Last September at the public meeting of the Old Home Week celebration in the Congregational Church, Charles Elliot Mitchell of New Britain, said, referring to that game: "In 1859, I was half dead with excitement lest Bristol should be defeated. Now possibly because I have lived in New Britain so long, my sentiment is, 'May the best players win.'"

Governor Chamberlain, at the banquet in the Gridley House after the last game of wicket between New Britain and Bristol on September 4th of last year said: "I came to Bristol today as a citizen, simply because I wanted to come and couldn't think of giving it up. I had an enthusiastic desire to see this game and I have seen it. I remember playing wicket against Bristol in 1859. We got licked in good shape that day and I nearly lost heart. To those of this generation, wicket is tame, but to us old boys it's the delight of our lives."

The Govenor wrote the author of this article last week: "I have a vivid recollection of the game between New Britain and Bristol and of the great excitement and large attendance. Of course this is a game of my youth, of which I have very pleasant memories, but it seems to me a game where the interest is fully equal to that of baseball at the present time. I regret that the boys of this generation have not the opportunity of participating in a recreation so enjoyable."

On August 27, 1880, the Bristol Wicket Club went to Brooklyn, N. Y., and administered a decisive defeat to a club made up in that city. The team there had shown good work for some time and the result was a challenge to the one in Bristol. Some of the players that went to the city were:—Austin D. Thompson, Miles Lewis Peck, Harry S. Bartholomew, James A. Matthews, Albert M. Sigourney, Joseph H. Ward, Henry Peck, Henry B. Cook, George Bartholomew, Hiram Wilcox, Michael B. Rohan, Timothy B. Robinson, Harry W. Barnes, Adrian J. Muzzy, Wallace Muzzy, and Theodore D. Merriman.

There was a good deal of curiosity among the new York reporters over the game and the *Brooklyn Eagle*, in reporting it, remarked that there was a regular army of them watching the game from the start. The next day's issue of the *Eagle* contained a column and a half on this strange Yankee game which was played so deftly by the Bristol men. The newspaper said:—

"There were many greybeards on both sides, but what was most striking in the contest to the spectators present, accustomed to witnessing games and matches of all kinds in the metropolis, was the entire

(1) No. 4, Mrs. W. E. Barker *R*, Joe Terrien *R;* (2) No. 14, S. R. Goodrich *O*, C. A. Neal *R;* (3) No. 15, W. O. Goodsell *O;* (4) No. 22, O. C. Ives *R*, Geo. A. Askey *R;* (5) No. 27, A. Q. Perkins *O;* (6) No. 35, P. J. Crowley *O*, Martin Hahn *R*, James McWilliams *R*, Mrs. Andrew Karbaun *R;* (7) No. 26, C. W. Edgerton *R*, Miss Sarah Goodenough *R*, (8) No. 36, C. E. Hungerford *O*, Mrs. C. H. Muzzy *R;* (9) Mrs. Elizabeth Hart *O*.

absence of that spirit of partisan malice of continuous disputing and quarreling, which is so frequent at the local contests on the local ball fields. There was plenty of good-natured chaffing, but the behavior of the contestants throughout the game was that of educated, intelligent, American workmen. It is rather rough recreative exercise, well calculated to give a man a healthy old appetite after a match, besides making him sleep well that night."

The game commenced at ten o'clock and for the first half Bristol was apparently taking things easy, for it looked to the *Eagle* man as if they were to be defeated, but in the afternoon they went in to win and trimmed their opponents in good shape.

The Brooklyn paper made special mention of the fine playing of Cook, Bartholomew and Newell and said they really won the game by their hard hitting. After the game the clubs with their officials, went to the Brighton Beach Hotel, where they had a wicket supper, talked over old times and ended the day, as the *Eagle* says as joyfully as it had been commenced.

FAMOUS GAMES FOR THIRTY YEARS OR MORE.

Henry B. Cook has a book in which are the records of all the wicket games played in Bristol for the past thirty years. The first game recorded in the book was between Bristol and Forestville October 3, 1874. It was a three-inning game and there were the usual thirty men on a side. Bristol won 122 to 111. Among the high scores made were those of A. M. Sigourney, who made 14 runs, H. B. Cook 11, Gus Smith 10.

On the next page is a game played the year before at Wolcottville

(10) No. 57, George S. Reed's store, Harry Wing *R;* (11) No. 61; M. Chirrico *R;* (12) No. 63, A. E. Hare's *Old Homestead Bakery;* (13) No. 62, Searles & Osborne's Meat Market; (14) No. 68, Joe Perry *R,* Joe Foushear *R;* (15) No. 77, W. E. Hough *R;* (16) No. 79, Mrs. A. Bantot *R,* No. 81, Mrs. John Myers *R;* (17) No. 89, Franklin Ball, *R;* (18) No. 95, Arthur J. Hannah *R,* John Whitman *R.*

now Torrington, with the team of that place. The score that day was: Bristol, 312; Wolcotville, 109. A. M. Sigourney made 31 runs, H. B. Cook 14, I. P. Newell 31, S. D. Bull 22, Hiram Wilcox 21, H. S. Bartholomew, 16, J. H. Ward 14, Miles Lewis and Henry A. Peck each 13.

A game with Ansonia in that city September 24, 1873, resulted in a score for Bristol of 282, while Ansonia made only 45 runs. At that game Herbert Booth made 27 runs, M. L. Peck 26, S. D. Bull 24, George Hendricks 21, Hobart A. Warner 18, H. B. Cook 17, and Joseph Bradshaw and Gus Smith each 10.

In July, 1876, the Bristols tackled their old friends, the Waterburys on their home ground. At the end of two innings the score was even each scoring 147. The next inning abounded with fireworks and the Bristols won out, making 83 runs in that inning, thus defeating the men of the Brass City 230 to 193. John Ward made 23 runs, H. B. Cook 17 and James Matthews 13.

Bristol came so mighty near defeat at Waterbury that the members decided to do some practicing before they played a return game. Accordingly they played Burlington, July 29, 1876 and won, 305 to 135. The two clubs played again on August 5th of the same year and the farmers from the hill town got a worse whipping than before, the score being 409 to 109, the Bristols making so many runs they got tired of the sport. H. B. Cook made the star record of his life that day and piled up 47 runs, while Dewitt Stevens made 40, J. H. Ward 29, A. M. Sigourney 24, Henry A. Peck 23, Seth Barnes 20, M. L. Peck 18, H. A. Warner and James A. Matthews each 17. They played Forestville September 9th of the same year and won 153 to 130. The return game with Waterbury was in September; Bristol winning before a big audience, 318 to

(19) No. 105, James Freeman *O*, E. Chioniere *R;* (20) No. 108, John W. Moore *O*, Elmer Berg *R;* (21) No. 111, H. W. Hungerford *O;* (22) No. 119, George S. Reed *O;* (23) No. 118, Mrs. Rosa A. Smith *O*, Charles W. Peck *R;* (24) No. 128, Mrs. G. J. Schubert *O;* (25) No. 136, Louis Rindfleisch *O*, B. F. Whitman *R;* (26) No. 144, Chas. Freeman *R;* (27) D. A. LaCourse's Carpenter's Shop.

230. I. P. Newell scored 33 runs, C. H. Hotchkiss 30, H. B. Cook 24, George Bartholomew 22, M. L. Peck 21, Dewitt Stevens 19, John Ward and Frank Steele each 15, Theodore D. Merriman and "Gus" Smith each 13, J. H. Ward 12.

The next year there was a game between the married and single men of the town which was consequential from the fact that Gus Smith made the record of his life, and which is said to be the greatest record ever made in this or any other State. He made in two innings 54 runs.

Two games were played with Forestville during the next three years and the next big game was with Brooklyn. After this game seven years elapsed before the Bristols went outside the town to play.

On August 15, 1887, they went to Winsted and warmed that team to the tune of 184 to 100. J. H. Ward made 23 runs and Harry S. Bartholomew and H. B. Cook each 10. Winsted played a return game in Bristol in September, 1887 and lost again. The high stand men on that occasion were H. B. Cook, who made 26 runs, Thomas Steele 24, A. F. Alpress 21, J. H. Ward 20, T. D. Merriman 19, A. D. Thompson 15, S. D. Bull 11. Then during the next few years there were games between local teams in Bristol and the first out-of-town club to come here was Newington, which now seeks to take the laurels from Bristol. They played here October 6, 1892, and were defeated 280 to 164. H. B. Cook made 34 runs and S. D. Bull 19. Dr. Howard of the visitors made 29 and J. H. Fish 19.

The next game with Newington was on October 27th in Newington. Bristol being victorious,191 to 111. On August 18, 1893, Bristol again played to Newington, winning 164 to 125. On September 8, 1893, the Newingtons came here and came near winning. The score was: Bristol 84; Newington 80. On October 13, 1893, Bristol went to Torrington

(1) N. Miller O, Joseph Gorsky R; (2) Thos. W. Greeno O; (3) Heny Simpson O; (4) Oscar Linden O; (5) J. Cajkoski O, M. Hayes R; (6) John Lamb O; (7) Chas. Johnson R (first house built on Hull street); (8) Robt. Carlson O; (9) Carl A. Carlson R.

and won from that town 168 to 107. Newington played here again September 7, 1894 and lost 215 to 122. Bristol visited Newington again September 20, 1895 and won 79 to 76.

When Bristol had it Old Home Week celebration the idea of having a wicket game between Bristol and New Britain took tangible form and clubs were organized in each place. The New Britain men went into the matter with great earnestness and did a good deal of practice work during the month preceding the game. Governor Chamberlain readily assented to do the umpiring for the game and Miles Lewis Peck of Bristol was selected as the captain of the team. William H. Hart of New Britain and Captain Henry A. Peck, both survivors of the famous game of 1859 were selected as the judges.

The game was played on September 4, 1903, on the Center street baseball grounds. At 11:30 Governor Chamberlain walked over to the bench he was to occupy and the game commenced. "Gus" Smith who had been imported from the Soldiers' Home at Togus, Me., to do the bowling was on hand and threw the first ball. The first inning was won by Bristol 57 to 41. The first part of the game was concluded at 2:45 P. M., and then the players had lunch and rested for a time. The second half resulted in some of the players making fine scores, but New Britain was easily defeated 109 to 81. In the evening at the Gridley House there was a banquet at which over one hundred were present, the Governor occupying the seat of honor. Miles Lewis Peck was the toastmaster and those who spoke were Governor Chamberlain, William H. Hart, Mayor Samuel Basset of New Britain and John H. Kirkham.

In the next morning's *Courant* appeared the following from New Britain: "There is some talk of challenging Bristol for a return wicket game. The local players are not at all satisfied that the defeat of today could not be turned into a victory on another occasion. The local

(10) Herbert J. Smith *O;* (11) Henry Fleming *O;* (12) Arthur H. Porter *O;* (13) Bernard H. Fallon *O;* (14) James M. Scanlon *O;* (15) John Augdahl *O;* (16) Fred Nichol *O*, Fred Kriger *R;* (17) O. Taillon *O*, Philip Rondeau *R;* (18) Harry C. Wright *O*.

players lacked practice as a general rule, although there were several who played the game exceedingly well. Many of the team were accustomed to batting baseballs and spread their feet apart when striking at the ball. The ball rolling past knocked down the wicket and they were out." Bristol is still waiting for the challenge.

*Since this article was written, the following letter from Mr. Harry S. Bartholomew, in reply to an invitation to act as "judge" at a wicket game in Thomaston, has been found. It is very interesting and gives the rules in the famous "New Britain game."

BRISTOL, CONN., May 17, 1865.

* * * * * * * * * * * * * * *

Enclosed I send a copy of the rules that were adopted when we played with New Britain.

If nothing happens to prevent, than I know of at present, I will try to come to your place July 1st. It is not a very easy job for a single judge to watch and decide all matters in a game, and it often leads to hard feelings. But many times I have thought it best as it saved disputes and time. All that can be asked of a man is to be just and prompt.

RULES OF THE GAME OF WICKET.

1st.—The ball shall be from $3\frac{3}{4}$ to 4 inches in diameter and weigh from 9 to 10 ounces.

2d.—The wickets shall be 75 feet apart.

3d.—The wickets shall be six feet long.

4th.—The tick marks shall be six feet from the wickets.

5th.—The ball shall strike the ground on or before it reaches the center, to be a bowl.

(1) No. 107, Philip Allaire *O;* (2) No. 99, Chas. Stock *O;* (3) No. 98, Karl Helming *O,* Adolf Crowl *R;* (4) No. 77, B. J. McGovern *O;* (5) No. 75, Edmund O. Duquette *R;* (6) Dwight F. Russell; (7) No. 62; Edward Helman *O,* Stanley Heinze *R;* (8) No. 61, M. Aurocolette *O,* (9) No. 53, A. Walter Fish *O.*

6th.—The bowler must start from behind the wicket and pass over it in bowling.

7th.—The bowler shall be within ten feet of the wicket, when the ball leaves his hand.

8th.—A throw or jerk, is in no case a bowl, but the arm in bowling must be kept perfectly straight.

9th.—In ticking, the bowler must stand astride or back of the wicket striking it off from the inside, retaining the ball in his hand.

10th.—When the bowler has received the ball, it shall be bowled by him before it is passed to the other bowler.

11th.—The striker shall in no case molest the ball when it is being thrown in, so as to hinder the bowler from ticking him out.

12th.—There shall be no crossing the alley when the ball is being bowled.

13th.—There shall be no unnecessary shinning.

14th.—In catching, flying balls only are out. A ball caught before striking any other object but the catcher is out.

15th.—In crossing, the striker shall tick his bat down on or over the tick. Mark to have a cross count except when caught or ticked out.

16th.—No stricker shall strike a ball more than once except in defense of his wicket, neither shall he stop the ball with his bat and then kick it.

17th.—No one shall get in the way of a striker to prevent his crossing freely.

18th.—Lost ball may have four crosses run on it.

19th.—No one but the judge may cry "no bowl."

(10) ——— (11) No. 44, Frederick Beatson R; (12) No. 37, Chas. Benson O;, Wm. H. Greenwood R; (13) No. 34, Patrick Farrel O; (14) No. 28, James C. Parsons R; (15) No. 25, Anthony F. Paderewski R, Mrs. Josephine Paderewski R, Edward Mulhern R; (16) No. 19, Frank Moreau R; No. 21, Mrs. Mary J. Guckin O, P. O. Connell R.

Trinity Church

By Florence E. D. Muzzy

Sabba' Day morning 1727. The scattered settlers of New Cambridge living in the clearings of the primeval forest which covered these hills, are early astir—regardless of weather—in carts, horseback, perhaps afoot, for the eight-mile pilgrimage to the meetin'-house in Mother Farmington—there to worship duly as the fathers decreed. And again at dusk—back again, jolting over the rough forest trail—keeping out a wary eye for wild beasts and Indians.

For fifteen years did they patiently submit to this hardship piled upon innumerable other hardships. Then the General Assembly granted their urgent petition that at least during the severe winters, preaching at home might be allowed them. This was the entering wedge; and in 1743 an Ecclesiastical Society was organized and the parish named New Cambridge.

In 1747 the pastor, being a strong Calvinist, was bitterly opposed. And "here it must be noted," says the record, "that Caleb mathews. Stephen Brooks, John hikox, Caleb Abernathy, Abner mathews, Abel Royce, denell Roe, and simon tuttel, publickly declared themselves of the Church of England and under the bishop of london." These with Nehemiah Royce, founded the first Epicopal Society in New Cambridge and were soon followed by Benjamin and Stephen Brooks, Jr., and Joseph Gaylord. These churchmen, all men of prominence, were compelled to pay taxes to the Ecclesiastical Society, as well as to support their own which naturally caused great dissatisfaction.

The first Connecticut priests were missionaries until the American Revolution paid by the English Society for the Propogation of the Gospel in Foreign Parts; each missionary being required to send twice a year an account of his work home to England—these reports furnishing valuable information to the historian.

The first mission-priest at New Cambridge (then a part of the Simsbury Mission) was the Rev. William Gibbs—Harvard 1734—ordained in England, as were all priests of that day. A "true copy" of the "Declaration" of Mr. Gibbs, "to conform to the Liturgy of the Church of England in the Province of New England in America," September, 1744,—may be found in the Bristol Public Library; also a copy of the grant to Mr. Gibbs by " 'Edmund, London,' to perform the office of minister in said Province;" also copy of a document from the Society stating that Mr. Gibbs, upon examination, "appears to be a person duly qualified for promoting ye good work . . . . And whereas, he is by ye Right Rev. Father in God, Edmond, Lord Bishop of London, a member of ye sd. Society, at their request Licenced and appointed to perform all ye Offices of his sacred function at Cymsbury in Connecticut in the province of N. England in America. . . . . We grant him an annuity of ye sum of £30 on consideration yt. ye. sd. Wm. Gibbs doth without delay. . . . . Transport, or cause himself to be Transported to Cymsbury aforesaid." Mr. Gibbs is then recommended to the protection of God and also to "the countenance of his Excellency the Governor of the Province and the Good Will of all Christian People at Cymsbury."*

In a letter to the Society, 1749, Mr. Gibbs says of the New Cambridge churchmen: "the dissenters do oblige them to pay to the dissenting minister, and which they have refused and for the refusal were, four of them committed to the Hartford gaol, in a place where they keep malefactors, upon which they then paid . . . . six more are now threatened." Six months later Mr. Gibbs writes that these men having paid, he himself "demanded the money of the collector, which refused the same, and which put me upon sueing him before one of his Majesty's justices of the peace in Simsbury town, for my Churchwarden's rate of Caleb Matthews, but was cast, and for my refusing to pay the cost . . . . I am . . . . brought to Hartford gaol . . . . where I now am. Thus presumptuous and bold are these men in these parts." Episcopal Mr. Gibbs was also compelled

TRINITY CHURCH, HIGH STREET.

to pay taxes from his own scanty income to support the Congregational ministry. Owing to his ill treatment at the time of his arrest and the shock to his nerves, he afterward became insane and suffered under this cloud till his death twenty-five years later.

About this time a compromise was effected by which the Churchmen were to pay half rates to the Standing Order, until they had a priest of their own to support.

Mr. Gibbs probably retired about 1750; as in a letter dated 1751, the Rev. Dr. Samuel Johnson "the Father of Episcopacy in Connecticut," speaks of the New Cambridge people as having "put themselves under the protection" of Mr. Mansfield of Waterbury—that parish being much nearer than Simsbury.

Rev. Richard Mansfield—Yale 1741—ordained by the Archbishop

of Canterbury 1748—in October of that year took charge of Derby, Waterbury and West Haven. To these were afterward added Oxford, Westbury (Watertown), Northbury and New Cambridge, 1750. If the Rev. Richard Mansfield could have found time between sermons and lonely horseback trips through the woods to record his ministerial experiences, they would make interesting reading in these days of electricity and divided labors. He writes: "I visit them as often as the care of my large Missions will permit." It has been written of him: "The aged . . . . speak with delight of the alacrity with which he would make a journey of twenty miles or more, over an extremely bad road to perform any extra parish duty." After his retirement in 1759, he continued to live in Derby until his death, having been rector of one parish for seventy-two years. These two are but examples of the stuff of which early New England was made.

"It was in 1754, during his ministry that the Churchmen of New Cambridge built their first church upon a lot deeded to the Society by Stephen Brooks. This held four acres and was at the north of the Training Ground, or The Green. The church opened June 10, 1754, with Abel roys and Stephen brooks chosen church wardens. Caleb mathews chosen clerk" The site of this First Church has been marked by Mr. George Dudley Seymour with a boulder of rose-quartz from Chip pin's Hill. Five of the original nine members lie buried in the old yard near. A few of the windows used in this first church are still in existence.

In 1759 upon Mr. Mansfield's retirement, the churches of Waterbury, Northbury, Westbury and New Cambridge petitioned the English Society to appoint Mr. James Scovil—Yale 1757—as Missionary, three churches having been built and membership greatly increased. He accordingly began work at once, settling in Waterbury. His charge consisted of 110 church families and 150 communicants. In less than a year these increased to 117 families and 172 communicants. In New Cambridge in 1760 there were 23 church families and 47 communicants; though in 1772 there were but ten families more and no increase of members. In 1763-4 a large decrease was recorded—probably caused by the removal of younger members to new settlements. Towns were like beehives in those days—always a swarm to newer fields.

In 1762 Farmington was added to this charge. Mr. Scovil in his letters says he officiated every fourth Sunday in New Cambridge, unless hindered by other duties. There seems to be no mention of vacations. He reported that most of the adults in the parish were regular communicants and living in harmony with the dissenters. His first salary was £20 a year, increased in 1764 to £30; but—poor man!—it is once recorded that, "At a vestry meeting . . . . held December 10, 1765, voted to give Mr. Scovil fifteen pounds for the year ensuing, and that we might have the liberty of paing it in pork and grain at the market price." Seventy-five dollars a year, to be paid in pork and grain—collected from five towns, separated by steep hills and unbroken forests! In 1766 he mentions casually that his duties were "full enough for two clergymen if any method could be found for their support." It appears not to have occurred to any economical parishoner that Mr Scovil "go halves" on his produce and cash.

In 1771 Mr. James Nichols graduated from Yale, and being native of Waterbury, he probably assisted Mr. Scovil as lay-reader.

In 1774, "the Rev. James Nichols, a gentleman well recommended, hath lately been ordained" to the parishes of Northbury (Plymouth) and New Cambridge (Bristol) these having "voluntarily engaged to support their own minister." Mr. Nichols was the last man from Connecticut to take holy orders from England and the Society voted him a gratuity of £20, in lieu of the salary usually paid by them—"£60 sterling per annum, and a glebe of forty acres of very good land", was the salary voted by Northbury and New Cambridge; while the records for 1773 says that New Cambridge voted him £40 lawful money yearly "for our part of his stated salary." Also:—"voted, that we would raise

REV. WILLIAM HENRY MORRISON, PRESENT RECTOR OF TRINITY EPISCOPAL CHURCH.

25 pounds to carry him home (to England) to be raised upon our lists at two pence half penny upon the pound." Mr. Nichols was the first priest to live at New Cambridge.

The relations between Congregationalists and Churchmen appear now to have become more friendly for a time, the rates being fairly divided and the Churchmen taking part in nonecclesiastical matters. But when the war came on, the "Church of England" sympathized almost entirely with the Mother Country, and friendliness gave way to active hostility in many places. Shortly after the Declaration of Independence, the clergy of the state held a meeting to decide whether or not to pray that the King "might be victorious over all his enemies." They feared to omit the prayer—they feared to use it; so they shrewdly avoided the issue by suspending services for a few months, when the war would doubtless be over. It is told that one absent-minded clergyman did pray for "our excellent King George"—hastily assuring the Lord an instant later that he "meant George Washington."

Rev. Nichols was an ardent loyalist and his people agreed with him. "Chippin's Hill became a rendezvous for Tory gatherings from all over the state, where soldiers enlisted for King George, and information went forth to New York." The famous Tory Den is not far rom here.

In 1776 Mr. Nichols baptized five; in 1777 but one, in 1780, four. One of these would seem to have been Moses Dunbar, the only loyalist hung in Connecticut during the war; as he was a "recent convert under the teachings of the persecuted ministers, and was a devoted and fearless supporter of the royal cause."

In the State Records, Vol. I, page 259, are the names of seventeen loyalists who were imprisoned on suspicion of being unfriendly to America and who pray for release, testifying that they "had been much under the influence of one Nichols, a designing church clergyman, who had instilled into them principles opposite to the good of the States." At least fifteen of them were Churchmen. Others were punished also in various ways; and it is said that Mr. Nichols was tarred and feathered. It is upon record that he was indicted for treason before the Superior Court, Hartford, in 1777, but escaped conviction. He was some of the time in hiding, and church services were discontinued.

After the war the church building was unfit for use, but meetings were held in private houses for a time. Mr. Nichols was again in New Cambridge, and probably reorganized the church, tho he died in another state, about 1829.

In 1784 it is recorded:—"that we are willing to meet again in the church which hath lain desolate . . . on account of the persecution of the times; and, voted that we would repair the church house." Also: "Voted a penny tax on ye pound on the list of Aug. 1784 . . . . for the purpose of hiring preaching to be paid in wheat, rie or otes." In November the reorganized parish contained 29 voting members; but finding the burden too great, in 1790 they "Voted, That we was desirous of having the east part of Northbury (Plymouth) and the south part of Harwinton to join with us in making up a Society." This new combination petitioned the General Assembly to establish a church at East Plymouth, central to all. This is the well-known, old, "East Church" built in 1791. The New Cambridge Church building was sold to Abel Lewis, who made it over into a barn. Services were discontinued in New Cambridge, until 1834 when "Trinity Church, Bristol" was organized.

The "Second Episcopal Church" built upon land bought from Ira Dodge, was named St. Matthews.

The records, long lost sight of were afterward recovered. They date from 1747 to 1800. They are not complete, but still much fuller than those following 1800.

We find this item: "The present church edifice was built in 1791, finished in 1794, consecrated by Bp. Seabury Oct. 21, 1795. The same day the Rev. Alex. V. Griswold was ordained priest. The next day was consecrated St. Mark's church, Harwinton. These were the last official acts of Bp. Seabury of which there is any record . . . . There were present in convocation 15 of the clergy of Connecticut." It would seem by this that Harwinton had ambitions of her own, and did not take kindly to union for strength. The records bear the inscription: "Fear God and Honor the King."

There seems to have been no especial name of any saint applied to the First Church, situate on the Green of Federal Hill. In 1792 the committee appointed to dispose of the old church is directed on the records to turn over the effects to the "new church in Northbury." This same year delegates were sent to "attend the State Convention at New Haven"—no longer a meeting in a Tory Den!

The meetings of 1793-4-5, give names of choristers, delegates, church officers; the fixing of rates, etc. In 1796 the record states that the "Vestry dissolved." Also in 1796 Mr. Cyrus Gaylord and Caleb Matthews, Jr. were "chosen to assist in reading services and sermons as occasion may require." This was during the ministry of Rev. Alex. Griswold, who also officiated at neighboring towns, and taught school winters. Moreover he was a mighty fisherman. Mr. Welton tells tales of Mr. Griswold in his note book. In 1805, he resigned to accept a call to Bristol, R. I., where he afterward became Bishop of the Eastern Diocese. He wrote, later: "No years of my life have been more happy than the ten I passed in these parishes. . . . . The people were mostly religious and all comparatively free from vice."

From 1797 to 1800, vestry meetings are noted, but little done except regular choice of officers. A "List of vessels belonging to the church in New Cambridge" is given and judging by the names of the givers they were of early date:

PLYMOUTH EAST CHURCH IN 1907.

> "one beacker given by lieut. John row,
> one platter given by Nehemiah roys,
> one bason bought with the church's money,
> one tancut (tankard) bot with church's money,
> A cution (?) given by Caleb mathews,
> Mr. Abel roys, Nehemiah roys,
> one beakcer given by Simon Tuttle."

After Mr. Griswold, the next permanent rector appears to have been the Rev. Roger Searle, from 1809 to 1818. He went from East-Plymouth to "New Connecticut" in the Western Reserve, as a pioneer missionary, and was the founder of the first Episcopal Parish in Cleveland, Ohio. From 1820 to 1829 Rev. Rodney Rossiter officiated, and then resigned, "believing a dissolution of my pastoral connection . . . expedient." This was received with much regret; and somewhere about 1832-3 Rev. Horatio Potter, afterward Bishop of New York, preached at St. Matthews. Following him came students from Washington College, Hartford. Then, in 1834, Rev. George C. V. Eastman occasionally officiated at evening.

About this time, "owing to the arbitrary conduct of a prominent layman at East Church" the subject of reorganizing the New Cambridge (now Bristol) Society was agitated. Several families, descendants of the original founders of the 1747 Mission joined in this movement. This loss of so many liberal supporters lead eventually to the rapid decline of St. Matthews.

The new church was built at the "North side" of Federal Hill, not far from the site of the original church. Mr. Eastman was chosen rector and the church was named "Trinity."

In Mr. X. A. Welton's copies of the old records including those of both First and Second Early Churches, is a list of officiating clergymen, beginning with the unhappy Mr. Gibbs. The dates do not fully coincide but are not far astray. Some of these names were doubtless those of assistants to the rector or "supplies:"

```
  Rev. William Gibbs........................1747 to 1753
{ Rev. Ichabod Camp (converted dissenter)....1753 to 1755
{ Christopher Newton (converted dissenter)...1755 to 1759
  Rev. Richard Mansfield........................to 1759
  Rev. James Scoville...........................to 1773
  Rev. James Nicholls (occasional)..............to 1784
  Rev. Samuel Andrews (of Wallingford) (occasional)...1785
  Rev. James Scoville (occasional)..................1785
  Rev. Ashbell Baldwin.....................1785 to 1793
  Rev. T. Bronson—once in.........................1793
  Rev. Seth Hart—four times in....................1794
  Rev. Alex. V. Griswold...................1795 to 1805
  Rev. David Butler—once in........1795 and once in 1797
  Rev. N. B. Burgess...............................1807
  Rev. Joseph Davis Welton.........................1808
  Rev. Roger Searle........................1809 to 1818
  Rev. Nathan B. Burgess...........................1819
  Rev. Rodney Rossiter.....................1820 to 1829
  Rev. Alpheus Geer................................1829
  Rev. Palmer Dyer.................................1830
  Rev. Norman Pinney...............................1831
  Rev. Allen C. Morgan.............................1832
  Rev. Allen C. Morgan.....................1831 to 1832
{ Rev. Drs. Wheaton and Totten..............
{ Rev. Drs. Wheaton and Totten..............
{ Revs. Horatio Potter, Tyler, Keeler & Purdy...1832 to 1834

  Rev. James Keeler................................1833
  Rev. Geo. C. V. Eastman..........................1834
```

The St. Matthews' list after 1834, when Trinity Church was founded in Bristol, is as follows:

Rev. Fred. B. Woodward.................1839 to 1842
Rev. John H. Hanson.........................to 1843
Rev. S. Sevilious Stocking....................to 1844
Rev. John M. Guion—½ in......................1845
Rev. Henry V. Gardner..................1846 to 1847
Rev. Collis J. Potter—6 mos. in...................1848
Rev. Frederick Holcomb..................1850 to 1852
Rev. James Morton........................1858 to 1860
Rev. Isaac Jones................................1856
Rev. Daniel Burhans............................1857
Rev. Joseph Covell.........................
Rev. Fred. B. Woodward..................1864 to 1867
Rev. Alanson Welton—3 Sundays in............ 1868
    and later, from Nov. 1874 to July 1877 as assistant to Rev. Collis Potter, a native of the town though non-resident, elected rector without salary.
Rev. Collis J. Potter...
Rev. Wm. Everett Johnson, rector of Trinity Church, Bristol, Mission Services about
                              1882 to 1886
Rev. Thos. S. Ockford, a few times autumn of........1898
Rev. J. D. Gilliland..................................

A list of the Society's Church Wardens, Vestry, Committees, and so on, is given in this record, in which many familiar names appear. It may be well to supplement here this list, with that of the Rectors of Trinity, before continuing the account of the Church:

VIEW ON MAIN STREET BEFORE GRADE CROSSING WAS ABOLISHED.

LIST OF RECTORS OF TRINITY CHURCH.
(Time approximately given.)

Rev. Geo. C. V. Eastman	1834 to 1836
Rev. Joseph S. Covell	1836 to 1845–6
Rev. Joseph H. Nichols	1846 to 1847
Rev. Samuel J. Evans	1848 to 1850
Rev. Henry Fitch	1850 to 1859
Rev. Nicholas J. Seeley	1859 to 1867
Rev. A. E. Bishop	1867 to 1870
Rev. Wm. G. Wells	1870 to 1872
Rev. W. J. Piggott, 9 months	1872 to 1873
Rev. J. D. Gilliland	1873 to 1878
Rev. James L. Scott	1878 to 1881
Rev. Wm. Everett Johnson	1882 to 1886
(Lay reader, 1881–2.)	
Rev. E. C. Johnson	1886 to 1889
Rev. J. H. Fitzgerald	1890 to 1897
Rev. Wm. H. Morrison	1897

(July 7, 1907, the Rev. Mr. Morrison is the present incumbent, at whose suggestion this account is written.)

Upon the first page of Trinity Church Records appears a copy by H. A. Mitchell, of the Incorporation of Trinity Church Society, Town of Bristol, Diocese of Connecticut, Sept. 22, 1834. In this the old family names re-appear, together with newer members. It is signed by: Constant L. Tuttle, Ephraim Downs, Daniel Hill, Jeremiah Rice, Herald J. Potter, Nathaniel Matthews, Jr., Thomas Mitchell, Lazarus Harte, Merriman Matthews, Henry A. Mitchell, Elijah A. Shelton, Wm. E. Booth, Attest, Henry A. Mitchell, clerk.

Follows a list of members, with autograph signatures, beginning Sept. 2, 1836. Opposite most of these is written "dead" or "removed," up to 1873. A few may be living—not many. It is believed that but three descendants of these Founders attend service in their Fathers' church today—so vast have been the changes in the town.

After 1873, the signatures are more familiar and include those now in active work. Quotations from this old book itself will give a better insight than anything else could to the history of the church.

At a Vestry Meeting, Oct. 4, 1834, held at the office of (Judge) Henry A. Mitchell, a committee was appointed to "solicit subscriptions for building a church." Note here that "tax rates" have disappeared and no mention is made of Hartford goal.

Dec. 1834—Committee appointed to report on "the most eligible place" for church . . . . Vestry authorized committee to purchase "the lot of Dr. Titus Merriman, near the dwelling house of Alanson Richards . . . and not to pay over two hundred dollars for said lot." . . . . A committee was appointed "with full powers to make contracts for the erection of the church . . . . and receive all monies subscribed."

Feb. 1835—Voted that the church should not cost "over twenty-two hundred dollars, exclusive of the land."

Sept. 1835—"Voted to offer for sail all the slips in Trinity Church, with the exception of the two front slips in the square body, and two back wall slips" . . . Also in a striking commentary on the changes of the past forty years,—at this early meeting of the new society, it was "Voted that thanks be returned to the Cong. Society for the privalidge of holding meetings in their Conference room, and presented by the Clerk."

"Received of the Committee . . . . three hundred and fifty Dollars in full for two Years' service ending August 20th, 1835.—G. C. V. Eastman." Ponder a while on that! Donations possibly not included.

TRINITY CHURCH, BEFORE ITS REMOVAL TO PRESENT SITE.
From Photo loaned by Bristol Public Library,

Here is a curious entry: "I do hereby certify that I consider myself as belonging to Trinity Church, Bristol, and that I calculate to bare my proportion in support of the same.—Samuel Allen."

Meetings of 1837-8, name officers, etc.; and one reports a "bill dew Mr. Covell" of $160.00.

Meeting of Dec. 8, 1838 records:—"Voted that the Societies Committees be authorized to sell all the land on the hill belonging to said Society not occupied by Graves, reserving the right of passage. Voted that the money raised from the sail of the sale of land and Jeremiah Rice Note dew the Society be appropriated to the payment of the dit of the Church. . . . Voted to apply the offering of the Church to the payment of the rearag due Mr. Covell."

1840—"Voted to engage the parochial services of the Rev. Joseph S. Covell the whole of the time for the ensuing year."

1841—"Voted to give leave to any member of this Society to erect Sheds on the west end of the Land belonging to Society." . . . . Voted to build a fence around the Society's grounds.. . . . Balance in Treasury of $62.08.

1842.—As certain members had built sheds on the north end of the land next the church,—"therefore voted to grant, establish, and continue to them the use of the ground on which the sheds are built." Mr. Covell is voted a salary of four hundred Dollars this year.

1843.—The Society finds itself "in debt twenty-seven & 93-100 Dollars"—yet they still continue Mr. Covell's extravagant salary . . . . but—"the Society to have the benefit of the Christian Knowledge Society's money if they vote us any and the meeting was difsolved."

1844—"As near as we could get at the Debts the Society were in Debt between thirty & forty Dollars there fore voted to take sixteen Dollars of Communion funds, provided we could raise Sixteen Dollars more by Subscription & pay up the old Debts. . . . . Voted to apply our Monthly offerings towards paying Mr. Covell's Salary if we do not Raise it without"—the said salary to be increased to $475.00— "and from that up to five hundred Dollars if we can raise it." Cautious, shrewd old fellows—our ancestors! They did not "raise it"—and long-suffering Mrs. Covell doubtless turned again her Sunday silk, and again pieced down the youngster's garments. They voted also to start a subscription to paint the church "but no one to be holden unless we can raise Eighty-five Dollars." This was done in June; and in July they raised enough besides to pay all debts up to Easter previous; besides "the sum of thirty Dollars to buy A Bafs Viol." It is here noted that the year before they had placed a Lightning Rod on the church, and a Chain Fence in front of it—all the modern improvements.

1845—"Voted to apply tenn Dollars Communion offerings to Pay for Lamps Provided we could raise twenty Dollars More Which was raised on the spot." Remember all this was but sixty short years ago; and contrast the bass viol with the organ; the lightning rod with modern fire protection; the chain fence with the lawn; the lamps—successor to tallow dips—with electricity.

1846—Good Mr. Covell goes on a strike:—Voted to engage Mr. Covell, "provided we can raise a salary to his acceptance and also "Voted to give Charles Covill Three Dollars for making fires the past winter." They offered Mr. Covill $450.00, but he had accepted a call to Essex, and so they made him a parting gift of $98.64.

In 1847—Rev. Joseph H. Nichols is reported as accepting a call to the church; but a month later they "Pay Mr. Jones his expenses to New York amounting to ten Dollars to see The Rev. Mr. Cushing." No record of the services of either of these is given; though elsewhere Mr. Nichols is said to have served some time in one year.

1848—Rev. Henry Fitch was invited "to becom permanently our Rector at a Salary of $500.00 pr. Annum"—but Mr. Fitch declined; and they then called Rev. Frederick B. Woodard, who also declined.

"OVERSHOT" WATERWHEEL, FOR MANY YEARS IN USE BY DUNBAR BROS ON SOUTH STREET. PHOTO BY GALE STUDIO.

They paused now long enough to vote to get three Cords of good Maple Wood Cut and Pile for seasoning for the stove for the coming Winter." The lack of punctuation leaves doubt as to which was to be seasoned—wood, or stove by the wood. Then four successive and perhaps stormy meetings "opened and adjourned." At the fifth they agreed to call the Rev. Samuel J. Evans of the Diocese of New York—salary $550.00. Mr. Evans accepted. He had perhaps, city ideas, for at once the pulpit was repaired and altered; the "Church proper" somewhat rejuvenated; and a vestry was "attached to the rear of the church."

As a result, in 1849, the church is reported $100.00 in debt.

1850—Mr. Evans resigned and a second call was extended to Mr. Fitch—salary $500.00 "and give him three Months Notice if we did not wish him longer." This was accepted, and there be some to remember him today.

1851—The bass viol was supplemented by an organ before this, for it was ambiguously voted to "afsume the debt of George Jones on the organ, by his paying Ten Dollars and voted that this Society pay Interest on the Organ."

1852—"Voted that the vestrymen keep the stove pipes from leaking."

1853—"Voted to circulate a subscription paper for paying for the Organ in part or all." The elections of regular church officers, delegates and committees are reported each year, and their names may be found in the Record.

1854—"It was motioned and seckonded to raise the salary of the Rev. Henry Fitch."

1855—Mr. Fitch received $600.00. "When the bills are collected there will be enough to pay the debts of the Parish."

1856—"Parish in debt $165.64—with $177.50 due the parish."

1857—"Voted to have the Communion and Monthly offerings Payed to the Treasurer."

1858—"Voted to shingle the South Roof."

1859—Mr. Fitch's letter of resignation evidently because of the low state of parish finances, is preserved in the records. Voted to call a clergyman "on such terms as the Society will be able to meet." The Rev. Nicholas J. Seely became rector about this time and his monument remains even now, in the church built by his efforts.

1860—"Monthly offerings not otherwise appropriated are to be paid into the Treasury to defray ordinary expenses."

1861—Herald J. Potter, Merriman Matthews and H. A. Mitchell were appointed a Committee of Enquiry in regard to moving church or building new, "in the vicinity of what is called Bristol South Side."

1862—"Voted to Secure the Lot of one Acre and Three Roods on which the House stands known as the late Joseph Ives place."—"Voted, Franklin Downes,* and Herald J. Potter to be a Committee to confer with Henry A. Seymour and secure sd. lot," and Committee appointed to Solicit Subscriptions for new church.

At a Special Meeting, 1862, the purchase of said house and lot was authorized—(boundaries and descriptions fully recorded); the Clerk instructed as to loans and mortgage deed; instructions issued for the sale of "present lot and church building;" clerk empowered to execute proper deed of conveyance if sold; building committee appointed "with full power to contract for, & superintend the erection of a new church building . . . . and use the name of the Society in all contracts"—etc, etc. This Building Committee consisted of: H. A. Mitchell, H. J. Potter, Nathaniel Matthews and Franklin Downes. They were authorized, if funds would allow, to "purchase a New Organ;" and

---

* Son of Ephraim Downes and father of the writer.

three well-remembered musicians of the church (Burritt Darrow, Elmore Welton and Eugene Matthews) were requested to advise with the Building Committee on this head.

1863—A Special Meeting was called in March "at the old Church Building" to consider finances as applied to the now completed new Church Building. The 1863 Annual Meeting was "legally warned and held at their New Church," on Easter Tuesday.

The first service was held the Sunday before Easter. The votes of 1863 cover much ground. "Voted not to pay a Delegate to Convention his expense as has been the custom. . . . . Voted to take any moneys now collected to pay up back arrearages of the past year. . . . . Voted to accept the use of the Organ upon the terms proposed by the owners thereof . . . . to erect horse sheds . . . . to Sell the old Bell and get the 1279 lb. Bell that Mr. Reed saw in New York . . . . to ceil the Bell Tower over head at top of the windows . . . . . to sell Nathaniel Matthews the old Book Case for three Dollars which he has paid for grading . . . . to grade the church grounds" . . . . Finance also occupies considerable time in these 1863 gatherings.

1864—Slips No. 11, 65 and 77 are voted to be given to Mr. Burritt Darrow, organist, Miss Dora Williams, soprano, and Miss Electa Churchill, alto, for musical services. These two ladies with Franklin Downes, bass, and Eugene Matthews, tenor, formed probably the first quartette choir in Bristol; broken only by the early death of Mr. Matthews. Mr. Darrow is the only member now living (1907).

Rev. N. J. Seeley wrote in 1898 that the entire cost of the new church, together with furnishings, organ, grading, fence, etc., "was something over Ten Thousand Dollars." A small note book in the possession of the writer gives a long list of contributors to this fund. A legacy was left the church this year by Daniel Hill.

A BIT OF WEST CEMETERY—SHOWING THE BROCKETT AND WELCH MONUMENTS.

1865-1866—Witnessed quietude and, let us trust, rest from money collections.

1867—There was a call to "supply a rector," Rev. Mr. Seeley having accomplished his task and resigned. The old church was later sold to the Methodists and moved by them to Forestville where it was afterward burned.

1868—Rev. A. E. Bishop accepted a call.

1869—The "Pledge System" inaugurated; and vote passed to take two "contributions" each Sunday. The Weltons were here interested in the music together with various church members—Holt, Olcott, Downes, Prior and others in turn, seldom mentioned on records.

1870—In April Mr. Bishop resigned; and in Sept. the Rev. Wm. G. Wells succeeded him—a pastor beloved throughout the town as well as in his own church.

On April 18, 1870, Herald J. Potter, who had served as Clerk for twenty-eight years, and attended every meeting, with the exception of three, in April 1858—made his last entry in the old Record, and passed on to the Beyond.

1872—Rev. Mr. Wells resigned—and his loss was universally regretted. Rev. Mr. Piggott was called, and remained nine months.

1873—Church land sold to Savings Bank at north of church.—Vote of thanks to Ingraham Co., for gift of clock.—Rev. J. D. Gilliland called.

1874-5-6-7—The entries run smoothly. Names familiar today appear on the record. A few are recalled here—though there were others equally well known for which time for research fails. Some are as follows: Sutliffe, Griffin, Linstead, Funck, Muzzy, Barnum, Olcott, Holt, Woodward, Steele, Welton, Morgan, Pennoyer, Bradley, Sherman, Reed, Downes, Bassett, and so on . . . . Groups of workers in different periods stand out clearly, each group

CANDEE MONUMENT, WEST CEMETERY.

related to its own day—founders, officers, committees, delegates, societies, collectors (the former unhappy "rate gatherer"). It is a pity these all cannot be listed as they worked . . . . .

1878—Rev. Mr. Gilliland resigned; and the Revs. Ockford, Pratt, Rogers and Nichols appear on the baptismal records for one service each.

1879—Seats assigned—not sold.

1880—Owing to infirmities of age, Rev. Mr. Scott who succeeded Mr. Gilliland, resigned. Reference to public printing and insurance policies show changes from the early days. Mr. W. E. Johnson officiated as Lay Reader.

1881—S. R. Goodrich engaged as salaried organist, and certain collections reserved as Musical Fund.

1882—Voted to call Rev. W. E. Johnson as "Rector Elect from date of his ordination." Call accepted. This year the Wardens are authorized to "take such action as they think expedient in regard to the running and switching of trains on Sundays, to the annoyance of members of Trinity Parish." Shades of ye early Church of England—that such a vote should be needed! . . . . A Committee on Repairs was authorized to consider cost of moving the church to High Street . . . . . $5,000.00 offered Church Society for property on High Street—declined. . . . . Committee appointed to lay concrete walk, grade yard, paint church, where it is, and add appliances to obtain more heat"—(this in lieu of "seeing that the stove pipe does not leak!") . . . .

1883—The first Rector's Vacation noted—four weeks, without rebate of salary.. . . . Legacy left church by Mrs. Betsey Hills. . . . . New horse sheds erected . . . . same to be leased on week days, reserving Sunday use for persons attending service.

1884—Special musical action. Prof. Stubbs voted salary to instruct a vested boy choir, and hire Miss Youngs as organist.

MERRIAM MONUMENT, WEST CEMETERY.

1885—Organ moved from loft to chancel and choir seated therein. . . . First record of paid sexton. . . . Voted to "buy presents for boys in choir," and paint rectory.

1886—First record of appointment of usher. Rev. W. E. Johnson tendered resignation; but was requested to reconsider "and devote his entire time to Trinity Parish" (probably in reference to Mission work). Declined, because of previous engagement.

Rev. W. H. Watkins (former Lay Reader) called, but declined. A committee was appointed "to ascertain the availabilities and capabilities of Mr. ——, and others." Mr. Shepard appointed to read during vacancy.

Rev. E. C. Johnson called and accepted. Negotiations with Railroad Co. concerning sale of land, for "a new highway."

1887—"Voted to lease the Church Building for two religious services a week provided the consent of the Bishop be obtained thereto." New concrete walk and stone gutter ordered.

1888—Resolutions of sorrow upon the loss of Hon. Henry A. Mitchell, are entered this year. Voted to sell land upon which church now stands to Wm. Linstead, for the sum of Ten Thousand Dollars (the original entire cost of land, church and all).

1889—Voted either to sell church building or to move, remodel and refurnish present edifice. In the Committee's report we find references to modern improvements, parlor, dining-room, kitchen——such as would have delighted the heart of the New York rector of 1848, who asked but a vestry and repairs! The Committee to move and re-model, consisted of Adrian J. Muzzy, Wm. Linstead and George Steele. Mr. Linstead and the Society each donated a strip of land five feet wide to form a mutual driveway. In July 1889, a cordial invitation from the Official Board of the Methodist Episcopal Church to use their Church Building on Sunday afternoons during the removal of Trinity, was unanimously accepted with hearty appreciation. Voted that the

THE WELCH MONUMENT, WEST CEMETERY.

following articles be .... deposited in corner stone of church on High street:—

"1. All articles .... taken from old corner stone, laid in 1862, and redeposited this day, Sept. 9, 1889, as follows: (Here comes list of Church and Daily papers, etc., of 1862, Bible, 1859, Common Prayer Book, Brief History of Records from 1754 to 1862, etc.)

"2. New articles added: Centennial Celebration of Bristol, 1885, View of Bristol, Daily papers of New York and Hartford, 1889, Bristol Press and Bristol Herald, Church Record, Coins and Fractional Currency, Cover of old lead box in corner stone of 1862, Brief History of Trinity from 1862 to 1889, Rectors and present officers, Dates, etc." The box was deposited in the northeast corner of the Church Building, at the ceremony of the laying of the corner stone, prior to placing the church building in its present location on High Street.

THE SESSIONS MONUMENT IN WEST CEMETERY

This year St. John's Mission of Forestville joined with Trinity Parish..... Rev. E. C. Johnson resigned. Rev. J. C. Linsley called and declined..... Rev. Alfred Lee Royce has vote of thanks for his gift of a Prayer Desk, in memory of his father.

1890—Strip of land sold to Savings Bank. .... Committee of four appointed to welcome strangers. .... Rev. S. S. Mitchell called, declined. .... Rev. J. H. Fitzgerald called, accepted. .... Vote of thanks to Mrs. W. E. Sessions for her gift of a Lecturn to parish. .... Vote of thanks to Mr. Rogers for gift of Prayer Book and Hymnal. .... Rules of Order for Vestry Meetings adopted. .... Memorial Altar to the late Henry A. Mitchell purchased by vote of Vestry. .... New Rectory built facing High Street, east of church, upon old rectory garden. .... Agent appointed to represent Society at Hearing in regard to change of R. R. grade crossing.

1891—"Voted that we sign the testimonial of Charles N. Shepard to the Standing Committee of the Diocese of Connecticut."

1892—Voted instructions to cover chancel window from the intense colored light . . . . dispose of horsesheds, etc. . . . . Ladies' Aid Society offers to be responsible for half choir salaries, which is "fully appreciated" by Vestry, but declined, tho the Ladies' Aid agrees to pay the Quartette. . . . . At the first meeting noted as "held in the Guild Room," a legacy from E. E. Shelton is gratefully acknowledged. . . . . Vote of thanks to Mrs. Hannah Griffin for gift of $125.00 to purchase a Flagon. . . . . Other gifts to the church are: The Bishop's chair and cushion from Mrs. C. Adeline (Downes) Perry; Reading Desk for Altar in memory of Mrs. Dora (Williams) Jacobs, from the Ladies' Aid Society, two brass Super-Altar Vases from Adrian J. Muzzy and Augustus Funck, inscribed in memory of departed ones; memorial windows; Altar Rail; stone baptismal font and cover; a set of Altar Linen; besides other gifts for use, beauty or memory, not all recorded in the book.

1892—Voted to sell the "corner lot"—Main and High Streets— to Mr. Linstead.

1893—Church lighted by electricity.

1894-5-6—Minutes of several stormy meetings at one of which Bishop Williams was present. . . . . Record of several cash gifts.

1897—Rev. J. H. Fitzgerald, resigned. . . . . Rev. John Nichols offered his services as supply without salary during the vacancy. This was accepted with grateful appreciation. . . . . Mr. Geo. Dudley Seymour was authorized to "do such work as he shall deem proper" in the old Episcopal burying ground on the hill near the site of the First Church." (The old burying ground was put in repair and a boulder later was placed upon the site of the First Church by Mr. Seymour.) . . . . On Oct. 6, 1897, it was voted to extend a call to the Rev. William H. Morrison. This was accepted and Mr. Morrison continues in the office at this date, July, 1907.. . . . . He is one of the six Rectors who have remained for a period of about ten years, during the one

LEVITT MONUMENT, WEST CEMETERY.

THE HULL MONUMENT IN WEST CEMETERY.

hundred and sixty odd years of the Parish existence. Great good has been accomplished under his leadership, especially during the period from 1902 to 1907. Membership has increased. .... In 1898 the amount raised by the Parish for church expenses was $892.00; in 1906, a little less than $4,000.00.

1905-6-7—The improvements show the work of an active Parish. Among them are noted: Painting of church building; church newly carpeted; Sunday school rooms (The Guild) re-decorated; a new brass pulpit and new chancel; and a beautiful Memorial Organ presented by Mrs. Margaret Sutliffe in memory of her husband, Samuel M. Sutliffe and of her mother, Mrs. Hannah Griffin. .... For many years Miss Inez Beckwith is noted on the records, as organist; with Mrs. Florence Leigh as leader of the Vested Choir. .... The Rectory, during these years has been improved by the introduction of electricity and gas, a far cry from candles, and fire-wood cut early "to season." .... New concrete walks are laid and grading is also done, in these recent records. .... The Ladies' Aid Society has always been a most important factor in the life of the church; and for many years has helped to lift the burdens of a struggling Parish.

Of the usual "church troubles" Trinity has had only its allotted share; but until all men are so constituted that all think alike there must be that difference of opinion, which, in the end is all good, for it spells progress, after all.

Since 1860 the record shows year by year, the name of the beloved and venerated Bishop Williams, side by side with the Confirmation Lists. Following him comes our Bishop Brewster and twice only does the name of Bishop, other than these, appear: Bp. Seabury and Bp. Niles of New Hampshire. . . . . Partial lists of marriages and baptisms appear elsewhere—tho seemingly very incomplete. . . . . The Clerks of the Parish were: H. A. Mitchell, 1834; Elijah Shelton, 1835-1842; H. J. Potter, 1842-1871; A. H. Barnum (supply), 1871; S. M. Sutliffe, 1872-1880; A. J. Muzzy, 1880-1895; Geo. T. Waterhouse, 1895-1897; A. J. Muzzy, 1897 to date, 1907. It would be of great interest had these records all been writ fuller—personal relations of pastor and people—the life of those who made the Church; but as each entry is complete or lacking according to the whim of the Clerk who recorded, it is only left for the student of human nature to read between the lines, and then shrewdly guess the history of those old days—the toil of those bygone people—their self-denial, service, and weary struggles, all for conscience sake.

GENERAL VIEW OF THE OLD NORTH CEMETERY.

NOTES ABOUT THE FIRST EPISCOPAL CHURCH.

The Burning of the First Episcopal Church and Some Otems Items of Early History.

By Mrs. Ellen Lewis Peck.

THE First Episcopal Church stood on the Federal Hill Green on the spot where is now a boulder placed by Mr. George D. Seymour to mark the site. Its adjacent burial ground was directly east of the building, where it still remains.

Mr. Abel Lewis, my grandfather, who had built a house in 1793, on the corner and kept an inn, bought the Church after it had ceased to be used for religious purposes and used it as a barn. One day, Mr. Lewis's brother, who lived near the north burying ground saw a steady line of smoke rising from the back end of the barn and mounting his horse rode down to see what it meant. There had been blasting near there and it was supposed a spark of fire went through a knot hole into the hay. The windows and contents of the barn excepting the hay were removed, but the heavy oak timbers and hay burned constantly for over three weeks. Water was impossible to be got on the Hill, but finally a long rain came and nearly put it out, but it smouldered for some time longer.

The windows were afterwards put into a gambrel roofed house, which Mr. Lewis built as a dwelling-house and store for Mr. George Mitchell, who had been a clerk for Mr. Thomas Barnes in a store near his dwelling-house opposite the Bristol House. Mr. Mitchell lived in the east part of the building and the store was in the west end. After his removal the store was continued by Mr. Lewis till he removed to the foot of the Hill at the end of Maple street, after the Hartford and Danbury Turnpike, now North street and Farmington avenue, was opened. The south half of the second story of his house on the Hill had a nice ball room, where numerous balls and dances were held and he furnished suppers and also sold beer and other liquors and cakes.

On public occasions, as training days, etc., the Green was the center of festivities. One Fourth of July, tables were set on the Green for 500 guests at once, who had a generous dinner of turkeys, chicken pies and all accompanying "fixin's." The tables were screened by a row of trees set as an arbor by the young men of the town. The church bells were rung in the early morning and an oration and address delivered.

There was no road running east and west between Lewis and Federal streets till the turnpike was cut through, when Mr. Hinman built a rival tavern at the foot of Maple street. Mr. Lewis bought him out and moved into that house in order to keep the stage passengers and horses which he did until his death in 1820. After his death his daughter ran the tavern for a while and the store on a small scale till her death in 1853. The store and house were known as Aunt Roxa's for many years.

Old Episcopal Cemetery

THE accompanying material was kindly furnished by Judge Epaphroditus Peck, and his letter of October 14, 1897 to the *Bristol Press*, will prove of great value in supplementing the information obtained by the Rev. Charles N. Shepard.

Editor of the Bristol Press:

"Mr. George Dudley Seymour, who had lately cleaned up the old Episcopal Cemetery on the hill, has handed me the following copy of the inscription on the stones made by Rev. Charles N. Shepard in 1891:

The fragments last mentioned are shown by a list of stones made by Miss Kezia A. Peck in 1851, to belong together, and to be a stone to the memory of Lent Price, who died 1809, aged 42."

Perhaps here it will not be out of place to express the earnest hope that in the immediate future, steps will be taken to permanently preserve this historic old burying place. A simple iron fence would afford the needed protection, and future generations will point to this spot as the most historic place in the town. To the editor, it seems almost a sacrilege that it is left in its present unprotected condition. Who will do this little labor of love!

Inscriptions from the remaining tombs in the burying ground of the Pre-Revolution Episcopal Church of New Cambridge, copied by Mr. Charles N. Shepard of Bristol, April 20, 1891.

In Memory of Mr
Jarard Alling Hoo
Departed This Life
September The 12 1794
in the 24 year of His
Age

you yong companians all
of the dere youth
That by his deth are cold
read this truth
That suddin you may die
AWay your soul may fly
Into eternity
Which hath no end.

(This stone appears to be the first work of a youthful amateur.)

Here lies ye Body of
Mrs. Phebe Wife of
Mr. Thomas Beach she
died Aprl ye: 30th 1758
in ye: 91st year of
her Age.

The graves chown in the illustration are numbered, and are as follows:

No. 1. Mrs. Athildred Carrington.
No. 2. A. B. Carrington.
No. 3. Salmon Mathews.
No. 4.
No. 5. Mrs. Hannah Hill.
No. 6. Mrs. Ruth Mathews.
No. 7. Rhoda Royce.
No. 8. Maurice Mathews.
No. 9. Mrs. Nehemiah Royce.
No. 10. Stephen Brooks.
No. 11. Jarard Alling.
No. 12. John Hickox.
No. 13. Abel Roys.

Here Lieth Interr'd
the Body of Mr
Stephen Brooks
Who Departed this
Life May ye 16th AD
1773 in the 71st year
of his Age

Behold & see as you Pass by
As you are now so once was I.
As I are now so you must be
Prepare For death & follow me.

A. B. Carrington
departed this life
June 2, 1824
AE 29.

(Footstone, marked A. B. C.)

In
Memory of
Mrs. Athildred
wife of
Mr. Lemuel Carrington,
who died
Dec. 10th, 1811
In the 58th year
of her age.

A pleasing form, a generous gentle heart,
A good companion, honest without art,
Just in her dealings, faithful to her friend,
Belov'd in life, lamented in the end.

Hear Lies the
Body of Mr JOSEPH
GAYLORD Who
Departed This Life
Octr ye 20th AD 1791
In the 70th year of
His Age.

In Memory of
Mr Cornelius
Graves Junr who
Departed this
life October the
7th 1781 in the 25
Year of his
Age.

(Footstone marked Cornelius Graves.)
Probably the father of the noted Stephen "Graves" of the Tory Den.

Here lies
ye Body of
Hannah wife of
Cornelius Graves
She died Novmr
ye 17, 1759 in
ye 34 year of
her Age.

In Memory of
Mr John Hickox
he died Febry 14th
1765 in ye: 68th
year of his Age.
(Footstone marked J. H.)

In Memory of Mrs
Hannah Hill ye: Wife
of Mr Dan Hill
She Died Febry ye
13th 1766 in ye:
29th year of
her Age.
(Footstone marked Hannah Hill.)

In Memory of Capt
Caleb Mathews
Who Departed this
life April ye 7th 1786
In the 83d year of
his Age.
(Footstone marked Caleb Mathews.)

In Memory of
Mrs Ruth Consort
of Capt Caleb
Mathews. Who
Departed this life
November 3d
1785 In the 73d
year of her Age.
(Footstone marked Ruth Mathews.)

In Memory of
Mamre Daugtr of
Capt Caleb & Mrs
Ruth Mathews She
died April ye 25th
1759 in ye 14th year
of her Age.
(This stone is almost illegible, but I think I have deciphered it correctly. The grave is short and the footstone marked M. M.)

Iu Memory of
Mr. NATHANIEL MATHEWS
who died Feb. 15, 1806
aged 78 years
"Blessed are the dead who die in the Lord.
(Footstone marked N. M.)

In
Memory of
Mr. Salmon Mathews,
Son of Mr Nathaniel &
Mrs. Martha Mathews,
who died
Dec. 27th 1803
aged 35 years.

Death is a debt to nature due,
Which I have paid and so must you.

In Memory of Mr
Abel Roys he Died
Septr ye 6th 1769 in ye 69th
year of his Age.
Behold and se as you pass
by as you are now so once
was I

(Footstone marked A. R.)

Here Lies the Body of
Mr NEHEMIAH ROY
CE Who Departed This
Life Feb (?)—
AD 1791   In the
69th Year of His Age

Behold and see, as you pass by
As you are now, so once was I.
As I am now so you must be,
Prepare for death and follow me.

(The inscription on this stone is in very poor condition; the latter part of the fourth line is wholly gone and the figures of the year and age (except the *6*) are very indistinct, and I may have read them wrongly. The footstone is marked Nehemiah Royce.)

Here Lies Buried, the Body
of Mrs RHODA ROYCE
the Wife of Mr Nehemiah Ro
Royce, Who Died August
29th AD 1786: in the 61st
year of her Age.

(Footstone marked Rhoda Royce.)

The top of a marble slab in two pieces inscribed:

In
Memory of
NT RICE

Another marble fragment possibly of the same slab marked:

AE 42
Ten tender plants
To mourn my dear
O may we meet
When Christ from dea

Oct. 27, 1899, Rev. Alfred Lee Royce identifies this fragment as belonging to the above stone, by the age and the mention of ten children.

It appears from record of inscriptions in the old yard made by Miss K. A. Peck in 1851, that this stone is to *Lent* Rice, who died 1809, ae 42.

Brightwood Hall*

By Fred. Calvin Norton

Passengers on the Highland Division, passing through Bristol, notice as they look out of the car windows an imposing castle of granite on the hill west of the town, within sound of the busy hum of Bristol's industries. It stands as a sort of sentinel over the thriving town of commerce much as did the old English castles over the more peaceful towns of England and Scotland 500 years ago.

Brightwood Hall, the name of the castle, is more interesting to the traveler when he is told that the owner, Mrs. Helen Atkins-McKay, daughter of Bristol's millionaire clock manufacturer is deterred from finishing the structure on account of ill health and that the finishing touches will probably be made after her death.

For years she planned, worked and thought over the erection of this magnificent country seat and its completion was one of the great aspirations of her life; but the erection of castles of this sort entail much arduous study and planning. Mrs. Atkins-McKay is now well along in

BRIGHTWOOD HALL

* Published in Hartford Courant, May 27, 1904.

years, her health is poor and she will probably be an invalid the remainder of her days, so that the completion of the granite pile, the aim and thought of her life will have to be left for others. She has spent on the estate to date at least $150,000 and its completion means that $75,000 more will have to be spent.

Brightwood Hall, had it been completed, would have been a sort of monument to the Welch family of Bristol, of which Mrs. Atkins-McKay is a member. Her father was the late ex-Senator Elisha N. Welch, who commenced his business life here wheeling iron in a small foundry on North Main street but ended as the millionaire clock manufacturer of Connecticut. He was born in East Hampton and came to Bristol when a young man and bought out the old Brown clock factory in Forestville. He did not know anything more about clock making then than any other shrewd Yankee did; but he built up a business that was not equalled in the state during his life. His clocks were known all over the world and he died in Bristol not so many years ago, possessed of an estate estimated at $3,000,000.

He left several children, the oldest of whom was Mrs. Atkins-McKay the castle builder. Her old home was for many years on West street in Bristol and there she was born in what is now known as the Gaylord house. Her father lived there when a young man and in that neighborhood he saw the first early successes of his busy life. When Mrs. Atkins-McKay became older she gained the idea that she wanted a fine country seat in the neighborhood of her youthful home and with this in mind she planned for years towards its realization. A woman of more than ordinary ability, of wide reading and scholarly inclinations, she travelled in all parts of the world. Fourteen times she crossed the Atlantic Ocean. She visited the art galleries of Venice, Milan, Rome and other cities, studied their treasures and gained much information about her scheme of erecting a castle in her native town.

She visited Abbotsford, the home of Sir Walter Scott, studied the medieval castles in both England and Scotland and was a student of classical architecture for many years before she consulted an architect about the building of her house.

At length she decided on what she wanted to do and coming to her old home here purchased from the Tracy Peck estate about sixteen acres of land which was directly across the street from where she lived as a girl. The tract of land is on a hill west of the town and is one of the best locations for a country seat that one will find short of the Berkshires. It is on an elevation of 500 feet from the sea level and from the grassy slopes in front of the castle, can be seen all but the lowland district of the busy town. To the north and south stretch the ranges of green hills that make Bristol so beautiful. To the southeast can be seen Meriden Mountain and South Mountain in Bristol which divides New Haven and Hartford Counties.

About eighteen years ago the owner first commenced the work of transforming her purchase into a baronial estate and it has gone forward each year until within a short period when ill health compelled her to desist from further effort. First she caused to be erected a granite wall four feet high around the front portion of her estate. A lodge for the superintendent was erected at one corner, after the English fashion and at the top of the grassy slope the foundations for the castle were laid. The architect who drew the plans was H. Neil Wilson of Pittsfield, Mass., but Mrs. Atkins-McKay's was the real planning mind of the whole structure. The granite for the noble pile was taken from the town much of it was quarried on the estate she bought and it is of particularly fine color and effect. And the stone was cut and fitted on the grounds.

A Frenchman, Adrian Taillion, who had come from Canada a few years previous, built the castle. Without any training except what he gave himself, he started the work and carried it on until it was stopped

RESIDENCE MRS. ATKINS—MCKAY—BRIGHTWOOD.

a few years ago. He had a big gang of experienced masons at work on the castle but it is said of him that he always laid more stone than any two of the men laboring for him. The work of constructing the mammoth structure was slow and only a small portion was done each year. It is now completed so far as the outside is concerned and the interior is partitioned off so that one can get an idea of the grand proportions of the hall.

The main building is of Gothic design, principally, although Mrs. Atkins-KcMay told the writer that it belonged to no particular school of architecture but that it was a combination of several. It is about 150 feet long and 50 feet wide, is really three stories high and has an ell part erected in the rear which is 40 by 30 feet. The whole building is of granite which is of a light color. The illustration accompanying this article shows the castle facing the east and the main entrance to the hall is shown in the center.

At the left of the illustration is the tower with the English battlements from which one obtains a fine view. Below this is the porte cochere, where the visitor alights from his carriage to enter the hall. At the left hand corner under the tower is the entrance, a grand affair of massive granite. The interior is divided into three rooms of large dimensions, each being at least forty by thirty feet in size. The reception hall is the first room as one enters and this is designed for a drawing room also as was the custom in the baronial castles of England. At the further end is a great fire place and in the south end of the reception hall is an alcove twenty by twenty feet which is designed for the library of the hall. The ceiling of paneled oak is very high and the windows of modern size. Two large doors lead to the hall proper as was the case in the old castles of England. This baronial hall is one of the most impressive rooms in the whole building.

Over the main entrance to the hall is the coat of arms of the family, the Latin inscription on which is "Auspice Numinee." The tablet which is of granite and cleverly executed was made in England and brought to Bristol by Mrs. Atkins-McKay. The hall reaches across the castle and overhead to the extreme top of the big building. It is modeled after the old style so that the ceiling of the hall is the roof of the castle. This admits of a fine effect inside, with a grand staircase winding up to each side of the broad galleries surrounding the hall. This reminds one of the pen pictures of the galleries in the baron's hall of old England, and of the festal occasions which so often took place around them.

The hall is large enough to hold a troop of horsemen and an assemblage of people numbering several hundreds, could find easy accommodation inside. One Bristol contractor said not a great while ago that the completion of this hall alone meant an outlay of at least $10,000. The whole building is on a grand scale and no expense has been spared thus far to make it a thing of beauty and of massive elegance.

From the hall the visitor walks through another great portal into the banquet hall of the castle which is a huge room with high ceiling. as large as the reception hall at the left of the illustration. Doors open from the banquet hall to the quarters of the maids and butlers and in the rear of the castle is the servants quarters. The kitchen is back of the banquet hall. The floor is of cement and tile was to have been laid in it. A great oven large enough for a New York hotel occupies a prominent place.

After seeing the first floor one ascends to the second by the great staircase which is a work of art so far as stair-building is concerned. A wide hallway extends across the rear of the chambers which are six in number and all of such size as castle chambers should be. The tower chamber is one of the pleasantest in the castle and there is still one

LOG CABIN ON FALL MOUNTAIN.
(*Photograph by Milo Leon Norton.*)

THE OLD SAMUEL LADD HOME—PEACEABLE STREET.
Since destroyed by fire.   *Photo loaned by Mrs. Bassett.*

above this which makes that portion of the building three stories high. The attic is so arranged that one may go there and walk out on the battlements to enjoy the view. The whole structure impresses one as European and makes one realize more than ever the grand homes of old England.

The stable is of similar construction to the castle and is not far from the main building. There are quarters for the stablemen and coachmen and the ceiling of the stable is finished in quartered oak, representing a large outlay of money. In a large chest in the harness-room is a fine bear skin rug which Mrs. Atkins-McKay purchased in Stockholm a few years ago. This is said to be worth at least $1,000 and was originally designed to decorate the hall of the castle.

Mrs. Atkins-McKay erected in the summer of 1888 about the time work was commenced on her castle, a cottage in the rear of the big structure which she intended for a summer residence during the time her great house was building. She has occupied this at different periods since but most of her time has been spent in traveling abroad. She is now and has been for some time at her cottage which she calls Brightwood cottage and will probably always remain there. In the south range of mountains a few miles away stands a log cabin that was erected by her a few years ago and this is on an elevation of nearly 1,000 feet above the sound. From this place the views are grand and are probably not exceeded in the state.

THE TOWN BUILDING, NORTH MAIN STREET.

Bristol's Early Industries

By Hon. Noble E. Pierce.

The following is a compilation of Roswell Atkins' Notes on the early industries of Bristol, other than the clock business, by Hon. Noble E. Pierce. One or two unimportant changes are placed in brackets.

THE early history of the manufacturing enterprises of the town is for the most part extremely vague as to location and dates. The earliest ventures in that line seem to have been confined to the immediate necessities of the people—the grist mill to fit the grain for consumption, the spinning wheel and loom, the fulling mill, the tannery and the shoe shop, the tin shop in which was made the ovens, sometimes called Dutch ovens, to set before the large fireplace to bake meat and bread, at the same time the potatoes and other vegetables were boiling over the fire or roasting in the ashes beneath.

Previous to the incorporation of the town (1785) only tradition and the assessment rolls give any clues to the occupations of the inhabitants. This is indicated by the imposition of what was called a faculty tax, apparently because certain men were able to command more compensation than from farming alone. Thus we find in 1760, in addition to the farms and stock assessed to Benjamin Churchill, twenty-four pounds faculty tax. He had a saw-mill but what beside that is not known. Abel Lewis 1775, fifteen pounds, he was a merchant; 1765, Samuel Deming twenty pounds, and in 1775, thirty pounds—this was for a grist mill; Zebulon Frisbie and Thomas Hungerford ten pounds,

VIEWS OF TERRY & ANDREWS CLOCK FACTORY, 1856.
Factory was built on ruins of old Terry Factory, burned about 1840. From Ambertypes taken by William A. Terry.

they had tanneries; Josiah Holt, 1776, fifteen pounds, he was a doctor; James Lee eighteen to twenty pounds, his business was blacksmithing; James Stoddard 1760, thirty-five pounds, business unknown; Seth Roberts twenty-five pounds, probably for a store; Gideon Roberts twelve pounds, probably for the manufacture of clocks. In 1779, Abel Lewis was assessed seventy-five pounds, innkeeper and merchant. These taxes were not always the same for different years, nor does the list state the ground on which the faculty tax was laid, and the amounts vary from one to thirty-five pounds.

These taxes were continued in a similar form, giving the occupation and substituting the decimal system for the pounds up to about 1849. In 1823 there were forty-nine persons assessed from five to seventy-five dollars; in 1810 doctors were assessed thirty-four to one hundred dollars; taverners twenty dollars, blacksmiths seventeen dollars; grist millers thirty to forty dollars; sawmills ten to thirty dollars. carpenters and joiners ten to thirty dollars; clothiers forty dollars; tinners fifteen to fifty dollars; tanners and shoe makers seventeen dollars; silversmiths seventeen dollars; attorney-at-law one hundred and sixty-seven dollars.

The first gristmill built within the parish limits was, as far as can be known, owned by Joseph Plumb in 1741 on the south side of the river from the Pierce homestead, followed soon after by the sawmill on the north side opposite where a clothing shop was also built, about the same time Samuel Deming owned the gristmill called the Langdon or Downs mill, which was erected soon after the other.

Tanneries and shoe shops were also located in different sections soon after the middle of the century. Jabez Roberts in 1750 tanned leather by the old English processes until it would withstand attacks of water for any reasonable time, the local forests furnishing the material from which to extract tannin suitable for the different uses, hemlock for the sole leather, oak for the uppers, and sumac for the linings and finer soft leathers.

Wood turning was also established, the forests furnishing abundance of the best materials for making articles for household use. trenchers or plates, clothes pins, rolling pins, mortars and pestles, faucets for the cider and vinegar barrels, awl handles, pin boxes, lather boxes, which were made of different woods to suit the fancies of the customers, and a lookingglass was inserted in the cover of the box. combs were manufactured quite extensively made from wood or the horns of cattle and there were several shops for their manufacture; numerous spinning-wheels required in order to furnish clothing, demanded a supply which was made by the mechanical skill of our fathers. and the whole outfit from the growing of the wool upon the body of the sheep and the pulling of the flax in the field to the finished cloth or stocking was provided for by local manufacture, and specimens of this handiwork are still numerous in the garrets of our farm houses with the initials of the makers' name branded on them—J. B. for Joel Baldwin, who made a foot lathe for turning the several parts; he lived at what is now called the "Crittenden place" in Stafford district. (Joseph Byington, also made spinning wheels on Fall Mountain, and some of the "J. B.'s" are his initials.)

Tin shops seem to have been quite numerous in different parts of the town, one of two on red stone hill, one on the south mountain, one on the corner of School and West streets and in other places. In 1804, there were in all eleven tin shops, together with two cloth manufacturers, four tanners and shoe makers, two gristmills, three sawmills, two carding mills, four blacksmiths, one silversmith, two merchants, two doctors, one lawyer, and several taverns.

The tin shops sent their production far and wide over the country until the Yankee tin peddler was known throughout the whole country, they were not all from Bristol, but Bristol supplied its full quota. These tin peddlers also sold the wooden trenchers and other wooden articles before mentioned.

Attempts to develop the iron industry of the town were early entered upon. Beside the blacksmith, search was made for iron ore, and the most prominent place was on north Chippin's Hill near the Burlington line. This was leased by Luke Gridley who experimented upon the ore which was pronounced of excellent quality, and in order to work it successfully he applied to the Legislature for the privilege of a lottery to raise about three hundred pounds, his petition was endorsed by about forty of the principal business men of the surrounding towns, the petition was referred to a committee who made a favorable report thereon. It is said that some of the ore was reduced and it is probable that it was reduced at what was called the forge, which was situated at what is now known as Pequabuck Falls near the Plymouth line. This forge was established before 1785 as part interests therein were sold from time to time until 1807, John Rich sold his interest to Sherman Johnson, retaining the use of one fire sufficient to make one ton of iron per year for five years; that this was not a blacksmith shop is evident, as mention is made of one on the same premises "located near the forge."

The clock industry created a demand for castings for weights, also bells, which was met by the establishment of a casting shop or foundry, and there were two of this kind as early as 1831. Orrin Judson and Lord S. Hills established one on what is now Union street, east of the brook where Claytons' shear shop stands, and another was established on what is now West street by George Welch, the former of these was not long used as it was not easily reached and was probably sold to Welch and Mr. Hills was taken into the employ of Mr. Welch. It is also said that Mr. Hills at one time had a small foundry on what is now Valley street for a short time.

GILDING ROOM, "BRICK SHOP," MAY. 1888.
From Photo loaned by Mrs. Gilbert Lyon.

The Welch casting shop passed into the hands of Elisha N. Welch who removed it to North Main street, where it was managed by him until about 1852, when Mr. Welch entered into partnership with Mr. Harvey Gray and bought out the machine business which had been established by Atkins, Allen & Co. on West street, of which Mr. Gray was superintendent, and removed it to a shop built for the purpose adjoining the foundry. In this shop machinery was made suitable for making clocks. Presses adapted for the particular uses of clockmaking, lathes for turning the several parts, so that every one of a thousand should be a duplicate of its fellow. The foundry business was carried on in this place under different names until the National Water Wheel Co. took possession of this plant for the manufacture of water wheels.

The Bristol Foundry Company followed and conducted the foundry business for a time on the ground where Eaton's elevator and the brick shop of the J. H. Sessions & Son, factory are now located, the business being conducted by Gray & Bentley, and later by Gilbert Bentley and Andrew Terry, the ground where the foundry was located having been held by them under a lease from 1873 until 1876, when they bought the land on Laurel street and removed the foundry thereto, greatly enlarged it, and in 1879 sold out to John H. Sessions, who associated with him his son, William E. Sessions, and they conducted the business under the name of the Sessions Foundry Co. at that place until 1895, when the building of the present plant of the Sessions Foundry Co. was completed, which is now the largest and best equipped foundry plant east of Chicago. [*End of the Atkins Notes.*]

Concerning the old forge, which was the forerunner of the present extensive iron works of the Sessions Foundry Co., the writer has information obtained from his grandfather, who was familiar with the plant, and who was well acquainted with its proprietors. Ore was brought from the Salisbury mines by teams, unloaded at the top of the hill, near where the railway embankment now is, or a little east of where the railway emerges from the hills and parallels the road near the Devil's Backbone. The old road was obliterated for some distance when the railway was built, but can be traced for a short distance at the top of the hill, at about the same height as the railway. It was lowered about twenty feet by the railway company, and about twenty feet more by the tramway company, when the Terryville trolley line was built. The ore was conveyed to the forge which stood on the bank of the river, through a chute, and was there wrought into rods by means of trip-hammers, to be sold to blacksmiths. In digging for the foundations of an enlargement of the buildings, iron ore was discovered, and some of it worked into bars. One of the workmen told the grandfather of the writer, that he could always tell when he was forging iron from this ore, as it was far superior to the Salisbury product. It was not obtained in large quantities, however, and its working was only experimental. The cost of hauling the ore over the Litchfield hills, was the principal reason for the abandonment of the enterprise.

So valuable a water privilege could not escape the notice of the thrifty manufacturers of Bristol. A natural dam, consisting of a spur of rock, covered with a thin layer of soil, and forest trees, which extended in the remote ages across the valley, at this point not more than a hundred yards in width, the only connecting link between Fall Mountain and Chippens Hill, was gradually eaten away by the river, until a chasm was made through which the lake above was eventually drained. So narrow was this natural dam it was possible to sit astride of it, and because of its resemblance to the spine of some imaginary monster, it was dubbed by the early settlers, the Devil's Backbone. It was not until 1837, however, that the privilege was utilized, after its abandonment by the Forge Company. In that year, inspired no doubt by the organization of The Bristol Manufacturing Co. and the building of the South Side satinet mill, a knitting company was formed, known as

The Bristol Falls Co., to whom Ebenezer Miller and Hiram Camp conveyed their interest in the property, which included the water privilege, factory and other buildings standing thereon. The company was not recorded as an organization until 1839, with a capital of $20,000; Richard Peck, President, Ebenezer Miller, and Joshua I. Taylor, Directors. Chauncey and Noble Jerome, and other leading business men of Bristol, were stockholders. Reports were made as required by law in 1839 and 1840, but there is no further report. It is understood that it was a short-lived affair.

In 1853 The Ames Shovel Co. was organized by Bristol capitalists, John Birge, President, with a capital of $10,000, acquiring the buildings of the Falls Co., and manufacturing shovels, spades, scoops, hoes, forks and other farm implements. The stockholders were John Birge, Theodore Terry, Edwin Ames, E. L. Dunbar, Winthrop Warner, Alphonso Barnes, Thomas Barnes, 2d, and Wallace Barnes Annual reports were made in the years 1854, 1855 and 1856, when they ceased. The business was wound up, and put into the hands of S. R. Gridley, as Receiver. After standing idle a number of years the buildings were torn down, sometime in the sixties. It was understood that Edwin Ames, the Secretary of the Company, was taken into the business principally to secure his name, and to thus profit by the reputation of the firm of the same name in Massachusetts. It was not a success.

It may not be generally known that the Stafford oil well was not the first effort made to strike "ile" by Bristol capitalists. In 1865, the Pequabuck Oil Co. was organized, with a capital of $12,000; Noah

THE OLD INGRAHAM CLOCK-CASE SHOP ON POND STREET. FRONT PART WAS OLD CONGREGATIONAL CHURCH, BURLINGTON.

Pomeroy, President, S. R. Gridley, W. H. Nettleton, H. A. Seymour and Wallace Barnes, being the other stockholders. A well was bored in the oil regions of Pennsylvania, Mr. Seymour superintending the work, but no oil was found.

In 1869 The American Coal Barge Co. was organized in Bristol, with Elias Ingraham, as President. A coal barge was constructed at New Haven, after a design by a Mr. Preston, of that city, which was calculated to load and unload coal mechanically, obviating the expensive process of hand shoveling which had been previously employed. The barge was a success, coal being taken on at New Jersey ports, transported to New Haven and unloaded there, at a great saving of expense. The hard times coming on, about that time, discouraged the investors, and the business was sold. The Consolidated road is now practically following the same method in transporting and unloading its coal supply.

RAILROAD VIEW, 1863.   *Cut loaned by Milo Leon Norton.*

THE BRISTOL PRESS

A. S. BARNES.

THE founder, editor and for seventeen years proprietor of *The Bristol Press*, was C. H. Riggs. The first number of *The Press* was published on March 9, 1871. *The Press* was started in a small way upon prepaid subscriptions and borrowed money with very insufficient material and machinery, but it made the best of circumstances and held on its course.

The paper owed its origin to the suggestion of Rev. W. W. Belden, then pastor of the Congregational Church, and to the helping purses of Messrs. N. L. Birge, Elias Ingraham, J. H. Sessions and Josiah T. Peck, each of whom advanced forty dollars in aid of the enterprise. All were repaid out of the first year's profits. The subscription list at first consisted of about two hundred and fifty names.

The first office occupied by the paper and connected job printing business was the second story of a frame building twenty feet square, adjoining Seymour's block, next to the railroad. Here, with a Washington hand press for newspaper work, and a Novelty job press, the editor started a five-column folio "patent outside" paper, the type for the inside being mostly what had been worn out and thrown aside in an office in New York state.

The editor had gained some knowledge of type-setting and printing while teaching school, but was far from being expert in the art. However, with the assistance of a girl, who was greener at the business than he was, he resolutely set to work, and in the face of difficulties, he entered upon his new career.

Before the first year was ended new quarters were secured in S. E. Root's factory on lower Main street where with power presses, the business greatly increased. In 1877 a building was erected by H. S. Pratt on Main street, opposite Muzzy's corner and to this building the business was removed, Mr. Pratt becoming a partner.

Mr. Pratt remained in the partnership less than two years, when Mr. Riggs resumed the entire ownership. In 1880 another office was built in the rear of what was then Gale's studio on the east side of Main street. This building about 1890 was removed to Riverside avenue where *The Press* was published for seventeen years.

In August, 1888, Mr. Riggs the founder of the paper, disposed of the business to Messrs. Haviland & Duncan, of Southington. Mr. Thomas H. Duncan became editor and manager and remained as such until December, 1891, when the Bristol Press Publishing Co., with a capital stock of $10,000, purchased the business. The first officers of the company were: O. F. Strunz, President; J. H. Sessions, Jr., Vice President; S. K. Montgomery, Secretary; Richard Baldwin, Treasurer. Mr. C. H. Riggs was employed as editor and manager until April, 1893, when he was succeeded by Mr. H. H. Palmer of New Haven. Mr. Palmer remained with *The Press* less than a year when Mr. Wallace H. Miller took charge of the paper as editor and manager.

Mr. Wallace H. Miller continued as editor of *The Press* and manager

The photograph herewith reproduced, represents Mr. Riggs and his office force, probably in 1882. At the left are Walter H. Royce and Miss Bertha Evans. In the door at the right stands George A. Fish; farther in front is Herbert E. Garrett, and seated by Mr. Riggs is Sidney M. Card. In the doorway at the left stands Rev. Asher Anderson, the pastor of the Congregational Church at that time.

of the Bristol Press Publishing Co. until February, 1901, when he was succeeded by Mr. Chas. F. Olin. Mr. Olin remained with *The Press* as editor until June, 1907, but in March, 1902, he was succeeded by Arthur S. Barnes as manager. Mr. Barnes is a Bristol boy and was born on March 12, 1871, the very year and month in which *The Press* made its initial appearance before the people of Bristol.

Under Mr. Barnes' management *The Press* has been increased from a six column to a seven column paper and the number of pages from eight to ten, twelve and sometimes sixteen. Associated with him in carrying on the work are Wallace H. Miller as editor and Thomas A. Tracy as assistant. Mr. Miller returned to *The Press* in June, 1907. The officers of the Bristol Press Publishing Co. are—President, Gilbert H. Blakesley; Secretary and Treasurer, Arthur S. Barnes; Directors, Gilbert H. Blakesley, Otto F. Strunz and Arthur S. Barnes.

In January, 1907, the land on Riverside avenue occupied by *The Press* building was sold to Mr. Wm. E. Sessions and a plot 53 by 90 feet was purchased from Mrs. Edward E. Newell on Main street, the former site of S. E. Root's factory. A two-story brick building has been erected there, and in September, 1907, *The Press* removed to its new home. This new building is 74 by 36 feet and is of mill construction throughout, and is situated on the very same spot where *The Press* was quartered in S. E. Root's factory from 1872 to 1877.

The Press considers it as its first duty to faithfully chronicle local events in Bristol and to reflect public opinion on local affairs. In politics it is independent, believing that such is the only course that a local paper can take. It strives always to live up to the commendation of one of its former editors who spoke of it as "a high-grade, influential home newspaper, one that always works for the welfare of the town and its best interests."

MAIN STREET, 1868.

The Yankee Clock Industry

Edited by Milo Leon Norton.*

THE late Roswell Atkins devoted much time to the search of records, and all other available sources of information, in pursuit of knowledge as to events in the early history of Bristol.

Mr. Atkins was careful, painstaking, and cautious, in his investigations, and what he committed to writing was the result of as thorough investigation as it was possible to make. The sources of information as to the earliest industries are extremely meagre, the business enterprises of the eighteenth century being conducted on so small a scale as never, in the opinions of the active participants, likely to become of interest to future generations. In the preparation of this work it has been thought best to give Mr. Atkins' notes on the clock industry in full, substantially as he wrote them, making only such minor additions to them as may be thought necessary.

Ephraim Downs Clock, 1825.

---

*It was the intention to fully illustrate this article, but after mature consideration it was thought advisable not to attempt to do so in the limited space at our disposal—as to do justice to the subject hundreds of clocks would have to be shown.

In a preliminary way it may be of interest to say that the first Yankee clock-making, as a business, was undoubtedly established in Bristol by Gideon Roberts, a soldier of the Revolution, son of Elias Roberts, who was a victim of the Wyoming massacre in 1778. His home was the house now owned by Asher C. Bailey, on the Fall Mountain road, afterward the residence of his son, Hopkins Roberts, and known a generation ago as the Hopkins Roberts place. The house itself has a historic interest as occupying the site of one of the first houses in that section of the town, built by Moses Lyman, in 1736. The Roberts house was built by Alvin Cole, a brother of Katherine Cole Gaylord, and came into the possession of the Roberts family by purchase.

One of the several tin shops that were in active operation in Bristol prior to the Revolution, stood on the west side of Wolcott street just north of the residence of the late Alonzo Rood. When the grading for the lawn in front of the house of Edward Bradley was done, the open cellar hole of this old shop was filled up, having existed until that time, about twenty years ago. This shop was purchased by Gideon Roberts, as his business had increased, and was moved by him to the southwest corner of his front yard, where it was used by him as a clock shop, and may be accorded the distinction of being the first clock shop in the United States. This probably took place not far from the year 1800. The building is still standing, having been purchased by Asahel Hinman Norton, and attached to the east side of his house, now occupied by Jason H. Clemence. Mr. Roberts made the first clocks by the aid of a foot lathe, and such hand tools as the saw, dividers, hand drills, etc., from wood, the first clocks not being cased, but bracketed to the wall. Some of his later movements were cased in the tall cases in fashion at that time. His method of disposing of these clocks was to take three or four of them with him upon horseback, to New York and Pennsylvania, where he sold them at twenty-five dollars apiece. It was in Pennsylvania that he became acquainted with the English cherry, which the thrifty Quakers had transplanted from British soil, and he brought pits of the cherry home with him, planting the same and distributing to his neighbors. There are cherry trees still standing which are the descendants of these original trees, but it is doubtful if one of the originals is left. The Fall Mountain cherries were long famous, and were in great demand. But the cherry was not the only acquisition that he made from the Pennsylvania Quakers; he adopted their religion as well, and also the peculiar dress and quaint speech of the Society of Friends. He died in 1813, and it is said that his business of clock making had increased at that time so that he had four hundred movements in the works.

NOTES ON THE CLOCK BUSINESS,

By Roswell Atkins.

The earliest manufacturers of clocks seem to have been confined to the Roberts family, so far as the records show, and though the date of 1790 is given, it would seem as if it might have been even earlier. But soon after the opening of the new century others turned their attention that way, and in 1808, Barnes & Waterman, Levi Lewis, Sextus O. Newell; in 1809-1811, Joseph Ives, probably in company with Manross, and located on the Self Winding Clock Co.'s site; Chauncey Boardman and Butler Dunbar, at the Ashworth shop just south of the burner shop; Amasa and Chauncey Ives, at the Hiram C. Thompson shop; and Elias Roberts & Co., on the brook near the Dana Beckwith place; made clocks. This last shop was used for different purposes: German silver combs, tinder boxes on the plan of the lock and flint, also the wheel and flint, prior to the introduction of lucifer matches. These were made by the Iveses, Joseph and Shailer, and later by Bryan Richards, in this shop. Others soon engaged in the clock business, some making cases and buying movements, putting their own names inside. In 1821, Barnes

& Johnson, also Chauncey Boardman and Col. Joseph A. Wells, in the east part of the town, near the turnpike. This shop was first used for wood clocks, later brass clocks were made there, and the tools were sold to Mr. Ingraham. Cutting boxes for cutting hay, were also made there by Wells, Barnard & Co. Seymour & Churchill also made movements, also some rules.

In 1821, Chauncey Jerome bought of George Mitchell a house and land on South Street, to be paid for partly in clocks. He afterward bought a small shop built by Treat, Lee & Alle, on the north side of the river, west of what is now Main Street, for making any article connected with the business, and in 1824 entered into partnership with Elijah Darrow and his brother, Noble Jerome and they, in 1826, secured the laying out of Main Street. They then bought land on the east side of the new street; erected a shop on the west side, for making cases, about where the Ives meat market stands; a movement shop where the spoon shop is, but closer to the road; and, soon after, a finishing shop on the west side opposite; and a large barn on the north side of the river, for stabling the horses necessary for the economical prosecution of their business. There was no other means of transportation of merchandise to New Haven or Hartford, until the completion of the canal in 1826 or 1827; and as the canal was useless during the winter, horses had to be employed until the completion of the railroad to Plainville, in 1847, and to Bristol, in 1848.

The coming of Mr. Jerome gave an additional impetus to the clock industry, and this was followed by the location of Ephriam Downes, an experienced clock maker, in 1825, he having also purchased of George Mitchell the property on which was a small shop, and which has since remained in the family until its purchase by the Liberty Bell Co. This property was to be paid for in clocks for Mr. Mitchell, who supplied peddlers with various articles of manufacture.

In May, 1828, Samuel Terry, of Plymouth, a brother of Eli Terry, bought the old grist mill property south of Pierce's, on which, beside the mill, was a small shop owned by Simeon Johnson, and also a tannery. The mill was converted into a clock manufactory. Charles Kirk, about this time, made clocks in a shop on the north side of the river from the mill, soon after buying the shop on Race Street, and carrying on the business a number of years, when he sold out and removed to Wolcott, where, with his sons, he invented and manufactured musical clocks.

Samuel Terry, was succeeded in the clock business by his sons at the old stand, for some years, followed by Terry & Andrews; and the shop owned by C. E. Andrews, and used as a manufactory of light hardware, was built by them. Auger bits were made there, and that line of business is still followed. Of the sons of Samuel Terry, Theodore removed to Ansonia, for a time, and was also located in Pequabuck, where Scott & Co.'s mill stood. William A. Terry still resides here, a man of scientific attainments in any line in which he becomes interested. He is the inventor of a calendar which is absolutely perpetual, taking up the leap-year changes, automatically. He was for many years one of the most skillful photograghers the country afforded; and his microscopic discoveries in the realm of diatoms, have given him a world-wide fame.

George W. and Eli Bartholomew, commenced making wood clocks in Edgewood, about 1829, and continued till about 1843, a part of the time in connection with cabinet making. The site they occupied had been formerly used by Martin Byington, and Isaac Graham, as a gristmill, a sawmill, and a distillery. Since 1855, bit braces have been made continuously by the Bartholomews.

In 1830, George Mitchell, Rollin and Irenus Atkins, bought the old Baptist meeting house (the second church edifice was built that year), and moved it northwest to the location of the shop where they had carried on wood turning and comb making since 1819. Clock making was conducted in it by different firms: Mitchell & Atkins; Atkins & Downs (Anson, a brother of Ephraim); and R. & I. Atkins, for a number of years, until the saw business was established in 1836, under the name of Frost, Merriman & Co. A dam was built by this firm some distance above Hickory Park, a raceway dug, and a shop erected near the building occupied as an isolation hospital during the smallpox visitation a few years since. This was used as a grinding shop for saws, but was abandoned and the shop removed to the top of the hill, opposite the stone house, on Divinity Street, where it became the residence of Constant Welch, for many years. In 1857 the firm name was changed to I. Atkins & Co. An extensive business was done by this concern, who made cotton gins, and other machinery. The firm failed about 1858, in the saw business, and it was conducted by the Jessups, of New York, for four years, then for two years more by H. Porter, who removed it, in 1864, to the melodeon shop, where The Porter Saw Co. was succeeded by The Penfield Saw Works. In 1851, the manufacture of clocks was recommenced by the Atkins Company, and continued until 1880. Barnes Brothers continued the business for a few years, when the business was abandoned, and the shop was finally burned.

In 1835, Alden A. and E. G. Atkins, and Noah E. Welton, bought the Churchill sawmill, and built a shop for the making of clocks, principally, also making spool stands, work-boxes, etc. Norman Allen afterward took the place of N. E. Welton, and the firm name became Atkins & Allen. The business was conducted until about 1846, when the shop was sold to Smith & Goodrich, afterward passing into the hands of The Bristol Brass & Clock Co., through the J. C. Brown interest. After two fires, the present shop is known as the Burner Department of the Bristol Brass & Clock Co.

In 1833, J. C. Brown, W. G. Bartholomew, and William Hills, of Farmington, who were jointly engaged in the business of cabinet making in Bristol, bought the land where the Sessions Clock Co. is now located, on the south side of the river, and secured the privilege of building a dam, and of thus creating a water privilege, of the owners of the north side of the stream, erecting a factory for making clocks. There were some changes in the firm, previous to the erection of the shop, and a company, consisting of William Hills, Lora Waters, J. C. Brown, Chauncey Pomeroy and Jared Goodrich, known as The Forestville Manufacturing Co., commenced the manufacture of brass clocks in the spring of 1835. There was then no highway nearer than Pine Street, until Church Street was opened to and across the river, afterwards extended eastward to the factory, and southward to Pine Street. The business continued to increase until in 1845 their establishment was turning out more finished work than any other in town. About this time F. S. Otis built the shop called the Otis shop (recently removed), and made a fancy case inlaid with pearl. This being something new in the market, increased the sale of clocks, as every dealer was bound to have the latest styles. In 1853, the shops of J. C. Brown & Co. were consumed by fire, which involved so much loss that an assignment became necessary, not only of that company, but of others with which they were connected. Elisha N. Welch, being the largest creditor, purchased the entire plant, together with the Otis shop, The Forestville Hardware Manufacturing Co., erected in 1852, and the Elisha Manross factory, of the assignees, and combined the business under one management. In 1864 the E. N. Welch Manufacturing Co. was organized. In 1868, the Welch, Spring & Co., firm was organized, which occupied a factory that stood on the site of the present electric power house of the Sessions Co., and also the factories recently occupied by the Codling Manufacturing Co. Since the Welch Company was organized, all the factory buildings except two, have been destroyed by fire, but have arisen some of them from their ashes, in larger and better proportions for the economical production of the different varieties of clocks produced by the Company. (This was written by Mr. Atkins prior to its acquisition by the Sessions Company.

How, after the death of Mr. Welch, in 1887, the extensive plant went into the hands of a Receiver; was reorganized, with J. Hart Welch, at the head; and how, after his death, it was acquired by the Sessions Company, who have largely increased the plant and its output are matters of recent history, too well known to need definite mention.)

Elias Ingraham, the founder of The E. Ingraham Co., came to Bristol from Hartford, where he was working at his trade as a cabinet maker, in 1828, and entered into the employ of George Mitchell, in the old building long used by the Ingrahams as a case shop, on the site of the Turner Heater Co.'s plant. Mr. Mitchell was desirous of introducing a new style of case equal to, or superior to, the bronze pillar, invented by Jerome. Mr. Ingraham designed a very handsome case, with carved columns, having lions' paws at the bases, and fret work at the tops. They proved to be excellent sellers. The movements were made by Ephraim Downs. The old factory referred to, was originally the Congregational Church of Burlington, and was used as a cotton mill after its removal to Bristol. After working for Mr. Mitchell for about two years, he commenced work for Chauncey and Lawson C. Ives, at what is known as the Eureka shop, continuing in their employ until 1836, when he contracted to make cases for Davis & Barbour, who were shipping cases and movements separately to the south, where they were put together, thus saving the payment of the heavy state licenses. In 1843 the firm of Brewster & Ingraham was formed; Epaphroditus Peck, and after his death, Noah L. Brewster, representing the firm in England. In 1848, the firm was dissolved, and the firm became E. & A. Ingraham, by the admission of his brother Andrew into partnership. Their shop was burned in 1855, which stood on the site of the old movement shop, and the business was afterward continued by Mr. Ingraham in the old cotton mill, which was enlarged from time to time as more space was needed. About 1860, the old hardware shop, which stood on the corner of Meadow and North Main Streets, was purchased and moved to the site of the burned factory, and was made the movement department of the firm of The E. Ingraham Co., until the completion of their new and commodious movement factory. Edward Ingraham became a partner in his father's business in 1859, and the joint-stock company was formed in 1881, consisting of Mr. Ingraham, his son and grandsons, becoming one of the largest establishments for the manufacture of clocks in the country. Mr. Ingraham was born at Marlborough, in 1805, and died in 1885. His son Edward died in 1892.

In 1843, The Bristol Clock Co. was organized, with a small capital, for the purchasing and vending of clocks; consisting of Chauncey Jerome, Elisha Hotchkiss, Edward Fields, Elisha Manross, E. C. Brewster, Joseph A. Wells and Augustus S. Jerome. This company was organized, primarily, for foreign trade, reporting that in 1844, $1,935 worth of clocks had been shipped to China, and that their expenses had been $400. In 1852, The Brewster Manufacturing Co. was organized, for the purpose of making and vending clocks. It consisted of E. C. Brewster, Wm. Day, Augustine Norton and Noble Jerome. These firms were principally for the purpose of extending the sale of clocks of American manufacture to other countries, the outgrowth of which has added largely to the success, financially, of the clock industry. At the first venture in this line, Mr. Jerome shipped a cargo of clocks to England, in charge of Epaphroditus Peck, accompanied by his son, Chauncey Jerome, Jr. This attempt was considered unwise by many, and failure was predicted. But the prices at which they were invoiced for entry at the custom house, though high enough to be very remunerative, excited the suspicion of the customs officials that they were being priced at too low a figure, and so they exercised their right to add ten per cent. to the invoice price, and seize the whole cargo. Another cargo was despatched as quickly as possible, and was also seized in the same way. After that the officials concluded to let the Yankees sell their own clocks, which they did, with the result that the foreign trade in clocks was thoroughly established, and a good deal of money has been brought into town thereby, especially at times when, without it, business would have been very dull if not dead.

The Bristol Clock Case Co. was organized in March, 1854, with a capital of $20,000. It consisted of thirty-five of the prominent business men of that time, as follows: J. C. Brown, Walter Williams, W. W. Carter, Eli Barnes, H. E. Merriman, George Merriman, Almon Lewis, Daniel Lardner, Henry Beckwith, W. McCracken, Erastus Foster, Benjamin Ray, H. M. Burnham, J. U. Doolittle, S. P. Burwell, Hopkins Stephens, Roswell Webster, Geo. Goodrich, J. T. Peck, Ashel Butler, D. P. Spear, Samuel Beckwith, Robert Beckwith, N. L. Birge, E. N. Sexton, Anson Beckwith, J. A. Sweetzer, E. C. Goodwin, Tracy Peck, S. P. Newell, H. K. Hotchkiss, Jr., Richard Peck, A. P. Goodrich, Carlos Welton, and W. D. McClenithan. Most of them were residents of the north village, and a number of them were clock-case makers as well. A large shop was built at the North Side, at Doolittle's Corner, near the railroad, on land now owned by The Sessions Foundry Co., north of the road. The enterprise was soon abandoned, and the shop stood idle for a number of years. In 1861, it was taken down and put up in Forestville, taking the place of the old Alden Atkins clock shop, destroyed by fire, and was used for the manufacture of lamp burners, and also for the manufacture of mechanical and other toys of tin.

Other people have, at different times, been engaged in the manufacture of clocks: Byington & Graham, located west of the Bartholomew shop, at Edgewood, made cases; Terry, Downs & Co., at the Ephraim Downs shop; Beach, Hubbell & Hendrick, at the Manross shop; Atkins & Porter, at the Merritt Atkins shop, Stafford; Barnes, Hendrick & Hubbell, at the old (original) Manross shop, afterward becoming the property of Laporte Hubbell, which firm made the first marine clocks, invented by Bainbridge Barnes; Solomon C. Spring, at the Codling & Co. factories, who made the same rolling-leaf pinion movement for clocks and regulators, as were made by the Atkins Clock Co., until the business was merged with the Welch company, and removed to Forestville; A. S. Platt & Co., where the Wallace Barnes plant is now located; Noah Pomeroy, at the H. C. Thompson shop, and others.

The early clock industry, in its development, necessitated the establishment of numerous separate shops for the manufacture of parts which could not be economically made in one factory at that time; and the making of verges, pendulum rods and balls, wire bells, and later, of lock-work, for the striking mechanism, and pillars, ratchets and pinions, became important industries. W. H. Nettleton conducted the business of lock-work making for many years successfully, which afterward passed into the hands of George Jones, and, finally, was absorbed by the Ingraham company. Albert Warner made clock verges for many years, up to the time of his death in 1888. All these separate industries were gradually acquired by the large clock concerns, and the small manufacturers went out of business, or took up other lines.

Col. E. L. Dunbar was a pioneer in the manufacture of clock springs of steel, purchasing of S. Burnham Terry the process of tempering coiled springs in 1847. About the same time John Pomeroy succeeded in tempering them by another process, and these inventions cheapened the cost of clock springs, which had formerly been imported from France at a cost of from one to three dollars each, so that the manufacture of cheap clocks became possible. The Dunbar spring business has been continued up to the present time, and is one of our substantial industries, though the original business of clock-spring making has given place to the manufacture of springs for many other purposes.

Wallace Barnes commenced the manufacture of clock springs in 1857, on the site of the present factory, and the business has been conducted there continuously ever since. In 1858, in company with Col. E. L. Dunbar, under the firm name of Dunbar & Barnes, steel springs for hoop-skirts were extensively made there, the upper story of the shop being used for the braiding department, in which the flat steel springs were covered with cotton, starched and finished ready to be made up into crinoline. During the life of this firm the building then known as Crinoline Hall, afterward known as Town Hall, was built. At first the lower story was used as a wood shed for storing the pine wood used for tempering the springs, but was afterward closed in and occupied as a furniture warehouse and for other purposes. After the dissolution of the firm of Dunbar & Barnes, the hoop-skirt business was conducted about two years by Benjamin & Doremus, of New York, wire braiders and finishers; and by John Fairbanks, who wove the tapes, and made up the wire and tapes into the finished skirts. The shop was burned in 1866, when the hoop-skirt business was discontinued. Since the death of Wallace Barnes, in 1893, the spring business has been increased to its present immense proportions through the able management of C. F. Barnes.

SUPPLEMENTAL NOTES.

This concludes Mr. Atkins' notes on the clock industry. From other sources we learn that among the early makers of clocks, in Bristol, John Rich made wood clocks in a shop which stood just back of the James Holt place. Levi Lewis, mentioned by Mr. Atkins, had a shop near the Chandler Norton house, on Cog. Hill, "Cog." being an abbreviation of Cogswell, a family once resident there. Lewis had, at one time, 1500 movements in the works, which fact created much excitement in the community, as well as doubts as to his sanity. Indeed, when, in 1803 Eli Terry, the founder of Terryville, and the father of the American clock industry, commenced to manufacture two hundred clocks a year, people thought him crazy and prophesied that he could not sell so many, as the country would be overstocked! In the fall of 1837, a year of financial disaster, and especially hard for the struggling clock manufacturers, Chauncey Jerome was collecting what he could of debts and scattered clocks, throughout Virginia and South Carolina, when, one night, in his room in a hotel at Richmond, Virginia, he conceived the idea of making a cheap, one-day, brass clock. That idea, put into practical shape by his brother, Noble, who made the first one-day, brass movement, revolutionized the clock business, and put new life into the industry, and fortunes into the pockets of the men who followed Jerome in their manufacture. The old wood clocks, while good timekeepers, could not be shipped across the water, as the wheels would swell, and become worthless. But Jerome saw an opening for the sale of the cheap, brass clocks in England, and determined to make the venture, with gratifying results. The introduction of the clocks in England, however, was attended with much difficulty, the dealers believing them to be worthless because so cheap. One merchant went so far as to turn Mr. Jerome's agents out of doors for trying to induce him to have anything to do with the Yankee clocks. England made clocks for the world, and for these presumptuous Yankees to send their cheap toy clocks over there filled the English dealers with indignation. But finally, one merchant in London was persuaded to permit two of the clocks to be left in the store, saying that he did not believe they would run at all. The clocks were set running, and the next day when the agents called they found that they had been sold, and were told to leave four more. They were sold in a few hours, when the sale was increased to a dozen, and it was not long afterward that the same merchant bought two hundred at a time! Sylvester Root carried on the business of making wood clocks, in the Ephraim Downs shop, for about two years, 1842–4. It was a common saying at that time, that Root would go into the woods in the morning, cut down a tree and have it made up into clocks before night. That was intended as a compliment to his celerity, but how little the originator of the pleasantry realized what quantities of clocks would be turned out in Bristol in after years! Mr. Downs thought that three thousand clocks a year was a large output, and so it was in his day. From 1844 until 1851, the Downs shop remained idle, but in the latter year a company consisting of Ralph Terry, Elias Burwell, George and Franklin Downs, commenced the manufacture of a brass marine clock, invented by Ralph Terry, and eight-day clocks designed by Ralph Terry, and Hiram Camp of New Haven, formerly with Chauncey Jerome, when he was located at Bristol. After two years they bought out Mr. Burwell, when the firm name was changed from Terry, Downs, Burwell & Co., to Terry, Downs & Co. The business was discontinued in 1856. David Matthews, in company with Lyman Jewell and Samuel Botsford, made clock movements in a small shop east of the James Holt place, afterwards occupied by the Claytons. They made marine movements for the Litchfield Clock Co., until that concern failed; also for E. O. Goodwin, who cased them in a shop which he put up for the purpose on High Street. The Jewell & Matthews shop was originally fitted up as a turning shop by Andrew, a brother of Chauncey Jerome. It was afterward used by Lyman Jewell, for the manufacture of clock trimmings, daugerreotype case hooks, etc., previous to the formation of the firm of Jewell, Matthews & Co. Besides clock movements, Jewell, Matthews & Co., made galvanic batteries, of several patterns, much used in those days in therapeutics. Matthews afterward was associated with Elmore Horton, in the manufacture of toy drums, from 1860 until 1862. The firm failed, and the later years of Mr. Matthews were spent in the employ of the E. Ingraham Co. Clock calendars were introduced in Bristol by Benjamin B. Lewis, who came here in 1859, with a calendar invented by a man named Skinner. Not succeeding in placing the contract for their manufacture, he commenced to make them himself, in the Manross shop. The calendar failed to sell well, and in 1862, Mr. Lewis contracted with Burwell & Carter, to manufacture a calendar of his own invention. for five years. This calendar was a great success. He afterward entered the employ of Welch, Spring & Co., as foreman, which position he held for many years. Daniel J. Gale of Sheboygan Falls, Wis., brought an astronomical clock here, of his own invention, which Welch, Spring & Co. commenced to manufacture in 1871. But the clocks were not in demand, and the first five hundred made were never sold. Wm. A. Terry, also invented a calendar, which has no superior, and is absolutely perpetual. It was made by The Atkins Clock Co., and by George A. Jones, early in the seventies. It was previously made at Ansonia. The clock business was once conducted on Peaceable Street, in a small shop south of the brick house once owned by Edward M. Barnes, on the same side of the road. Deacon Charles G. Ives was the proprietor, who did a small business. He was succeeded by Orrin Hart, who bought out Deacon Ives, in 1820, and who continued the manufacture of clocks until John Bacon bought him out, in 1833. A shop was built on the opposite side of the road, where, in company with E. M. Barnes, cases were made, the movements being purchased of Chauncey Boardman. After eight years the partnership was dissolved, and both made clocks separately for three or four years more. Then Mr. Bacon sold the shop to Mr. Barnes, who made candlesticks, tin spoons, etc., up to the time of his death, in 1871. Neither of these shops is now standing. John Birge was associated, early, with Erastus and Harvey Case, in the manufacture of clocks, which were sold, for the most part, in the South. He was associated also with Ransom Mallory, a biographical sketch of whom appears elsewhere, under the firm name of Birge & Mallory. Joseph Ives, better known as "Uncle Joe Ives," and, probably, the greatest inventive genius in the clock line ever resident in Bristol, commenced manufacturing in the old Manross shop, near the Hubbell factory, in 1811. He was afterward associated with his brothers, Ira, Amasa, Chauncey and Philo, as early as 1816, who made wood clocks near the Dana Beckwith place. Mr. Ives made a metal clock, in 1818, the wheels of cast brass, and the plates of iron. The clock required a case five feet long, and was made by a company in which Lot Newell, Thomas Barnes, and others were interested. The place where the manufacturing was done was in the shop which stood on the site of the present Dunbar spring factory.

He went to Brooklyn, N. Y., where he made clocks for a few years, became involved and was imprisoned for debt. John Birge relieved him and induced him to return to Bristol, taking him into partnership, and manufacturing the rolling pinion movement invented by Ives, the best clock ever made at that time. The shop stood near the late Codling Manufacturing Co.'s plant. The writer has seen one of these clocks which had run continuously for forty years, and had never been repaired, nor had it struck wrong during that time. Mr. Birge paid Ives $10,000 for the patent of this clock, and the partnership was dissolved. Ives going to Plainville, where his usual misfortunes overtook him, which was always the case whenever he undertook the manufacture of clocks alone.

About 1832 Lawson and Chauncey Ives built the "Eureka" shop, now the Homestead Bakery, making a movement invented by Mr. Ives. E. C. Brewster, also became interested, about 1860, in a new invention of Mr. Ives, called the "rolling pinion, rolling escapement" clock, intended to so diminish friction as to make oiling unnecessary. But the business was not successful. Many other improvements in the construction of clocks were made by Mr. Ives, who was too much absorbed in them to ever find time to secure a competency for himself. A co-operative concern called The Union Clock Company, from which we have Union Hill, and Union Street, made clocks for a short time in the Waters shop, on the site of the Clayton Brothers' factory. They sold their clocks in New York at cut prices, but were soon put out of business by the other manufacturers combining against them.

Whigville, which was always so intimately connected with Bristol as almost to be considered a suburb, was also a clock-making village. The old red shop, known as the Jones shop, was built by Thomas Lowrey, of Red Stone Hill, for a cloth mill. His sons, David and Alfred, made clocks there, and were succeeded in the clock business by E. K. Jones and George Langdon. Edwin Bunnell erected what it now the Mills turning shop for a clock factory, also another shop farther north, on the corner. The large shop where the D. E. Peck Manufacturing Co. conducted a large turning business for many years, was built for a clock shop by Stever & Bryant, about 1845. They failed in a short time.

Among other manufacturers of clock trimmings and parts mention should be made of S. E. Root, who commenced to manufacture clock dials and sash, of metal, in 1846, in a small room in Chauncey Boerdman's shop, later occupied by the Ingraham Company. In 1851, he entered into partnership with Edward Langdon, and occupied a portion of the spoon shop, later removing to the shop which stood on the site of the present Dunbar factory. In the fall of 1853, ground was broken for the large three-story factory which stood for half a century on the corner of Main and School Streets. In 1855 the firm of Langdon & Root was dissolved, Mr. Root conducting the business alone thereafter. In 1866, he commenced to manufacture marine and pendulum clocks, purchasing the Manross machinery. In 1859 he invented and patented the paper clock dial, for use in small and fancy front timepieces. After his death in 1896, the business was continued a few years by his son-in-law, E. E. Newell, and was then sold to the Fitzpatrick Brothers, who built a shop on the Terryville road, and removed the machinery there. The old Root factory was converted into tenements. Joel H. Root, a brother of the preceding, commenced to manufacture clock trimmings in 1850. For many years he occupied a room in his brother's shop, but, in 1868, put up a small shop on what has since been called Root's Island. Since his death in 1885, the business has been conducted by his son, Charles J. Root, whose life, together with that of his aged mother, his aunt, Miss Candace Roberts, and his sister, Miss Mary P. Root, was terminated by a horrible grade-crossing accident, at Ashley Falls, Mass., August 18, 1907. Mrs. Root and Miss Roberts were granddaughters of Gideon Roberts, the pioneer clock-maker.

Company D, First Infantry, C. N. G.

BY FIRST LIEUTENANT R. K. LINSLEY, C. N. G., RETIRED.

LT. RAY K. LINSLEY, C. N. G. (RETIRED).

THE movement which resulted in the organization of the present "Co. D" started in the summer of 1899. In earlier days Bristol had been represented in the old militia regiments, but for a long period there had been no part of the State Military located here. A company in the "Guard" had been talked of at times but it was not until 1899, when the disbanding of Company D in New Britain, left a vacancy in the First Regiment, that these movements took definite form.

A petition for the organization of the company was put in circulation in September, 1899, and quickly filled with more than enough names of would-be soldiers. The Hon. A. J. Muzzy at that time representing this district in the State Senate, took a very active part in the work by securing the approval of Governor Lounsbury and Adjutant-General Cole, and lending his own influence to the movement. General Schulze, then Colonel of the First Regiment gave the movement his most hearty approval and in due time an order was issued from the Adjutant-General's office, accepting the petition and organizing the signers into a military company to be located in Bristol, and known as Company D, First Regiment, Connecticut National Guard. Colonel Schulze was ordered to take the necessary steps to muster the company into service.

A meeting of the signers was held in the old Borough Office in Linstead's Block, during October. Several military men were present from Hartford, and elsewhere. Speeches were made by Senator Muzzy, Colonel Schulze, Captain Johnson, then adjutant of the First, and others. The writer, who was at that time a private in the Hartford City Guard, and one of the signers of the petition spoke briefly of military life as an enlisted man.

At the suggestion of Colonel Schulze, it was decided to form a temporary organization, to take charge of matters, until the company should be mustered into service and have regularly appointed officers. The meeting then named as a committee, Ray N. Linsley, President; Herbert E. Newport, Vice President; Ora A. Colby, Secretary; John C. Page, Treasurer. All of them, but recently settled in Bristol, yet all signers of the petition and all heartily in favor of the project.

As soon as active steps toward enlistment began, it was discovered that very few of the original signers of the petition were willing to join the company. When confronted with an enlistment blank, they all made excuses the most common being, "I supposed I was only asking that a company be organized and had no intention of joining it." So the committee faced a harder task than was expected and it was only after hard personal work that the required number of members were finally secured and examined by the surgeons, and the following order issued:

HEADQUARTERS FIRST REGIMENT, C. N. G.
HARTFORD, CONN., Jan. 6, 1900.

SPECIAL ORDERS
No. 1.

In compliance with Special Orders, No. 278, Adjutant General's office, dated Hartford, Nov. 17, 1899, the enrolled members of Company D, 1st Regiment C. N. G., are hereby directed to assemble at the Total Abstinence and Benevolence Hall, North Main Street, Bristol, Conn., on Friday evening, January 12, 1900, at 7:45 o'clock, then and there to be mustered into the service of the Connecticut National Guard, and to nominate by ballot, a Captain, a First Lieutenant and Second Lieutenant.

By order of
COLONEL SCHULZE.

Official:
FRANK E. JOHNSON,
    Captain and Adjutant.

At the appointed hour the company assembled and was "mustered in" with almost full ranks. It is interesting to note that there were only ten of the signers of the original petition mustered into the new company. One more, the writer, joined as soon as the necessary transfer papers could be sent through.

The nomination of officers resulted in the choice of Herbert E. Newport, Captain; Clifford Bronson, First Lieutenant and Ernest E. Merrill, Second Lieutenant. These nominations were the practically unanimous choice of the company and were at once approved by headquarters, Captain Newport assuming command immediately. The appointment of noncommissioned officers followed quickly in Special Orders, No. 4, from Regimental Headquarters.

I. Appointments in Company D, First Regiment, C. N. G. are hereby made as follows:

To be First Sergeant,	Ray K. Linsley.
To be Quartermaster Sergeant,	Edward S. Busch, Jr.
To be Second Sergeant,	Ora A. Colby.
To be Third Sergeant,	Edgar S. Soule.
To be Fourth Sergeant,	Frank A. Haviland.
To be Fifth Sergeant,	Nathan B. Richards.

FIRST REGIMENT ARMORY, NORTH MAIN STREET.

INTERIOR OF FIRST REGIMENT ARMORY, DECORATED FOR A FAIR.

EP-CAPTAIN ERNEST E. MERRILL.

To be Corporals: Joseph J. Quinn, Charles M. Carrington, John Stotz, Louis L. Burg, John C. Page, James F. Douglass, James O'Connell, Jay J. Merrill, all with rank from Feb. 11, 1900.

Arms, uniforms and equipments all being perfectly new, were soon supplied and drills began.

Thus "Company D" became an established fact and took its place among the institutions of Bristol. I do not recall any member of the company at that time, other than myself, who had seen any previous service, yet all took hold with a will and when the first Field Day parade was held, May 25, 1900, the company made quite a creditable showing. On this occasion the Company marched to Hickory Park and spent the day in drill and guard practice, having dinner on the grounds and entertaining as the guest of honor A. J. Muzzy for whom the name "Muzzy Guards" had been assumed. The following Memorial Day the Company turned out as an escort to the Grand Army Veterans. Drills were kept up nearly all summer in order that the Company might be in shape to make a fine appearance at their first camp. Lieutenant Bronson left the Company soon after organization and on July 31, 1900 Lieutenant Merrill was promoted to the First Lieutenancy and Sergeant Ora A. Colby was appointed Second Lieutenant. Under these officers the Company joined the regiment and appeared at Niantic for the first time. A novel experience for most of the men, but thoroughly enjoyed by all. A special effort was made for honors, especially in the review on Governor's Day and we were informed that several compliments were given our work. On Oct. 4th, 1900, the Company went to Hartford and participated in the dedication of "Camp Field Monument."

Lieutenant Colby moved out of town soon after Camp leaving a vacancy which was filled by the nomination of Sergeant Linsley, Nov. 9, 1900. Sergeant Richards was promoted to the First Sergeancy and a number of other changes occurred among the noncommissioned officers at this time.

An element of discord arose in the Company about this time, and a committee of which the writer was chairman, was elected to take up the matter of complaints regarding certain features of Company management. The committee recommended that the matter be dropped and things were smoothed over but effects were not so easily altered and showed up at later times.

The writer felt obliged to tender his resignation the next February which was accepted. The nomination of Sergeant Blodgett, failing approval the Company nominated myself to fill my own vacancy, a manifest impossibility. This action was duly appreciated by the writer. Before this vacancy was filled Captain Newport's resignation, as he was preparing to leave town, placed Lieutenant Ernest E. Merrill in command, and left him the only commissioned officer. When nominations were ordered, Lieutenant Merrill was promoted to the captaincy and I found myself named for First Lieutenant with Sergeant J. C. Page for Second. Following lead of others, Lieutenant Page immediately left town and I do not recall that he ever drilled with us as a Lieutenant. Sergeant John J. Quinn was nominated for the position and held it several months when he was followed by Corporal Frank E. Kennedy. Under these officers the Company settled down to three years of solid hard work. They paraded at Hickory Park for Field Day and Inspection, May 17, 1901, and went to Camp McLean in August, taking part in the march across from Lyme to Niantic. Camp of shelter tents was pitched the first night out in a cold, drizzling rain. The next May the Field Day parade took place on Colt's meadows in Hartford. the Company taking enough camp outfit to cook their dinner on the grounds. The Company was at Camp Keeler, Niantic, the next Angust, when

FUN IN CAMP. DINGWELL IN THE AIR.

COMPANY D'S FAMOUS "TUG OF WAR" TEAM.

we received another practical lesson in marching, camping and outpost duty, spending two days in the special field campaign. On Sept. 25, 1902 the Company paraded in Hartford with the regiment on the occasion of the dedication of the monument to the 1st Heavy Artillery C. V. The old mortar known as the Petersburg Express, being mounted on the capitol grounds.

It was on the first of February, 1903, that Company D boys were called to the most trying service that has yet been their lot. It will be remembered that it was Sunday when the Governor decided to order out troops to stop the lawless rioting of the street car strikers in Waterbury. And further that it was but four and one-half hours after the orders were issued that the regiment was on duty in Waterbury. As none of the officers were handy to telephones, the orders were necessarily delayed in reaching us and with the Company scattered far and wide for a Sunday afternoon rest, it was no easy task to get them out, but when the train came through on its way to Waterbury, Company "D" was ready with nearly full ranks. Owing to trouble in getting a team, our baggage did not get on board and the boys were without blankets and other comforts the first night making things worse than necessary. But the service was well and promptly rendered, a credit to the Company.

The usual Field Day in Hartford and week at Camp Chamberlain, Niantic, followed in routine in 1903.

Then during "Old Home Week" in September, 1903, Company D entertained as its guests the entire First Regiment which came here to take part in the big parade which was one of the chief features of the week. Dinner was served on improvised tables set up in the new shop of the E. Ingraham Co., which had not then been occupied. The entire

Company acted as waiters and served their guests. The occasion was one that will long be remembered by all who took part.

The next spring the writer felt obliged to relinquish military life asked to be retired from active service, which was granted. Very soon after this Captain Merrill also gave up military for other duties and was the second to be placed on the retired list.

Captain Merrill was a very popular officer and the esteem in which he was held by the Company was shown by the presentation of a handsome gold watch, after he had left the service. This popularity was justly earned by hard work and careful judgment. Taking a Company of almost raw recruits, ignorant of military rules, he had made of them a Company which could hold its own with any in the regiment. Second Lieutenant Frank E. Kennedy was promoted to the captaincy with Corporal Daniel J. Breshnahan and Sergeant Frank S. Merrill for lieutenants. Under these officers the Company made a memorable tour of duty with the regulars at Mannassas, Va.

The next fall (1905) found the Company under new officers again, Lieutenant Frank Merrill having become Captain with Chester E. In-

COMPANIES D AND I OF THE FIRST INFANTRY, C. N. G., COOKING IN THE STREET, IN WATERBURY, DURING THE STREET CAR RIOTS, IN FEBRUARY, 1904.

EX-CAPTAIN FRANK KENNEDY.

CO. D IN CAMP AT NIANTIC, CONN.

graham and William Van Ness as Lieutenants. This was the year of "Regimental" at Camp Roberts, Niantic. 1906 brought another change. Lieutenant Ingraham resigned and Lieutenant Van Ness was promoted with Sergeant Clark as Second Lieutenant. Under these officers the Company is now doing good work and making new records.

It was under Captain Kennedy's administration that the old Springfield rifles were discarded for the more modern weapon "The Krag" with the knife bayonet.

Company "D" has entered a team in the regimental rifle shoot nearly every year and a number of individual prizes have been won by the members though they have not captured the chief honors.

Many a pleasant evening has been passed by the Company at the Armory entertaining friends and guests with suppers and dances.

Company "D" today is prepared for active warfare, armed and equipped in accord with the regular army rules. With capable and efficient officers and full ranks ready if duty calls, while we all hope its services may not be needed.

The members have also had a hand in athletics, producing a champion tug of war team and fine basket ball and baseball teams at different times.

CO. D., 1ST INFANTRY, C. N. G., IN CAMP AT HICKORY PARK.

OFFICERS OF FIRST C. N. G. INFANTRY IN CAMP AT MT. GRETNA, PA., 1906.

1, J. Linnehan; 2, Chas. Nagle; 3, Jas. Blodgett, Q. M. Sgt.; 4, A. Garrett; 5, W. Gould, Corp.; 6, J. Weiberg; 7, A. Moquin; 8, W. Costello, Mus.; 9, M. Canfield; 10, W. Grown; 11, Frank Merrill, Capt.; 12, C. Hill, Cook; 13, M. Ryan; 14, J. Gaffney; 15, A. Medley; 16, A. Gustafson; 17, Geo. Rowe; 18, J. Lass; 19, W. Johnson; 20, C. Peterson, 21, W. Stoltz; 22, A. Gartman; 23, J. Breshnan, Mus.; 24, F. Herold; 25, H. Emerson; 26, L. Griswold, Corp.; 27, W. W. J. Reynolds, Sgt.; 28, Thos. Costello, Corp.; 29, D. Haskill, Corp.; 30, C. Spencer; 31, G. Colgrove; 32, F. Zink; 33, L. Noble; 34, W. Smith; 35, J. Strup, Corp.; 36, W. Bennett.

Owing to unavoidable delays, we are obliged to show the rest of the members of Co. D on page 425.

Rev. Thomas J. Keena.

St. Joseph's Church

By Rev. Bernard M. Donnelly

REV. BERNARD M. DONNELLY.

FAR off, in the north-eastern part of the town, at the Copper Mines, in the waning years of the "forties," were sown the seeds which afterwards ripened into the present large and flourishing plant of St. Joseph's Church.

This little band of early Catholic settlers were mostly Irish emigrants; for Irish emigration was, at that time, at its height. The dark years of famine had passed over the fair face of Ireland; persecution had followed in its train, driving to this land of promise, men and women, as strong in faith as they were in physique.

A small band of these—about twelve families in all—found their way to the Copper Mines. Here they were in a strange country. Between them and their homes lay thousands of miles of water, which represented months of travel in slow-sailing vessels, exiles they were,

ST. JOSEPH'S CHURCH AND RECTORY.

INTERIOR OF CHURCH SHOWING CHRISTMAS DECORATIONS.

cheered only by occasional messages from home, or, sometimes, by the visit of Father Daly, who came amongst them to attend to their spiritual wants.

Few as they were, they were self-reliant and looked to the future with confidence. No hardships daunted them; for they had come to stay, to cast their lot with their fellow colonists from other lands, and to assist, as far as they could, in laying, deep and strong, the foundations of what is now a prosperous community.

In 1849, there were but nine priests to administer to the wants of the Catholics throughout the State of Connecticut!

Truly, those were days that tried priests' souls, and the names of these heroic and apostolic men should, for all time, be held in grateful remembrance by Catholics.

One of these was the Rev. Luke Daly, then pastor of St. Mary's Church, New Britain. His spiritual charge comprised New Britain, Farmington, Berlin, Bristol, Forestville, Collinsville, New Hartford, Simsbury, Tariffville and Rainbow.

REV. M. B. RODDEN.

Owing to the extent of the territory covered by the above places, the scattered condition of the Catholic flock, and the hardships of the jounrey imposed on the traveling priest, Catholic worship could not be had with any degree of regularity. Mass was offered at the mines about once a month, and the few Catholics of Bristol Centre went there.

When the copper mines closed, the construction of the railroad began, and the Catholics finding employment at the work, settled at Bristol Centre in larger numbers.

At this time, Catholic services were held in the house of the Roche family on Queen Street, not far from the present church site; later on, at the South Side, in the home of one Michael McGovern, until, when the congregation became more numerous, its members worshipped in the old Gridley Hall, which is now the store of Mr. Cleveland, and was then situated south of the old Town Building.

In 1855, the present church was built by Rev. Father Daly. At that period, the Catholic population had reached the number of two hundred souls.

On October 1, 1864, Bristol was made an independent parish, with the Copper Mines and Forestville as missions. The first resident pastor of the new parish was the Rev. Michael B. Rodden. Here he remained for four years, until 1868, when, on account of ill-health, he was appointed pastor at Greenville, R. I. Rev. Christopher Duggett succeeded him at Bristol. Fr. Duggett sold the old rectory, which was located on the corner of Prospect Place and Maple Street, and purchased St. Joseph's Cemetery and the site of the present Catholic rectory.

In 1872, Rev. Fr. Rodden returned to Bristol, reappointed pastor of St. Joseph's Church—a pastorate which he retained continuously for twenty-nine years!

Twenty-nine years of pure, priestly life—years of honest devotion to the poor, to the weak, to the little ones of God's Kingdom. Twenty-nine years of earnest effort to do God's work in a mild, unpretentious way, have made Father Rodden's memory sacred. His sterling qualities of mind and heart, manifested throughout this long term of years, have caused him to be beloved by his own charge; while his priestly zeal, his gentle, courteous manners, and his public-spirited actions, have earned for him, regardless of creed or nationality, the esteem and respect of all who knew him.

Realizing that the infirmities of age were rendering him incapable of attending to the growing needs of the Bristol parish, he resigned, May 1st, 1901, to accept the lighter charge of St. Catherine's Parish, Broad Brook.

He survived his removal only one year, and died in Broad Brook towards the end of May, 1902. His remains were brought to his own beloved Bristol, where, in St. Joseph's Cemetery, under the shadow of the church he served so long and so well, they are interred with others of an earlier day and generation, who strove and made sacrifices to propagate on earth the teaching of Christ.

Father Rodden had for assistants: Rev. James Walsh, Rev. Chas. McGoon, Rev. Frank M. Murray, Rev. Maurice Sheehan, Rev. Terence Smith, Rev. Patrick J. O'Leary, Rev. John Brennan and Rev. John Clark, in the order given.

Rev. Thomas J. Keena, the present incumbent, assumed charge of St. Joseph's parish, May 1, 1901. He set himself at once to the task of erecting a parochial school.

A Catholic laity responded to his efforts with good will and generosity. In the space of two years, he purchased the land on the extension of Center Street, moved the old rectory, transforming it into a convent, built and furnished the school and the present new rectory, and purchased the new St. Thomas' Cemetery.

On May 24, 1902, Right Rev. Bishop Tierney of Hartford blessed the new cemetery and dedicated the parochial school. The sermon was preached by Rev. Wm. H. Rogers of St. Patrick's Church, Hartford.

The presence of the Right Rev. Bishop and upwards of 100 priests from all parts of the diocese, the demonstration of strength and number made by the children and the societies connected with the church, rendered that day a memorable one for Catholics in the history of Bristol.

Co-operating with the priests of St. Joseph's parish is a strong and united force of Catholic laity, formed into societies under the auspices of the church, for the promotion of temperance, as well as for benevolent and charitable purposes—we give them in the order of their foundation, viz.: the Ancient Order of Hibernians, The Knights of Columbus, St. Joseph's Young Men's Temperance and Benevolent Society, St.

SCENES IN OLD CATHOLIC CEMETERY.

ST. JOSEPH'S PAROCHIAL SCHOOL AND CONVENT.

Joseph's German Society, St. Jean Baptiste Society, and the Polish Society. Societies for women are: the Ladies' Catholic Benevolent Legion, Ladies' Auxiliary, A. O. H., Young Ladies' Sodality, Young Ladies' Temperance Society, besides confraternities for younger members. These societies are in full vigor and representing, as they do, the best in layman and womanhood, they are strong aids in the promotion of church work.

In the new parochial school, 375 children are receiving instruction under the fostering care of the Sisters of St. Joseph in charge of Sr. M. Carmella. These good women, who bring to their vocation virtue and talent, instruct their pupils in all the branches of education taught in the public schools. While doing so, they also teach them in a broad and efficient manner, that religion must be an ever-present factor in their lives, and that all earthly ambitions must be made subordinate to the end for which alone man was created.

Rev. T. J. Keena, the present pastor is a native of Hartford, Conn. He received his early education in St. Peter's Parochial School. His college studies were pursued at St. Charles' College, Baltimore, Md., under the direction of the Sulpitian Fathers. He entered the Grand Seminary, Montreal, Canada, to study philosophy, but completed his philosophical and theological studies in the Ecclesiastical Seminary, Troy, N. Y., where he was ordained to the priesthood, Dec. 19, 1885.

His first appointment was to St. John's Parish, Stamford, where, for 12 years, he labored faithfully and with great success until he was appointed as pastor to St. Lawrence's Parish, Hartford, Nov. 21, 1898. Here he remained for 3 years, until he was transferred by Bishop Tierney and made pastor of St. Joseph's Church, Bristol.

Associated with Father Keena in the work of St. Joseph's, was Rev. John Clark from May 1 to Oct. 6, at which date he was called to Montville to act as pastor. He was succeeded by the Rev. Bernard M. Donnelly of Stamford, Conn., the present assistant.

Father Donnelly completed his preparatory studies at St. Charles' College, Maryland, pursued the study of philosophy and tehology at the Grand Seminary, Montreal, Canada, and was ordained to the Priesthood, July 30, 1899, by the Rt. Rev. Michael Tierney, in St. Joseph's Cathedral, Hartford. After a year of post-graduate study, spent in Rome, Italy, he was assigned to duty, for short periods, in Hartford, Bridgeport and New Haven, before coming to Bristol.

Thus the Catholic population has increased in 50 years from 200 souls to more than 3,000. St. Joseph's is a parish of composite character: its different elements are drawn from many branches of the human family, so that the native American worships side by side with the Irish, the French-Canadian, the German, the Pole, the Lithuanian, and the Italian.

Thus, in a short span of years, the little seed of Catholicity sown at the Copper Mines, has grown up and branched forth into a great tree, which offers spiritual shelter and a peaceful haven to so many of the wandering children of the different nations of the earth.

What a distinguished churchman once said about the Catholics of this State might be appropriated to fit the situation in Bristol—"Catholics have ever manifested a deep interest in whatever concerns the welfare of the town. Zealous in guarding her fair name and in upholding her prestige, they join willing hands with their fellow citizens of all other denominations in laboring for the common weal. Knowing their duties, and grateful for the blessings which they enjoy, they have become closely identified with whatever tends to the advancement of the town's and State's interests."

Y. M. T. A. B. BALL TEAM.

SCENES IN NEW CATHOLIC CEMETERY.

ST. JOSEPH'S ALTAR BOYS DRUM CORPS.

REMINISENCES OF YOUTHFUL PASTIMES

By Roswell Atkins.

OUR ancestors were a reading people, and early in the 19th century organized circulating libraries, one of which was a part of the old Scott Swamp library, but soon changed to the Farmers' Library. This library was composed of standard works: Rollins, Ancient History, in eight volumes; memoirs of prominent men; histories, etc., so far as they could be obtained. This was in the east part of the town, and in the west part of Farmington. This library was sold sometime in the thirties, as newspapers became more numerous and easily obtained.

While our ancestors were of necessity a pastoral people, they were not unmindful of the finer arts and embellishments of life which were within their reach. Of course the common school was regarded as a necessity, and was established in different localities as the different hamlets became large enough to warrant it.

Music was also given considerable attention, teachers were hired, and the young men and women, on saddle and pillion, or in wagons without springs, hied away to the singing school in the center of the town, and the grand old anthems of Mozart, Clark, Whittaker, Mason, Kent, Stephens, Handel, and many others in the Bridgewater Collection, were made to yield their rich melodies to the listening congregations, with only the pitch pipe to give the key, and the wand of the leader to keep time, in some instances; in others, the flute, clarionette, violin and bass viol gave support to the voices, until the introduction of the church organ. The first band for out-door music was composed of clarionettes, bassoons, fifes, piccolos, bugle or French horn, cymbals and drums. Only one man is now living who participated in this band, Elias Burwell. This was followed very soon by the brass band, composed of the Kent, or C bugle, the E-flat or tenor horn, cornopean, trombone, ophicleide and drums. These were followed by the modern band instruments.

The town was not without its holidays. The spring gathering of the militia was a gala time for the boys as they watched the evolutions of the red-coats, every man from eighteen to forty-five being required by law to have a suitable gun, length and calibre being given, and to do duty as warned. There were three companies in town; regulars, a rifle company, and an artillery company, with two field pieces; also part of a cavalry company, the other part being composed of Southington men. This made quite a display. The annual regimental review, generally held in Plainville in the fall, made another day for sight-seeing and ginger-bread sale.

Athletics were in common repute in the state, and the town was not without its representatives at either wrestling or kicking; and the spectacle of a man standing on his head on the ridge-pole of a building frame was not unknown; or kicking an object six inches above his head, while standing on one foot, kicking with that foot, and returning to the original position without touching the other foot to the ground, was one of the

OR "NEW CAMBRIDGE." 377

ST. JOSEPH'S ALTAR BOYS DRUM CORPS.

REMINISENCES OF YOUTHFUL PASTIMES

By Roswell Atkins.

OUR ancestors were a reading people, and early in the 19th century organized circulating libraries, one of which was a part of the old Scott Swamp library, but soon changed to the Farmers' Library. This library was composed of standard works: Rollins, Ancient History, in eight volumes; memoirs of prominent men; histories, etc., so far as they could be obtained. This was in the east part of the town, and in the west part of Farmington. This library was sold sometime in the thirties, as newspapers became more numerous and easily obtained.

While our ancestors were of necessity a pastoral people, they were not unmindful of the finer arts and embelishments of life which were within their reach. Of course the common school was regarded as a necessity, and was established in different localities as the different hamlets became large enough to warrant it.

Music was also given considerable attention, teachers were hired, and the young men and women, on saddle and pillion, or in wagons without springs, hied away to the singing school in the center of the town, and the grand old anthems of Mozart, Clark, Whittaker, Mason, Kent, Stephens, Handel, and many others in the Bridgewater Collection, were made to yield their rich melodies to the listening congregations, with only the pitch pipe to give the key, and the wand of the leader to keep time, in some instances; in others, the flute, clarionette, violin and bass viol gave support to the voices, until the introduction of the church organ. The first band for out-door music was composed of clarionettes, bassoons, fifes, piccolos, bugle or French horn, cymbals and drums. Only one man is now living who participated in this band, Elias Burwell. This was followed very soon by the brass band, composed of the Kent, or C bugle, the E-flat or tenor horn, cornopean, trombone, ophicleide and drums. These were followed by the modern band instruments.

The town was not without its holidays. The spring gathering of the militia was a gala time for the boys as they watched the evolutions of the red-coats, every man from eighteen to forty-five being required by law to have a suitable gun, length and calibre being given, and to do duty as warned. There were three companies in town; regulars, a rifle company, and an artillery company, with two field pieces; also part of a cavalry company, the other part being composed of Southington men. This made quite a display. The annual regimental review, generally held in Plainville in the fall, made another day for sight-seeing and ginger-bread sale.

Athletics were in common repute in the state, and the town was not without its representatives at either wrestling or kicking; and the spectacle of a man standing on his head on the ridge-pole of a building frame was not unknown; or kicking an object six inches above his head, while standing on one foot, kicking with that foot, and returning to the original position without touching the other foot to the ground, was one of the

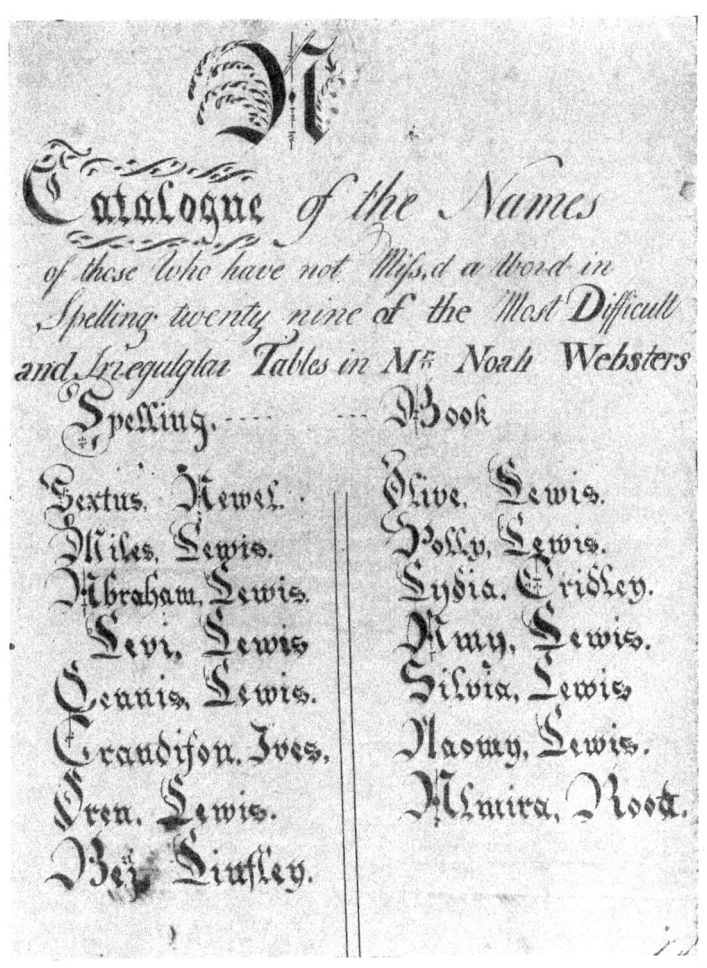

This Diploma was given as a prize to the scholar who stood at the head of the spelling at the close of the winter term. It must have been in the early 1790's. You will see that ten of the fifteen names are Lewis—all descended from one grandfather. MRS. ELLEN L. PECK.

feats reported. Rivalry between towns was ordinarily decided by a wrestling match between chosen champions, and even fistic encounters decided the division lines between towns.

Human nature was much the same then as now, and if work could be turned into play it seemed all the easier; so the husking to assist the farmer in storing his corn crop made the barn echo with laughter, as red ears were found, and forfeits were claimed of the fair sex. The apple-paring bee, to aid the farmer's wife in preparing her winter store of apple sauce, turned many a cold, fall evening into a scene of merriment. Busy hands with sharpened knives passed deftly around the bright, red apples. Circling the unbroken paring two or three times around the head and then dropping it to the floor to see if it formed the initials of the one whom it was hoped would be a life companion, was one of the pastimes of the occasion. The evening's sport was closed by the young people, hand in hand, with the old-time plays and songs:

> The needle's eye, it doth supply
> The thread that's running through;
> It hath caught many a smiling lass,
> And now it hath caught you.

This was accompanied by the usual suiting of the action to the words of the song, and the not unwilling osculation that closed each melodious act. Another of the old jingles ran:

> Pretty Pink, I s'pose you think,
> I cannot do without you;
> But I'll let you know, before you go,
> I care but little about you!

The hearty smack that followed this verse would not be very convincing to the fair maiden involved, as to the sincerity of the poetical utterance.

The close of the winter's term of school was often accompanied by an exhibition in which declamation, recitation and dialogue, from

> You'd scarce expect one of my tender age,

to

> The boy stood on the burning deck,

the Indian Chief, and selections from Shakespeare, with all the accompaniments of sword and bugle blast. For want of better theatre a barn, with a temporary floor laid over the bay, now empty of hay, for the stage, carpeted and hung with quilts; the barn floor seated for the pit, and the loft over the stables for a gallery; the violin orchestra to fill in the time between acts, afforded a good deal of pleasure to the participants, as well as to the parents of the rising generation.

THE CURFEW BELL.

THE curfew bell, which for so many years has tolled its ninety-and-nine strokes at nine o'clock, formerly did duty at the copper mine, in calling the men to their work and dismissing them at noon and night. It was purchased by Col. E. L. Dunbar, when the old mine buildings were dismantled, to be placed in the belfry of his new spring shop, which was built upon the foundations of the burned factory of the Union Spectacle Co., and other concerns. But this was not the first nine o'clock bell in Bristol, by any means. The old Congregational church, previous to 1795, was without a steeple. It was then that the time seemed propitious for raising the amount necessary to add this desirable feature to the meetinghouse, and liberty was secured, at a meeting of the society, to build a steeple. In 1796 a tax of one cent on the dollar was levied for the purpose of procuring a new bell for the steeple. George Mitchell, David Granniss and Gideon Roberts were appointed a committee to procure the bell. In 1797 a tax of eight mills was laid to pay arrearages on the steeple, any surplus remaining to apply on the bell. On the eighth of January, 1798, the following vote was passed at a society meeting:

"REGULATION FOR RINGING THE BELL."

(Copied by Roswell Atkins.)

"*Voted*, that the bell shall be rung at nine o'clock every night in the year, except Saturday night it is to be rung at eight o'clock; and in the months of July and August it is to be rung at twelve o'clock, or midday, in the room of nine at night. To be rung each Sunday, Thanksgiving and Fast, one hour before the time of exercise, and to ring until the Priest comes in sight south of Mr. Royce Lewises, and then to toll until the Priest enters the Meeting House. To be rung at the public meeting one hour before the time of meeting, and at the time of entering on business until the meeting is opened. To be rung and tolled at funerals. That the bell be rung at Society's cost till the next annual Society meeting."

That the youthful American may have had an existence even in those Puritan days, may be conjectured from the following vote, passed December 14, 1797: "*Voted*, a fine of 50 cents on any one who shall ring the bell after this date without orders from the Society's Committee, and applied to the use of the Society."

It may be possible that the new bell of 1796 was too small to be heard over the entire township, with its sparse and scattered population, for on February 29, 1808, the odd day of leap year was utilized for the purpose of holding a Society meeting, at which it was "*Voted*, to procure a Meeting House bell that will weigh about 650 pounds."

As affording a glimpse into the methods and requirements of the past, the following report of a Society's Committee may be useful. The report bears the date of January 8, 1798:

We, the subscribers, being appointed a committee by the inhabitants of the First Ecclesiastical Society of the Town of Bristol, to examine the certificates lodged with the clerk of said Society, and having attended to the business of our appointment, beg leave to report that having examined the law respecting certificates, are of the opinion that the statute is calculated to give the most free and ample liberty to the good people of this State, to worship God in that way that is most agreeable to the dictates of their own conscience, while, at the same time, it is wisely guarded against exempting any from (omitting) the joining and attending public worship in some religious congregation of Christians allowed by law in this State; and that in order to exempt a person from being taxed by the located societies, there must not only be a joining to some other denomination of Christians, but a common and ordinary attendance at the public worship of God with such denomination of Christians; and that having examined the certificates as aforesaid, lodged in the Society Clerk's office by John Hendricks, Jacob Lindsley, Doctor Josiah Holt, Seth Roberts, William Rich, Thomas Yale, James Stone and Elias Wilcox, do not come within the meaning of the statute, but are liable by law and ought to be taxed by the inhabitants of this Society for the support of public worship; but, as lenient and mild measures are always preferable to more harsh and coercive, and as we earnestly wish for peace and harmony among all the inhabitants of this Society, we beg leave to recommend it as our opinion that it is best to cancel all the taxes that are already become due from all or any of the above named persons, and at the same time we would let them know that we consider them to be holden for the payment of all taxes which may become due at any future period; all which is humbly submitted by your most obedient humble servants.

ASA UPSON,
ZEBULON PECK,
STEPHEN DODGE,
ENOS IVES,
Committee.

SOME BRISTOL PUPPIES.

Photo by Moultrope.

German Evangelic Lutheran Zion Church

By Rev. G. Gille, German Lutheran Pastor. Translated from the Original German Manuscript.

REV G. GILLE.

THE German Evangelic Lutheran Zion Church in Bristol, Conn. was founded under the name of German Lutheran Church on August 19, 1894, by Rev. H. Weber, after a religious service in the Temperance Hall. The first officers were Mr. Curell, president, Mr. Wahl, secretary; Mr. Blank, treasurer and Mr. J. Rindfleish, elder. As there were extraordinary difficulties in the way of erecting a church edifice, it was decided to hold services in the above named hall.

Under the leadership of the third pastor, Rev. G. Brandt, the second being Rev. Handel, a church was erected on School street in the year, 1896.

As fourth pastor, the late Rev. Gross of New Britain officiated. His three predecessors had preached in the spirit of the great reformer,

GERMAN EVANGELIC LUTHERAN ZION CHURCH.

Dr. Martin Luther, and his fellow workers. Their doctrine is still preached and has been preached in all Lutheran churches of Germany for nearly four hundred years. Rev. Gross, on the contrary, was a member of the so-named Lutheran Missouri Synod and he introduced, without the knowledge of the congregation, the doctrine of the above named synod. The point on which these two doctrines differ is the question of predestination. According to this doctrine, since eternity God has chosen a certain number of human beings and decided that these should and must become saved; that salvation through Christ is offered to all, but only by the chosen ones does God guarantee that they surely grasp it and never lose it. On the other hand, it is impossible for those who are not chosen to become saved.

Luther, and with him the Lutheran church of all lands and times, has pronounced this doctrine unbiblical and affirms that God has chosen all human beings to be saved and that He does all to help them gain this end; that it is the fault of man if he does not grasp it.

That these differences should be put out of the way, a conference was held in St. Paul's Church, Middletown, Conn., on April 8, 1901. A number of ministers of both doctrines were present. The same did not lead to an understanding.

The successor of Pastor Gross still officiates in Bristol and on the ground of the doctrine of Evangelical Lutheran Missouri Synod, so-called.

For various reasons, confessional reasons, a few of the original members were not allowed to attend the Lord's Supper and since the year, 1899, attended the St. John's Church in New Britain, until they built a church of their own and formed an independent congregation. When they did form such a congregation they looked upon it as a restoration of the original congregation.

With the constitution of St. John's Church of New Britain as a constitution the following officers were chosen: Henry Redmann, president; Joseph Rindfleish, elder; Michael Rindfleish, treasurer; Fred Stanke, secretary; John Grünewald, trustee.

Rev. M. W. Gaudian was given a call to act as pastor. As places of worship the W. E. T. & W. Hall and then the A. O. U. M. Hall were used. The president of the Prospect Methodist Episcopal Church kindly offered them the use of the basement of their church, which the congregation then gratefully accepted.

In a regular meeting, in which the forty-five members of which the congregation consisted were present, on the 26th of May, 1902, it was decided to build a new church. The kind offer of Mr. W. E. Sessions to present them with a building lot on Judd street and plans of a church, were thankfully accepted. The contract was given to Contractor Thompson. The manner in which the citizens of Bristol came forward with pecuniary help, the congregation always will gratefully remember; how a strange people of strange tongue extended the friendly helping hand.

With glad courage and thanks to God, the congregation laid the cornerstone of this church on June 25, 1906, and on October 12, 1906, it was dedicated. On both occasions, many of the American citizens of Bristol were present. The sound and clear words of the English sermons apparently made a deep impression upon them and gave them a glance into the deep soul and spirit of the Germans and their church, showing, at the same time, their value to religion and learning in America.

As expected, the congregation, which was bound heart and soul to its new church, grew very well. Almost every month new members joined them. As the most of these were young unmarried people, many of them often changed their place of residence to other towns, but in spite of this, the congregation grew steadily.

At this time their pastor, Rev. K. Riebesell, followed an urgent and repeated call to Englewood, N. J. Almost at the same time, their capable first president, Henry Redmann, was taken from them by death. From June, 1905, to July 1, 1906, at which time their present pastor, Rev. G. Gille accepted a call, the congregation could not get, that is keep a minister. Rev. O. Konrad, after staying with them three months followed a call to the larger congregations of Seymour and Shelton. It will be readily understood, when it is said that these misfortunes dampened the courage and hope in the congregation.

Under the leadership of the present pastor, who is on the ground of a new constitution, at the same time president of the congregation, matters have acquried a brighter outlook. Apparently the congregation have great love and faith in him and there is, with God's help a good future before them, both in material and spiritual matters.

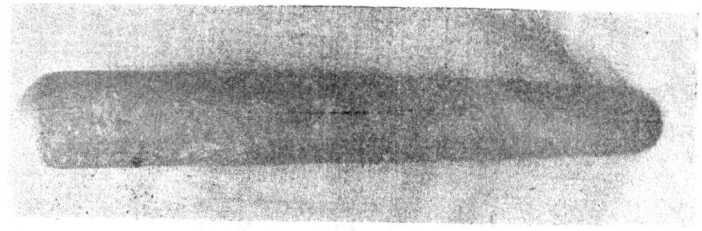

BEAUTIFUL SPECIMEN OF INDIAN PESTLE.
Found on Chippen's Hill by Frank J. Smith. Now in collection of A. E. Kilbourn, So. Windsor, Conn.

The Swedish Congregational Church*

The Swedish Congregational Church was organized in Bristol the 7th of February, 1890, with a membership of nine.

Rev. E. G. Hjerpe of New Britain, Conn., was invited to attend when the church was organized.

On account of the small membership the church could not afford to have a regular pastor, but depended upon the ministers of nearby towns to preach in turn for them. Rev. Hjerpe of New Britain being near to Bristol took special interest in the church, for which the church thanked him most heartily.

REV. P. G. FALLQUIST.

Pastors of nearby towns preached here in rotation until 1893, when Rev. A. Abrahamson, who had charge of the Swedish in the Chicago Theological Seminary, arrived here to take charge of the church.

He told the congregation that they should have a regular pastor. Money being scarce, they decided to appeal to the American people in Bristol for help, and had very much success. Rev. Abrahamson remained here until November, 1893, when he resigned.

Rev. Otto Svenson then took charge of the work and under his leadership a church was built. Until this time the church meetings were held in halls. The church was dedicated December 29, 1895, the

[*This article was written by Mrs. Johnson of Goodwin Street and translated by George Malmgren.]

same year that it was built. Under the leadership of Rev. Svenson the church took great strides towards increasing its membership and prosperity. Rev. Svenson resigned the 10th of March, 1896.

The church was without a pastor until July of the same year, when Rev. H. Palmer arrived here. Rev. Palmer was well liked by the congregation and there was very much regret when he resigned in the latter part of the year, 1902.

Rev. A. G. Nyreen came here the first of December, 1902. He stayed but a short while, leaving Bristol in the month of October, 1903.

The congregation then voted to call Kenneth A. Bercher, who arrived in Bristol on Thanksgiving Day, 1903. He remained here a little over a year, leaving in December, 1904.

Until this time Bristol and Plainville churches had been combined, but now decided to each work by themselves.

Rev. David Brunstrom of Yale College then preached in Bristol until March, 1906, when Rev. Avel Olson came here and remained for three months.

On the first of October, Rev. P. G. Fallquist came and at the present writing is still pastor.

The congregation at this writing has a membership of 25.

THE SWEDISH CONGREGTIONAL CHURCH, QUEEN STREET.

THE SWEDISH LUTHERAN LEBANON CONGREGATIONAL CHURCH.

By Rev. Nimrod Ebb.

THE Swedish Lutheran Lebanon Congregation of Bristol, Conn., was organized October 20, 1887, with fifty-six communicant members. The church was built in 1891 and has a seating capacity for two hundred persons. The cost of the church and parsonage is $9,200.00. At the present time the congregation consists of 220 members.

REV. O. NIMROD EBB.   *Photo By Elton*

The first Swedish ministers who visited and preached at Bristol were Rev. Ludwig Holmes, D. D., now at Portland, Conn., and Rev. O. W. Ferm, now at Sioux City, Iowa. Rev. A. F. Lundquist was the first local pastor and came here in the spring of 1893. In 1903 Rev. Lundquist resigned his charge of this church and moved to McKeesport, Pennsylvania, and was succeeded by Rev. E. C. Jesseys, who moved to Kiron, Iowa, in May, 1906. The present pastor, Rev. O. Nimrod Ebb, B. D., was called from Duquesne, Pennsylvania and took charge of the congregation, September 30, 1906.

THE SWEDISH LUTHERAN LEBANON CONGREGATIONAL CHURCH.

SWANSTON'S ORCHESTRA

ORGANIZED in 1903, is now in its fourth season. With Chas. A. Swanston, first violin and leader, Robert H. Woodford, clarinet, Fred C. Galpin, cornet, Lucien E. Rouse, trombone and Walter H. Porch as pianist, the personelle is the same as when organized with the exception of Mr. Porch, who succeeded Mrs. Florence Tucker after the first season.

With a reportorie of standard and popular concert and dance music, they have been heard at almost all of the clubs, societies, and assemblies in town, also High School "Class Nights" and graduation. Music at basket ball games for two seasons were furnished by them

They do not aspire to the ranks of professionalism, but rather for the sake of congenial fellowship among themselves, and the love of music. They hold rehearsals every week. The financial remuneration from engagements being sufficient to create and maintain an interest that has brought them to a state of proficiency that is very creditable to an amteur orchestra and with the five "regular" men they can at short notice procure musicians in town to make a good orchestra of eight to ten pieces.

SWANSTON'S ORCHESTRA.   *Photo by Elton.*

Natural History Photography*

By Geo. E. Moulthrope.

During 1902-1903, I was engaged supplying photographs and data for several Ornithological and Natural History Publications and soon found I had attempted by far the most difficult, as well as the most interesting branch of photography.

The ordinary camera and lens not being equal to produce the objects large enough, the extreme long focus instrument, with the most powerful lenses are required, which, with the various other articles used, made an equipment which carried for 8 or 10 hours on a trip through brush, swamps, briars, over stonewalls and barbed wire fences, makes one aware of the fact that he had well earned a week or two's salary, even if, as often was the case, it was acquired in a single day.

On my first outing I was requested to secure pictures showing a phœbe, also her nest and eggs. The scene began at the Log Cabin on Fall Mountain, on a beautiful May morning. A Phœbe was found to have constructed her nest on a beam under a shed facing the north.

Of course photographing a live bird under these conditions, was out of the question, and I had to resort to some way of throwing sunlight under the shed onto the nest and bird thus lighting it sufficiently to admit of a snapshot.

I had in the outfit two mirrors, about two feet square, one of which I placed outside at the correct angle to throw the light on the desired place. What a change this made. The nest and woodwork surrounding it was transformed from a dark shed into a spot of dazzling brightness.

---

*The following is a description of cuts on Page 391,

(1) KING BIRD'S NEST IN AN OLD APPLE TREE.
(2) LIVE QUAIL ON HER NEST.
(3) GREEN HERON'S NEST IN MAPLE TREE.
(4) CROW'S NEST IN PINE TREE. PHOTOGRAPHED 60 FEET FROM THE GROUND. CAMERA AND ARTIST HAD TO BE STRAPPED TO THE TREE IN TAKING PHOTO.
(5) BANK SWALLOW'S NEST IN SAND BANK. PART OF BANK HAD TO BE DUG AWAY TO SHOW NEST.
(6) BLUE JAY'S NEST IN A DENSE PINE TREE.
(7) WHIP-POOR-WILL'S EGGS ON GROUND. THEY BUILD NO NEST.

All of these were photographed in their natural location and with the exception of the Bank Swallow's, were undisturbed and that only slightly. As I had to furnish data regarding the nests, birds, etc., as well as the photos, I made several visits to most of the nests.

The eggs all hatched in due time, and in case of the quail, 15 little fuzzy balls, a little larger than bumble bees, darted away at my second visit to their home.

What bird would have the hardiness to return under such changed conditions!

Before trying the old bird I thought it would be a good idea to secure photos of the nest and eggs, but here another difficulty.

The nest was situated above my head and close to the roof of the shed so that the eggs could not be seen. I could easily photograph the nest on the beam, but I had to furnish photographs showing the eggs also.

The second mirror helped me out of this difficulty and after I had placed it in position above the nest I made the exposure and secured the photo shown here.

A barn swallows' nest was photographed from the top of a 30 foot ladder with the aid of the mirrors and reflected sunlight, later in the season in the same manner.

The Phœbe's nest I secured and printed here is shown right side up, but immediately upon handing the photo to anyone they invariably quickly turn it around as if afraid the eggs might fall out, and it takes a little explanation on my part to show them that they are not looking at the eggs but only at their image in the mirror placed over them.

Now to the old bird. The second mirror was removed and after attaching several yards of rubber tubing to my camera shutter, I hid myself and with the aid of my field glasses I watched and waited for

YELLOW HAMMER'S NEST—IN HOLLOW TREE.

the old bird's return. The shifting sun made it necessary to adjust the mirrors about every five minutes, which undoubtedly delayed the Phœbe in her decision to return to her nest, although she made several hundred attempts during the next few hours. She finally settled on the nest for a fractional part of time, the instant was the one I had been watching and waiting five long hours for and the click of the shutters announced that I had won in my contest with the phœbe, two first class photos being secured, showing the bird in two positions.

During the next two years several hundred photos were secured under similar circumstances, including birds, nests, game, and hunting scenes. The subjects varying in height from the ground, as in case of the quail on her nest, and whip-poor-will photos, to the crow's nest, which was photographed 60 feet from the ground in the top of a swaying pine. In this instance, as in others, I had a large limb to stand upon, but having to use both hands in the taking of the photos, I had to strap myself to the tree, draw up my outfit with rope, securely strap it to the tree and then proceed with taking the photos.

It is needless to say that this line of photos is in a greater demand by many publications than any other. A few of the photos I secured are reproduced here.

VIEW OF PHOBBE'S NEST. *Photographed with the aid of mirrors.*

Present Industries of Bristol

THE SESSIONS CLOCK COMPANY.

THE Sessions Clock Company is one of the leading industries of the town, and is located at Forestville which is another village and post office in the town of Bristol, about three miles east of the borough on the direct line of travel to New Britain and Hartford. The company which they succeeded was founded by Elisha N. Welch in 1855. He was for a generation a very prominent manufacturer of the town and interested in many of its leading manufacturing industries. Mr. Welch bought the property and business of the assignee of J. C. Brown, who was a large clock manufacturer until 1855. He also purchased the factories of F. S. Otis and the Forestville Hardware Co., all of which he devoted to the manufacture of clocks. In 1864 he organized the E. N. Welch Mfg. Co., associating his son James Hart Welch and his son-in-law, George Henry Mitchell, with

VIEWS OF THE PLANT IN 1907.

him as officers in the company. The business was conducted by them, manufacturing of clocks in large variety until after Mr. Elisha N. Welch's death in 1887. In the meantime they had merged into the company the business of Welch, Spring & Co., which had been conducted by Mr. Solomon Spring and Mr. Elisha N. Welch in the manufacture of fine regulator clocks. Mr. George Henry Mitchell died in 1886 and Mr. James Hart Welch in 1902.

WHIP-POOR-WILL WITH EGGS

After Mr. Welch's death in 1887 the company went out of business for some time on account of financial reverses. The company was reorganized in 1897 under the same name, the E. N. Welch Mfg. Co., by George W. Mitchell, James Hart Welch, Mrs. George H. Mitchell, Edward A. Freeman, A. H. Condell and a number of others and conducted by them until the summer of 1902, when on account of the death of James Hart Welch, which occurred in the spring of the same year, they were financially embarrassed, and Mr. William E. Sessions, president and principal owner of the Sessions Foundry Co., was persuaded to interest himself in the business and did so largely in order to save the company from bankruptcy, and the village of Forestville from another period of adversity. He was elected President of the company, Mr. Albert L. Sessions, his nephew, was elected treasurer and Edward A. Freeman of Plainville secretary. The Messrs. Sessions secured a control of the stock of the company and within a few months purchased practically every share of stock, when the name of the company was changed to The Sessions Clock Co.

Since that time, although the old company had rebuilt the case shop and movement shop with new modern brick buildings and equipped them with modern machinery, on account of fires which had destroyed the old buildings, the new company have erected still other large new brick buildings of modern construction and equipped them with the best machinery and appliances, which include the black enameling department, finishing department, power plant including new engine and boilers and brick stack, kiln drys, warehouse and shipping department, lumber sheds and railroad sidings and made very large improvements at a cost of a large sum of money. Since the Messrs. Sessions took up the enterprise the business has developed rapidly and employment has been given to more than double the number of hands that had been employed for a number of years previously. The output of the company in eight day pendulum clocks compares favorably with that of the other leading manufacturers, and the prospects for the continued success of the company are well assured.

The Sessions Foundry Company

There is no more complete plant of the kind in the world than the establishment of the Sessions Foundry Company, begun in August, 1894, and finished in December, 1895. It is a model in all respects. In it the Messrs. Sessions have met and solved the problem of economical production by the construction of the plant in such a manner that the raw material on its way to the finished product, can be handled at the least possible expense and the least number of times. The works embody the best practice of the present time in design, arrangement and appliances. The members of the company have had long practical experience and are intimately acquainted with every detail of the business. This enabled them to so plan and construct as to provide for the most economical production of both large and small castings. Every department exhibits careful forethought and thorough knowledge of the business.

After an extended experience in the wood turning and trunk hardware business John H. Sessions bought out the foundry business of the Bristol Foundry company in 1879, and took his son William into partnership, the business being conducted under the name of Sessions Foundry Company. Since the start the business has been under the direct management of William E. Sessions, and has developed from a small plant having but ten thousand dollars capital stock and a force of about eighteen men to its present proportions.

BIRSEYE VIEW OF SESSIONS FOUNDRY. *Cut loaned by Company.*

WILLIAM E. SESSIONS.

In July, 1896, the company was changed from a partnership to a corporation, under a special charter by the Legislature. The officers are John H. Sessions, president; William E. Sessions, treasurer; Geo. M. Eggleston, a graduate of Wesleyan University of Middletown, Conn., secretary, and Joseph B. Sessions, assistant secretary.

The plant, which includes some thirty acres, and is the largest plant of the kind east of Chicago, is about one mile from the center of Bristol, and is bounded on one side by the tracks of the N. Y., N. H. & H. R. R.

Provision has been made for any growth that may become necessary in the future, as the works are located near the center of the tract owned by the company. At the entrance, which is at the south side of the grounds, is the main office building, to the rear and connected with which is the pattern storage building, containing the superintendent's office and pattern rooms. To the east of this is a large storehouse for inactive patterns, surplus castings and general storage. Directly north of the pattern storage building, and connected thereto, is the shipping department, to the west of which are the heater rooms, sorting room, tumbling barrel room and power house, while to the east are the shipping and cleaning rooms and carpenter and machine shops. Still further north is the large foundry or moulding room, on the south side of which is the foreman's office and foundry pattern repair room, and on the north side are the cupolas, core rooms and mold drying ovens. North of the foundry are molding sand bins and stockyard. To the east of these are the slag tumbling barrels.

The standard gauge track system, of which there is about two miles inside the grounds, is most complete, and every building is approached from the main line. This, in connection with the narrow gauge system of tracks, of which there is three-fourths of a mile, which traverse the buildings and yards, provides for the rapid and easy handling of supplies and material, and for the convenient shipment of the finished articles. The business is of such magnitude as to demand the services of two locomotives, which are owned by the company. The track enters the yard at the southwestern corner, and branches eastward to the shipping department, power house, cleaning rooms, and to the eastern end of the foundry, which it enters, so as to handle the heaviest castings.

Handling the Work.

When cars enter the property, their contents are weighed before being dumped into the bins, and a record is kept by the weighmaster of the amount of material in each bin and of the amount that is taken to charge each furnace. The furnaces are supplied by push cars, which after being weighed, are run over a trestle to the charging platform of the furnaces, which is on the level of the storage bins and about ten feet above the floor of the foundry.

The foundry building is six hundred and thirty feet long and one hundred and twelve feet wide, and is divided into three aisles by two interior rows of columns. The roof trusses in the wings are eighteen feet above the floor, while the trusses over the central aisle are forty feet above the floor.

Located against the north wall are four cupola rooms, each cupola room being arranged for two cupolas having a capacity of fifty tons each. Each cupola is supplied with a blast from a blower driven by a by a twenty-five horse-power electric motor.

Between the middle cupola rooms is a wash room for the workmen and a core room, the latter containing two core ovens. The small cores are made in a room one hundred and six feet long by twenty-three feet wide above the wash and core baking room. For about three-quarters of the length of the foundry building, a sand wall five feet high is constructed, with openings for the car tracks. Benches are constructed along both sides of this sand wall and along the south wall of the building, and it is upon these that all of the smaller molds are made.

MAIN OFFICE.

At the eastern end of the foundry there is a pit forty-five feet wide and eighty feet long, and in this all of the heavy castings are made. This pit is three feet deep and is paved with brick. Two twenty-ton Morgan traveling electric cranes traverse the center aisle of the foundry for one-third its length, while on opposite corners of the pit are located four six-ton hydraulic jib cranes. The larger sized ladles are handled by the traveling and jib cranes.

Steam from the engine boilers is carried to a large coil of pipe where it is driven through large galvanized flues to all parts of the buildings by the Sturtevant blower system, making an overhead heating arrangement that is sufficient and that gives the most perfect ventilation, the entire air of the buildings being subject to change once in twenty minutes. This is a very important feature in a foundry. The flues which run overhead in all the rooms are large, tapering down to smaller sizes required by the smaller rooms. The flue which leaves the blower is seventy-eight inches in diameter and goes directly into the great foundry room, giving a large radiating surface. When the pouring is going on the heat is not needed and is shut off, or turned to other rooms.

The cleaning and shipping building is three hundred and twenty-three feet long and L-shaped. The west portion, containing the tumble-barrel room and sorting room, is fifty-three feet wide, and the east portion, containing cleaning and shipping room, is ninety-eight feet wide. A special feature of the shipping room is that eight cars can be placed in the building, the doors tightly closed, and the cars loaded at pleasure, avoiding any possible inconveniences in inclement weather.

When the smaller castings have been made they are taken to the tumbling barrels, of which there are fifty, and there cleaned. From thence they are taken to the sorting room and then to the shipping room adjoining, and after being packed and weighed are loaded on cars. The floor of the cars is on a level with the floor of the shipping room. The heavy castings are lifted from the pit by the cranes and put on the flat cars and taken to the cleaning room, where a pickling vat is provided. The castings are cleaned and any machine work that is necessary is done in the adjoining machine shop, the castings being run in upon cars. A 10-ton electric travelling crane traverses the east end of the shipping and cleaning room for handling and loading heavy castings.

The carpenter and machine shop is a separate two-story building, about one-half of the lower floor being occupied by the carpenter shop and the other half by the machine shop. The upper floor contains the pattern shop. All patterns are stored in the two-story building specially provided for the purpose.

The office building is a handsome structure of Roxbury granite, two stories high, with a south and west frontage looking out upon a large grassed lawn. This office building is conveniently arranged and equipped for the rapid transaction of business, having two long-distance telephone systems which can be used alternately, an independent local telephone system reaching to twenty-four localities in the works, for immediate communication with all the departments, and a pneumatic-tube system connecting with the shipping office for the transmission of orders and documents.

The gate-house, which is also the time keeper's office, is fitted up with self-registering time clocks. Each employe of the company has to pass through the gate-house upon entering or leaving the foundry.

The best proof of the interest taken in the employes is what has been done for their comfort and convenience. The toilet rooms are samples. They have received attention from a sanitary standpoint, as well as that of utility. The washbowls are provided with hot and cold water supply. Employes have individual lockers in which their clothing and belongings can be kept. The time-honored custom which regards a foundry as inevitably associated with dirt, smoke and smudge, is upset at the Sessions foundry.

CLEANING ROOM.
ENTRANCE TO SHIPPING BUILDING.

PATTERN STORAGE.

SHIPPING ROOM.
MAIN FOUNDRY.

Along the south front of the plant runs a trout brook, as clear as crystal, and this has been turned to run by the roadside furnishing a natural boundary to the grounds and lawn in front of the plant. A handsome stone bridge across it furnishes entrance to the premises. In addition to the plant proper, the Sessions' company has purchased large tracts of land with buildings in the immediate vicinity which may be developed into a residence section for its employes. The company will not establish any tenement system but will sell to its employes at reasonable prices, having a view to encouraging them to form a model industrial community. All objectionable features will be excluded, and the workmen employed by the firm will not only have a comfortable factory in which to work, but opportunity for self-improvement as well, and that without anything that savors of patronage.

There were used in the building of this great plant seven hundred and sixty tons of structural steel, three million bricks, and four hundred tons of slate. There are three and one-half acres of floor space in the buildings, mostly on one floor.

Within this immense enclosure the Sessions Foundry company cast anything ordered from the smallest to the largest, its customers coming from the manufacturing trade of New England and near by. There is naturally an almost endless variety to the work turned out, but any one seeing this foundry room with its splendid equipment will be satisfied that whatever is wanted can be turned out with rapidity and with the greatest possible economy.

TOILET ROOM.

"JO-KEN"—SESSIONS FOUNDRY CO.'S YARD ENGINE.

This was the old Ingraham Movement shop, built for a hardware shop, corner Meadow and North Main Streets. For description see Atkins' notes, which also descripe the old case shop, later Turner Heater works. The building to left of shop was office of Ingraham Co. (upper floor) for many years.

HOBRO & ROWE.
Hobro & Rowe's Granite and Marble Works.

Alfred H. Hobro is well known to the people of Bristol, being formerly in the employ of Geo. C. Arms as his foreman from 1896 until entering into business for himself in 1906 at the same location formerly occupied by Geo. C. Arms, which was bought by William H. Rowe, member of this firm. Mr. Hobro first went to learn his trade with his father in 1890 at the well known firm of Thomas Phillips & Son of New Haven. After serving his time at the trade, he severed his connection with that firm to accept a position as foreman for the P. W. Bates Granite Works of Norwalk, Conn., which he held until 1896 when he accepted the position as foreman for Geo. C. Arms. His work can be seen on most of the monuments illustrated in this book. Many of which were erected by this firm. William H. Rowe is well known to most of the people of Bristol, being successfully engaged in the coal and wood business for the last thirteen years his sheds being located on side track in the rear of the Granite Works. On and after January 1, 1908 the granite and marble business will be conducted under the name of Alfred H. Hobro, he to buy out the interest of his partner, William H. Rowe. He expects to be located in a new building which is to be erected where the old shop now stands and will be equipped with latest machinery making a first class shop so as to handle his increasing business.

THE BARTHOLOMEW FACTORY, EDGEWOOD.

The factory called "Grinding Shop" was built by George W. Bartholomew, 1846, for use in the manufacture of table cutlery. The street was one of the pieces of abandoned road, called in the deed of 1828 to Asa Bartholomew, "Mill Road." Re-opened, 1846, and known as "The New Road," until 1882, when the first Bristol directory published the name "Warner Street." The cutlery business was closed when Mr. Bartholomew in the fall of 1848 went with his friends to California. In 1855 George W. and Harry S. Bartholomew, (father and son) formed the partnership under firm name G. W. & H. S. Bartholomew to manufacture bit stock braces, beginning their project in the "Grinding Shop." In the early sixties the business was removed to the former clock factories. Soon after the removal of the Bartholomews, a wood turning enterprise was started and conducted at this place by Alpress, Carpenter & Company (Charles H. Alpress, Wm. B. Carpenter, Jr. and Augustus H. Warner). There were changes in the personnel of the firm. C. H. Alpress' interest was bought by Henry A. Warner, father of Augustus (Carpenter & Warner). The second change was in the purchase by Mr. H. A. Warner of W. B. Carpenter's share in the business. The firm then was H. A. & A. H. Warner till their removal to District No. 8, after the burning of the first (Grinding Shop) and second (New Factory) built on its site. These fires were the beginning of a series of similar calamities sufficient to dishearten a common man. Ruin's mark the locality of the Grinding Shop and its successor (1907).

BARTHOLOMEW FACTORY FROM RARE SKETCH
(ORIGINAL IN COLORS)

The first manufacturer and builder known to have a business career at the location marked 61, was the remarkable beaver that built the first dam. Date of construction unknown. In 1788, Benjamin and William Jerome, 2d (brothers), purchased from Amasa Ives an interest in the gristmill which was increased in 1803. In 1809 William Jerome, 2d, was three-quarters owner with Isaac Graham owner of the remaining one-quarter. The mill was sold to (Byington and Graham (Martin Byington and Isaac Graham, Sen.), who conducted the mill for some years. William Jerome, 2d, died 1821. On the site of the gristmill or in it, George W. Bartholomew with his cousin Eli Bartholomew began to make clocks, 1828. G. W. Bartholomew continued the business alone until 1840. A second factory with bell was on the north side of the road(the bell was finally used in Bristol for a school-house), where decorating clock tablets and filling numbers for clock faces was done by young women.

The Winstons did a brisk wood turning business for five years. Possibly Allen Winston may have had for a short period an industry in this building. Some of the Winstons made at one time coffee roasters and Edward M. Barnes of Peaceable Street made candle sticks in the basement. Soon after 1860 G. W. and H. S. Bartholomew employed the Bunnell Brothers (Warren and Norris) of Burlington to move the bell shop across the street where it was joined to the first building to increase the room needed for the bit brace works. It was destroyed by fire 1884 when G. W. Bartholomew retired. Harry S. Bartholomew built anew and was identified with this business at the time of his death, February 19, 1902. His son Joseph P. Bartholomew who had relieved his father of all care for several years continued the business until sold to Stanley Rule & Level Company of New Britain. The factory is still in possession of heirs of H. S. Bartholomew.

VIEWS OF PLANT IN 1907.

THE E. INGRAHAM COMPANY.

The E. Ingraham Company was founded by Elias Ingraham, who was born in Marlborough, Conn., November 1st, 1805.

From 1827 to 1835 he made clock cases under contract for various parties, and in the latter year bought a shop with water privilege in Bristol, Conn., where the present factories now stand, and commenced making clocks on his own account. This he continued until 1843, in which year he and his brother formed a partnership with Elisha C. Brewster, under the firm name of Brewster & Ingraham. This firm was succeeded in 1848 by E. & A. Ingraham, who continued business until 1855 in which year the plant was entirely destroyed by fire. Two years later Elias Ingraham rented a shop and continued the manufacture of clocks, and in 1859 formed a co-partnership with Edward Ingraham, his son, which was continued until 1881. In that year a joint stock company was formed, comprising Elias Ingraham, Edward Ingraham and the three sons of Edward Ingraham, Walter A., William S. and Irving E.

Elias Ingraham died in August, 1885, and Edward Ingraham in August, 1892. The officers of the company and its managers at the present time are: Walter A. Ingraham, president; Irving E. Ingraham, vice president; and William S. Ingraham, secretary and treasurer.

The company is engaged exclusively in the manufacture of eight-day wooden case pendulum clocks and nickel alarms. The line of eight-day clocks comprises practically every style of wooden case clocks consisting of hundreds of patterns.

The plant at the present time consists of two main buildings, the case shop and movement shop, with the necessary auxiliary buildings, all built of brick and equipped with the most modern machinery for the manufacture from raw material of practically every "part" entering into the construction of a clock. The case shop is 400 feet long, four stories high, connected by an overhead passage with the movement

shop, which is 250 feet long, four stories high. The auxiliary buildings consist of engine house, boiler house, kiln dry, casting and plating shop, raw material warehouse, finished stock ware house (capacity 100,000 clocks) and other smaller buildings.

L. H. SNYDER & COMPANY.

The firm of L. H. Snyder & Company, was organized in January of 1902. They commenced business in the factory formerly occupied by The Codling Manufacturing Company, and continued operations there for one year. In 1903 they purchased the Churchill property on the corner of East Street and Riverside Avenue, which is their present location.

THE TURNER HEATER COMPANY.

The Turner Heater Company was organized September 18, 1890, as a joint stock company capitalized at $50,000, for the purpose of manufacturing and dealing in hot air heaters and other heating devices. The officers being: W. A. Ingraham, president, George S. Hull, vice president and S. K. Montgomery, secretary and treasurer. The company bought all the patents of L. W. Turner covering the Turner hot air heater and started business in the old case shop of The E. Ingraham Company which was bought for the purpose.

In 1892, S. K. Montgomery resigned as secretary and treasurer and G. W. Neubauer was elected to the position. Geo. S. Hull was elected president in 1893 and held the position until his death in 1906, when W. E. Fogg was elected to the position. The old case shop was destroyed by fire in 1904 and in spring of 1905 the present shop was built. Besides wholesaling and retailing furnaces the company does a jobbing business in smoke stacks, blowers and metal roofing.

PLANT OF BRISTOL PRESS—1907.

THE HORTON MANUFACTURING COMPANY.

The Horton Manufacturing Company, situated at No. 135 North Main Street, manufacturers of the famous Bristol Steel fishing rods, organized in 1887, has a capitalization of $100,000, with the following officers: Charles F. Pope, president, residing in New York; Charles T. Treadway, treasurer, and Willis H. Bacon, secretary.

The plant consists of a three story brick building and tower, forty by two hundred feet, of the best construction, a one story hardening shop, twenty-five by twenty-five feet, and a two story finishing shop, twenty by twenty-five feet.

The factory equipment is of the best, with latest improved ma-

chinery. About one hundred skilled workmen are employed the year round, producing a line of steel fishing rods ranging from the lighest fly tackle to the heavier styles used in deep sea angling, as well as a comprehensive line of rod mountings and sundries.

Rood & Horton, established in 1874, machine work and novelties, sold out in 1880 to New Haven Clock Company, Mr. Horton oing to New Haven.

In 1886 Mr. Horton came back to Bristol and started in the same line as before, and invented the steel rod in 1886 and 1887. The Horton Manufacturing Company was formed, and Mr. Horton eventually selling his interest in the rods and patents to them.

JEROME B. FORD MACHINE SHOP.

Jerome B. Ford Machine Shop was established in 1894. The shop contains 30 different machines for the manufacture of dies and tools, and special machinery. It is equipped with machinery for both large and small works of all descriptions.

INTERIOR, SHOWING MR. FORD AT WORK.

FLETCHER TERRY & COMPANY.

The firm of Fletcher, Terry & Company, located in East Bristol, was started in January, 1903, for the purpose of making and placing on the market a patented glass cutter. Meeting with good success, they have branched out into the standard styles also, and they are today making as large a line of glass cutters for all purposes as any other firm in the United States. Catering in particular to the glass

trade, they are making a cutter that is rapidly gaining a reputation for the firm among the large users.

The policy of the firm is for expansion, and already other departures in light hardware lines are contemplated.

The firm was started by Fred S. Fletcher and Franklin E. Terry, but later on two brothers of Mr. Fletcher were taken into partnership. They employ at present from three to seven employees and the prospects are that more help will be required in the near future.

THE PENFIELD SAW WORKS.

The business that bears this name was started in 1834 by the late Irenus Atkins; conducted by him for about 30 years, then removed to present location and organized as The Porter Saw Co., later as The Bristol Saw Co.

In 1879 it was bought by E. O. Penfield, and conducted by him until 1899, when it was acquired by the present owner, M. D. Edgerton, and since that time known as The Penfield Saw Works.

The saws made here are of high grade, adapted to cutting a wide range of material; those for various kinds of metal being special feature. Other goods are made including circular slitters for metal and paper, dial plates, cutting and creasing rule for folding box-makers use.

Selling is mainly direct to users.

TURNER & DEEGAN.

The individual proprietors of the works are: Messrs. Geo. H. Turner and Patrick H. Deegan. The business consists of the manufacture of bit braces, screw drivers and other light hardware.

This enterprise was established in March, 1894, at Forestville, in the factory known as the old Bit Shop, formerly used for the manufacturing of clocks, and located on the Pequabuck River. They continued business in this factory for about five years, when in the spring of 1899, March 13, Mr. Deegan, through an accident, received injuries from which he died, March 20.

Mr. Turner purchased of the estate Mr. Deegan's interest, continuing the business under the firm's name. During this year Mr. Turner purchased of A. H. Warner & Company their water privilege, located in northern part of the town in the village formerly called Polkville, now called Edgewood, and built a new factory and moved into it November of the same year. This gave them more room which they needed in the manufacturing of their goods, which has developed a demand for their products in all parts of the United States and foreign countries.

Before closing this subject the writer would like to call attention to the fact, as a matter of history, that this water privilege was built by Alexander and Edward Graham. Leasing the land that the pond is built on from David A. and Franklin Newell on May 23d, 1843. Term of lease 999 years. Just when the factory was completed is not known by the writer, but somewhere about 1843. For several years they made clocks and other house furniture.

Loring Byington became interested in the company during the year of 1843, and until about 1860, when on January 1st, 1862, H. A.

Warner and John H. Sessions purchased this property from the Bristol Savings Bank & Building and Loan Association. They entered the wood turning business and began the manufacture of cabinet furniture trimmings. They continued as a company until April 15th, 1865, when Mr. J. H. Sessions bought out Mr. Warner's interest and continued the business there until 1869; disposed of this property and built a new factory in the center of the town. George Turner purchasing this property on April 15th, 1869, began the manufacture of table cutlery and other light hardware until 1884, when this factory was destroyed by fire, Mr. Turner disposing of his property to Mr. E. F. Gaylord, December 2d, 1885, and on December 3d, Mr. Gaylord sold to H. S. Bartholomew.

In the spring of 1891 Mr. Bartholomew exchanged property with A. H. Warner & Company. They, building a new factory on this site, continued the wood turning business until 1896, when this property was again destroyed by fire. Then they moved their business to Plainville.

THE BRISTOL MANUFACTURING COMPANY.

The Bristol Manufacturing Company is one of the oldest establishments in Bristol, and its mills and warehouses are located on both sides of Riverside Avenue, a little east of Main street. The Company was organized in 1837 with a capital stock of $45,000, and manufactured satinet. Chauncey Ives and Bryan Hooker were respectively first President and Secretary. In 1856 the Company was reorganized and its capital stock was increased to $75,000, and John English chosen

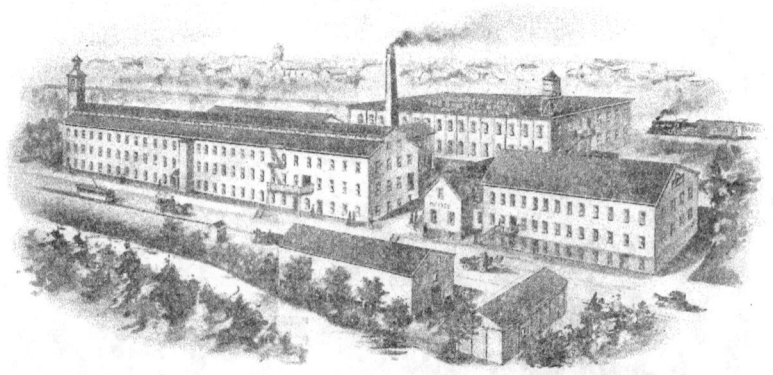

THE BRISTOL PLANT.

President with Harmanus Welch Secretary. They then gave their attention to the manufacture of knit underwear, in which the Company has ever since been successfully engaged. The growth of the Company in its new business has been steady, and its career has been prosperous, as its product has become very popular in the markets by reason of its superior quality and excellent finish.

In 1860 Mr. English retired and Mr. J. R. Mitchell was chosen President. He was succeeded by Elisha N. Welch who held the position until his death, in August, 1887, when Mr. Mitchell was again made President, and served until his death in May, 1899. Mr. Mitchell was followed by Mr. J. Hart Welch as President, until he died in 1902, when Mr. F. G. Hayward was elected President. Mr. Hayward has been with the Company since 1879, first as its Secretary, then as Treasurer and Manager, and now as its President. The present officers of the Company are, F. G. Hayward, President, Pierce N. Welch, Vice President, and A. D. Hawley, Secretary and Treasurer. The Directors are Pierce N. Welch, Henry F. English of New Haven, F. G. Hayward, Julian R. Hawley, Roger S. Newell, A. D. Hawley and C. T. Treadway of Bristol.

Besides the Bristol Mills, the Company owns and operates a large mill at Plainville, which was formerly conducted as The Plainville Manufacturing Company, and employs in the two mills about 350 hands.

THE PLAINVILLE PLANT

CLAYTON BROTHERS, INCORPORATED.

The business of this firm was founded by William Clayton, a native of Sheffield, England, who came to this country in 1849 and started a factory in Whigville, Conn., in 1866, occupying part of the Don E. Peck factory where he manufactured table cutlery handles of wood, bone and ivory, importing blades from England and hafting them in this country. After a short time he moved to Bristol and occupied the old Dunbar shop on Union street, now owned by H. C. & A. J. Clayton, where he continued the manufacture of table cutlery, and re-plating and re-finishing. In this business he was associated with his son under the firm name of Clayton Bros. & Son. In 1875 they purchased a shop and water privilege known as the Drum Shop, building a new dam and factory. At first little was done in the table cutlery line, the company engaging largely in the manufacture of screw drivers. About 1881 they commenced the manufacture of shears, which since then has continued to be their principle business. Mr. Wm. Clayton founder of the business died in 1883, and after his death the business was continued by his

sons under the firm name of Clayton Brothers. The two younger brothers, Frank and James, withdrew and started in business for themselves in the old Watrous Shop in the style of Frank Clayton & Co. This shop burned down in 1893, and the old firm of Clayton Bros., and Frank Clayton & Co. consolidated as Clayton Brothers, and built a new factory on the site of the Watrous Shop in 1893, where they manufactured steel laid, cast iron shears and tinner snips.

November 17, 1906, Clayton Bros. sold their business to W. M. Bowes of New York, who previously marketed their goods for a number of years, and S. L. Butler of Northampton, Mass. December 26th, Bowes and Butler incorporated the business under the firm name of Clayton Brothers, Incorporated. The plant has been added to from year to year, and they have recently completed a large foundry for turning out their grey iron castings. The business is growing rapidly.

THE H. C. THOMPSON CLOCK COMPANY.

This business was founded by Chauncey Ives, who, in 1849, sold out to Noah Pomeroy. Mr. Pomeroy continued the business, making clock movements only, until 1878, when H. C. Thompson purchased the plant and increased the business by adding new lines of manufacture.

In 1903 a joint stock company was formed and the name was changed to The H. C. Thompson Clock Company.

THE OLD FACTORY, PARTIALLY BURNED NOV. 20, 1906.

NEW PLANT ON FEDERAL STREET.

The business has grown and developed so that not only clock movements, but gas, water and electric meters, spring motors and various articles of similar nature are manufactured.

November 20, 1906, the plant was destroyed partially by fire. The old wooden shop was superseded by a modern brick structure, where business was resumed in May, 1907, with largely increased facilities.

A. H. WARNER & COMPANY.

The business now conducted by this company was established in 1865 by Charles H. Alpress and William B. Carpenter in the district since known both as Polkville and Edgewood. In the spring of 1866, Augustus H. Warner was admitted to partnership, the firm being known as Alpress, Carpenter & Company. The following fall, Henry A. Warner bought the interest of Mr. Alpress. Soon after, the business was moved from the factory of G. W. & H. S. Bartholomew to one of their own a little farther down the stream. The product was wood turning, mostly handles, and was entirely hand turning. In 1869, Mr. Carpenter sold out to the Warners and the name was changed to H. A. & A. H. Warner. A new factory was built in 1873.

After the death of H. A. Warner in 1890, Henry D. Warner went into partnership with A. H. Warner, his father, since which time the name has been A. H. Warner & Company. The factory burning in 1892, they rebuilt on ground formerly occupied by the business of H. A. Warner and J. H. Sessions and later by George Turner, now the site of the factory of Turner & Deegan. Later for three years the factory was in operation in Plainville but in 1900 was relocated in Bristol.

In 1904, the building called "The Dial Shop" was bought of The E. Ingraham Company, and was moved to Federal Street and refitted. Lathes for both hand turnings and machine turnings are operated and a general line of small wood turnings is produced. Among the specialties are wood faucets, base ball bats, bicycle grips, turned work and other work for the electrical trade, bath tub seats, etc. Especial attention is given to turnings in cocobola, rosewood, lignumvitæ, mahogany, and boxwood.

THE W. C. LADD COMPANY.

W. C. Ladd, maker of cathedral gongs, cast iron nuts, lantern holders and light hardware, succeeded the late Harry W. Barnes, who, at the time of his death in 1889, was located on Laurel Street.

Mr. Ladd built his present factory on Wallace Street in 1092. The

first floor is used for manufacturing purposes, the stock room being in the basement. It is equipped with hydraulic elevator. The power is furnished by a gas engine.

FISHERMAN'S (P)LUCK.

A SAD TALE OF INTENT TENT LIFE.

I belong to the West Hill Club,
And fish is my favorite grub,
Every year I camp out,
And catch numberless trout,
And bass, perch, pick'rel and chub.

Our canvas and baggage we load on the cars
And go to the woods to sleep under the stars,
Civilization and business we leave far be-
hind,
And we kick up our heels
just as free as the wind.

We are veterans all, wearing each a wool
shirt,—
A "biled shirt" in camp would show too
much dirt.
We can sleep on pine boughs or even the
ground,
But our sleep is at times not very profound,

The   surveys us from loftiest
height,
The   reconnoiters almost every
night,
The   serenades by   Luna's pale
light,
The   hoots in tree-tops away out of
sight,
The   o'er our faces doth venturesome
run,
(Or a   -ish tent-mate is up to
some fun,)
The   darts past in surprise that,
we've come,
Daring to venture so far from our home.

I belong to the West Hill Club,
And fish is my favorite grub,
Once a year I camp out,
And *attempt* to catch trout,—
But eat bullheads! and sunfish! and
chub!
(Or canned beef!)

Our ambition for fish is enormously great,
And expect to catch naught less than five
pounds in weight;
We carry no scales for each fish has his own,
And we're sure he's full weight if he isn't
half grown.
We judge of the weight by the trouble
we've had,
So every small minnow seems big as a shad;

I'm the typical Fisher-man,
I go with our caravan;
I camp on the hills,
By the lakes and the rills,—
And dig breakfast out of a can.

THIS

is what we expect,
This   is what we oft get,
And we're hungry as hungry can be;
Our Chicago canned beef is a wonderful
treat
When we've fished all day long and no
something to eat,
For hunger and we don't agree.

I belong to the West Hill Club,
But beef is substantial grub;
I'd eat lots if I could,
When I camp in the wood,
But if hungry I'd eat catamount cub.

THE ▨▨▨ HOTEL.

ITS RISE, PROGRESS AND FALL.

A half score years ago
I sat me down and thought—
"A splendid brick hotel
I'll build on this 'ere spot."

A house I moved away,
My plan was good throughout,
Some bricks I bought—and then
I kinder petered out (Luke 14 28

For several years or more,
A shanty marked the place
Where I did think to build,
Before I changed my base.

But time flew on, as time
Will always fly, you know,
And by-and by I thought,
"This thing bad oughter go."

More bricks I bought, and then
I shoved it with a rush,
And never, for its style,
Had reason e'er to blush.

A monument to me
I really meant it for,
To die and be forgot
I always did abhor.

A few years it has stood
An orn'ment to the town,
A splendid Brick Hotel—
But now it must come down.
  I love my Brick Hotel,
  As Moses loved Isaac;
  But surely, nevertheless,
  I'm going to sacrifice it.

Oft in the woods of Maine,
I go to fish and roam;
But lately 'taint much fun—
My Brick Hotel's at home.
  I love my Brick Hotel
  As Aaron loved Isaac,
  Notwithstanding, nevertheless,
  I'm "inspired" to sacrifice it

Against my interest, the town
Has voted herlicense,
Against which I protest
And call it an offense.

No temperance hotel
Shall be identified
With me or mine, so long
As I stay in this my hide.

As sure's Beelzebub
In Tophet lives, will I
Make this town sick—you'll see
And that before I die
  I love my Brick Hotel,
  As Jacob loved Isaac,
  But, nevertheless, you'll see
  I'm going to sacrifice it.

My Brick Hotel shall not
Be run without a bar,
Where thirsty men may lose
Their perpendicular.

And so I'll pull it down,
My beauteous Brick Hotel;
It's worse than pulling teeth,
Much worse than tongue can tell.
  I love my Brick Hotel,
  As David loved Isaac,
  But licensed it is not,
  And so I'll sacrifice it.

Ruins shall mark the spot
Where stately structure stood.

A home for bat and crow,
For rat, and snake, and toad.
  I love my Brick Hotel,
  But sure I'll sacrifice it;
  I'll pull it down as true
  As Abel murdered Isaac.

The pale new moon will look
With sadness on the place.
The cat a requiem sing,
With woeful, weeping face.

Good bye to all my hopes,
Good bye my loved Hotel;
Your stones and bricks within
My heart are treasured well
  I love my Brick Hotel,
  I hate to sacrifice it,
  But sure, without a bar,
  I only should despise it

THE WEST HILL CLUB AND THE BRICK HOTEL.

In the days when Mr. Charles H Riggs was editor of *The Bristol Press*, there occasionally appeared some original poems of local interest, written by the editor uniquely illustrated by the use of bits of type ornaments and little cuts. Two of these articles we reproduce with the accompanying explanatory data, which was kindly furnished by Editor Riggs.

WEST HILL CLUB organized 1878; disbanded 1906. Membership as follows:

George S. Hull, D. P. Pardee. Everett Horton, Hiram Wilcox, W.W. Thorpe, E. B. Dunbar, W. W. Dunbar, S. G. Monce, Thos. Barnes, George P. Barbour, G. H. Blakesley, H. C. Butler, Thomas T. Barbour, George W. Mitchell, H. B. Cook, A. J. Muzzy, H. W. Barnes, C. S. Treadway, William T. Smith, John J. Jennings, Lee Roberts, Charles A. Lane, Roger S. Newell.

"THE BRICK HOTEL."

The poem on "The Brick Hotel," or The Gridley House, was written by the editor and published in *The Bristol Press* in 1882.

A few words of explanation are necessary to an understanding of the poem. In 1871, Henry W. Gridley moved from the corner of Main and North Main Streets a frame dwelling for the purpose of erecting on the site a hotel. But before the work was commenced Seymour's and Nott's blocks, opposite, were destroyed by fire, and L. G. Merick, who had occupied a store in Nott's building, rented the vacant corner and erected a shanty for his grocery business, to be used until Mr. Nott could rebuild. After he vacated the shanty, Mr. Gridley allowed it to remain several years, renting it to different parties for various purposes. This shanty became popularly known as the "Brick Hotel," and was made the basis of a great deal of fun in the press and the community, as long as it was allowed to stand. Finally the owner bought a quantity of brick, preparatory to building, but just then the town gave a vote for no license, which so incensed Mr. Gridley that he sold his brick and allowed the shanty to remain a year or two longer. Finally in 1879, he concluded to carry out his design, and the Gridley House was built. He soon found a tenant and matters went along smoothly till 1882, when the town again voted no license, whereupon Mr. Gridley declared his intention of tearing down the hotel. This is what inspired the poem.

THE N. L. BIRGE SONS CO.

ONE of the old established industries of this city is the knitting works of the N. L. Birge Sons Co., manufacturers of men's fine knit underwear. This concern has long been an adjunct to the prosperity of the town, having been founded in 1850, when it was known as the "Bristol Knitting Company." After various changes, Mr. N. L. Birge became the sole proprietor and carried on the business until 1882, when he admitted his son, Mr. John Birge into copartnership, under the style of N. L. Birge & Son. In 1893 his second son, Mr. George W. Birge, was also admitted into the firm. Their new mill is a model efficiency throughout and the equipment of machinery and appliances is of the latest improved description, including two thousand spindles, five sets of cards, seven mules, forty-two sewing machines and thirty-nine improved circular rib knitting machines, also winder, loopers, etc. A seventy-five horse power engine drives the machinery, which has a capacity of producing over one hundred dozen

underwear daily, the mill affording steady employment to one hundred and twenty hands. The firm's goods are much preferred by the trade, being of such superior quality and splendidly finished. The New York office and salesrooms are located at No. 346 Broadway. Their goods are sold generally throughout the United States and stand today among the best in the market. Mr. N. L. Birge was a native of this city and was a director and vice president of the Bristol National Bank; was one of the original incorporators of the Bristol Savings Bank; and vice president of the Bristol Water Company. Mr. John Birge was also a native of this city, and was State senator from the fourth district. In the knit goods industry The N. L. Birge Sons Company have continued a prosperous career, the secret of their success being due to the manifest superiority of their products.

MARSHALL I. SMITH.

Die making and sheet metal stamping to order. This business was established in 1898 by Ira B. Smith who conducted it until August 1906, when it was sold to M. I. and R. M. Smith who formed a partner-

ship under the firm name of The Ira B. Smith Company and was conducted by them until July 1, 1907, when Marshall I. Smith became sole owner.

The Second Plate of Co. D Portraits will appear in the section of the book devoted to "Bristol Societies."

1. Hardening Department. 2. Patent Department in Bristol National Bank Building. 3. Foundry. 4. Patent Department, General Office. 5. Office of Chief Patent Attorney. 6. Patent Department Office. 7. Office of President A. F. Rockwell. 8. Office of Treasurer C. T. Treadway. 9. Accounting Department. 10. Advertising and Purchasing Departments. 11. Office of Secretary DeWitt Page. 12. Main Factory. 13. Printing Department. 14. Office of Superintendent. 15. Drafting Department. 16. Office of Outside Department and Laboratory. 17. Dipping Department. 18. Gas Plant, Interior. 19. Engine Room No. 1. 20. Buffing Room. 21. Engine Room No. 2.

THE NEW DEPARTURE MANUFACTURING COMPANY.

Through The New Departure Manufacturing Company, Bristol is known the wide world over. The New Departure coaster brakes and bicycle bells are sold and advertised in every large trade center on the globe. The company has offices in England, France, Germany and Denmark and its literature is printed in twelve or more languages. Whatever the language of the newspaper advertisement, circular or catalogue, the name of the company and its home town are in English, giving Bristol wider advertising than most American cities.

This broad market has consumed millions of Bristol made coaster brakes. It is safe to assume, after the extensive advertising this product has had in more than thirty countries, that today the number of bicycle users who do not know of New Departures, is indeed few.

The New Departure Manufacturing Company, while one of the

BRANCH FACTORY AT WEISSENSER, BERLIN, GERMANY

youngest of Bristol's principal manufactories, is the largest, employing at its Bristol and East Bristol factories, over six hundred hands and at its German factory, located at Weissensee (suburb of Berlin), over one hundred hands.

Less than eighteen years ago, this Company began its existence in a room sixty feet square, in the north end of the old H. C. Thompson clock factory on Federal Street. At the busiest times of the year, six hands were employed. Today, should its plants be combined in a one-story building forty feet wide, that building would extend nearly a mile in length.

The New Departure Bell Company was organized June 27, 1889, and incorporated with a capital of $50,000, for the manufacture of door, office and call bells, under patents taken out by Albert F. Rockwell, now president of the company.

The mechanism of the bell gave "electrical results without a battery" and was a unique and distinctive invention. This fact suggested the

1. Milling and Drilling Room, looking west, 2. Automatic Room. 3. Car and Fire Bell Department, 4. Machine Room. 5. Rivet and Screw Department. 6. Milling and Drilling Room, looking east. 7. Shipping Room. 8. Ball Filling and Testing Department. 9. Assembling Room. 10. Bell Department Factory, East Bristol: 10. Dipping, Pickling and Tumbling Department. 12. Enameling Department. 13. Grinding Room. 14. Cyclometer Department. 15. Ball Making Department. 16. Tool Room. 17. Press Room.

name of the company and throughout its career that name has been an apt characterization of its product—things new and ingenious.

Presently, a line of bicycle bells was marketed, adapting the same mechanical principles as in the other bells. The business of the company increased rapidly and it was not long before people outside of Bristol were calling it the "Bell Town." The original quarters were inadequate and the company purchased what was then known as the Jones factory on North Main Street. This building is now the smallest of the score that comprise the New Departure plant. The company removed to this building in less than a year from its organization.

The growth of the new industry was nothing short of marvelous. At one time, the product of the factory was ten thousand bells a day.

The manufacture and sale of bicycle lamps was also successfully undertaken and carried on for several years. This business was sold in 1897 to the Joseph Lucas Sons Company of Birmingham, England, who continue the manufacture of the lamps at the present time.

The year following the sale of the lamp business, the New Departure Company began the manufacture of New Departure coaster brakes, under patents of Albert F. Rockwell. The success of this manufacture has already been intimated.

Several years ago, the branch factory in Germany was established and January 28, 1907, the plant and business of the Liberty Bell Company in East Bristol was purchased. This plant has been enlarged and is now the bell department of the company.

In 1907 also, additional buildings were constructed at the main plant, principally the large four story steel construction building on Valley Street, for the manufacture of the New Departure "two-in-one" ball bearing.

Until the first of last August, John H. Graham & Company of New York had been the selling agents of the company. On that date this arrangement was discontinued and the company now markets its product direct from the factory.

The name of the company was changed some years ago from that of the New Departure Bell Company to the New Departure Manufacturing Company. At the last session of the General Assembly, the company was authorized to increase its capital to $1,500,000.

The present officers are:—President, Albert F. Rockwell; Vice President, George A. Graham of New York; Secretary, DeWitt Page; Treasurer, Charles T. Treadway. These, with Charles F. Pope and W. A. Graham of New York, constitute the Board of Directors.

THE WALLACE BARNES CO.

The Wallace Barnes company is busy installing the machinery in the large factory addition just completed. The new building is a four story brick structure, 40x140 feet, of mill construction, and containing all of the latest equipment for heating, automatic sprinkling, etc. The new factory gives an additional floor space of 22,000 feet, increasing the floor space of the concern to 55,300 feet and supplying the necessary room for the rapidly increasing business.

The whole of the new factory will be used for general manufacturing purposes. A large new hydraulic elevator is also being constructed on the south side of the new building. The first floor will be used as a press room and for other heavy work. The second floor will be utilized chiefly for bench work and machinery. The third floor will be taken up by the machine and die room, while the lighter work will be done on the top floor.

The factory is well lighted and sanitarily equipped throughout. A telephone system has been installed to facilitate the factory communication. Upon each floor an office space has been set off by grill work for the foreman of the room. A two story brick and concrete building, 25x25 feet, strictly fireproof, has been constructed for the die house.

The machinery, tools and stock are being moved from the factory building on Main street to the new building, and the old building will be occupied by the office, shipping room, and for storage purposes. The present office room will be greatly increased.

The Wallace Barnes company is this year celebrating its fiftieth anniversary. It was established in 1857 by Wallace Barnes. Shortly after he consolidated with E. L. Dunbar and the business was conducted under the firm name of Dunbar and Barnes, but in 1866 Wallace Barnes purchased the interests of Mr. Dunbar and conducted the business till his death in 1893. For the next four years the business was conducted as the Wallace Barnes estate. In 1897 The Wallace Barnes Company was incorporated and the business has increased and prospered under the management of Carlyle F. Barnes. During the past ten years the concern has increased its capacity and business from six to eight times its former size.

The company is engaged in the manufacture of all kinds of small springs, made of sheet steel, flat or round wire of either brass or steel. The company has also taken up extensively the manufacture of small screw machine products, and drop forgings. There are 225 employees at work at the factory at the present time.

The company gets its power from two steam engines and a generator which transmits power to motors which are placed upon each floor of the factory. The power plant is of 300 horse power capacity.

M. H. BARNARD.

White Rock Ice Cream has the reputation of being one of the purest and best Ice Creams on the market. We have one of the largest storage capacities of any concern in the state. We furnished the Sessions Foundry Co. with 4,100 individual boxes on July 10th, 1907, which was one of the largest orders ever filled in this State.

This is also the home of the celebrated Barnard Cattle Stanchion. This stanchion is conceded by all who have used it to be the most practical cattle fastener on the market. All parts are made in the factory from the raw materlai.

GEORGE C. ARMS' MONUMENTAL WORKS.

George C. Arms was born in Duxbury, Vt., March 2, 1827. He engaged in the marble and granite business in 1862 in Waterbury, Vt., with a branch shop in Montpelier, he also dealt in mowing machines, lumber and furs, buying and selling several thousand dollars worth of the latter each year. In all he did a large and successful business.

His many duties were wearing upon his health and in 1875, he sold his entire business.

He was employed by Governor Proctor as traveling salesman, wholesaling marble, covering the middle and western states. He refused a very flattering salary and discontinued this business on account of the death of a son while he was away. In May, 1880, Mr. Arms started the monumental business in Bristol and has succeeeded in building up a large trade, many monuments being shipped direct from the quarries to their destination. Being a man of sterling character and strict business

integrity, he has won an enviable reputation among the business men of the State, as well as the respect and esteem of the citizens of Bristol.

Mr. Arms has always striven to buy the most lasting material, furnishing the best of works, and selling at a moderate profit. This is substantiated by the fact that for fifteen years, not a stone was erected in Bristol by outside parties, and during the twenty-seven years he has been in Bristol he has placed nearly every job in our cemeteries, agents and dealers being frank to admit they could not compete with his prices.

He employs no agents, has never lost $100 during his business career of forty-five years and today, when nearly eighty-one years of age, can be found every day attending to his increasing business. His work, which is a standing advertisement can be seen in nearly every city and town in the State, as well as in New York City, Albany, Unadilla, N. Y., Springfield and many other Massachusetts towns, also Wisconsin, Florida, Pennsylvania, New Hampshire, Rhode Island, etc.

Among the monuments illustrated in this book, erected by Mr. Arms are the Hull, Candee, Levitt, Sessions and others.

Mr. Arms takes pride in telling of a number of expensive monuments which he has sold for one thousand to five thousand dollars each, when he was told to put up a monument from a certain design as large as he could for such a sum, no contract being required.

Mr. Arms always does what he agrees to, consequently no dissatisfied customers. His son, Howard G. Arms, has been with him thirty-six years (excepting from 1894 to 1907) when he occupied the office of Chief-of-Police, resigning April 1, 1907, to assist his father. January 1, 1907, Mr. Arms removed from his old location on North Main street to No. 15 Center street.

Mr. Arms has always been active in church work, being for twenty-two years treasurer of the church and serving as superintendent of the Sunday School of the Advent Church for eighteen years. It has been the writer's privilege to know him thoroughly for many years, a consistent Christian seven days in the week.

THE BLAKESLEY NOVELTY CO.

The company was organized in 1887, for the manufactory of round arm bands, and the "easy" arm band was their first product and is today a great seller. In the manufacture of arm bands this company is easily the recognized leader.

THE IDEAL LAUNDRY.

The laundry was started by Eli La Fabare, May 1, 1895, and for three years was operated under the name of "The Empire Steam Laundry." In 1898, the business was purchased by Card & Doudoin, who continued as proprietors until 1900, when the business was sold to E. E. Hart. Mr. Hart removed to Pearl Street, occupying the present quarters in the Brick Factory Building, erected by Joel T. Case, for the

manufacture of the "Case Engine." Mr. Hart conducted the business for five years, after which he leased the business for one year to Bennett & Clary of New Britain, who changed the name to "The Ideal Laundry" and Mr. W. G. Fenn managed the business for them. December 1, 1906, Mr. Fenn bought the business and has today one of the best equipped laundry plants in the State.

THE GIDDINGS' CARRIAGE, FORGING AND SHOEING SHOP.

The "Giddings" shop has for many years been a staid landmark on North Main Street. It was established in 1874, 33 years ago, by Watson Giddings, who came to Bristol from Terryville where he had run a shop for three years, and had previously run a carriage shop in Winsted for a term of years. The original shop building on North Main Street had a floor space of only 2,000 square feet, but by strict integrity, first-class work and honest dealing, the business has steadily increased, requiring additions being built on from time to time, having been enlarged no less than seven times, the plant now has a floor space of over 10,000 square feet, besides a two story storehouse on Foley Street of 2,400 square feet capacity.

F. W. Giddings, his son and the present proprietor, was admitted into partnership in 1886, twenty-one years ago, and has been continually identified in the business since that date. By building wagons of good material only, and of first-class workmanship, they have established a reputation for the durability of their work that reaches far beyond

the borders of the town, having built wagons and trucks for the Collins Company of Collinsville, the Echo Farm Company, and others of Litchfield and for parties in Ansonia, Waterbury, South Manchester, New Britain, and many other surrounding towns, also some light work for parties in Rhode Island. In April, 1901, F. W. Giddings bought out his father's interest in the business and has successfully conducted it since.

In 1905 he erected the storehouse on Foley Street and last fall found it necessary to still further enlarge the shop building, and this spring has installed a power hammer to do the heavier forging, and has also added other improved machinery. The Giddings' shop is now by far the largest and best equiped wagon and forging shop in the State, outside of the larger cities.

The painting department has been conducted by F. R. Mallory & Son since 1891, who have built up a large and increasing trade in that line.

THE FACTORY OF WILLIAM L. BARRETT.

This business was established in 1893 in what was known as the Root Shop at the corner of Main and School Streets, continuing there until the Root Estate went out of business in 1902, when quarters were secured in the Ira B. Smith factory on Parallel Street, remaining there until 1904, when the present factory was erected by Mr. Barrett.

Fifteen hands are here employed in the manufacture of glass cutters, of which about twenty-five different patterns are made. These goods are widely known and find sale in every civilized country on the globe

SOME BRISTOL GAME.

Photo by Moultrope.

The BRISTOL GUN CLUB.

The Bristol Gun Club was organized July 25, 1887, at a meeting called for that purpose at the residence of A. Q. Perkins, who was elected its first President; H. J. Mills, Vice President, and G. W. Barnes, Secretary, being the other officers. The club took the place of two clubs previously existing, known as the North Side Club, and the South Side Club. In 1891, H. J. Mills was elected President, holding the office for a number of years. The present officers are: President, C. E. Kittell; Vice President, W. Moran; Secretary, J. Z. Douglass. The club house, below the Golf Links, was erected in 1890.

MR. NEWELL MOULTHROPE, CELEBRATED COON HUNTER.

A MEMBER OF THE GUN CLUB—AFIELD.

AT THE MOUTH OF THE OLD COPPER MINE.

COPPER MINES IN BRISTOL.

BY MILO LEON NORTON.

IT WAS late in the eighteenth century that copper was discovered at a spring issuing from the southern end of a mountain, then known as Zach's mountain, from an Indian hunter who made it his hunting ground, by Theophilus Botsford, a farmer living east of the mine in a house occupied many years by the Gomme family. Attention was called to the matter by the green colored water issuing from the spring, also tinging the small brook flowing from it, and destroying the vegetation along the banks. Beyond scraping away some of the soil and exposing rich indications of ore, Mr. Botsford did nothing to develop the mine, and was succeeded by Asa Hooker, who, about the year 1800, leased the land of the owner, Widow Sarah Yale, but did little work upon it, transferring his interest to Luke Gridley, a blacksmith, who lived in the Stafford District, near the site of the Boardman clock shop. Gridley worked the mine a few years, smelting some of the ore in his forge, but accomplishing little.

The real history of the mine begins with the development of the rich deposit of ore, said to have been the richest in the world, by George W. Bartholomew, a resident of Edgewood, who, in 1836, drained the hole made by Gridley, opening a trench twenty feet long, ten wide and seventeen deep, revealing veins of variegated ore, ranging from sixty to eighty per cent. pure copper, and so rich that it had only to be trimmed with hammers to fit it for the smelting furnace. It was shipped in bags by canal to New Haven, whence it was sent to England to be smelted, and was a very profitable venture. Mr. Bartholomew organized, in 1837, the Bristol Mine Company, consisting of Andrew Miller, Harvey Case, Erastus Case, Sylvester Woodward, and himself. Miller was a practical miner from New Jersey, who soon acquired a controlling interest, selling a half interest in the mine to English capitalists for $28,000. Business prospered until the death of Miller by drowning in the Tunxis river, which was the first of a series of misfortunes that attended the subsequent working of the mine, eventually wrecking it. The original company failed in 1846, and the property passed into the hands of Richard F. Blydenburg, of New York, to whom Abel Yale leased the lands of the mine, and also the water privilege where a dam was afterward erected to furnish power for the machinery of the mine, for the period of nine hundred and ninety-nine years. Blydenburg sold two thirds of his interest in the mine to H. Bradford, also of New York, for $61,849.

To raise capital for extensively working the mine, the property was mortgaged to Dr. Eliphalet Nott, President of Union College, for $212,052. Blydenburg sold his third interest to Nott for $31,000, and he became the owner of the entire property. The mine was worked on a large scale, extensive drifts were made, large buildings erected, and ore of exceeding richness was taken out in vast quantities. Extravagance in management and expenditures soon exceeded the income from the mine, great as it was, and Dr. Nott got out of it finally, wiser, undoubtedly, but decidedly no richer for his mining experience. The property passed into the hands of John M. Woolsey, son of President Woolsey, of Yale College. Under the direction of Prof. Silliman, the most extravagant schemes and experiments, of a costly nature, were indulged in, the Professor being a fine theorist, but a very poor practical miner. Hundreds of thousands of dollars, from first to last, were poured into the mine, and, as the longest purse has a bottom, so in this case the bottom of the purse was reached, and the Bristol Mining Company, organized in 1855, became bankrupt in 1857, the year of the financial crash, although an income of $2,000 a month above necessary expenses was being received from the mine up to its closing. In 1858, Woolsey, having acquired the entire property by foreclosure of a mortgage, closed up the property, and for thirty years it remained idle. The extensive buildings, machinery, etc. were sold at what they would fetch, Colonel Dunbar purchasing the bell, which has never ceased to ring at nine o'clock since it was installed in his factory; the engine was placed in George Jones' clock shop, now the old building of the New Departure Co.; and the conical hopper, in which the crushed rock was placed to be ground still finer before separating, was removed to his farm in East Bristol by Lemuel Hollister, who utilized it, inverted, as the roof of an out-building, where it still stands. Some of the smaller buildings were moved away, and converted into dwelling houses; and the lumber of the large buildings was utilized by neighboring farmers for enlarging or repairing their farm buildings.

In 1888, the attention of Burton S. Cowles, who was then foreman in the box factory of Rev. B. Hitchcock, was called to the large quantity of crushed rock, from the workings of the mine, and from which not all of the copper had been extracted; and, being something of an amateur chemist, he experimented with the sand, extracting the metal by means of acid, depositing it upon scrap iron, from which it could be removed in a pure state. Mr. Cowles succeeded in interesting E. G. Hubbell of Pittsfield, Mass., who entered into the project, securing the co-operation of other capitalists, when the control of the mine and the lands connected with it, passed into their possession. The Bristol Copper and Silver Mining Co., was organized at Albany, with a capital of $500,000. The separation of the metal still remaining in the tailings of the old workings not proving practicable, the new company pumped out the old Williams' shaft, 240 feet in depth, and explored the old workings in every direction. New drifts were excavated, new shafts sunk, and the Williams' shaft sunk to a depth of 400 feet. The rich deposits of ore looked for did not appear, however, although immense quantities of low-grade ore were found. Much of this was hoisted to the surface, and crushed by the expensive machinery installed, of the most modern and approved construction.

In 1893, Col. Walter Cutting foreclosed the mortgage he held for money advanced, and acquired the title, in whose estate the title now remains. In 1895, becoming disgusted at the outlay of money, and the meager returns, owing partly to the low price of copper that prevailed, Col. Cutting closed the mine, which soon filled with water. The expensive machinery is rusting in the great buildings put up by the company, and the hoodoo which has attended the working of the mine from the first, seems to have succeeded at last in wrecking the fine property. which no doubt contains valuable ore, sufficient to pay good returns on the money invested, if practically and capably administered. The chapter of calamities that befell the mine property was fittingly closed in 1896, when, following a heavy downpour of rain, the waste weir of the great dam of the mine pond became clogged with ice, causing the dam to give way, precipitating a disastrous flood down the stream, washing away every bridge between there and Forestville, and wrecking a freight train on the railroad, by undermining the roadway. The privilege has since been procured by the municipality of New Britain, together with the water shed above, as an auxiliary supply to the city water works.

LAKE AVENUE CEMETERY,

The original plot of ground was deeded to the town of Bristol by Ezra Norton in 1841. Additional portions were added by his son in 1872. Restoration and improvements begun in 1899.

REV. GEORGE E. TYLER.

HISTORY OF THE ADVENT CHRISTIAN CHURCH.

The Advent Christian Church of Bristol, Conn., was organized on the 24th of February, 1858, with the following charter membership: Luther L. Tuttle, Henry L. Bradley, William O. Hough, John H. Sutcliff, George L. White, John W. Whiting and Edmond Tompkins. This number was materially increased by the addition of many new members during the months following.

For several years the public services of the society were held in various halls near the center of the town, and it was not until the year 1880 that a church building was occupied. In that year as the old Methodist Church at the North Side had been vacated the Adventists leased the building and continued to occupy it until it was totally destroyed by fire on the 5th of October, 1890. Steps were taken at once to build a new church on the same site which had now become the property of the Adventist people. The present building was dedicated with appropriate services on July 1, 1891.

Quite a heavy mortgage rested upon the property at the time of its dedication, but this has all been paid, important additions also have since been made and paid for, and besides the church has a permanent endowment fund of $2,000, the interest of which is applied to the current expenses.

INTERIOR VIEW—SUNDAY SCHOOL IN SESSION.

Since the organization the following clergymen have served as pastor of the church: Rev. Ralph Williams, 1860–62, Rev. Benajah Hitchcock, 1867–75, Rev. A. A. Hoyt, 1879–80, Rev. H. H. Tucker, 1880–83, Rev. J. C. St. John, 1884–88, Rev. George M. Tuple, 1889–91, Rev. J. C. St. John, 1891–93, Rev. L. F. Baker, April, 1894–July, 1894, Rev. William Gibb, Dec., 1894–July, 1897, Rev. George E. Tyler, March, 1898 to the present.

The membership of the church is about 175 and of the Sunday School about 125. The Young People's Society of Loyal Workers numbers 60. And there is also a Mission Society which is doing good work. The church is a mission church and has given large sums of money each year for home and foreign missions.

Three young people from the church have (in 1907) volunteered to go as missionaries to China and are training and preparing for the foreign field.

It is a principle with the church to raise all moneys for religious purposes by free will offerings and voluntary gifts. All expenses are met in this way. The pews are all free and strangers are welcomed to all services.

The present pastor, Rev. George E. Tyler, is now serving his tenth year as pastor and this is his third pastorate, the other two having been in Sturbridge, Mass. and Hartford. He is president of the United Loyal Workers of Connecticut, also President of the American Advent Mission Society whose headquarters are at Boston.

ADVENT CHRISTIAN CHURCH—WEST STREET.

THE PRUDENTIAL INSURANCE COMPANY. *Elton Photo.*

The Prudential Insurance Company of Newark, New Jersey, opened a branch office at No. 13 Prospect Street, in 1899. December 8th, 1902, Niels Nissen came here from Hartford, Conn., to take charge of the office and the agency has grown, under his management, so that he has an agency force of seven men and a stenographer.

The above is a photograph of Assistant Superintendent N. Nissee and his staff of agents working under him in April 1907.

Genealogical Section.

OWING to the limited space in a work like this we have been obliged to mention only a few of the prominent people of the past, who have been citizens of the town. These biographies have been written with much painstaking care, and with the utmost impartiality, and it has been thought best to make no attempt to arrange them in chronological order. This section of the work has been under the supervision of Mr. Milo Leon Norton, and the information given may be depended upon as being as correct as it is possible to make it.

EPHRAIM DOWNS.

FRANKLIN DOWNS.

DOWNS (OR DOWNES) FAMILY.

Ephraim Downs, one of Bristol's first clock makers, born in Wilbraham, Massachusetts, 1787, was son of David Downs and Mary Chatterton. His father was a soldier of the American Revolution. He was descended in several lines, from first New England settlers, and in six or more from original settlers of New Haven. The earliest of the name here was John, of New Haven, 1646 (of the same family as John Downs the regicide, who signed the death warrant of Charles I).

Ephraim began clock making in Waterbury, Connecticut, 1811.

In 1822 he married Chloe (spelled Cloe on her old sampler) Painter (daughter of Thomas Painter, revolutionary soldier) and settled at Hoadleyville, now Greystone, with Seth Thomas, Eli Terry and his brother-in-law, Silas Hoadley. He began the clock business for himself here, but in 1825 removed to Bristol, bought the property now known as "Downs' Mill," of George Mitchell, "paying half cash, and balance in wood clock-works, three dollars each"—his own make. The grist mill he rented on shares, "one half toll" being his own share.

From the old shop across the stream Ephraim Downs' Yankee clocks went to New York, New Jersey, Pennsylvania, Ohio, Missouri, Louisiana, Mississippi and elsewhere. An old letter states that clocks shipped to "Washington City," D. C., May 21, 1824 were received there June 17. These undoubtedly went by sailboat from New Haven. The "looking-glass" clock was a favorite. "Carved" and "bronzed" cases with "square" or "scroll" top were good sellers. One bill, 1831, gives an "alarm" eight dollars. Many are still in existence—fine examples of Bristol's great industry in its infancy.

In Ephraim Downs' day, notes were given almost entirely in settlement of accounts, but it is said that his name was never upon a note, except as endorsed for collection; and to this may be attributed the fact, that, of all the Bristol clock makers, he alone neither failed nor made assignment in the "hard times" of 1837.

In 1842-3 he retired from business owing to failing health. He was representative and first selectman, being a Jeffersonian democrat in politics. He was a prominent Mason and church worker. He died in 1860 at the homestead on Downes street, bought when he first removed from Plymouth. His children were Rosetta, Franklin, George, Robert, Adeline, Adelaide and Helen, none now living

Franklin Downs was born June 12, 1824, at Hoadleyville, now Greystone, from whence his father Ephraim Downs, one of our pioneer clock-makers, came to Bristol, about 1825. He worked at clock-making for a time with his father, but afterward became a miller and dealer in grain, Downs' mill being one of the most widely known stands in this section. He was also interested in the firm known as the Bone & Ivory Manufacturing Co., situated on the site of the original Downs' clock shop. He married Emeline M. Upson of old colonial and revolutionary ancestry, in Waterbury, in 1844. Their children were: Ella A., married Dr. Charles R. Upson; Florence E., married Sen. Adrian J. Muzzy; Fannie A., married Thomas F. Barbour; Frank Ephraim, married Mary Annetta Sprague; Mabel G., married Reese McCloskey. Their grandchildren numbered eight; living, Marguerite Barbour, Adrienne Muzzy Downs, Jean and Gail McCloskey. Franklin Downs died August 24, 1898.

RANSOM MALLORY.

One of the prominent business men of Bristol, of a generation ago, who helped to build the foundations upon which the prosperity of Bristol rests, was Ransom Mallory, a man of sterling integrity, quiet and unostentatious in his manner, a consistent Christian, and a valued citizen.

Peter Mallory, the first of the family in Connecticut, came from England to New Haven, where he joined the infant colony, and signed the Planter's Covenant in 1644. To him and his wife who came from England with him, were born twelve children, all of whom settled in New Haven and vicinity. Ransom was of the sixth generation, of the line of Thomas, second son of Peter, and was the son of David Mallory, a revolutionary soldier, who was with Washington when he crossed the Delaware, and who served through the war, undergoing the severest hardships unflinchingly, with a sublime confidence in the righteousness of the colonial cause. Ransom was born in Oxford, Conn., December 25, 1792. May 15, 1814, he married Lucy Candee, of Oxford, who was born September 26, 1790.

He learned his trade as carpenter and cabinet maker, in Oxford, serving seven years, as was the requirement at that time. During his apprenticeship he was employed on two different occasions upon the capitol, at Richmond, Virginia. He came to Bristol in 1821, and brought his family here the following year, living in the house then owned by Col. Botsford, afterward owned by Samuel Terry, and now owned by Frank Terry. His first work in Bristol was clock-case making, at a private house, since known as the Alfred Way place, on South Street. He was a contractor at the Jerome clock shop, for some years, and, while there, built the house which stood on the site of the Masonic building, and which was recently torn down to make room for the new bank at Muzzy's corner. It will be remembered as the Lord Hills place. He left the Jeromes to form a partnership with John Birge, under the firm name of Birge & Mallory, for the manufacture of clocks. Sheldon Lewis, Thomas Fuller and Ambrose Peck were also interested in the business. The shop stood on Riverside Avenue, near the factories formerly owned by Welch, Spring & Co., later by the Codling Manufacturing Company.

This was previous to 1837, for, while the hard times of 1837 caused

RANSOM MALLORY.

many failures, Birge & Mallory were able to continue their business uninterruptedly through the whole disastrous period, paying their indebtedness in full, notwithstanding the fact that their agent in the West had taken many deeds for land in payment for clocks, and most of these were spurious, resulting in an almost total loss to the manufacturers. Mr. Mallory continued in this firm until its dissolution. He bought the house now occupied as a parsonage by the Congregational Society, of Samuel B. Smith, in 1838. At this house he passed away, January 10, 1853.

Mr Mallory was a member of the Congregational Church, and was a man universally esteemed. In a letter to his daughter, Mrs. Catherine C. Hayden, recently removed to New York, Dr. Levi Barnes, of Oxford, who once taught in the academy on Federal Hill, wrote of Mr. Mallory as follows: "He was, as I remember him, a man universally esteemed, of great force of character, energetic in business, honest, and a staunch, quiet Christian man, upholding all good, including religion, education, and everything promotive of the public welfare. But no one could write a biographical sketch of your father better than a loving daughter, and then the half has not been told."

From Mrs. Hayden, now in her eighty-second year, these data concerning Mr. Mallory were received, necessarily condensed on account of limited space.

DEACON BRYAN HOOKER.*

Deacon Bryan Hooker was a descendant of the fifth generation from Rev. Thomas Hooker, one of the founders of Hartford, the line of descent being through Samuel, John, Hezekiah and Asahel of Woodbury. Asahel Hooker married Anne Parmeley and their third son Bryan, was born in Woodbury, August 15, 1764 and died in Bristol, July 22, 1826. He is buried in the North Cemetery.

Mr. Hooker came to Bristol in early life and established one of the first woolen manufactures in the state. His fulling mill was long known as the old yellow shop, near the bridge on the corner of East and South Streets. It was destroyed by fire in 1903.

Mr. Hooker first married Lydia Lewis, October 7, 1790, daughter of Eli Lewis of Bristol. She died without children April 20, 1804, at the age of thirty-nine. On October 7, 1804, he married the widow Nancy Lee Fuller, daughter of William and Elizabeth Gilbert Lee of Bristol. Mrs. Fuller had two children, the eldest daughter, Rhoda, married Samuel Augustus Mitchell, publisher of geographies; their descendants are now living in Philadelphia, Pennsylvania. The son Thomas Franklin, married Lucy Winston, and always lived in Bristol. He built the Saw Shop on Riverside Avenue for the manufacture of tinder boxes and curry combs. His daughter, Mrs. Mary Martin, and his grandchildren Mr. Carlyle F. Barnes and Mrs. Wyllys Ladd are at present well known residents of Bristol.

Mr. Hooker was a man of mark and influence both in church and state and filled many offices of trust. The town records tell us that he took the Freeman's oath in September, 1796. In 1806 and again from 1811 to 1820 we find continuously as the second item of business at the town meeting, the note "Voted and chose Bryan Hooker, Esq., Town Clerk for the year ensuing." When he was not Town Clerk he was often Moderator of the meeting.

He represented the town at the General Assembly in 1812, 1813, 1814, 1817, and on July 4th, 1818 was appointed "a delegate to meet in convention in Hartford on the fourth Wednesday of August next,

---

*This sketch was prepared by Miss Clara Lee Bowman. The likeness shown of Deacon Hooker was taken from a colored minature in the possession of Miss Bowman.

for the purpose of framing a Constitution of Civil Government for the people of the state."

In the records of this Constitutional Convention, we find Bryan Hooker always voting on the extremely conservative side and his report to his fellow citizens could not have been very favorable, as we find that "one hundred and five voted against the approbation and ratification of the Constitution of Civil Government framed for the people of the State by the said Convention, and ninety-five voted for its approbation and ratification."

He was chairman of many important committees such as the Inspection of Bridges and Highways, and appointed to make a draught of laws to prevent hogs, sheep, geese, turkeys, etc., going at large. He served several times as Selectman and was often on the Board of Relief. He filled the office of Justice of the Peace for some years and often held court in the large living room of his home on East Street.

He united with the Congregational Church, September 29, 1799, under the preaching of the Rev. Giles Cowles, a year in the church history "long to be remembered." Mr. Hooker immediately took an active part in church work and in 1801 he was elected deacon which position he held until his death in 1826. A rounded out quarter century of earnest Christian life. We find in the church records that he was often moderator in cases of discipline brought before the church, especially of Sabbath breaking, and his own views were so strict that he would stop people driving by his house on Sunday, in order to ask them who was sick and if they were going for the doctor.

His interest and sympathy for the poor and unfortunate were unbounded. As has been noted he frequently served on the Board of the poor relief and his private charities were numerous.

Mr. Hooker's first recorded purchase of land in Bristol was September 22, 1791, but on April 16, 1793, he bought from Reuben Thompson the fulling mill on East Street near the river and half of the little gambled roofed red house near by, which was his first home here. It has long given place to factories and store houses, but at the same time he brought ten acres of land on the opposite side of the street upon which he built his house on East Street in 1811, which is still occupied by his descendants of the fourth generation.

A carefully itemized bill of expense for the building of this house was found among his papers and may be interesting as a comparison of prices and orthography of the present day.

Bill of expense for building my house done in the year 1811:

Frame	$230.00
Brick 1100 at $8.34	91.74
Pine boards 12 000 feet	130.
transporting the same	66.
Shingles 16 500	49.50
transporting the same	8.
Ruff boards 2 000 feet at 75 cents	15.
Flour boards for the wood house and garret	12.75
other flour boards	55.00
Lath boards 5 000 feet at 67 cents	33.50
Lining boards 2 000 feet at 62 cents	12.40
Petition plank 1 200 feet at 1.60	20.
Joiner bills	363.
Daily & Churchels bill	75.84
Miles Lewis about 25 cotton bails 5	30.
Glas 48 dollars	48.
200 lb. cut nails	22.92
75 lb. raut nails at 12	9.37
Brads	5.
12 bbs. double tins	1.50
Mantletrys and Jams at Farmington	9.

Expense of cellar of the mason's bill	100.
Shingle nails	20.
4 casks Canan lime.	20.
8 casks lime	30.
Masons bill for plastering	36.
Making morter and tending mason	40.
Door hangers etc.	20.
Iron barrs for mantletrees	2.
Oil for painting 36 gallons	36.
White led 225 bb white led	37.
other paint about	8.
Johnsons bill for painting	21.50
Painting the inside paid the Rands & Co.	20.
House sink.	7.
Expense of raising	25.
My own time $50	50.
Board 156 dollars	156.
Rum and brandy	30.
	1947.00
Contingent expenses not recorded above	53.
	$2000.00

The farm which surrounded the old homestead, was a large one reaching from the river to the top of the hill and extending as far west as Main Street, which was not laid out until 1827, the year after his death. The farm was first cut into by the laying out of the road now Riverside Avenue and later by the railroad. He apparently bought land very extensively as his name appears twenty-one times on the record between 1791 and 1813, and after his death his estate figures as frequently in selling it off.

For those days Mr. Hooker was a prosperous man, but his modesty and humility were strong traits of character and his daily morning prayer always included the petition, "May we carry the cup of prosperity with a steady hand;" and another phrase long remembered by his children was "may we use this world as not abusing it, remembering that the fashion thereof passeth away."

The fulling mill required many hands and the apprentices all boarded at Mr. Hooker's house. Some of Bristol's prominent men were numbered among them. He always felt a responsibility for their spiritual as well as physical welfare, and would not allow any of them to read the writings of Thomas Payne while they were members of his family. He died at the age of sixty-two, lamented, revered and respected, a worthy representative of his name and generation. He left three children, Lydia, Lewis named for his first wife. She married Cyrus Porter Smith and moved to Brooklyn, New York, where her descendants are still living. Nancy, who married William Hill of Troy, New York, but who was a son of Gaius and Mary Wheeler Hill, of Chippin's Hill in this town. He lived but a few years and Mrs. Hill returned to the old homestead for the remainder of her long life. She died May 26, 1902, at the age of ninety-three. Her daughter, Mrs. George R. Bowman and granddaughter, Miss Clara Lee Bowman, still live in the old house at 60 East Street.

Mr. Hooker's only son, Bryan Edward Hooker, was for many years a resident of Hartford and deacon in the Center Church, where a memorial window has been placed to his memory. His son, Edward Williams Hooker, at present Hartford's representative in the Legislature, Thomas Williams Hooker, and a grandson, Joseph Hooker Woodward, are all well-known and influential men in the Hartford of today.

ELDER SAMUEL C. HANCOCK.

Samuel Cooley Hancock, widely known as "The Blind Preacher," and who was for many years a resident of Stafford District, was born at East Hartford, September 16, 1828. When about four weeks old he became nearly blind from inflammation of the eyes. At the age of nine years he was sent to the Perkins Institution for the Blind, at Boston, where he remained five years, receiving a thorough education in the ordinary English branches, and in music, in which he was an adept, both in instrumental and vocal music. After leaving the Institution, he resided at Meriden for some years, playing the organ of the Episcopal church, and teaching music. In 1851 he contracted the smallpox at Hartford, which resulted in the total loss of his sight, as, previous to that, he had been able to discern light, and plain colors. For several years afterward he was engaged in the sale of memorandum books and diaries, with a boy to lead him, visiting many towns in this and adjoining states. He was married to Susan D. Sims of Westerly, R. I., November 27, 1853, and resided, for a short time afterward at Farmington. He then purchased a small place two miles north of Forestville, where he resided up to the time of his death.

Mr. Hancock early united with the Methodist Episcopal church, of Meriden, but became convinced of the truth of the Advent doctrines, also of the observance of the seventh-day Sabbath. At a conference of the Advent denomination, held at Providence, R. I., December 1860,

he was ordained a preacher of that faith. During the remainder of his life he traveled extensively throughout New England and the Provinces, preaching the Gospel, sometimes laboring for months in a place, but more frequently journeying from place to place, as an Evangelist and vocalist. He was a composer of fine piano and vocal music, some of his hymns finding a place in the regular hymnals of the denomination After his death his devotional songs were compiled in book form and sold for the benefit of his widow, by Milo Leon Norton. They are now out of print. Mr. Hancock died at Springfield, Mass., August 23, 1874, in the 46th year of his age. He had but one child, Florence Eliza, who died in 1862. His widow survived him only a few years.

RODNEY BARNES.

Rodney Barnes was born in Burlington in 1818, of old colonial stock, in a house which stood near Monce's trout pond. His father was Sherman Barnes, who was an American soldier in the war of 1812. His mother was Miss Luanna Smith, daughter of Gideon Smith, and Rodney Barnes' parents lived for many years at the Milo Schriver place in Whigville. Here it was that Mr. Barnes spent his boyhood days except when living out with farmers of Burlington and other towns. As his father was a most versatile mechanic, being a millwright and machinest, it was not strange that the son would also have mechanical ability, and at the age of 18 years, Mr. Barnes entered the employ of Elisha Manross, who conducted a small shop near where the Laporte Hubbell brick factory now stands. In 1848 he was active in the formation of a company to manufacture marine clocks, the movement of which was a product of his brother's idea, Bainbridge Barnes. In company with Ebenezer Hendrick, Daniel Clark, Laporte Hubbell and his brother Bainbridge, Mr. Barnes succeeded in promoting the company which for many years continued in the clock industry. Afterwards Mr. Barnes sold out his interest to Messrs. Hubbell and Beach.

On February 27, 1842, Mr. Barnes was married to Miss Roxana Horton, an estimable daughter of Jared Horton of Wallingford. Of the eight children who blessed this union only two are now alive, Watson E. Barnes of Forestville and Roland D. Barnes of Bristol. Mr. and Mrs. Barnes celebrated their golden wedding in 1892 and congratulations were received from all the townspeople who realized that Mr. Barnes was one of those instrumental in building up Forestville.

After disposing of his interest in the clock industry, Mr. Barnes entered the real estate business for the purpose of developing and building up Forestville which in the days gone by was in many localities nothing but a forest of white burches. His energy and foresight was eventually rewarded as under his leadership houses sprang up in what was then considered isolated sections, and today in almost any part of Forestville houses can be pointed out that were built under the supervision of Mr. Barnes.

As the years grew on apace, Mr. Barnes was looked upon as an authority upon local history and genealogical matter. His fine retentive memory and cheerful consideration of the rights of others gained him the friendship of the citizens at large, and his death at the age of 80 years and eight months was deeply deplored. Although always prominent in town affairs Mr. Barnes refused to accept any pubic office except in 1873 and 1875 when he served on the board of selectmen.

After coming to Forestville in 1836, he, with the exception of one year, 1839, spent sixty three years of his life in Forestville, which he saw grow and expand from a few settlement houses to a commodious prosperous community.

EDWARD PRINDLE WOODWARD.

Edward Prindle Woodward, son of Asa C. Woodward, M. D., and Amanda Warner Woodward was born on February 5, 1837 in Litchfield, Conn., where his father was at the time a practicing physician. He first attended lectures in the Boston University School of Medicine, but completed his medical studies at the Yale Medical School. After graduating in 1860, he began practice in Cheshire, Conn., but a few years later removed to Bethany, where his father was then practicing. In the spring of 1868 he settled in Bristol, and there he gained the esteem and confidence of all classes, and for over thirty years had a large practice.

Upon the organization of Bristol as a borough in 1893, Dr. Woodward was elected the first warden and reelected the next year. This shows the esteem in which he was held, as he had not approved the change in form of government.

Dr. Woodward was a member of several lodges, Odd Fellows, Masons, Commandery and Shrine of Mystic Temple.

In the fall of 1900 he suffered a stroke of paralysis, but at length rallied sufficiently to be about the streets. He died at the home of his daughter, the wife of Dr. B. B. Robbins in Bristol, on March 19, 1904, at the age of 67 years.

He was a member of the Protestant Episcopal church. Burial was at Bethany in the family lot.

HERBERT N. GALE.

A native of Sheboygan, Wisconsin, where he was born April 2, 1859. When ten years of age he came here with his parents, Daniel and Lucy A. Gale, and attended the public schools. At the age of eighteen he took up the work of mechanical drafting, being employed at the office of James Shepard, Patent Solicitor, at New Britain. While there he learned the process of making blue-prints of drawings, which suggested to him the taking of photographs, which he took up, being self-taught, his first work being the making of stereoscopic views of local scenery, in partnership with W. H. Wright. From scenic photography, he took up portrait work, and, in 1878, in company with Elias Burwell, he opened a studio built for the purpose, on Main Street, just north of the present Masonic Temple. In two years he had prospered sufficiently to be able to buy out his partner, and became the leading photographer of the town.

Being an inventor, he introduced several improvements in the mounting of photographs, the Gale Glass Mount being a popular and profitable device. His death was hastened by an accident while taking a flash light picture of the employees of A. J. Muzzy & Co., on the evening of September 30, 1902. He was using a new flash lamp, which he was holding in one hand while preparing to flash it by blowing through a tube. W. E. Throop was operating the camera. In some manner the lamp exploded with tremendous force, shattering his hand so that the flesh hung in shreds. He was taken at once to the office of Doctor Griswold, where the hand was amputated above the wrist by Dr. Demarais, assisted by Dr. Robbins. He received other injuries of a less serious nature. The wounds were healing, and it was thought that he would recover, but Bright's disease set in and he died, October 21, 1902. The picture taken at the time was developed, and is presented herewith.

Mr. Gale was an inventor of much ability, some of his inventions proving useful and their manufacture profitable. Among the number, were the following: A trolley fork for electric tramways; a bicycle bell; a compact stationary engine, something after the model of the Case engine and a band-saw joint.

OR "NEW CAMBRIDGE." 457

IT WAS IN TAKING THIS PHOTOGRAPH THAT MR. GALE RECEIVED THE
INJURIES THAT LATER RESULTED IN HIS DEATH.

While very young, about fifteen years of age, with the assistance of Horace Campbell, a lad of about his own age, he built a working miniature locomotive and tender, which was a model of perfection in workmanship, and attracted much attention wherever exhibited. He purchased the second automobile owned in Bristol, a steam-driven car, in which he took much interest.

His wife was Lola M. Whitman, who survives him. His sister is the wife of Ex-Chief of Police, Howard G. Arms. The business has been continued by W. E. Throop the present proprietor, who, when compelled to move out of the original studio to make room for a new building, fitted up another in the second story of the Muzzy building, which was afterward moved across the street to make room for the new building of the Bristol Trust Company. It is equipped with all the modern improvements for taking portraits by night or by day.

EDWARD INGRAHAM.

Entered into partnership with his father in the clock business in 1859, and conducted the increasing business of the company until his death in 1892, with the assistance of his sons, who have increased the business and enlarged the plant materially since his death. A public-spirited man, genial and companionable, and one of the most potent agencies in developing Bristol's phenomenal prosperity, his death was greatly lamented by the entire community. The great plant of The E. Ingraham Co., is the most fitting monument that could be reared to his memory, for it speaks in unmistakable tones of his genius and business ability that developed from small beginnings so gigantic an enterprise.

EDWARD INGRAHAM.

LESTER GOODENOUGH.

Was born in Burlington, September 18, 1820. He worked for a time at clock-making in Whigville, and then came to Bristol, in 1837, working for Chauncey Boardman, and afterward forming a partnership with Asahel Hooker, in the brass foundry business, which Mr. Goodenough continued after the death of his partner, in 1865. Mr. Goodenough died December 26, 1898. He was never an office seeker though he held several positions of trust, and was a quiet, reliable citizen and business man, a model of integrity, and respected by all his townsmen.

FILBERT LEANDER WRIGHT.

Filbert Leander Wright was born in Southington, November 18, 1816. When a small boy he rode horse on the tow path of the raging canal, to New Haven. He was the son of Harvey Wright, who was a descendant of James Wright, of Milford, of English ancestry, whose son Joseph was born in Durham, November 1, 1713; his son Joseph, Jr., was also born in Durham, May 6, 1744, whose son Harvey, was one of the pioneers of clock making in Bristol. He married Esther Crissey, descendant in the sixth generation, from Rev. John Davenport, founder of the Colony of New Haven. Harvey Wright was a manufacturer of the olden-time wooden clock movements, the few tools at his command consisting of a good jack-knife, a file, a foot-lathe, and possibly a fiddle-bow drill; occupying a little shop which stood on the river bank near

the present Main Street bridge. Competition reduced the price of clocks to that extent that he abandoned the enterprise and moved his shop farther down the river, where it became the property of the Codling Manufacturing Co., now in the possession of the Sessions Co. There he carried on a wood-turning business for several years. The same pond is still there, and the willows on the south embankment were whips which Filbert Leander Wright picked and planted there in sport.

Filbert Leander Wright was married to Sabrina H. Merrill, of Nepaug, December 31, 1849. They had three children: Frank Merrill, born July 30, 1854, died November 12, 1888; Florence Esther (Mrs. W. E. Fogg), and Wilbur L., both of whom are now living. Mr. Wright was instantly killed by a switch engine, near the spot where the depot now stands, October 2, 1886. He was a member of the Congregational church, and a man much esteemed and respected by his fellow townsmen. For twenty-seven years he followed the profession of dentistry, most of the time in partnership with Dr. Wales A. Candee. He was for many years a clock-maker, and the designer of many improvements in machinery for manufacturing brass clocks.

SAMUEL AUGUSTUS MITCHELL.

Was the youngest son of William Mitchell, the first of the name in Bristol. He was possessed of literary as well as of business talents, and turned his attention to publishing, "The British Poets" being one of his productions. He also issued a line of texts book for common schools which were far in advance of any previous works of that kind, his Atlases and Geographies becoming standard works. He was born in Bristol, March 20, 1792, and died in 1868. He was located in Philadelphia where he conducted his extensive publishing business.

WARREN IVES BRADLEY.

Better known by his literary name of "Glance Gaylord," was cut off at the threshold of a brilliant literary career by consumption, at the early age of twenty-one years. He was born in Forestville, March 20, 1847, and died there in 1868, on the 15th of June. His mother was a daughter of Elisha Manross, a sister of Prof. Newton Manross, and he therefore came of a talented family. Of a retiring disposition, yet possessed of a brilliant imagination, he produced books for Sunday school reading in rapid succession, having published fifteen up to the time of his death. They were all stories for boys, of a high, moral tone, and were highly esteemed by youthful readers.

LAPORTE HUBBELL.

Was the son of William and Julia Hubbell, who lived near the Downs' place, East Bristol, and at twelve years of age commenced his life work as a clock-maker. In 1848 he became associated with Rodney Barnes and others in the manufacture of marine clocks, which business he conducted until near the close of his active life, when he was compelled to retire from business because of ill health. He died at his home in Forestville, September 4, 1889, aged 64 years and 9 months.

JULIUS R. MITCHELL.

Born January 8, 1821, was perhaps more widely known as merchant, politician, and citizen, and faithful adherent of the Baptist faith, than any other man in Bristol. Inheriting from his father, Hon. George Mitchell, superior business talents, he was identified throughout his lifetime with the mercantile and manufacturing interests of his native town. During the last few years of his life he suffered ill health, and passed away on the 19th of February, 1899. He thrice represented the town in the General Assembly, and the district in the Senate.

JULIUS R. MITCHELL.

HENRY WARD.

Was a native of Cornwall, England, where he was born April 29, 1834. He came to Bristol with his father's family, where he worked as a miner in the copper mine. He also lived in Pennsylvania, and was a gold miner in California. His last years were spent in Bristol, as a merchant, in company with Gilbert Penfield and A. H. West. He was also in the grocery business. He was married in 1869 to Estelle, daughter of Capt. Alvia Wooding, who, with three children, survive him. He died November 16, 1882.

NEWTON SPALDING MANROSS.

Son of Capt. Elisha Manross, was born in Bristol, June 20, 1825. Of a studious and scientific turn of mind he was given good educational advantages, graduated at Yale in 1850, studied in Germany, and received the degree of Doctor of Philosophy. He became a Professor of Chemistry and Botany at Amherst. He also visited Mexico and Central America and conducted explorations there. When the war broke out he commanded Company K, Sixteenth Regiment raised in Bristol, and was killed at Antietam, the first action in which his regiment participated, in 1862. He was married to Charlotte Royce, of Bristol, in 1857. One daughter resides in Orange, Mass.

JAMES HANNA.

Born in north of Ireland in 1848. Came to the United States at six years of age, and settled in Hebron, Conn. He was on the police force of New York, and in the street car service during the war. Shortly after the war he came to Bristol, and conducted the harness business until about five years before his death. He organized the Hook and Ladder Company in 1872, and was foreman a number of years taking great interest in the department, and was Chief Engineer. He was a member of the Episcopal Church, and married Mary Fieft, of Terryville, in 1878, who survives him. Mr. Hanna was the first member initiated into Ethan Lodge, K. of P. He was a charter member of the I. O. R. M., and belonged to the Veteran Fireman's Association of Hartford.

WALLACE BARNES.

Oldest son of Alphonso Barnes, was born December 25, 1827. He married Eliza Fuller, in 1849, and lived in Winsted a few years, where he was engaged in the drug business. In 1857 he engaged in the spring business which has been continuously conducted ever since at the same plant on Main street. One of the most active men in Bristol, he was constantly engaged in real estate and other enterprises. Two of his five children survive him—Carlyle F. Barnes, who now conducts the extensive business founded by his father, and Mrs. Wyllys C. Ladd. He died March 28, 1893.

SAMUEL EMERSON ROOT.

Was a native of New York, born in Broadalbin, Fulton County, October 12, 1820, of Connecticut ancestry. He was a nephew of Chauncey Ives, of Bristol, and at an early age he came to Bristol, and in partnership with Edward Langdon built the factory which so long stood upon the corner of Main and School streets. His specialty was clock dials, and other clock trimmings. His son-in-law, Edward E. Newell, continued the business until recently, after the death of Mr. Root, which occurred on April 7, 1896. Another daughter, became the wife of Judge Roger S. Newell.

SAMUEL E. ROOT.

JOEL H. ROOT.

A brother of the late S. E. Root, was also born in Broadalbin, near Saratoga, N. Y., December 5, 1822. He came to Bristol, when five years of age, and made it his home during the remainder of his life, which terminateff after a long period of suffering, on April 11, 1885. In 1867 he bought what is known as Root's island, and built a small factory there, where he manufactured clock trimmings, and where the business is still conducted by his son Charles J. Root. His wife, Catherine Roberts, was a granddaughter of Gideon Roberts, the pioneer American clock-maker.

LEONARD ANDREWS NORTON.

Was a life-long resident of Bristol, first seeing the light on August 9, 1813, at the Burton Allen place, on the Fall Mountain road. When a year old he moved to the old homestead on Peck lane, where he spent the remainder of his long life. He was by occupation a farmer and basket-maker. He was well informed concerning the early history of the town, was a self-educated man, botany being his favorite study, in which he was remarkably proficient. He died July 16, 1895. His widow and two sons, Milo L., and Manilus H., survive him. In 1897 the homestead was sold and is now occupied by W. H. Miller, formerly editor of the Bristol Press, and is known as "Fallmont."

COL. EDWARD L. DUNBAR.

Was a Scotch descent, and was for many years a prominent business man in Bristol. He was born in 1815, married Julia Warner, of Farmington, in 1840, and settled in Bristol. He became a manufacturer of clock springs, and was associated with Wallace Barnes during the period when hoop-skirts were worn, in the manufacture of crinoline. What is now the old Town Hall was erected by this firm for a wood-shed, and was called Crinoline hall. He represented the town in the Legislature in 1862, and was always keenly interested in the affairs of the town. He died in 1872.

COL. E. L. DUNBAR.

WILLIAM DAY.

Was born in Lanesboro, Mass., March 28, 1809. He learned the cabinet business in Pittsfield, and came to Plymouth Hollow where he worked on clock cases for Seth Thomas. He came to Bristol in 1841, and was employed in case-making until his retirement owing to ill health in 1880. He was chosen a deacon in the Congregational Church in 1855, and continued in that office until 1888. He married Emeline C. Hitchcock, of Southington, in 1836. He had two daughters, who survive him. He died November 14, 1899.

CHARLES CHURCHILL.　　　　　　CHARLES CHURCHILL, JR.

CHARLES CHURCHILL.

Was born in New Hartford, May 25, 1822, and died in Bristol, November 16, 1891, where he had been a resident for about fifty years. He married Miss Alice Celestia Phillips of Middletown, May 3, 1843. He was an active business man and was universally esteemed as an honorable and upright citizen, while his genial ways and fair dealings won for him many friends. For many years he was engaged in the coal and lumber business and many houses in town were built by him at that time. Afterwards he carried on the hay and produce business until the time of his death. He was for many years a Mason, a member of the Congregational Church, and a charter member of the Bristol grange. Mr. Churchill's only son, who lived to manhood, enlisted at the time of the Civil War and died in a rebel prison at the age of twenty years.

CHARLES CHURCHILL, JR.

Charles Churchill, Jr., was born August 27, 1844. He attended the Third District school, and when about eighteen years of age enlisted in Company K, 16th Regiment., Connecticut Volunteers. He died in a rebel prison at Florence, S. C., November 3, 1864.

NOAH POMEROY.

Was born in Somers, December 20, 1819. About 1840 he came to Bristol, and worked at clock-making. In 1849 he bought the shop formerly owned by Chauncey Ives, where he made clock movements until 1878, when he sold out to Hiram C. Thompson, the present principal owner. Since 1865 he resided in Hartford. He died while at San Francisco, California, June 9, 1896.

CHARLES E. NOTT.

Charles E. Nott was born in Bristol, August 17, 1845, where he attended the common schools until twelve years of age and then clerked for his father until the latter disposed of his store. He did no active business other than that of taking care of his real estate. He was married June 25th, 1884, to Miss Harriet J. Stoneburner, who was born in Pittsford, New York, July 5, 1850, but at the time of marriage was a resident of Brighton, New York, with her parents, John and Almira (McMinders) Stoneburner. Mr. Nott was a member of the Congregational Church. He died April 20, 1900.

JESSE GAYLORD.

Was born in Bristol, March 17, 1833, at the old Gaylord homestead on Fall Mountain, where he lived during the early years of his life, following the occupation of a farmer and wood dealer. He removed to Bristol, purchasing the old Welch homestead on West street in 1870, continuing the sale of wood, and was the first to introduce the sale of baled hay in Bristol. He was also the first to introduce street sprinkling. He was married to Julia E. Williams in 1862. She died in 1902. He had four children: Frank M., Mrs. W. G. Plumb, of Springfield, Mass., Mrs. W. H. Merritt, and Miss Emma L. Gaylord. He died July 15, 1880.

ELIJAH DARROW.

Was born in Plymouth, in 1800, and came to Bristol in early life. He was an enterprising business man, and one who commanded the universal respect of his townsmen. In company with Chauncey Jerome he was one of the first to manufacture brass clocks. After the dissolution of his partnership with Jerome, he conducted the business of clock-tablet making, from a process of his own, and other enterprises. He was chosen a deacon in the Congregational Church in 1855, which office he held at the time of his death, which occurred January 15, 1857.

ELIJAH DARROW.

FRANKLIN ELIJAH DARROW.

Was born in Bristol, at the Darrow homestead on South street, July 18, 1834. He was educated in the public schools, and succeeded to the business of the manufacture of clock tablets, carried on by his father, which he finally sold to the Ingrahams. He was married May 17, 1860 to Miss Amelia Whiting of Canton Centre. He organized the Darrow Manufacturing Company, for the manufacture of rawhide doll heads, and other goods, which did a thriving business for a number of years. After his connection with this business was severed he resided for three years at Rockport and Lynn, Mass., where he was superintendent in a factory. After his return to Bristol he became the chairman of the School Committee of District No. 3, which position he held with much credit for efficiency, until his death, January 8, 1882. He was also the first President of the noted society of B. B's.

EVITS HUNGERFORD.

Born in the town of Bristol, Conn., October 20, 1777, and was a lifelong farmer in that locality. He was also a blacksmith and worked at his trade for years. In politics he was an ardent Democrat, in religious faith a consistent Methodist and the first piece of timber for building the old Methodist Church was taken from his land. He was a charter member of the Franklin Lodge, F. & A. M. On September 23, 1810, he married Annah Peck of Burlington, Conn., who was born September 14, 1789. Children as follows were born to them: Leander G., William Ellis, Rev. Chas. Lyman (he died in 1845 in Brooklyn where he was a Methodist preacher), Louisa Amy and Caroline Sally. The father died September 17, 1867; the mother June 20, 1881.

HAVILAH THOMPSON COOK.

His early life was spent in Albany, N. Y., but resided in Bristol the greater part of his life. He conducted a large business as a shoe-maker and shoe-dealer at the North Side, while that was the center of the town, but followed the tide of population to the South Side where he located in Seymour's block. He was married to Sophia Crampton, of Cheshire, in 1835. He was an early and outspoken abolitionist, a radical temperance man. strictly honest and fearless in every line of duty. His son, Henry B., succeeds him in the same line of business. He had three daughters, Ellen, Ann Maria, and Ellen Maria. He died June 24, 1869.

GILBERT PENFIELD.

Born in Portland, in 1823; died at Bristol, in 1896. Nearly the whole of his life was spent in Connecticut, mostly in Bristol, where he was in business with his son-in-law, A. H. West, for twenty-two years, selling sewing machines, and later conducting a store for the sale of art goods, and many other articles. Many of those who see this book will recall the vision of the old wagon with its sewing machine, and the face of the merchant, who probably visited every house in the town and the near-by villages. Of a jovial, genial disposition he won many friends.

GILBERT PENFIELD.

CHARLES ANDREW STEELE.

Was born in West Hartford, October 19, 1814. Was a resident of Bristol for many years, serving the town in the capacity of Selectman, and the county as Deputy Sheriff. He was for many years station agent at Plainville, and afterward in Bristol, where he was retired by the railroad company because of advancing years. At one time he was Superintendent of the Bristol Manufacturing Company. He was an active member of the Methodist Church for many years, and was a very efficient and faithful man in the many responsible positions which he was called upon to fill. He died February 24, 1893.

DAVID SYLVESTER MILLER.

Was born in Torrington, July 27, 1823. Died in Bristol, February 26, 1895. He resided in Bristol from 1845 to 1856, the greater part of the time in what was then called Polkville. Returned to Bristol again in 1879, and resided here until his death in 1895. For years was the head book-keeper for J. H. Sessions & Son, retiring some time before his death.

JOHN HOUSE ADAMS.

Was born in Andover, December 5, 1812. He learned the trade of bookbinding in Hartford, in early life. He was married to Mary Noyes, of New London, in 1836, by whom he had three children, two of whom survive him—William H., and Mrs. Sarah M. Potter. He worked at his trade in New York for several years, came to Bristol in 1841, and was employed by Brewster & Ingraham, until 1851. He worked ten years for H. A. Pond, at candlestick making in the north part of the spoon shop on Main street, and in 1861 commenced work for S. E. Root, where he remained until he was compelled to retire by reason of old age. He died February 19, 1900. He was a member of the Congregational denomination for sixty years.

JOHN H, ADAMS.

WILLIAM GIBB.

Very few men left such a host of devoted friends, embracing the entire community, as did Rev. William Gibb, pastor of the Advent Society, who died in the morning of his life and usefulness, in Callander, Scotland, July 20, 1897, where he had repaired, with his devoted wife of a year, for the benefit of his failing health. He was a native of Glasgow, came to this country in 1893, and became a preacher of the Advent denomination, conducting evangelical services in Southington. His ordination took place in 1895, as pastor of the Bristol Church. He married Millie Arms, of Bristol, June 30, 1896. To such a sweet devoted, spirit as his these lines of Moore will apply:

"You may break, you may shatter the vase if you will,
But the scent of the roses will hang round it still."

JOSEPH SIGOURNEY.

Joseph Sigourney came to Bristol in 1845, and worked in the South Side knitting mill. Not long before the war he purchased a small fruit and confectionary store that stood near where Merrick's grocery store now stands, which he moved to the location now occupied by the New York clothing store on Main street, where he did a large and very successful business, using one store as a jewelry and variety store and the other for the fruit and confectionary business. He made a host of friends and was respected by all. He was a prominent member of the Methodist church. He married Miss Sibyl Dawson and had two sons. He retired from active business in 1881 and died June 17, 1887, aged 66.

JOHN H. SUTLIFFE.

Was born in Plymouth, October 4, 1810. In 1832 he married Harriet Warner, of Farmington, and to them were born three daughters, Mrs. Thomas Barnes, Mrs. Julia Barber of Indianapolis, Ind., and Mrs. Harriet Russell. He came to Bristol soon after his marriage, working for many years for the Atkins Clock Co., and later for the Welch-Spring Co., retiring a few years before his death, which occurred March 24, 1884. He was a man of sterling character, and a member of the Baptist Church for many years.

JOHN H. SUTLIFFE.

ANSON LUCIUS ATWOOD.

Mr. Anson L. Atwood, one of the oldest and most respected citizens of the town, has been for the greater part of his long life associated with the chief industry of Bristol, the clock making business.

He was born at Norfolk, Conn., June 12, 1816, and came to Bristol as a young man, in the fall of 1838. He began work with the clock firm of Birge & Mallory, which occupied the shop now known as the Saw-factory of M. D. Edgerton. These were the days of contracts or jobs.

Mr. Atwood took the job of turning parts of clock cases for Birge & Mallory, and when this was completed, continued in the same shop a short time longer, turning brass for clock movements.

In April, 1839, he engaged to work for Elisha Brewster at his clock shop on Race street, known in later years as the "Elias Burwell Shop." Not long after this Mr. Brewster became associated with Shaylor Ives in the manufacture of *spring* clock movements,—said to be the first made in this country.

Mr. Atwood continued with Brewster & Ives and except for a brief interval, with the succeeding firm of Brewster & Ingraham (formed in 1843), for several years. In 1845 he contracted with the latter company for the manufacture of their one-day clock movements. For this business he fitted up the factory known as "The Blue Shop,"—still standing near the bridge on North street. To this factory later,—during 1847,—the remainder of the clock movement business of this firm was removed. In April of this year, Mr. Atwood sold the house he had owned for several years on Federal street to Wm. E. Day and purchased a farm in Stafford District, thinking farm life would better suit his health. But during the years on the farm he was many times persuaded to take up his previous occupation. In the spring of 1848, he contracted with Brewster & Ingraham for the manufacture of all of their clock movements for the year (the last of their partnership), and a little later made a similar contract with Elisha Brewster, who continued the business for many years.

Mr. Atwood was next superintendent for a time of the clock shop of Captain Elisha Manross, at Forestville, which stood where the engine house now stands, and later for Manross Brothers, then occupying the factory known of late years as "The Bit Shop." He also manufactured movements for Elisha Brewster during the latter part of this stay on the farm.

Mr. Atwood returned to town in the spring of 1865, to start the clock movement business for E. Ingraham & Co. They purchased a building known as the "Hardware Shop" (where curry-combs and tin candlesticks had been made), which stood on the corner of North Main and Meadow streets, and removed it to a location just north of their present factory buildings.

Mr. Atwood fitted this factory with the necessary machinery for the manufacture of clock movements, and continued with E. Ingraham & Company as superintendent for twenty-two years, retiring in August 1887, at the age of seventy-one. This was made the occasion of a visit from the employees of the firm who presented him with a handsome gold headed cane as a token of their esteem and goodwill.

Mr. Atwood married Eliza Ann Hooker, daughter of George Hooker, who for a time just previous to this, 1840, manufactured stocks (neckwear) at the North Side. Their family of children consisted of one son and three daughters.

Mr. and Mrs. Atwood celebrated their golden wedding, November 18, 1890. Mrs. Atwood's death occurred April 1, 1902, and that of the son, who was a resident of Hartford, three years later. The daughters reside with their father at the home on Summer street. This house, built by Mr. Atwood in 1871, was the first house erected in all that portion of the borough included in Summer street and vicinity.

Although deeply interested in all questions of public welfare, Mr. Atwood has never cared to hold office. His chief interest, apart from business and family life, has centered in the Congregational church, of which he has been for sixty-six years an active member and up to the present time a constant attendant.

Mr. Atwood's ninetieth birthday was most happily marked by the presentation by his near neighbors and friends, of a beautiful silver loving cup, suitably engraved, accompanied by a handsomely engraved testimonial bearing tribute to "his high Christian character" and "to the power for good in the community of his long life of true and steadfast honor, uprightness and integrity." He died August 25, 1907.

EDWARD BUTLER DUNBAR.

EDWARD BUTLER DUNBAR.

(From *Bristol Press*, May 20, 1907.)

Edward Butler Dunbar was born in Bristol November 1, 1842 and was a son of Edward Lucien Dunbar and Julia Warner. He was descended from one of the oldest Scotch-American families in New England

Mr. Dunbar attended the public schools of the town and completed a course at the Williston seminary at East Hampton, Mass. At the age of eighteen years he went to New York and became associated with the late William F. Tompkins in the mangaement of the New York office of the "crinoline" or hoop skirt business of Dunbar & Barnes, then an extensive Bristol industry. Two years later Mr. Tompkins resigned and Mr. Dunbar succeeded to the sole management of the office. He continued in the position three years, when the fashion for hoop skirts had materially subsided and the New York office was given up.

Returning to Bristol in 1865, Mr. Dunbar entered the employ of his father who had that year established the small spring factory at the present location of Dunbar Brothers. He resided here continuously since. In 1872 the elder Dunbar died and the following year a partnership was formed between the brothers, Edward B., William A., and Winthrop W. for carrying on the business under the firm name of Dunbar Brothers. The partnership continued until 1890 when because of ill health, W. A. Dunbar sold out his interest to his brothers and retired from the firm.

The business thrived under the management of the new firm and became one of the leading manufacturing houses of the town. The original factory building is still in use and one of the landmarks of the town. Since the death of the elder Dunbar, and by his express wish the old bell is tolled every night of the year ninety-nine times at 9 o'clock.

Just previous to the death of the subject of this sketch the firm of Dunbar Brothers was incorporated, with C. E. Dunbar as a member of it. E. B. Dunbar was the largest stockholder and president of the firm.

Mr. Dunbar's life was an active one, and he found time to devote much time, energy and thought to worthy public enterprises and institutions.

He served his town two terms as representative in the general assembly, in 1869 when but twenty-seven years old and again in 1881. He served the old Fourth senatorial district in the upper branch of the general assembly in 1885 and was re-elected in 1887. Subsequently he was urged to accept a nomination for Congress but declined.

For thirty years he was the Democratic registrar of voters in the First district of the town and borough, and the first election he failed to attend in all those years was the borough election held a few days ago.

He was one of the active promoters of the project which provided Bristol with a High school and was chairman of the High school committee from its establishment until four years ago when he resigned, because of the press of other duties. It was under his direction the present sightly school building was constructed. His interest was ever intense for maintaining high standards at the school, giving it a standing and efficiency beyond that of similiar schools in towns the size of Bristol.

For a number of years Mr. Dunbar was a member of the board of school visitors and for more than a quarter of a century, was a member of the district committee of the South Side school.

Mr. Dunbar had been the executive head of the Bristol fire department since 1871, the date of the establishment of the board of fire commissioners. He was deeply interested in the progress of the department and within his administration saw it grow from the old hand engine equipment to its present modern apparatus.

In 1891 when the Free Public library was suggested as a solution of the question of what should be done with the library of the then defunct

Y. M. C. A., Mr. Dunbar was very active in behalf of the movement for the town institution. He was chosen president of the board of library directors which position he held to the time of his death. He was a member of the special committee of the board appointed to solicit for the building fund and during the absence of Mr. Ingraham from the town acted temporarily as a member of the building committee.

Mr. Dunbar was also active in the interests of the movement for the establishment of the Bristol National bank and from the first has been a director in that institution, For a number of years he was its vice president. In 1905, following the death of President Charles S. Treadway, Mr. Dunbar was chosen his successor and filled that office with characteristic faithfulness and ability to the last days of his illness.

He was also a director and vice president of the Bristol Savings bank since 1889.

Mr. Dunbar united with the First Congregational Church July 7, 1867, and since October 11, 1901 had been a faithful deacon in that church.

He was a member of the Bristol Business Men's association, Reliance Council, Royal Arcanum and the Central Congregational club.

In former days he was president of the Bristol Board of Trade and of the Young Men's Christian Association. being particularly interested in the Boys' branch of that institution.

Every position held by Mr. Dunbar was regarded by him as a channel for service to the community and his fellows. Faithfulness and ability and self sacrifice characterized his administrations, throughout his long career of usefulness.

Mr. Dunbar married Miss Alice Giddings, daughter of Watson Giddings, December 23, 1875 and three children were born to them:— Mamie Eva, who died in 1881; Marguerite, wife of Rev. C. N. Shepard, professor of Hebrew at the General Theological seminary, New York City, and Edward Giddings Dunbar who is at present attending a preparatory school at Stamford.

Mr. Dunbar is survived by Mrs. Dunbar and five brothers and sisters:—Winthrop W. Dunbar, William A. Dunbar, Mrs. Warren W. Thorpe, Mrs. Leverett A. Sanford and Mrs. George W. Mitchell. Mr. Dunbar's death took place May 13, 1907.

HENRY ALBERT SEYMOUR.

Henry Albert Seymour was born in New Hartford, January 22, 1818. He was married in Bristol, in 1844, to Electa Churchill of New Hartford. In 1847 he removed to Stafford District where he engaged in clock-making in the Boardman & Wells shop in partnership with his brother-in-law, John Churchill and Ebenezer Hendrick of Forestville. Conflicting with patents controlled by Noble Jerome, he relinquished this business and moved to Bristol, where he built a small factory, now used as a tenement house on Riverside avenue, and began the manufacture of ivory and boxwood rules, which business he sold to The Stanley Rule and Level Company of New Britain. In 1851 he built the first of the Main street buildings known as Seymour's Block, where he conducted a jewelry and watch repairing business for several years. He sold all his Main street property, homestead included, in 1896, to the New York, New Haven & Hartford Railroad Company. Mr. Seymour served the town as Selectman, Assessor and in other capacities. He was one of the organizers of the Bristol Savings Bank in 1870, was elected its first president, and served in that office continuously until his death, a period of nearly twenty-seven years. He died April

6, 1897. Mrs. Seymour died December 10, 1873. Their surviving children are: Laura E., of Bristol; Henry A., of Washington, D. C.; Mary, wife of Miles Lewis Peck, of Bristol; Grace, wife of William S. Ingraham, of Bristol and George Dudley Seymour of New Haven.

ALLEN BUNNELL.

Was born in Burlington, February 7, 1802, and died in Bristol, May 20, 1873. His schooling was received at the Center district of his native town until fourteen, when he gave seven years to learning the trade of wagon making of "Boss" Hale of the same town. At twenty-four he was married to Rhoda Atwater, of Bristol, and raised a large family of intelligent, active children, too well-known as prominent citizens of Bristol, to need designation. Except for a period of three years spent in Ohio and Illinois, his long life was spent in Burlington and Bristol. He was one of the earliest and most outspoken of the abolitionists, and burned a keg of powder when his three boys were at the front, in celebrating the freedom of the slaves.

ELISHA C. BREWSTER.

Was a son of Capt. Elisha Brewster, of Middletown, and a descendant of Elder William Brewster, of the Mayflower. He was a clothmaker by trade, but became interested in the sale of clocks as a "Yankee clock peddler," in the South, selling the clocks made by Thomas Barnes of Bristol. In 1843 he became a partner of Elias and Andrew Ingraham, afterward associating himself with William Day and Augustine Norton. He retired from business in 1862. His son, N. L. Brewster, represented the London, England, branch of the business for twenty-one years. He was a prominent man, a deacon in the Congregational Church, and much respected as a man and citizen. He died January 28, 1880.

GEORGE W. BARTHOLOMEW.   HARRY S. BARTHOLOMEW.

GEORGE W. BARTHOLOMEW.

Descended from the first settlers of the town. Mr. Bartholomew became, indeed, a representative man. His father was born in the old "Bartholomy" tavern, near the Burlington line, Peaceable street, March 25, 1776. Mr. Bartholomew was born June 19, 1805. He lived many years in Polkville, now Edgewood, but in early life traveled extensively in the South and in California. He was one of the first to open the Bristol copper mine; and in company with his son, Harry S., was engaged in manufacturing up to the time of his death, which took place May 7, 1897.

HARRY S. BARTHOLOMEW.

Son of George W., was born in Bristol, March 14, 1832. He married Sabra A. Peck, of Whigville, in 1860. He was a student of Simeon Hart's noted academy, in Farmington, went to California in 1854, but returned in 1855, and commenced the manufacture of bit braces, in company with his father in Polkville, in which business he continued to the end of his life, which took place February 19, 1902, in the South, where he was seeking to benefit his health by a change of climate.

CHARLES BEACH.

Was born at Burlington, August 8, 1816. His parents were John and Betsey (Curtis) Beach. He came to Bristol in his boyhood, engaging in various employments in his earlier years, but was for many years preceding his death an efficient and faithful employe in the clock factory, his specialty being varnishing. He was twice married; first to Miss Mary Granniss, of Southington, Conn., who lived but a few years. In 1845 he married Miss Abigail Clark, of Sandisfield, Mass. He was a faithful member of the M. E. Church for over sixty years, and a constant attendant upon its various services until failing health compelled him to stay at home. He died December 3, 1894.

CHARLES BEACH.

ORRIN BURDETTE IVES.

Was born in Bristol Aug. 2, 1830. His first experience in his mercantile career was as a clerk with George Merriman at the North Side. After living in Boston and other places he formed a partnership with Andrew Shepard, in the store now owned by the Muzzys. Mr. Ives took the grocery department about 1862, and carried it on separately for a time. On the death of Mr. Shepard he took the entire business, selling out to A. J. Muzzy in 1875. He was in South Norwalk for several years where he conducted a dry goods store. After disposing of his store to Mr. Muzzy, he was engaged in the feed business, and harness business, and finally the glass and crockery trade which he sold to Lee Roberts, who has since conducted it. His death occurred while returning from Florida, where he had been for the benefit of his health, which had long been delicate, at Aiken, S. C., April 18, 1896.

CONSTANT LOYAL TUTTLE.

Constant Loyal Tuttle, the subject of this sketch, was born in Bristol, Conn., January 28, 1775, the son of Ebenezer and Eunice Moss Tuttle (I mention the year as it accounts for his strange name.) He was their sixth child. October 21, 1798, he married Chloe, daughter of Caleb and Annah Carrington Matthews. They commenced housekeeping at East Plymouth and in 1812 returned to her home on Chippin's Hill to care for her parents in their declining years. Nine children were born to them. Two died young, seven grew to maturity and married. He had twenty-seven grandchildren and twenty-two followed him to his grave.

Mr. Tuttle was a prosperous farmer. He built a tannery north of his house where they tanned leather making a portion of it into shoes and harnesses. Here was a cider mill and distillery, for in those days it was not considered wrong to make and drink brandy. That was given up long before his death in 1858.

He was a church man and helped build the Episcopal Church at the North Side and with Mr. Ephriam Downs built and owned the rectory. He was Justice of the Peace and was a man thoroughly respected. He was a Free Mason previous to the Morgan trouble and his name is mentioned as treasurer in 1819.

JOHN HUMPHREY SESSIONS.

John Humphrey Sessions, in whose death at Bristol, September 10, 1899, the community lost one of its most valued citizens, was a native of Connecticut, born March 17, 1828, in Burlington, Hartford County.

The Sessions family, with which our subject was connected, had its origin in Wantage, Berkshire, England, which place was visited in 1889 by a member of the Connecticut line, who found none of the family there. However, in the adjoining country of Gloucester, there is a family by the name of Sessions, which, there is little doubt, came from the same stock, in fact, it was the only one of the name to be found in England. The head of this Gloucestershire family, Hon. J. Sessions, at the age of eighty years, was Mayor of the city of Gloucester, and his three sons were associated with him in a large manufacturing business in both Gloucester and Cardiff (Wales), the style of the firm being J. Sessions & Sons. There is also a daughter who is actively engaged in benevolent and reformatory work, while the mother established and built a "Home for the Fallen," which is managed and cared for by members of the family. They all belong to the "Society of Friends," and Frederick Sessions, although at the head of a large business, gives his entire time, without salary, to reformatory work, lecturing and organizing Sunday Schools, and temperance and other beneficent societies.

The crest of the English Sessions family is a griffin's head. This mythological creature was sacred to the sun, and, according to tradition, kept guard over hidden treasures. It is emblematical of watchfulness, courage, perseverance and rapidity of execution—characteristics of the Sessions family to the present day.

*   *   *   *   *   *   *   *   *   *   *

John Humphrey Sessions, born March 17, 1828, in Burlington, Conn., was married April 27, 1848, to Miss Emily Bunnell, born in Burlington, January 30, 1828, a daughter of Allen and Rhoda (Atwater) Bunnell, also of Burlington. Children born to John Humphrey and Emily (Bunnell) Sessions were as follows: (1) John Henry, born February 26, 1849; (2) Carrie Emily, born December 15, 1854, married December 24,

1871, George W. Neubauer of Bristol; (3) William Edwin, born February 18, 1857.

John Humphrey Sessions received a common school education, such as the district schools afforded in his boybood days, and at an early age began to work in the wood turning establishment of A. L. & L. W. Winston, Polkville, a suburb of Bristol. In 1858 he entered into partnership with Henry A. Warner, under the firm name of Warner & Sessions. The venture proving a success, he in 1869 removed the business to the center of the town. About 1870 he purchased the trunk hardware business that had belonged to his deceased brother, Albert J. Sessions, and the business was a success from the commencement. In 1879 Mr. Sessions bought the property of the Bristol Foundry Co. on Laurel St., and together with his son Wm. E. Sessions, formed the Sessions Foundry Co. This business, like the others, proved a great success, and in 1896 they moved into their present plant on Farmington avenue.

All his life Mr. Sessions was identified with important concerns of the town. In 1875 he was one of the founders of the Bristol National Bank and was elected its first president, a position he held until the time of his death. He was president of the Bristol Water Company at the time of his decease. He was one of the original stockholders of the Bristol Electric Light Company and was its president until it merged into the Bristol & Plainville Tramway Company; was a stockholder in the Bristol Press Company.

"Besides being a most important factor in financial life of the town, he was no less a potent force in its moral and religious life." A brief sketch of his connection with the Prospect M. E. Church is given in the article about the Church, on page 283.

JOHN HENRY SESSIONS.

Eldest son of John Humphrey Sessions, born in Polkville, February 26, 1849, and received a liberal education at the schools of Bristol. In 1873 he was admitted into the firm of J. H. Sessions & Son, trunk hardware manufacturers. He was a director of the Bristol Water Company at its organization and at the death of his father became its president. At the time of his father's death he was elected vice president of the Bristol National Bank. Mr. Sessions, though a staunch Republican, took no active part in politics. In 1883 he was elected secretary of the Bristol Board of Fire Commissioners. On May 19, 1869 he married Miss Maria Francena Woodford, who was born September 8, 1848, a daughter of Ephraim Woodford, of West Avon, Conn., and one son was born to them, Albert Leslie, born January 5, 1872.

ALBERT JOSEPH SESSIONS.

Was born in Burlington, June 11, 1834. At the age of twelve he left home to work for a farmer for his board and clothes, attending school in the winter. At sixteen he started out in the world for himself. In 1857 he engaged in the manufacture of trunk trimmings, in Southington, in company with his brother, the late Samuel W. Sessions, of Cleveland, Ohio. In 1862 the business was moved to Bristol, and conducted by him until his death, when it was acquired by John H. Sessions. He died June 25, 1870. He was an active member of the Congregational Church, President of the Y. M. C. A., and interested in all the affairs of the town, political and otherwise.

HERVEY ELLSWORTH WAY, M. D.

Hervey Ellsworth Way, M. D., the subject of this sketch, was born in Meriden, Conn., January 17, 1828. He was the son of Susan and Samuel Way.

He received a common school education and studied medicine under the instruction of Gardner Barlow, M. D., of Meriden and later under John B. Newman, M. D. of New York City, after which he took a course of study in the University of the City of New York, from which institution he graduated in the year 1849.

He commenced the practice of medicine in Westbrook soon after graduation, where he remained but a short time. While in Westbrook he married Lucy Ann Kirtland, daughter of Philip M. Kirtland of that town. From Westbrook he removed to Cheshire remaining a few years and in 1857 came to Bristol where he was in active practice until two years before his death which was caused by heart trouble.

Dr. Way was upright and honorable in his dealings with men, conscientious to a very marked degree and highly regarded by all with whom he came in contact. He ranked high in his profession and was often called in consultation. He was first of all a student and his library contained many choice works, the study of which was to him a pastime.

He died in Bristol, July 29, 1892, survived by his wife, daughter, son and granddaughter and a large circle of friends and patrons mourned his loss.

EX-SENATOR ELISHA N. WELCH.
From Bristol Press, August 4, 1887.

Elisha N. Welch died at his home in Forestville at noon on Tuesday, August 2d, in his 79th year. He had long been in feeble health, and of late, for the most part confined to the house. The immediate cause of his death was *angina pectoris*.

Mr. Welch was born in Chatham, East Hampton Society, February 7, 1809. During his minority his father moved to Bristol, having bought the house on West street, now owned by Mrs. H. Bradley.

He became of age on a Sunday and the next day entered upon a business career in connection with his father. The business in which they engaged was that of casting clock weights. The scale on which they began this enterprise would hardly entitle it to the dignified name of a business in these days, for their facilities were exceedingly limited. The blast for their cupola was produced by a blacksmith's bellows worked by hand, and the cupola itself is still humorously spoken of by the old residents of Bristol as a "porridge pot." The weights were sold to clock makers, and payment taken in finished clocks. They were disposed of to such customers as they could find, some of them being carried to Philadelphia by the younger member of the firm. Old iron was frequently taken in exchange. As the business grew, other branches of it were added, and in a few years the father and son, who started in so small a way, were possessed of $20,000, which in those days was considered a large fortune.

Later he had as a partner in the foundry and machine business, for many years, the late Harvey Gray, and this firm did a large business. Much of their work was for the Bristol Copper Mine Company. Mr. Welch withdrew about 1856, and Mr. Gray continued alone until burned out a year or two later.

As a result of the business panic in 1857, the clock business of J. C. Brown at Forestville came into Mr. Welch's hands, and he organized the E. N. Welch Mfg. Co., which has had a most successful career, and is today one of the largest clock concerns in the country. Mr. Welch was also founder of the Bristol Brass and Clock Co., in 1850, which has also been a great financial success. This company has a rolling mill for the manufacture of sheet brass, located between Bristol and Forestville; a lamp burner factory at Forestville, and a spoon and fork factory in Bristol. Mr. Welch was also principal stockholder in the Bristol Manufacturing Co., manufacturing knitted underwear. Of these three companies he has been the president for many years. He was also a large stockholder in manufacturing concerns in Waterbury, New Britain, Plainville and other places. He was also one of the five stockholders of the First National Bank of New Haven, of which his brother, H. M. Welch, is president. Each of the five stockholders put in $50,000 when the bank was instituted. Mr. Welch was also a director in the Bristol National Bank, and in the Travelers and National Insurance Companies of Hartford. He has also had some interest in mines in Montana. His financial success in all of his undertakings has been very great and his estate is estimated at $3,000,000.

Mr. Welch was a member of the Baptist Church in Bristol, and its principle financial supporter, and contributed very largely to the building of a new church edifice and parsonage a few years since. He represented Bristol in the Legislature in 1863 and 1881, and was Senator from the Fourth District in 1883 and 1884. In politics he was a Democrat.

In 1829 Mr. Welch married Miss Jane Bulkley of Bristol, who died in 1873. Their children were four, one of whom, Mrs. Frederick N. Stanley of New Britain, is deceased. The others are Mrs. A. F. Atkins, Mrs. G. H. Mitchell, and James H. Welch. In 1876 he married Mrs. Sophia F. Knowles of Canandaigua, N. Y., who survives him. Two brothers and one sister also survive him, H. M. Welch of New Haven, H. L. Welch of Waterville, and Mrs. J. R. Mitchell of Bristol.

JULIUS NOTT.

Was a native of Rocky Hill, where he was born June 11, 1819. Learned the trade of stonemason and bricklayer prior to 1840. Came to Bristol and in 1843 began to work at his trade here, and in other towns. While at work on the knitting mill in Plainville in 1857 he sustained injuries from a fall that prevented him from following his trade. He opened a small grocery in Bristol, in 1858, in the basement of the building that he afterward owned, where the Main street railroad bridge now is, where he accummulated a competence, though twice burned out. In 1872 he sold the business to H. & L. G. Merick. He served the town faithfully as Selectman and Representative; and was a Director in the National and Savings Banks, from their organization. His death came from an accident at the railway crossing on Prospect street, January 2, 1877.

GAD NORTON.

Gad Norton, son of Parrish and Betsy Rice Norton, was a descendant of John Norton, the founder of the line known as the "Farmington Nortons," who was also one of the eighty-four proprietors of that town.

He was born in Southington, October 24, 1815, and married Mary A., daughter of Solomon and Olive Comes Wiard of Wolcott, October 23, 1839. He died May 4, 1898.

His ability and worth were early recognized in his native town. He served as selectman of Southington a number of years, represented his town in the Legislature several terms, and occupied other positions of responsibility and trust.

As a resident of Bristol he was elected a member of the School Board and was a director of the Bristol National Bank and the Bristol Savings Bank. On June 4, 1875, through a petition to the Legislature, his homestead and adjoining lands were set off from the town of Southington to the town of Bristol, thus making him a resident of the latter place. The property thus transferred was a portion of the original allotment of Southington land made in 1722 to John Norton, son of the pioneer ancestor and has been in the family through seven generations.

Mr. Norton inherited, with his farm the Lake Compounce property which had belonged to the family since 1787 and developed it as a summer resort in the years previous to 1850, later instituting several of the permanent organizations which meet there annually.

BENJAMIN F. HAWLEY.

Mr. Hawley was born in Farmington, Conn., December 7, 1808. He came to Bristol at about fourteen years of age, his father buying the house still standing at the corner of West and Pleasant Streets. Here he lived for a number of years. He made good use of the educational advantages he had received and taught school for two or more years in Stafford District. At the age of twenty-seven he went to Michigan where he taught for a year. Returning to Bristol he taught for many years in District No. 1. February 3, 1852 he was married to Mary C. Seaverns of Dorchester, Mass. They had three children all of whom are still living. In 1850 he was elected to the office of Town Clerk, serving as such from 1850 to 1854, again from 1857 to 1861 and from 1864 to 1887. He was elected Judge of Probate from 1858 to 1875. In 1862 he was elected Town Treasurer and treasurer of the town deposit and town school funds which offices he held during the remainder of his life. He also served for several years on the board of school visitors. The length of time that he filled these different offices showed his fitness for them and the confidence reposed in him. He was twice sent to the Legislature. In politics he was a life-long Democrat. While he may have had political opponents yet there were none but who loved and respected him. His thirty years of official life open always to public view, was passed without a blot. He was for years active in church and Sunday school work until such time as he resigned on account of failing health. It may be truthfully said that Judge Hawley "died in the harness." He went to his office in the forenoon of the last day that he ever went out of the house, after that he conducted such business as could be done in the quietude of his own home. His death occurred August 23, 1887. Though his life filled so large a place in the activities of town and church it filled a still larger place in the hearts of those whom he loved best.

BENJAMIN B. LEWIS.   SAMUEL M. SUTLIFF.

BENJAMIN BENNET LEWIS.

Was a native of Athens, N. Y., where he was born October 30, 1818. At nine he was left an orphan, and after a short experience as a clerk in a store in New York City, went to sea at fifteen and worked his way up to the position of Commander. In 1840 he went to Huron, Ohio, and engaged in the drug trade, also dealing in jewelry, clocks and watches, and while there he invented the calendar which brought him to Bristol, where he manufactured them in company with the late William W. Carter. He afterward entered the employ of the Welch, Spring & Co. and was foreman for many years. He died in 1890.

SAMUEL MORSE SUTLIFF.

Was born in Southington, January 28, 1828. In 1860 he married Margaret Griffin. In early life he came to Bristol, and for ten years was bookkeeper at the knitting mill of the Bristol Manufacturing Co. Under Lincoln's administration he was the postmaster. Afterward conducted a grocery store where Cook's bakery is now located. During the last seventeen years of his life he resided in Florida, where he had a large orange grove. He was a member of the Episcopal Church, and a man of marked business ability. His death occurred at his home in Hawthorn, Fla., in January, 1899.

ISAAC PIERCE.

One of the most genial and popular men of our town, was born in the old Pierce homestead, November 21, 1815. He spent nine years of his life in Alabama, from 1833 to 1842, returned to Bristol and went to California in search of gold in 1849. He returned to Bristol in 1850, and secured a half interest in Lake Compounce in 1851, retaining his interest there until his death which occurred July 28, 1897. He represented the town in the Legislatures of 1861 and 1868. In 1864 he married Catherine Degnan, by whom he had four children, of whom three are now living: Edward, Julius and Mrs. Stanton Brown. He lived to see the Lake connected with the outside world by electric cars and become one of the most popular resorts in Connecticut.

ELIAS INGRAHAM.

Was born in Marlborough, November 1, 1805. He was a cabinet-maker in early life, and worked at his trade in Hartford coming to Bristol about 1827, and working for George Mitchell. He made clock cases by contract until 1843, when the firm of Brewster & Ingraham was formed by the admission of Deacon Elisha C. Brewster. The E. Ingraham Co. was formed in 1881, and the present immense plant is the outgrowth of good business management and excellence of product. He died in 1885.

DANIEL PIDCOCK.

Was born in Sheffield, England, July 10, 1823, where he learned the saw trade. He came to the United States in 1847, and worked for R. Hoe & Co. and Henry Disston, in New York and Philadelphia, coming to Unionville and then to Bristol in 1862, where he remained during the rest of his life, except four years spent in British Columbia, on the Pacific coast. He was employed by the Atkins Saw Co., the Porter Saw Co., and E. O. Penfield. In 1848 he married Sarah A. Hales, of Brooklyn, N. Y., by whom he had three children, only one of whom is now living, Mrs. Ida May McGar, of Prospect street.

ELIAS INGRAHAM.

DANIEL PIDCOCK.

ELISHA MANROSS.

Was born in Bristol, May 11, 1792, and became one of the pioneers of brass clock-making in America, making the first jeweled movements ever made here. He was a Captain in the war of 1812, and commanded a company of one hundred men to guard the coast at Fort Killingly. He was also Captain of the Bristol Artillery Company. He was a deacon and long a member of the Congregational Church in Bristol. Three of his sons were in the Civil War, Captain Newton, Sergeant Elias, and John. He was an extensive land owner in Forestville, and conducted a large clock business. In 1821 he married Maria Cowles Norton. He died September 27, 1856.

HIRAM C. THOMPSON.

The subject of this sketch was born in Bristol, October 25, 1830. He came of Revolutionary stock, his grandfather and great grandfather having been soldiers in the patriot army during the war for independence. His grandmother reached the remarkable age of one hundred years, two months, and twenty-three days.

He was educated in the common school and academy in his native town. At the age of thirteen, having been in school continuously from the age of three and one half, he obtained permission of his parents to enter one of the shops and learn clock making. He continued this employment a year for two dollars a week, working eleven hours per day. He then gladly resumed his studies, attending the academy until he was sixteen. At that age he again entered a clock factory, and after working in various shops in Bristol and elsewhere, he entered the employ of Noah Pomeroy in July, 1862. He was soon promoted to the foremanship of the business, and held this position until he bought out Mr. Pomeroy, November 20, 1878. He carried on the business until his death.

Mr. Thompson joined the Bristol Congregational Church in 1849, and was during the remainder of his life one of its most active and zealous members. He was for many years interested in the Y. M. C. A. work, and served one year as its president.

In politics Mr. Thompson was a Republican, standing with that party from its birth, and was a member of the First Republican Town Committee.

GEORGE S. HULL, M. D.

George S. Hull, M. D., was born in Burlington, Conn., March 31, 1847, where he received a common school education. He attended the Connecticut Literary Institute at Suffield, Conn., taking a preparatory course before entering the Yale Medical College, where he spent one year. Later he attended a course of lectures at the College of Physicians and Surgeons in New York, and graduated from the New York Homeopathic Medical College in the spring of 1872.

On October 23, 1883, he was one of the charter members of Ethan Lodge, K. of P., of Bristol, Conn., and its first Past Chancellor. He was instrumental in forming the Hull Division, No. 5, Uniformed Rank K. of P. The same year, at their first field day held in Hartford, he was elected surgeon of the First Regiment, which office he held until 1890, when he was appointed surgeon of the Second Regiment. A few weeks later he received the appointment of Assistant Surgeon-General on Brigadier General E. F. Durand's staff. In 1888 he was appointed G. M. A. at the Grand Lodge session of that year; in 1889 was elected G. P.; in 1890 was made Grand Vice Chancellor; in 1891, at the Grand Lodge session held at Wallingford in February, was elected Grand Chancellor, and was obligated in the Supreme Lodge at its session in Washington.

On March 27, 1872, he located in Bristol, Conn., where he was continuous in the practice of his profession until his death.

In the spring of 1872 he became a member of Franklin Lodge, F. and A. M. of Bristol, Conn., and early in the next year of Pequabuck Chapter. He was also a member of the Doric Council of New Britain, Conn. In 1888 he joined the Washington Commandery, Knight Templars, of Hartford, and later was made a member of Pyramid Temple of The Mystic Shrine of Bridgeport. During 1889 he became a thirty-second Scottish Rite Mason of the Sovereign Consistory of Norwich, Conn.

WALES A. CANDEE.

Son of Woodruff Candee, a well-known farmer of Chippen's Hill, was born in Oxford, in 1825. When ten or twelve years of age he went to sea as a cabin boy with his uncle, and visited all parts of the globe. At twenty-five he was a gold seeker in the California mines for two or three years, when he took up dentistry, and became a very skillful dentist. He returned to Bristol, and practiced his profession. During the war and afterward he traveled extensively as a magnetic healer. In 1869 he built the "Blue Cottage" on Prospect street, where his office was located. For many years he was in partnership with his pupil, Dr. F. L. Wright. He was twice married, and his widow survived him. He died July 24, 1883.

SAMUEL P. NEWELL.

Was born in Scott's Swamp District, Farmington, November 16, 1823, the son of Roger Newell, an honest, intelligent farmer of that place. He was graduated from the Yale Law School, and selected Bristol as his residence, where he became the leading lawyer for many years. He was married to Martha J. Brewster, in 1854, to whom five children were born, his son, Roger S. Newell, Judge of Probate, succeeding to his father's practice and partnership with the late John J. Jennings. He died suddenly, much regretted, in 1888.

SAMUEL P. NEWELL.

CHARLES S. BAILEY.

 Charles S. Bailey was born in Thompson, Conn., February 20, 1811. At nineteen years of age he removed to Bristol and as an apprentice to the joiner trade, first worked upon the house owned by the late E. O. Goodwin and used by Pastor Leavenworth as the Congregational parsonage. His next work was upon the present Congregational Church. In 1836, Mr. Bailey was married to Louisa Peck of this town. An acre of land was purchased by him near the head of Main street and on this he erected one of the first houses on Main street. Mr. Bailey was sexton of the Congregational Church and served for a number of years as night watchman at the factory of the Bristol Manufacturing Company. In 1866, Mr. and Mrs. Bailey celebrated the fiftieth anniversary of their wedding. Mr. Bailey died August 23, 1890.

JOHN J. JENNINGS.

Cut loaned by the Bristol Press.

Was born at Bridgeport, in 1835; died in Bristol, April 1, 1900. Graduated from Yale in 1876. Taught school in Bristol and elsewhere for a few years. Studied law with the late Samuel P. Newell. Was admitted to the bar in 1882 and practiced law till his death. He married Elizabeth Naomi Newell, the daughter of his preceptor and partner. Mr. Jennings had attained a large practice in the State and United States courts. He always took a great interest in education and was Acting School Visitor for many years. He left two sons at his death, Newell Jennings and John Joseph Jennings.

JOHN BIRGE.

The subject of our sketch is the son of John Birge of Torrington, Conn., and was born in that town in the year of 1785. Having completed his education, he was taught the trade of a carpenter and builder and assisted in the building of Harwinton church.

Removing later to Bristol, he commenced business in the town as a wagon builder, in the north part of the town, near the Sheldon Lewis place, and also as a practical farmer, owning an extensive farm adjoining the Gad Lewis farm and taking special interest in agricultural work until his death. He carried on the wagon business for a number of years and was very successful.

He afterwards purchased the patent of the rolling-pinion eight-day brass clocks, and having purchased the old woolen factory in the east part of the town, a portion of which afterwards was used by the Codling Mfg. Co., he commenced to manufacture clocks which made for him a reputation throughout the United States and Europe. He sent out peddlers to the south and west and a very extensive business was done. Quite a number of these clocks are to be found in Bristol today. He continued in the clock business and farming until a few years previous to his death.

In politics he was an Old Whig, and was a very active politician. He also served in the War of 1812. From his first coming to Bristol until his death, in 1862, he was a member of the Congregational Church.

NATHAN L. BIRGE.

Nathan L. Birge, the son of John Birge, was born at his fathers farm in Bristol, August 7, 1823; was educated and graduated from the High School, Bristol, and entered Yale College at the age of sixteen years.

After leaving college he was engaged for two years as teacher in the Albany Academy. Among his pupils were the Rev. Morgan Dix, General Massey and also the son of Secretary Seward. He afterwards entered the law office of Stevens & Cagger, Albany, where he studied law. Later he entered into partnership in a dry-goods store in New York. On the death of one of the partners this business was given up. He then went to London, England, to superintend the clock business there for his father, a very extensive trade being done both in England and France. He returned in 1848 and joined a gentleman on a trading expedition with the Indians on the Arkansas river, dealing in furs, skins and general merchandise, and succeeded in doing quite a large business with them.

In 1849 he started out for the gold mines in California, traveling overland. This journey, which occupied seven months, was of a varied description. The party had to swim across the Colorado river about ten times; all their baggage had to be taken across on rafts. Arriving at San Francisco the place was besieged with miners, and finding that food and every requisite was very scarce and expensive, he decided to spend the winter on the island of Hawaii. He returned to the mines in California in the spring and spent the summer in the gold mines, after which he came home, settled in Bristol, and commenced business at the knitting factory, which was carried on at the north side of the town, assisted by his two sons, John and George W., under the name of N. L. Birge & Sons.

Mr. Birge married Adeline, daughter of Samuel B. Smith of Bristol. The members of the family are John, Ellen S., George W. and Frederick Norton; none now living except Ellen S.

Mr. N. L. Birge was vice-president of the National Bank of which he was one of the original corporators; a director of the Savings Bank; and vice-president of the Bristol Water Company. He died October 29th, 1899.

HON. JOHN BIRGE.

Son of Nathan L. and Adeline M. Birge, was born August 25, 1853; began his education in the common schools and finished with an academic course at the Lake Forest Academy, Lake Forest, Ill. Active business early engaged his attention. For this he had predilections and uncommon ability. He was a member of the firm of N. L. Birge & Sons, one of

the leading manufacturers of Bristol. He was always active in politics;
was Senator for the Fourth district, and has been a member of the Republican state central committee for the Fourth district. In this important place he discharged his duties with great efficiency, being an
excellent judge of men and means. He was a believer in pure politics
and also in the young men's movement. He was president of the Young
Men's Republican Club, which is associated with the state league and
was chairman of the Republican town committee for several terms.

    He is a descendant in the tenth generation from the author of our
New England system of town and municipal government, the Rev.
Thomas Hooker, settler and first minister at Hartford in 1636. Senator
Birge is also descended in the eighth generation from William Smith,
a settler at Huntington, L. I. and again through the maternal line, in
the ninth generation, from George Smith of the New Haven colony of
1638, and Theophilus Smith, who was a soldier in the Revolution. He
is also a descendant of Samuel Terry, who made and put in the large
wooden clock in the steeple of the Congregational church, Bristol. The
Birges are descended from the Puritans, who came over on or about the
time of the Mayflower.

    Senator Birge married Miss M. Antoinette Roote, daughter of S. E.
Root of Bristol, in 1874. She died April 25, 1891, leaving four children,
Adeline, Nathan R., Marguerite and J. Kingsley, all of whom are living.
In 1893, Senator Birge married M. Louise Loomis, of Portsmouth, New
Hampshire. He died October 20, 1905.

GEORGE W. BIRGE.

    The third child and second son of N. L. and Adeline M. Birge, was
born in Bristol, June 8, 1870; graduated from the High School, Bristol,
and afterwards went through a course at Huntsinger's Business College,
Hartford. He prepared for Yale but was unable to enter on account
of weakness of eyes. He married Eva May Thorpe, October, 1898. A
daughter Rachel, was born September 8, 1899. He continued as Secretary of company up to the time of his death, September 22, 1901.

    In 1893 he was admitted partner in the firm of N. L. Birge & Sons,
of which he was the junior member.

NATHAN R. BIRGE.

    The eldest son of Senator John Birge was born in Bristol, in June,
1877. He graduated from the Bristol High School in 1896, and was a
student at the Worcester Polytechnic Institute. He then went to
Lynn and now occupies a responsible position with the General Electric
Company, Schenectady, N. Y. He is also president of the N. L. Birge
& Sons Company. He was married September 14, 1904, to Bertha
Elizabeth Haight, of Schenectady, A son, John Cornell, was born No-
vember 3, 1905.

    After the death of Geo. W. Birge, William F. Stone, Jr. who has
been with the company since its incorporation was elected Secretary
to fill his place and continued in this capacity until the death of John
Birge when he was elected Treasurer and General Manager which position
he holds at the present time.

HENRY ALEXANDER MITCHELL.

Was born in Bristol, Nov. 25, 1805. His father was Thomas Mitchell, son of William, the founder of the family. He graduated from Yale, the Military Institute at Norwich, Vt., and the famous law school at Litchfield, where he was a classmate of John C. Calhoun. He was admitted to the bar, and became a judge of the Superior Court and represented his town in both houses of the Legislature. He edited the *Hartford Times* during the campaign of 1840, and sold it to Mr. Burr, the famous editor of that journal. He was a faithful member of the Episcopal Church, a man of good judgment, and strict integrity of character. He died March 17, 1888.

LEVERETT GRIGGS.

Born in Tolland, November 17, 1808, died January 28, 1883. Dr. Griggs was a graduate of Yale College, and tutor there for two years, and many years later received the degree of Doctor of Divinity from his alma mater. His first pastorate was in North Haven, then in New Haven, Millbury and Bristol. He was pastor of the First Congregational Church of Bristol for fourteen years. He then was compelled by failing health to relinquish his charge. He was much interested in the public schools and after partially regaining his health, was acting school visitor in Bristol for ten years. Dr. Griggs was a very lovable man, and seemed to take every one that came to Bristol into his smiles. He was endeared alike to people of all religious faith.

DR. LEVERETT GRIGGS.

WILLIAM CLAYTON.

A native of Sheffield, England, served an apprenticeship of seven years at the cutler's trade. He came to America in 1849, and worked for the John Russell Cutlery Co., of Massachusetts. In 1866 he came to Whigville, where he occupied a part of the D. E. Peck factory, in the manufacture of table knives. He came to Bristol six months afterward and established the business now conducted by his sons on Union street. In 1875 the shop was built on the site of the old drum shop, which plant was enlarged, and occupied until it was destroyed by fire. The old Waters' shop was also occupied by them, and that being burned' the present shop was erected. Since the death of the father, in 1883, the business has been conducted by his sons under the firm name of Clayton Brothers.

GEORGE JOHN SCHUBERT.

Was born in Bavaria, Germany, October 2, 1836, and became a resident of Bristol in 1853, holding for years the position of contractor in the works of the E. Ingraham Co. He served in the army during the Civil War, and was an Orderly Sergeant in Company I, Twenty-fifth C. V. He became a member of the Grand Army, of which he was Commander; organized with George H. Hall, George Merriman and George C. Hull, Ethan Lodge, K. of P., which was long known as under the rule of the Georges; and was also an Odd Fellow. In whatever he undertook he put the whole energy of his nature, and no more faithful or efficient member, in any position to which he was called, ever entered a lodge room. He died, respected by all, December 31, 1901.

THOMAS BARNES, JR.

LOT NEWELL, DIED 1864.

NAOMI, WIFE OF LOT NEWELL.

WALTER ADAMS.

Was born in Wethersfield, May 3, 1810. Died at Bristol, June 22 1880, where he had spent the greater part of his life. He was identified with the clock business in Bristol during his residence here, except while serving his country in the Civil War. He led a quiet, peaceful and industrious life, and was much respected for his candor and integrity of character. For many years he worked for Chauncey Boardman, and later for the Atkins Clock Company.

THOMAS BARNES.

Was born in Bristol, August 1, 1773, married Rosanna Lewis in 1798, by whom he had two children, Eveline, who became Mrs. Dr. Charles Byington; and Alphonso. His second wife was Lucy Ann Candee. He was a merchant and manufacturer, building a factory on the site of the present Dunbar factory, and made carriages. He was instrumental in opening Main street to the river, at his own expense, and built a button shop on the ground now occupied by Cook's bakery. It is little realized how much of Bristol's prosperity is due to the energy of Thomas Barnes, and a few others, possessed of the true Yankee spirit of enterprise and thrift. We do well to honor their memory. He represented the town in 1826. He died in 1855.

WILLIAM RUSH RICHARDS.

William Rush Richards was born October 16, 1816, in a log cabin in Peru, N. Y. When he was very young his father, who was a goldsmith, died, and at eight he was bound out to a farmer in Harwinton, Conn. At sixteen he was apprenticed to learn the carpenter's trade, and at the completion of his apprenticeship went to St. Louis, and later to St. Paul, where he worked at his trade. At the end of two years he came East. When he reached Chicago he found a village consisting of 14 houses. September 26, 1840, he was married to Sarah C. Champion, in Winsted, and soon after removed to Bristol, and was employed in the clock business; afterward becoming a partner in the firm of Birge, Peck & Co. During his last years he was employed by Welch, Spring & Co. His death occurred March 15, 1885, and his only son, William C. Richards, survived him.

WILLIAM CHAMPION RICHARDS.

One of the best known residents of Bristol, and one who was interested in all that pertained to Bristol, his native place, past, present or future, died suddenly on the evening of March 6, 1908, of apoplexy. He had just started for his office and stopped a moment to talk to Henry B. Cook, a life-long friend, and passed on a few steps, when Mr. Cook saw him supporting himself by a tree, hurried to his assistance, and reached him just as he sank lifeless to the pavement.

Mr. Richards was born in Bristol, August 3, 1845. He was educated in the common schools of the town, and at Eastman's Business College, Poughkeepsie, N. Y., and was a veteran of the Civil War, serving in a New Jersey regiment. For many years he was engaged in mercantile pursuits, as merchant and salesman, and for nearly thirty years as a physician in company with Dr. F. H. Williams.

Mr. Richards devoted much of his leisure to the study of microscopy, and had a fine collection of diatoms and other microscopic specimens. He was an enthusiastic local historian, and also a collector of Indian and other relics, taking great interest in the historical collection of the Bristol Historical Society, one of the best collections in the state, due largely to his untiring energy in its behalf.

He was the owner of considerable remunerative real estate near the center of the borough, and part owner of the four-story block in which his office was situated. He was a member of the Masonic Fraternity, and of Gilbert W. Thompson Post, G. A. R.

Mr. Richards was for many years a staunch Spiritualist, and a man of very pronounced opinions, ready at all times to give a reason for the faith that was in him. No man living, probably, enjoyed the perpetration of a practical joke upon some one, in a harmless way, than he, and some of his escapades will long be remembered by his more intimate friends. He was married in 1870, to Miss Lizzie Graham, who survives him, as do four children: Nathan B., of South Manchester; Mrs. Mortimer Clarke, and Mrs. Charles T. Treadway, both of Bristol; and Miss Christine, of Maryland.

WILLIAM GAYLORD.

William Gaylord, son of Billy* Gaylord, was born in Burlington, Conn., 1819. His father engaged in the manufacture of cloth in Burlington in the year 1826. William was thus early trained in all of the branches of cloth-making and succeeded his father in the business about the year 1850, where he remained until 1864. In 1865 he removed to Bristol, and there spent the remainder of his life. For twenty-four years he performed the duties of sexton in the West Cemetery.

*—This was not a nickname, but his full name.

AUTO TRAGEDY.

[* From the Bristol Press, August 22, 1907.]

During its thirty-six years of activity the Press has chronicled many sorrowful events, but not in all its history has it been called upon to record so sad and tragic an affair as that in which Charles J. Root, his aged mother and aunt were killed and his sister fatally injured.

No happier party, comprising Charles Root, his mother, Catherine R. Root, Miss Mary P. Root, Miss Candace Roberts and Miss Catherine Root, a fourteen years old niece, left Bristol last Sunday, Aug. 18, 1907, and not many people enjoyed automobile riding so much as these people.

They were bound for the Berkshire Hills in Massachusetts. A few hours later the family was practically annihilated, only the little girl escaping.

The accident constitutes the most tragic and sorrowful one in the annals of automobiling in this country, and Bristol was saddened as it has never been before. The news of the disaster was so overwhelming that it was some time before it was given credence. The people whose lives were so suddenly obliterated had for years been so active in so many ways in the life of Bristol that their deaths brought keenest grief to almost the entire community.

The party left here soon after nine o'clock Sunday morning. Mr. Root and Miss Roberts occupied the front seat of the big Stanley steam touring car. The other three were on the rear seat. The route led through Torrington and Norfolk which was reached about noon. From there the route was to Ashley Falls in Massachusetts. Near the Ashley Falls station the fine, hard highway runs parallel with the railroad tracks for perhaps a mile and is only a few feet distant. While the Root automobile was speeding along this road an overdue express train came in sight at terrific speed. The highway crosses the track at an abrupt angle. Express train and auto reached the fatal crossing almost at the same moment. Just how it happened can never be known but the automobile struck the train, probably the baggage car, a glancing blow and was instantaneously and completely wrecked. The occupants were hurled out with awful force, apparently striking their heads against the train, and were then carried some distance. All were frightfully mangled. Mr. Root and Miss Roberts were killed instantly. Mrs. Root had her skull fractured and died while being taken to Great Barrington. Miss Root had her skull fractured and her right shoulder crushed. She was removed to the House of Mercy in Pittsfield.

The only one to escape was Miss Catherine Root, and the manner in which she came through the crash is little short of miraculous. She was buried beneath the wreckage of the machine which for some unaccountable reason did not take fire. She was taken to the home of a friend in Great Barrington. She was dazed but appeared not to be seriously hurt, and was brought to the home of her parents, here, Mr. and Mrs. Theodore Root, on Monday.

The train, which was in charge of Engineer Arthur Strong and Conductor William Jaqua, stopped and all possible assistance was given. Medical aid was quickly secured, and all that was possible was done. The knowledge of the accident was received by Frederick C. Norton to whom a telegram was sent asking him to notify the relatives. Mr. Norton had declined an invitation to accompany the party. The telegram was received at half past one o'clock. Within an hour Representative A. F. Rockwell and wife and Mr. Norton went to the scene in Mr. Rockwell's automobile. Soon after Dr. A. S. Brackett, W. H. Bacon and R. A. Potter, a cousin of Mr. Root, also went to the place in Mr. Bacon's auto, and took charge of the bodies, which were cared for and brought to the home here Tuesday morning.

CHARLES J. ROOT. MISS MARY P. ROOT. MISS CANDACE ROBERTS.
MRS. JOEL H. ROOT.
"FRITZ"

This photo was taken by John Berkin, June, 1905, on the lawn of the Root home. The dog "Fritz" was a great pet and died about August 1st, 1905.

It was the saddest home coming ever known here. There were few dry eyes among those who gathered at the station when the caskets arrived and were taken to the desolated home.

The passengers on the train, among whom was Fred H. Barnes, a son of Seth Barnes of Bristol, heard the crash and realized that an accident had happened.

The only eye-witnesses, aside from the engineer and firemen, were two young girls Josephine and Anna Tinkever, who live near the crossing. Their testimony is not very clear. The engineer insists that he repeatedly blew his whistle to give warning of the crossing.

Miss Catherine Root, when able to talk about the affair, said that no one in the car had the least intimation of danger and she can recall only a sudden collapse, the cause of which she cannot realize.

Mr. Root, as well as his sister and mother, were extremely deaf. He was a skilled operator of his machine and often ran it at high speed, but his friends had entire confidence in his ability to control it. He had met with minor accidents, but never showed any inclination to avoid responsibility and always showed consideration for others who might be inconvenienced. He was an enthusiast and loved his machine as most men do their spirited horses. On this fatal trip the canopy was on the machine, and the gasoline tank whistle was out of order, making a continuous noise. His friends are confident that he never for a moment realized his danger and turned for the crossing, dashed into the train and to the death which came to him, without warning. They say that had he known his imminent danger he could and would have kept a straight course and taken his chances with the fence and bank into a meadow.

Miss Mary P. Root, who sustained a fractured, skull, broken shoulder and other injuries, was removed at once to the House of Mercy in Pittsfield where she died without regaining consciousness.

Miss Root was one of Bristol's most talented women. She was a graduate of Vassar, class of '80, and was known all about the state and New England as a prominent D. A. R. worker.

At the time of her death Miss Mary P. Root had a biography of Gideon Roberts in preparation for this work, and her article, "The Founders and Their Homes," appears on page 193.

The family was one of the best known in town. Its members have long been prominent in business, social, religious and intellectual affairs. The father of Charles and Mary, was Joel Henry Root. He was born in Broadalbin, near Saratoga, N. Y., December 5, 1822. He was the third son of Samuel Root, an elder in the Presbyterian church of Mayfield, N. Y., and Philotheta Ives of Bristol, Conn.

On the early death of his parents, he came, a boy of five years, to live in Bristol, in the home of his uncle, Joel Root, whose wife was Piera Ives, the sister of the young Joel's mother. His grandparents, Amasa and Huldah Shaylor Ives were among the earliest settlers in Bristol and lived on Federal Hill. His grandfather, Moses Root of Meriden, was a soldier in the Revolution, enlisting when only seventeen years of age, who married at the close of the war, Esther Mitchell, daughter of Moses Mitchell, of Meriden.

Joel H. Root's boyhood was spent partly in Bristol and partly in Whitesborough, N. Y. In the latter place he attended the Oneida Institute of Science and Industry, an institution founded in 1827, perhaps the first school in the country established "to blend productive manual laber with a course of study." Before he was thirty he went into business for himself.

In 1867 he bought the land known as the Island, and erected there a factory where, for the remainder of his life, he engaged in the manu- of piano hardware and of brass butt hinges.*

Mr. Root was married, August 4, 1852, to Catherine Roberts, daughter of Wyllys, and granddaughter of Gideon Roberts, and in 1859, he purchased the property on High street which has ever since been the home of the family. He died April 11, 1885.

His children were Charles J., and Theodore, and Miss Mary P. Root. The home on High street was a delightful one and many warm friends enjoyed its charming hospitality.

THE ROOT FACTORY ON ROOT'S ISLAND.

R. N. Blakeslee of the Bridgeport Post writes to the Press as follows:—

"The news of the shocking death of Charles J. Root, his mother and aunt has cast a heavy pall of gloom over every one who has known this estimable family. To the writer the death of Charles J. Root is especially saddening. I remember him more intimately of course during our childhood and young manhood days. As school chums we were inseparable and our vacation days were spent together. Charlie, as we always called him, was a splendid fellow, always cheerful and full of fun. He was upright, clean and a perfectly moral young man, and a true friend. These qualities won for him a host of friends. The attachments formed in our younger days have always remained although for more than twenty years we have been but little in each other's company. We bow in humble submission to the "Reaper" who respects no human ties and in silent prayer seek that preparation which is needful in the hour of human extremity."

*After Mr. Root's death the business was formed into a joint stock company.

MRS. CATHERINE ROBERTS ROOT.

The death of Mrs. Catherine Roberts Root, although she had lived the alloted age and was eighty years old last January, brought the greatest sorrow to the scores of friends in Bristol who had known and loved the woman for many years. Her life was one of great profit to those who knew her, and their remembrance of the fine old lady will be a precious heritage in the future. Few women have lived in this or any other community who possessed the rare qualities of character that graced Mrs. Root. Born in Bristol, she was the daughter of Wyllys Roberts, a substantial resident of this town, and the granddaughter of Gideon Roberts, who, coming home from the Revolutionary War hung up his old gun and powder horn and started the great American clock industry. He it was who first manufactured clocks in the town of Bristol, and he usually made up enough during the winter season to last him on a trip through the Southern states in the summer; and this small sized industry started away back in the eighteenth century is what developed into the great clock factories of the Ingrahams and the Sessions to-day. All honor is due the memory of Gideon Roberts; and Bristol will not soon forget his work here.

Mrs. Root spent all of her long life here and Bristol was glad she did, for few women have lived in the town who possessed more gentle manners and solidity of character and intellectual attainments. Her education was obtained in Bristol and in early womanhood she taught school in different places, one of which was in the town of Simsbury where she "boarded around" as was the custom in those days. Her success as a teacher was eminently successful. She was a great reader of books all her long life, and although she did not receive a college education she had a fund of knowledge that would reflect credit in a graduate of Vassar or Wellesley.

In 1852 she was married to Joel H. Root, for many years one of the solid and prominent business men of the town. They moved into the house on High street in 1859, where they have lived ever since and which was one of the very first houses to be built on that street. Several children were born to the couple and their married life was an extremely happy and successful one. Her husband died in the spring of 1885 and her son Charles, then only a young man, took hold where his father left off and not only increased the estate left by the elder Root, but made one for himself as well.

Mrs. Root was a talented and thoroughly intellectual woman. Among those well qualified to judge she was considered a person of acute and unusual intelligence; her knowledge of history and philosophy was accurate and complete, while the general fund of knowledge she always possessed was of the character that embraced a wide range of polite literature and political history. It was a pleasure to sit and talk with the rare old lady on any of these subjects and hear from a woman who had not been able herself to read a book for a dozen years or more, her opinions of current topics and recent books. Her daughter and Miss Roberts, her sister, used to read to her hours at a time as she was unable to do so herself on account of failing eyesight.

Mrs. Root's life will be long remembered. Her dignified manners and thoroughly lovable Christian character will long be the pride of those who were fortunate enough to be her close and intimate friends. Of great or famous deeds, this woman did none; but the simple story of her fine, noble life is enough to inspire a love for the things that amount to something in this life.

CHARLES J. ROOT.

Charles J. Root was born in Bristol 48 years ago. He had long been identified with Bristol's manufacturing business and mercantile interests. Early in life he assumed the management of the factory on Root's Island and developed a profitable business in making automatic counters, piano hinges and novelties. Only a few days ago he let the contract for a new brick factory to Messrs. Fogg and Currie. In recent years he had given a good deal of attention to real estate matters and had done much to develop the town. Some years ago when the street grades were changed at Gridley House corner, after a long railroad fight, he purchased the Gridley House property and spent thousands of dollars in remodeling it and conventing it into a modern building.

Some years later he purchased the old Ebers building and site adjoining the Gridley House, tore down the ram shackle wooden buildings and erected one of the finest business blocks in town, as well as in this section.

One of his earliest enterprises in the building line was the erection of the Grand Army Hall on North Main street. In addition he owned a number of houses on the Island and other property about town.

Mr. Root's activities were many and far reaching. Quite a number of years ago he became interested in orange growing in Florida and had a fine grove and winter home in Rockledge, Florida, where he, with the family, spent portions of nearly every winter. He was also one of the early promoters of Sachem's Head, where he had an attractive summer home. He was greatly interested in mining enterprises, especially in Butte, Montana. He was one of the heavy stockholders and a director in the Raven Mine of that city. His interests included other mining properties to a considerable extent. Mr. Root was an enthusiastic automobilist. He was one of the pioneers in that line here, and was one of the first to bring a machine into town. He was an auto expert and few men derived as much pleasure as he from one. He delightd in inviting friends to ride with him and share in the pleasure. He often took long runs about the country, always with members of his family or friends. While afflicted with extreme deafness, his friends felt that he was an unusually competent operator because he seemed always to have good judgment and a clear head, as well as perfect control of his machine.

While very active in business affairs, devoted to the town of his birth, and contributing much to its upbuilding, he cared little for political or public life. His membership in Bristol organizations was confined to the Bristol Social Club and the Business Men's Association.

Mr. Root had a comprehensive knowledge of and liking for mechanics. Before he was twenty-one years of age he invented an automatic counter from which he realized considerable money, and which he manufactured afterwards. He possessed great determination as well as business acumen and his large fortune was made mostly within the past twelve years, by his own unaided efforts. He handled his large business affairs with skill and ability, and had he lived a few years longer would undoubtedly have become one of the wealthiest men in town.

He was modest and unassuming, and found his chief pleasure in his home life and in the company of his intimate friends. He had a keen sense of humor and was a delightful companion and host. His untimely death is a sad ending to a busy, useful life, and brings keen sorrow to many a heart.

MISS CANDACE ROBERTS.

Miss Candace Roberts, daughter of Wyllys Roberts, and sister of Mrs. Joel H. Root, was also a native of Bristol, and had spent most of her life in this town. She also received her education in the schools of Bristol and spent a good deal of her early life in teaching school. She taught successfully in East Haven and lived in that town for some years. Many years ago she removed to Bristol and has lived in the family of her sister, Mrs. Root, for the last thirty years.

Miss Roberts was a quiet, unassuming woman of fine tastes, good intelligence and an almost invaluable assistant to her afflicted sister. For many years Miss Mary Root and Mrs. Root were quite deaf, and during these years she had charge of the household. She had a lovable and attractive disposition and endeared herself to everybody with whom she came in contact. Her friends in Bristol were legion. She was a thoroughly good, Christian woman.

She was a member of Katherine Gaylord Chapter, D. A. R., as her grandfather was an officer in the Revolutionary War. She was a long time member of the local Congregational church, and also a member of the Delta Reading Club. She was interested in all the things that went for the advancement and intellectual culture of the town.

RESIDENCE FREDERICK CALVIN NORTON, STEARNS STREET.

THE SCHOOLS OF BRISTOL

BY MILO LEON NORTON

THE early history of the schools of Bristol is so thoroughly treated in the various historical articles in this book, that more than a brief mention is unnecessary. Quoting from an article written for the *Bristol Magazine*, of November, 1906, it was there stated:

"If it were asked what were the two leading traits of the Puritans who founded Connecticut, the answer would be: first, an all-pervading devotion to religion; second, a deep interest in education. Their first care was set up religious worship, and their next duty that of establishing schools for the mental training of their youth. For the establishment of these two institutions, the church and the school, they freely taxed the slender resources at their command, and voluntarily and cheerfully bore the burdens incident to their maintenance. . . . .
In New Cambridge, after the establishment of the first ecclesiastical society in 1744, and the building of the first meeting-house, in 1747, it was voted, December 4, 1749, 'that [we] would have a school kept in this society six months, *viz.*, 3 months by a master and 3 months by a dame. Josiah Lewis, Benjamin Gaylord, Joseph Adkins, and Caleb Abernethy, were chosen a committee to order the affair of said school.' This was the first actual school board of the town. It was not until 1790 that a regular school board was organized and no official act of the board was recorded until 1796. In 1766, five districts were formed, and in 1798, Fall Mountain district was added to the number. In 1842,

FEDERAL HILL SCHOOL.

BRISTOL HIGH SCHOOL.

PEACEABLE STREET SCHOOL AND SCHOLARS. 1907

thirteen districts, as they now exist with some modifications, were organized and their boundaries defined."

In 1854, the school board voted to consolidate Districts Nos. 1 and 2, but upon the presentation of an urgent petition from the voters of No. 2, the vote was rescinded. Soon after Districts Nos. 3 and 4 were consolidated, and a new schoolhouse built, about 1856. This has been twice enlarged. The old schoolhouses of Districts 3 and 4 are still standing, remodeled; one occupied by Deborah Sanford, on West Street, the other by Thomas J. Lane, on South Street.

At present there are eleven school districts, the number four having been omitted since the consolidation. The Copper Mine District has also been merged with the Edgewood, or ninth district. There was tabulated in the last annual report of the Board of School Visitors (1907), an enumeration of 2,682 children of school age in the town of Bristol. Of these 2,090 were registered at the various district schools, 437 attended private schools, including St. Joseph's parochial, and the German Lutheran schools, and 174 attended the High School. The total expense of conducting the public schools for one year, was given as $47,884.02. Deducting what was paid for books, apparatus and repairs to buildings, the actual expenses amounted to $43,772.18. Of this amount $25,686.15 was paid from the proceeds of town taxation, $7,284.75 from the State, and other sources, the balance being made up by districts 1, 2, 3 and 13. The High School is conducted at an expense, in round numbers, of $10,000 per annum.

The Board of School Visitors consists of Noble E. Pierce, chairman; Arthur S. Brackett, Mrs. Edson M. Peck, Carlton B. Ives, Michael B. O'Brien, Charles L. Wooding, Secretary.

The Bristol High School was established in 1883, F. A. Brackett, Principal, graduating its first class in 1886. High School departments were also maintained in the schoolhouse of District No. 1 and at Forestville in the schoolhouse of No. 13. But the princpal school was that in

SCHOOL AT PINE STREET CORNER.

the No. 3 schoolhouse. The present, elegant High School building was erected in 1892. At first a spacious hall for entertainments, lectures, etc., was provided on the second floor, but as the attendance kept increasing it became necessary to fit up the hall as a schoolroom. At present the attendance is so large that the building is entirely inadequate for the needs of the school, and its enlargement is an imperative necessity, plans for which have been prepared by an architect, at an estimateed cost of $27,000. The present attendance is about 216, including pupils from out of town, and is increasing from year to year.

SCHOOL DISTRICT No. 10

BY MRS. DAVID BIRGE.

School District No. 10 of Bristol is situated in the western part of the town, adjoining the town of Plymouth. The boundary line between Bristol and Plymouth is also a part of the line between Hartford and Litchfield Counties.

One square mile of this land was granted to three brothers bearing the name of Matthews. The schoolhouse is situated on the northwest corner where Matthew's and Hill streets cross. The original schoolhouse stood a few rods north of the present site, in a piece of heavy timber, where now is a smooth, nice meadow.

Shall we go from the schoolhouse a few rods south to the Matthews' homestead, where a large family of boys and girls were trained in the rigid ways of our forefathers? One of the sons, inclined to oratory, found a dead fowl, and placing it upon a board, called an audience of

SCHOOL HOUSE AND SCHOLARS, DISTRICT NO. 10. 1907.

his brothers and sisters, then mounted the fence and took for his text the first chapter of bar-post and second hole. The father listened to the remarks and exhortation (unknown to the youthful preacher), and at the close gave the boy a sound flogging for trifling with serious matters. Four generations of Matthews lived here, and about 1870 the property was sold to Mr. Eri Scott, who came with his small family from Meriden and lived in the old long-roofed lean-to house a few years, then built the house that is now owned and occupied by his daughter, Mrs. Willis Roberts, and her son Otis and family.

Next south of the Matthews' place we come to the Lemuel Carrington farm where Mr. Ezekiel Carrington, son of Lemuel, built the house that for many years was the home of Silas Carrington, who, tiring of our severe winters and wishing to make his home in Florida, sold the home of his ancestors to Reverend Farrel Martin of Waterbury.

Down the street a few steps, and we come to a branch in the road; taking the right hand road we soon reach the old Litchfield and Hartford Turnpike and see the Captain Norton place, where our late townsman, Mr. Augustine Norton, was raised with a large family of brothers and sisters. The Nortons moved away and the place was rented. For a short time it was the home of a family by the name of Crittenden, then of the Lovelaces and Keeneys, and about 1848 was bought by Mr. Woodruff Candee of Harwinton. After the death of Mrs. Candee, in 1892, the place was sold to Mr. C. C. Weld, who now occupies it.

Going west about a quarter of a mile we turn south from the "Pike"

(1) Aaron C. Dresser, Mathews street; (2) At present used as lodgings for R. R. workmen; (3) John B. Mathews *O*, Edgar Wm. Cahoon *R*; (4) George Bresnahan *R*, Mathews street; (5) Mrs. Walter E. Cook *O*; (6) J. B. White *R*; (7) Michael Ristock, Perkins street, formerly the "Tommy" Roper Place, built by Nathaniel Mathews, about 1845; (8) Frank E. Pond *O*, Perkins street, once the Lehman Stevens Place. House built by Lehman Stevens; (9) Allen Manchester *O*, Elmer J. Stone *R*, Perkins street, formerly the Evits Hungerford Place, built by Harvilla Hart.

SILAS H. CARRINGTON.

and soon reach the Barlow homestead, that for a long time was the home of Mrs. Chloe Daniels and her sister, Mrs. Jane Culver, who sold to Mr. Anton Weigert, the present owner.

West from here, over a crooked, hilly road, we come to the Ittai and Sally Curtis place, later the home of Mr. Miles Welton, who, when the road was changed, built the new house on the knoll north of the old and nearer the new, straight road. The place changed owners often after Mr. Welton went west, and for a short time was the home of a Mr. McWilliams, a contractor on the railroad that was building between Hartford and Waterbury. Mr. Amos Webster of Harwinton bought and occupied it several years. Later, a Mr. Birge was there, and Mr. Homer Cook of Terryville. Mr. Amzi Clark and family lived there several years, then moved to Terryville, and soon the house burned down. The old house that was abandoned so many years ago has been repaired and is the comfortable home of a family of foreigners.

North from here, and crossing the old turnpike, we come to another portion of the Matthews' property, owned for many years by Mr. Merriman Matthews, then later by his daughter, Mrs. Henry Reed, who sold to Mr. Frank Mix who soon tired of fancy farming and sold to his tenant, Mr. John Tanner, and after a few years he moved to Plymouth, and a Mr. Sahlin bought and occupies it. North a few rods and west, we come to a house built by Mr. Horace Munson and now the property of Mr. Charles Barber.

West from here and down a winding hill, we reach the last house in the west side of the district, as this stands near the Plymouth line which is a part of the Litchfield County line also. The house was built by Mr. Simeon Matthews, who was not a "carpenter and joiner" but planned his house, cut the trees, hewed out the frame and the men at the raising said the joints worked together and everything was as true as if a professional brain and hand had done the work. I heard some one say only a few years ago, that the red paint on the house at that time was the paint that Mr. Matthews used when the house was built, but cannot certify to the fact. Here a large family was raised, and of those who lived in this vicinity during their lives were our late townsman, David Matthews and his sister Betsy, the wife of Mr. Ira Churchill of Forestville. Several of the family moved to Illinois when young. The only living member of the family of twelve is Mrs. Eliza, widow of Mr. Harrison Elwell, who lives with her son Edwin in Worcester, Mass. After the death of Mr. Matthews his widow married Mr. Cyrus Gaylord, and the following nuptial agreement was made between them.

Mr. Samuel Benham bought the place and after his death it became

Bristol September 21st 1844
This is to Certify That Cyrus Gaylord of Plymouth and Rhoda Matthews of Bristol are soon to be married And that both of them agree not to claim each others Property any farther than Said Gaylord is to Support Said Rhoda Matthews during his natural Life
David Matthews
Sally Matthews   Witness,   Cyrus Gaylord

FAC SIMILE MARRIAGE AGREEMENT BETWEEN MR. CYRUS GAYLORD AND MRS. MATHEWS.

the property, by inheritance, of Mrs. Horace Munson; and now it is owned by Mr. J. J. Jee.

We shall have to turn and retrace our way back to the Merriman Matthew's corner, then down the hill towards the east to the Isaac Shelton place, said to have been a resting place for Tories. Later it was the home of Mr. Thomas Mitchell, the father of Judge Henry Mitchell, late of Bristol, then of Mr. Eli Ely of Harwinton, and after his death the place was bought by Mr. Levi Moulthrop, and now is owned and occupied by Mr. Chauncey Atwood. A new house across the road from the old is the home of Mr. and Mrs. Edwin Gaylord, Mrs. Gaylord being a daughter of Mr. Atwood. A little way east and we are at the schoolhouse corners once more. Shall we cross Hill street and go towards town until we reach the top of the long hill where in winter we get a fine view of Bradley Heights and the houses in that part of the town with the farther hills?

Here we find a house that was a carpenter's shop on the Darrow place, directly north of its present location. It was bought and moved across the fields to this place and made into a dwelling house by Henry Reeder, an Englishman. After his death it had several tenants and is now the property of Fred. Ristoch. Leaving the road we cross the fields towards the east, and come to a small house built by Mr. Nathaniel Matthews for his hired man, Tommie Roper, who was one of the first Irishmen that came to Bristol to work in the copper mine. He tired of mining and farming and for several years was a handy man at the railroad station, depot it was called then. Mr. Michael Ristoch is the present owner.

Passing through the woods north of Mr. Ristoch's a half mile or less we come to a road leading west, where stands the Darrow place. The old house was on the south side of the street, but one of the sons, Mr. William Darrow, a carpenter and joiner, built the new house about 1834, on the north side, "facing the sun," and built it for the use and comfort of his family. Here a large family of boys and girls grew up, and Mr. Burritt Darrow of Norfolk, Conn., is the only one living. For fourteen years Mr. Williams Darrow was the first selectman of Bristol, and North Main street was laid out and built under his administration. When Mr. Darrow was arranging to sell his place Mr. Sylvester Saxton, who helped build the house, remarked to his wife that he knew how that house was built and would try and get it. He bought and moved there, and very soon died leaving two small boys who grew to manhood under the influence of a good mother. Our worthy townsman, Mr. F. A. Saxton, is the only surviving member of this family. Mrs. Saxton sold the place to Mr. Edson Downs and later it became the property of Mr. Fred. Hubbard, and the old pine tree gives it the name of Pinehurst.

Once more we will retrace our steps to the corner where was an old lean-to house that had never been painted and was past repairing, and had been the home of a family by the name of Woods. Mrs. Clara Woods, wife of Capt. Elijah Darrow of South street, was one of the daughters. Mr. and Mrs. Leaman Stevens, familiarly known as Uncle Leaman and Aunt Celestia, lived in the old house several years, then built the house that is now standing. At their death it passed into the

(10) Louis Lagase O, Hill street, The Sidney Hough Place; (11) Joseph Bleau O, Hill street, The Hiram Curtiss Place; (12) Wm. O. Miller O, Wm. Janecka R, Hill street, The Andrew Hough Place; (13) John Spielman O, Hill street, The Stephen Russell Place; (14) Fred, Hellman O, Hill street, The Samuel Jones Place, was built by Mr. Jones and the original window panes were of American made glass, probably among the first used in Bristol; (15) Chas. Schroder O, built on the George Stone Place, known before that as the Hill Place, built on the site of Noble Hill's Clock Shop. This shop was afterwards altered into a dwelling house; (16) Charles Tong O, Hill street, house was originally the boarding house at the Fall's Factory, later called (Satinet cotton warp and wool filling) *Old Shovel Shop* on the Terryville Road. Was moved to its present location by Nathaniel Mathews, and Hanford Pennoyer. This was located in the site of the widow Hill Place, by Thaddeus Bristol; (17) James McWilliams R, Charles Katzung R, Hill street, built by Harrison Gould, and then known as the Harrison Gould Place; (18) Geo. N. Minor O, Hill street, built by Mr. Daniel Hill.

possession of their nephew, Mr. Ira Gaylord, who sold to Mr. C. C. Welch, and he in turn sold to Mr. Forster, and now Mr. Frank Pond is the owner.

Going north a few rods we find the Hungerford place, where Uncle Evits and Aunt Anna lived many years. Late in life, and warned by the infirmities of old age, they sold the dear old home to Mr. Harvilla Hart, and spent the remainder of their days with their daughter, Mrs. Lockwood Tuttle, who cheerfully ministered to their wants and comforts. Mr. Hart built a new house and enlarged his farm, buying back the homestead of his parents (that had passed out of the Hart family), but joined the Hungerford farm on the east and north. He sold the place to Mr. Henry Pond and it was owned by his family until a year ago, when it was sold to the Manchester brothers. Just north of this place the road branches and we come to the land owned many years by the Hart family. Just east of Perkins street on the cross road through the Hoppers to Peacable street is an old cellar place, where once was the Asel Hart home, and on Battle street, at the foot of the steep hill and on the east side of the way was an old lean-to house, the home of Mr. Seth Hart. On the west side of Battle street, at the foot of the hill, where the old road (that was closed by the town authority a few years ago) joined Battle, is an old cellar and the stone underpining to a barn, showing that there has been a large house and out-buildings, the home of another Mr. Hart. It seems reasonable to suppose that they had a grant of land the same as the Matthews brothers.

We are near the northern boundary of the district now and must

CHIPPINS HILL

(19) Built by Caleb Mathews, for many years The (Squire) Constant Loyal Tuttle Place, Mathis Hintz O; (20) Pinehurst, built by Mrs. Williams Darrow, Fred Hubbard, O; (21) The Hanford Pennoyer Place; Mrs. David Birge R: (22) Maple Crest Farm, Chauncey Atwood O, (23) Sunny Side, E. L. Gaylord, O; (24) Maple Corner, Fred Sahlin O, (25) Breezy Nook Farm, formerly the Horace Munson Place, Charles H. Barber O, (26) The Simeon Mathews Place, Joseph J. Gee O; (27) "Maple Lawn Farm," originally the Nathaniel Mathews Place, Mrs. Ellen Roberts O.

either cross the lots or climb the Battle street hill past the line, until we reach a short road across to Hill street, and from here we go south past the Samuel Jones' and the Widow Hill's places and come to the first house in the district on the north side. The old house was built first for a clock shop for Mr. Noble Hill, but failing in this it was made into a dwelling house and occupied by Mr. George Stone and his wife Nabby, many years. A Mr. Charles Schraeder bought it and soon it burned down and was replaced by the stone house now standing. A little farther south we come to the old Gaylord homestead. The first house was built on the west side of the street, but the newer house was built by one of the sons, Esq. Phillip Gaylord, who sold to a Mrs. Gould and her son Harrison and by inheritance it became the property of Mrs. Carrington, the mother of Silas. It had several owners and at one time was owned by Mr. Andrew Terry of Susanville (the grandfather of Mr. Charles Terry Treadway, who wanted a place where he could have his ideas of farming carried out by hired hands. He soon tired of this scheme and sold the place to Uncle Billy Gaylord of Burlington, a nephew of the builder. For several years it was the home of Mr. Ira Gaylord, now of Summer street, who sold the farm to Mr. Frank Atwood. It is now the property of Dr. A. S. Brackett and occupied by a Mr. McWilliams.

A little to the south of this and commanding a wonderful view, stands the house built by Mr. Darrow for Mr. Daniel Hill. After the death of Mr. Hill his son William lived there with his mother until he tired of driving over the road between his home and Bristol, saying the hills were no shorter or less steep than when he was young. He sold to Mr. Mark Miner of Wolcott, who, with his grand-son, Edson Downs, lived there several years. After the death of Mr. Miner, Mr. Downs sold to a Mr. Winton of Woodbury. Later Mr. Frank Atwood bought it and lived there until the great blizzard in 1888, when he sickened and died. Mrs. Atwood sold to Mr. G. N. Miner, grand-son of "Uncle Mark," who is the present owner.

NORTH CHIPPIN'S HILL SCHOOL.

SQUIRE CONSTANT LOYAL TUTTLE PLACE.

Now leaving Mr. Miner's we will go down the steep hill until we come to a little resting place where there is another Matthews' homestead built by Mr. Caleb Matthews over a hundred years ago and was owned by the family until after the death of Mr. Nathaniel Matthews in 1863, when it passed into the hands of strangers. In the house are two chambers with a "swinging partition" between them, a partition that could be lifted up and fastened to hooks in the ceiling above, making a large room where the Masons held their meetings in the early part of the Eighteenth Century. It was also used as a ball-room, and the neighbors gathered there for their quilting parties.

After the death of Mr. Matthews a Mrs. Blanchard and her son from Northfield bought and occupied the place several years, then Mr. Henry Forster of Hartford, and after changing owners several times, is now in the possession of a Mr. Heintz.

At the foot of the hill below the Esquire Tuttle place is an old house said to have been built by Mr. Enos Ives, and about 1840 was bought by Mr. Tuttle for his son Hiram, who about 1850 sold it to his brother-in-law, Mr. Hanford Pennoyer, who lived there until 1899, when he died at the age of 94 years and a few months. His wife, Emily Tuttle, daughter of Esquire Tuttle, died two weeks earlier, aged 87.

The house is now occupied by two of Mr. Pennoyer's daughters, the only descendants of the old settlers now living on the hill.

If we go south from here to the old turn-pike and turn towards town we shall find a comparatively new house just east of Mr. Weld's that was built by Charlie Blanchard, son of Calvin and sold by him to Mr. Edson Smith. Towards Bristol and at the top of Pine Hollow Hill we come to the Castle place, afterwards the home of Stephen Russell and of Timothy Hill, son of Daniel and of William Webster, and of Harvilla Hart, who built the new house and sold to Mr. Calvin Blanchard. It is now owned by Mrs. Farnham.

AN OLD TIME VIEW OF THE NORTH SIDE SCHOOL.

THE NORTH SIDE SCHOOL DISTRICT, No. 2

By Arthur S. Barnes.

District No. 2 is not one of the old school districts of the town of Bristol. Before this district had a separate existence, the children of that portion of the town attended school at the south end, at a schoolhouse located near the old Baptist church, or went to the school on Federal Hill. Probably the children living at the foot of Chippins Hill attended school in the South Chippins Hill District as both the South Chippins Hill and the North Chippins Hll Districts were separate districts before what is now known as District No. 2 had an individual existence. The thirteen school districts of the town were designated and numbered at a Bristol School Society meeting, held on January 19, 1842.

In the earlier days North Main Street was not cut through, and there was no cross roads between West Street and Federal Hill and Queen Streets, except Center Street. Center Street was used principally by residents of the southwestern section of the town and people from Fall Mountain in traveling to the Congregational Church on Sundays.

What is now known as District No. 2 was set apart at a meeting of the Bristol School Society on December 14, 1837, and was known as the West Center School District. Walter Williams was the first committee. Land was purchased of Daniel, Nelson and Nancy Roberts in the rear of the Methodist Church, and on this a school building was erected. This plot of ground was bounded on the north and west by land of grantor, east by the Methodist lot, and south by land of Eli Barnes.

The length of the school year at this time was evidently six months, as we find on record a vote passed October 7, 1839, "instructing the district committee to employ a female teacher for 6 months to commence as soon as a suitable teacher could be found." That the district insisted on having the very best teachers that could be secured is evidenced by the following vote that "the committee be instructed to employ a female teacher and requested to obtain one second to none in Hartford County."

The schoolhouse being situated in the rear of the church, there was more or less friction between district authorities and the Methodist Society, on account of the doings of some of the school children. There is a record of a special meeting held in 1849, in which it was voted to pay a bill of the Methodist Society for $1.08 for broken window glass, and at this same meeting it was made a standing rule of the district that the committee ascertain whose children broke glass in the windows of the Methodist Church and report the same, and that the expense of the repairs be added to the rate bill of the parents of these children.

In 1854, the question of uniting with District No. 1 was considered at a number of special meetings. The vote was finally passed to unite with District No. 1 and build a graded school, but this action was never carried out.

The Methodist Society needed more room for horse sheds, and in 1860 it was vated to sell to the Society a part of the district lot, the schoolhouse to be moved to the rear, about a quarter of an acre of land additional having been purchased from Daniels Roberts. The deed for this land was dated October 12, 1863. In 1877, an addition of about fourteen feet was added to the rear of the school building, which was the first addition made to the building since it was erected in 1838.

In 1882, it had become necessary to take further steps toward enlarging the accommodations as the number of children in the district had so increased that this one room would not accommodate them. A special meeting was called to consider consolidating Districts Nos. 1, 2 and 3. This special meeting was held on May 31, 1882, and it was voted that "It is not deemed expedient to consolidate with other districts." The district committee were instructed to call a meeting to consider enlarging the schoolhouse or building a new one. After receiving an offer from Lawson Wooding, the district voted "to exchange the present property for the so-called Mitchell property, the price not to exceed $1000.00 as a difference in exchange." This Mitchell property was the old George Mitchell homestead on the site of the present schoolhouse. The Mitchell house was removed from its location, and is now standing on Williams Avenue, and is used as a residence. The ell part of this Mitchell home was removed to a plot of ground in the rear of the church by the side of the old schoolhouse, and that also is still standing and used as a residence.

The district appointed a building committee, consisting of Lester Goodenough, Seth Barnes, Henry Hutchinson, Edward Graham, and J. M. Peck. They were empowered to sell the old schoolhouse, and to build a new one on the new site. $4000.00 was appropriated for this purpose, and this amount was afterwards increased by $600.00, making a total of $4600.00.

A two room building was erected, and was first occupied in the spring of 1883, Mr. Burton A. Smith and Miss Sarah Goodenough being the teachers. Mr. Smith finished that school year, and was succeeded by Clarence A. Bingham who came to District No. 2 at the beginning of the fall term in 1883. With the completion of the present school year (1907-1908) Mr. Bingham will have served 25 years as the principal of the North Side School. During these years he has rendered faithful and intelligent services to the District, and has been looked up to by his scholars as a man who could be respected and trusted. He has seen the school grow from an average registration of about 95 to 325 pupils. There are now in attendance many children of his former pupils. The coming of Mr. Bingham marks the transition of District No. 2 from a country district school to a graded school of the town. It was formerly a rare thing to have a teacher remain a whole year, and the ordinary custom was to change teachers every term. Whether this "movable feast" in the line of school-teachers was brought about by the desire of the district committee to have some real work to do in the appointment of teachers, or whether it came from the teacher's opportunity to get more pay, or whether the teachers were driven out by the unruly pupils is a matter which does not at present concern us.

The schoolhouse as erected in 1883 was occupied without change or addition until 1889 when an addition was built of two rooms, and later in 1900 another addition was built of one room for kindergarten work which makes a present equipment of five rooms in the school building.

The names familiar in the early days of the district were Peck, Carrington, Burwell, Barnes, Mitchell, Smith, Birge, Goodrich, Foster, Sheldon, Blakesley, Plumb, Phetzing, Burnham, Way, Stevens, Williams, and Ingraham. These families have now for the most part either moved away or passed on.

In "Connecticut Historical Collections" by John W. Barber, published in 1838 there is a very interesting picture of the town of Bristol. The picture is sketched from the hill back of the Methodist Meeting house and inasmuch as it is largely of this section now known as the Second School District, the following quotation is interesting:

"This is a manufacturing town, and the inhabitants are distinguished for their enterprise and industry. There are at present sixteen

North End School that stood on West St. near Terryville Ave. It is now in back of Advent Church and used as a dwelling. The teacher standing in center is Mr Jennings. This picture was loaned by Mrs. Lyons of West St.,

clock factories, in which nearly 100,000 brass and wooden clocks have been manufactured in a single year. The manufacture of buttons is also carried on.

"The principal part of the village is built at the base of a circular hill, the buildings being mostly on ar oad which passes round the hill in somewhat of a semicircle. The most conspicuous building is the Methodist Church, erected in 1835. To the right of this in the distance, and on the summit of the hill is the Congregational Church. The Episcopal Church is situated on the northern descent of the hill, near the forest. The Baptist Church is on the road passing by the Methodist Church, a little distance to the south."

The Methodist Church referred to is the original Methodist Church erected in 1835, and afterwards sold to the Advent Society and burned to the ground in 1890.

We do not find that many men who have written their names high in the hall of fame have received their education at District No. 2. Perhaps the most prominent are Hon. Chas. E. Mitchell of New Britain, former U. S. Patent commissioner, and Tracy Peck, head of the Latin Department at Yale. But District No. 2 has turned out a goodly number of intelligent American citizens, men who have done and are doing their day's work as their hands find it to do.

The memory of our days in the district school is always with us, and twice happy is he whose memory goes back to the days in the little white schoolhouse behind the church.

> Rough, bleak, and hard, our little State
> Is scant of soil, of limits strait;
> Her yellow sands are sands alone,
> Her only mines are ice and stone!
>
> From Autumn frost to April rain,
> Too long her winter woods complain;
> From budding flower to falling leaf,
> Her summer time is all too brief.
>
> Yet on her rocks, and on her sands,
> And wintry hills, the schoolhouse stands,
> And what her rugged soil denies,
> The harvest of the mind supplies.
>
> .   .   .   .
>
> Nor heeds the sceptic's puny hands,
> While near her school the church-spire stands;
> Nor fears the blinded bigot's rule,
> While near the church-spire stands the school.
> —WHITTIER.

THE MOUNT HOPE CHAPEL.

A small Sunday-school was organized in 1884 in the North Chippins Hill district near the Burlington line, by Miss Hattie O. Utter, school teacher in that district. Miss Utter organized the school because the children of her day school were non-attendants of any Sunday-school. She conducted the Sunday-school successfully for a year when her engagement closed and she left the school to return to her home and be married. She was greatly beloved by the people of the district, and only lived about a year after her removal. At her earnest request Mr. William E. Sessions and Mr. B. S. Rideout, who was General Secretary of the Y. M. C. A. in Bristol, continued the school, beginning in June, 1885. The first Sunday only three little girls, sisters, Mary, Sarah and Lizzie Goodsell, were present. Mr. Rideout was only able to continue for a few months. Mr. Sessions conducted the school for four years in the schoolhouse, and has conducted it in the chapel ever since. There was a large and increasing attendance which outgrew the accommodations of the schoolhouse, and in 1889 the Mount Hope Chapel was built by voluntary contributions of the people and friends.

The chapel was dedicated by the Rev. A. C. Eggleston, who had been the pastor of the Prospect Methodist Episcopal Church in Bristol, but was at that time pastor of the First Methodist Episcopal Church in Waterbury.

The school was named Mount Hope by Mr. Rideout, who has been for many years a Congregationalist minister at Norway, Maine. Among the prominent workers and teachers in the early years were Mrs. Louisa Tuttle (deceased.), Mrs. W. O. Goodsell, Mrs. Frank H. Perkins and Mr. Charles S. Smith. The Sunday-school has been kept up continuously and frequently sermons have been preached by ministers of different de-

MT. HOPE CHAPEL.

nominations, some prominent and noted speakers having spoken there, including Bishop McCabe, familiarly known as Chaplain McCabe, Bishop Moore and Bishop Cranston, all of the Methodist Church, President Raymond of Wesleyan University, President Spencer of the Women's College, Baltimore and Fanny Crosby, the hymn writer, and others.

The school has always been conducted as a union or non-sectarian Protestant Sunday-school. Mr. Isaac T. Rowe has been assistant superintendent for many years. Many of the young people who formerly lived in that neighborhood have removed to Bristol and to other points throughout the country, but often return to visit the school.

In 1906 an arrangement was made with Mr. H. S. Coe to bring an omnibus load of children and young people from the East Church District every Sunday. Since that time Mrs. Coe has been an efficient teacher and worker in the school. For many years the school has supported a missionary native pastor-teacher school in India, called The Mount Hope School, and annual reports are read from the pastor-teacher.

A remarkably large attendance for such a scattered district has been maintained throughout the entire period and many families who live remote from any church enjoy the privileges of the Sunday-school. Annual excursions are held and the Christmas tree and exercises are always a pleasing feature.

The anniversary of dedication is celebrated every October, and a large number of former members are accustomed to attend. It is estimated that at least four hundred to five hundred people have been members of the school in the 23 years of its history.

A THOROUGHBRED MORGAN COLT.
OWNED BY DR. G. T. ELLIOTT. V. S., 1907.

THE BRADLEYITES

By Milo Leon Norton.

There are always dissenters from established opinions, be they political, religious, or commercial, and the world owes much of its progress to this fact. Someone is discovering a shorter route, or a better system, or is advancing a step ahead of his contemporaries, constantly; often persecuted, ridiculed and censured, but eventually gaining followers, and establishing a new standard of faith and practice.

Early in the last century, David Bradley, of Hampden, became dissatisfied with the doctrines of the Congregational church of which he was a member, separated himself from that denomination, and, being a student for the ministry, received baptism and ordination from the Baptists, though he never joined that communion. Gradually gathering together a small body of believers, a chapel was built for him at Mount Carmel, where he preached for many years, baptising converts, administering the sacrement, and performing all the functions of the Christian ministry. He attracted to his meetings such as considered the orthodox, or regular denominations, too narrow, or too widely, and who wished to lead a more spiritual life than they thought it possible to do in the churches; besides enlarging the boundaries of their fellowship to include every sincere believer in Christ, of whatever name or creed. After his death in the fifties meetings were held at the chapel, but there was a gradual scattering of the little flock, and eventually the meetings were discontinued there, and the chapel converted into a blacksmith shop, about 1870.

Among this little company of people, who were sitgmatized Bradleyites, agitators of various beliefs labored and secured some converts, notably John Humphrey Noyes, founder of the Oneida Community. The Advent movement of 1843, and subsequently, made some inroads into the membership; but on the whole, the original members remained true to the principles taught by their first and only pastor, for no one succeeded him in the pastoral relation.

During the two decades ending about 1870, occasional protracted meetings were held by this people, who were still called Bradleyites because of the prominence among them of Dr. H. I. Bradley, of New Haven, a physician and druggist, the son of the former pastor. These meetings were held in various places, at private houses, and were continued for from one to three weeks. All were welcome, of whatever religious belief, and perfect liberty was given for the expression of individual views, without opposition. A more heterogeneous body of Christians it would have been difficult to get together. The home of Asahel Mix, who lived in a house now abandoned, at the eastern end of a glacial knoll in the level meadows to the east of Edgewood, was one of the places where these people met on several occasions; also at the home of his son, Judd Mix, on Jerome Avenue; and at Ephraim Maltby's, in Stafford District. Most of the Bristol people who met with them were Millerites, or Second Adventists; and some of them, including the families of Ashael Mix, Mr. Maltby, and S. C. Hancock, the blind preacher, were Seventh-day Adventists, the converts of Mrs. Ellen White, who labored among them in 1848 and 1849, securing a number of adherents, but who never united with the sect of that name which she founded, with headquarters at Battle Creek, Michigan. The Hamden people, for the most part, were not believers in the literal coming of Christ; and there were others from Hartford, including the wife of the Mayor of the city, from New Haven, Southington, Cheshire, and other places, having almost as many distinct religious views as there were individuals.

They had one common ground of agreement, however, and that was the opposition to any church organization, or leadership. With the Quakers they believed in the leadership of the "Spirit," under which it was considered proper if one was speaking, and another wished to speak, for the second person to notify the first of his desire, when the first speaker sat down and waited for the second to deliver his message. They believed in the "gifts" mentioned in Scripture, including the "gift of tongues," when one would be "moved" to speak in an unintelligible gibberish, which, sometimes, another would be moved upon to interpret. Of course cranks of various kinds took advantage of the liberty of speech given in these meetings, and were patiently listened to, and tolerated. If they became violent or abusive, as they sometimes did, they were usually successfully squelched by the united determination of the level-headed persons present, without recourse to force or violent opposition. Sometimes there were heated and uncharitable discussions, but usually there was perfect tolerance, and the utmost patience with discordant elements noticeable. Sometimes there were "exercises," when persons would be apparently under "control," like a spiritualist medium, and in a semi-conscious state. When in this state personal messages were delivered to those present, believed to emanate directly from God. Admonitions were also given, warnings, and rebukes to offensive or disturbing elements. There seemed to be much discernment of inharmonious and disturbing influences, and their quick detection and exposure. Some of these instances were truly marvelous, and would almost surpass belief if related.

One of the most notable of these intruders into the little gathering of believers, who called themselves "Come-outers," because they had come out of the various churches to which they formerly belonged, was a Quaker from New Bedford, Mass., name Frederick Howland. He was a dentist by profession, and a remarkably skillful one, considering the crude instruments in use at the time, which was prior to 1860. He first appeared in Bristol as a lecturer, having a chart illustrating prophecy as he understood it. It developed that he regarded the Advent movement of 1843, and succeeding years, as applying to himself, finally announcing that he was the Holy Ghost. There is no claim so absurd that will not find acceptance, and in Massachusetts, at Worcester and Athol, he gained adherents who accepted him as the visible manifestation of the Paraclete. But the Bristol people did not take kindly to his pretentions, and when he came to Ashel Mix's house with his followers, half a dozen men and women in 1863, and asserted his power to kill, and to raise the dead, and to work miracles, he was promptly suppressed. His desire was to establish a community upon Mr. Mix's broad acres, but the scheme fell through, and he took his departure. One of his peculiarities was the observance of a vow never to perform any manual labor. This he rigidly observed. At Petersham, Mass., he established a community, over which he held absolute sway, until 1874, when he was accidentally killed. The community lingered a few years, dissolved and passed away. At one time it numbered twenty-five members, and was prosperous.

Ashael Mix, one of the most peculiar characters of his time, was a native of the Mine District, where he spent his early life, at the house which stood where H. I. Muzzy's house now stands. At early convern to Millerism he at once became a marked man, and the subject of many false accusations. About the time of the expected coming of the Lord, in 1843, his well-sweep, which was attached to a large pine tree in front of the house, got out of order, and he climbed up into the tree to repair it. Of course that was all that was necessary to start the story, believed to this day, that he climbed the tree, arrayed in "ascension robes," ready to be caught up to meet the Lord in the air. The old pine was blown down a few years ago, and until that time the iron rod upon which the well-sweep was hung, could be seen in the fork of the tree. Afterward Mr. Mix removed to the house before mentioned, where he spent the remainder of his life. He was the owner of a vast amount of real estate in Bristol, Burlington, and other places, mostly woodland, and was a dealer in horses and cattle, Occasionally but not often he was worsted in a trade. He was inclined to take things philosophically, as may be seen by the following incident, which illustrates his shrewdness also: He sold a cow to a Southington man, who enquired particularly if the cow was unruly. Mr. Mix replied that she never troubled him. The cow proved to be very unruly, and the purchaser demanded to know why this matter had been misrepresented to him. Mr. Mix replied that he never said the cow was not unruly. He said she never troubled him; he did not let such things trouble him. The purchaser was not satisfied with the explanation, sued for damages, and was beaten, the court sustaining Mr. Mix's philosophical view of the case. The incident was related to the writer by the purchaser, years afterward, who was much amused at the shrewdness of Mr. Mix, notwithstanding the fact that he was the loser by the transaction. There used to be a story current, at Mr. Mix's expense, related by a Bristol man, who professed that he dreamed one night that he met a well-dressed stranger on Main Street, and got into conversation with him. He said to the strange gentleman, who appeared to be a man of culture and refinement, "You seem to be a stranger hereabouts; might I enquire your name?" The gentleman addressed replied that he was Satan. The Bristol man was incredulous, believing that the stranger was joking; but when he parted the tails of his long frock coat, there was a forked tail which had been concealed there; when he lifted his tall, silk hat, horns protruded from his brow; and when he extended his foot, lo, it was cloven! When the Bristol man recovered from his surprise, he ventured to ask the stranger where he kept himself. "Up to Asahel Mix's," was the reply. "What on earth are you doing up there?" asked the Bristol man. "Helping the old gentleman trade horses and cattle," replied Satan. "Keeps me so busy that I haven't had time to come up town before in several weeks." Mr. Mix had to deal with all sorts of crooked characters, in his trading business, and it is believed that his unerring judgment, and native shrewdness, made it unnecessary for him to require any assistance from His Satanic Majesty.

FORESTVILLE

By Joseph Francis Dutton.

WE HAVE still with us an honored few who were young when Forestville commenced to thrive. Much of their hair has gone and what is left is whiter than it used to be. But the old fire of intelligence and energy that was largely responsible for the building up of Forestville remains, and for them we append a few notes of old-time days in Forestville.

What follows is not intended for a chronological history of Forestville, but a brief sketch of men and conditions that existed in the bygone days. It is eminently proper that these records be entered upon the history of New Cambridge, for although Forestville is but a village of Bristol, nothing relating to the latter could be considered without reference to the former.

In the early revolutionary days, Forestville was the hunting grounds of the Tunxis tribe of Indians, whose reservation was in old Farmington.

ST. MATHEWS' ROMAN CATHOLIC CHURCH.

Where commodious houses and civilization now exist, here too the Indian hunter pursued the panting deer.

The section through which Poland Brook runs was also a favorite camping spot for the Indians, and in the layout of the Stafford District in 1721, the white settlers respected the claims of the Indians to the Poland section.

The first settler in Forestville was Nehemiah Manross, who came here from Lebanon, this state, in 1728, and built a small house almost opposite the Felix Holden homestead in East Bristol. Sonn afterwards he migrated eastward, and erected a small home on the edge of what is now known as Spring's Ditch. The exact spot is now unknown, and today nothing remains to mark its existence.

Nehemiah Manross was the great, great-grandfather of Elijah Manross of Garden street, who, today, in his eighty-first year is the oldest man now living, who was born and bred in Forestville. Nehemiah and his two sons, Elijah and Elisha, were the forerunners of a long-lived family, whose descendants in the years to follow exerted a powerful influence in the building up of the community. Tradition states that a young Nehemiah Manross, was ambushed and eventually put to death by the Indians in Poker Hollow, or near the present day homestead on the back road to Plainville. It is interesting to record that in the stirring days of 1775, Elisha Warren, who at that time lived in a small cabin standing close to the edge of the Merritt's pond in the Stafford District, contracted smallpox while visiting his two sons at the Continental Camp near Boston. Mr. Warren's death followed, and he was buried in the swamp that runs westward towards the Barnard estate. A fragment of a stone marks his resting place, but otherwise this old hero of the early days lies unremembered by the present generation.

The first manufacturing industry was started in the year 1811, when Joseph Ives commenced making clocks in a little structure where the present Laporte Hubbell shop now stands. This was soon afterwards moved to Bristol, and the first permanent industry began in 1813, when Chauncey Boardman commenced making clocks of a primitive wall pattern in an old building that stood across the street from the Timothy Collins place in the Stafford District. The shop was close to the old Boston and Albany turnpike road that connected Hartford with the Bristol post office which was then under the management of a man named Mitchell.

Soon after this, Elisha Manross, father of the present Elijah, started to make the wood parts for the Boardman Company. The Manross shop stood just north of the present Hubbell factory and the same dam that was used to generate the water power is still doing duty for the present manufacturers. At one time the company had finished up twenty-five clocks in advance of the trade, and it was feared that this large stock order would ruin the concern. A salesman was started out on horseback and eventually succeeded in disposing of the goods. Prosperity followed and the future of the Company was assured.

In the olden days matches were an unknown luxury, and at the Manross factory an implement was manufactured to produce fire. It consisted of a tin cup fitted to the hand. There were two compartments, one full of brimstone, the other of tinder. A wheel on a shaft like an inverted wheelbarrow completed the outfit. A string would be wound around the arbor of the wheel and when a light was needed, the string would be pulled, while a piece of flint would be held close to the flying wheel. This resulted in sparks flying downward to the tinder, which consisted of some slightly burnt cotton cloth. A match saturated with brimstone would be dipped into the tinder and a small blaze created. One can imagine the predicament of some of the present day youths, if they were obliged to do likewise in order to enjoy a fragrant Havanna.

In 1837, Alden Atkins and Elizeur Welton commenced making wooden spools, faucets and inkstands in a little shop that stood on the site of the present burner factory.

THE OLD M. E. CHURCH, DESTROYED BY FIRE.
PARSONAGE AND PORTRAIT OF WILLIAM. T. HILL.

At this time the roads of Forestville were few in number. One ran from the Buell house on King street eastward. This was the old turnpike road that entered into Plainville. Another ran north from where Deming's store now stands through the Stafford District to the Boston and Albany division. There was also another old country road leading from the Ralph Terry place down through the Dublin section. This road goes up over the West Mountain and underneath is an old worn-out copper mine.

The buildings were also conspicuous by their absence. The present Cramer house on Stafford Heights marked the beginning in that section. Then came the Uncle Lot Jerome, or Amos Sage place, the Gardner Hall home, then known as the Byran Churchill place, an old saw mill north of the present burner factory, and the Ira Churchill house to the south of the Roland Douglass house. From the west, commencing with the Buell house, then came the Valentine Atkins place, built by the Manrosses, and now occupied by George Doherty, an old shop where Lyman Ashworth afterwards drew wire, the Manross homestead standing on the site of the late Dan A. Miller place; a little red house owned by Mrs. Lafayette Hill, the Thomas Hollister place near the top of Buckley Hill, and the Hendrick place which still marks the turn to the Plainville camp grounds.

A small building afterwards used as a saloon stood just north of the present bridge. It is somewhat singular that intoxicating liquors are still dispensed from a saloon standing practically on the old site.

A small shop stood near where the present Sessions Clock Company present plant is. Eight day movements clocks were made here under a company afterwards known as the Forestvillle Clock Company. The prime movers were Lowrey Waters, William Hills, Jared Goodrich, Chauncey Pomeroy and J. C. Brown. The section where the shop stood was even then known as "Mud Row," a cognomen it enjoys at the present time. There were no roads hereabouts and in order to get across the Pequabuck River, one was obliged to use a boat. Eventually a big tree that stood to the west of the Forest House was felled, and

OIL WELL IN STAFFORD DISTRICT.

SCHOOL AT STAFFORD DISTRICT.

for many years did duty as a bridge. Even now, when the water is a shallow, the old gnarled tree stump can be seen lying close to the river edge as a vivid reminder of the primeval days.

A small lane, long known as "Hen Coop Alley," ran from "Mud Row" up to a large pine tree that marked the intersection of the Dublin Road.

With the formation of the eight day clock company it was decided to select a name for the rapidly growing community, and it naturally "slid into its name of Forestville" as its sponsors were even then surrounded by a great forest that stood forth in all its grandeur.

A few years previous to the War of the Rebellion, the citizens united, and after securing land from Elisha Manross, built the present Church street connecting the upper section with the center. In 1864, the E. N. Welch Company secured control of the Forestville Clock Company which was then owned by J. C. Brown, and only a few years ago, after a long manufacturing career, the Welch interests were absorbed by new people, resulting in the formation of the present successful manufacturing corporation known as the Sessions Clock Company.

Following close upon the panic of 1837 came a feeling that all the energies of Forestville should not be confined to one branch of industry, and this idea in 1850 resulted in the formation of the Bristol Brass and Clock Company, with a small factory located on the site of the old Atkins and Welton toy shop, which was built in 1836. From a small beginning the Bristol Brass and Clock Company has succeeded in building up one of the greatest industries in the town. During recent years a silver department has been added to the large burner factory and the future of the concern is very bright. The original Bristol Brass and Clock Company is now incorporated under the title of the Bristol Brass Company with important branch industries in Bristol and East Bristol, in addition to the plant at Forestville.

In 1902, great excitement prevailed in the usual quiet village due to the alleged discovery of oil at the Taylor farm in the Stafford District.

Oil could easily be seen working its way through to the surface, and real estate in that section commenced to assume perpendicular prices. Visions of another Standard Oil monopoly with Forestville as the center were seen on the horizon. Oil experts from the various oil fields of the country visited the little hole in the ground, and would quietly depart, leaving behind them an air of mystery.

A local company was formed and active operations commenced to mine the petroleum. A shaft was sunk to an immeasureable distance, but beyond the first indications of slimy liquid that permeated through the ground, no oil was ever found, at least in paying quantities.

Elijah Manross of Garden street tells an interesting story of how in the early February of 1836, the natives were almost scared to death by the snow suddenly turning to a deep crimson color. Mr. Manross, who was then in his tenth year, was bringing the supper to the men employed in his father's little shop when the change took place. He hustled forward in great fear and tumbled in through the shop door. One workman, who was just getting over the effects of a protracted spree, seeing the blood-red snow through the open door thought that the end of the world was at hand, and that judgment had been passed on him. No satisfactory explanation was ever given of this curious incident, which has never been repeated in the history of Forestville.

Marine clocks were then unthought of, but in 1848, Brainbridge Barnes, a brother of the lamented Rodney Barnes, succeeded in perfecting a marine movement that gave good results. A company was at once formed with headquarters at the old Manross factory. No time was lost in getting the goods on the market and thus it is that Forestville enjoys the distinction of having made the first marine clock that the world ever had. After several changes the original marine clock company came into the possession of Laporte Hubbell, now deceased; and it was due largely to Mr. Hubbell's individual efforts that a big business was eventually built up.

An organization that made Forestville famous was the Forestville Cornet Band, which was organized in 1854, with sixteen members. Of these only four are now alive, Alphonse Boardman of Brooklyn, N. Y., Clay Hubbell of Hartford, Elijah Manross, and Hiram M. Osborne, both of Forestville.

This band was in great demand and ranked next to the Dodsworth Band of New York City. The band disbanded during the Civil War and the instruments were purchased by musicians residing in Wolcottsville, which is now known as Torrington.

Hiram Osborne, who was instrumental in organizing the Forestville Cornet Band, still resides in a house on Academy street that he purchased in 1860. At one time this house stood in the midst of a great forest of white pine birches, which extended in all directions.

Close by, stood the Forestville schoolhouse, which with the exception of a few additions and alterations is still doing duty. This school was built about seventy years ago, the land being donated by the Manross family on the condition that it revert back to the Manross estate if it ever be used for other than educational purposes. Miss Nellie Hills, the present efficient principal, is a daughter of Mrs. Eliza H. Hills of Garden street, who attended the first day's session of school.

Another building that is regarded by the present generation as a landmark is the store now occupied by the J. S. Deming and Company. It was built in 1852 and was first used by George Pierpont for a general store. Upstairs was a large hall that in those days was considered very fine. This hall was used for public purposes of a religious, political and social nature.

The Methodist Church Society that was organized in 1854 held its first public services here under the leadership of Rev. Mr. Whittaker. In 1864, the Methodists purchased the Maple street Episcopal building in Bristol, and removed it to the site of the present church. The old

OLD TIME FORESTVILLE SCHOLARS

edifice was used for church purposes until it was destroyed by fire, and the present commodious tabernacle built in 1900, and the congregation is now in a most flourishing condition, The present pastor is Rev. John T. Hamilton, who is universally respected by all.

As far back as 1840 the Roman Catholics of this section journeyed northward to assist at the devotions held at the old copper mines. Later when the mines were abandoned, the faithful were obliged to go to the parish church in Bristol until 1881, when Rev. Michael B. Roddan commenced celebrating mass each Sunday in the old Firemen's Hall, Forestville, that was afterwards destroyed by fire. This practice was continued until 1891, when Rev. Henry T. Walsh of Plainville assumed charge and erected the present splendid edifice to the service of the Almighty. In the year 1901 the Episcopalians of Forestville banded together and erected a neat little church, which has been consecrated for religious purposes.

The Swedish population which during the past decade has increased rapidly, is even now centering its efforts upon the erection of a large new church, which, it is hoped, will be in use before the snow flies.

One man who contributed largely to the building up of Forestville was Rodney Barnes. Mr. Barnes opened up roads in various sections and was the pioneer in building in several sections that are now thickly populated.

Another well-known citizen was Dan A. Miller, who in days gone by was regarded as a legal expert on many things. Although not a lawyer and devoting most of his time to practical business purposes, Mr. Miller was continually in demand to pass upon judicial questions and many of the old time deeds and instruments were drawn by his advice.

No sketch of Forestville would be complete without a reference to the lamented Charles W. Brown, better known as Hube. A skilled brass worker, Mr. Browne's favorite pastime was writing and his humorous articles were quoted by all the leading papers of the east. His death in 1903 robbed Forestville of a loved citizen and an honorable man.

The first post office was located in the East Bristol section, opposite the "old store" on land now owned by Wilson Potter. The first postmaster was Theodore Terry, an uncle of Franklin E. Terry, who now resides on Middle street. The exact date of the opening of the office seems lost to history, but it was early in the year of 1847, At this time East Bristol seemed destined to be the center of the village, as three of the shops with the post office and a general country store were in its midst.

The extension of the railroad through to Forestville in 1850, marked the beginning of a prosperous future. Despite strenuous efforts of the East Bristolites the railroad station was established at Forestville and the post office soon followed. A large part of the original "Terry post office" has been converted into a dwelling-house owned by Thomas O'Brien and now stands the second house west of Davitt's crossing.

For many years afterwards the post office was located near where the present railroad station stands. The building now used by Douglass Brothers for a business office was for many years used for post office purposes. Here it was that J. Fayette Douglass, who was first appointed postmaster under President Grant, remained in office for seventeen years, and today ranks as one of the oldest ex-postmasters now living in the State.

At present the Forestville post office is under the efficient management of Postmaster James F. Holden, who enjoys the distinction of having served under both Democratic and Republican Presidents. Forestville is also well served politically, having two of the town selectmen in its midst, as well as a representative to the General Assembly. Through the Honorable William J. Malone, Forestville is honored by having the only representative from the town of Bristol who ever presided as speaker of the House of Representatives. Representative Malone is also judge of the Bristol Police Court, thus giving unto Forestville both excellent judicial and legislative representation.

FORESTVILLE ATHLETIC CLUB.

Thus it is that the Forestville of today is very much in evidence. Its factories are rushed with orders, it possesses an up-to-date educational institution, the railroad facilities, both steam and trolley, are unexcelled, and the water supply for both private and public uses is good.

The citizens of the present, although planning for the future, always enjoy looking back upon the golden past and the men and women who made it possible for the Forestville of today to be.

FORESTVILLE ATHLETIC CLUB.

As large oaks from little acorns grow, and big streams from little rivulets flow, so too, has the Forestville Athletic Club increased in numbers and reputation until it has become an abiding institution and will go on, the members trust, like Tennyson's brook, "Forever and ever."

The nucleus of the club was formed on December 10, 1903, when a band of young men of Forestville met in the Firemen's hall to consider the formation of an organization for the purpose of promoting athletic sports and to foster a more sociable spirit among the youth of the town.

These young men had previously presented a minstrel overture, and the amateur thespians realized that if they could secure the same "hits" on the diamond, that they had before the footlights, their future success was assured.

A permanent organization was perfected in February, 1904, with about twenty-five charter members with rooms in the Porter building, the home of the F. A. C. boys ever since.

The first officers of the club were: President, Geo. C. Doherty; vice-president, Henry R. Warner; secretary, William Armitage; treasurer, Charles P. Roberts. A committee consisting of T. F. O'Connell, James L. Murray, H. V. McDonald and H. E. Myers drafted by-laws of the club that are still in force

Of the minstrel troupe, of which the club is an offspring, only four members are now enrolled under the red and white banner of the F. A. C. This quartet consists of Stephen Lambert, John Carroll, James L. Murray and William J. Roberts. The others gradually fell away and their places were taken by younger aspirants for athletic and social distinction, and the club grew and continued in a very prosperous condition.

The Forestville Athletic Club is the oldest existing organization of its kind in Bristol. Many strenuous contests have been waged upon the athletic field in various kinds of sports. Throughout all the games both at home and abroad the club has always endeavored to maintain a record for clean sports.

The social functions given under the auspices of the club have always been popular and well patronized. Big delegations would be in attendance from the adjacent towns and although at times defeated in athletic contests, the hospitality always captivated both friend and foe, thereby making the local boys victorious in the end.

The present officers of the club, President, Charles Brennan, vice-president, Robert Miller, treasurer, Henry Davitt, and secretary, Joseph Dutton, have not only succeeded in putting the club in a good financial condition, but have made every social event an overwhelming success also.

Sporting Bristol.

By Charles T. Olin.

Bristol has always been friendly to sports. The reputation of the town in this particular is not a recent acquisition. For more than a century Bristol has been known as being alive athletically.

First it was wicket, the exciting days of which are fully set forth in another chapter. Then came baseball. The New Departure Manufacturing Company was the father of the national game in this town, and for several years maintained a crack team known as the "Bell Ringers' and giving the town the name of the "Bell Town," a name that has stuck ever since.

For a time Bristol was in the state league, acquitting herself handsomely at the box office and on the diamond, notwithstanding the comparatively small population of the town. For one year the Bristol team won the pennant. But largely because of the chagrin of the cities on losing to "little Bristol" as they called us, the honor was a matter of record only. The championship flag was never turned over to Bristol. But when the state league wanted a capable president it elected W. J. Tracy, who was practically the owner of the team, and chose J. E. Kennedy, who was associated with Mr. Tracy in promoting championship baseball, for its chief of umpires.

Polo, basketball, football and all of the faddy sports have thrived in Bristol, the announcement of a game of anything ensuring an audience. Perhaps the most unique chapter in the history of local sports was the organization of basketball teams by fraternal societies of the town, combining in the Bristol Fraternal Basketball league for a championship series of games. Nearly all the players were green at the start but in the course of a few weeks considerable talent developed and each contest was witnessed by large and wildly enthusiastic audiences.

After a time the basketball constituency wanted the fastest in the land and the Bristol Delphis were the result, under the management of Charles Barker. This team for two seasons played the crack teams of the country on the armory floor, winning 80 per cent of its games. In the second year a series of championship games was arranged with Winsted. The rubber was played in New Britain and Bristol lost. Bristol's failure, however, was almost completely due to lack of management in providing a strengthened team. This was the end of professional basketball in Bristol.

The Bristol High school latterly has developed basketball teams that have played in championship form. Baseball and football are also features of the athletic interests of the High school.

FRATERNAL LEAGUE, BASKETBALL MANAGERS.

BRISTOL WHEEL CLUB POLO TEAM,

FRANKLIN LODGE, F. & A. M. BASKETBALL TEAM

FRIENDSHIP LODGE, SONS OF ST. GEORGE, BASKETBALL TEAM
CHAMPIONS SEASON 1904-'05.

STEPHEN TERRY, I. O. O. F. BASKETBALL TEAM CHAMPIONS SEASON 1903-'04.

BASKETBALL TEAM RELIANCE COUNCIL, ROYAL ARCANUM

BRISTOL GRANGE BASKETBALL TEAM.

PEQUABUCK LODGE, I. O. O. F. BASKETBALL TEAM.

ETHAN LODGE, K. OF P. BASKETBALL TEAM

A BRISTOL BASKETBALL TEAM PLAYING OUTSIDE TEAMS.

BRISTOL HIGH SCHOOL BASKETBALL TEAM, SEASON '06-07.

BRISTOL BASKETBALL TEAM, STATE CHAMPIONS

ONE OF BRISTOL'S MANA JUVENILE BASEBALL TEAMS.

Fraternal Bristol

Bristol is said to have more fraternal organizations, pro rata, for its male citizens than any other place in the United States. A whole volume the size of this work could be used to advantage in recording their various histories, but in the space at our command the subject must of necessity be but casually treated. As far as possible we have endeavored to present a photographic reproduction of the officers of the various organizations. Unless otherwise stated these group photographs were all made at the Elton Sutdio. The data given in this section brings the various subjects to June, 1907, and necessary allowances must be made for any changes made since that time.

Bristol as a whole is proud of its civic organizations, and the eligible citizen who is not enrolled in one or more of the various societies is an exception ra her than a rule.

OFFICERS COMPOUNCE TRIBE, NO. 15, IMPROVED ORDER OF RED MEN.

COMPOUNCE TRIBE, No. 15, IMPROVED ORDER OF RED MEN.

Compounce Tribe, No. 15, Improved Order of Red Men, was organized on December 11, 1890, with the following charter list: W. H. Merritt, F. C. Meder, J. H. Glasson, D. W. Abrams, G. N. Wright, E. E. Merriel, J. Edwards, G. A. Gowdy, W. C. Spring, C. E. Kittell, F. A. Hubbell, C. H. Curtiss, F. Wright, D. W. Hull, S. T. Nichols, H. W. Hinman, A. W. Granniss, B. Fallan, W. C. Smith, E. S. Marden, J. B. Churchill, E. S. Stocking, F. S. Parsons, J. Hanna, C. H. Tiffany, W. H. Carman, L. S. Burg, G. A. Sweetland, F. W. Jacobs, F. D. Knickerbocker, H. S. Judd, G. A. Warner, T. H. Duncan, V. Matthews, W. H. Card, S. D. Bull.

The degrees were conferred by Tunxis Tribe, No. 10, of Waterbury, in the O. U. A. M. Hall in Linsted's Block. Like all new organizations, the Tribe flourished for a few years, when reaction set in and for a few years not much work was done, but in 1901, Past Sachem Chas. J. Phelan started a revival, and through his efforts the Tribe has grown steadily until now it numbers 165 members on the roll and dispenses charity among its members with a lavish hand, which is recognized by words of praise from the Great Council of Connecticut, and the townspeople of Bristol.

The present officers are: Sachem, Albert M. Judd; Senior Sagamore, S. Edwin Green; Junior Sagamore, Geo. F. Scherr; Prophet, Wm. L. Casey; Chief of Records, F. C. Stark; Keeper of Wampum, Alfred L. Beede; Collector of Wampum, Thos. A. Tracy; Trustees, Jos. H. Glasson, Geo. A. Warner, and Ernest E. Merrill.

The Tribe meets on Tuesday evenings in G. A. R. Hall, where the members take great pride in showing visitors a large Indian picture presented by the Great Council of Connecticut for the exemplification of the Chief's degree before the officers of the Great Council of the United States at Waterbury, where the Great Incohonee John W. Cherry of Norfolk, Va., stated that the work done by the Tribe of Connecticut was the best that it had been his pleasure to witness.

A GROUP OF RED MEN, OLD HOME WEEK.

THE ONEIDA CLUB.

THE ONEIDA CLUB.

Among the social organizations consisting of young men exclusively, the Oneida Club is without question the leader. This society was instituted by a few young men for the purpose of promulgating a fraternal intercourse on strictly high grade lines, and to provide suitable rooms for mutual enjoyment and benefit.

The primary steps of organization were taken on September 10, 1906, and officers formally elected as follows: President, Dwight H. Hall; Vice President, Charles Green; Secretary, Arthur J. Wasley; Treasurer, Harry Andrews.

Arrangements were immediately made to secure proper and convenient quarters which were obtained and fitted out with good and substantial furniture, in a suite located on the second floor of the "Bristol Savings Bank," on September 15, 1906.

Rules, Regulations and By-Laws were duly prepared and adopted, so that a congenial atmosphere. free from all unhealthy influences, should at all times prevail, and the Club attained its high aims and position in the social world of the Bristol borough.

The penant consists of a triangular banner of royal blue, inscribed with the word "ONEIDA" in white letters, while the club pin contains similar colors and is shaped in the form of a diamond.

Entertainments are periodically provided in "Assemblies" or dances, and in whist parties, admission to which is afforded by invitation only, and in these the members endeavor to produce attractive conceptions in order to impress the recipients with a due sense of originality, and it goes almost without saying that the young ladies who are fortunate enough to be invited, are perfectly justified in anticipating a royal good time.

OFFICERS ORDER OF VASA.

THE ONEIDA CLUB.

Among the social organizations consisting of young men exclusively, the Oneida Club is without question the leader. This society was instituted by a few young men for the purpose of promulgating a fraternal intercourse on strictly high grade lines, and to provide suitable rooms for mutual enjoyment and benefit.

The primary steps of organization were taken on September 10, 1906, and officers formally elected as follows: President, Dwight H. Hall; Vice President, Charles Green; Secretary, Arthur J. Wasley; Treasurer, Harry Andrews.

Arrangements were immediately made to secure proper and convenient quarters which were obtained and fitted out with good and substantial furniture, in a suite located on the second floor of the "Bristol Savings Bank," on September 15, 1906.

Rules, Regulations and By-Laws were duly prepared and adopted, so that a congenial atmosphere. free from all unhealthy influences, should at all times prevail, and the Club attained its high aims and position in the social world of the Bristol borough.

The penant consists of a triangular banner of royal blue. inscribed with the word "ONEIDA" in white letters, while the club pin contains similar colors and is shaped in the form of a diamond.

Entertainments are periodically provided in "Assemblies" or dances, and in whist parties, admission to which is afforded by invitation only, and in these the members endeavor to produce attractive conceptions in order to impress the recipients with a due sense of originality, and it goes almost without saying that the young ladies who are fortunate enough to be invited, are perfectly justified in anticipating a royal good time.

OFFICERS ORDER OF VASA.

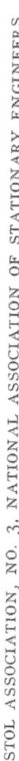

BRISTOL ASSOCIATION, NO. 3, NATIONAL ASSOCIATION OF STATIONARY ENGINEERS

ORDER OF VASA.

A member of the New Britain Order of Vasa, Mr. Card Bergendahl, became interested in starting a branch of this lodge in Bristol, so with the help of a few of the most popular local Swedes he finally succeeded. In order to obtain a charter, 17 men must sign, so a meeting was called October 5, 1906, to which the necessary amount of men responded and signed. At this meeting all preliminary steps for an organization were taken up and the following officers were elected: Past Master, Carl Almquist; President, Victor Modien; Vice President, George Gustafson; Recording Secretary, J. W. Johnson; Financial Secretary, Alfred Erickson; Treasurer, August Erickson; Sermon Master, Axel Johnson; Chaplain, Alfred Carlson; Inside Guard, Gustave Anderson; Outside Guard, Pat Anglewood. The name of the lodge was also adopted, it being "Carl XII Order of Vasa."

Since then the organization has been in a prosperous condition, starting with 17 members, and with a total membership now numbering 90, with more coming in.

The following are the charter members: Victor E. Modien, Pat Anglewood, J. W. Johnson, Alfred Carlson, George Gustafson, Anthon Anderson, August Erickson, Gustaf Anderson, Oscar Anderson, Carl Armquist, Axel Johnson, Alfred Erickson, Fred Ryding, Victor Lofgren, Amandus Shvan, Axel Anderson, Justus Johnson, August Molien, Erick Anderson, Charles Olsen, Hjalmar Anderson, Charles Holmberg, Harry Gustafson, Anthon Chelberg, Charles L. Johnson, Albert Anderson, Jacob Benson, Huldah Benson, Olga Beorkman, Hanning Nelson, Abrin Lindquiss. Teckla Gustafson, Carl Emanielson, Elen Carlson, Hadrick Modien, Charles Erickson, Axel Aspolien, John Johnson, Mrs. Carl Armquist, John Carlson, Alma Johnson, Frank Johnson, Axel Olson, Hanna Palm, Alfred Anderson, Charles Peterson, Peter Gustafson, Pattline Anderson, Jennie Peterson, Martin Pierson, Matildah Johnson, Nils Wm. Johnson, Emma Linden, Jons Lindvahl, Elen Gustafson, Bernt Liga, Malcolm Svenson, Lilly Lindien, Axel Carlson, Ansel Wieberg, Joseph Anderson, Wensent Quisberg, Helen Angdahl, William Carlson, Augusta Anderson, John Engdahl, Alme Lindquist, Christiana Lorsen, Ester Anderson, Jennie Lorsen, Annie Johnson, Johnas Johnson, Elsie Anderson, John Ludirckson, Earnest Aspolien, Hanning Armquist, Easter Armquist, Oscar Ecklund, Carl Carlson, August Johnson, Charles Lorsen.

BRISTOL ASSOCIATION No. 3, NATIONAL ASSOCIATION OF STATIONARY ENGINEERS.

Organized in O. U. A. M. Hall, corner of Main and Prospect Streets, Linstead's block, April 8, 1899. Instituted by Wm. E. Norton and Fred McGar. Organized by Edward L. Murphy and Alex. Rich of Meriden, Conn.

Preamble:—This Association shall at no time be used for the furtherance of strikes, or for the purpose of interfering in any way between its members and their employers in regard to wages; recognizing the identity of interests between employer and employe, and not countenancing any project or enterprise that will interfere with perfect harmony between them.

Neither shall it be used for political or religious purposes. Its meetings shall be devoted to the business of the Association, and at all times preference shall be given to the education of engineers, and to securing the enactment of engineers' license laws in order to prevent the destruction of life and property in the generation and transmission of steam as a motive power.

First board of officers of Bristol, No. 3, N. A. S. E.: President, Wm. E. Norton; Vice President, Fred. McGar; Treasurer, B. A. Brown; Recording Secretary, H. W. Simons; Financial Secretary, F. A. Warley; Conductor, H. B. Norton; Doorkeeper, A. E. Moulthroup; Trustees, L. D. Waterhouse, Theodore Schubert, Jr., J. P. Garrity; Association Deputy, Wm. E. Norton.

Present officers, June, 1907, National Association of Engineers: President, E. E. Merrill; Vice President, E. A. Porter; Treasurer, P. J. Murray; Financial Secretary, O. A. Thomas; Recording Secretary, Wm. E. Norton; Conductor, J. P. Garrity; Doorkeeper, Fred McGar; Trustees, H. W. Simons, J. P. Garrity, L. D. Waterhouse; Association Deputy, Fred McGar.

State Association of National Association of Stationary Engineers convened at Bristol on July 14th, 1896, and delegates from all over the State were present. The delegation was welcomed by Local Deputy Fred McGar and was responded to by State President James L. Band of Ansonia, Conn.

Present members of National Association of Stationary Engineers: P. J. Murray, J. P. Garrity, Martin Keeting, E. E. Merrill, H. B. Norton, L. D. Waterhouse, A. E. Moulthroup, Wm. Coe, Fred McGar, Wm. E. Norton, H. W. Simons, O. A. Thomas, W. G. Rood, C. N. Parsons, Geo. W. Thompson, R. R. Wellington, E. A. Porter.

OFFICERS COURT FOREST, NO. 40, F. OF A.

COURT FOREST, No. 40, F. of A.

This court was instituted December 13, 1888, by Court Wolfe Tone of Waterbury, Deputy Grand Chief Ranger John D. Bolan, and a large delegation of Brother Foresters from Waterbury and other towns.

The following were installed as its first officers: Chief Ranger, A. J. Brannon; Sub Chief Ranger, W. H. Dutton; Financial Secretary, M. B. O'Brien; Recording Secretary, J. F. Holden; Treasurer, M. J. Dalton; Sr. W., W. K. Parker; Jr. W., W. J. Hyland; In. B., T. McCormick; Jr. B., Wm. Wilson.

The court has a membership of 70 members and is in a good financial condition, having a treasury of one thousand dollars. Thirteen of its members have passed away since its institution. The court pays a weekly sick benefit of $5.00 a week for 13 weeks, and $2.50 for 13 more weeks if sickness continues, the services of Court Doctor, medicine and an allowance of fourteen dollars a week for nurse.

Its meetings are held on the first and third Tuesdays after the first and third Mondays, at Foresters' Hall, Central Street, Forestville.

The court prides itself on being one of the oldest benefit societies in town, as well as the most generous to needy brothers.

Its present officers are: Chief Ranger, A. J. Brannon; Sub Chief Ranger, G. P. Dutton; Financial Secretary, M. B. O'Brien; Recording Secretary, J. P. Moran; Treasurer, M. McCormick; Sr. W., C. Daley; Jr. W., W. H. Roberts; In. B., W. J. Roberts; Jr. B., G. B. Lewis; Janitor, W. H. Roberts.

OFFICERS FEDELIA CIRCLE, NO. 166, C. OF F.

FEDELIA CIRCLE, No. 166, C. of F.

The first meeting of Fedelia Circle, No. 166, C. of F., was held in the old Firemen's Hall, May 16, 1892. It was instituted by Circle Ever Ready, No. 84, of New Britain, with a membership of fifty-five.

The first board of officers elected were: Chief Companion, Miss Margaret Bower; Sub Chief Companion, Miss Julie Keating; Past Chief Companion, Thomas McCormick; Financial Secretary, Miss Louise Beeman; Treasurer, Miss Mary O'Brien; Recording Secretary, Miss Della Hyland; Right Guide, Miss Margaret Burdy; Left Guide, Miss Mary Gormley; Inside Guard, Mrs. Michael Emmett; Outside Guard, Miss Abbie Foran; Deputy, John W. Daley; Trustees, Miss Annie Gillew, John W. Daley, Thos. McCormick; Auditors, Miss Julie Dutton, Miss Eliza McKane, Miss Della Hyland; Circle Physician, Dr. John J. Wilson; Apothecary, William Reynolds.

The present board of officers are: Past Chief Companion, Mrs. Fred Hayden; Chief Companion, Mrs. Emily Brown; Sub Chief Companion, Mrs. Mary Roberts; Recording Secretary, Miss Etta Brannan; Financial Secretary, Mr. P. J. Murray; Treasurer, Miss Katie Ford; Right Guide, Miss Mary Lambert; Left Guide, Miss Agnes Dutton; Inside Guard, Miss Mamie Murray; Outside Guard, Miss Elizabeth Hoylen; Deputy, Mrs. Ernest Hamlin; Physician, Dr. W. R. Hanrahan; Apothecary, William Madden; Trustees, Mrs. Matthew McCormick, Miss Julie Dutton, Miss Nellie Lambert; Finance Committee, Miss Mary Lambert, Miss Agnes Dutton; Auditing Committee, Miss Agnes Dutton, Miss Mamie Lambret, Miss Julie Dutton.

Since the institution of the Circle it has paid for sick benefits, $3,898.58. The running expenses have been $1,573.96, and the total receipts $6,306.82, leaving a balance of $834.24 at the present time, having a membership of fifty-seven and lost three members by death during a term of fifteen years.

Our motto is S. S. and C.

OFFICERS ADELPHI LODGE, NO. 12, N. E. O. P.

ADELPHI LODGE, No. 12, N. E. O. P.

Adelphi Lodge, No. 12, of the New England Order of Protection was organized in Bristol, December 15th, 1887, and was the second lodge of the Order to be established in Connecticut, the first, Ida Lodge, No. 10, having been organized in the city of Bridgeport a few evenings before. Its charter list of thirty-three members contains the following names, the greater portion of whom came over as a body from a lodge of "The Knights and Ladies of Honor." Elizabeth M. Sikes, Albert C. Loomis, Harriet J. Loomis, Lucy C. Adams, Will B. Adams, Martha R. Russell, Harriet E. Simons, Hiram W. Simons, Noble C. Sparks, Helen U. Sparks, Homer W. Welton, Nellie A. Welton, Adelbert D. Webster, Harriet E. Webster, Delbert W. Abrams, Ella A. Abrams, George B. Chapin, Minnie J. Chapin, Mary J. Merriman, Libbie F. Bennett, Fred E. Burr, Susie M. Burr, Alice C. Olcott, Charles E. Russell, Roland T. Hull, Dr. Maurice B. Bennett, Ellen M. Crane, Albert Munson, Sarah E. Munson, Lewis H. Smith, Edward I. Bradshaw, Walter S. Jones, Dr. Edward P. Woodward. This lodge of the Knights and Ladies of Honor desired a New England Jurisdiction and prospects of obtaining same seeming remote, they found in the New England Order of Protection, which had been organized in Boston the previous month, the opportunity for the realization of their desire in this respect.

At the installation of the lodge the word "Adelphi" was adopted as its name and is supposed to have been derived from the word Adelphia, meaning brotherhood.

Of these thirty-three charter members, twenty applied for insurance of $1,000 each, three for $2,000 each, and five for $3,000 each, making at the start a total insurance of $41,000, five remaining social members. Their average age was about forty years. Out of this number thirteen have either died or withdrawn from this lodge, leaving twenty of the original list still retaining their membership.

Hiram W. Simons was the first Past Warden of the lodge and Albert C. Loomis the first Warden; Elizabeth M. Sikes, Vice Warden; Harriet E. Simons, Recording Secretary; Fred E. Burr, Financial Secretary; Susie M. Burr, Treasurer; Martha R. Russell, Chaplain; Adelbert D. Webster, Guide; Harriet E. Webster, Guardian; George B. Chapin Sentinel; Hiram W. Simons, Adelbert D. Webster, and Roland D. Hull, Trustees.

For a few years the lodge met in Woman's Christian Temperance Union Hall, which was located on North Main Street, in a building adjacent to the Gridley House. They then removed to the G. A. R. Hall where at the present time they hold their meetings the second and fourth Wednesday in each month.

The present officers of the lodge are as follows: Edward I. Bradshaw, Jr., Past Warden; Josie M. Glasson, Warden; Rosa D. Bechstedt, Vice Warden; Geo. A. Bechstedt, Recording Secretary; John J. Merrills, Financial Secretary; Franklin E. Terry, Treasurer; Elizabeth M. Sikes, Chaplain; Grace R. Bechstedt, Guide; Fred E. Burr, Guardian; William Allport, Sentinel; Franklin E. Terry, Richard L. Prothero, and William C. Glasson, Trustees. The Treasurer and Financial Secretary are under bonds of $300 each, and the Trustees, of $100 each. In early years these bonds were given by the members of the lodge, but at the present time they are secured in Guarantee Companies.

The Adelphi Lodge, through its almost twenty years of existence, has paid from its general fund large sums of money in aiding its sick and disabled members, and has a considerable amount invested for future purposes.

The total number who have joined since the organization of the lodge is one hundred and ninety-three. Of this number, twenty have died who carried a total insurance of $37,000 and thirty-three have either withdrawn or transferred to some other lodge, leaving the present membership one hundred and forty.

OFFICERS PALOS COUNCIL, K. OF C.

PALOS COUNCIL, K. OF C.

Palos Council, No. 35, K. of C., was instituted March 11, 1886, by District Deputy Grand Knight P. J. Markley, under the provisions of the following charter:

SUPREME COUNCIL KNIGHTS OF COLUMBUS,
STATE OF CONNECTICUT.

To all whom it may concern—Greeting:

WHEREAS, it having been made known to the officers of the Supreme Council, Knights of Columbus, of the State of Connecticut, located in New Haven, that a sufficient number of eligible men residing in Town of Bristol, in Hartford County, State of Connecticut, having duly petitioned that they be chartered and authorized to organize and maintain a Subordinate Council of our Order within said Bristol, and appearing to be for the benefit of said Supreme Council and cause of Charity as well as for the proposed brethren that their petition be granted.

Therefore, be it known, that we, the undersigned members of the Supreme Committee of the Knights of Columbus, by and with the consent of Supreme Council, hereby authorize and direct the following named gentlemen to assemble and work as a regularly constituted Council of the Knights of Columbus, to be designated and known by the name of Palos, No. 35:

Thomas H. Brown, James Kane, Thomas Harrigan, Owen C. Kilduff, Frank J. Emmett, John Missett, Michael B. Kilduff, Richard Murray, David Griffith, Patrick Foran, James Holden, Enos B. McMullen, Michael Conlon, Stephen Sullivan, James Missett, John Drury, Michael Tracy, James H. Kilduff, James D. Whipple, Michael O'Brien, Laurence Fitzpatrick, Michael Emmett, Maurice Toley.

In testimony whereof, we have hereunto affixed our names, under the seal of the Supreme Council.

Attest:

JAS. T. MULLEN,
JAS. McCARTHY,
HENRY T. DOWNS,
Committee.

Given this 11th day of March, 1886.

DANIEL COLWELL,
Secretary of Supreme Council.

A large delegation was present from New Britain, Hartford, Unionville, and Southington. Eighteen members were initiated and the following officers installed: Grand Knight, Thomas H. Brown; Deputy Grand Knight, James Kane; Chancellor, Bernard Fallon; Treasurer, Thomas Harrigan; Financial Secretary, Frank J. Emmett; Recording Secretary, Owen C. Kilduff; Warden, John Missett; Inner Guard, Stephen Sullivan; Outside Guard, David Griffith; Lecturer, Michael B. Kilduff; Chaplain, Rev. M. B. Roddan; Trustees, Patrick Foran, J. F. Holden, M. B. Kilduff, Wm. Scott.

Council held its meetings in Knights of Labor Hall in J. R. Mitchell's building on Main Street, until August of the same year, when it transferred to G. A. R. Hall on North Main Street, the present quarters.

Since the institution of the Council fifteen members have died. The Council is in excellent financial standing with a membership of eighty.

The Council has had ten Past Grand Knights, including the following: T. H. Brown, J. A. Kane, M. N. Kelly, B. M. Holden, J. F. Gleeson, F. J. O'Brien, L. H. Missett, D. J. Heffernan, S. O'Connell, P. W. Salmon.

Present officers are: Grand Knight, J. D. Whipple; Deputy Grand Knight, J. F. Gleeson; Chancellor, M. B. Kilduff; Treasurer, J. A. Kane; Financial Secretary, M. B. O'Brien; Recording Secretary, J. N. Laudry, Jr.; Warden, L. H. Missett; Advocate, T. H. Brown; Inner Guard, John Enghart; Outside Guard, Dennis Sullivan; Chaplain, Rev. T. J. Keena; Trustees, J. F. Holden, M. J. Dalton, J. E. Hayes.

Council holds regular meetings on second and fourth Thursdays.

OFFICERS ROYAL NEIGHBORS OF AMERICA.

ROYAL NEIGHBORS OF AMERICA.

Ladies' Branch of Modern Woodman of America, first Camp in Connecticut, was instituted by Mrs. Wm. E. Norton and organized on March 12th, 1905, in No. 1 Hose Company's hall on School Street, by Mrs. Mode M. Pierce, state deputy, with a charter list of twenty-six members.

Present officers, Royal Neighbors Camp, No.   : Jennie Johnston, Oracle; Mrs. Margaret Kennedy, Vice Oracle; Margaret Kennedy, Recorder; Catherine Kennedy, Finance Keeper; Ellen Walch, Chaplain; Margaret Burns, Inside Guard; Catherine Whelan, Outside Guard; Agnes Heffman, Trustee; Catherine Lonergan, Trustee; Lillian Hayes, Trustee; Margaret Norton, Camp Deputy.

Present membership:
: Margaret F. Kennedy, Margaret C. Kennedy, Margaret Simmons, Margaret Burns, Mary Smithwick, Rebecca Smithwick, Bridget Swift, Agnes Heffernan, Catherine Mansel, Ella Doyle, Catherine Bergh, Anna Scanton, Ellen Walch, Catherine Whelan, Mary Crowley, Jennie Johnston, Lizzie Hannan, Bridget Doley, Catherine Sullivan, Minnie Judd, Agnes O'Brien, Mary O'Brien, Rose Ryan, Nora Delay, Lizzie Mansel, Katherine Murphy, Katherine Hayes, Annie Delay, Catherine Kennedy, Lillian Hayes, Catherine Lonergan, Nellie Minery, Margaret Norton, Catherine Lambert, Susan Holden, Bridget Daley, Johanna Hummell.

Members of the Fur, Fin and Feather Club, at their club house on Wolcott Mountain.

OFFICERS FRANKLIN LODGE, F. AND A. M.

FRANKLIN LODGE, No. 56, F. and A. M.

Franklin Lodge, No. 56, F. and A. M., was instituted January 7, 1819, and have had their lodge home in various halls of the town until the erection of the present Masonic Temple, which was dedicated November 16, 1892. The membership at the present time numbers about 320, and the lodge has had forty masters since its charter was granted. Following is the list of masters: Geo. Mitchell,* 1819, '29, '30, '31, '32, '33, '34, '36, '37, '38, '39, '41, '42, '44, '45; Philip Gaylord,* 1821, '24, '35; Asa Bartholomew,* 1822; Orra Martin,* 1823; C. B. Andrews,* 1825, '26, '28; Irenus Atkins,* 1827; Henry A. Mitchell,* 1853; C. I. Elton,* 1854, '57, '58; S. W. Squires,* 1855; J. H. Austin,* 1856; Dan A. Miller,* 1850; J. H. Root,* 1860, '61; Lester Goodenough,* 1862, '63, '64, '65, '69, '70; Roswell Atkins,* 1866; Edw. Ingraham,* April, 1866; Gilbert Penfield,* 1867, '68. J. E. Ladd, 1871, '73; S. M. Norton,* 1872, '74, '87; S. M. Suthill,* 1875; H. A. Peck, 1876; Seth Barnes, 1877, '78; H. K. Way, 1879, '80; M. H. Perkins,* 1881, '82; W. E. Bunnell, 1883; S. W Forbes, 1884, '85, '86; A. Q. Perkins, 1888; J. R. Holly, 1889, '90; G. W. Wooster, 1891, '92; John Winslow,* 1893; A. F. Rockwell, 1894, '95; J. C. Russell, 1896, '97; M. L. Lawson, 1898; F. A. Southwick, 1899; C. W. Stewart, 1900, '01, L. L. Beach, 1902; C. L. Wooding, 1903; A. D. Wilson, 1904; C. N. Parsons, 1905; A. G. Beach, and H. A. Vaill.

---

*—Deceased

Officers Ethan Lodge, Knights of Pythias.

Ethan Lodge, Knights of Pythias, was organized October 25, 1883, with 22 charter members, with the following officers: George Hall, C. C.; Wm. H. Nott, V. C. C.; Wm. B. Coulter, P.; Walter G. Austin, K. of R. S.; George Schubert, M. of E.; Frank Dutton, M. of F.; Lewis Smith, I. G.; Fred Crane, O. G.. Present officers named as they are grouped in the photograph from left to right: H. C. Wright, Outer Guard; J. W. Bidwell, Prelate; Wm. J. Parker, Master of Work; H. C. Rockerfeller, M. of E.; Wm. F. Porter, M. of F.; Wm. S. Elwin, Chancellor Commander; C. S. Lasher, V. Chancellor; L. H. Lasher, Inner Guard; H. N. Law, K. of R. S.

NATHAN HALE COUNCIL, No. 18, O. U. A. M.

Officers Nathan Hale Council, No. 18, O. U. A. M., reading from left to right: Councilor, W. E. Throop; Vice Councilor, A. E. Barnes; Recording Secy., A. B. Judd; Financial Secy., J. D. Burgess; Inductor, Arthur Bristol. (*Photos by Mr. Throop, Gale Studio.*)

Nathan Hale Council, No. 18, O. U. A. M., was instituted June 30, 1885. The following were the charter members: H. M. Simons, Theo. Schubert, J. R. Holley, John Seaman, W. E. Throop, F. Dresser, N. A. Robinson, C. D. M. Clark, W. J. Stone, E. H. Yale, W. E. Shelton, John D. Monaghan, E. P. Woodward, W. R. Coe, Wesley J. Thomas, Joseph Reynolds, J. F. Clark, A. G. Clark, M. R. Keeney, George H. Elton, A. C. Dresser, C. A. Hart, C. E. Munson, J. H. Swift, C. E. Woster, Geo. Angeling, Edward Barnes, George F. Cook, George A. Gowdey, Charles E. Ingraham, A. P. Stark, Alfred Brockway, Nath. Peck, Robert Hall. The meetings are held in the old Masonic hall at the corner of Laurel and North Main streets.

The following are the first officers of the council: Councilor, H. W. Simonds; vice-councilor, Theo. Schubert; recording secretary, J. R. Holley; corresponding secretary, John Seaman; financial secretary, W. E. Throop; treasurer, F. Dresser; indentor, N. H. Robinson; examiner, C. D. M. Clark; inside protector, W. J. Stone; outside protector, E. A. Yale; trustees, John Seaman, M. E. Shelton and John Monoghan.

After a few years they fitted up a nice hall at the corner of Main and Prospect streets, and occupied it for ten years and at the expiration of their lease moved to their present quarters, in the G. A. R. hall, North Main street.

This order stands for everything pertaining to the interest of the American people and is purely an American order and should be supported by all good American people. The present officers are: Councilor, W. E. Throop; vice-councilor, E. A. Barnes; recording secretary, A. B. Judd; assistant secretary, H. Bancroft; financial secretary, J. D. Burgess; treasurer, Wm. Van Ness; inductor, A. Bristol; outside protector, J. Swift; junior ex. C., W. E. Neston; senior ex. C., A. T. Clark; trustees, G. T. Cook, W. E. Nestor and A. Bristol.

Officers Turner's Society, 1907

BRISTOL TURNER SOCIETY.

The Bristol Turner Society was organized August 2, 1903, for the development of the body and athletics in general. Inaugurated April 6, 1904, with a public exhibition of gymnastics and a grand ball. The present officers (March 1, 1907) are: President, Paul Stein; Vice-President, Frank Gallousky; Recording and Corresponding Secretary, Oscar A. Jörres; Financial Secretary, Charles Kutz; Treasurer, Henry Quanz; Turnwart, August Gerick; Collector, Aug. Stichtenoth; Hallenwart, Arthur Kleefeld; Hall Agent, Charles Kutz.

The charter membership was as follows: Simon Cossick, Gustave Frohlich, William Frohlich, Otto Frohlich, Karl Frohlich, August Gerick, Baker Hummel, Wm. Herrman, B. Heppner, Chas. Kutz, Arthur Kleefeld, Thomas Luchsinger, Ernst Nurnberger, Armand Pons, Henry Quanz, Theodore Quanz, Pius Schussler, Wm. Schonauer, Paul Stein, O. F. Stromz, Tommy Casey, Fred Sigmund, James McKiernan, Dr. Deichman, Ignatz Bachman, Ch. Hoffmann, Tom Casey, Simon Cossick.

Monthly meeting every second Sunday, 2 p. m. at old Town Hall.

Gymnastics every Monday and Thursday, 8:10 p. m., at old Town Hall.

Ladies' Turn Society, organized April 2, 1906. Its present officers are: President, Pauline Nurnberger; Vice-President, Bertha Gallowsky; Recording and Corresponding Secretary, Bertha Ehlert; Financial Secretary, Mary Heppner; Collector, Mary Heppner; Treasurer, Hattie Jorres.

OFFICERS RELIANCE COUNCIL, R. A.

RELIAMCE COUNCIL, No. 753, R. A.

Reliance Council, No. 753, Royal Arcanum, was instituted April 3, 1883, with twenty charter members. Their names were: H. F. Henderson, T. F. Barbour, W. B. Adams, H. B. Cook, T. D. Merriman, D. DeWolf, H. S. Goodale, W. J. Geer, G. S. Hull, W. W. Dunbar, Geo. Merriman, G. J. Bentley, H. W. Barnes, C. E. Russell, C. T. Olcott, T. B. Robinson, G. W. Baker, C. H. Riggs, A. M. Sigourney, S. R. Goodrich. Of these twelve are still members, three have died. Since the council was instituted, twelve members have died, eleven being insured for $3,000, and one for $2,000. The present membership is 135.

The Order of the Royal Arcanum was chartered by the legislature of Massachusetts in 1877. It is primarily a fraternal life insurance organization, and now has a membership of over 243,000. It has paid out in death benefits, over $105,000,000 within the 31 years of its existence, and payments are usually made in from one to three weeks after death. It has an emergency fund, which was not started until 1898, which now (1908) amounts to more than $4,000,000.

All the securities of this fund are lodged with the Treasurer of the state of Massachusetts, as the laws of that state require.

Reliance Council has a loan fund, in the hands of the Collector, from which the assessments of delinquent members are temporarily paid. By such accommodation their membership is kept good, and for it a small fee is charged.

There are 12 regular assessments each year, and an extra assessment has never been called.

Officers Pequabuck Chapter, No. 32, R. A. M.

Pequabuck Chapter, No. 32, R. A. M.

Pequabuck Chapter, R. A. Masons, was instituted May 22, 1866 with Rev. Brother Arza Hill as High Priest. The officers (March, 1907) are as follows: Louis L. Beach, Secy.; J. M. Buskey, Tyler; Wm. R. Russell, C. of H.; H. Austin Vaill, R. A. C.; Stanley D. Gwillim, C. of 1st V.; John W. Bryce, K.; Morris L. Tiffany, P. S.; C. Norton Parsons, H. P.; J. Fay Douglass, C. of 3rd V.; Joseph C. Russell, Treas.; Geo. F. Brown, C. of 2d V.; Jas. T. Case, S. The names of the above are given in the order that they appear in the picture, reading from the left to the right.

Daughters of Rebekah, "Magnolia" Lodge, No. 41, I. O. O. F. was instituted November 21, 1895. Meets second and fourth Tuesdays of each month. Present membership, one hundred and forty. Officers named as they appear in the photograph, reading from left to right: Mrs. Anna M. Pfening, Treas.; Mrs. Frances Swanston, Trustee; Miss Bertha Ruic, Rec. Sec.; Mrs. Martha Nearing, Financial Secy.; Mrs. Ida M. McGar, Noble Grand; Mrs. Edna Robbins, Vice Grand.

Officers Ruth Rebekah Lodge, I. O. O. F.

Ruth Rebekah Lodge. No. 24, I. O. N. F.

Ruth Rebekah Lodge, No. 24, I. O. O. F., was organized May 22, 1888, with 48 charter members. The present membership is 90, with the following officers (March, 1907) : Noble Grand, Lena Nystrom; Vice Grand, Bessie Griswold; Past Grand, Stella Simmons; Inside Guard, Mercy Clinton; Warden, Flora Bailey; Left Supporter, C. B. Smith; Sitting Past Grand, Alice Clark; Treasurer, Mrs. James Mathews; Financial Secy., L. E. Cucel; Recording Secy., Louise Miller; Chaplin, Lottie White; Left Supporter of N. G.; Mrs. E. H. Brightman.

ST. ANN'S LADIES' T. A. B. SOCIETY.

ST. ANN'S LADIES' T. A. B. SOCIETY.

St. Ann's Ladies' T. A. B. Society of Bristol was organized May 24th, 1904, by County Director Brother Wm. O'Mara of New Britain, with a membership of twenty.

The following were elected officers: President, Mary Grisner; Vice President, Julia Fitzsimons; Recording Secretary, Anna Daley; Financial Secretary, Nellie Coughlin; Treasurer, Mayme Mulligan; Marshall, Lauretta Simmons; Sentinel, Elizabeth Mulligan.

The object of this society is to provide for each other's temporal welfare by giving relief in case of sickness or accident and aiding in the burial of deceased members. Also to cultivate a social and fraternal spirit among young ladies.

The society has grown very rapidly for the last three years, having been admitted to the State Union in February, 1906.

They have had many public entertainments, which were very successful, as well as social affairs among the members.

This society has two meetings a month, the second and last Tuesday, and pays a weekly benefit in case of sickness.

BRISTOL GRANGE, No. 116.

Officers Bristol Grange, No. 116, reading from left to right: Burdette A. Peck, J. B. Mathews, Master; Harry Tuttle, Overseer; Mrs. Edna Robbins, Lecturer; Harry S. Elton, Lecturer; Chas. Pond, Steward; Mrs. Ella Freeman, Chaplin; Mrs. Ella M. Gaylord, Treas.; Raymond Perkins, Asst. Steward.

Bristol Grange, No. 116, was organized April 16, 1890, with thirty-three charter members. The first Master was Elbert Manchester, who took a dimit from Whigville Grange and rendered very efficient service in organizing this Grange. Whigville Grange has many times furnished by dimit, valuable members for Bristol Grange. B. A. Peck, Past Master of Bristol Grange and present Overseer of Connecticut State Grange, being among the number.

The other officers elected were: Overseer, J. M. Peck; Lecturer, Mrs. Ellen F. Judson; Steward, George R. Tuttle; Assistant Steward, George B. Evans; Lady Assistant Steward, Mrs. Annie E. Bailey; Chaplain, Titus C. Merriman; Treasurer, H. C. Butler; Secretary, Emerson F. Judson; Flora, Miss Mary Wilcox; Pomona, Mrs. James Williams; Ceres, Mrs. William Hotchkiss; Gate Keeper, C. S. Blanchard. Since then the following have served as Masters: Elbert Manchester, Johnathan M. Peck, B. A. Peck, Elbert W. Gaylord.

The losses by death since its organization have been: Wallace Barnes, George R. Tuttle, (charter members) Charles Churchill, Emily G. Bailey, Henry E. Way, M. D., Mrs. E. D. Lamb, Mrs. Minnie B. Ramson, Mrs. Rosa M. Judd, Edward L. Linker, Sarah L. Judson.

Along social lines the Grange ranks well in the long list of the fraternal organizations of the town.

Bristol Grange for a number of years enjoyed the distinction of being the largest Grange in the State of Connecticut. The present membership is two hundred and twenty-eight.

The present officers are: Master, John B. Matthews; Overseer, Harry Tuttle; Lecturers, Mrs. Edna Robbins, H. S. Elton, Allen Manchester; Steward, Charles Pond; Assistant Steward, Raymond Perkins; Chaplain, Mrs. Ella Freeman; Treasurer, Mrs. Ella M. Gaylord; Secretary, Mrs. Mary C. A. Perkins; Gate Keeper, Mrs. Emma Hills; Ceres, Mrs. Edith Cook; Pomona, Mrs. F. Edith Williams; Flora, Mrs. Emily Cleveland; Lady Assistant, Miss Gertrude Tallis.

WHIGVILLE GRANGE. No. 48, P. OF H.

Whigville Grange, No. 48, P. of H., was organized June 2, 1886, by State Master J. H. Hale of Glastonbury. Its organization was the outcome of what had been called "The Farmer's Club," composed of farmers and their wives from West District, Farmington, Burlington, of which Whigville forms part, and the north part of Bristol. At these meetings debate and research in best farm methods with domestic subjects for the wives of the club men, made a good foundation for the after-work in the Grange, where like subjects, as well as music, literature the drama and history.

Whigville Grange was organized June 2, 1886. Worthy Master Hale was assisted by Brothers Baker and Barnes of Cawasca Grange and Kimberly and Patterson of Hope Grange. The charter members were forty in number, and were as follows: Mr. and Mrs. B. Emory Barker, Mr. and Mrs. Edwin M. Gillard, Mr. and Mrs. Edwin H. Gillette, Mr. and Mrs. Augustus A. Lowrey, Mr. and Mrs. Hiram P. Lowrey, Mr. and Mrs. Lester L. Lowrey, Mr. and Mrs. Charles H. Matthews, Mr. and Mrs. Dwight E. Mills, Mr. and Mrs. Charles E. Morris, Mr. Byron Matthews, Mr. George W. Atwood, Mr. and Mrs. Burdette A, Peck, Mr. and Mrs. Don C. Peck, Mr. and Mrs. George W. Hart, Mr. and Mrs. A. W. Saunders, Mr. and Mrs. Mark B. Stone, Mr. and Mrs. Frank Thompson, Mr. and Mrs. Ira Taft, Mr. and Mrs. James Webster, Mrs. Maria Thompson, Mrs. Sarah Bradley, Mrs. Celia Wilcox, Mr. Samuel D. Newell. Of these charter members, twenty-nine are living.

Bristol Grange is a daughter of Whigville, many of the charter members of the former, belonged to the latter. At first Whigville Grange

Officers Whigville Grange, No. 48, P. of H., reading from left to right: Master, Ernest W. Hart; Overseer, Dwight E. Mills; Lecturer, Ruth G. Atwater; Chaplin, Lester L. Lowrey; Steward, Augustus A. Lowrey; Asst. Steward, Geo. M. Henry; Treas., Arthur D. Carnell; Secy. Robert S. Carnell; Gate Keeper, Wm. Saunders; Ceres, Mrs. Cora Broadbent; Pomona, Mrs. Abbie Mills; Flora, Miss Genevieve Thorpe; Lady Asst., Miss Ruth Morris.

Photo by Throop, Gale Studio.

met in "School Hall," but early in 1893, decided to build a hall of their own, on land given by L. L. Lowrey. Largely aided by the late Edward F. Gaylord, an enthusiastic Patron, the "Grange Hall" was built and dedicated in June, 1893. It cost about $1,100, largely raised by contributions from its members.

The Grange has had for Master the following persons:

1886–'88.	E. M. Gillard, now residing in Bristol.
1888–'94.	L. B. Pond, now residing in Unionville.
1894–'96.	E. F. Gaylord.
1896–'97.	Mrs. Sara Bradley of Whigville, showing the Grange to be up-to-date, with "The New Woman" in the chair of the chief executive. Mrs. Bradley was the first lecturer of the Grange, and held the office seven years.
1897–'98.	E. F. Gaylord.
1898–'00.	D. E. Mills.
1900–'02.	E. F. Gaylord.
1902–'04.	L. L. Lowrey.
1904–'05.	E. F. Gaylord. Mr. Gaylord's death in May, 1905, was a great loss to the Order; one that is felt keenly today. His term was filled out by
1905–'06.	E. S. Gillette.
1906–'07.	A. D. Carnell.
1907–'	E. W. Hart. Mr. Hart represents the younger portion of the Grange, as did Messrs. Carnell and Gillette.

Whigville Grange has been well represented in the higher degrees of the Order, different officers in Central Pomona, No. 1, have been from its members and Mrs. E. F. Gaylord was State Grange Ceres for several years.

The first officers of Whigville Grange were: Master, E. M. Gillard; Overseer, A. W. Saunders; Lecturer, Mrs. Sara Bradley; Chaplain; Chas. H. Matthews; Treasurer, L. L. Lowrey; Secretary, B. A. Peck, Steward, H. P. Lowrey; Assistant Steward, M. B. Stone; Gate Keeper, E. H. Gillette; Ceres, Mrs. E. M. Gillard; Pomona, Mrs. James Webster; Flora, Mrs. D. E. Mills; Lady Assistant Steward, Mrs. C. E. Morris.

The present officers are: Master, Ernest W. Hart; Overseer, Dwight E. Mills; Lecturer, Ruth G. Atwater; Chaplain, Lester L. Lowrey; Steward, Augustus A. Lowrey; Assistant Steward, George Henry; Treasurer, Arthur D. Carnell; Secretary, Robert S. Carnell; Gate Keeper, William Saunders; Ceres, Mrs. Cora Broadbent; Pomona, Mrs. Abbie Mills; Flora, Miss Genevieve Thorpe; Lady Assistant, Miss Ruth Morris; Pianist, Mrs. A. D. Carnell.

The present membership of Whigville Grange, No. 48: Ruth G. Atwater, Arthur W. Barker, Mrs. Annie Barker, Mrs. Edna Barnes, Mrs. Sara Bradley, Archibald H. Bradley, Mrs. Mary Bradley, Mrs. Cora Broadbent, Laura Brainhall, Paul Brainhall, Walter S. Beach, Rose Beebe, Myron L. Butler, James L. Byington, Mary Byington, Arthur D. Carnell, Mrs. Jennie G. Carnell, Robert S. Carnell, John A. Carlson, Earl B. Curtiss, Mrs. Amy R. Cleveland, Mrs. Sarah E. Curtiss, Mrs. Effie J. Curtiss, Wellington L. Curtiss, Mrs. Louise Curtiss, Edwin H. Elton, Mrs. Veronica C. Elton, George H. Elton, Bessie Elton, Sylvia Elton, James E. Elton, George A. Edwards, G. Elton Edwards, Mrs. Addie Edwards, Estella R. Ender, Charles E. Gaylord, Mrs. May Gaylord, Mrs. Martha Gaylord, Mrs. E. H. Gillette, E. Samuel Gillette, Mrs. Miriam C. Gillette, W. O. Goodsell, Mrs. W. O. Goodsell.

Maida Green, Ruth E. Gardner, Mrs. Jane Hart, Ernest W. Hart, Salmon G. Hart, Mrs. Helen Hart, Arthur J. Hanna, Bertha Hanna, Mrs. Minnie Hanna, Gilbert Hatch, Mrs. May Hatch, Virginia Hatch, Olive R. Hatch, George W. Henry, Grover Henry, Ernest Hinman, Ida Hough, Maude Huntington, Jennie Hurley, Maurice Hurley, Isaac Juliff, Hiram A. Jones, Kitty M. Jones, Henry Joy, Mrs. Luna C. Kennedy, Alfred Krappatsch, Edward Krappatsch, Elizabeth LaMont, Matthew LaMont, Mary LaMont, Augustus A. Lowrey, Mrs. Ida Lowrey,

OR "NEW CAMBRIDGE." 599

Mrs. Elnora Lowrey, Hiram P. Lowrey, Mrs. Delia Lowrey, Edwin W. Lowrey, Lester L. Lowrey, Mrs. Lillie Lowrey, Annis Lowrey, Mrs. Fannie Matthews. Edwin A. Matthews, Mrs. Etta Matthews.

Arthur Messenger, Mrs. Delia Messenger, Dwight E. Mills, Mrs, Abbie Mills, Elmer A. Mills, Harrison B. Mills, Francis A. Mills, Robert S. Morse, Chas. E. Morris, Mrs. Annie Morris, Ruth L. Morris, Partha G. Norton, Herman J. Ockels, Ernest Peterson, Agnes Peterson, Arthur Reed, William W. Reed, A. W. Saunders, Mrs. L. S. Saunders, Arthur Saunders, William Saunders, Charles Saunders, Sarah Scoville, Wheaton Scoville, Sherman B. Scoville, Mrs. Flora B. Scoville, Joseph D. Slocum, Mrs. Ina Stone, William Stone, Rachael Spencer, Charles Snow, Mrs. Daisy Snow, Edgar J. Stuart, Mrs. Annie Stuart, Theodore L. Thomas, Mrs. Eliza W. Thomas, Eugene H. Thomas, Genevieve Thorpe, Mrs. Harriett Tuttle, Duane Webster, Mrs. Alvira Webster, Mrs. Celia Wilcox, L. Cecil Wilcox, Ruben Wellington, George Wells, K. H. Wollman, Ella M. Winston, FrankWinston.

A group of Bristol Police, reading from left to right: Ernest T. Belden, Chief; Thos. F. Gucking, Capt.; Clarence Lane, James O'Connell; Fish; Geo. Schubert; A. Legasse; C. Hough; Daniel McGillicuddy; A. Breault. (*Photos by Mr. Throop, Gale Studio.*)

BELL CITY ARIE, F. O. E.

Bell City Aerie, F. O. E., organized February 16, 1907, present membership 250. Officers March, 1907, named in the order in which they appear in the photograph, reading from left to right: John J. Welsh, Trustee; John Burns, Inside Guard; John Johnson, Outside Guard; Fred B. Michaels, Treas.; Thos. O'Brien, Secy.; Thos. Glucking, Trustee; J. H. Davis, Pres.; John Lonergan, V. Pres.; W. R. Hanrahan, M.D., Doctor; Wm. A. Hayes, Chaplin.

Officers Bell City Aerie, F. O. E.

EAGLE DEGREE TEAM. (1907)

Officers St. Jean Baptiste Society.

The St. Jean Baptist Society was organized on the 10th of November, 1886, by the following: Adrien Taillon, Amedie, Fregeau, Odilace Taillou, Pierre Allaire, Augustin Cote, Leandre Brault, Leon Lacourse, Oliva Landry, Fanie Lupieu, Athanase Dumaine, Joseph Phaneuf, Octave Lacourse, Joseph Bechard, Napolean Brault, Jean B. Isabelle, Etienne Quisonault.

The charter was issued about two years later, on the 19th of October, 1888. The motive of this society is to unite under one banner the French-Canadians of our city and vicinity. To be a member of this society one must profess the Roman Catholic religion, be not less than 15 and not more than 45 years of age.

The sick benefit is $5.00 a week during twelve weeks in twelve months. The society to-day numbers 115 members and is increasing rapidly.

SCANDINAVIAN SICK AND DEATH BENEFIT SOCIETY.

Officers (March, 1907)

With a view to mutual protection in the time of sickness and death, twenty-seven well-known men of the town, who were natives or descendants of Scandanavia, assembled on November 11, 1882, and organized the Skandanavian Sick and Death Benefit Society. The society was established as a purely local organization, having no affiliations with State or national bodies.

The objects of the organization are charitable—to bring aid to the members in the time of sickness and bereavement and also to respond to any cry of distress among the members. Its membership is not confined wholly to men, but ladies are also enrolled.

From its institution, under careful officers, the society has had a steady and healthy growth. The present membership numbers eighty. With the increase of membership, the treasury has kept apace and the society is in a good financial condition. The society has met all of its obligations promptly, and furnishes a nurse in extreme cases of illness.

John Berg was its first president, and after eleven successful years the society was incorporated under the laws of the State of Connecticut in 1893. The members are now planning a big jubilee celebration in honor of the twenty-fifth anniversary in the fall.

The society meets the fourth Saturday of each month at the lecture room of the Swedish Lutheran Church. All communications to the Order should be sent to Algot Nelson, 9 Stewart Street. The present officers of the society are: First President, John M. Bergh; Second President, Joseph Lindholm; Third President, Mrs. Maria Carlson; Secretary, Edgar Gustafson; Assistant Secretary, John L. Anderson; Financial Secretary, Algot Nelson; Treasurer, Victor Lindholm; Chaplain, H. A. Wiberg; Inside Guard, Benjamin Gustafson.

The One Hundred Men Sick Benefit and Burial Society "Star," was organized 1892 and incorporated 1903. The following are the officers at present (March, 1907) named in the order they appear in the photograph reading from left to right. B. Gustafson, Guard; Chas. Anderson, Secy.; Chas. Vallin, 2d Trustee; Edward Gustafson, V. Pres.; Nils Pierson, Rec. Secy.; Chas. Benson, Treas.; Martin Pierson, President; Edward Olson, Fin. Secy.

Officers Order Sons of St. George (March, 1907).

St. Joseph's Sick Benevolent Society was organized April 18, 1892, with seventeen charter members, as follows: Joseph Blum, Rudolph Bachman, Eugene Blum, John Engbert, Enos Bachman, Joseph Aulbach, John Griesner, Bernard Kather, Joseph Ehlert, Anthony Grove, Joseph Fries, August Rerich, Anton Heppner, Adam Spielman, Roman Bachman, Damian Fries, William Engels. The installing officers were: Thomas Kunkel and E. Wachner of Bridgeport. Receipts since organization, $1,950.00; expenditures, death and sick benefits, $1,547.54; balance in treasury, $402.46. Present membership (March 1, 1907), twenty-five, with the following officers: President, Arthur Clayvelt; Second President, August Gerrick; First Secretary, John Englert; Second Secretary, Rudolph Bachman; Treasurer, John Greisner; Trustees, W. Englert, Julius Bachman.

Officers Societe des Artisans Canadiens Francais.

Societe Des Artisans Canadienes Francais

Societe Des Artisans Canadiens Francais, was organized in May, 1903. The following are the officers at prseent (March, 1907), named as they appear in the picture, reading from left to right: Osias Lebeau, Napoleon Landry, Emanuel Rondeau, Aime Millite, Napoleon Dube, Rodolphe Beaudoin, Joseph Landry, President, and Dosithe Breault.

THE SWEDISH TEMPERANCE SOCIETY LODGE "FRIHET,"*
No. 40.

This society was founded November 11, 1905, with eight charter members, as follows: President, Axel Sjogren; vice-president, Carolina Larson; secretary, Gustave Johnson; collector, Jöns Lindvall; sermon master, C. E. Johanson; chaplain, Kristina Larson; inner door watch, Jennie Larson; treasurer, Elizabeth Johnson.

The first ordinary meeting was held November 18, 1905. At this meeting fifteen joined the society and from these the rest of the officers were elected, which are as follows: Lodge invisar, Gustave Johnson; representative, Alfred Johnson; assistant secretary, Josephina Carlson; outer door watch, Joseph Anderson; assistant sermon master, Selma Persson; past president, Mary Pasmusson.

This society was formed to fight the use of intoxicating drinks, and anyone who can talk the Scandinavian language may join the organization. This is a world-wide society and its headquarters is in Stockholm, Sweden. Frihet, No. 40, is a branch of the England Grand Lodge of Hartford, Conn.

Our lodge meets every Friday night in the new T. A. & B. Hall on North Main street. We now have forty members all of good standing up to April 12, 1907. The above picture shows who are officers now.

President, C. E. Johnson; Vice-President, Jons Lindvall; Representative from Young People's Templar, Gustave T. Lundahl; Secretary, Vincent Quistberg; Collector, Anton Chellberg; Treasurer, Ester Anderson; Sermon Master, Arthur Anderson; Chaplain, Henney Nelson; Inner Door Watch, Joseph Anderson; Outer Door Watch, John Carlson; Assistant Secretary, Harry Linden; Assistant Sermon Master, Lilliam Linden; Past President, Per Lindell; Lodge Invisar, Gustave Johnson.

---

*—"Frihet" or Liberty.

OR "NEW CAMBRIDGE". 609

Officers of "Freheit" Lodge, No. 40.

Thomas A. Tracy, First Exalted Ruler

BRISTOL LODGE, No. 1010, B. P. O. ELKS.

Late in the year of 1906 several young men who were affiliated with the lodges of the Benevolent and Protective Order of Elks in the neighboring cities, conceived the idea of organizing a lodge in Bristol. The idea met with the immediate approval of every Elk residing in the town. A dispensation was applied for to Grand Exalted Ruler Robert Brown, by the following brothers: W. J. Tracy, C. H. Tiffany, F. C. Stark, J. F. Gleeson, P. H. Condon, W. J. Madden, T. A. Tracy and C. D. O'Connell.

The preliminary work was completed so that the new lodge was instituted at the Opera House on Wednesday evening, January 24, 1906, by District Deputy Dr. James H. Kelley of New Haven, in the presence of 800 visiting Elks from all parts of this State and Massachusetts. The initiatory work was conferred by the degree team of New Britain Lodge, No. 957.

After the initiatory work and institution, the members and guests adjourned to the Armory where a banquet was served, followed by addresses by Editor A. C. Moreland, of the *Elks' Antlers*; Alexander Harbison, of Hartford; Dr. James H. Kelley, of New Haven; Thomas L. Reilley, of Meriden; John D. Shea, of Hartford; Patrick McGovern, of Hartford; George E. Bunney, of New Britain; William J. Malone, Noble E. Pierce, Roger S. Newell, Adrian J. Muzzy, D. Brainard Judd, Burdette A. Peck, and George A. Beers, all of the new lodge. The program was also generously interspersed with musical numbers.

The new lodge was instituted with a membership of sixty-two, with the following officers: Exalted Ruler, Thomas A. Tracy; Esteemed Leading Knight, Roger S. Newell; Esteemed Loyal Knight, James F. Gleeson; Esteemed Lecturing Knight, William J. Malone; Secretary, F. Clinton Stark; Treasurer, Charles R. Riley;. Tyler, Harry C. Rockefeller; Esquire, Charles H. Curtiss; Inner Guard, William L. O'Connell

Chaplain, Rev. William H. Morrison; Trustees, D. Brainerd Judd, Patrick H. Condon, and Dewitt Page.

The charter list of the lodge consisted of the following: H. G. Arms, B. O. Barnard, A. S. Barnes, D. M. Barry, G. H. Blakesley, G. A. Beers, H. G. Brown, T. H. Brown, H. D. Brennan, W. S. Buckingham, W. H. Carpenter, P. A. Cawley, G. E. Cockings, J. J. Coughlin, C. H. Curtiss, C. H. Deming, A. W. Griswold, W. A. Hayes, J. H. Hayes, D. J. Heffernan, W. T. Hofsees, D. B. Judd, F. P. Kennedy, W. J. Lambert, M. Loughlin, W. J. Malone, C. V. Mason, P. J. McCue, J. McGinnis, J. D. Monaghan, F. E. Meder, W. H. Morrison, W. C. Morgan, A. L. Morse, H. G. Murnane, A. J. Muzzy, F. C. Norton, H. B. Norton, N. Nissen, R. S. Newell, M. O'Connell, T. G. O'Connell, D. W. Page, B. A. Peck, N. E. Pierce, I. E. Pierce, M. E. Pierson, C. R. Riley, G. L. Roberts, A. F. Rockwell, J. D. Rohan, E. L. Shubert, F. T. Thoms, B. P. Webler.

The following came into the new lodge by demit from New Britain and other lodges: T. A. Tracy, W. J. Tracy, F. C. Stark, C. H. Tiffany, P. H. Condon, J. F. Gleeson, C. D. O'Connell and W. J. Madden.

The new lodge has had a steady, healthy growth and increased its membership to 100 during its first year. The present officers of the lodge are: Exalted Ruler, Charles H. Curtiss; Esteemed Leading Knight, Henry E. Myers; Esteemed Loyal Knight, William L. O'Connell; Esteemed Lecturing Knight, William C. Holden; Secretary, F. Clinton Stark; Treasurer, S. Edwin Green; Tyler, Richard T. Lambert; Trustees, D. Brainerd Judd, Patrick H. Condon, and Dewitt Page.

The lodge at present meets each first and third Monday evening at Pythian Hall, but expects within a few years to have an Elks' home of its own.

Bristol Band, Old Home Week.

Group of
Officers and members of Co. D., Hibernian Rifles, (March, 1907).

BRISTOL DIVISION, ANCIENT ORDER OF HIBERNIANS.

Bristol Division, No. 1, Ancient Order of Hibernians, ranks high among the benevolent organizations of Bristol. This division was organized on December 27, 1887, with eleven charter members; of the original members only two are now left, Michael J. Cawley and William Kane.

The installation exercises were held upstairs in the old Mitchell building on Main street, where Cleveland's store now stands.

As the division increased in numbers and reputation, it moved to various meeting places in order to accommodate the constantly increasing lodge. The old Y. M. C. A. building, with the Skelly block, were among the places where the lodge met. Eventually headquarters were secured in the commodious hall of the Y. M. T. A. B. society and here, at regular meetings, the lodge holds forth in large numbers. The membership is rapidly approaching the two hundred mark, and when the society celebrates its twentieth anniversary in December of the present year, it is confidently expected that the double century mark will be reached.

It is interesting to note that Michael J. Cawley, the original president of the division, who was instrumental in organizing the society, has held every office possible, and is still active in the affairs of the lodge. He has also been present at every state and county convention held since the organization of the local division.

An idea of the excellent work done by the division can be gleaned from the fact that over $10,000 has been expended for benevolent purposes. The division has always been active in supporting the church affiliation of its members and has many handsome trophies awarded for popularity. A magnificently mounted silver loving cup stands in a conspicuous place in the lodge room, as a striking example of the division's triumph over other fraternal organizations in a recent friendly contest.

The last county convention of the order was held in Bristol, and the delegates were entertained in true Bristol style. The present officers of the division are: President, Jeremiah McCarthy; vice-president, Thomas Hackett; treasurer, Thomas Moran; financial secretary, David Kelley, and recording secretary, John J. Donnelly.

Bristol Division enjoys the honor of having had one of the first uniformed degree teams in Connecticut, and it is in constant demand at various meetings throughout the state.

The present finances of the division are excellent, and the outlook for the future is bright.

The Ladies' Auxiliary, A. O. H., Division No. 23, of Bristol, was organized Sunday, June 30, 1901, by State President Mrs. Eleanor McCann of South Manchester, and County President Miss Nellie Turley of Hartford, with the following members: Mrs. P. Swift, Mrs. C. Smithwick, Mrs. M. Carey, Mrs. J. Foley, Kathryn Foley, Flora Foley, Hannah Foley, Mary Griffith, Annie Diniene, Minnie Diniene, Mary McMahon, Anna O. Harrigan, Rose Linnehan, Annie Mansel, Ellen Mansel and Kathryn Jones.

The following officers were nominated and elected: President, Mary McMahon; vice-president, Anna Harrigan; recording secretary, Rose Linnehan; financial secretary, Minnie Diniene; treasurer, Maude C. Smithwick; sergeant-at-arms, Annie Diniene; sentinel, Mary Griffith.

The charter closed September 6, 1901, with 131 members enrolled.

During the first year, as well as the years following, we had several social hours, which helped to promote good fellowship among the members.

In March, 1902, the five officers of our division, attended their first convention, held at Meriden.

The first anniversary of the society was held in June, 1902, at T. A. B. hall, the members of the First Division and also the Ladies' Auxiliary of New Britain, being present.

An event of great importance to our auxiliary was the County Convention, which was held in the Pythian hall, October 13, 1904. This was attended by all the division officers of Hartford county.

The society has a well trained degree team, and during its six years of existence it has been to Thomaston, Southington and Terryville to exemplify the first, second and third degrees.

The present membership of the society is one hundred and fifty-six.

During the life of the order the angel of death has entered into our presence, taking six of our beloved sisters to their eternal home, and although we miss them we know they are safe in their heavenly home.

The auxiliary has been prosperous and has helped the various charities which called upon it for assistance.

The present officers of the society are: President, Anna C. Harrigan; vice-president, Mary Casey; recording secretary, Mayme Harrigan; financial secretary, Nellie Doyle; treasurer, Mrs. Fitzsimons; sergeant-at-arms, Annie Diniene; sentinel, Agnes Murray.

A. O. H. Tug-of-War Team.

COMPANION COURT GENEVA, NO 99.

Companion Court Geneva, No. 99, was organized November 27, 1904 by J. B. Vallee of Waterbury, Conn. The officers installed for the year 1907 are: Court Deputy, Geneva Berchard; Ex-Chief Ranger, Marie Moquinn; Chief Ranger, Eglantin Cote; Vice Chief Ranger, Josephine Bechard; Treasurer, Delia Lufieu; Financial and Recording Secretary, Oglore Lufieu; Orator, Elize Vauasse; Organist, Valeda Cote; Senior Woodward, Alphonsine Jodoin; Junior Woodward, Pomela Dube; Senior Beadle, Dora Buell; Junior Beadle, Melecie Vanasse. Companion Court Geneva is one of the only French Companion Courts in Bristol, was organized with a membership of 20 and now numbers 45. It is a very prosperous little court. Meetings are held in the French parish hall on the 2d Thursday of each month.

The charter members are Josephine Bechard, Geneva Bechard, Delia Duval, Virginia C. Benoit, Bertha Marcotte, Alphonsine Jodain, Marie Moquin, Milicie Vanosse, Dora Lemaine, Marie L. Dauphinois, Emma Duval, Virginia C. Bensit, Bertha Marcotte, Alphonsine Jodain, Marie A. Jodoin, Mauthe Carriguan, Angelina Alexandre, Valido Grenier.

L'UNION SAINT-JEAN-BAPTIST D'AMERIQUE.

The local lodge was opened Sept. 9, 1906. The first lodge of the order being organized in Woonsocket, R. I., May 7, 1900, and while the order is young, it is rapidly growing. The fundamental principle is fraternal insurance.

BRIGHTWOOD CAMP, No. 7724, M. W. of A.

Brightwood Camp, No. 7724, M. W. of America, was organized in February 15, 1899 in T. A. B. Hall with fifteen charter members, the society has a steady and healthy growth and to-day numbers over one hundred members. Since the organization of the society there has been eight deaths and every claim paid promptly. The head office of the Modern Woodmen of America is in Rock Island, Illinois and numbers over 1,000,000 members on its roll. It is an insurance order and offers protection to American citizens at a very low cost. The society meets the 3rd Friday of every month in the G. A. R. Hall on North Main street. It is the largest fraternal insurance organization in the world; also the cheapest.

OLIVET CHAPTER, No. 29, O. of E. S.

Olivet Chapter, No. 29, Order of the Eastern Star, was organized February 14, 1888, with a charter membership of forty. The present membership (Mar. 1, 1907) is one hundred and eight, with the following officers named as they appear in the photograph, reading from left to right: Mary Parsons, Ruth; Anna Schmelz, Electa; Estelle Ely, Chaplin; Mary Buck, Warder; Bertha Beede, Organist; Ellen F. Judson, Secretary; Ida McGar, Esther; Josie Elwin, Conductress; Maude Bryce, Associate Matron; Emily Brown, Worthy Matron; George Brown, Worthy Patron; Lelia Coe, Marshal; Rachel Brown, Adah; Bessie Warner, Conductress. Clara B. M. Douglass, Martha, and Judson Buskey, Sentinel, do not appear in the group.

Officers of Companion Court Geneva.

Officers L'Union St. Jean Baptiste de La Amerique

Officers Brightwood Camp, M. W. No. 7724. of America.

Officers Olivet Chapter No. 29 EastrenStar.

Katherine Gaylord Chapter, D. A. R.

Organized April 19, 1894. Present membership (April 1, 1907), 129. Charter members: Florence Emlyn Downs Muzzy (Mrs. Adrian J.), Mary Harriet Seymour Peck (Mrs. Miles L.), Mary Jane Atwood, Charlotte Stearns Griggs, Grace Brownell Peck (Mrs. Epaphroditus), Laura Electa Seymour, Clara Lee Bowman, Pierce Henderson Root-Newell (Mrs. Edward E.), Lucy Hurlburt Townsend Treadway (Mrs. Charles S.), Mary Elizabeth Brewster Brainard (Mrs. Wilbur F.), Alice M. Bartholomew, Edith Barnes Ladd (Mrs. Wyllys C.), Angie Manross Sigourney (Mrs. Albert M.), Minnie Louise Tuttle, Louise Griggs Goodwin (Mrs. Willard E.), Ida Cook Chidsey (Mrs. John T.), Annie Whiting Darron, Grace Ella Seymour Ingraham (Mrs. William S.), Ellen Amy Peck, Iva Clarissa Darron, Anna Clarke Tuttle, Katherine T. Curtiss (Mrs. Harrison).

The officers April 1, 1907, were: Regent, Mrs. Carlyle F. Barnes; vice regent, Mrs. William S. Ingraham; recording secretary, Miss Mary C. Peck; treasurer, Mrs. Chas. M. Kent; registrar, Mrs. Mary F. Martin; corresponding secretary, Mrs. Wilbur F. Brainard; historian, Mrs. Edson M. Peck.

North Cemetery Committee—Miss Clara L. Bowman, Miss M. Jennie Atwood, Mrs. Miles Lewis Peck and Mrs. Mary F. Martin. South Cemetery Committee—Mrs. Adrian J. Muzzy, Miss Mary P. Root and Miss Mary C. Peck. Advisory Board—Mrs. Geo. W. Mitchell, Mrs. Albert L. Sessions, Mrs. Harry W. Barnes and Mrs. Chas. T. Treadway. Foreign Citizens' Committee—Mrs. E. E. Newell, Mrs. Miles L. Peck and Miss Ella A. Upson. Music Committee—Mrs. Charles T. Treadway. Auditor—Mrs. S. Waldo Forbes.

Officers
INDEPENDENT ORDER OF FORESTERS.
(Companion Court, Victoria, No. 146.)

Companion Court was instituted January 13, 1905 with the membership of 35. The charter members were as follows: C. Deputy, Agnes O'Brien; P. C. R., Mary Farrell; C. R., Malinda Lange; V. C. R., Nellie Coughlin; R. S., Hannah Shaw; F. S., Lottie E. White; Treas., Julia Fitzsimmons; Orator, Edith Shaw; S. W., Lucy Letomneau; J. W., Laura Letomneau; S. B., Elizabeth Hynds; J. B., Mary Mills; Physicians, Dr. O. J. Beach, Dr. H. D. Brennan; S. J. C., Bessie Day; Organist, Mary O'Brien; the rest of the charter members were: Ellen Collins, Stella Russell, Wilhelimina Gleeson, Anna Aulback, Nellie Gloade, Amelia Leary, Ellen Leary, Emma Robey, Bertha Ochler, Mary Sawe, Mary Moriarity, Margaret Moriarity, Mary Buskey, Rosie O'Brien.

Installation Officers Pequabock LODGE, NO. 48, I. O. O. F.   (March 1907)

PEQUABOCK LODGE, No. 48, I. O. O. F.

Instituted February 8, 1883, by the following Grand Lodge officers: L. I. Munson, Grand Master; Harry Andrews of No. 52, Deputy Grand Master, pro tem.; Thomas E. Templeton, Grand Sentinel, pro tem.; George Barry, Grand Marshall; William Terry, Grand Inner Guard; Joseph A. Peck of No. 5, Grand Warden, pro tem.; Frederick Botsford, Grand Secretary.

Five members of good standing, living in Bristol, having asked for a charter, a meeting of the Grand Lodge was called to order in the afternoon and the following officers elected and installed: Noble Grand, Charles H. Steel; Vice Grand, Dr. E. P. Woodward; Secretary, A. H. Stahm; Treasurer, William C. Daab, who with Charles C. Steele had asked for the charter and after being installed the meeting was adjourned to evening when the following named persons were taken in and given all the degrees:

A. H. Stahm, R. A. Crothers, Geo. J. Shubert, Fred A. Crane, J. C. Christinger, J. W. Hickey, E. Alderman, A. Lane, H. Holt, E. J. Brose, C. H. Warren, Charles H. Steele, Dr. E. P. Woodward, Wm. C. Daab, Geo. H. Olmstead, Charles F. Micheal, Theo. Dresher, I. W. Tyler, E. Mohler, O. A. Jones, C. E. Raymond, M. L. Perkins.

Pequabock Lodge, No. 48, has in its twenty-four years of life contributed its share in the building up of Odd Fellowship in Bristol, as many of its members can testify to, and as the following detailed report will show

Amount received for dues	$23,452.20
Paid out in sick benefits	7,769.78
Paid for the care of members of other Lodges	863.99
Paid for the relief of widows	288.73
Watching	924.17
(For many years the Brothers watched with a Brother.)	
Money paid for paraphernalia	1,3C0.00
Money deposited in bank	1,409.17
Number initiated	294
Present membership	182
Number of Past Grands	40

I. W. Tyler was appointed our first district deputy in 1893-94, Charles J. Anderson in 1901, C. B. Smith, 1905-07, I. W. Tyler was the first to receive the Grand Lodge Degree, was our first deputy and is still active in the Lodge. Of the charter members, I. W. Tyler, Fred A. Crane, Charles F. Michael, E. G. Brose, M. L. Perkins, father of our present Noble Grand, C. E. Perkins, are at the present time members of Pequabock Lodge.

Philip Pond, father of the present Grand Master, was initiated in old Pequabock Lodge, No. 48.

Respectfully submitted in F., L. and T.,
C. B. SMITH,
F. A. GRISWOLD,
FRANK SMITH,
FRED WILLIAMS.

Present Officers of Pequabuck Lodge.

Past Grand, A. Stephenson; Noble Grand, C. E. Perkins; Vice Grand, Geo. B. Michael; Secretary, F. Wilder; Permanent Secretary, W. T. Tyson; Treasurer, F. A. Griswold; Warden, E. P. Choiniere; Conductor, Geo. Scherr; Inside Guard, W. Burnham; Outside Guard, Paul Nichols; Right Supporter Noble Grand, C. F. Michael; Left Supporter Noble Grand, A. A. Lilgren; Right Supporter Vice Grand, Frederick Miles; Left Supporter Vice Grand, J. Johnson; Right Scene Supporter, Jos. Galipo; Left Scene Supporter, Chas. Dickinson; Chaplain, F. J. Smith.

Degree Team Pequabuck Lodge No. 48, I. O. O. F.

STEPHEN TERRY LODGE, No. 59, I. O. O. F.

Stephen Terry Lodge, No. 59, I. O. O. F., was instituted April 15th, 1892, by George H. Cowell, Grand Master, assisted by Charles B. Ware, Deputy Grand Master, Frederick Botsford, Grand Secretary, and John W. Smith, Grand Treasurer.

The following are the names of the charter members: Seth W. Beebe, Henry M. Cadwell, Geo. M. Howes, Chas. H. Kimberly, B. T. Lyons, Henry W. Morgan, Chas. C. Morgan, John H. Simmons, G. T. Steele, Adolphus D. Washburn, Arthur F. Woodford, Chas. R. Wood.

At the close of the ceremonies of institution, the charter members were called to make a choice of officers, with the following result: Noble Grand, Henry M. Cadwell; Vice Grand, Chas. H. Kimberly; Recording Secretary, L. D. Waterhouse; Permanent Secretary, A. D. Washburn; Treasurer, W. H. Merritt. The above named officers were installed by Grand Master Cowell. A team from Nosahogan Lodge, No. 21, then initiated forty-eight candidates.

At the close of the first term ending December 31, 1892, Stephen Terry Lodge numbered 84 members. At the present time, May, 1907, our roll numbers 358. We have lost by death 16 members.

Since the lodge was instituted, we have paid in benefits and relief, $10,114.40. Amount of invested funds, $3,000, and furniture and paraphernalia which is insured for $2,500.

Some Officers Stephen Terry Lodge, No. 59, I. O. O. F.

Present officers: Noble Grand, Samuel W. Howe; Vice Grand, B. B. Robbins; Secretary, J. G. Beckwith; Financial Secretary, W. B. Chapin; Treasurer, Ira L. Newcomb; Right Supporter Noble Grand' Charles Johnson; Left Supporter Noble Grand, E. M. Church; Warden Roland D. Barnes; Conductor, S. E. Dunning; Right Scene Supporter, Leon Barnum; Left Scene Supporter, James Hinchcliff; Outside Guard, Clarence Mallory; Inside Guard, John Beaton; Chaplain, Arthur C. Jewett; Right Supporter Vice Grand, Henry Soule; Left Supporter Vice Grand, William W. Grant.

Officers Victoria Lodge, No. 13, D. O. H.

VICTORIA LODGE, No. 13, D. O. H.

Victoria Lodge, No. 13, D. O. H., was organized Mar. 22, 1891, with twenty charter members. Present membership (March, 1907), forty-four. The following are the present officers (March, 1907), named as they appear in the picture, reading from left to right: Mrs. Louisa Geisweit, Trustee; Mrs. Rose Lucksinger, Vice-President; Mrs. Johanna Hummel, Treasurer; John Englert, District Deputy; Mrs. Louisa Schreck, Secretary; Mrs. Augusta Bachmann, President; Mrs. Magdalena Englert, Financial Secretary.

GUTTENBERG LODGE, No. 570, D. O. H.

The above named lodge was organized January 27, 1889. There were twenty-two charter members, as follows: First President, Anthon Wolfe; Second President, Louis Bachman; Treasurer, Lawrence Matz; Secretary, Amandus Bachman; Joseph Aulback, Frank Bachman, Damian Fries, Fred Herold, John Ott, John Ronalter, John Spielman, Erwin Salg, Fred Zang, Joseph Zang, Bruno Gerth, Oscar Jorres, Theodore Tresher, August Stamm, Joseph Blatman, Charles Wieget, Chas. Wolfe, John Warenburger.

These members were installed the same day, which was January 27, 1889, by State Deputy, George Shultzer of Hartford; President, John Row of New Britain; Secretary, George Mischler of Meriden, and Treasurer, Gustave Whaler of Rockville.

Present officers are: Debitor, Rudolph Bachman; First President, Lawrence Spieler; Second President, Roman Bachman; Secretary, Joseph Aulback; Financial Secretary, Amandus Bachman; Treasurer, Enos Bachman.

BRISTOL SUB-DIVISION, NATIONAL RED CROSS.

A group of the members of The Bristol Sub-Division American National Red Cross: 1 Julian McGar, 2 James Burgess, 3 Leroy Green, 4 Claude Griswold, 5 Lester Sigourney, 6 Robt. Lee, 7 Harry Daniels, 8 Gilbert Smith, 9 Raymond Cook, 10 Harvey Wilder, 11 Kenneth Abbott, 12 Frederick Beatson, 13 Elmer Whittier, 14 Lawrence Steele, 15 Chas. F. Olin, 16 Ira Smith, 17 Irving Wasley, 18 Eric Waldo, 19 Samuel Steele, 20 Clarence Thomas, 21 Clarence Bond, 22 Walter Wade, 23 Paul Pelky, 24 Gustave Lundahl.

SESSIONS LODGE, No. 44, K. of P.

Sessions Lodge, No. 44, Knights of Pythias, was organized Mar. 1, 1905, with a charter membership of thirty. The mebership in March, 1907 was fifty. Names of officers as they appear upon the picture, reading from right to left are as follows: E. N. Bunnell, master at arms; J. H. Warner, past chancellor; Arthur Potter, master of finance; J. W. Bunnell, keeper of records and seal; W. B. Crumb, master of exchequer; Fred Percival, prelate; H. E. Lawrence, outer guard; C. W. Daniels, past chancellor; F. G. Osborne, master of work; H. N. Downs, chancellor commander; C. J. Foster, past chancellor; W. C. Warner, inner guard; J. W. Yale, past chancellor; C. W. Taylor, vice chancellor.

A Group of Members of Bristol Sub-Division, American National Red Cross.

Officers Sessions Lodge, No. 44; K. of P.

Ionic Council, No. 33, R. & S. M., was granted its charter May 11, 1904, and started with 19 charter members, who were formerly members of Doric Council, No. 24, of New Britain.

The membership now numbers over 50 and has had three masters: C. Norton Parsons, 1904; Frank L. Mathes, 1905 and 1906, and Louis L. Beach for 1907.

Officers Guttenberg Lodge, No. 570, D. O. H. (See page 628)

BRISTOL FIRE DEPARTMENT.

From Notes by Roswell Atkins

Fire Dept. Chief Engineer, Harlan B. Norton; 1st Asst. Engineer, Mathew McCormick; 2d Asst. Engineer, John M. Hayes.

Previous to 1853 the Town of Bristol had no other protection from the ravages of fire than the unorganized bucket line, notwithstanding repeated demonstrations of the necessity for something had been oft repeated, especially in 1845, by the total destruction in a few short hours of the largest manufacturing establishment in the town, consisting of three large shops with out buildings, located on Main Street between School street and Riverside avenue, belonging to the Chauncey Jerome Clock Co., resulting in the removal of the entire plant to New Haven, and about the same time the Terry Clock shop, located near the Pierce bridge, was destroyed, under the excitement of which a charter was obtained for a fire company, consisting of forty-five men, thirty-five of whom might be military subjects, but as no apparatus was provided, after several attempts to organize a company, the matter was dropped until in 1853, the business men residing in the south part of the village, headed by Edward L. Dunbar, Alanson S. Platt and Alphonso Barnes, took the matter in hand systematically and raised by subscription something over two thousand dollars, built an engine house on School street near Main, purchased a hand engine and a hose cart, such as were in use at that day in most of the cities, and five hundred feet of leather hose, secured a charter for a company of sixty men, as Bristol Engine and Hose Co., No. 1, to be located within one half mile of the bridge over the Pequabuck river on Main street, and in September of that year the first fire company was duly organized and the property placed in their care, thus forming the nucleus of the present department.

The first action of the town in reference to the matter was in 1856, by an appropriation of six hundred dollars for the purchase of hose, at which time the property on School street, which had been bought by individuals, was deeded to the town, since which time repairs have been paid for by the town, previous to this the members paid for them from their own pockets, except occasionally upon solicitation manufacturers assisted them, their only remuneration being exemption from poll and military taxes.

In 1870, those living in the north village, having witnessed the effectiveness of even one hand engine in confining the destruction by fire to the single building in which it was discovered, and learning that a good engine of the same capacity as No. 1, could be secured at a reasonable price of the City of Norwich and also a hose cart, raised by subscription a sum of money sufficient to secure them, and also erected the building now known as Engine House No. 2, on North Main street. In this matter Mr. Wm. W. Carter and Lester Goodenough were particularly active. And a charter was granted as Uncas Engine and Hose Co. No. 1 (that being the name of the engine), with an allowance of seventy men, and in October, 1870, a company was organized and placed in possession to care for and use the property for the purpose designed.

It soon became apparent that in many instances ladders, axes and hooks were needed in order to successfully cope with the element, and in 1872, a light truck with several ladders, the longest being forty feet, were purchased, and the No. 1 engine house lengthened to receive it, and a charter having been obtained for a company consisting of forty members at any time as Zealot Hook and Ladder Co. No. 1, a company was organized and occupied these quarters for about two years, when a building was erected on Meadow street (its present location) in order to have it more centrally located.

In 1881, the citizens of Forestville, having purchased a steam fire engine and a hose carriage, obtained a charter for a company allowing one hundred men as Welch Steam Fire Engine and Hose Co. No. 1, of Forestville, a company was organized and the town erected a suitable building for the storage of the apparatus and the use of the company. In the same year the town appropriated the sum of seven thousand five hundred dollars ($7,500) for the purchase of a steam fire engine to be located with the hook and ladder truck on Meadow street, and Hon Edward B. Dunbar, Samuel P. Newell, Esq., and John H. Sessions, Jr.' with the chief engineer and the selectmen were appointed a committee to procure the same.

After a thorough canvass of the matter this committee came to the conclusion that the interests of the town would be better served by the purchase of two lighter engines, located as the hand engines were, and so reported.

This decision was approved by the citizens generally, and two La France rotary engines were purchased, and the results have proved the decision to have been a wise one by the quickness of the arrival of one engine at a fire in any part of the village.

This outfit did good service until the introduction of a system of water works in 1885 rendered the use of engines for the most part unnecessary wherever hydrants could be reached. Soon after one of the rotary engines took the place of the apparatus in use in Forestville, and the other was placed with the truck on Meadow street for use in case of emergency. One of the hand engines and the old steamer in Forestville were sold. The original No. 1, Hand Engine, was retained as a relic or survivor, it having been built for the town in 1853 by A. W. Roberts & Co. of Hartford. A new hook and ladder truck with extension ladders was purchased in 1889, and the old one sold.

In 1871, the town for the first time, appointed a Board of Fire Commissioners, consisting of five members, to have a general supervision of the department, and the appointment of a Chief Engineer and assistants, and in 1875, compensation of twenty cents per hour was voted the members of the department for services at fires.

In 1881, the number of Commissioners was increased to six, and instead of annual appointments, two were to be elected each year to serve for three years, and a code of by-laws was adopted for the regulation of the department.

The following persons have served as commissioners, most of them until death or resignation: Dr. James H. Austin, James E. Ladd Josiah T. Peck, Julius Nott, Wm. W. Carter, Laport Hubbell, Edward B. Dunbar, Julius R. Mitchell, Edward Ingraham, Roswell Atkins, George H. Miller, John H. Sessions, Sr., John Birge, Samuel D. Bull, George W. Mitchell, George H. Hall, Charles H. Deming, John H. Sessions, Jr., and the following have served as chief engineers: William W. Carter, Henry A. Peck, William A. Dunbar, Roswell Atkins, James Hanna, Joseph T. Bradshaw, George H. Hall, Howard G. Arms, most of them having served in other capacities previously.

The department by its promptness to respond to alarms, whether in summer's heat or winter's cold, at noonday or dead of night, its skill and tenacity of purpose to leave nothing undone to secure safety of life and property, has won a reputation at home and among insurance adjusters, of which they are justly proud, having frequently been complimented for their successful control of fires in exceedingly close and dangerous conditions, and the harmony which exists throughout the department is a matter of congratulation.

Engineer Fred McGor.   Stoker Fred Mitchell.

Group of
Officers and members of Bristol Engine and Hose Co., No. 1, (Mar., 1907).

BRISTOL ENGINE AND HOSE CO. NO. 1.

In 1853 the business men residing in the south part of the village, headed by Edward L Dunbar, Alanson S. Pratt, and Alphonzo Barnes, raised by subscription something over $2,000, built the engine house on School street, near Main, purchased an engine and hose carriage, such as were in use at that time in most of the cities, also 500 feet of hose, secured a charter for a company of sixty men, as Bristol Engine and Hose Co. No. 1, to be located within one-half mile from the bridge over the Pequabuck river on Main street, and in September of that year the first fire company was duly organized, and the property placed in their care, thus forming the nucleus of the present department. The first action of the town was in 1856, by an appropriation of $600 for the purchase of hose, at which time the property purchased by individuals on School street was secured by deed and bill of sale to the town, since which time repairs have been paid for from the town treasury, previous to which the members paid for them from their own pockets, or solicited from the property holders, their remuneration being exemption from poll and military taxes only. The illustration on the opposite page shows the officers and men March, 1907.

No. 1 Hose Company's Tug of War Team.

Officers and members of Zealots Hook and Ladder Co., No. 1, (March, 1907).

ZEALOTS HOOK AND LADDER CO. NO. 1.

In 1872 a light truck with several ladders, the longest being forty feet, was purchased, and the No. 1 engine house lengthened to receive it. A charter having been granted to James Hanna, James A. Matthews, Thomas Parsons, William Root, and William Curtis, and associates, as Zealots Hook and Ladder Co. No. 1, to the number of forty at any one time, a company was organized occupying these quarters for about two years, when a building was erected on Meadow street (its present location), in order to have it more centrally located. The half-tone illustration on the opposite page shows the officers and men March, 1907.

Zealot Hose Campany's Running Team, 1906.

UNCAS FIRE COMPANY.

It had been argued that there should be located at the North End of Bristol, then growing very fast, a fire company, as much valuable property would be lost in case of fire, if too much dependence was placed upon the only fire company in town, which was doing a great deal of good, but was located at the south end of the town. So, through the efforts of William Carter, O. D. Warner, James E. Ladd, Harry Henderson, J. T. Peck, George Lewis and H. L. Beach, a company was organized and petitioned the General Assembly to incorporate them into a fire engine company.

In May, 1870, the General Assembly granted a charter to the above named men and others who were interested, for a fire company.

At this late day it is impossible to give an accurate history of the old company which disbanded May 30, 1894, when the new company was organized under the efforts of Howard Arms, who was then chief of the department.

The first meeting of the present company was held May 30, 1894, with Chief Arms in the chair, and on July 5, 1894, the following officers were elected: Foreman, Joseph Conzelman; first assistant, C. R. Goodenough; second assistant, E. O. Porter.

It has always been a matter of comment, not only of the citizens of the town, but of visitors, of the quick response to fires of the entire department. It has been the custom of the Uncas Company to start immediately with cart, without waiting for the truck and horses which are located at the south end of the town, and which would cause, if waited for, the loss of valuable time at fires.

The following is a copy of resolutions presented to the company after a hard and disastrous fire:

"At a meeting of the Board of Fire Commissioners held November 16, 1905, it was unanimously voted that a letter of thanks should be written each company, relating to their efficient services at fires; and in behalf of the town the commissioners do hereby thank you all for your loyalty and bravery in the work. We trust that the drenching which many of you often receive of ice cold water will not cool your ardor, but that you will continue the good work in the future as in the past."

The Uncas House is always open to its active and honorary members in which there are card tables and pool room, with which to amuse oneself. A phonograph has also been bought and is at the disposal of members, and is in constant use, especially on Sunday afternoon and evenings. Clam suppers have become a noted event with the friends of the company. The first clam supper was held in December, 1895, and since that time the company has given from three to eight in a season. It has been customary to invite the town and borough officers, as well as the Fire Commissioners, at least once a year to enjoy a steamed clam supper with the members.

The company have held several lawn festivals and concerts on their spacious lawn. The first of these was held in May, 1897, which proved so successful that others have been given with same degree of success.

The only fair the company has given was held in the Opera House in January, 1902.

In November, 1895, the company paid a visit to the Plantsville Company in Plantsville and presented the company with a pitcher. On April 19, 1898, the company was presented by the members of the former company, three large elegant silver trumpets, which have ornamented the parlors as well as being very useful to the officers.

On March 1, 1897, the company fitted out a room that had been set aside, into very elaborate parlors, which is the pride of the company.

Officers and Members of Uncas Hose Company.

It has a full set of leather seated chairs and tete-a-tete, a lounge, oak table, ak secretary's desk and a very handsome chandelier.

On March 4, 1897, the members opened the house to the public for their inspection and the company received very high praise in the tastefulness of the decorations and the general interior.

On August 2, 1898, the Fire Commissioners and honorary members were given a reception in the parlors.

The company has been to several of the surrounding towns and participated in parades. The following towns are among those visited by the company: Plantsville, Thomaston and Torrington.

The cart decorations have been most elaborate, the young ladies of the north end have taken a great deal of interest in the company and on all of its parades have spent evening after evening decorating the cart with flowers.

The company has had two different uniforms; the first was a blue used by a great many of the city departments. On April 21, 1901, the uniform now worn by the company was adopted and has been the cause of very high praise for the company. The first time the new uniforms were worn was at the parade held in Torrington, August 10, 1901. The first time the company appeared in the uniforms in Bristol was at the annual inspection of the department held in September, 1901.

The company has in the basement an apparatus for washing hose, which is the only one like it in use. It was gotten up and built and patented by members of the company and with a few men a thousand feet of hose can be thoroughly washed in ten or fifteen minutes.

It is very sad to look back over our records and find that some who were once active in our circle have been taken by death. The first of our members who have died was George Van Ness who died March 16, 1896. On December 12, 1901, Walter Pond died. On September 23, 1904, Walter Hill died.

Uncas Hose Company.

Officers and members of Welsh Steam Fire Engine and Hose Co., No. 1, (March, 1907).

WELCH STEAM FIRE ENGINE AND HOSE CO. NO. 1.
(Of Forestville.)

In 1881 the citizens of Forestville, having purchased a steam fire engine and hose carriage, and a charter having been granted George H. Mitchell, Laport Hubbell, Chauncey L. Hotchkiss, Isaac W. Beach, Hobart Booth, and Samuel D. Bull, and associates, to the number of 100 men at any one time, as Welch Steam Fire Engine and Hose Co. No. 1, of Forestville, a company was organized and the town erected a suitable building for the storage of the apparatus and the use of the company. The company has prospered since its very beginning, and is at present in first class condition, being splendidly equipped and having a fine personnel. On the opposite page is shown a group picture of the officers and men in March, 1907.

GILBERT W. THOMPSON POST No. 13, G. A. R.

Gilbert W. Thompson Post, No. 13, Department of Connecticut, G. A. R., was organized December 6, 1882, with the following charter members:

Nelson Bronson, 1st lieut. U. S. Army, retired; Grove E. Castle, private, Co. C., 8th Conn. Vols.; Wm Hubbell, private, Co. K., 16th Conn. Vols.; Walter H. Hutchinson, private, Co. C., 12th Conn. Vols., and 1st lieut. 99th U. S. Vols.; George Merriman, Jr., private, Co. K, 16th Conn. Vols.; Irving W. Tyler, private, Co. K, 20th Maine Vols.; Merwin H. Perkins, corporal, Co. E, 20th Conn. Vols.; Augustus Lane, private, Co. I, 1st C. V., H. Art.; Henry H. Riggs, private, Co. C, 8th Conn. Vols.; Franklin Ball, musician, Co. C, 10th Conn. Vols.; James S. Reynolds, private, Co. I, 97th N. Y. Vols.; Gilbert S. Richmond, private, Co. I, 25th Conn. Vols.; George J. Schubert, corporal, Co. I, 25th Conn. Vols.; Silas M. Norton, 1st sergeant, Co. K, 16th Conn. Vols.; Wm. W. Dickens, wagoner, Co. A, 11th Conn. Vols.; Theodore Schubert, bugler, Co. A, 1st Conn. Cav.; W. E. Shelton, private, Co. D, 5th Conn. Vols.; Clifford D. Parsons, private, Co. A, 8th Conn. Vols.; Wm. H. Adams, sergeant, Co. M, 1st Conn. Cav.; Asa Dillaby, corporal, Co. A. 18th Conn. Vols.; Burnham W. Francis, private, Co K. 16th Conn. Vols.; Aldelbert D. Webster, corporal, Co. ', 2nd C. V., H. Art.; Fred W. Crane, private, Co. A, 16th Conn. Vols.; Sereno T. Nichols, private, Co. I, 25th Conn. Vols.; Henry A. Peck, captain, Co. I, 10th Conn. Vols.; Gilbert J. Bentley, sergeant, Co. B, 37th Mass. Vols.;

Some Members Gilbert W. Thompson Relief Corps, March, 1907

Past Commander Franklin Ball.

Newell Moulthrop, private, Co. H, 23d Conn. Vols.; George H. Bates, corporal, Co. D, 2d C. V., H. Art.; Chas. E. Russell, private, Co. A, 20th Conn. Vols.; Samuel R. Terrell, private, Co. D, 2d C. V., H. Art.; Mortimer R. Keeney, corporal, Co. B, 13th Conn. Vols.; David W. Hall, captain, Co. H, 4th Engrs.; Wm. C. Hillard, hos. steward, U. S. army; Arthur S. Parsons, private, Co. G, 16th Conn. Vols.

ROSTER JANUARY 1, 1907.

Roster January 1, 1907.

Wm. Hubbell, Walter H. Hutchinson, Geo. Merriman, Irving W. Tyler, Franklin Ball, Theodore Schubert, Wm. H. Adams, Henry A. Peck, Newell Moulthrop, Geo. H. Bates, David W. Hall, Wm. C. Hillard, Arthur H. Parsons, Austin D. Thompson, Henry B. Cook, Gilbert H. Blakesley, Geo. B. Chapin, Timothy B. Robinson, Wm. C. Richards, Harrison S. Judd, Wm. H. Nott, Henry S. Avery, Z. Fuller Grannis, Marvin L. Gaylord, Albert C. Loomis, Elbert Manchester, Asahel A. Lane, Heman A. Weeks, Wm. L. Weeks, Augustus H. Funck, George H. Grant, Fairfield Dresser, Napoleon B. Neal, Chas. B. Upson, Aaron C. Dresser, Amzi P. Clark, Hiram W. Simons, Walter Fish, Chas. H. Johnson, Watson N. Smith, George T Cook, Thomas Bunnell, Clarence H. Muzzy, Hubert D. Royce or Rice, Wm. L. Norton, William W. Cone, Ira B. Smith, Homer W. Griswold, Sylvester P. Harrison, Isaac W. Judd, Nathan L. Bartholomew, John Walton, Francis Williams, Edward H. Allen, Epaphroditus Harrison, James B. Sanford, Stephen C. Robbins, Geo. F. Nichols, Clifford D. Parsons, Leroy T. Hill—total, 60.

LIST OF OFFICERS, MARCH 1, 1907.

Post Commander, George T. Cook; S. V. Commander, George H. Bates; J. V. Commander, Harrison S. Judd; Surgeon, Henry A. Peck; Chaplain, Franklin Ball; Officer of Day, Hiram W. Simons; Officer of

Guard, Walter Fish; Quartermaster, George B. Chapin; Adjutant, Ira B. Smith; Sergeant-Major, Walter H. Hutchinson; Quartermaster-Sergeant, Thomas Bunnell.

LIST OF POST COMMANDERS.

George Merriman, Walter H. Hutchinson, Franklin Ball, Wm. Hubbell, Irving W. Tyler, Wm. C. Hillard, Timothy B. Robinson, Z. Fuller Granniss, Albert C. Loomis, Heman A. Weeks, Ira B. Smith, John Watson

GILBERT W. THOMPSON RELIEF CORPS

On the 2d day of January, 1884, Gilbert W. Thompson Relief Corps, No. 4, of Bristol, was organized, Mrs. Elizabeth C. Keifer of Wadhams Corps, Waterbury, acting as the instituting and installing officer. The number of charter members was 27, viz.: Emma Parlin, Ellen Morse, Ellen Grant, Mary Norton, Mary Nott, Minnie Chapin, Sophia Schubert, Mary Merriman, Fannie Stone, Augusta Judd, Henrietta Thompson, Rebecca Hall, Martha Russell, Althea Hutchinson, Parmelia Holmes, Susan Traver, Hattie Webster, Emma Arnold, Sarah Potter, Alice Cook, Eva Yale, Ellen Dickens, Minerva Hungerford, Ida Stillman, Jennie Riggs, Betsey Downs, Jennie Williams. The first officers of Thompson Corps were: President, Emma Parlin (who is now Emma Wright of New Britain, where she has since been President of Stanley, No. 12); Senior Vice-President, Henrietta Thompson; Junior Vice-President, Minnie J. Chapin; Secretary, Mary B. Nott; Treasurer, Sophia M. Schubert; Chaplain, Ellen Morse; Conductor, Ida Stillman; Guard, Jennie Riggs.

Old Town Hall.

Officers of Gilbert W. Thompson Relief Corps.

Newton S. Manross, Women's Relief Corps.

WOMAN'S RELIEF CORPS.

Newton S. Manross Woman's Relief Corps, No. 9, Auxiliary to Manross Post, was organized December 10, 1884, with a charter membership of twenty, including Forestville and Plainville ladies.

Its first officers were: Sarah E. Reynolds, President; Kate F. Hills, Senior Vice President; Mary L. Tinker, Junior Vice President; Alice E. Wilson, Secretary; Jennie B. Atkins, Treasurer; Sarah J. Graves, Chaplain; Georgiana Newell. Conductor; Laurie E. Frisbie, Guard.

The meetings were held in the old Firemen's Hall until it was destroyed by fire, the Corps losing its original charter and organ. A new charter was procured and in spite of losses and the incompleteness of instructions in these early years, these loyal, faithful women, who were its charter members and an equal number who had joined its ranks labored on, and its present success is largely owing to their courage and faithfulness.

At the present time it has a membership of 67, and is now as in its first years striving to be a help to the veterans and to the Post to which it is auxiliary.

Some of the Members of Manross Post.

BRISTOL TRUST COMPANY.

The new building is a substantial structure composed of pure white marble. Its exterior outlines are sharply defined angles, while its stalwart and symmetrical columns relieved by beautiful carving, classic in every line, impart stateliness and dignity to its appearance.

The tiled roof with its red and green and copper tints affords a striking contrast with the white walls beneath.

The building is the embodiment of substantiality and practical service, as well as architectural strength and beauty. Its style combines those qualities of ancient Greek architecture which appeal so strongly to the modern mind, that even its resurrected masterpieces are the marvel of modern architects. This style requires the most skilled workmanship and gives assurance that the building will permanently retain its beauty and command admiration in after years.

The building is surrounded by an attractive lawn provided with a profusion of plants and shrubbery after the Italian garden style, with an Italian garden bench at the concave corner.

Set in an ample green space, the white walls and red crowned roof of this building will inspire and develop esthetic ideals in the mind of even the most indifferent observer.

Four stately fluted columns guard the entrance which leads into an attractive vestibule, richly decorated in gold tints. From the vestibule one enters the public corridor where at once the entire main banking room is in view. The domed ceiling rises out of the large fluted Ionic pilasters with ornamental cornices and the floor is of Italian marble with green serpentine borders, and the side walls are wainscoted with polished Paonazzo marble, characterized by dark green veins. The woodwork is Honduras mahogany of the finest fibre and the highest finish.

The decorators of the building were Mortensen and Holdensen of Boston. Both Mr. Mortensen and Mr. Holdensen have had a thorough art education, having studied at the Royal Academy at Copenhagen and the Imperial School of Design in Vienna, and have worked with the best decorative artists of the continent.

The greater portion of the bank building is composed, of course, of the main banking room, devoted to the public and the transaction of the bank's regular business .

The walls of this room are of Empire blue, and the architectural features are gilded and toned down to a general impression of old gold.

The room occupies the whole height of the building, which gives space for an impressive coved ceiling.

The decoration in this cove is French renaisance with a leaning toward the classic. The four sides of the cove are decorated with emblems representing, respectively, Finance, Agriculture, Industry and Commerce, to harmonize with the larger decorations painted by Mr. Vesper L. George, which occupy the center of the sides, and which are enclosed by frames of laurel.

The public corridor occupies the heart of the building and is of octagonal shape with the paying and receiving tellers' and bookkeepers' windows facing it, and framed off from it by the metallic screen which guards the banking force at work. The building is thoroughly modern, absolutely fire-proof and is damp-proof and water-proof throughout.

The vault is directly in the rear of the working space and conveniently located with reference to the booth rooms which are used by patrons of the bank in examining their valuables that are stored in the Safe Deposit Boxes. The vault is of the most modern construction, equipped with every device for absolutely safeguarding important papers and valuables against fire, burglary or other danger or loss, and contains the Safe Deposit Boxes, and the safe provided for the cash, securities and other important holdings of the company.

OFFICERS.

The officers are: William E. Sessions, president; Charles L. Wooding, vice president; Francis A. Beach, secretary and treasurer; George S. Beach, assistant secretary and treasurer; executive committee, the president, hte vice president, the treasurer; directors, William E. Sessions, president, The Sessions Foundryy Co. and The Sessions Clock Co.; Charles L. Wooding, secretary and treasurer, Bristol Water Co.; A. J. Muzzy, real estate; M. E. Weldon, merchant; Albert L. Sessions, president J. H. Sessions & Son; Joseph B. Sessions, vice president, The Sessions Foundry Co.; Francis A. Beach, treasurer, The Bristol Trust company.

Old Library Building, corner Main and High Streets.

BRISTOL'S NEW FREE PUBLIC LIBRARY.

(From Notes in Bristol Press Aug. 15, 1907.)

The formal dedication of the New Library took place Aug. 14, 1907. Callers were welcomed by Judge Epaphroditus Peck, Librarian Charles L. Wooding and assistants Miss E. J. Peck, Miss A. W. Darrow and Miss Emma Winslow. In the evening the following program was rendered:

William S. Ingraham,·
Chairman of the Board of Library Directors, presiding.

Music,	Selection from "Martha,"	Flotow
	Miss Olcott's Orchestra	
Address,	Epaphroditus Peck,	
	Secretary of the Board of Library Directors	
Address,	Miss Caroline M. Hewins,	
	Librarian of the Hartford Public Library	
	Secretary of the State Library Commission	
Dedicatory Prayer,	Rev. A. H. Goodenough	
Singing,	America	
Music,	The Great Divide,	Maurice
	The Orchestra	

Every seat in the assembly room was taken. Judge Peck's address was in part as follows:

Among the different causes of satisfaction in our new library building, and in the library which it contains, the one most frequently expressed is that it is not a gift from some world-famous plutocrat, or even from some single wealthy citizen of Bristol, but that it represents the general effort and the general interest of our entire community.

Over four hundred persons have taken part in the erection of this building by the contribution of larger or smaller sums, the smaller sums doubtless representing as much real sacrifice as the larger, and of these nearly all are residents of Bristol, and the few others are persons interested in Bristol by former residence or family connection.

It is interesting to note that the course of events out of which this library grew was not the beginning of the public library idea in Bristol. I hold in my hand a book in which are pasted three book-plates; one of the "Reformed Library in New Cambridge," one of the "Mechanics Library in Bristol," and the third our own book-plate.

The first book-plate reads as follows:

No. 61. This book belongs to the Reformed Library in New Cambridge. All books must be returned on the first Mondays of Oct., Nov., Dec., Jan., Feb., March, May, July and last Monday of August, on forfeiture of six-pence, one penny for every day's neglect afterwards. One penny for turning down a leaf. Other damages estimated by the inspecting committee.

The second plate is as follows:

No. 79. Price $1.25. This book belongs to the Mechanics Library of Bristol. All books belonging to this library must be returned on the first Thursday of every month, on penalty of fine of five per cent (probably meaning five cents), and one per cent for every day's neglect afterwards. Two cents for turning down a leaf, twenty-five per cent for lending books to non-proprietors, and other damages estimated by the inspecting committee.

Now the name Bristol was given to this community when it was incorporated as a town in 1785, and the use of the older term "New Cambridge" as well as the use of the English currency, indicate that the earlier library must have been formed some years before 1800. The written inscription on the fly-leaf, "Newell Pyington's book bought October 28, 1816, of the New Cambridge Reformed library," probably shows that at that time the library association had broken up and was selling its books, and we may infer that the Mechanics Library was organized afterwards.

The existence of still a third library, the "Philosophical Library," and perhaps a fourth, in the late eighteenth and early nineteenth centuries, is shown by a record book which has lately come into the possession of the library from Miss Kezia A. Peck. This book contains in one end the "Rules and regulations of the public library in the first society in Bristol," (Burlington was then the second society in Bristol), dated December 19, 1792, and signed by forty-three proprietors, whose names probably give a good census of the solid and intelligent men in the Bristol of that day, headed by that of the Congregational minister, Giles Hooker Cowles.

At the other end of the book are the records of the Philosophical library, organized on December 5, 1803, with twenty-eight subscribers. The record of annual meetings of this society continues till 1812, after which twenty pages or more are torn out. On a later page is the first invoice of books bought for this library; Adam's Defense, 2 vols., Morse's Geography, 2 vols., History of the French Revolution, 2 vols., Ramsay's American Revolution, 2 vols., Trumbull's History of Connecticut, 1 vol., Adam's View of Religion, 1 vol., The Farmer's Dictionary, The Rambler, 4 vols., Franklin's Life and Letters, and President Jefferson's Notes on Virginia.

The Rambler is the only book in this list that could by any possibility be classed as light literature, and we may safely guess that the works of Anthony Hope and James Barr McCutcheon would have little favor with the purchasing committee, even if there had been any books of that class to buy.

Putting together the information gathered from these two book-plates, and that afforded by the record book, we can clearly identify at least three successive libraries. First, the "Reformed Library," of the older book-plate, which may be identical with the unnamed "publick library" of 1792, or may be (and more probably is) a still earlier one; second (or third) the Philosophical library of 1803, and third (or fourth) the Mechanics library of the later book-plate.

The series of events that have led directly to our present library began about 1845, with the organization of a sewing society by the ladies of the Congregational church to raise money for a new carpet for the church. This was officially called the "New Carpet Society" but popularly the "Old Maids' Society." When the carpet had been bought and laid down, the ladies found their association so pleasant that they decided to keep up their meetings and to use their earnings for a library for their common use. They bought books from time to time, and some member kept the collection at her own house. In 1868 this library had grown to 445 volumes and the society had also sixty dollars in its treasury.

In that year some public-spirited men were just organizing a Young Men's Christian association for the benefit of the young men of the town. They were naturally seeking attractions for their rooms, and I suppose that the "Old Maids'" library had reached such size as to be rather burdensome to its owners. A contract was accordingly made by which the ladies placed their library with the accumulated cash in the hands of the Y. M. C. A., the most important part of the agreement being as follows: "The library shall be kept in Bristol as a circulating library, open to all persons who shall pay the fees and conform to the rules, and no portion of it or its funds shall be appropriated to any other purpose."

The only survivors of this ladies' society, so far as I know, are Mrs. Ann North, Mrs. Ellen Lewis Peck, Miss Lucy Beckwith and Miss Ophelia Ives, all still residents in Bristol.

New Library Building in Process of Construction.

The Young Men's Christian association maintained a somewhat checkered existence here for twenty-three years, but during all that time it housed and cared for the library, twice replaced it after fires (in which all the original books but two were destroyed,) and faithfully devoted all subscription fees to its increase. By this means, the library had increased to 2,528 volumes in 1891.

Mrs. Norton's bequest to the town of $5,000 for library purposes, and her own fine private library of almost a thousand volumes, came at the critical moment, in the summer of 1891, when the Y. M. C. A. had voted to disband, and the library was left homeless. A project was immediately set on foot for the establishment for a free town library, a circular advocating it and signed by fifty leading citizens was mailed to every voter, and at the annual town meeting in October, 1891, by a vote of 489 to 130, the town voted to permanently appropriate for library purposes a three-fourths mill tax.

That was before the establishment of the state library commission; and I think I am right in saying that Bristol was the first town in Connecticut to establish a free library, supported and managed wholly by the town.

Another most pleasant surprise came in 1893, when we were notified of the bequest to the town by Mrs. Julia M. Tompkins of Chicago of $5,000 for library purposes.

These two bequests, both totally unexpected, each given by a lady who had long since removed from Bristol, were certainly striking pieces of good fortune, and well calculated to stimulate the people of our own town to do their share.

I may add that Mr. Dunbar, then Chairman of the Board of Libarry Directors, was connected with the making of this bequest in much the same way as I had the good fortune to be with the Norton gift. Mr. Tompkins, who had been a shopmate of Mr. Dunbar in his young manhood, and who in the latter years of his life had desired to express his interest in Bristol by some gift, had consulted with Mr. Dunbar and been advised, first, to make his gift to the Y. M. C. A. and afterward to make it to the public library; and this purpose of Mr. Tompkins was carried out by his wife, who survived him.

The town library was opened in the modest second story of the Ebers Block on January 1, 1892, with Mr. T. H. Patterson as its librarian. Mr. Patterson laid the foundations of the library on sound and workmanlike lines, but later in the year he resigned the office to resume his school work. I shall ever recall, as another of the fortunate events in our library history, the coming into my office of Mr. Wooding, then a newly fledged graduate of Yale, with a most modest inquiry as to whether he would be deemed eligible for the position of librarian. I preserved a due severity during the interview, but after he went out I shouted (metaphorically) for joy in the conviction that we had found the right man. That was just fifteen years ago; and you will agree with me that our confidence was not misplaced.

In 1896 the wooden dwelling house on this lot was offered for sale. It seemed to the Board most important to secure this lot, the most desirable in town for library purposes, and we used the Norton and the Tompkins bequests, which had been allowed to accumulate on interest, some $11,000 in all, to buy the house and lot, and to fit the old house up for the temporary service which it performed for nine years and a half. We moved into it on December 1, 1896, and it was torn down to make room for this building just one year ago, in August, 1906.

Now as to the present building. During the ten years that we occupied the old building, our library increased from 6,200 to over 14,000, and the annual circulation from 34,000 to 46,000. This great increase, both in the size and in the use of our library, made it evident several years ago that the old building would before long become wholly in-

New Library Building.

sufficient. The problem was discussed and its solution postponed from year to year until early in 1905, when the time seemed for various reasons propitious, and the Board appointed a committee to make a general canvass for a library building fund. Mrs. Augustine Norton had in 1901 made a bequest to the library of over $4,100; nearly $1,000 of this had been used for the printing of our present catalogue, but the rest had lain on interest, and up to July first of this year amounted to exactly $3,800.12. Mr. C. S. Treadway, who as a member of the Board had always taken a warm interest in our building plans, had died just before the definite launching of the project, leaving in his will a gift of $1,000 to the library. Your committee have received subscriptions from living doners aggregating $40,171; from the sale of the old building $200, and from interest on early payments over $120, making a total building fund to date of $45,368.10.

One item of importance we have not yet, however, fairly approached. Most of you know of the interesting historical collection which for some years was kept together in the Linstead Block, and of which a considerable part is now stored in the High School building. Dr. Williams has also presented to the town his fine collection of Indian and prehistoric relics, certainly one of the best private collections in the United States.

When the Board appointed its building committee, consisting of Messrs. Ingraham, Wooding and Peck, we were all agreed that the library of an old New England town, situated on residence streets, shaded by stately and beautiful elms, ought to be of that quiet and dignified style popularly known as "colonial," which is really an adaptation of the classic forms of Greece and Rome to modern purposes. A library, also, made to contain chiefly book-cases and reading-tables, is almost of necessity rectangular in design; and the necessity in a small library, of having all parts of the library under the direct observation of the librarian or attendant at the desk, make it essential that the working library rooms shall all be on one floor.

A comparatively low, rectangular building, of Colonial design, was therefore called for by the essential requirements of the situation.

The choice of an actual design was made from many plans submitted in competition, and the one which has been carried out, prepared by Mr. Wilson Potter, of Bristol and New York, was chosen by a unanimous vote, both of the committee and of the entire Board. We have no occasion to comment further upon the design, so far as its aesthetic qualities are concerned; the building is before you for your condemnation or approval.

It contains book-cases sufficient to hold over 30,000 volumes; a second tier of shelving, for which there is abundant height in the stackroom, would add 25,000 more; and a third tier in the basement, which is entirely practicable, gives us a possible total book capacity of 80,000. We certainly feel that that is ample provision for an indefinite future.

And if the voters of the town, a constituency somewhat different, and yet to a great extent of the same, shall in October grant us the permanent tax for which we ask, we shall feel that we have received a double vote of confidence which surely ought to stimulate us all to continued and better efforts in this field of public service.

I cannot close these remarks without referring to the fact that since this movement was initiated, two members of the Board, both of whom had been members since its establishment, were deeply interested in the building project and contributed generously to it, and would have rejoiced in the dedication of the completed building, have passed away; Mr. Charles S. Treadway and the Honorable Edward B. Dunbar.

Street Department at Work.

RIVERSIDE AVENUE PLANT OF JOHN H. SESSIONS & SON.

JOHN HUMPHREY SESSIONS & SON.

In November, 1854, Mr. John Humphrey Sessions, a young man of 26 years, formed a partnership with Henry A. Warner, and rented a small factory in Polkville (Edgewood, as it is now called), in which to conduct a woodturning business. The small capital which he invested was the result of his hard labors, for early in life he had been thrown entirely upon his own resources.

This partnership was dissolved in 1865, Mr. Sessions continuing in his own name the business, which at first consisted mainly of wood turnings for the various clockmakers in the vicinity, and which grew rapidly from the beginning.

In 1869 he bought a plot of ground on North Main street, Bristol, and built the main wooden building, now standing, and moved his plant to Bristol.

In 1857, Albert J. Sessions and Samuel W. Sessions, brothers of John Humphrey, started in a very small way to make trunk hinges, at Southington, and in 1861 this business was moved to Bristol, growing prosperously until June, 1870, when Albert J. Sessions, who was then the sole owner, died, and at this time John H. Sessions bought out his brother's trunk hardware business, combining it with his own. In 1873 he admitted his son, John H. Sessions, Jr., as a partner, which partnership continued until the death of the senior Sessions, on September 10, 1899. A younger son, William E. Sessions, was a co-partner for a short time until he left to develop the foundry business with his father. During the steady growth of the business numerous additions were made to the plant, the large brick storehouse now standing being erected in 1883. The increasing trunk hardware business constantly required more of the available room in the factory, so that the woodturning department was eventually discontinued.

In 1904 the plant on Riverside avenue, which had been recently occupied by the Codling Manufacturing Company, and which was formerly owned and used by Welch, Spring & Company, as a clock factory, was bought and occupied until a new plant could be erected. The modern plant on Riverside avenue was completed and occupied in 1907, and gives its owners the largest and most complete plant for the manufacture of trunk hardware in the country.

After the death of John Humphrey Sessions, a grandson, Albert L., was admitted into partnership by his father, John H. Sessions, Jr., and this continued until the death of John H. Sessions, April 2, 1902. This co-partnership was succeeded in 1905 by a corporation, J. H. Sessions & Son, chartered by a special act of the Connecticut legislature, all the stock of the company being owned by its officers, Mrs. J. H. Sessions, Albert L. Sessions and Mrs. Albert L. Sessions, so that the business is being carried on under the name used so many years.

Mills Box Shop.

H. J. MILLS.

Among the flourishing manufacturing establishments of Bristol, built up from small beginnings, is the paper box manufactory of H. J. Mills on Church street.

The business had its origin about 1865, at which time Elder Benajah Hitchcock commenced the manufacture of matches on a small scale near the school-house in Stafford district, in the east part of the town. In order to supply himself with boxes for his matches, Mr. Hitchcock commenced making them by hand in a very primitive fashion. It was at the suggestion of the late Don E. Peck of Whigville, that Mr. Hitchcock purchased a scorer and undertook the business of general box making. His first boxes were made for Don E. Peck, and other firms soon gave him their patronage.

Herbert J. Mills, a nephew of Mrs. Hitchcock, entered his employ about 1867, and has been connected with the business almost continuously ever since. In 1872 Mr. Hitchcock purchased his present place of residence in Divinity street, and fitted up and enlarged the barn for box making.

In 1887 Mr. Mills and his cousin, David Mix, leased the business. Mr. Mills purchased his partner's interest the same year, and continued the business until 1891, when he bought the entire business of Mr. Hitchcock and built his present factory.

The shop is thirty by one hundred, two stories high, fitted up with steam power, and the most modern and improved box-making machinery.

BOROUGH OF BRISTOL.

The General Assembly of the State of Connecticut, January session, 1893, passed an act incorporating the Borough of Bristol, same was approved March 23, 1893. Committee appointed to secure the charter were the following named citizens of the Borough, viz: George S. Hull, Edward B. Dunbar, Frank G. Hayward, Jonathan M. Peck, Charles S. Treadway and William Linstead.

At a meeting of the voters of the Borough upon the adoption of the charter the total number of votes cast were 564; for the charter, 441, against the charter 123; majority for the charter, 318. William A. Dunbar was moderator of the meeting and declared the charter adopted and approved.

The first election of borough officers was held May 23, 1893, and the following named persons were elected to the several offices, viz:

Warden, Edward P. Woodward.
Burgesses, George S. Hull, William Linstead, William S. Ingraham, William E. Sessions, Charles F. Michael, James W. Williams.
Clerk, Roger S. Newell.
Treasurer, Charles S. Treadway.
Sheriff, Howard G. Ames.
Collector, Silas M. Norton.
Assessors, G. Perry Bennett, Wm. R. Strong, Herbert J. Mills.
Auditors, Julian R. Holley, Wyllys C. Ladd.

January 26, 1895, it was voted: That for the purpose of constructing a system of sewers in the Borough, bonds to the amount of $50,000 be issued, the total cost of the sewer being about $95,000.

The following named persons have served the Borough as wardens, viz:

Edward P. Woodward, one year, 1893-4; *Ira N. Bevans, six months 1894; Miles Lines Peck, one year six months, 1894-5-6; Henry A. Carrington, one year, 1896-7; Lemuel L. Stewart, two years, 1897-8-9; Wilfred E. Fogg, one year, 1900-01; * John F. Wade, three years, 4 months, 1901-02-03-04; Joseph H. Glasson, eight months, 1904-05; Gilbert H. Blakesley, two years, 1905-07; Charles A. Lane, present incumbent, 1907.

The following named citizens have served the Borough as Burgesses from the date of first election to the present time:

George S. Hull, William Linstead, Wm. S. Ingraham, Wm. E. Sessions, James W. Williams, Charles F. Michael, Frank G. Hayward, Ira B. Smith, Solomon C. Spring, Edward O. Penfield, Anson Q. Perkins, Patrick H. Condon, Charles S. Yeomans, Lemuel L. Stewart, George W. Neubauer, William W. Russell, Herbert J. Mills, Watson Giddings, Wilfred E. Fogg, William T. Shepard, William J. Tracy, Stephen N. Mason, Charles A. Lane, John F. Wade, Martin E. Pierson, Thomas N. Brown, Charles W. Roberts, Frank N. Saxton, Joseph H. Glasson, Gilbert H. Blakesley, Frank W. Dutton, Frank Griffith, James O'Connell, Eliphalet L. Hall, George A. White, George W. Duxbury, Byron P. Webler, Carlyle F. Barnes, Charles W. Edgerton, John Lonergan.

The following named citizens have served the Borough as Clerk, viz: Roger S. Newell, one year, 1893-4; Burdette T. Lyons, two years, 1894-6; John Winslow, two years, 1896-8; Daniel J. Heffernan, present incumbent, ten years, 1898-1907.

*Warden Bevins resigned October 2, 1894; and Miles Lines Peck was elected to fill vacancy. Warden Wade resigned August 23, 1904, and Joseph H. Glasson was elected to fill vacancy.

The following named citizens have served the Borough as Treasurer, viz: Charles S. Treadway, seven years, 1893-1900; Leveritt G. Merrick, one year, 1894; Morris L. Tiffany, present incumbent, seven years, 1901-1907.

The following named citizens have served the Borough as Collectors, viz: Silas M. Norton, one year, 1893-4; Robert A. Potter, one year, 1894-5; Seth Barnes, two years, 1895-7; Benjamin F. Judd, six years 1897-1903; William F. Benoit, Jr., two years, 1903-1905; Edward L. Carrington, present incumbent, three years, 1905-1907.

The following named citizens have served as Sheriff, viz: Howard G. Arms, one year, 1893-4; Albert L. Morse, fourteen years, 1894-1907.

The following named citizens have served the Borough as Assessors, viz: G. Percy Bennett, William R. Strong, Herbert J. Mills, Lester Goodenough, Daniel J. Heffernan, Theodore H. Kerins, Silas K. Montgomery, William A. Dunbar, George H. Hall, Marclius H. Norton, Leon M. Case, George W. Duxberry, George A. Beers, Frank R. Graves, Seth Barnes, William J. Connelley.

The following named citizens have served as Auditors, viz: Julian R. Holley, Wyllys C. Ladd, Carlyle F. Barnes, Frederick Dovery, Russell Losher, Morris L. Tiffany, John T. Chidsey

The following named citizens are now serving the Borough for the present year, viz:

Warden, Charles A. Lane.
Burgesses, Thomas H. Brown, Frank W. Dutton, Byron P. Webler, Carlyle F. Barnes, Charles W. Edgerton, John Lonergan.
Clerk, Daniel J. Heffernan.
Treasurer, Morris L. Tiffany.
Sheriff, Albert L. Morse.
Collector, Edward L. Carrington.
Assessors, William A. Dunbar, Seth Barnes, William J. Connelly.
Auditors, John T. Chidsey, Julian R. Halley.

―――

WELCOME TROLLEY.

By Milton Leon Norton.

From the Bristol Press, of August 8, 1895, on the completion of the the Bristol-Plainville Tramway.

Ere our fathers came no pathway,
  But a well-trod Indian trail,
Led out westward through the wildwood
  From the shadowy Tunxis vale;
When the red man, venison laden,
  Homeward wending from the chase,
Sought the lowly, skin-thatched wigwam,
  That he made his dwelling place.

Then there came the early settler,
  Who, on every sabbath day,
Mounted on his pillioned saddle,
  Toward the sunrise rode away;
While his good wife sat behind him,
  And their thoughts dwelt on the text,
And on questions theologic,
  Questions knotty and perplexed.

Next there came the cumbrous ox-cart.
  'Twas our fathers' coach and chaise.
Well the sleek and gentle oxen
  Served them in those early days.
From the encircling hills and mountains,
  Came they into church and store,
While the patient oxen, waiting,
  Chewed their cuds beside the door.

Then there came a great sensation!
  'Twas the talk of all the town,
When from Hartford the first stagecoach
  To the tavern rattled down.
Eager eyes were early watching,
  When, on every night and morn,
Rang out over hill and valley,
  Cheerily, the driver's horn.

Later came the locomotive,
  Snorting, puffing on its way.
Old men said, "An age of wonders!
  Glad we lived to see this day."
Then it was the old stage-driver,
  Grieving, hid his ruddy face,
And the stagecoach, and the toll-gate,
  Disappeared and left no trace.

Then good people sought the Scriptures,
  Read of flaming torches there,
Nahum's chariots, rattling, jostling
  In the highways, everywhere.
And they said, "Of this the prophet
  Spake"; and many a tale and song,
Told the locomotive's prowess,
  Sang its praises oft and long.

But one day the locomotive
  Screamed in anger, loud and shrill,
"What is that I see approaching,
  Climbing swiftly up the hill?
Surely that must be the trolley!"
  Quoth the engine in its wrath;
"I will crush, annihilate it,
  Should it ever cross my path!"

But the peaceful trolley answered
  Not a word, but skimmed along,
Like a swallow o'er the meadow,
  Or a sweet, idyllic song.
By the river and the forest,
  By the lakeside and the rill,
Through the streets of town and borough,
  Over plain and over hill.

And we welcome thee, O Trolley;
  Welcome, royal welcome give;
Take thee to our township's bosom,
  Hoping there thou long may'st live.
And our hearts thrill like the current
  Flowing through thy pulsing heart.
Long and happy be our union;
  Long be it ere we shall part!

SWEDISH EVANGELICAL LUTHERAN BETHESDA CHURCH AT FORESTVILLE, CONN.

The first Swedish families moved into Forestville as early as 1871. Three years later the first service in the Swedish language was held when Rev. T. O. Linell, pastor at Pontiac, R. I., stopped here while on a mission tour through the state. After this time services were held off and on by itenerant ministers traveling for the Lutheran Mission.

The 16th of February, 1880, a congregation with a communicant membership of twenty-five was organized by Rev. J. Melander, and the constitution of the Lutheran Augustana Synod was adopted. The Bethesda Congregation was the second Swedish church organized in Connecticut. From 1882 to 1885 Rev. C. O. Landell of New Britain was pastor of the church, and during the years 1886-1887 Rev. Ludvig Holmes, D.D. of North Grosvenor Dale, filled the pulpit. On the 23d of August, 1886, the congregation unanimously decided to build a church. Rev. L. Holmes and Mr. N. A. Johnson were appointed to have the work in charge, and in the fall 1886 the little church on Academy Street was ready and dedicated to the Lord. Rev. O. W. Ferm of New Britain became the successor of Rev. Holmes, and continued the work until the congregation at Bristol and the Forestville church, jointly called Rev. A. F. Lundquist, who became first stationary pastor of the church in July, 1893. In 1903 Rev. Lundquist moved to McKeesport, Penn., and was succeeded by Rev. E. C. Jessup, who moved to Kiron, Iowa in May, 1906. The present pastor, Rev. O. Nimrod Ebb, B.D., was called from Duquesne, Pennsylvania, and took charge of the congregation Sept. 30, 1906. The present church building was erected in 1907 and cost $5,000. It is 50x30 feet, the basement walls are of stone and shingle finish above. The seating capacity is one hundred and fifty. The congregation has one hundred and thirty-one members.

Forestville Athletic Club Base Ball Team, March, 1907.

Bristol Homes

The publishers would have been pleased to have shown a photographic reproduction of every home in Bristol. This, of course, was not possible or practicable, but enough are represented to give a correct idea of the architecture of the town. In most cases the pictures are numbered 1, 2, 3, etc., and in the description of the photographs these same numbers appear giving, on streets that are numbered, the house number as well. O signifies that the resident is owner and R indicates resident. This data has been carefully compiled, and while it is probable some mistakes may have been made, the information is given in the way that we received it.

FEDERAL STREET.

STEARNS STREET.

WOODLAND STREET.

WOODLAND STREET.

OR "NEW CAMBRIDGE" 671

WOODLAND STREET.

GOODWIN STREET.

GOODWIN STREET.

GOODWIN STREET.

WOODLAND STREET.

GOODWIN STREET.

GOODWIN STREET.

GOODWIN STREET.

FEDERAL STREET.

(1) No. 117, M. H. Smith *R;* (2) No. 111, H. A. Reynolds *R*, No. 113, Irving Schubert *R;* (3) No. 105, Arthur R. Osborne *R*, No. 107, Howard U. Sparks *R;* (4) No. 75, Wm. O'Connell *R;* (5) No. 56, Harriett E. Day *O;* (6) No. 47, Chas. Letourneau *R*, M. A. Perkins *R;* (7) No. 32, James Cairns *R*, S. H. Smith *R;* (8) No. 31, C. D. O'Connell *O;* (9) No. 8, J. W. Fairchild *R*.

STEARNS STREET.

(1) F. C. Norton *O;* (2) No. 27, B. L. Burton *R*, Arthur Ingraham *O;* (3) No. 31, D. Gwillim *O*, A. D. Wilson *R;* (4) No. 43, J. Donnelly *O;* No. 45, F. A. Mitchell *R;* (5) No. 49, E. Erickson *R;* No. 51, C. Neilson *R;* (6) No. 55, W. Muir *R*, C. Larson *O*, E. E. Nichols; (7) J. F. Mather, Jr. *R*, A. B. Way *R;* (8) No. 83, Katherine Sheehan *R;* (9) A. Skelskey *O*.

WOODLAND STREET.

(1) No. 20, Mrs. John Birge *O;* (2) No. 23, Calvin E. Fuller *O;* (3) No. 24, E. W. Cahoon *O;* (4) No. 38, G. E. Gillette *O;* (5) No. 42, Mrs. E. W. Spencer *O;* (6) No. 35, E. B. Case *O;* (7) No. 49, A. L. Norton *O;* (8) No. 56, Mrs. Sarah Allport *O*, Wm. Allport *R;* (9) No. 50, Arthur G. Nearing *O*.

(10) No. 62, Henry B. Wilcox *O;* (11) No. 74, Joseph Lindholm *R;* (12) No. 65, Frank Curtiss *R;* (13) No. 77, L. L. Stewart *O;* (14) No. 77, Wm. H. Nott *O;* (15) No. 80, F. B. Colvin; (16) No. 85, Henry Wilcox *R;* (17) No. 102, Wm. Merrill *O;* (18) No. 105, John W. Carroll *O*.

WOODLAND STREET, ETC.

(19) No. 114, G. H. Elton *R;* (20) No. 113, H. E. Markham *O;* (21) No. 126, Wm. M. Sheeran *O*, Alfred K. Carlson *R;* (22) No. 125, J. F. Kearns *R*, No. 127, C. J. Heisse *R;* (23) Anton Schrade *O*, Chas. Johnson *R;* (24) Wm. E. Troope *O*, Oakland St.; (25) No. 11, Bradley St., Patrick T. Martin *O;* (26) Bradley St., W. E. Wightman; (27) Grove St., Joel T. Case.

GOODWIN STREET.

(1) No. 210, Mrs. W. L. Clark *O;* (2) No. 207, Victor Johnson *O*, D. S. Page *R;* (3) J. F. Gleeson *R*, Robt. B. Codling *R;* (4) No. 190, E. A. Barnes *O*, John Tonkin *R;* (5) No. 180, L. Larson *O*, C. A. Peterson *R*, A. Anderson *R;* (6) No. 163, Christina Lundhal *R;* (7) No. 153, I. D. Rowe, *R;* (8) No. 147, L. H. Snyder *R;* (9) No. 141, Edw. Reardon *O*.

(10) Arthur Page *O;* (11) No. 108, O. Dahlgren *O;* (12) No. 107, Mons Larson *O;* (13) Bernard Johnson *O;* (14) No. 100, John Carlson *O;* (15) No. 99, Wm. Johnson *R;* 101, Oscar Johnson *R;* (16) Olaf Wieberg; (17) Mrs. Pensauet *O*, Richard Baldwin *R;* (18) No. 44, G. W. Whittemore *O*.

(19) No. 43, N. Peson *R*, W. Boutelle *R;* (20) No. 35, A. G. Calvin *R*, G. C. Bidwell, Lester J. Root *R;* (20) No. 38, W. B. Adams *R*, Lewis Langham *R;* (22) Chas. Doolittle *R;* (23) No. 29, C. P. Waterman *R;* E. R. Simmons; (24) No. 24, M. S. Hughes *R*, F. T. Thoms; (25) No. 25, G. J. Funck *R;* (26) No. 19, H. A. Warner *R*, Mr. Slade *R;* (27) No. 20, Mr. Whittlesey.

STEWART STREET.

WOODING AND STEWART STREETS.

JUDD STREET.

QUEEN STREET.

QUEEN AND HARRISON STREETS.

BLAKESLEE STREET.

UNION STREET.

UNION STREET.

STEWART STREET.

(1) No. 7, N. C. Sparks *R*, No. 9, Algot Nelson *O*; (2) No. 36, Chas. W. Stewart *O*; (3) No. 42, Chester Ingraham *O*; (4) H. L. Sherwood, W. C. Morgan; (5) No. 56, A. B. Lockwood *R*; (6) No. 57, C. Statz *R*, R. Herman *R*; (7) No. 59, John Johnson *R*, No. 61, John Nelson *O*; (8) No. 66, Mrs. Frank H. Marshall *R*, Nellie M. Hills *O*; (9) No. 70, Gustave Jaschembowski *O*.

WOODING AND STEWART STREETS.

(1) No. 20, John B. Page *O*; (2) No. 19, Edwd F. Connelly *R*, Wm. Richardson *R*; (3) No. 25, Alfred Erickson *O*; (4) No. 31, Chas. Parcell, Wm. Rowe; (5) No. 37, Albert Eaton *O*; (6) Guy Clifford; (7) No. 52, John Leahy *O*; (8) No. 111 Stewart St., D. J. Morey *O*, No. 113, Jas. Prendergast *R*; (9) Stewart St., Adolph ush, Adolph Putz.

JUDD STREET.

(1) No. 20, Mrs. A. Casey *R*; (2) No. 28, G. Bachand *R*; Alfred Richards *R*; (3) J. Elert *R*, H. C. Downs *R*; (4) No. 38, L. Lapierre *R*; (5) No. 51, S. E. Stockwell *R*, Sidney Morse *R*; (6) No. 63, Alex. Anderson *R*; (7) David Girard *R*, W. Steward *R*, Geo. Shafrick *O*; (8) Chas. Munson *R*; (9) No. 123, Wm. Brunt *R*, John Brunt *R*.

QUEEN STREET.

(1) No. 124; (2) J. F. McCarthy *R*; (3) No. 85, C. Mallory *R*; (4) No. 83, L. E. Rouse *R*, N. Neal; (5) No. 68, S. W. Steele *O*; (6) No. 62, Edw. M. Gillard *O*; (7) No. 54, Mrs. Ericson *R*, A. M. Judd *R*; (8) A. D. Weeks *R*; (9) M. Richtmyer *R*, F. A. Kennedy *R*.

QUEEN AND HARRISON STREETS.

(10) No. 38, Queen St., N. C. Guiden *R*; No. 36, J. J. Merrill *O*; (11) No. 14, Queen St., W. I. Reynolds; No. 16, John Green; (12) No. 17, Queen St., Francis Williams *O*; (13) No. 10, Queen St., Arthur G. Muzzy *O*; (14) No. 12 Harrison St., Mrs. R. A. Ryan; No. 14, John Hughes; (15) No. 20, E. J. Meed *O*; (16) No. 32, John A. Edman *O*; (17) No. 34, Edwd. Hansen *O*; (18) Rudolph Miller *O*.

BLAKESLEE STREET.

(1) A. P. Stark *O*; (2) Miss Sidney E. Tracy *R*; (3) John Palmen *R*; (4) Thos. Grantville *O*; (5) James Daley *O*; (6) Nelson Decker *R*; (7) (empty); (8) John Fingelton *O*; (9) P. J. Kilduff *O*.

UNION STREET.

(1) No. 14, A. G. Hodges *R*, No. 16, Geo. Thomas *R*; (2) No. 22, Mrs. Flora Clark *O*, Mrs. Fannie Clayton *R*; (3) No. 26, Wm. Glasson *O*; (4) No. 32, Julius Grossman *R*, No. 34, Stanley Heintz *R*; (5) No. 35, Peter Alexander *R*, Wm. Archambault *R*; (6) No. 39, Peter F. Gorman *O*; (7) No. 50, John F. Neil; (8) No. 66, Frank M. Moski *R*; (9) No. 62, Lepold Kamiski *R*.

(10) No. 72, Richard Odlum; (11) No. 65, Robt. Campion *R*; (12) No. 73, Mrs. Ida M. Gateley *R*; (13) No. 83, Geo. Dalger *R*; (14) No. 82, Mrs. M. S. Quinlan *R*; (15) No. 88, Wm. Moulthrope *O*; (16) No. 97, Amandus Swan *O*, E. Bessell *R*; (17) Aug. Lomberg *O*, Geo. Thompson *O*; (18) John Ryan *O*.

CHURCH AND UPSON STREETS.

PLEASANT STREET.

PLEASANT AND OAK STREETS.

PRATT STREET.

OR "NEW CAMBRIDGE." 681

PRATT AND LOCUST STREET.

CHESTNUT STREET.

682 BRISTOL, CONNECTICUT

SUMMER STREET.

FARMINGTON AVENUE.

CHURCH STREET.

(1) Baptist Parsonage, Rev. H. Clarke *R*; (2) No. 23, Daniel Casey *O*; (3) No. 18, C. B. Ives *O*; (4) John Kelley *O*; (6) No. 24, Russell Lasher *O*, W. Elwin *R*; (7) No. 45, G. F. Pingpauke *R*, N. F. Marion *R*; (8) No. 63, Samuel Howe *R*, L. A. Gaylord *O*; (9) Richard Bromige, Upson street.

PLEASANT STREET.

(1) No. 9, Mrs. Wise *R*; (2) No. 18, H. W. Pease *R*; (3) No. 24, C. M. Woodford *O*; (4) No. 21, Miss Emmett *O*; (5) No. 31, Mrs. Eunice Judson *O*, Mr. Freeman *R*; (6) No. 28, The Misses Hitchcock, Miss Woodford *R*; (7) No. 34, W. A. Hayes *O*; (8) No. 39, Geo. H. Grant *O*.

PLEASANT STREET.

(10) No. 50, P. Boland *R*, Jas. McDonald *R*; (11) No. 55, J. B. Barnes *R*; (12) No. 64, A. H. Wilcox *O*; (13) No. 67, M. Fitzgerald *R*.

PRATT STREET.

(1) J. P. Landry *R*; (3) W. M. Whitely *R*, G. De Rosier *R*; (4) W. J. Keough *R*, Murray *R*; (5) No. 6, W. H. Mills *O*; (6) No. 14, E. H. Whelan *O*; (7) No. 13, Frank Davis *O*; (8) No. 17, Walter Mills *O*; (9) No. 19, A. E. Edwards *O*.

(10) No. 20, J. S. Steward *R*, A. Maynard *O*; (11) C. E. Hotchkiss *O*; (12) O. Johnson *O*, Mr. Dickson *R*.

LOCUST STREET.

(13) Edw. Lowney *O*; (14) E. G. Waterhouse *O*; (15) Chas. Kasmina *R*; (16) A. Vanoni *R*; (18) No. 10, Jos. Gervais *O*.

CHESTNUT STREET.

(1) No. 129 West St., W. H. Cleveland *O*; (2) No. 19, John Hintz *O*; (3) No. 27, M. Coveity *O*; (4) No. 41, Everett Brown *O*; (5) No. 49, Martin Van Allen *O*; (6) No. 51, Philip Lheureux *O*; (7) No. 38, Mrs. W. F. Perkins *O*; (8) No. 56, D. E. Mauke, Mrs. Turk *O*; (9) No. 57, Edw. Beillette *R*.

SUMMER STREET.

(1) No. 17, Miss H. L. Lounsbury *R*; (2) No. 21, S. C. Grant *R*; (3) No. 29, E. F. Mull *R*; (4) No. 35, A. E. Whittier *R*; (5) Mrs. Wightman *O*; (6) No. 49, E. A. Parter *R*; (7) No. 44, Chas. F. Olin *R*, M. Loughlin *R*; (8) Chas. Gordon *O*, Mrs. Russell *R*; (9) No. 68, Hobart S. Goodale *R*.

FARMINGTON AVENUE.

(1) Jos. W. Fries *O*; (2) C. Collins *O*; (3) L. M. Lawson *O*, Albert Johnson *R*; (4) Fred. Kowalski *O*; (5) N. Nelson *O*; (6) Mrs. Eliza J. Crittenden *O*; (7) Joseph Lindquist *O*; (8) A. B. Ackerman *O*; (9) Andrew J. Johnson.

RIVERSIDE AVENUE.

LAUREL STREET.

SOUTH ELM STREET.

PROSPECT PLACE.

NORTH MAIN STREET.

PROSPECT STREET.

DIVINITY STREET.

DIVINITY STREET.

DIVINITY STREET.

FIELD STREET.

PROSPECT PLACE.

(1) A. F. Rockwell R; (2) No. 106, H. L. Beach O; (3) No. 62, P. M. Holley O; (4) No. 52, Mrs. Merriam; (5) A. J. Muzzy O; (6) No. 38, C. F. Barnes O; (7) No. 37, M. L. Seymour O; (8) No. 31, Mrs. M. Perkins O; (9) No. 30, F. A. Beach R.

SOUTH ELM STREET.

(1) No. 109, Mrs. Kathrina Kaizer R, Mrs. Maggie Bushey R; (2) No. 99, Joseph Rich O; No. 97, Michael Pendel R; (3) No. 89, Joe Connell O; No. 87, Mary Pallen R, Fiorito Alzejio R; (4) No. 83, John McCann R, No. 85, Martin Strupp O; (5) No. 75, Jas. Labelle R, No. 75, Tony Kryzenski R; (6) No. 84, Augusta Zurell O, No. 82, J. W. Moshier R; (7) No. 74, Edmund Cook R, No. 72, W. A. Judson R; (8) No. 69, Michael Cavallir O; (9) No. 66, Elijah Williams R, No. 64, Walter Brown R.

DIVINITY STREET.

(1) Henry Gosselin, E. Campbell, Landry St., (2) Lyman C. Fuller, Landry St., (3) J. Loman, Landry St., (4) No. 28, P. Lupien O; (5) No. 38, John R. Hess R, Miss Jennie Thomas R; (6) Arthur Pion O; (7) Joseph Tebo R; (8) Joseph Courville O; (9) No. 60, Adam Jobes O, Wm. Robinson R.

(10) No. 66, Mrs. A. Benoit R; (11) No. 68, Geo. J. Pepler R; (12) No. 74, H. W. Perkins R, Newton Montrope R; (13) No. 87, G. Sandstrom O; (14) No. 86, Mrs. James Miles O; (15) No. 88, Hayard Plumb- R; (16) No. 96, J. W. Greeno O; (17) No. 93, Henry Steadman R; (18) No. 104-106, Celista Diemo O.

(19) No. 101, Chas. E. Hanchett O; (20) No. 105, Almeron Pond; (21) No. 113, Frank Miles O; (22) No. 124, H. B. Dodge O; (23) No. 113, Mrs. Solomon Spring O; (24) No. 144, Eliada S. Tuttle O, Lewis Tuttle R; (25) No. 129, Mrs. Charlie Spring O; (26) No. 162, Jos. H. Ryals R, Miss Julia Norton O; (27) No. 155, Thos. O'Brien O.

FIELD STREET.

(1) Gideon Gamache O; (2) G. K. Keith O; (3) Wm. A. Ryan; (4) Anton Stenger O; (5) E. Salg O; (6) Amandus Bachman; (7) Adam Diener; (8) Pius Bachman; (9) L. Spieler.

MEADOW STREET.

(1) No. 17, Louis Dimeo; (2) No. 21, Mrs. A. Coughlin R, No. 23, Mrs. Arthur Leport R; (3) No. 53, Mrs. Henry P. Corless; (4) No. 73, F. E. Banning; (5) No. 92, Peter King R; (6) No. 79, Geo. Troland, No. 81, John Fagan, No. 83, W. B. Stone; (7) Frank A. Pfennig; (8) No. 103, A. A. Smith O; (9) No. 102, Chas. H. Hyde.

MAIN STREET.

MEADOW STREET.

Forestville Homes

MAIN STREET.

(1) N. E. Riley R; (2) Forestville Branch Bristol Public Library; (3) W. W. Winston R; (4) Mrs. Marilla N. Woodruff O; (5) A. J. Brennan, C. F. Norton; (6) Mrs. H. D. Mitchell O; (7) C. B. Sanford R; (8) Geo. Warren R; (9) W. C. Granger R, Mrs. M. M. Keys R.

MAIN STREET.

(10) Mrs. S. M. Potter O; (11) F. A. Brennan R, Fred Wright R; (12) Ralph G. Rigby R; (13) Mrs. S. A. Belden O, Mrs. S. L. Atwood R; (14) Preston St., D. G. White R; (15) E. H. Perkins' Lunch; (16) Chas. S. Jones R; (17) Broad St., Chas. A. Palmer R, Robt. Clark R; (18) Mitchell St., Mrs. Wilson Potter.

CENTRAL STREET.

(1) P. Kenney O, C. Daley R; (2) Thos. H. Dalton R; (3) W. P. Weed O, L. Jacobs R; (4) Mrs. H. Daley O; (5) J. Walsh R; (6) Fred Hayden; (7) Nobel D. Jerome R, O. P. Downs R; (8) Lawson A. Taplin O; (9) F. A. Warner's Barber Shop, Quarters Forestville Athletic Club.

CENTRAL STREET.

(10) Post Office, J. F. Holden P. M.; (11) R. P. and J. V. Burns' Cafe; (12) Gate House; (13) R. R. Station; (14) Douglass Bros. Store and G. A. R. Hall; (15) Forest House, M. O'Connell Prop.; (16) J. Segla; (17) S. R. Kidder; (18) Mrs. Wm. Lambert O, T. A. Lambert R.

CENTRAL STREET AND PLEASANT STREET.

(19) L. B. Allen R, N. A. Alexander R; (20) J. P. Garrity O; (21) Jas. Dalton O; (22) F. N. Manross O; (23) Mrs. S. McDermott; (24) Pleasant St., W. C. Pride R; (25) Mrs. A. Dutton; (26) H. J. Avery R; (27) S. W. Wooster O.

GARDEN STREET.

(1) W. E. Allen O; (2) E. S. Chase O; (3) Y. P. Birdy O; (4) W. L. Bradshaw R; (5) W. E. Conlon R, W. H. Roberts R; (6) Thos. Kenney R; (7) W. B. Crumb O; (8) W. H. Plummer O; (9) J. F. Holden P. M.

ACADEMY AND VERNON STREETS.

(1) Mrs. W. L. Glidden R; (2) 13th. District School; (3) Frederick A. Crane R, Vernon St.; (4) (5) Fred Niles O; (6) C. Critchley; (7) J. O'Connell; (8) Geo. Sessions R; (9) Miss E. H. Merrill R.

WASHINGTON STREET.

(1) Miss Emily O, (the Truman Beach Place), Geo. J. Angerbower R; (2) M. F. Spelman O, D. Leonard R; (3) H. G. Ashton R, H. Spencer R; (4) John Percival R; (5) H. Austin Vaill R; (6) F. R. Warner R; (8) W. C. Buckley O; (9) Mrs. Geo. Fellows O, Mortimer C. Hart R.

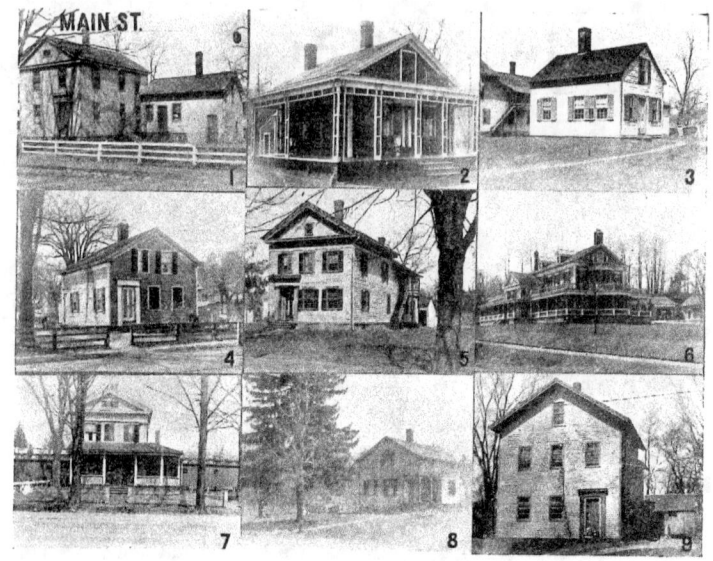

MAIN STREET.

MAIN STREET.

OR "NEW CAMBRIDGE." 693

CENTRAL STREET.

CENTRAL STREET.

CENTRAL AND PLEASANT STREETS.

GARDEN STREET.

ACADEMY AND VERNON STREETS.

WASHINGTON STREET.

WEST WASHINGTON STREET.

PINE STREET.

WEST WASHINGTON STREET.

(10) Frank Myers *O;* (11) Chas E. Winchell *R;* (12) E. D. Holley *O;* (13) Mrs. N. M. Burr *O*, E. M. Burr *R*; (14) E. D. Curtiss *O;* (15) H. L. Norton *R*, Chas. A. Johnson *R;* (16) Academy St., Hiram N. Osborne *R;* (17) Washington St., Miss Kate McCormack *R;* (18) Washington St., Miss Alice Hills *O*, C. E. Trewhella *R*.

STAFFORD AVENUE.

(1) Thomas; (2) Henry M. Taylor *O*, Edwin A. Taylor *R;* (3) Joseph H. Tredinnick *O;* (4) A. Larson *R*, E. Johnson *R;* (5) A. Peterson *R;* (6) M. Polis *R;* (7) H. V. Palenius *O*, J. D. Tapailius *R;* (8) Fritz W. Johnson *O*, Carl Ebb *R;* (9) J. Fayette *O*.

STAFFORD AVENUE.

(10) Richard Walton *R*, Mrs. Alice Powell *R;* (11) E. C. Fowler *O;* (12) L. Fitzpatrick *O;* (13) W. D. Garlick *O;* (14) H. Stone *O*, Thos. Barry *R;* (15) C. C. Scoville *O;* (16) Wm. H. Dutton *R;* (17) W. E. Bunnell *O;* (18) H. W. Scoville *R*.

STAFFORD AVENUE.

(19) Mrs. Shepard *R;* (20) *Burner Shop, Am. Silver Co.;* (21) Alfred Tallis, Sr. *O;* (22) Simeon Fox *O;* (23) W. G. Atkins *O;* (24) John H. Juliff *O*, The Deacon Lloyd Atkins Place—and birth place of Roswell Atkins; (25) Mrs. M. L. Hotchkiss *O;* (26) W. C. Bramhall *O;* (27) Maltby Ave., Henry Juniver *O*.

PINE STREET.

(1) H. Brown *R;* (2) Mrs. E. MacDonald *O;* (3) Mrs. C. D. Hough *O*, M. B. Brennison *R;* (4) F. H. Perkins *O;* (5) M. B. O'Brien *O;* (6) A. F. Dresser *O;* (7) J. Cafferty, Jr. *O;* (8) Thos. Roberts *O;* (9) W. C. Dean *R*.

NEW, BROOK AND KING STREETS.

(1) Aug. C. Stichtenoth, New St.; (2) Mrs. Margaret Kenny *O*, Brook St.; (3) Darwin S. Reade *O;* (4) Commodore M. Broadwell *O*, Brook St.; (5) Mills H. Barnard *O*, Brook St.; (6) S. M. Barnard *O*, Brook St.; (7) Felix Holden *O*, King St.; (8) Oscar Anderson *O*, King St.; (9) Patrick J. Curran *O*, King St.

698 BRISTOL, CONNECTICUT

STAFFORD AVENUE.

STAFFORD AVENUE.

STAFFORD AVENUE.

FARMINGTON AVENUE.

NEW, BROOK AND KING STREETS.

OFFICERS OF WORKMEN'S SICK AND DEATH BENEFIT SOCIETY, NO. 120.
Ernst Nurnberger, President; Wm. Schoenhauer, Financial Secretary; Pius Schoessler, Secretary.

OFFICERS LADIES' TURN VEREIN.
Pauline M. A. Nurnberger, President; Hattie Joerres, Vice-President; Emma Aulback, Treasurer; Bertha A. Ehlert, Corresponding Secretary; Mae E. Heppner, Financial Secretary.

THE NORTH SIDE HOTEL—FEDERAL AND NORTH STREETS.

THE BRISTOL HOUSE—SOUTH STREET.

LONGEST TAILED PONY AND TALLEST TROTTING HORSE IN THE WORLD FORMERLY OWNED BY J. W. SKELLY.

Lieutenants Clark and Van Ness, and Members of Co. D, 1st Infantry, C. N. G. See page 52

FRONT VIEW DUNBAR BROS. FACTORY—SOUTH STREET.

AN OLD TIME VIEW OF THE GALE STUDIO.

List of Advance Subscribers

C. B. Abell,
Mrs. S. J. Allport,
E. E. August,
Peter Alexander,
E. J. Arnold,
Geo. C. Arms,
H. G. Arms,
Chas. Benson,
H. I. Arms,
Wm. J. Andrews,
J. Aulbach,
Hjalmar Anderson,
W. G. Atkins,
A. B. Ackerman,
C. O. Anderson,
Sarah L. Atwater,
C. N. Atwood,
Elbert Atwood,
O. Almquist,
C. Anderson,
F. Aliano,
Forestville Athletic Club,
J. Anglebower,
Geo. Atkins,
G. L. Anderson,
W. B. Adams,
G. Avolt,
H. S. Avery,
J. E. Andrew,
C. H. Allen,
F. C. Alger,
Emily Allen,
Oscar Anderson,
Victor Avery,
C. J. Anderson,
E. Bradley,
Mrs. S. H. Bartholomew,
R. D. Barnes,
Mrs. J. Birge,
D. Alexander,
G. C. Arms,
G. Bresnahan,
W. E. Broadwell,
P. Buchner,
P. Buckner,
A. Bachmann,
C. F. Barnes,
Mrs. J. Brady,
J. L. Barnum,
Mrs. H. A. Booth,
E. R. Brightman,
R. Beaudoin,
M. Bechard,
J. Breshnan,
E. W. Bengthman,
G. B. Bacon,
H. R. Barnum,
F. Beaton,
H. C. Beach,
Jas. A. Brunt,
Adolph Busch,
Geo. T. Bachand,
J. M. Buckly,
W. R. Brunt,
Walter Bennett,
J. M. Blodgett,
C. H. Beaudoin,
S. P. Bartholomew,
Seth Barnes,
Margaret Burns,
H. Brown,
H. P. Brockett,
W. H. Burns,

A. L. Bassett,
N. D. Bushkey,
Mrs. W. L. Beach,
R. D. Buhstedt,
S. M. Barnard,
C. M. D. Broadwell,
L. Bachmann,
M. H. Barnard,
Mrs. D. Birge,
C. L. Bachand,
R. N. Buell,
W. Brown,
H. R. Beckwith,
V. Bettna,
A. A. Bunnell,
T. H. Brown,
B. L. Bennett,
J. F. Bristol,
C. L. Birdsall,
Jos. Bechard,
W. F. Brainard,
Mrs. Julia Burns,
Herbert Booth,
E. J. Bradshaw,
A. S. Brackett,
D. Bresnahan,
W. R. Burkan,
W. W. Buys,
W. P. Ball,
Mrs. J. Bryce,
A. J. Brennan,
J. D. Burgess,
F. Ball,
J. Bride,
P. W. Barnum,
N. Beaudoin,
F. E. Burr,
A. H. Buskey,
W. E. Barker,
E. Bruce,
W. L. Barrett,
Edw. Balch,
J. M. Bergh,
H. L. Bradley,
E. Bailey,
F. Bruen,
Irving Bruce,
T. Barry,
W. E. Boughton,
W. P. Birdy,
W. C. Buckley,
W. F. Bradshaw,
H. Beach,
W. J. Benoit, Jr.,
E. N. Burr,
Mrs. Mary Bates,
W. E. Bunnell,
W. C. Bramhall,
H. C. Butler,
W. H. Bacon,
L. Belden,
C. L. Belden,
S. Bunnell,
Rev. C. H. Buck,
W. L. Bradshaw,
Mrs. S. R. Butterick,
E. Burwell,
E. A. Barnes,
R. Barnes,
Miss C. L. Bowman,
E. T. Belden,
G. L. Bush,
O. J. Bailey,

A. C. Bailey,
A. F. Bunnell,
E. Bradley,
R. Bachman,
A. L. Bud,
A. D. Blair,
C. H. Barr,
F. Bruen,
S. Barnes,
Mrs. J. E. Burns,
Misses Blakeslee,
J. W. Bryce,
Miss A. Burzler,
P. Bissemey,
T. H. Coffy,
Robt. Carlson,
F. B. Calvin,
J. W. Clark,
C. M. Carrington,
W. J. Connelly,
F. J. Costello,
G. Cari,
J. Coughlin,
E. F. Connelly,
J. J. Cunningham,
H. P. Corless,
F. Cleveland,
W. Clayton,
T. Chagnon,
A. Chouiniere,
J. Chouiniere,
C. R. Carlson,
W. H. Cleveland,
G. C. Canfield,
G. T. Colegrove,
E. Chouiniere,
O. M. Coffin,
J. H. Cafferty,
D. W. Collins,
Mrs. J. Carroll,
Wm. Casey,
W. J. Calkins,
C. F. Cable,
Chas. S. Cook,
W. L. Casey,
C. Critchley,
J. H. Carroll,
W. R. Coe,
J. Chagnon,
A. M. Curtiss,
W. E. Conlon,
F. A. Crane,
H. B. Cook,
F. S. Chase,
E. D. Curtiss,
H. C. Cottle,
Achille Croye,
P. J. Crowley,
S. E. Curtiss,
W. Chapin,
G. Clayton,
S. B. Chapin,
G. Crowther,
W. Coons,
J. H. Clarence,
Mrs. M. H. Carroll,
O. H. Calkins,
A. L. Calvin,
A. M. Clarke,
W. W. Clark,
D. Y. Clark,
W. Cook,
E. J. Cullen,

BRISTOL CONNECTICUT.

Mrs. J. Conlon,
P. F. Curran,
P. Casey,
A. Carlson,
B. H. Curtiss,
Miss M. Carnell,
E. Cote,
Mrs. E. C. Christensen,
C. Collins,
E. J. Crittenden,
J. A. Christenger,
F. B. Curtiss,
W. W. Clark,
Mrs. Camp,
J. G. Cairns,
H. B. Cook,
E. Curtiss,
Dunbar Bros.,
C. F. Duchmann,
Jas. Dingwell,
Geo. Dalger,
L. E. Cucuel,
M. Carey,
J. R. Cairnes,
J. T. Case,
A. J. Calkins,
C. Doolittle,
G. H. Dennison,
L. Dimeo,
S. Driver, Jr.,
J. E. Doyle,
Mrs. F. E. Darrow,
J. B. Degnan,
J. Douglass,
O. P. Downs,
C. W. Daniels,
C. B. Dailey,
T. H. Dalton,
W. H. Dutton,
C. H. Deming,
W. C. Dean,
H. E. Day,
Mrs. R. C. Downs,
T. J. Dwyer,
J. H. Davis,
N. Dube,
H. S. Dutton,
O. B. Dayton,
R. Dutton,
G. H. Button,
E. S. Doune,
A. F. Dresser,
S. Dutcher,
E. J. Dutton,
C. E. Dunbar,
M. Dresser,
R. E. Dillon,
Geo. H. Day,
W. W. Dunbar,
Dr. Desmarais,
H. M. Davitt,
J. Dalton,
J. J. Deegan,
T. F. Doyle,
L. A. Downs,
W. W. Dunbar,
C. H. Dickinson,
Thos. Dienneen,
A. Diener,
M. Driscoll,
W. J. Daly,
P. Deegan,
C. H. Daniels,
Mrs. E. Duffy,
Mrs. E. Donahue,
E. S. Dunbar,
F. J. Davis,
Eg. Dunbar,
J. F. Douglass,
Mrs. E. B. Dunbar,
W. J. Day,
E. Edwards,
G. H. Elton,
W. E. Elwin,
E. H. Elton,
Rev. Nimrod Ebb,
Alfred Erickson,
August Erickson,
J. Englert,
E. J. Emmett,
S. C. English,
H. S. Elton,
A. S. Eaton,
J. E. Edwan,
G. T. Elliott,
M. D. Edgerton,
A. E. Edwards,
H. J. Forsyth,
J. Fries,
F. P. Flescher,
J. Fitzsimmons,
W. G. Fenn,
B. H. Fallon,
J. Frey,
M. Farrell,
J. Fingleton,
H. J. Farnnam,
E. C. Fowler,
J. W. Fries,
Mrs. W. F. French,
A. A. Ferry,
Nettie A. Fogg,
J. L. Fitzpatrick,
L. Fitzpatrick,
J. Freeman,
S. Fox,
J. B. Ford,
G. B. Frolich,
G. J. Funck,
C. E. Fuller,
G. W. Fenn,
Winifred E. Fogg,
R. W. Ford,
J. Geisner,
C. N. Gordon,
J. Gasske,
G. S. Goddard,
L. W. Goodsell,
Chas. A. Garrett,
W. O. Goodsell,
Mrs. I. M. Gateley,
W. C. Glasson,
W. Gould,
Ralph Gerth,
A. Gartmann,
S. T. Goodspeed,
C. W. Greenough,
Mrs. E. T. Gaylord.
C. E. Gaylord,
W. D. Garlick,
W. C. Granger,
Mrs. S. C. Goodenough,
Mrs. W. Giddings,
J. W. Gray,
L. L. Griswold,
A. H. Gosslein,
F. W. Giddings,
C. Gray,
H. E. Garrett,
C. Grant,
W. W. Grant,
S. E. Green,
G. C. Graham,
E. J. Gaudreau,
F. Gaylord,
W. D. Gorlick,
S. R. Goodrich,
Mrs. D. B. Goldsmith,
A. C. Golpin,
A. W. Griswold,
T. J. Gewillim,
G. E. Gillette,
A. H. Hobro,
E. W. Gaylord,
A. J. Garrette,
J. P. Garrity,
Geo. Gustafson,
C. H. Grant,
C. F. Gage,
A. J. Gerigk,
Miss Geissweit,
W. E. Gumme,
Mrs. M. Guckin,
D. Girard,
W. Grant,
E. Gustafson,
M. B. Granfield,
J. J. Gee,
Bruno Gerth,
F. B. Hartranft,
E. Horton,
J. F. Gleason,
H. A. Hannum,
Mrs. J. B. Hamilton,
C. D. Hills,
D. Haskell,
W. R. Hough,
C. E. Hotchkiss,
J. M. Hart,
S. B. Harper,
A. Harper,
J. S. Hare,
M. Hahn,
A. J. Hanna,
P. F. Hurley,
N. E. Hare,
M. C. Hart,
D. J. Heffernan,
Mrs. M. Hanna,
Mrs. M. Hutchington,
F. Herold,
G. W. Hull,
F. Hayes,
E. M. Hare,
L. P. Hannum,
D. N. Hawley,
F. S. Hyde,
W. A. Hayes,
D. H. Hall,
Mrs. A. J. Hamlin,
Perry N. Holley,
D. Hare,
J. Hyland,
S. P. Harrison,
P. J. Holden,
G. W. Hall,
H. Huhn,
J. E. Hinchcliffe,
M. F. Harney,
F. A. Hubbell,
Jas. Hurley,
G. C. Herman,
C. A. Hough,
W. A. Hayes,
Mrs. B. Hammond,
M. Hause,
F. A. Haviland,
L. P. Hayden,
F. H. Holmes,
A. Harman,
J. V. Heffernan,
W. Hotchkiss,
Mrs. M. L. Hotchkiss,
P. M. Hubbard,
Thos. F. Hackett,
C. E. Hungerford,
Mrs. P. J. Holmes,
S. W. House,
J. H. Hayes,
H. W. Hungerford,
Dr. Hanrahan,
W. S. Hart,
P. Hassett,

OR "NEW CAMBRIDGE." 707

C. E. Hotchkiss,
J. Hiritz,
W. H. Hutchinson,
A. D. Hawley,
R. T. Hall,
F. Hayden,
F. A. Horton,
F. G. Hofsess,
Geo. Hall,
E. D. Holley,
W. H. Hoylan,
Mrs. E. M. Hough,
J. F. Holden,
C. B. Ives,
F. Ives,
C. E. Ingraham,
W. A. Ingraham,
Mrs. E. L. Judson,
H. H. Judd,
J. H. Johnson,
B. Johnson,
C. J. Johnson,
B. F. Judd,
H. M. Johnson,
J. W. Johnson,
F. H. Judd,
N. D. Jerome,
G. Johnson,
A. Josolowitz,
F. N. Jacobs,
W. Jerome,
E. F. Judson,
N. Johnson,
O. A. Jones,
H. C. Jennings,
A. Johnson,
J. N. Juliff,
W. Janecker,
F. E. Johnson,
W. E. Johnson,
Rev. T. J. Keener,
J. E. Kennedy,
Geo. Klimek,
D. A. Kelly,
A. Kleefeld,
Mrs. K. C. Kelly,
P. F. King,
C. Katzung,
F. P. Kennely,
W. H. Kelsey,
H. Kunt,
A. Kallstrom,
S. R. Killer
A. E. Knickerbocker,
Thos. Kennedy,
W. F. Kilmartin,
Emile Kohle,
P. Keefe,
Chas. Kimberly,
J. F. Kearns,
F. Lebeau,
C. Larson,
A. Larson,
F. Kowalewski,
J. Lindquist,
John Lamb,
W. H. Lugg,
H. Law,
C. T. Lane,
T. Large,
N. A. Lamphier,
R. Lasher,
M. Lawlor,
J. J. Lass,
Mrs. E. M. Lowrey,
H. A. Loomis,
A. Larocquse,
D. Larson,
M. L. Lawson,
Rose Luchsinger,

W. C. Ladd,
C. A. Lane,
Jos. Lebeau,
H. W. Layassay,
J. Lanly,
R. K. Linsley,
M. J. Lyons,
A. F. Lincoln,
H. Lafayette,
Geo. Lawley, Sr.,
Geo. Lawley, Jr.,
Aug. Landburg,
D. Leonard,
L. H. Loomis,
H. Lawrence,
Theo. Lockenwitz,
A. F. Lawson,
Geo. J. La Course,
L. La Course,
L. H. Lardner,
T. Leavett,
A. Lupier,
F. Lupien,
G. Lewis,
L. Larson,
J. Lonergan,
Mrs. L. H. Linsley,
A. A. Lilgren,
T. A. Lambert,
Miss L. Lange,
Antoine Lupien,
C. Lundgren,
G. P. Lyons,
L. Lasher,
G. E. Littlefield,
G. B. Lewis,
A. Legase,
T. J. Lane,
S. A. Ladd,
O. Linden,
Louis La Pierre,
J. McKernan,
Jas. McKernan,
W. Y. McMullen,
F. McGar,
J. McNabola,
J. J. McDonagh,
E. E. Merrill,
E. McCue,
M. T. McCormack,
C. McCarthy,
J. H. McWilliams,
J. McLaughlin,
J. McDonald,
W. McDermott,
M. K. McCormack,
B. J. McGovern,
N. H. Merrill,
G. O. Mosley,
Mrs. G. C. Manchester,
J. W. Moshier,
A. Morin,
A. Manchester,
W. E. Mills,
A. Z. Maynard,
Jas. Mondeau,
Geo. Mitchell,
C. E. Mitchell,
Mrs. A. J. Muzzy,
A. F. Matthews,
G. H. Miles,
Rev. W. H. Morrison,
F. S. Merrill,
C. B. Moody,
Moses Medeley,
Mary F. Martin,
P. F. Martin,
F. Moreau,
W. W. Merrill,
W. W. Morley,

H. I. Muzzy,
M. Munn,
Geo. N. Minor,
B. Munson,
J. K. Mulford, Jr.,
L. Merz,
C. E. Mallory,
A. H. Medley,
F. B. Michael,
C. F. Michael,
J. J. Merrill,
J. A. Mathews,
A. G. Muzzy,
A. C. Mills,
D. J. Mahoney,
J. Muelleins,
A. L. Moses,
J. B. Matthews,
A. Munson,
V. E. Modin,
E. H. Moulthrope,
O. Melacon,
W. H. Merritt,
F. A. Mitchell,
J. D. Monaghan,
Mrs. C. H. Muzzy,
F. Moulthrop,
Geo. B. Michael,
H. E. Meyers,
J. W. Moore,
J. P. Moran,
R. J. Miller,
J. Murphy,
E. A. Matthews,
E. Manchester,
R. C. Manchester,
H. J. Mills,
E. L. Miner,
W. S. Moore,
Mrs. H. D. Mitchell,
Chas. Messenger,
Mrs. J. Myers,
B. H. Mason,
S. Murphy,
J. T. Mather, Jr.,
M. J. Malone,
J. D. Maynard,
W. H. Miller,
D. Mason,
F. C. Norton,
A. J. Norton,
N. Nissen,
Mrs. C. E. Nott,
Wm. H. Nott,
Mrs. F. A. Noble,
B. G. Nichols,
G. O. Northrop,
H. L. Norton,
Mrs. C. Nelson,
T. Nichol,
A. R. Nettleton,
N. B. Neal,
J. G. Nichols,
E. E. Nichols,
W. E. Norton,
C. Nagel,
E. Nurnberger,
C. N. Nagel,
H. B. Norton,
W. M. Norton,
A. Nelson,
J. A. Norton,
Jno. A. Norton,
L. B. Norton,
N. Nelson,
Florence S. Norton,
E. E. Newell,
P. C. Nicholls,
G. F. Neale,
A. G. Nearing,

S. F. Nichols,
Mrs. Robt. Norton,
L. S. Norton,
Roger S. Newell,
N. E. Nystrom,
Edw. Olsen,
G. E. Olcott,
J. T. O'Brien,
M. B. O'Brien,
D. T. Ogden,
Mrs. M. E. O'Brien,
M. O'Connel,
J. O'Connell,
Wm. O'Connell,
Thos. O'Brien,
J. T. O'Connell,
M. L. Peck,
G. A. Peters,
DeWitt Page,
J. A. Peckham,
C. Peterson,
A. S. Poas,
F. E. Pond,
J. C. Parsons,
E. H. Perkins,
E. Peck,
U. C. Parsons,
Mrs. A. E. Pettibone,
Nils Pierson,
Fred Perry,
N. C. Parsons,
H. S. Pratt,
M. E. Pierson,
Jos. Perry,
C. Peterson,
W. O. Perkins,
H. J. Peck,
J. Peterson,
N. E. Pierce,
C. A. Parsons,
A. H. Parsons,
J. T. Palmer,
Mrs. J. A. Pond,
E. M. Peck,
B. A. Peck,
C. E. Perkins,
H. B. Plumb,
C. F. Pettibone,
A. S. Parcell,
C. E. Parcell,
Mrs. J. B. Page,
A. Peterson,
Mrs. L. Poam,
Mrs. J. B. Pender,
A. Peterson,
M. Polis,
J. E. Pierce,
Mrs. E. L. Peck,
E. Prenez,
A. C. Perkins,
Mrs. E. S. Piper,
Thos. Perry,
F. Percival,
Mrs. S. M. Potter,
W. N. Plummer,
A. Q. Perkins,
A. E. Parker,
Miss E. Jennie Peck,
Miss Helen A. Peck,
F. E. Pond,
C. A. Palmer,
F. R. Parsons,
Geo. J. Pepler,
J. M. Peck,
B. R. Plumb,
N. Peck,
Mrs. W. Potter,
J. J. Quinn,
R. N. Quinion,
O. Roberts,
W. A. Ryan,

A. Richards,
W. W. Roe,
Mrs. P. J. Riley,
C. Ryan,
Darwin Read,
R. L. Rigby,
E. L. Royland,
Mrs. H. C. Rockefeller,
W. C. Richards,
J. A. Royce,
A. L. Roberts,
H. T. Roberts,
J. H. Rals,
P. Riquist,
R. Ronalter,
N. E. Riley,
W. H. Roberts,
H. C. Rancor,
R. J. Rigby,
G. S. Reed,
A. F. Reed,
W. R. Russell,
C. E. Rottger,
J. Riley,
W. W. Russell,
H. Redmann, Jr.,
Geo. A. Rowe,
Robt. F. Ryan,
W. Roberts,
H. S. Richemeyer,
J. W. Reynolds,
A. J. Rawson,
M. B. Rohan,
C. E. Russell,
T. C. Root,
H. E. Russell,
Dr. B. B. Robbins,
W. C. Robinson,
H. A. Reynolds,
Wm. H. Rowe,
G. L. Roberts,
G. B. Roberts,
L. E. Ponse,
J. D. Reeve,
W. J. Roberts,
W. C. Rechtmeyer,
P. J. Reddy,
Miss M. Roberts,
J. H. Ryals,
W. I. Reynolls,
J. W. Skelly,
Mrs. F. Schubert,
Mrs F. B. Scudder,
H. J. Smith,
E. J. Sheeky,
Mrs. Geo. J. Schubert,
T. Schubert,
A. Stephenson,
J. F. Streigle,
A. P. Stark,
L. Spieler,
A. L. Sessions,
F. A. South,
Mrs. L. E. Seymour,
E. Spencer,
Mrs. M. G. Sutliffe,
A. Schafer,
Mrs. F. Smith,
L. A. Sanford,
E. P. Sanborn,
J. L. Shields,
W. E. Sessions,
Mrs. A. Sampson,
H. W. Soule, Jr.,
J. L. Strup,
W. Stolz,
F. Sigourney,
W. W. Sharpe,
J. Skelsky,
C. Stock,
J. Scarritt,

C. H. Stock,
B. Smith,
A. L. Strichteneth,
Mrs. M. G. Sutliffe,
E. E. Stockton,
W. L. Smith,
M. S. Soule,
Paul Stein,
G. Schubert,
C. Spencer,
P. Schussler,
H. Sweeney,
W. Schoenaner,
W. F. Smithwick,
D. C. Stevens,
Mrs. C. C. Smith,
A. J. Sjogren,
E. E. Smith,
E. S. Soule,
J. Seaman,
Mrs. J. H. Swift,
Rev. C. N. Shepard,
C. B. Sanford,
F. Sahlin,
W. T. Smith,
C. J. Swenson,
Roy Stone,
M. L. Sullivan,
F. H. Saxton,
W. R. Strong,
H. W. Simmons,
J. J. Sullivan,
Michael Schilling,
Mrs. A. Spring,
A. F. Stawart,
L. H. Snyder,
J. E. Stewart,
S. W. Steele,
O. F. Strunz,
C. A. Swanston,
G. F. Scherr,
F. Shields,
M. J. Smith,
F. Salery,
C. C. Scoville,
Mrs. G. Shepard,
H. Stone,
H. W. Scoville,
J. Segla,
S. N. Sheldon,
F. Steele,
W. E. Spicer,
H. W. Scoville,
L. Scheidel,
W. F. Stone,
F. A. Schaffer,
Mrs. C. Treadway,
G. F. Thomas,
G. Tong,
G. W. Thompson,
H. W. Tuttle,
A. J. Tollis, Jr.,
J. Troye,
R. V. Tomlinson,
H. W. Taylor,
L. F. Thomas,
T. L. Thomas,
H. M. Taylor,
F. H. Thomas,
J. Tredennick,
Mrs. Sidney Tracy,
E. S. Tuttle,
Thos. Treloar,
Mrs. H. C. Thompson,
A. Theureaux,
J. Theureaux,
W. J. Tracy,
D. Theureaux,
W. A. Thewhella,
Mrs. J. Tywell,
O. H. Thomas,

T. A. Tracy,
J. Tregauza,
Mrs. N. Turk,
Joseph Terrien,
Mrs. L. A. Taplin,
C. E. Trewhella,
G. H. Turner,
W. Thomas,
G. F. Thomas,
W. H. Thomas,
J. H. Thomas,
F. E. Terry,
J. W. Tracy,
E. L. Tolan,
C. I. Treadway,
Mrs. G. R. Tuttle,
A. J. Tymerson,
E. Thomas,
C. H. Terry,
W. A. Terry,
Ella A. Upson,
Dr. C. R. Upson,
Mrs. H. Umphrey,
R. Unwin,
M. Van Allen,
W. Van Ness,
Mrs. J. S. Voorhees,
A. H. Vaill,
G. W. Veubana,
A. Vanasse,
F. W. Vickers,
F. Valentine.

C. W. Vosberg,
P. Vanoni,
C. L. Wooding,
H. O. Webler,
B. P. Webler,
D. S. Wadsworth,
L. L. Whittlesey,
J. Wheeler,
F. A. Weeks,
J. J. Welsh,
R. Walton,
Geo. W. Waterhouse,
Dr. J. S. Wilson,
M. E. Weldon,
E. H. Whelan,
B. Williams,
P. J. Welsh,
F. S. White,
J. D. Whipple,
J. M. White,
B. White,
R. H. Woodford,
H. N. Wilcox,
G. A. White,
G. W. Wooster,
F. A. Warner,
J. Wise,
H. Willman,
George Weeks,
Mrs. W. L. Weeks,
W. P. Weed,
J. Walsh.

H. J. Wilson,
Mrs. S. E. Weed,
A. M. Warner,
G. R. Webster,
Jno. Walton,
Mrs. H. S. Wilson,
Mrs. N. S. Whightman,
E. Williams,
G. W. Whittemore,
N. J. Walsh,
J. W. Williams,
W. E. Whightman,
George Warren,
F. E. Wilcox,
Mrs. J. L. Wilcox,
C. C. Weld,
B. S. Warner,
T. West,
F. B. Wasley,
F. A. Wasley,
Mrs. C. E. Winchell,
H. C. Wright,
F. W. Wright,
H. R. Way,
E. J. Weed, Jr.,
D. J. Webster,
S. N. Young,
F. Zink,
A. Zarn,
G. Zahnke.

INDEX

	Page
Arms, Geo. C., Mounmental Works,	432
Barnard, M. H.	431
Barnes Co., The Wallace	430
Barrett Factory, The Wm. L.	436
Bartholomew Factory, The Edgewood	405
Birds, Rambles Among the Bristol,	217
Natural History, Photography	392
Same Bristol Game	437
Berge Sons' Co., The W. L.	424
Blakeslee Novelty Co., The	433
Bradleyites, The	540
Brightwood Hall	333
Bristol in 1721	21
Centennial Address, Peck, 1885	25
"New Cambridge"	30
Mr. Newell Installed	31
Petition for Eccles. Incorporation,	30
Incorporation	38
Borough of Bristol	663
Bristol Mfg. Co., The	416
Bristol Press, The	345
Bristol Homes	668
Bristol Trust Co.	652
Cemetery, The Old Episcopal	328
Churches, Ecclesisatical, etc.	
Advent Christian	443
Baptist	43, 213
Congregational, The First	170
Earliest Preaching	28
Early Ecclesiastical Controversies	30
Early Episcopal	34
Episcopal Church, The First	327
German Ev. Lutheran	383
Methodist Episcopal, Prospect, 45,	283
Methodist Episcopal, Forestville. 46,	545
Mount Hope Chapel	538
St. Matthew's Roman Catholic	543
St. Joseph's Church	369
Swedish Congregational Church	386
Swedish Lutheran Lebanon	388
Swedish Ev. Lutheran, Forestville	666
Trinity Church	306
Clayton Bros. Inc.	417
Clocks, Early Days of Industry, 49,	140
Co. D., C. N. G.	357
Copper Mines of Bristol, The	440
Curfew Bell, The	380
Diatomes of Bristol	278
Dunbar, Moses, Loyalist	141
Early Industries	46, 339
Fall Mountain, History of	125
Fire Department, 633, 637, 639, 641, 645.	
Ford Machine Shop, The J. B.	412
Forestville	543
Founders and Their Homes	193, 227
Fraternal Bristol—	
A. O. H.	613
Brightwood Camp, M. W. of A.	615
Bristol Grange	595
Bristol Turner Society	589
Companion Court Geneva	615
Daughters of Rebekah	593
Eagles	593
Foresters	575
F. & A. M.	585
Fedelia Circle	577
Gilbert Thompson Post	646
I. O. O. F.	623, 626
Katherine Gaylord Chapter, D. A. R.	620
K. of C.	581

	Page
K. of P.	628
L'Union S. J., Baptist D'A.	615
Manross Post	651
National Assn. Stationary Engineers	573
N. E. O. P.	579
One Hundred Men Society	604
Oneida Club	569
Order of Vassa	571
Order of E. S.	615
O. U. A. M.	587
Red Men	587
Red Cross	628
R. A. M.	593
Royal Arcan m,	591
Royal Neighbors of America	583
Ruth Rebekah Lodge	595
Scandinavian Sick Benefit	603
Societe Des Artisans, etc.	607
Sons of St. George	605
St. Jean Baptiste Society	602
St. Joseph's Sick Benevolent	606
Swedish Temperance Society	608
Whigville Grange	599
Gaylord, Katherine, Heroine,	61, 134, 620.
Geneological Section (see also pages 227, 526, 534.)	
Adams, John H.	476
Adams, Walter	512
Atwood, Anson L.	479
Barnes, Rodney	454
Barnes, Thos	511
Barnes, Wallace	465
Bailey, Chas. S.	503
Bartholomew, Geo. W.	486
Bartholomew, Harry S.	486
Beach, Chas	486
Birge, John	505
Birge, Geo. W.	507
Birge, Hon. John	506
Birge, Nathan L.	505
Birge, Nathan R.	507
Bradley, Warren I.	460
Brewster, Elisha C.	485
Bunnell, Allen	485
Candee, Wales A.	502
Clayton, Wm.	509
Churchill, Chas.	469
Churchill, Chas. Jr	469
Cook, Havilah T.	473
Darrow, Elijah	471
Darrow, Franklin E.	472
Day, Wm.	468
Downs (or Downes) Family	447
Dunbar, Edw. B.	481
Dunbar, Col. Edw. L.	467
Gale, Herbert N.	456
Gaylord, Wm.	515
Gaylord, Jesse	471
Gibb, Rev. Wm.	477
Griggs, Dr. Leverett	508
Goodenough, Lester	488
Hancock, Elder S. C.	453
Hawley, Benj. F.	496
Hanna, Jas.	464
Hooker, Deacon Bryan	450
Hubbell, Julius R.	461
Hull, Geo. S., M. D.	501
Hungerford, Evits	473
Ingraham, Edw.	457
Ingraham, Elias	498
Ives, Orrin B.	487
Jennings, John J	503
Lewis, Benj. R.	497
Mallory, Ransom	448
Manross, Elisha	499

OR "NEW CAMBRIDGE." 711

	Page
Miller, David S.	476
Mitchell, Hon. Alex	508
Mitchell, Julius R.	461
Mitchell, S. A.	460
Newell, Lot and Naomi	511
Newell, Samuel P.	502
Norton, A. L.	467
Norton, Geo.	495
Nott, Chas. E.	471
Nott, Julius	494
Penfield, Gilbert	475
Pidcock, Daniel	498
Pomeroy, Noah	470
Pierce, Isaac	498
Richards, Wm. C.	514
Richards, Wm. R.	513
Root, Chas, J.	516, 521
Root, Mrs. Catherine R.	520
Root, Miss Mary P.	516
Root, Samuel E.	465
Roberts, Miss Candace	516, 522
Schubert, Geo. J.	510
Sessions, Albert	491
Sessions, John Henry	490
Sessions, John Humphrey	489
Seymour, Allen	485
Satliffe, J. H.	479
Sigourney, Jos.	478
Steele, Chas. A.	475
Sutliff, S. M.	497
Thompson, H. C.	500
Tuttle, Constant L.	488
Way, Harvey E., M. D.	492
Welch, Elisha N.	493
Woodward, Edw. P.	455
Wright, E. L.	459
Gidding's Carriage, Forging, etc.	485
Hobro & Rowe	404
Horton Mfg. Co., The	411
Hotel, The Brick	423
Ideal Laundry	434
Indians of Bristol and Vicinity	9
Ingraham Co., The E.	407
Indian Names	13, 26
"Compound" (Compounce)	16, 17
Tunxis	25

	Page
Prehistoric Remains	79
John Humphrey Sessions & Son	381
Ladd Co., The W. C.	421
"Leather Man," The Old	162
Mills Box Shop	662
Mount Hope Chapel	538
Natural History Photography	392
New Departure Mfg. Co.	426
Peck, Abigal, "The Bear Girl"	59
Penfield Saw Works	414
Pequabuck River, The	166
Police	599
Prehistoric Remains	79
Present Industries of Bristol	395
Public Library	654
Reminiscences of Youthful Pastimes	378
Schools of Bristol	523
First School Houses	35
History of School Dist. No. 9	227
History of School Dist. No. 10	526
North Side School Dist. No. 2	534
Sessions, Clock Co., The	395
Slave Bill of Sale	33
Sessions Foundry Co., The	397
Slave Girl	57
Sporting Bristol	353
Smith, Marshall J.	425
Snyder Co., The L. H.	408
Swanston's Orchestra	390
Taverns	42
Terry & Co., Fletcher	413
Thompson Clock Co.	418
Turner & Deegan	414
Turner Heater Co., The	409
War—Revolutionary	36, 37
French and Indian	36
Civil	53
Warner Co., The A. H.	419
West Hill Club	422
Wicket, The Srtnage Yankee Game of	292
Welcome	664
Witchcraft	44
Whigville Grange	599

ERRATA

Page 58. It has been inaccurately stated that Zebulon, the *father* of Abigal, was a deacon in the Congregational Church. Zebulon Peck, his son, the *brother* of Abigal filled that office. *Note by Miss A. M. Bartholomew.*

Page 140, line 12, should read "*Capt. Alvah Wooding, Horace Moultrop, etc.*"

Page 342, all of the matter following line 26 was written by Mr. Milo Leon Norton.

Page 388. The title of the article should read "The Swedish Lutheran Lebanon *Congregational* Church.

Page 247. Line under photograph should read, "*Branch Factory at Weissensee, Berlin, Germany.*"

Page 497. The lines under the two photographs are transposed, making Mr. *Sutliff* to appear as Mr. *Lewis* and *visa versa*.

In the article "History of School District No. 9," commencing on page 227, the following corrections and changes are necessary.

Page 231, line 21, should read "*after 1860, James, son of etc.*"

Page 234, line 10. *Anteitam* instead of *Bull Run*.

Page 236, lines 28 and 29, read "*Yale, married Edward Root, they had two daughters Jane and Mary.*"

Page 237, line 34, should be *Josiah Jr.*, instead of *Josiah*.

Page 238, first line under photograph, *No. 55* instead of *No. 35*.

Page 243, line 16 should be *Methodist* Episocpal, etc.

Page 245, line 19, "*Fox, widow of William, etc.*"

Page 246, line 10, *Muzzy* instead of *Muzay;* line 25, *Funck*, instead of *Frinck*.

Page 247, 6th line from the bottom, *Asahel* instead of *Asabel*.

Page 250, 2nd line under photograph *1807* instead of *1867*.

Page 252, line 27, "*or before*" instead of "*to 1870.*"

Page 256, last line "*he purchased of Amasa Ives Jr., etc.*"

Page 270, line 15, read "*Miranda*" for "*Mary.*"

Page 274, 8th line from bottom, read "*age five years; Charles H. Alpress (2), b. Dec. 31, 1835. Unmarried, lives at Hot Springs, Ark.*"

Page 263, lines 50, 51, 52, 53 and 54 read "*George Welles Bartholomew, born June 19, 1805, married Jan. 14, 1829, Angeline, daughter of Dea. Charles G., and Parthenia (Rich) Ives, born Mar. 20, 1807, died Mar. 13, 1861. He married 2nd Mrs. Julia (Marvin) Cole, Jan. 27, 1864, she had one daughter Hettie Julia, b. May 17, 1856.*

It was the original intention to print a number of biographies of prominent living citizens of Bristol, but the limited space prevented. It is with pleasure that we show here the photograph of one of the oldest and best known residents of the town, Wilfred H. Nettleton.

VIEWS ON THE PEQUABUCK RIVER—(SEE POEM *The Pequabuck River*).

The Old Downs' Mill, Riverside Avenue.

Photo by W. E. Throop.

www.ingramcontent.com/pod-product-compliance
Lightning Source LLC
Chambersburg PA
CBHW071213290426
44108CB00013B/1173